ALSO BY JAMES MacGREGOR BURNS

Guam: Operations of the 77th Infantry Division (1944)
Okinawa: The Last Battle (co-author) (1947)
Congress on Trial (1949)
Government by the People (with Jack Peltason
and Thomas E. Cronin) (1951, 1984)
Roosevelt: The Lion and the Fox (1956)
John Kennedy: A Political Profile (1960)
The Deadlock of Democracy: Four-Party Politics in America (1963)
Presidential Government: The Crucible of Leadership (1966)
Roosevelt: The Soldier of Freedom (1970)
Uncommon Sense (1972)
Edward Kennedy and the Camelot Legacy (1976)
Leadership (1978)
The Vineyard of Liberty (Volume I of The American Experiment) (1982)
The Power to Lead (1984)

The Workshop
of Democracy

THE
AMERICAN EXPERIMENT · VOLUME II

The Workshop
of Democracy

By
James
MacGregor
Burns

Alfred A. Knopf

19   85

NEW YORK

THIS IS A BORZOI BOOK
PUBLISHED BY ALFRED A. KNOPF, INC.

Copyright © 1985
by James MacGregor Burns
All rights reserved under
International and Pan-American Copyright Conventions.
Published in the United States
by Alfred A. Knopf, Inc., New York, and simultaneously in Canada
by Random House of Canada Limited, Toronto.
Distributed by Random House, Inc., New York.

*Grateful acknowledgment is made to Harmony Books, for permission
to reprint verses from the song "Brother, Can You Spare a Dime?,"
in 100 Best Songs of the 20's and 30's. Lyrics by E. Y. Harburg
and music by Jay Gorney. Reprinted by permission.*

*Owing to limitations of space, all acknowledgments of permission to use
illustrations and maps will be found following the index.*

Library of Congress Cataloging in Publication Data

Burns, James MacGregor.
The workshop of democracy.

(The American experiment)
Includes index.
1. United States—History—1865–1921.   2. United
States—History—1919–1933.   I. Title.   II. Series:
Burns, James MacGregor. American Experiment (Alfred A. Knopf, Inc.)
E661.B97   1985   973   85–8002
ISBN 0–394–50546–8

Manufactured in the United States of America
First Edition

For Kurt Tauber
and my other Williams College colleagues
who teach in the tradition of
Mark Hopkins and Robert L. Gaudino

Here, then, was the explanation of her restlessness, discontent, ambition,—call it what you will. It was the feeling of a passenger on an ocean steamer whose mind will not give him rest until he has been in the engine-room and talked with the engineer. She wanted to see with her own eyes the action of primary forces; to touch with her own hand the massive machinery of society; to measure with her own mind the capacity of the motive power. She was bent upon getting to the heart of the great American mystery of democracy and government. She cared little where her pursuit might lead her. . . .

Democracy, by Henry Adams

I have seen America spread out from th' Atlantic to th' Pacific, with a branch office iv th' Standard Ile Comp'ny in ivry hamlet. I've seen the shackles dropped fr'm the slave, so's he cud be lynched in Ohio . . . an' Corbett beat Sullivan, an' Fitz beat Corbett. . . . An' th' invintions . . . th' cotton-gin an' the gin sour an' th' bicycle an' the flyin'-machine an' th' nickel-in-th'-slot machine an' th' Croker machine an' th' sody-fountain an'—crownin' wurruk iv our civilization—th' cash raygister.

Mr. Dooley, 1897

Contents

PART V · The Culture of Democracy

PART I
The Crisis of
Democracy

CHAPTER 1

The War of Liberation

BELCHING clouds of steam and hazy blue smoke, the stubby little locomotive chugged along the iron rails that wove through the low Allegheny Mountains. While the fireman heaved chunks of walnut and cherry into the roaring firebox, the engineer looked out through his narrow window past the small boiler, the polished brass fittings, the stovepipe-shaped smokestack, watching for the village stations along the way: Relay House, Lutherville, Timonium. . . . In a rear coach sat Abraham Lincoln, regaling cronies with droll stories and listening imperturbably to politicians who climbed aboard to exhort and complain, while a little party of diplomats silently watched this loose-framed man who, with his seamed face, deep-sunk eyes, and rough cut of a beard, appeared in mourning even as he told his small-town anecdotes.

Love's Station, New Freedom, Jefferson Station, Hanover Junction . . . "This is all very pleasant," Lincoln told his listeners, but he had to work on his speech. Retiring to a closed drawing room in the rear of the coach, he sat watching the red-brown mountain slopes and hollows slip by his window. He could see farmers still harvesting grain in the lush Pennsylvania fields. Few young men were visible; these farmers and their fellows all across the North had seen their sons off to war. Lincoln could share their feelings: a year before, his own Willie had sickened and died, while he just now had left his second son, Tad, ill in the White House with Mrs. Lincoln almost hysterical with worry and memories.

That morning—November 18, 1863—the President had left a capital deeply enmeshed in the business of war. At the War Department, Secretary Edwin M. Stanton was following telegraphed reports from the Union forces in Virginia, which were cautiously advancing, and from those in Tennessee, which were readying an attack. The Ordnance Bureau announced that it would accept bids for the manufacture of 71,000 heavy-artillery shells. Navy Secretary Gideon Welles was working on his annual report to Congress. Chief John Ross, whose Cherokee tribe had been exiled for a quarter century in Oklahoma, visited the Indian Bureau with reports and petitions. The Treasury Department announced the next issue of new national banknotes, this time with better printing and paper. The

3

President himself had just proclaimed a place in the city of Omaha as the starting point for the Union Pacific Railway.

Now, in the swaying compartment of the presidential train, Lincoln scratched some more words on a sheet of foolscap. He was bound for Gettysburg, the battlefield where 40,000 Northern and Southern men had been lost to death or wounds less than five months before. He had not much looked forward to the occasion, had found it difficult to compose his thoughts, and his Cabinet had not been keen to accompany him. Secretary of State Seward had come; Treasury Secretary Chase, who was being talked up as Lincoln's likely antagonist in the 1864 election, remained in Washington. People seemed to be playing old-fashioned politics and economics in this dire crisis.

Had Americans become so engrossed in the everyday business of running the war, the mechanics of war, that they had forgotten the goals? Had they lost sight of the values that were being tested, of the purpose of the great experiment that Washington and Hamilton and Jefferson had launched eighty-seven years before? Forced like the Founding Fathers to play politics, Lincoln would transcend the routine play of the political game. Confronted at a cemetery by common people who had lost fathers and brothers, sons and husbands, he would ask them to renew the American experiment in liberty and equality. Asked to dedicate a battlefield, he would reconsecrate a nation.

It was dusk when the presidential special pulled into Gettysburg, which already was overflowing with thousands of visitors. Lincoln and his party were driven to the home of Judge Wills, where they met up with Edward Everett, who was to give the main address. Everett was everything Lincoln was not: a Harvard graduate, governor of Massachusetts, Minister to the Court of St. James's, president of Harvard, senator from Massachusetts, and a member of Boston's social elite. He was also not President, having run on the tail end of John Bell's Constitutional Union ticket in 1860. Now he was best known as probably the most brilliant of Union orators. After chatting with Everett and the other distinguished guests, Lincoln retired, only to be summoned to his window by revelers who wanted a speech. Lincoln offered a few words so self-deprecating that the grumbling crowd headed off in search of Seward to coax a few purple passages from him. Lincoln meantime resumed copying the second draft of his closing sentences.

Next morning, what was to be a grand parade of pomp and pageantry turned into a struggling procession of democracy. Lincoln, dressed in black and wearing a tall hat and white gauntlets, his huge frame draped over a little horse, led the procession, behind blue-clad soldiers; soon he was slouched down, sometimes shaking the hands that were extended to him, at other times appearing to be lost in thought. Then came politicians, dignitaries, religious committees, telegraph men, a hospital corps, Knights Templar, Masons, Odd-Fellows, literary and scientific representatives, the press, firemen, and citizens. Soldiers with bandages and crutches limped alongside. After an hour the bloated and disorganized column had wound its way uphill to the cemetery. Then there was more confusion when Everett could not be found. While bands played, Lincoln waited patiently and people milled about. Everett finally showed up, the meeting started, the invocation was offered. Then America's most respected orator rose.

With rolling periods and many a classical allusion, Everett re-created the drama of the three-day battle. He could see the battlefield itself over his listeners' heads. There ahead, on that fateful July morning, in the distance, Union cavalry on Seminary Ridge had begun the fighting. A little closer lay the town itself, through whose twisting streets the blue-clad infantry had fled as the first day's fighting ended. A sweep of Everett's left arm took in the Peach Orchard, where reinforcements in blue and gray had clashed on the second day. There, on the slopes of Little Round Top, boys from Maine and Alabama had rushed up to club one another. There, amidst the rocks of Devil's Den, other men had been blown to pieces by cannons firing point-blank.

Glancing right, the orator could see Culp's Hill, where Ewell's Louisianans had almost turned the Union flank that second day. And ahead, beneath that copse of trees visible a half mile away, the battle had reached its climax. Fifteen thousand Virginians, led by ringlet-haired George Pickett, had stormed across the wheatfields, across the lower slopes of Cemetery Ridge and Hill, up, up toward the center of the Union lines. Shells, canister, bullets cut down the charging Confederates, but here the survivors broke through. And then they wavered. Assailed from front and flank, they finally turned to flee. The last great assault of Robert E. Lee's army had washed back down from the crest, and now Edward Everett stood there, speaking at the high-water mark of the Confederacy.

While a hymn was sung, Lincoln drew from his pocket the two pages of his own speech and adjusted his spectacles. The dignitaries behind him shifted in their seats. Then the audience quieted.

"Fourscore and seven years ago our fathers brought forth upon this continent a new Nation, conceived in Liberty, and dedicated to the proposition that all men are created equal."

Lincoln's words, spoken in a high, almost metallic tone, carried to the farthest reaches of the crowd. He held his manuscript in both hands but hardly glanced at it.

"Now we are engaged in a great civil war, testing whether that Nation or any Nation so conceived and so dedicated can long endure. We are met on a great battle-field of that war. We are met to dedicate a portion of it as the final resting-place of those who here gave their lives that that nation might live."

The President's words were carrying over the crowd to the battlefield itself, still littered with broken guns, scattered bits of uniforms, shattered caissons, stripped trees, thousands of spent bullets, the carcasses of un-buried horses. The air stank of rot and death.

"It is altogether fitting and proper that we should do this. But in a larger sense we cannot dedicate, we cannot consecrate, we cannot hallow this ground. The brave men living and dead who struggled here have conse-crated it far above our power to add or detract." Here the President's voice broke, and his hands seemed to tremble. "The world will little note nor long remember what we say here, but it can never forget what they *did* here.

"It is for us, the living, rather to be dedicated here to the unfinished work that they have thus far so nobly carried on. It is rather for us to be here dedicated to the great task remaining before us, that from these honored dead we take increased devotion to that cause for which they here gave the last full measure of devotion; that we here highly resolve that the dead shall not have died in vain; that the nation shall, under God, have a new birth of freedom; and that Government of the people, by the people, and for the people, shall not perish from the earth."

Manning the Front

Twenty-eight months earlier, in July 1861, Lincoln had peered out the White House windows at pale ghosts of soldiers, caked with the grime of battle, stumbling along Pennsylvania Avenue toward the Capitol, at glassy-eyed cavalrymen swaying slack in their saddles—a beaten army, reduced almost to a rabble. These were the bloodied survivors of the first battle of Bull Run. During the next few days, as he sat in the cabinet room talking with generals and foot soldiers or tossed fitfully at night on the sofa in his office, the President had penciled the rudiments of a grand strategy. Before then, he and his generals had not bothered much with broad war planning, for the struggle was expected to be brief, but Northern illusions had died on that battlefield soaked with the blood of hundreds of Billy Yanks.

Tighten the blockade of Southern ports—drill and discipline the exist-ing volunteer forces—hold insecure, divided Baltimore with a "gentle, but firm, and certain hand"—step up organization and operations in the

West—reorganize the forces in northern Virginia as rapidly as possible: these were the essentials of the President's immediate strategy. Behind it lay a grand strategy for a massive, collective military and economic effort: simply to overpower the South along the vast land and sea fronts, ultimately to divide and dismember it. Topography dominated Northern strategy. Sprawling from northern New England to northern Alabama, the vast Appalachian chain cut the eastern states into two huge theaters of combat, with few connections between them for large armies; to the west, across the Mississippi, lay another theater.

In the Confederate capital at Richmond, planning and calculating in his own "White House," President Jefferson Davis had fully understood the advantages topography gave the South. Union troops would have a hard time fighting their way south through the bristling Virginia defenses, across six muddy rivers running west-east, while Confederate forces could easily move west and north along the wide Shenandoah Valley, a natural route of invasion toward Pennsylvania and Maryland. Farther west, on the other hand, the river and valley system favored the Union. "The Cumberland and Tennessee rivers were highways of invasion into Tennessee, northern Mississippi, and northern Alabama," in James McPherson's summation, "while the Mississippi River was an arrow thrust into the heart of the lower South." Southern generals were also superior to Northern, Davis felt. And he could hardly avoid comparing the two commanders-in-chief —he with his West Point training, background in Southern military exploits and traditions, Mexican War combat, secretaryship of war, as against Lincoln's three months of inglorious service against Indians—which Old Abe himself mocked.

Above all, Davis would exploit the South's military advantage in not needing to invade the North or destroy its armies. He could stand on the defensive—the Yanks had to come to him. "We seek no conquest," he had told the Confederate Congress in the first days of the war, "no aggrandizement, no concession of any kind from the States with which we were lately confederated." He seemed to find a moral superiority in the South's defensive posture. "All we ask is to be let alone."

To preserve the Union—his highest immediate goal—Lincoln could not let the secessionists alone. Month after month he had pressed his generals to carry the fight to the enemy in Virginia and Tennessee. By the beginning of 1863, after a series of ferocious encounters, capped by a second battle of Bull Run that again sent the Union forces reeling, the war had settled into a bloody stalemate. Union naval squadrons had closed most Southern ports, but numerous small vessels slipped through, and a handful of Confederate cruisers harried Northern merchant ships on the high seas. All three main Union armies were bogged down in the winter mud, far from their objectives. The Army of the Potomac sprawled in its northern Virginia camps after its most recent rebuff. In central Tennessee, the Army of the Cumberland lay at Murfreesboro, decimated by a "victory" in which a quarter of its ranks had fallen. And on the Mississippi, the Army of the Tennessee, which had advanced farthest into the Southern heartland, seemed the most hopelessly mired. The blue-clad soldiers shoveled, shivered, and sickened in the Mississippi swamps, while their commander vainly sought a way around the Confederate stronghold at Vicksburg.

Northern prospects had seemed bright enough toward the end of 1862 for Lincoln to move ahead on his supreme political act of the war—emancipation. But even as the President was readying his final proclamation of January 1, 1863, Lee's men at Fredericksburg had virtually massacred a much larger Union force, arousing the anger of Northerners against their own military and political leadership. Exclaimed Lincoln, on hearing the outcome at Fredericksburg, "If there is a worse place than Hell, I am in it."

In the North, talk had grown of compromise and peace. "Copperheads," as their detractors called them, organized to resist the draft and force Washington to end the war. On the floor of the House, Clement Vallandigham of Ohio charged Lincoln with despotism and failure. A wave of desertions swept through the Northern armies. Some of the farmboys-turned-soldiers resented Lincoln's Emancipation Proclamation. Why should they fight and die for "niggers"? Some soldiers felt their officers were incompetent. Finding the war meaningless as well as miserable, and knowing the heavy burdens falling on their womenfolk on the farm, thousands simply walked away from camp and headed home. The Army of the Potomac alone reported 85,000 men absent. Some were caught, and gunfire occasionally punctuated the quiet of the Union camps throughout the winter of 1862–63 as alleged deserters were shot.

Would spring mean new hope? Northern power was mounting as masses of men and matériel were thrown into the fray, but somehow superior numbers and munitions did not bring victory. The problem was leadership. Lincoln had run through a string of generals—McDowell, Pope, McClellan, Burnside. He wanted a man who could *fight* and *win.*

Such a commander was emerging in the West. Stumpy, plain-dressed, constantly smoking or chewing on a cigar, forty-one-year-old Major General Ulysses S. Grant hardly cut a heroic military figure. To some he was known mainly as a sometime drunk within the army and a failure outside it. Rival generals dismissed his February 1862 victory at Fort Donelson, the North's first striking success in the war, as a fluke; scandal-hungry reporters overlooked his calm courage at the battle of Shiloh and charged him with being drunk on the field.

Urged that Grant be removed from his western command, Lincoln answered with jokes, but to a Pennsylvania politician he responded with feeling: "I can't spare this man—he fights." A Confederate general took the measure of the man: not a genius, but "clear-headed, quick and daring." One of Grant's officers summed him up as neither bully nor bon vivant, but only a "plain business man of the republic." As 1863 dawned, the next piece of business was seizing the fortress of Vicksburg.

Vicksburg in early 1863 was still a frustrating target. Perched on a bluff above the east bank of the Mississippi, the city was protected by swamps and strong fortifications to the north, while shore batteries seemed to block any assault via the river. As the last Confederate stronghold on the Mississippi—even more, the last link between the eastern and western halves of the Confederacy—it was fully manned. Still, General John Pemberton held Vicksburg with a force slightly smaller than the Union besiegers, which made it all the more galling for the Northern commanders that during the winter they had tried six different means of getting at Pemberton's army and all had failed. In despair, William Tecumseh Sherman of the Army of the Tennessee had suggested a retreat back to Memphis for regrouping, but Grant had demurred. The Northern people, Grant said, would not countenance another setback. "There was nothing left to be done," as he later put it, "but to *go forward to a decisive victory.*"

Sometimes fortune favors the bold. This time Grant would move *south* of the fortress and then try to beat the Rebels in detail. The notion of deliberately marching troops deep into enemy territory, with an insecure supply line and with two enemy columns ready to pounce on them, appalled Sherman and his fellow officers, but they had confidence in Grant. As the rains began to ease off in mid-April, the Army of the Tennessee moved down the muddy roads of the west bank, opposite the fortress. Admiral David Porter, after running his gunboats past the Confederate batteries at night, ferried the Union army piecemeal across the river.

In trapping the enemy had Grant and Porter become trapped? Some thought so: the Unionists were on the dangerous side of the river, under Confederate guns. But Grant was just where he wanted to be—on dry ground and within grappling reach of the enemy. He pushed his army, a compact triangle of about 43,000 men, forward between Pemberton and the veteran Rebel general, Joseph Johnston, who commanded a newly assembled force in Jackson, to the east. On May 14 one prong of the mobile triangle stabbed into Jackson, putting Johnston to flight. While a Union detachment stayed behind destroying rail lines and military stores, the other two prongs of Grant's main force cut back to grasp Pemberton, who was advancing cautiously out of Vicksburg. After twice pushing their foe back toward the fortress, Grant's men attacked Vicksburg itself.

The assault failed, but the battle had been won. Pemberton's army now was trapped in Vicksburg; Johnston's reinforcements were scattered on roads and troop trains for many miles around; the Army of the Tennessee, now resupplied, had a tight grip on the river stronghold. Sherman, riding with Grant to inspect the lines, was jubilant: "This is a campaign; this is a success if we never take the town."

The war was more than a campaign, however; it was a conflict in many theaters, and back on the eastern front the Federals were floundering after another defeat. In late April a refurbished Army of the Potomac, under a breezily confident new commander, Joseph Hooker, had marched forth to do battle once again with Robert E. Lee's Army of Northern Virginia. Hooker hoped to maneuver behind Lee, trap him at Fredericksburg of recent sad memory, and then crush him with the Union's superior numbers. Instead, Lee met Hooker's thrust head-on, blocking it for a time near the hamlet of Chancellorsville. At first, the Union men seemed to be winning the fight as the gray-clad troops slowly fell back through thick forest and tangled underbrush.

Lee, badly outnumbered, seemed at last to be cornered, but he was setting a trap of his own. While his men slowly retreated, Lee sent "Stonewall" Jackson with 28,000 men on a fourteen-mile march, circling far around Hooker's right flank. At dusk on May 2 Jackson's men burst screaming out of the shadowy underbrush, routing an entire Union corps and knocking the Federals back toward the Rappahannock. Darkness, Northern reinforcements, and the accidental wounding of Jackson by his own men stopped the attack. Hooker still had strong forces left, but Lee simply outgeneraled him during the next two days, and the remaining Federals pulled back to the north bank of the Rappahannock.

"My God!" an ashen-faced Lincoln had exclaimed on getting the news of Chancellorsville. "What will the country say?" Once again the South felt a surge of pride, tempered by the news of Stonewall Jackson's death after the amputation of an arm and the onset of pneumonia. Lee's textbook victory made him the military hope of the Confederacy. A son of Henry "Light-Horse Harry" Lee of Revolutionary War fame, a West Point graduate, married to the great-granddaughter of Martha Washington, a gallant officer in the Mexican War, Lee had seemed the natural choice as commander of Virginia's armed forces when he chose his native state over the Union at the start of the war. He had directed such a slow and fumbling campaign in western Virginia during the first months of the war, however, as to be called "Granny Lee" and almost lose his reputation before he could win it. But then, in battle after battle, he had developed such qualities of resourcefulness, mobility, audacity, imagination, resoluteness, and an almost intuitive understanding of enemy plans as to make him the supreme tactician of the war.

A tactician—but now the South needed a strategist. Grant had Vicksburg in his grasp, thus threatening to cut the Confederacy in two. The blockade was tightening. Union forces were threatening to attack in central Tennessee, even launch a joint army-navy operation into Charleston. Now, in May 1863, Confederate leaders took anxious counsel together. Some wanted to strike west, liberate Tennessee, and break Grant's grip on Vicksburg and the Mississippi. But Lee pressed for a more daring plan—to reinforce the Army of Northern Virginia and then strike north through the Shenandoah Valley into the fertile Pennsylvania countryside, thus lightening the pressure on Richmond and forcing the Union to pull troops from the west; this would inspire the Peace Democrats in the North, perhaps win recognition from European powers, and possibly even result in the capture of Washington. The tactician had turned strategist.

In June, in search of the decisive victory of the war, Lee slipped his army toward the Shenandoah Valley and plunged northward. Things went handily at first. Confederate columns scattered Union detachments in the valley, crossed the Potomac, speared through Maryland and southern Pennsylvania, and reached the outskirts of Harrisburg. Hooker proposed to the President that, while Lee moved north, the Federals should move south and seize Richmond; Lincoln responded drily, "I think *Lee's army,* and not *Richmond,* is your true objective point." Still looking for a fighter, the President accepted Hooker's resignation and chose George Gordon Meade as commander of the main Union forces in the East. In Pennsylvania, Lee was already finding that instead of encouraging Peace Democrats, his advance—especially his seizure of livestock and food, and the capture of Pennsylvania Negroes and dispatch of them south to slavery—had aroused Northern anger to a new pitch.

So stupendous odds had turned on the outcome of the battle that erupted in the little town of Gettysburg on July 1, as commanders deployed their troops and sent them forward into a cauldron of noise and heat and smoke, of fear and pain and sudden darkness; as artillery pounded away, soldiers shot and stabbed and clubbed one another on Little Round and the Wheat Field and Cemetery Ridge, and famous regiments once a thousand strong melted away. Waiting in the War Department's telegraph room, Lincoln finally received the message he so desperately wanted: Lee was defeated, his troops moving back toward Virginia. Then came word from the Army of the Tennessee: Vicksburg had surrendered to Grant on the Fourth of July. Telegraph lines flashed the news across a joyous North.

"We have at last got the harpoon into the monster, but we must now look how we steer," Lincoln had said earlier, "or with one flop of his tail he will send us all into eternity." His words seemed more apt than ever as Meade allowed the bulk of Lee's troops to retreat south. Gideon Welles had never seen the President so upset and discouraged. "We had them in our grasp," Lincoln kept saying. "We had only to stretch forth our hands and they were ours." Further confirming his fears, the seesaw of war again teetered as autumn neared. General William Rosecrans's Federals captured Chattanooga in southeast Tennessee, but Braxton Bragg's Confederates counterattacked at Chickamauga, cracked and broke the Union line, pushed the Union forces back to Chattanooga, and laid the city under siege.

The whale's tail was still flopping, but the Northern harpoon was sinking deeper. Given command of the armies of the west, Grant drove Bragg's men off Lookout Mountain and then off Missionary Ridge, in a battle won by soldiers who stormed the ridge on their own, ahead of orders. Lincoln got the news a few days after returning from his Gettysburg Address trip. With Union ships once again plying the Mississippi, Bragg's troops retreating into Georgia, and Grant's divisions poised to break through the mountains and advance on Atlanta, the President was on the eve of achieving his great strategic aim of breaking the Confederacy in two.

Confederate hopes ebbed after Gettysburg and Vicksburg. "We are now in the darkest hour of our political existence," Jefferson Davis said. Wrote a Confederate private captured at Vicksburg: "We have Lost the Mississippi and our nation is Divided and they is not a nuf left to fight for." A Southern veteran of Gettysburg wrote his sister: "We got a bad whiping. . . . They are awhiping us . . . at every point." He hoped the South would make peace so that he could "get home agane" alive.

In Richmond the Confederates' diarist-at-large, Mary Chesnut, began her January 1, 1864, entry, "God Help My Country." She had almost become used to social occasions attended by men without arms, without legs, men unable to see, unable to speak. "Gloom and unspoken despondency hang like a pall everywhere." As she looked out on the endless Richmond rain, her main hope now was that the enemy would become bogged down. "Our safeguard, our hope, our trust is in beneficent mud, impassable mud."

General Mud. But there was also General Industry, General Supply, General Transport, General Manpower—and General Grant.

FORGING THE SWORD

Late in the afternoon of March 8, 1864, a train carrying Ulysses S. Grant, his teenage son, and two aides steamed into the Washington railroad station. No one was on hand to greet the man who was about to take command of the most powerful army the world had ever seen—and who had never set foot in his nation's capital or met his commander-in-chief. Making his way to Willard's Hotel on 14th Street, the general waited there until after nine in the evening, when he left for the White House. There, at one end of the Blue Room, Lincoln was greeting guests at one of his large receptions. Hearing a rising buzz of conversation at the other end, the President moved through the crowd toward the man who had just entered. "Why, here is General Grant!"

While the two men exchanged a few amiable words, other guests crowded in around them or climbed chairs and tables to get a better view. If some were disappointed in the appearance of this small scrubby man of forty-two, with his slight stoop and the wart on his right cheek, they did not show it. They needed a hero, and here was the Hero of the West. The next day the President commissioned Grant a lieutenant general, commanding all the armies—the rank previously given in full only to George Washington.

Leaders choose strategies, and strategies choose leaders. Grant was not only a proven fighter and winner but a general who could be counted on to carry out Lincoln's long-frustrated strategy of attacking the enemy on all fronts simultaneously. Grant also could be expected to wage a continuous battle of attrition: instead of engaging the foe in one major struggle at a time and then pulling back to prepare for the next encounter—the pattern so far of the Civil War and of most wars—he would hammer the Confederates unceasingly, hanging on like a bulldog, grinding and wearing down the South to the point of exhaustion.

Southern leaders had taken their measure of the man. "He fights to win, that chap," they were saying in Richmond. "He is not distracted by a thousand side issues. He does not see them. He is narrow and sure, sees only in a straight line."

As Grant came to grips with Lee in Virginia during the spring of 1864, the new general-in-chief found not only that a strategy of attrition was correct but that he had no alternative. For the new strategist-in-chief under Lincoln could not outgeneral the master tactician. Time and again Lee outmaneuvered Grant, and when the two armies came to grips with each other—in the horrifying Battle of the Wilderness, at Spotsylvania, at Cold Harbor—the Union's casualties totaled nearly 60,000 men, almost twice the Confederate losses. By mid-June Grant was moving his troops south of the James River to Petersburg, where he planned to cut Lee's transport to the south and attack Richmond from the rear. When Petersburg fought off the Union attacks, inflicting heavy Federal losses, Grant settled down to a long siege. It would last nine months. Meanwhile, strong Union attacks continued in the west.

*   *   *

Lincoln's strategy of exerting pressure on all fronts, combined with Grant's bulldog tactics, required a massive Northern effort in production, manpower, and transport—and called forth a forceful Southern response. Since the early months of the war, when men had first streamed to the colors on a three-month or (in the South) twelve-month basis, both commands had been struggling to keep their ranks filled. Facing threatened Yankee offensives in the spring of 1862, the Confederate Congress moved boldly to make all able-bodied white males between eighteen and thirty-five liable to military service for three years. Only a year later did the United States Congress pass a draft act, which made all men twenty to forty-five liable to military service, unless they paid a $300 commutation fee or found a substitute who would enlist for three years. These and later measures on both sides were heavily inegalitarian, allowing both Northerners who were wealthy enough and many Southerners with upper-class occupations—including the owner or overseer of any large plantation—to avoid the draft.

"A rich man's war and a poor man's fight," some had grumbled, and now they felt they had proof. To fight the war for the rich man—and even worse, for the "niggers" who were already taking jobs from whites—aroused muttering across the North. Nowhere did the first drawings catalyze feeling more than in the simmering working-class districts of Northern cities and the "secessionist" areas of the Midwest. In Manhattan, mobs of working people, mainly Irish, roamed the streets for four days, burning draft headquarters, pillaging homes, attacking Greeley's New York *Tribune* building, putting the Colored Orphan Asylum to the torch, and hunting down, torturing, and lynching blacks. Troops had to be brought in from the Gettysburg campaign to quell the riots.

"No measure of the war was a more stunning disappointment" than the North's conscription of 1863, Allan Nevins concluded. Inequitable and inefficient, the draft fostered a hive of bounty jumpers, substitute brokers, emigrant runners, collusive doctors. The draft act did, however, stimulate "volunteering," so, paradoxically, a small fraction of the Union army finally was supplied through this measure. In the South the draft met little open resistance, but as Confederate fortunes sagged, men took to the hills or woods instead of reporting, or hid with family or friends. Some Southerners contended that conscription was unconstitutional, a threat to personal liberty and states' rights, the very things they were fighting for. Several governors defied Richmond's efforts to enforce conscription within their borders. Still and all, both North and South mobilized an immense number of men—about a million and a half in the Union army, it is estimated, and almost a million in the Confederate.

To supply these men was, in some respects, an even more exacting task. Suddenly in 1861 there were hundreds of regiments to begin to equip— five hundred on the Union side alone. The records of a high quartermaster officer in the Army of the Potomac showed him, according to Nevins, "receipting within a short period for 39 barrels of coal, 7-1/2 tons of oats, 23 boxes of bandages, 31 of soap, 4 of lanterns, 80 beef cattle and 450 sheep, 180 mules, a miscellany of ropes, nails, rags, forges, lumber, and wagons, rolls of canvas, shipments of stoves, parcels of wire, 'sundries,' and sacks—how the army needed sacks!"

Despite enormous confusion, incompetence, and corruption, the rich agricultural North could easily supply such needs; by the end of 1864 Lincoln could report that the national resources "are, then, unexhausted, and, as we believe, inexhaustible." The economic expansion of the 1850s had laid the foundation for a factory as well as a farm spurt. A prime need was shoes, the things that armies literally travel on. By 1860 over 100,000 persons worked in the boot and shoe industry, in their homes or in factories where machines sewed the seams of the uppers, which were then sewn by hand, or pegged, to the sole. A Massachusetts inventor, Lyman Reed Blake, developed a machine to sew the soles to the uppers, then he traveled through New England teaching workers how to use it. Within two years of Sumter the new machines had stitched 2.5 million shoes. The Confederacy lagged behind, resulting in its troops often going bootless into battle— though Union men too, on occasion, had to march and fight without shoes.

Beset by the loss of Southern goods and markets and with swiftly changing needs, some Northern industries faltered early in the war, then experimented, improvised, and recovered. While cotton textiles declined, woolen mills hummed away, soon doubling production. Both iron and coal production dropped at first and then rose to the highest levels ever. Here again, the South fell behind badly. "The South lacked factories, raw materials, machines, managers who knew how to organize production, and skilled laborers," in T. Harry Williams's summation. "The largest ironwork in the section, and the only big installation of any kind, the Tredegar plant in Richmond, Virginia, had to operate at half or less of its capacity throughout the war because it could not procure sufficient supplies of pig iron," and because it was also short of trained workers.

The Northern munitions industries experimented and innovated as they expanded lustily. Armies and armories throughout the North and South had about half-a-million smoothbore muskets when Sumter fell, and 30,-000 or so rifles or rifled muskets. Immensely outproduced, Richmond was in many respects more innovative and daring than Washington in both spurring and undertaking war production. Needing desperately to make up for their industrial disadvantages, the Confederates centralized war production to a degree that would not be seen again until 1917. Their war and navy departments in Richmond directed rail traffic, spurred iron production, constructed ships—including twenty-two ironclads and an experimental submarine—and built up vast stocks of munitions. Even the home spinning of cloth by Southern women was coordinated by local quartermaster depots. Ironically, the Confederacy would run out of funds before it ran out of bullets.

With the Harpers Ferry armory lost when fighting began, the North had only its small federal establishment in Springfield, Massachusetts. A wild scramble for rifles on the part of competing states and armies produced a spate of orders for foreign arms and a burst of production at home. Slowly production was shifted from smoothbores to rifles, from the old muzzle-loaders to breech-loaders, from single-shot carbines to repeaters, amid much confusion, skepticism in the Ordnance Bureau, and wasted time. Artillery too was improved, but infantrymen on both sides often preferred their supporting gunners to use old-fashioned canister or grape that could mow down advancing enemy troops like a "huge sawed-off shotgun."

Moving these immense masses of men and munitions put enormous demands on boats, trains, and—all along the front—horses. After the lower Mississippi was cut off early in the war, river transport expanded to support the Union armies above Vicksburg, and west-east grain and other traffic grew so robustly that the Erie Canal carried a quarter more tonnage than in the feverish fifties. Ship builders at the same time were able to double their production of merchant tonnage for the high seas. At the other end of the long transport lines, quantities of horses were needed to draw wagon trains, ambulances, and artillery. By late 1862 the Army of the Potomac was receiving 1,500 horses a week and demanding more.

It was the iron horse, though, that most consequentially joined the colors, to a degree never before known in war. Despite all the other demands on iron and machinery, and despite the destruction of vast stretches of track in the South, the four years of war added 4,000 miles to the railroad network, though growth was slower than in the 1850s. Railroad men double-tracked major lines, built hundreds of bridges, standardized railroad gauges, fashioned efficient new terminals for transferring freight and passengers. Whole new railways were built, most notably the Atlantic & Great Western, which cut through Pennsylvania and Ohio to points west. Patriotism was not the only motive. "At no former period," Horace Greeley's *Tribune* noted, "has the whole Northern railroad system been so prosperous."

Nothing seemed to daunt the railroad builders. After the Confederates had destroyed a key bridge, Herman Haupt, a forty-five-year-old railroad genius, set to work to span Potomac Creek at top speed. Soldier-workmen labored in a bone-chilling rain. "While one crew hoisted and locked up the notched crib logs, others went into the dripping woods to cut and trim selected saplings and fetch the long poles to the bridge site," George Edgar Turner wrote. "Men, tools and time were too scarce to strip them of their bark. Above the cribs three stories of trestlework were to be erected. . . . At the second-story level of the trestle a new difficulty presented itself. Very few of the men had the ability or the courage to clamber about on the wet and slippery ropes so far above the rock-strewn bed of the gorge." Some men had to climb farther up to the eighty-foot level. But within two weeks the track was laid and the first engine pulled across inch by inch with ropes to see if the wooden crosspieces would hold up. They did.

Visiting the bridge, Lincoln seemed almost ecstatic. "That man Haupt has built a bridge across the Potomac Creek 400 feet long and nearly 100 feet high," he told war officials on returning to Washington. "Upon my word, gentlemen," he added, "there is nothing in it but beanpoles and cornstalks."

Men, matériel—and money. War's appetite for the last was as voracious as for manpower and munitions. Ultimately the war would cost the Confederacy $2 billion, the Union more than $3 billion—unimaginable figures at the start of the conflict. At war's outbreak, money seemed short everywhere: the federal government was running a deficit, the seceding states had tiny financial resources, businessmen north and south suffered from disrupted trade, and even private citizens lacked cash. By the end of 1861 Ralph Waldo Emerson was complaining that his plight was as hard as that of his fellow countrymen.

"The 1 January [1862] has found me in quite as poor plight as the rest of the Americans. Not a penny from my books since last June—which

usually yield 5, or $600.00 a year," he wrote his brother William. "The
Atlantic Bank omitting its dividends: My Mad River & Lake Erie Bonds
(Sandusky) which ought to pay $140. *per ann.* now for several years making
no sign. Lidian's Plymouth House now for 3 years has paid nothing and
still refuses. . . . Then lastly, almost all income from lectures has quite
ceased. . . ." They were economizing, and he was trying to sell a woodlot.
But better this "grinding" than any peace restoring the "old rottenness."

Expecting a short war, both Richmond and Washington had improvised
desperately during the first years of the struggle. Inexperienced in finance,
Chase had resorted to short-term funding, plunging into a huge loan
program and then into the issuance of greenbacks, as they would come to
be called, through the Legal Tender Act of February 1862. He opposed
the one device that would have permitted a pay-as-you-go strategy—heavy
income and excise taxation—and only strong congressional leadership had
produced by August of 1861 an income tax of 3 percent on incomes over
$800 and 5 percent over $10,000. Southern lawmakers, wary of general tax
measures, relied first on bond issues and then on the issuance of several
hundred millions in treasury notes—an invitation to soaring inflation.

By mid-1863 Northern finances had considerably improved, after extensive experimenting driven by iron necessity. Greenbacks steadily de-
preciated in value, but not nearly so much as Richmond's treasury notes.
The Confederate Congress at last passed a general tax bill, embracing an
8 percent sales tax on consumer goods, a 10 percent profits tax, and even
a graduated income tax, but these taxes were highly unpopular and poorly
enforced. In the North, by contrast, the income tax was producing almost
20 percent of total federal receipts, and manufacturers' and sales taxes
were bringing in even more, by the end of the war. Still, the Northern
public debt was heading toward almost $3 billion by mid-1865.

This colossal expansion virtually transformed the nation's finances. Before the war, operating in what Bray Hammond has called a "jungle" of
laissez-faire, 1,600 state banks circulated several thousand different kinds
of banknotes. But the old Jacksonian hostility toward a centralized banking
structure could not survive the heavy demands of near-total war. Early in
1863 Congress passed the National Bank Act, a vital first step toward a
national banking system. Backed, predictably, by most congressional
Republicans and opposed by virtually all the Democrats, the measure
provided for the chartering of national banks, with authority to issue bank
notes up to 90 percent of their United States bond holdings. Toward the
end of the war, Congress drove state banknotes out of circulation through
a 10 percent tax on them. Soon national far outnumbered state banks.

A spate of other national measures reached into people's lives to an

unprecedented degree. The 1862 Homestead Act granting citizens—virtually free—160 acres of surveyed public domain after five years of continuous residence; the Morrill Act giving each loyal state 30,000 acres for every
member of its congressional delegation in order to endow agricultural and
mechanical colleges; the Pacific Railway Acts authorizing a transcontinental railroad and providing huge grants of land for railroad rights-of-way;
a homestead bonus for soldiers—these and other measures, combined
with state and city actions, were propelled both by wartime necessity and
by private interests vigorously represented in the Capitol and White House
lobbies. For the first time—and it would be for only a short time—the
federal government became a presence in people's lives.

Few escaped the long reach of near-total war. Booming war industries
absorbed tens of thousands of immigrants still flooding into American
ports. Many thousands of women went to work in textile and other factories, hospitals, government offices, and Sanitary Commission projects in
the North. During the war, it is estimated, the proportion of women in the
manufacturing labor force—mainly textiles and garment-making—rose
from about a quarter to at least a third. As usual, women's wages lagged
behind men's. Toward the end of the war, a New York City woman using
a sewing machine and furnishing her own thread, working fourteen hours
a day, made 16 3/4 cents a day, while a male "common laborer" could
make $1.25.

To the newcomers threatening their jobs—especially to immigrants and
youths—white male workers reacted with fear and anger, all the more so
because of the sharp decline in real wages during the war. In the first heady
days, whole local unions of workers had gone off to war. "It having been
resolved to enlist with Uncle Sam for the war," the secretary of a Philadelphia local recorded in the minutes, "this union stands adjourned until
either the Union is safe or we are whipped." Later in the war, unionists
were marching off to picket lines as well. Some of their strikes helped white
males to keep ahead of inflation; a few were broken up by Union troops.

So feverish was much of the nation's activity during the war, both north
and south, that it spawned a grand myth: the Civil War as the economic
"takeoff," as the creator of a new industrial nation, as the "second American revolution," as indeed "a social war," in Charles Beard's words, "ending in the unquestioned establishment of a new power in the government,
making vast changes in the arrangement of classes, in the accumulation
and distribution of wealth, in the course of industrial development, and in
the Constitution inherited from the Fathers." More sober analysis has
shown that the war brought mixed and uneven development. Some economic activity was spurred, some depressed; some people's earnings—

especially makers of war goods—rose, those of others dropped; some moneylenders prospered, most did not. On the whole, industrial capitalists thrived, finance capitalists suffered, from wartime inflation. The great decade of innovation and expansion had been that of the 1850s; in the sixties the war brought relatively few key technological advances, uneven expansion of production, but in some cases—such as boots and shoes—rapid mechanization, often involving interchangeability of parts.

Yet, about halfway through the war, the nation seemed to pass from one economic and social watershed to another. By this time—mid-1863—soldiers by the hundreds of thousands were mixing with men of different origins, backgrounds, religions; the public's attention was riveted on a national effort as never before; newspapers were giving more attention to far-off battle actions than local dogfights. The mystic chords of union were being fashioned along the endless supply lines and battle lines, north and south. Sections of the economy were being accelerated, modernized, consolidated, if not revolutionized. Change was both slow and dynamic, always uneven and chaotic. The Confederacy experimented with various forms of state control, the North encouraged or permitted extremes of laissez-faire, including extensive private-enterprise trading across enemy lines. Perhaps if one word, *improvisation,* sums up the national effort during the first half of the war, *mobilization* sums up the second—a social and economic mobilization that had its roots in the 1850s and before, and its chief impact during the stupendous economic expansion that would come in the North after the war.

Just as old soldiers chinning in veterans' halls would later argue which campaign or strategy had been decisive, so historians have searched for the decisive causal forces in Southern indomitableness and final Northern success. In the seamless web of history, every effort was critical. Yet some factors are more critical than others, and the supreme paradox of the Civil War is that agriculture was probably most critical. The economy was still founded on agriculture; no sector of the economy was not linked in some way with agriculture. Farm boys provided much of the soldiery on both sides, and countless farm women took their places in the fields. Farm products were still the main source of vitally needed foreign revenue. The great canal and railroad networks had been shaped to meet agricultural needs. And if agriculture was decisive positively in the North, it was negatively so in the South. The shortage of farm labor was more acute there. Unlike his Northern counterpart, the Southern farmer found labor-saving machinery cut off; so were his outlets to Europe as the Northern blockade tightened.

While the war was becoming increasingly a mobilization of men, money, machinery, and munitions, to an astonishing degree it was finally won and lost on the grain fields of the North and the cotton fields of the South.

THE SOCIETY OF THE BATTLEFIELD

As for his spirits, Private John N. Moulton wrote his sister from his camp near Vicksburg early in 1863, "I cannot Boast of their being very high. There is the most down cast looking set of men here that I ever saw in my life. . . ." Six weeks later he felt no better. "I am lonesome and down hearted in Spite of my Self. I am tired of Blood Shed and have Saw Enough of it."

A soldier in Nashville reflected bitterly, "When we Enthusiastically rushed into the ranks at our Country's call, we all Expected to witness the last dying struggles of treason and Rebellion Ere this." But his hopes had been dashed. "Over 200,000 of our noble soldiers sleep in the silent grave. Almost countless millions of treasure has been Expended in the Unsuccessful Effort of the Government to put down this Rebellion. But after all this sacrifice of valuable life and money, we are no nearer the goal . . . than we were at the first booming of Sumter's guns."

From a camp opposite Fredericksburg, M. N. Collins, a Maine officer, wrote: "The newspapers say that the army is eager for another fight; it is false; there is not a private in the army that would not rejoice to know that no more battles were to be fought. They are heartily sick of battles that produce no results."

Soldiers railed against their leaders. The men, said Moulton, were beginning "to talk openly and to curse the officers and leaders and if the[y] go much farther I fear for the result. they are pretty well divided and nothing But fear keeps them under. . . ." Wrote a Maine soldier stationed in Virginia just before Christmas 1862, "All though I am wel and able to do duty I am in a very unhapy state of mind." His "delusive fantom of hope" had at last vanished. "The great cause of liberty has been managed by Knaves and fools the whole show has ben corruption, the result disaster, shame and disgrace." He was always ready to do his duty but "evry thing looks dark, not becaus the south are strong but becaus our leaders are incompitent and unprincipled." A Massachusetts private wrote of "incompetent leaders & ambitious politicians."

What were they fighting for? For Union and patriotism, but this did not seem enough. Lincoln's Emancipation Proclamation did not help most white soldiers. He was thoroughly tired of the war, a Pennsylvanian wrote in February 1863, and if he had known that the issue would become freeing the slaves, as it seemed to have become, he "would not have mingled with the dirty job." An Illinois soldier belittled the Administration's yielding to radicals favoring emancipation and Negro recruiting: "I have slept on the soft side of a board, in the mud & every other place that was lousy & dirty . . . drunk out of goose ponds, Horse tracks &c for the last 18 months, all for the poor nigger, and I have yet to see the first one that I think has been benefited by it." Other soldiers' comments on emancipation were even harsher.

If most Southern soldiers were fighting against emancipation, and few Northern men fully supported it, black people north and south were enlisted in the struggle, and on both sides. The drain of white manpower to the front made Southern agriculture heavily dependent on slave labor, while nearly 180,000 former slaves enlisted in the Union armies. Organized into separate "Colored" regiments officered mostly by whites, the black soldiers appeared to suffer fewer morale problems than whites— doubtless because they saw their stake in the outcome more clearly. "When God made me, I wasn't much," one black recruit said, "but I's a man now."

Many white soldiers desperately sought a way out. Some shot off their toes or trigger fingers, until discharges were no longer given to self-maimers. Others hoped for a compromise peace, any kind of peace that would enable them to go home. Even in his regiment, out only five months, wrote a Massachusetts man, "I don't believe there are twenty men but are heartily sick of war & want to go home." Wrote the Nashville soldier: "Many of the boys here are in favor of a Compromise, some are of the opinion that the Southern Confederacy will soon be recognized by the U.S. Alas! for our beloved Republic!"

Just about the time this Yankee in Nashville was exhibiting his brand of defeatism, a Confederate soldier from Alabama was displaying his. "If the soldiers were allowed to settle the matter," John Crittenden wrote his wife, "peace would be made in short order." On the average, Confederate spirits were probably a bit higher than Unionist, but from the early flush days of martial ardor and Southern pride, morale fell as the months and years passed. A Georgian home on sick leave wrote his brother that if he did not receive a third extension of his furlough he would stay home anyway. "There is no use fighting any longer no how," he wrote, "for we are done gon up the Spout the Confederacy is done whiped it is useless to deny it any longger." The men from North Carolina, another Georgian wrote his wife from his post with Lee's army, were threatening to rejoin the Union and "the men from Ga say that if the enemy invade Ga they are going home. . . ." Perhaps the worst blows to Confederate morale came from wives' letters telling of hunger and cold at home.

How to persuade such men to reenlist when their terms expired? President Davis and other leaders visited the camps to boost morale. Grand parades and even sham battles were held, patriotic speeches intoned. While a conscription law was ultimately passed, compelling reenlistment, some officers wanted to carry on the spirit of volunteerism. A favorite stratagem, Bell Wiley found, was to assemble men for dress parade, deliver a patriotic speech, move the Stars and Bars up a few paces ahead, and then urge all the patriots in the ranks to step up to the colors and reenlist for the duration. Few could resist such blandishments—but many regretted their action later.

On both sides it was the wretched life in camp, rather than the days of combat, that crushed soldierly spirit. For most soldiers the Civil War was both an organized and a disorganized bore. Days of dull routine, during which the men could at least build tiny nests of creature comforts, were punctuated by sudden and often inexplicable departures, followed usually by long marches to a new camp and the old tedium. Rain was the enemy —rain that seeped through tent sides and shed roofs, turned campgrounds into quagmires, penetrated every boot and uniform. A Union colonel, John Beatty, recited the daily routine of his camp—and of all camps: reveille at five, breakfast call at six, surgeon's call at seven, drill at eight, recall at eleven, dinner at twelve, drill again at four, recall at five, guard mounting at five-thirty, first call for dress parade at six, second call at six-thirty, tattoo at nine, taps at nine-thirty. "So the day goes round."

Soldiers occupied their spare hours in time-honored ways: grumbling, gambling, sleeping, reading, foraging, cleaning equipment, washing clothes. Confederate men, it was said, had a special love for singing. Eating was another diversion, but not a very pleasant one. During the early years of the war, soldiers lived mainly on the old army ration of salt pork or beef, hard bread or hardtack, coffee, dried peas or beans, and in the South, grits. Hardtack was a grim joke; it could hardly be broken by teeth or hand, and was best mastered by soaking in soup or water. Especially in the North, as the Union commissary became better organized, the old rations were supplemented with vegetables and fruit. After authorities sent appeals throughout the Northwest for food to prevent scurvy, hundreds of barrels of vegetables, jellies, and dried fruit were soon on their way down the Mississippi to Grant's regiments. Both Yanks and Rebs lived off the country, picking berries in season, stealing from orchards and gardens, buying from the ever-present sutlers. Cooking was often improvised.

Improvising, indeed, was the test of the good soldier—resourcefulness in adjusting to new conditions, ingeniously rigging up devices for keeping warm, cooking food, procuring clean water, washing clothes, warding off insects. He was a jack-of-all-trades, mending his clothes, tending to horses, cutting wood, digging fortifications, rigging up shelters, keeping his rifle clean by greasing it with a piece of bacon. Sometimes he had to rise to heights of inventiveness, as when Pennsylvania volunteers ran an entire mining operation, from surveying the ground to setting the charges, or when other infantrymen—mostly landlubbers—took over an enemy river-boat and ran it.

The army, above all, was a school for practical affairs, where men learned the arts of survival through organization, self-discipline, leadership, fol-lowership, collective and cooperative effort. The war had an immense nationalizing and homogenizing impact, bringing together not only West-erners and Easterners but farmers and industrial workers, teachers and storekeepers, college students and common laborers. The war was a geog-raphy lesson in which men from Maine occupied islands off Texas, men from Florida marched through the fields of Pennsylvania, men from New Orleans discovered snow and snowballs. The war was a regional exchange in which accents, attitudes, habits collided, coexisted, even coalesced. To a degree the war was a leveling process, though racial and class conflicts persisted and occasionally erupted. Ultimately habits and outlooks were reshaped that would prove indispensable in the organization of the na-tion's industrial and financial life in later years. Future workshops of peace were being shaped in the workshops of war.

*   *   *

Well before dawn, sergeants roused men lying in tents and hutments or in the open. Soldiers stumbled about in the dark as they choked down hardtack, collected their rifles, buckled on their cartridge boxes. Slowly, in thick underbrush, in ravines, out on open fields, men came into forma-tions, answered roll calls, made contact with flanking units. Behind, can-nons began to rumble, firing into the darkness ahead. Men waited, fear collecting in their stomachs.

As dawn broke, officers galloped along the lines. They wheeled about to bring regiments in line, paused to exhort the soldiers standing with rifles at the ready: "Do your duty today like brave men." Then the com-mand: "Load at will—load." The roar of battle mounted, sweeping down the lines like the rush of thundershowers across the hard ground of a stubble field, a soldier remembered.

Then the command to attack. The infantrymen moved out, at first almost perfectly dressed as officers and noncoms ranged back and forth, herding them like sheep. Soldiers' hearts strengthened as they marched onto the field of battle and saw endless formations of their comrades to the left and right, moving, as one noted, in great billowing waves, their gun barrels and bayonets shining like burnished steel.

It was after watching such a scene as this at Fredericksburg—in the rear, row after row of artillery spurting flame and smoke, columns of thick black smoke rising far up into the sky, "the massed formations of more than a hundred thousand infantry," in Nevins's words, their uniforms and rifles glistening in the sun, with "endless orderly parks of white-topped wagons and ambulances" behind—that Lee remarked to General James Long-street, "It is well that war is terrible, or we would grow too fond of it."

As the attackers marched toward the enemy and fell, officers continued to dress the lines in order to keep contact and intensify the shock effect on the foe. As enemy fire intensified and the attacking lines broke, officers organized short rushes and little flanking attacks. Rarely did men get close enough to use the bayonet. Under withering fire soldiers crawled into holes, pulled back in panic, disappeared in the smoke and dust of battle. Panting, cursing, shouting, their faces caked with sweat and grime, men cried out to one another, but few words could be heard in the inferno of gunfire, cannon roar, whinnying horses, shrieks and groans of wounded men. Soon the battle broke down into numberless tiny encounters in the dust and smoke, without apparent shape or meaning. "Nobody sees a battle," a soldier reflected.

In this hell the rifleman was king. Heavy artillery usually failed to soften up defenses—though small pieces on the line spewing out canister could be effective, and cavalry attacks were dramatic and might turn an enemy's flank. But nothing could substitute for the foot soldier. He did not feel like a king, except that as the struggle swayed back and forth, he tried to build a tiny realm of his own by scooping out a shallow hole or kneeling behind a tree. Here he had a chance to rearm his muzzle-loader by pulling a paper-wrapped cartridge from his box or pouch, tearing open the paper with his teeth, pouring the powder down the barrel and pushing a bullet after it, punching both down with his ramrod, then half-cocking the hammer, put-ting a percussion cap on the nipple, cocking the hammer, aiming, firing. Most of this he might do while lying on his back, amid the whine of bullets.

By evening the once-virgin fields, now reeking of the stink and smoke of battle, were littered with discarded rifles, cartridge boxes, knapsacks, mess kits, canteens, parts of uniforms—were strewn also with dead and wounded men and stricken horses. The only sign of earlier formations might lie in the disposition of the dead; at Gettysburg a Confederate officer was sickened to find seventy-nine of his comrades "laying dead in a straight line . . . perfectly dressed . . . the feet of all these dead men were in a perfectly straight line," though some had fallen forward and some back.

Through the night, wounded men begged piteously for water and succor. But help to the wounded was slow to come, and heavy-handed when it did. Battlefield treatment was chaotic, according to McPherson. "Regimental musicians (many of them younger than eighteen), cooks, teamsters, and other noncombatants were detailed as stretcher-bearers; and civilians were frequently employed as ambulance drivers. More often than not, these men and boys bolted in panic when the fighting became hot, leaving the wounded to lie untended for hours or days." But nothing could match the torment awaiting those who needed surgery. Amid flickering candles in borrowed wagon sheds or cow barns, men lay on stretchers or on the floor, the cut, maimed, and dying mixed together, some with open wounds covered with flies or maggots, some crying "help" or "doctor" or "God," others silent but following the doctors' movements with their pleading eyes. Off to the side stood the surgeons, their gowns and bare arms soaked in blood, cutting and sawing away flesh and bone, as assistants held the patients down and applied ether, chloroform, or whiskey. To the side lay little piles of fingers, feet, legs, arms.

Gangrene often developed from battlefield conditions, infected instruments, pus-stained coats, sheets, surgical silk. Even with all these battlefield deaths, however, twice as many soldiers died of diseases as in battle. Camp conditions were often atrocious—bad water and food, mosquitoes, poor sanitation. Flies and rats abounded. Soldiers relieved themselves in an open trench or a few feet from their tents. Knowing little if anything about bacteria, officers and men allowed garbage, slops, refuse, horse manure to pile up around camps. Men would go weeks without changing their clothes or even bathing. Countrymen suffered more from illness than city boys, evidently because the latter had already been exposed to more diseases, and the death rate from disease was almost twice as high among black soldiers as white.

Soldiers' health improved toward the end of the war, but far more in the North than in the South. The key to this difference was the work of the United States Sanitary Commission, and central to the Commission was the work of women. No mere "sanitation" agency but a huge national effort embracing thousands of local auxiliaries and led by men of such diverse talents as Henry W. Bellows and Frederick L. Olmsted, the Commission raised millions of dollars, recruited nurses and doctors for army hospitals, bought and distributed huge quantities of food, clothing, and medicine, staffed and operated hospital boats and trains—and taught soldiers why and how to use latrines and purify water. Organized in the teeth of hostility from some of the "old army" functionaries but applauded in Congress and in the ranks, the Commission led in the modernization and vast extension of the hospital and ambulance system and in the appointment of an outstanding Surgeon General, William A. Hammond.

Inspired by the dauntless Florence Nightingale of the Crimean War—a bloodletting in which the ratio of disease to battle deaths was four to one—American women brooked male and female hostility, army bureaucracy, and the dangers of hospital life to bring both professionalism and compassion to the care of sick and wounded. Over 3,000 women served as army nurses in the North, despite an edict by the first head of female nurses, Dorothea Dix, longtime reformer of insane asylums, barring all applicants for nursing who were under thirty and not "plain of appearance." While slave women served in Southern army hospitals from the start, the Confederacy was slow to authorize women nurses. Roman Catholic Sisters of Charity trained a host of nurses for the Northern army.

Women worked in general hospitals and—more glamorously and dangerously—in field hospitals just behind the front. Eliza Howland helped convert the Patent Office in Washington into an improvised general hospital. Women nurses and their aides made beds out of large tables, spreading mattresses also on the floors, amid glass cases filled with patent churns, cogwheels, waterwheels, clocks, and mousetraps. Provisions had to be hoisted up outside the building, and Washingtonians gaped at baskets of vegetables and huge chunks of bread creeping up the marble face of the building. Inside, on a Sunday afternoon, Eliza Howland nursed a soldier through a delirium during which he called her Betty—"and, to our surprise, got well, went home, and at once married the Betty we had saved him for."

If soldiers north and south feared anything more than becoming wounded, it was being taken prisoner—unless it was being wounded *and* captured. All the usual miseries of poor sanitation and shortages of food, shelter, and medicine were compounded in the prisoner-of-war camps. About 15 percent (30,000 men) of the Union prisoners died in their foe's camps, about 12 percent of the Confederates. Part of this difference was due to declining Confederate supplies during the course of the war. Exchanges of prisoners ran up against fierce Southern opposition to treating black Federals as prisoners of war; rather, Richmond warned, they would be turned over to state authorities for possible execution. Toward the end of the war, however, exchanges mounted to almost a thousand a day, and the desperate Confederacy began to enlist slaves in its own armies.

Lurid tales of prison conditions north and south inflamed passions on both sides. Thirteen thousand Union men died of exposure, malnutrition, disease, and neglect at the most notorious prison, Andersonville. Mainly, though, prison life was nasty, dull, brutish, and long. There were occasional moments of hope, even euphoria. Union soldiers in Libby Prison in Richmond had been thrown into despair on hearing from their jailers that the Confederates had won a great victory at Gettysburg. Then a black man bringing in food whispered that in fact the Union had won, leaving the enemy scattered. As the joyful word raced around the room, prisoners leaped to their feet in a paroxysm of delight, shouting and embracing one another. Chaplain Charles McCabe had read Julia Ward Howe's new "Battle Hymn of the Republic" in the *Atlantic Monthly*. Raising his powerful voice, he began:

Mine eyes have seen the glory of the coming of the Lord:
He is trampling out the vintage where the grapes of wrath are stored;
He hath loosed the fateful lightning of his terrible swift sword:
His truth is marching on.

Men were joining in the chorus, faces aglow as McCabe rendered the mighty lines: the "fiery gospel writ in burnished rows of steel . . . sifting out the hearts of men before his judgment seat . . . Oh! be swift, my soul, to answer Him! be jubilant, my feet." Then:

In the beauty of the lilies Christ was born across the sea,
With a glory in His bosom that transfigures you and me:
As He died to make men holy, let us die to make men free,
While God is marching on.

"Let Us Die to Make Men Free"

By mid-1864, with Grant's and Lee's troops locked in tortured embrace around Petersburg, audacious generals on both sides broke loose elsewhere for spectacular forays.

Hoping to take some of the pressure off the Northern siege of his Richmond-Petersburg bastion, Lee had sent his fellow Virginian, General Jubal A. Early, into the Shenandoah Valley, where Early routed a Union army and found his way open to the North—and Washington. Breaking through light Federal defensive forces, Early with 14,000 hardened troops crossed the Potomac and neared the northwest defenses of the Union capital. On an appeal from Lincoln, Grant dispatched a heavy force to drive the invaders out of the area; the President himself rode out to watch the impending battle and came briefly under fire. But Early, like a cool fox, retired with his strength largely intact, after levying a $220,000 tribute on Hagerstown and Frederick and burning Chambersburg when its citizens refused to cough up half-a-million. Appointed to a new Shenandoah com-

mand, General Philip Sheridan caught up with Early's forces in the early
fall, striking severe blows, and then proceeded to carry out Grant's orders
to ravage the Shenandoah.

On May Day 1864 another general who preferred dash and maneuver,
William Sherman, had stood poised five hundred miles southwest of Richmond behind a steep ridge twenty-five miles below Chattanooga, facing a
smaller army under Joseph Johnston. Suddenly Sherman struck, not at the
strongly entrenched Confederates but around them. There followed one
of the most masterly campaigns in the history of war. Manipulating three
armies as lightly as bayonets, feinting Johnston out of position, cutting
back from right to left to center to right again, sideslipping around the
enemy's flanks but never too far from the little single-track railroad that
meandered toward Atlanta, Sherman repeatedly forced Johnston to fall
back toward the key economic and political center of Georgia. By mid-July,
Sherman's men were nearing the capital.

Furious over Johnston's retreats, fearful that this Confederate general,
with whom he had long feuded, would give up Atlanta without a real fight,
Jefferson Davis sacked him and named a more aggressive commander,
John Bell Hood, thirty-three years old and already half crippled from
earlier battles, to hold the line. Hood struck forcefully at Sherman's approaching columns, but to no avail. Soon Union troops enveloped Atlanta
by swinging fifteen miles to the south of it, and occupied this key hub. But
now it was Sherman's turn to be frustrated. Although Sherman wired
Washington, "So Atlanta is ours, and fairly won," Hood managed to keep
his force intact and eventually moved north of Atlanta, where he threatened Sherman's railroad line. By early fall it seemed to many in the North
that Sherman was as tied down in the Atlanta area as Grant was in Petersburg.

But the view from Richmond was far from sanguine. Grant's and
Meade's troops were being held east of Petersburg—they had blown a
tremendous hole in the Confederate lines with four tons of gunpowder,
only to bungle their attempt to rush through the breach—but the men in
blue were slowly edging their way across Lee's communication lines south
of the city. The Union blockade of Southern ports grew ever tighter.
Inflation raged throughout the South; civilian morale sank; the men in gray
lacked clothing, food, even shoes. By September President Davis admitted
that two-thirds of his soldiers were absent, most of them "without leave."
Davis was threatening the vaunted liberties of his countrymen by stepping
up suspensions of habeas corpus, and shocking them by proposing the
arming of slaves.

And in the major cities, the endless trains arrived bearing the dead and dying and wounded. Mary Chesnut was now back in her native state of South Carolina and worked mornings in the Columbia hospital. She could hardly stand the sight of the "loathsome wounds, distortion, stumps of limbs exhibited to all and not half cured." But she marveled at the men's spirit. When she told one soldier, his arm taken off at the socket, that he should quit the army, he flared: "I am First Texas. If old Hood can go with one foot, I can go with one arm. Eh?"

Nor could Lincoln in the White House escape the anguish of war. Day after day onto wharfs along the Potomac, boats disgorged the walking, tottering wounded, followed by men carrying pine coffins or stiff forms under sheets. There they were swallowed up among throngs of anguished relatives, ambulance men and volunteer nurses, undertakers looking for business. From the river and from the train stations, ambulances carried the wounded to a dozen or so makeshift hospitals, where nurses and surgeons waited. One of the volunteers was Louisa May Alcott, working in an old Georgetown hotel. Like Mary Chesnut, she was repelled by the running, pus-ridden wounds and the amputations without ether, but she carried on. Walt Whitman wrote his mother about the soldiers broken down after years of exposure and bad food and water. "O it is terrible, & getting worse, worse, worse."

Thin, gaunt, his face deeply lined and his eyes shadowed, Lincoln himself seemed one of the casualties of war by the summer of 1864. This fourth year of the war had been expected to be a time of culmination for the President and his cause, but it had turned out a period of dashed hopes, frustration, war weariness, and widespread gloom. Lincoln had a special anxiety—this was an election year. Not a single respected voice had been raised against the fantastic notion that the people should actually pass judgment on their commander-in-chief—should fire or rehire him—at the height of a war for survival. Certainly Lincoln, a republican to the core, would not have dreamed of it. Still, by late 1864, it seemed likely that he would lose the battle of the ballots if not that of the bullets—so likely, indeed, that the President himself took out a sheet of stationery late in August and wrote: "This morning, as for some days past, it seems exceedingly probable that this Administration will not be re-elected. Then it will be my duty to so co-operate with the President elect, as to save the Union between the election and the inauguration; as he will have secured his election on such ground that he can not possibly save it afterwards." Thus Lincoln was reaffirming a noble democratic idea—peaceful transfer of power to the succession, even a hostile succession.

Was it conceivable, though, that a President at the height of his powers —a commander-in-chief who seemed finally to be winning the war though still losing some battles, the leader who embodied Northern hopes and expectations—that this man could lose an election in which the old southern bastion of the opposition Democratic party could not even vote? The fact that Lincoln was a masterly operator of the governmental and party machinery only sharpened the question.

Lincoln's political management was based on the strategy of balance, in which he alone acted as master balancer. He had built a Cabinet and Administration in which radicals were counterpoised against moderates. When that balance threatened to collapse during the dark days of late 1862, the President had secured letters of resignation from both Secretary of State Seward and Treasury Secretary Chase, and then retained both Cabinet members, exclaiming to a friend, "I can ride now. I've got a pumpkin in each end of my bag." Foes of the Secretary of State continued to arouse public pressure against him by gaining signatures for petitions demanding "reconstruction of the cabinet," but Lincoln fended them off. He had just the balance he wanted in his official family.

The President strove for this balance throughout his Administration. He pitted general against general, governors of border states against radical senators, party faction against faction, congressional bloc against bloc, border states against the "Solid North." He coached his subordinates on being balancers themselves, instructing a new general that if either both local political factions "or neither shall abuse you, you will probably be about right. Beware of being assailed by one and praised by the other." He used patronage and other presidential resources expertly to maintain the balance. He knew how to be ambiguous when need be; he knew how to time his actions, waiting for political forces to become identifiable and measurable before striking. He knew how to slow down, taking one problem at a time. He was a political acrobat, proceeding step by step along a swaying tightrope, balancing a pole along which danced politicians, generals, lobbyists, officials, businessmen.

Nowhere was Lincoln's managerial touch more delicate than in foreign policy. In the first year of the war, after Navy captain Charles Wilkes stopped the British mail steamer *Trent* on the high seas and seized two Confederate envoys on their way to Europe, the President had given a conciliatory reply to a British demand for an apology, amid an anti-British uproar throughout the North. Lincoln was not about to war on the South and on Britain at the same time. Rather, he concentrated on his key objective—persuading Britain and France not to recognize or aid the Confederacy. Lincoln's policy began to pay off within a few months of Union victories at Vicksburg and Gettysburg. The British government forbade Confederate "Laird rams"—floating fortresses with formidable wrought-iron "piercers"—under construction in Liverpool to leave that port, and Napoleon III ordered several naval vessels under construction for Richmond to be sold to European governments. By 1864, as Union fortunes rose, Confederate hopes for foreign recognition faded.

So, as a practical manager of captains and kings, of ships and shoes and cabbages and many other things, Abraham Lincoln had shown endless dexterity and persistence. Hence it was all the more remarkable that the President by 1864 had lost the confidence of some key leaders in his own party. The "most striking thing is the absence of personal loyalty to the President," Richard Henry Dana reported earlier from Washington. "He has no admirers, no enthusiastic supporters, none to bet on his head." Republican critics, David Donald was to note, called the President unfit, a political coward, a dictator, timid and ignorant, pitiable, too slow, uneducated, dazed, utterly foolish. Many important Republican leaders, Donald found—Chase, Sumner, Greeley, Thaddeus Stevens, Thurlow Weed, among others—doubted the advisability of a second term for Lincoln.

The criticisms came from all sides and often were mutually inconsistent. Some flayed the President for being ignorant of economics, diplomacy, the military arts; others for meddling too much. Some wanted a stronger hand on the tiller, others charged tyranny. Charles Francis Adams, Lincoln's minister in London, called Jefferson Davis "in some respects superior to our President." Fierce criticism erupted not only from Peace Democrats and War Democrats, but from radical Republicans. To them, Lincoln's resourcefulness was feckless improvisation, his deliberateness was indecision and drift, his balancing sheer juggling. Above all, they differed with Lincoln over postwar reconstruction—especially over his plan to recognize Southern state governments as soon as 10 percent of the 1860 electorate took the oath and the state agreed to emancipate; and when Lincoln pocket-vetoed the Wade-Davis Bill embodying their own plan of requiring a *majority* of each state electorate to take an oath of *past* as well as future loyalty, the radicals' hostility rose to white heat.

Above all, Republican leaders feared losing office. Could a man in Lincoln's political straits win both nomination and reelection? The ease with which the President dominated the Republican presidential convention in Baltimore in June was a revealing indication of the reach of his balancing and managing skills. So adroitly had he handled the considerable patronage at his disposal, so delicately had he steered through intrastate factional politics, that Lincoln easily headed off booms for Chase and for the colorful and controversial general Ben Butler. More threatening had been a radical thrust behind General John C. Frémont, the 1856 Republican candidate; the President parried this by favoring a platform plank that called for continuing the war until the South's "unconditional surrender." Almost as easily as he won his own renomination, Lincoln put through the vice-presidential nomination of Andrew Johnson, his military governor in Tennessee, a stalwart Unionist and War Democrat.

The choice of Johnson symbolized Lincoln's strategy of a Unionist coalition against the Democrats. In typical major-party fashion the Democrats, convening in Chicago late in August, tried a different kind of coalition—a War Democrat running on a peace platform calling for cessation of the war "with a view to an ultimate convention." The Democrats chose a formidable candidate in General George B. McClellan, still a hero to many Northerners, but he was fatally compromised by a platform that, in the view of the Richmond *Examiner*, "floats between peace and war." It did not help the general that Clement Vallandigham, the notorious Ohio leader of the "Copperheads," as Peace Democrats were called by their foes, had made his way back into the North via Canada after Lincoln had banished him to the Confederacy. In vain did the general shift from his "peace before reunion" position to reunion as a *condition* for peace. The Northern voters had moved ahead of him.

Lincoln's popular-vote victory in the fall, 2.2 to 1.8 million, resulted from a number of factors beyond his control—the absence of the Southern states, the grass-roots strength of his party, the tendency of voters to coalesce behind their leadership during wartime. His victory also was due to a number of forces over which he had partial control: his selection of Grant, the military mobilization of the country, and the exhilarating September announcement that Atlanta at last had fallen. Not least was victory due to the willingness of the commander-in-chief and his generals to grant soldiers timely furloughs by the tens of thousands, enabling them to cast a vote that all knew would be heavily pro-Lincoln.

But beyond all this, Lincoln won a victory over himself greater than his victory over McClellan. All his life a unionist who had put the Union before every other issue, including emancipation, he had come to realize that union could not be an end in itself but must be a crucial means to the nobler ends of liberty and equality. "From 1861 to 1865," McPherson says, "Lincoln had moved steadily to the left: from limited war to total war; from gradual, compensated emancipation to immediate, universal abolition; from opposition to the arming of blacks to enthusiastic support for it, . . . from the colonization of freed slaves to the enfranchisement of black soldiers and literate blacks." From union first and *then* emancipation, to union *and* emancipation and indeed union *for* emancipation—that was Lincoln's supreme strategic shift.

Perhaps Lincoln's finest moment as a leader came during his darkest hour, about the time he expressed the August surmise that he probably would not be reelected. Henry J. Raymond, chairman of the Republican National Committee and editor of the *New York Times,* had urged him to appoint a commission to offer Richmond peace on the sole condition of reunion, with all other issues—notably slavery—to be settled afterward. Sorely tempted, the President drafted a letter in effect feeling out Jefferson Davis on reunion, with the slavery question to be adjusted later. But Lincoln never sent the letter nor appointed the commission. Such a move, he decided, would be bad politically, for it would alienate antislavery Republicans but, even more, it would be wrong morally, for it would violate the "solemn promise" of the Emancipation Proclamation.

So, in the end, when all his famed political wiles had won him the support of his party, it was his capacity to transcend bargaining and brokerage and to embrace a politico-military strategy, to stick with it, to find the right men to carry it out, and to win with it, that characterized Lincoln's leadership. A fox by training and instinct, in the end he rose to the stature of Herodotus's hedgehog which knew one big thing—and of Machiavelli's lion that could command followers and frighten wolves.

*   *   *

Once again fortune seemed to favor the bold. Hardly were all the election returns in when Sherman struck from Atlanta toward the sea. He had won the reluctant consent of Grant to conduct a campaign that shocked the orthodox military mind as even madder than the Vicksburg gamble. Convinced that his armies must crush the Confederates' morale and economy in order to make them "sick of war" for generations to come, Sherman would cram his soldiers' knapsacks with rations, restrict his regiments to one wagon each, cut his troops loose from their Atlanta base, and march two hundred miles toward Savannah on the coast, in a campaign of total war. And this is precisely what he did, after leaving General George Thomas to hold Hood northwest of Atlanta. Cutting a swath sixty miles wide, Sherman's men engulfed military stores, cotton gins, farms, factories, warehouses, railroads, all the time foraging, burning, pillaging, destroying. By the new year, 1865, they were consolidating their position on the sea. Then Sherman turned north to rampage through South Carolina.

By Lincoln's second Inaugural Day on March 4, the Confederacy lay prostrate, cleft in two places but still fighting valiantly, its armies, always semi-autonomous, protecting their state bastions. The Union blockade was still tightening, especially after Admiral David Farragut's defiance of Confederate torpedoes and his dramatic sortie into Mobile Bay the previous August, and the closing of the key North Carolina port of Wilmington in February. Thomas had virtually destroyed Hood's army in Tennessee. Sherman's men were roaring through South Carolina, leaving Columbia in flames, capturing Charleston intact, making "Sherman neckties" out of rails by heating them over bonfires and wrapping them around trees. As Sherman drove northward, closing in on Johnston's defense forces, Lee tried to break through Grant's besieging army by attacking east of Petersburg. After an initial penetration his drive failed. The men in gray could still hold off the men in blue when on equal terms, but now the Union forces had such overwhelming numbers that they could check the Confederates on a broad front and still send powerful forces around the flanks.

Cornered, General Lee slipped out of Petersburg and Richmond toward the west, with 35,000 men, in a desperate effort to link up with Johnston's forces to the south. Grant's 80,000 men followed in hot pursuit, with General Philip Sheridan's cavalry and mobile infantry corps racing on Lee's left to prevent him from turning south. In a sharp engagement Lee lost 7,000 men captured, with minimal Federal casualties. "My God, has the Army dissolved?" Lee exclaimed as he watched the action. By now his hopes had, and his supply lines were cut. On April 9, he met Grant at Appomattox Courthouse.

It was a poignant encounter between the two adversaries, Lee with dress sword and red sash, Grant in faded campaign blouse and muddy boots—two old soldiers who had met during the Mexican War but not seen each other since. Because Grant would offer only terms of surrender and Lee knew he had no choice, the parley went smoothly, except when Lee asked that his cavalrymen and artillerists be permitted to keep their horses, which they owned. Grant demurred; only officers, he said, were allowed to keep their "private property" under the terms. Then he relented, reflecting that most of the men in the ranks were small farmers who would need their horses to put their spring crops in.

News of the meeting sped through both armies. Some on both sides disbelieved that Lee had actually surrendered. Said a Union colonel who had fought in Virginia for three years, "I had a sort of impression that we should fight him all our lives."

Grant telegraphed Lincoln: "General Lee surrendered the Army of Northern Virginia this morning." The President and Stanton threw their arms around each other; the austere Secretary of War, someone reported, "was trotting about in exhilarated joy." The booming of guns aroused Washingtonians in the morning. Newspapers appeared with huge headlines. Welles wrote in his diary, "Guns are firing, bells ringing, flags flying, men laughing, children cheering, all, all are jubilant." Lincoln had a few days of celebration as he spoke to hundreds gathered around the White

House, turned his thoughts to reconstruction, granted some pardons and reprieves, joyously greeted General Grant, and had him meet with the Cabinet. The President had never seemed more cheerful than on that day of the Cabinet meeting. His son Robert was back after serving on Grant's staff; the President and First Lady planned to attend the theater in the evening. It was Good Friday, April 14.

The next day telegraph lines clacked out the dread news—the President in the rear of the box, the audience intent on *Our American Cousin,* the shot ringing out in the dark, the wild-looking man in black felt hat and high boots leaping from the box and catching his spurs on a regimental flag, the tumult in the theater, the President breathing laboriously, carried across the street to the house of a tailor, the room crowded with spectators, the slow death. And then the legend—of the Great Emancipator, of Father Abraham, of the ungainly fellow who told crude stories to relieve the tension within him, of the practical politician who had come to believe in union *and* liberty, of the men who hated him, including a man named Booth, of the unerring course of the assassin's bullet, of a threnody by Whitman, and the grief of a people.

Guns were still booming as Lincoln's funeral train set out for the north and west, but soon Johnston and the other Confederate generals surrendered. The Confederacy was dead, and with it an experiment that few in the South had time to mourn and few in the North wanted to. It had been an experiment in extreme decentralization, in radical states' rights, in a *con*federation in which each state was sovereign. The central government could not impose tariffs or make internal improvements or of course interfere with slavery, except perhaps in wartime. Other powers, such as levying export duties or making appropriations not requested by the executive board, it could not exercise without a two-thirds vote of both houses of Congress. It was the great misfortune of the confederationists that they had to run such a dispersed system under the pressing conditions of war, which on the one hand tended to compel central direction and control and on the other aroused, temporarily at least, feelings of state rather than Confederate solidarity. President Davis was chronically in despair over the refusal of sovereign states to cooperate in the war effort, and South Carolina, living up to the heritage of John Calhoun, virtually nullified an act of the Confederate Congress authorizing Richmond to impress goods and services.

The North was ending an experiment too—in stepped-up national power. Upon the secession of the South and the departure of Southern Democratic members of Congress, Republicans and War Democrats controlled the White House and Congress. Thus they were able to put through the Homestead Act and other great measures including, early in 1865, the vital Thirteenth Amendment outlawing slavery. Could Northern Republicans and antislavery Democrats sustain their power through the harsh trials of reconstruction that seemed almost certain to lie ahead? In his second Inaugural, Lincoln had said in his compelling peroration: "With malice toward none; with charity for all; with firmness in the right. . . . let us strive . . . to bind up the nation's wounds" to achieve "a just, and a lasting peace." Could the national government, however, keep a creative balance between firmness and compassion? Could it extend the fruits of liberty and equality to millions of freed men and women?

But as Lincoln's funeral train wove its way through Manhattan and up along the Hudson and across New York State to Cleveland, to Indianapolis and Chicago, and then at last to Springfield, Americans were not asking these questions. They were simply pouring out their grief, none more so than Walt Whitman:

> When lilacs last in the dooryard bloom'd,
> And the great star early droop'd in the western sky in the night,
> I mourn'd, and yet shall mourn with ever-returning spring. . . .

> Here, coffin that slowly passes,
> I give you my sprig of lilac.

CHAPTER 2

The Reconstruction of Slavery

OWN by the bush spring on a Virginia plantation a young black woman jumped up from the ground, crying out, "Glory, glory, hallelujah to Jesus! I's free! I's free!" She looked around fearfully, then rolled on the ground and kissed it, calling out her love and thanks to "Masser Jesus." A few minutes before, in the mansion, she had found the white family in tears over a rumor that Jefferson Davis had been captured. After getting permission for another black servant to wait on table while she fetched water from the bush spring, she had walked tight-lipped, then run all the way to the spring, flung herself to the ground, and indulged in a paroxysm of rejoicing. To her, freedom meant one overwhelming hope—that she could rejoin her husband and four children, sold several years earlier to a slave dealer.

Other jubilees were more public. When reports of Lee's surrender reached Athens, Georgia, blacks danced around a liberty pole in the center of town, until whites cut it down in the evening. In Charleston, several thousand black people paraded through the streets, while other thousands of blacks cheered. A mule pulled a cart carrying two women, beside whom a mock slave auctioneer shouted, "How much am I offered?" Then came sixty men tied together like a slave gang, followed by another cart carrying a black-draped coffin with letters proclaiming SLAVERY IS DEAD. Blacks from many trades—carpenters, tailors, butchers, masons, wheelwrights—along with Union soldiers and religious leaders, made up the long procession that slowly wound its way through town.

Many years later, freed people would often recall "just like yistiday" the moment they heard that freedom had come. For most, however, the day of jubilee was more a day of confusion, worry, and uncertainty. How and where they heard the news of final Southern defeat, who told them and when, not only varied widely but carried omens of future frustration and tragedy.

Often blacks heard the news from Union soldiers passing through the neighborhood. "We's diggin' potatoes," remembered a Louisiana ex-slave, "when de Yankees come up with two big wagons and make us come out of de fields and free us. Dere wasn't no cel'bration 'bout it. Massa say us can stay couple days till us 'cide what to do." Sometimes a black who was "a good reader" would report the news from a newspaper. Most often slaves were assembled and told of their new freedom by their masters. Some masters in more remote areas waited weeks, even months, before informing their blacks, meantime using them to bring in the crops. Some planters accompanied their announcement with threats and warnings, demanding in some cases that the blacks stay and work and in others that they clear out at once. Occasionally a Union officer arrived to proclaim liberty; one such Yank had hardly left a Louisiana plantation when the planter's wife emerged from the house to tell the newly freed blacks, "Ten years from now I'll have you all back again."

Nor did the freed people always greet the news with jubilation. After the dashed hopes of recent years, they were above all wary and uncertain. Talking gravely among themselves in their quarters, they discussed rumors —that the federal government would not back up their newly found freedom, that the Yankees might sell them to Cuba in order to pay for war costs, that the whole thing was a giant piece of deception. "You're joking me," Tom Robinson told the master who said he was now a free man. He spoke with some slave neighbors to see if they were free too. "I just couldn't take it all in. I couldn't believe we was all free alike." But above all the blacks felt confused and disoriented. "We jes' sort of huddle 'round together like scared rabbits," an Alabama woman remembered about hearing the news, "but after we knowed what he means, didn' many of us go, 'cause we didn' know where to of went." Some blacks stayed on to help their former master or mistress, out of a feeling of compassion, affection, or obligation. Few exacted any real vengeance, but many were hostile. A story came down through generations of one black family about their great-grandmother Caddy, who had been badly treated.

"When General Lee surrendered," so the story went, "that meant that all the colored people were free! Caddy threw down that hoe, she marched herself up to the big house, then, she looked around and found the mistress. She went over to the mistress, she flipped up her dress and told the white woman to do something. She said it mean and ugly. This is what she said: *Kiss my ass!*"

The attitudes and actions of the newly freed were closely affected by those of the planters, who were variously angry, heartsick, resigned, vengeful, helpless, and helpful. Many were already grieving over sons, plantations, and fortunes taken by war; losing their blacks was the final heartbreak. Some masters whipped and even shot and hanged blacks who asserted their freedom. "Papa Day," a Texas planter, told his hands, after reading the official proclamation, that the government did not need to tell them they were free because they had been free all along, that they could leave or stay, but if they left, most "white folks would not treat them as well as he had."

Myrta Lockett Avary, daughter of a Virginia slaveholder, could never forget how her father had assembled his people one evening in the backyard. "You do not belong to me any more," her father said in a trembling voice. "You are free. You have been like my own children. I have never felt that you were slaves. I have felt that you were charges put into my hands by God and that I had to render account to Him of how I raised you." Looking out at a sea of uplifted black faces, illuminated by flaring pine torches, the master reminded them how he had fed them, clothed them, housed them, nursed them, taken care of their babies and laid away their dead. He wanted to keep them on by paying wages, but he hadn't finished thinking things out. He wanted to know how they felt. "Ben! Dick! Moses! Abram! line up, everybody out there. As you pass this porch, tell me if you plan to stay. . . ." All indicated they would remain. "Law, Marster!" said Uncle Andrew the patriarch, "I ain' got nowhar tug go ef I was gwine!"

Other slaveholders were glad to be rid of at least some of their slaves so that they need *not* take care of them; they would keep the good workers and turn out the very old and the very young, the ill and the inefficient—just like the Yankee capitalists!—to "root, pig, or die."

Many planters hardly knew how to liberate; many slaves hardly knew how to be liberated. Master and slave had lived in mutual dependency too long. Some planters almost felt relieved—they felt that their slaves had owned *them*—but others seemed to sicken and die. Mistresses in particular felt helpless when their servants disappeared. It was even harder for the blacks. "Folks dat ain't never been free don' rightly know de *feel* of bein' free," said James Lucas, a former slave of Jefferson Davis. "Dey don't know de meanin' of it. . . ." An old slave rejected the idea of a wage: "Missis belonged to him, & he belonged to Missis." Blacks knew how to work hard, said one of them, "but dey didn't know nothing 'bout how to 'pend on demselves for de livin'." Parke Johnston, a former slave in Virginia, recalled "how wild and upset and *dreadful* everything was in them times. It came so sudden on 'em they wasn't prepared for it. Just think of whole droves of people, that had always been kept so close, and hardly ever left the plantation before, turned aloose all at once, with nothing in the world, but what they had on their backs, and often little enough of that; men, women and children that had left their homes when they found out they were free, walking along the road with no where to go."

Still, it was far more a time of hope than fear. "That the day I shouted," a former slave in Texas remembered. "Everybody went wild," a Texas cowpuncher recalled. "We all felt like horses. . . . WE was free. Just like that, we was free."

Out in Bexar County a cowpuncher heard blacks singing:

> Abe Lincoln freed the nigger
> With the gun and the trigger;
> And I ain't goin' to get whipped any more.
> I got my ticket,
> Leavin' the thicket,
> And I'm a-headin' for the Golden Shore!

BOUND FOR FREEDOM

In the lush green spring of 1865 the Golden Shore seemed to stretch just across the horizon. An intoxicating sense of freedom filled the air. Defeated and despairing Southerners could at least be free of Northern assaults on their homeland and burnings of their cities. Whatever their continued suffering, black people still could hold high hopes for the future. Liberated from military duty and disciplines, soldiers and sailors were returning home by the tens of thousands. Onetime farm boys, having mastered the great engines of war, were drifting back to the simpler tasks and the old rhythms of the arcadian world they had known.

Many Northerners felt free in a more positive sense. They had beaten the enemy on the transcendent moral issue of the time. They could face up to the burdens of freedom not only with enhanced military and economic power, but with a formidable array of leaders. Out of the conflicts of the 1850s and the crucible of war had emerged politicians, generals, agitators, intellectuals, journalists tested by adversity, hardened by experience, committed to making the system work for freedom—a system they now controlled.

In the vanguard of the moral leadership of the nation stood Charles Sumner. After his heavy caning by Preston Brooks and his long, self-imposed exile, the Massachusetts senator had returned to Washington with the somewhat insecure status of minor martyr. But he soon reestablished his moral standing through his burning conviction about the responsibility lying on the Republican party, his absolute commitment to protecting the rights of freed people, and his uncompromisingly radical stand on the central issues. He was fifty-four years old at war's end, and the mass of nut-brown hair that hung loosely over his massive forehead, shading his deep blue eyes, was turning an iron gray; but he was still a commanding presence in the Senate as he rose to his full six feet two, broad of chest and a bit heavy of paunch. Many senators loathed the man from Boston for his eternal pomposity, his endless hectoring, his thunderous self-righteousness. Many respected him for his intellectual grasp and political integrity—and for his uncanny capacity for being right several years ahead of others. No one could ignore him.

At the opposite end of the long Capitol building, Thaddeus Stevens led the Radical Republicans in the House of Representatives with the same moral fervor as did Sumner in the Senate. Now seventy-three years old, the Pennsylvanian had climbed to the top after a long career in politics: anti-Mason state representative; two-term Whig member of Congress; an organizer of the Republican party; Republican member of the House of Representatives since 1858; and chairman of Ways and Means, the tax committee. Just as friends of Sumner speculated that the senator's boyhood inability to meet the demands of an exacting father and unloving mother had left him eternally dissatisfied with his own—and his associates' —endeavors, so people wondered if Stevens's clubfoot, his early poverty, and his desertion by a jobless and alcoholic father had produced a need both to compensate for a sense of inferiority and to chastise deserters, whether of the Union or of himself. Others had simpler explanations: both men found leadership against slavery morally fulfilling and politically rewarding.

Other congressional leaders were often more effective than Stevens or Sumner in the give-and-take of legislative politics. Benjamin F. Wade, Massachusetts-born and -bred, had moved to Ohio at the age of twenty-one, joined the abolitionist ranks, and after thirty years in politics won his Senate seat in 1851. Now a veteran of the upper chamber, he was still a bit rough in manner and coarse in speech, but politicians liked him for his honesty and affability. Zachariah Chandler of Michigan was another New Englander who had moved west and prospered, in his case as a merchant banker and land speculator. A founder of the Republican party, he seemed to feel no strain between his conservative business interests and his close association with radical Republicanism. One of the ablest leaders of the moderate Republicans was Senator Lyman Trumbull, an old friend and foe of Lincoln in Illinois politics, firmly opposed both to slavery and to a radical reconstruction policy, and a powerful voice on both issues as chairman of the Senate Judiciary Committee. To Trumbull's right stood Orville H. Browning, the man who had succeeded to Stephen Douglas's seat—a longtime critic of Lincoln, consistently opposed to abolitionism in the old days and now equally opposed to a strong reconstruction program.

In the House, Stevens had some equally capable associates in such men as George W. Julian of Indiana—successively a Whig, Free-Soiler, and

Republican, but always a firm egalitarian—and William D. Kelley of Philadelphia, a zealous humanitarian who would become an ardent protectionist. Julian was notable among these men for his firm belief in equality
between the sexes. These men and the other Republican leaders quarreled
with one another and sometimes despised one another but, in Martin
Mantell's words, collectively they "were able to define new basic policy
positions that met the needs of rapidly changing times while maintaining
the essential unity of their own party organization." In the forcing house
of Reconstruction the Republicans were shaping a party loyalty that would
tilt the balance of American politics for decades to come.

The great unknown in the existing balance, in the spring of 1865, was
the new President, Andrew Johnson. A Tennesseean who won attention as
the only Southern senator to speak out against secession, a slaveholder
who boasted that he had never sold slaves but only bought them, the
running mate of Lincoln in 1864 but lacking in ties to the Republican party,
a believer in both equal rights and states' rights and hence caught in the
tension between them, Johnson had risen to fame outside of the social and
political establishments—and he was proud of it. He boasted of his
plebeian Carolina origins, though somewhat less of his father, a hotel
porter who had died without reward after rescuing two boozing gentlemen
from an icy stream. As an impoverished young man, hardly literate, Johnson had moved with his mother and stepfather, their scanty belongings in
a two-wheeled cart, to Tennessee, where he had set up as a tailor and
moved successfully into politics. Yet his mudsill origins seemed to oppress
him, provoking a resentment in particular against the pontificators, like
Sumner, who wore their learning on their sleeves. He had had a bad press,
especially after he gave a rambling, drunken vice-presidential inaugural
speech, in which he had scolded the attending Diplomatic Corps for its
"fine feathers and gewgaws." He had always been, on the national stage,
a secondary, even shadowy figure. Now he was President.

What kind of President? On the day after Lincoln's assassination Wade,
Chandler, Julian, and other Radical Republicans met in Washington to
reassess the situation and plan strategy. They grieved over the loss of their
friend the commander-in-chief, but they seemed to share a sense of relief.
Lincoln had brilliantly held the Union together, even while emancipating
the slaves, but he had seemed to many Radicals too conservative on the
question of postwar Negro rights, too conciliatory toward the South. Johnson appeared to be a different breed: tough, uncompromising, a fiery foe
of Southern "aristocrats," a champion of the small white farmer in the
South, a firm and even zealous war governor of Tennessee. Radicals visiting the new man in the White House came away vastly reassured. He

seemed one of them. Even Sumner overrode his usual suspiciousness. Wade was almost euphoric.

"Johnson, we have faith in you," he greeted the President on one occasion. "By the gods, there will be no trouble now in running the government!" Responding in kind, Johnson said, "I hold that robbery is a crime; rape is a crime; murder is a crime; *treason* is a crime, and *crime* must be punished."

Prepared to mobilize behind a firm and comprehensive reconstruction policy was a relatively solid phalanx of Republican radicals and moderates. Often differing over means, they were fundamentally united over ends—to dissolve the old Confederate leadership, to provide national protection for the civil and political rights of freed people, to give the black people a chance to make out on their own. In seeking these goals, Radicals had extensive support among the electorate and powerful support from the intellectual leadership of the day—from thinkers and scholars like Ralph Waldo Emerson and John Lothrop Motley; from editors like Horace Greeley and Whitelaw Reid; from poets like Whittier, Whitman, and Lowell; from theologians and scientists; from leaders of the movement for women's rights. The Radicals had also the advantage of long reflection over Reconstruction issues. From the start of the war they had been anticipating difficulties, analyzing ways and means, debating political strategies. They had collected extensive information about Southern conditions from newspaper reports, government investigations, military intelligence, the Freedmen's Bureau, the resources of Northern universities.

The Republican leaders had, it seemed, one other signal advantage in organizing Reconstruction: they could proceed without constitutional constraints to a degree not possible since the founding days. Not only did the Constitution of 1787 authorize and even require the federal government to guarantee basic rights of American citizens, but the Republicans, through their large majorities in Congress and most of the Northern state legislatures, were able to put through constitutional amendments as long as these changes satisfied both moderate and radical Republicans. The Republican Administration and the Republican Congress, in short, possessed an extraordinary battery of military, political (especially party), economic, intellectual, and constitutional resources to make a whole new beginning for democratic republicanism in the South. These advantages were, it is true, offset by grave institutional and intellectual weaknesses. But when Charles Sumner, the political curmudgeon incarnate, could leave the White House beaming over Johnson's militant posture on Reconstruction, even the most pessimistic could indulge in high hopes for the future.

Within six months these hopes were dimming. Within one year the President and the Republican leadership were at odds. Within three years a President was being impeached, the North was aroused, the South inflamed. Within a decade a great experiment in liberty and equality was coming to an end, the blacks abandoned. By century's end the freed people were restored to a condition of virtual servitude, Northern blacks were still suffering discrimination, Northern whites had turned away from the quest for equality, Southern whites had won a Pyrrhic victory, the South was still mortgaged to the past, and racism lay like a blight across the land.

* * *

What happened in late 1865 and early 1866 to disrupt a Northern leadership apparently united on Reconstruction, and to turn the freed people of the South—and indeed all Southerners—back toward the path leading ultimately to reconstruction of the old racial tragedy? The question has long been debated. Since the first histories are usually written by the victors, the early postwar historians laid the blame largely on Johnson and the men immediately around him, on their alleged ineptness, narrowness, conservatism, vindictiveness, even wickedness. A later generation of historians shifted the blame to the Radical Republicans, accusing them of the same failings, plus extreme fanaticism. Still later, the failure was seen to stem from psychological, economic, institutional, and other complex sources, or even from sheer stupidity—the notion that the politicians of the 1860s happened to comprise a leadership generation of unusual ineptness.

All these factors doubtless had some part to play, for the great wrenching movements of history spring out of a profusion of forces. But the more recent historians, rising above the passions of olden times, have pointed to the psychological and other forces that tend directly to shape the actions of political leadership. The crises of the late 1850s and early 1860s brought to the top leaders of bounding political hopes and expectations and of considerable political skill. Not only had these men learned to operate the machinery of groups and parties, nominations and elections, legislatures and bureaucracies, and to calculate in terms of the arithmetic of nominations and elections; they possessed as well a heightened sense of the geometry of politics—of the new policy that had arisen during the Civil War, of a new nationalized and centralized system that, in Morton Keller's words, created and allocated power as the economy allocated and created wealth. Even more, they would act openly and boldly on the basis of values and purposes that had been hardened in the fires of civil conflict.

Andrew Johnson possessed more power than any of these men, but less grasp of the strategic factors. In the spring of 1865 he had much the same political advantage that Lincoln had held four years earlier—he could take the initiative in an unresolved political situation until Congress convened in December. He had an unparalleled political opportunity, if he would but grasp it—to follow a conciliatory mid-course between Radical Republicans and old-time War Democrats, enabling him to "command the center" and isolate his rivals on each flank. Then he could dismantle the old Southern secessionist leadership—men he had long hated—and mobilize a new leadership acting for the people he had always loved, the Southern white yeomanry, at the same time protecting the civil rights of Southern blacks, as he was pledged to do. Ultimately he could reunite South and North on a new basis of popular democracy. "The only safety of the nation," he said, "lies in a generous and expansive plan of conciliation."

Perhaps Johnson could have become the "great unifier," even if this required building a regenerated Union party that would unite moderate Democrats and Republicans, incidentally giving him a presidential term "in his own right" in 1868. It was not clear, though, that he had the comprehensive vision, the political skill of isolating politicians and playing them off against one another, the finesse at political management of his own followers, or the ability to rise above his seething resentments over the slights of "aristocratic" Southerners and of moralizing, condescending Northerners, to bring off such a realignment of parties and leaders.

He got off to a quick start in the late spring of 1865, leaving congressional leaders on the sidelines. In a series of proclamations and executive actions he struck at the old Southern leadership by granting amnesty to Confederates who took the oath of allegiance, except for large property holders and other influentials. Members of such excepted categories could, however, apply for special pardons. The President empowered provisional governors to call conventions made up of delegates elected by eligible voters; the conventions would then arrange elections for state offices and for Congress. Conspicuously absent from this plan was any provision for black suffrage.

Congressional Republicans were by no means idle during these spring days of 1865. With Congress out of session, they could not shape grand strategy, but at first they felt little need to because of their continuing confidence in Johnson. Sumner himself was so untypically trusting that he wrote to a friend that on *"the question of colored suffrage the President is with us."* Indeed, one of the Radicals' main reservations about Johnson at this time was that he was *too* vengeful toward the old Southern leaders. Many Radicals felt that the issue was far less the punishment of Confederate "traitors" than the combining of civil, political, social, and economic reforms as necessary for the freed people truly to achieve freedom. The more

Johnson remained silent on these crucial matters, the more uneasy many party leaders became. And the more he seemed to be following a policy of vengeance against the old Confederate leadership, the more he appeared to be astride two horses that were beginning to buck in opposite directions.

Which horse would Johnson stick with? As it turned out, he was left with little choice, for his increasing involvement with Southern leaders and Northern conservatives entangled him in a "pro-Southern," pro-states' rights constellation of forces, while it was temperamentally impossible for him—and, he doubtless felt, politically unrewarding—to work with the Radical leaders whom, in his hierarchy of hatreds, he loathed even more than most Copperheads. As he moderated his policies in the South, as he recognized Southern state governments that met his requirements, as he received endless delegations pouring out their grievances and playing on his vanity, as he issued thousands of special pardons to onetime Confederate leaders, he slowly became tied to the Southern structure of leadership and power that he had hated. He became, in Kenneth Stampp's words, virtually the prisoner of the men he had set out to destroy. Thus he lost his chance to mobilize a new leadership among Southern yeomanry and Unionists.

And Southern leadership was ready to assert itself. As provisional state governments were established under Johnson's plan, their legislatures, elected by whites only, began to pass "Black Codes" that gave freed people some basic legal rights, such as to marry and make contracts, but that also included vagrancy and apprenticeship provisions designed to keep blacks virtually in a condition of peonage. If Johnson felt politically embarrassed by the Southern leadership, he hardly showed it. He urged the legislatures to liberalize their racial policy, but he barely demurred when they defied him. Nothing was done for the Negro's basic needs and education. Carl Schurz, whom the President himself sent on a fact-finding tour of the South, reported that hundreds of times he was told that "learning will spoil the nigger for work" and that the elevation of the blacks would be the "degradation" of the whites. Johnson ignored his reports.

Sumner visited Johnson just before Congress convened. For two and a half hours the men sparred warily. Complaining that the "freemen" of Georgia and Alabama were mistreated by the "rebels," Sumner accused the President of throwing away the victories of the Union army. Johnson bridled.

"Mr. Sumner, do murders ever occur in Massachusetts?"

"Unhappily yes, Mr. President."

"Do people ever knock each other down in Boston?"

"Unhappily yes, Mr. President, sometimes."

"Would you consent that Massachusetts should be excluded from the Union on this account?"

"No, Mr. President, surely not." The breach between the two men was unbridgeable—especially after the senator, on leaving, picked up his silken tophat from where he had laid it on the floor and discovered that Johnson, in his excitement, had used it for a spittoon.

*   *   *

By the time Congress convened in early December 1865, the South was busy reconstructing its old political, social, and economic system and the President was actively abetting it under the banner of states' rights. Moderate as well as radical Republicans were furious—but no longer frustrated, for now they could take the initiative away from the White House. The legislators did so through the classic weapons of parliamentary battle: controlling entrance into their own ranks, holding up the executive's program, and using congressional investigations as a form of attack. At the opening of the session, the Clerk of the House simply omitted from the roll call the names of men elected from formerly seceding states. Now it was the Southerners who were furious—and helpless.

The Republicans, solidly in control of both chambers, proceeded to set up a fifteen-member Joint Committee on Reconstruction to plan and assert the role of Congress in Southern policy. The President could do nothing to stop this. Under the stinging parliamentary whip of Stevens and the moral lash of Sumner, the Radical Republicans along with many moderates began to act with unprecedented unity on procedure. On policy Republicans as a whole were still fundamentally divided, as later events would demonstrate; probably the only major issue on which *all* of them agreed was the end of slavery, and it was symbolic that the Thirteenth Amendment, passed earlier by two-thirds majorities in House and Senate, and then ratified by three-fourths of the state legislatures, was proclaimed in effect two weeks after Congress convened. At last, black emancipation was part of the United States Constitution.

Emancipation—but not freedom. And on this distinction turned some portentous differences among Republicans. Some felt that simply eradicating slavery was enough, while the vast majority recognized that the federal government must guarantee the freed people's legal and civil rights. A lesser number of Republicans would protect the blacks' political rights, especially their right to vote. Some Republicans—mostly Radicals—were eager to provide land, sustenance, and education on the premise that in the long run the blacks' civil and political liberties had to be buttressed by social and economic freedom; to some Republicans this notion was radical and dangerous. These differences over the substance of policy were multiplied by differences over the execution of it—whether the federal or state governments should direct Reconstruction, whether Congress or the President should control federal policy, how much power should be granted the Freedmen's Bureau or other bureaucracies, how much authority should be left in the hands of federal and state judges.

With all these permutations and combinations, it was a tribute both to the resolve of the Republicans and to the strength of their caucuses that the party remained united in the early months of 1866. Moving quickly to protect the freed people's civil rights through the use of military courts, Congress voted to extend the life of the Freedmen's Bureau and enlarge its powers. Though moderate Republicans favored the bill and radicals felt it was far too limited, the President vetoed it. Earlier, Congress passed a Civil Rights Act granting citizenship to the newly freed—thus overturning *Dred Scott*—and granting equal civil rights to all persons born in the United States, with the notable exception of Indians. Johnson vetoed this bill as an invasion of states' rights. Congress passed both bills over his vetoes.

Thus were the great constitutional catapults of Congress and President wheeled into position; the test now, as debate among press, politicians, and public rose to white heat, was one of leadership. Politicians were already maneuvering for advantage in the congressional elections of 1866, which they viewed as both an immediate sounding of public opinion and as a prelude to 1868 and beyond. Bypassing the President, the Joint Committee drew up a proposed Fourteenth Amendment in order to secure blacks' civil rights and to thwart any effort by the Supreme Court to invalidate the Civil Rights Act. This proposal was a supreme test of the Republicans' solidarity—especially over the issue of states' rights, for the proposed amendment barred the states from passing laws "which shall abridge the privileges or immunities of citizens of the United States" or from depriving "any person of life, liberty, or property, without due process of law," or of the "equal protection of the laws." Republican ranks held firm, but at a price—the amendment did not firmly grant the black man the right to vote.

Excluded from the Joint Committee at the start for his "extremism," Sumner infuriated congressional Republicans by opposing the amendment on highly political grounds—he had to deal with moderate Republicans back home—but he redeemed himself with a fervent five-hour address, "The Equal Rights of All," which concluded: "Show me a creature, with erect countenance looking to heaven, made in the image of God, and I show you a MAN, who, of whatever country or race, whether darkened by equatorial sun or blanched by northern cold, is with you a child of the Heavenly Father, and equal with you in all the rights of Human Nature. . . . It is not enough that you have given Liberty. By the same title that we claim Liberty do we claim Equality also. . . . One is the complement of the other. . . ."

The state of liberty and equality in the South three years after the Emancipation Proclamation was not good. At the end of April 1866, following three months of almost daily hearings, the Joint Committee on Reconstruction reported its findings. Well over a hundred witnesses, including Freedmen's Bureau agents, Southern unionists, and a few black men, had testified that floggings and killings of freed people continued, with many of the crimes not prosecuted or even disclosed. The celebrated Clara Barton, reporting with a nurse's precision, testified that a young woman, black and pregnant, had come to her for help; she had been whipped for not "spinning properly"—whipped with a "lash half as large as my little finger," whipped to the bone, the flesh completely cut out along most of the gashes. Southerners charged the committee with bias, but Northerners were horrified, and they were further aroused by news of race riots in Memphis and New Orleans; in each case more than a hundred blacks were killed or injured by white police and civilians who had gone on a rampage of shooting, stabbing, burning, and lynching.

Johnson watched in dismay as the country polarized, for the mounting division threatened his "middle way." But instead of dampening the fires, he poked them up with intemperate statements. Responding to a group of serenaders on the White House grounds, he branded the Joint Committee as an "irresponsible central directory"; he had fought traitors in the South, he thundered, and was prepared to fight them in the North. Goaded into naming names, he listed Stevens, Sumner, and Phillips. He could not veto the Fourteenth Amendment, but he could and did urge Southern states not to ratify it. As moderates as well as radicals broke away from him, he tried all the harder to rally the forces of the center. He not only replaced moderates in his Administration with more conservative types—including the supplanting of postmasters by the hundreds—but he summoned a National Union Convention to meet in Philadelphia to launch his new party. The convention made a fine show of unity, symbolized by Massachusetts and South Carolina delegates marching into the hall in pairs, but potential Democratic supporters held back, largely because they wanted to protect the standing of their state and local parties in the North. The still potent New York Democracy, in particular, preferred to concentrate on electing its own to state offices rather than backing an apostate Republican President.

Johnson fought on. In August he set out on a daring venture—a "swing around the circle"—to arouse support. Warned by a supporter, Senator James R. Doolittle, that he would be "followed by the reporters of a hundred presses who do nothing but misrepresent you"—who indeed might report one of his "outbursts"—the President was undeterred. He assembled a glittering presidential party headed by Secretary Seward, General Grant, and Admiral Farragut. The party took the old "presidential route" to Baltimore, Philadelphia, and New York, journeyed by yacht up the Hudson, then turned west for stump speeches along the Erie Canal. In the Eastern cities Johnson attracted huge, fervent crowds, who emboldened him to new attacks on the rump Congress, disunionists and "traitors," the "subsidized and mercenary press." But in the Midwest, as Johnson gave his one set speech over and over again, the press grew bored and hostile and crowds turned ugly, Grant deserted the presidential party, the President fell into shouting matches with hecklers, riots broke out, platforms collapsed, Seward came down with cholera and almost died. The "swing" was judged a disaster; the President had fired up issues without defining them, asked support for pro-Administration candidates without naming them, sought some kind of middle way without explaining it.

Most "off-year" elections, lacking the focus of a presidential contest, produce sketchy results; 1866 turned out to be a dramatic exception. Republicans carried every gubernatorial contest and every state legislature in the North. They would command huge majorities in the Fortieth Congress—42 to 11 in the Senate, 143 to 49 in the House. To the jubilant radicals, the results were as meaningful as they were decisive. The campaign had been vituperative on both sides, but it had sharply defined the lines of conflict. After years of isolation and frustration the radicals not only had a mandate; with their two-thirds majorities in both houses of Congress they now had *power*.

A REVOLUTIONARY EXPERIMENT

For a brief fleeting moment in history—from late 1866 to almost the end of the decade—radical senators and congressmen led the Republican party in an audacious venture in both the organization and the goals of political power. To a degree that would have astonished the constitution-makers of earlier years, they converted the eighty-year-old system of checks and balances into a highly centralized, majoritarian system that elevated the legislative branch, subordinated the executive and judicial branches, and suspended federalism and "states' rights" in the South. They turned the Constitution on its head. The aims of these leaders were indeed revolutionary—to reverse age-old human and class relationships in the South and to raise millions of people to a much higher level of economic, political, social, and educational self-fulfillment. That such potent means could not in the end produce such humane and democratic ends was the ultimate tragedy of this revolutionary experiment.

This heroic effort was not conducted by men on white horses, but rather by quarrelsome parliamentarians—by a Congress that seemed to one of its members as never "more querulous, distracted, incoherent and ignoble." In the Senate, Sumner had good reason to be distracted, for he had married a woman half his age shortly before the election and was preoccupied first by marital bliss and very soon by marital distress as he and his wife found themselves hopelessly incompatible. His colleagues found him more remote and unpredictable than ever. In the House, Stevens worked closely with his Radical allies, but he was now desperately anxious to move swiftly ahead, for he knew that time was running out for him and perhaps for his cause. Rising on the House floor, he now presented the countenance of death, with his dourly twisted mouth, deeply sunken eyes, parchment skin, and a body so wasted that he often conducted business from a couch just outside the chamber. But the old man never lost his ferocious drive to dominate; as he spoke, his eyes lighted up in a fierce gleam and his croaking voice turned thunderous, while he stretched his bony arm out in a wide sweep and punctuated his arguments with sudden thrusts of his long yellow forefinger.

The strength of the Republican party lay in the advanced positions of these two men but even more in the quality and commitment of other party leaders in both houses. Some of these men—John Sherman, James A. Garfield, James G. Blaine—would gain fame in the decades ahead. Others, with such names as Thomas D. Eliot, John A. Bingham, James M. Ashley, Samuel Shellabarger—would fade into the mists of history. Occupying almost every hue on the party rainbow, these men differed sharply and disputed mightily, but they felt they had a clear election mandate to establish civil and other rights in the South; they had a strong sense of party solidarity; and they had the backing of rank-and-file senators and representatives and of party organizations throughout the North.

They also had a common adversary in Andrew Johnson. The President stewed over his election defeat, but he would make no fundamental change in his political and legislative strategy. Setbacks seemed only to mire him more deeply in his own resentments. Karl Marx had noted that behind Johnson's "affectation of severity against single persons," such as Jefferson Davis, he tended to be "extremely vacillating and weak in substance"; certainly Johnson was more flexible in day-to-day tactics than in overall strategy. He received little independent advice from his Cabinet, which appeared to believe that the beleaguered President needed above all their loyalty. Stanton dissented on occasion but, characteristically, Johnson did not wholly trust him. As the President stuck to the disintegrating political center and the Republicans moved toward a radical posture, the legislative stage was set for drama and conflict.

The upshot was a burst of legislative creativity in the "hundred days" of winter 1866–67:

December 14, 1866: Congress enacts black suffrage for the District of Columbia, later reenacts it over Johnson's veto. *January 7, 1867:* the House adopts Ashley's resolution instructing the Judiciary Committee to "inquire into the conduct of Andrew Johnson." *January 22:* Congress grants itself authority to call itself into special session, a right recognized until now as belonging only to the President. *March 2:* all on the same day, Congress passes a basic act laying out its general plan of political reconstruction; in effect deprives the President of command of the army; and enacts the Tenure of Office Act barring the Chief Executive from removing officials appointed by and with the advice of the Senate, without Senate approval. *March 23:* Congress passes a supplementary Reconstruction Act requiring military commanders to start registering "loyal" voters.

The heart of congressional strategy to democratize the South lay in the first Reconstruction Act of March 2, 1867, as clarified, strengthened, and implemented in later acts. With the ostensible purpose of restoring social order and republican government in the South, and on the premise that the existing "Johnson" state regimes there could not realize these ends or even protect life or property, the South was divided into five military districts subject to martial law. The commanders were empowered not only to govern—to suppress disorder, protect life and property, remove civil officeholders—but to initiate political reconstruction by enrolling qualified voters including blacks, and excluding the disloyal. To be restored to the Union, the Southern states must call new constitutional conventions that, elected under universal manhood suffrage, in turn must establish new state governments that would guarantee black suffrage and ratify the Fourteenth Amendment. These states would be eligible for representation in the national legislature only after Congress had approved their state constitutions and after the Fourteenth Amendment had become part of the Constitution.

It was a radical's dream, a centralist's heaven—and a states'-righter's nightmare. Congress held all the governmental strings in its hands. No more exquisite punishment could have been devised for secessionists than to make them conform to national standards in reconstructing their own state governments and gaining restoration to the Union. Congress did not stop with upsetting the division of powers between nation and states; it overturned the separation of powers among the three coordinate branches of the national government. Radicals could defend the Tenure of Office Act against this charge by contending that its main purpose was not to undermine presidential power in general but to thwart any effort of Johnson to sack Secretary of War Stanton. But the effort of Congress to interfere with the hitherto near-sacred independence of the judiciary left little question as to the willingness of the Radicals to experiment with changes in the checks and balances.

Under Salmon P. Chase, the old-time abolitionist leader and Lincoln's Treasury Secretary until appointed Chief Justice in 1864, the Supreme Court had recovered some of the moral standing and political influence it had lost under Roger Taney. In general, the Chase Court had upheld national and congressional power, but in April 1866, just before the congressional Republicans took control of Reconstruction, the justices, in a preliminary ruling, struck down resort to martial law where the civil courts were operating. If it were possible to bring a civilian before a military court in a state that was not a theater of war, the Court ruled in *Ex parte Milligan*, "there is an end of liberty regulated by law." Stung by this decision, Stevens called it more dangerous to the "lives and liberties of the loyal men of this country" than even *Dred Scott*. Radicals recognized that the decision might hamstring Reconstruction, for the Court's argument, in William R. Brock's words, would now apply directly in the South, where war no longer existed, the civil courts were functioning, and the jurisdiction of military courts had been enlarged.

Radical fears rose again in the spring of 1867 when the Court invalidated a wartime measure requiring lawyers practicing before federal courts to take loyalty oaths. When the Republican leaders learned that the Court had agreed to review a case much like *Milligan* but involving a military court in Mississippi, Congress took direct action through a measure depriving the Court of jurisdiction over this kind of case. Some members of the Court wished to mobilize judicial power against congressional; but Chase, experienced in the balances and nuances of power, called them off, warning against a "collision" between Court and Congress. The Court then rebuffed two Southern states seeking to enjoin executive enforcement of the Reconstruction Acts. Once again the legislature emerged triumphant.

The most potent and dramatic congressional weapon against the President lay tucked away inconspicuously in Section 3 of Article I of the Constitution: "The Senate shall have the sole Power to try all Impeachments. When sitting for that Purpose, they shall be on Oath or Affirmation.

When the President of the United States is tried, the Chief Justice shall preside: and no Person shall be convicted without the Concurrence of two thirds of the Members present. Judgment in Cases of Impeachment shall not extend further than to removal from Office, and disqualification to hold and enjoy any Office of honor, Trust or Profit under the United States: but the Party convicted shall nevertheless be liable and subject to Indictment, Trial, Judgment and Punishment, according to Law."

No President had been impeached; the congressional weapon lay unused, a loaded gun neither cocked nor fired. Perhaps it was unfortunate that Congress had not seriously considered impeaching a President, for the ancient process had not been tested as part of the constitutional checks and balances. Some hoped that now it would be. When impeachment of Johnson neared, a friend of Congressman Garfield wrote him that the "next great question to be decided in our history is this—is the National Legislature to be as omnipotent in American politics as the English is in English politics. The struggle through which we pass in reaching an answer to that question will be the parallel to that through which the British people passed in the time of the Stuarts. . . . May we not anticipate a time when the President will no more think of vetoing a bill passed by Congress than the British crown thinks of doing the same thing?" Others were quick to point out that the Framers had devised an American system of separated powers rather than a unified one like the British. But this question had not been directly faced or tested.

Impeachment could also have been used as a grand confrontation between President and Congress over the fundamental strategy and substance of Reconstruction. In essence Johnson wanted a soft, conciliatory posture toward the South, with full deference to states' rights. Republicans, both moderates and radicals, wanted a hard policy, to be shaped and enforced by national power. The most clear-cut difference on substantive issues between the President and the Republican leadership was over federally guaranteed or sponsored black suffrage, although Johnson camouflaged his opposition to "niggers" voting by leaving it up to the (Southern, white-dominated) states. There were other grave issues. But impeachment failed to pose them in a manner that encouraged rational debate either in Washington or in the country at large.

The decision to impeach had come far more in response to personal and political events than to a desire to clarify constitutional and policy issues. It was clear after the 1866 congressional elections that legislature and executive would follow divergent reconstruction strategies, but most members of Congress shrank from the perilous experiment of impeachment. They feared making a martyr of Johnson, opening up new wounds among the Republicans, and giving Senator Benjamin Wade, a Radical, a soft-money man, and a supporter of women's rights as well as black suffrage, a leg up on the 1868 presidential nomination, for Wade as Senate president *pro tem* would move to the White House if Johnson should be removed. During 1867, an effort to recommend impeachment to the House failed, amid general ridicule. Even after the President in December pugnaciously told Congress that in certain cases he "would be compelled to stand on his rights, and maintain them, regardless of consequences," the House voted down an impeachment resolution two to one.

It was Johnson himself—a man with the courage of his convictions and the conviction of his innocence—who precipitated the battle of '68. He did so by sacking his Secretary of War, Edwin Stanton. The President had suspended Stanton in August 1867, and thus kept within the letter of the Tenure of Office Act. Now he flagrantly defied that act—and Congress. The House responded by resolving, 126 to 47, "That Andrew Johnson, President of the United States, be impeached of high crimes and misdemeanors in office."

The impeachment and trial of Andrew Johnson might have been the climactic stages of a great political and constitutional drama, but not one of the acts of this drama was well conceived or well played. When Johnson suspended Stanton, the President induced General Grant to serve as the temporary Secretary of War, on some kind of understanding that the general would help him make the Tenure of Office Act into a great constitutional test case. When, however, the Senate expressed disapproval of Stanton's ouster, Grant withdrew in favor of the sacked secretary, amidst mutual recriminations that brought out the worst in each man. After Johnson found an alcoholic, foppish general to serve as Secretary of War, Stanton held on to his job by posting a guard and barricading himself all night in his office.

Rumors circulated that Johnson would suppress Congress through a military coup—or that the Radicals would take over the White House with the help of their friends in the military. There was much whispering of money passing hands for the conviction or exoneration of the President.

Probably the most sordid episode was the resurrection of the case of Mary E. Surratt. The mother of a man who had been implicated in the Lincoln assassination plot and then fled the country, Mrs. Surratt had been convicted on flimsy evidence and in large part, it seemed, on the hope that her son would return when he heard of her imminent hanging. He did not and Mary Surratt, fainting and sobbing, was led to the gallows within sight of her open grave. Now, over two years later, a War Department subordinate of Stanton's abetted publication of a statement that President Johnson had signed her death warrant with a clemency recommendation from the military court staring him in the face. As the statement was blazoned across the nation's front pages, Johnson reacted with wrath and vengefulness against Stanton. Many believed that this incident precipitated Johnson's first move against the secretary.

The last act of impeachment was played out in the Senate starting on March 5, 1868, still without high drama. The chief protagonist, the President of the United States, was not present. He was well represented by William M. Evarts, a leading New York attorney, assisted by an ex–Supreme Court Justice and Johnson's just-resigned Attorney General. The President was fortunate too in the low caliber of the impeachment managers appointed by the House. Stevens was feebler than ever, and the prosecution fell into the hands of Ben Butler, whose prosecutorial manner, courtroom bombast, and general highhandedness did his cause little good. Moreover, the managers had a hard case to present, for the House had impeached Johnson on a farrago of charges ranging from preventing the execution of the Tenure of Office Act to bringing "disgrace, ridicule, hatred, contempt and reproach" on Congress. If Johnson's foes were trying the old prosecutor's trick of "throwing everything in the book" at the President with the hope that something would stick, the tactic failed, for senators were able to use the sheer variety of charges as means of evading them.

The pseudo-drama was robbed even of a final suspenseful scene, for it was widely expected that the President would win a narrow exoneration. Narrow it was, as the Senate, on the critical eleventh article—whether the President was guilty of high misdemeanors as charged—voted 35 for conviction and 19 for acquittal, one vote short of the two-thirds necessary for removal. Not only was the close acquittal predictable, it was probably contrived; and some senators, favoring acquittal but feeling the pressure to convict, voted against the President in the expectation of acquittal. Nor was there much Senate heroism on display, notwithstanding later efforts to glorify the seven Republican senators who voted to uphold Johnson despite intense constituency pressure. Several of the "Republican Seven" were subsequently denied reelection, but others felt that their political positions had been strengthened by their independent stand.

Thus ended a political struggle masquerading as a judicial performance. Were great constitutional stakes involved? "Once set the example of impeaching a President for what, when the excitement of the hour shall have subsided, will be regarded as insufficient cause," said Senator Trumbull, one of the "Republican Seven," "and no future President will be safe who happens to differ with a majority of the House and two-thirds of the Senate on any measure deemed by them important." Quoting these words, Kenneth Stampp disputed them, on the ground that Johnson's ouster, if achieved, would more likely have been a curiosity of American political history than a precedent for future action. In later years, following another struggle between President and Congress, the verdict on impeachment might shift again.

At the time, at least, the struggle left unchanged the paramount question of legislative versus executive authority over policy. It left unchanged even the lesser question of the political and moral authority of a President who had been chosen Lincoln's running mate as a former Democrat and present Unionist—and who had then come into office by chance—against the authority of a Congress that had very recently been elected to office. But there was little further debate about impeachment in 1868 as politicians turned away from it with relief, to more pressing matters of politics and policy. Many, indeed, would soon repent of their actions, but not Johnson. He served out his term as contentious as ever, but taking care not unduly to provoke Congress. He won his way back to the Senate in 1875—appropriately, as a Democrat—gave one major speech in the Senate against his old enemy Grant, and died the same year. He was buried, as he requested, with his head on a copy of the Constitution. It was his personal copy of the Constitution, very much thumbed and worn—very much his Constitution.

*   *   *

Johnson's near-removal had left Ulysses S. Grant as the most prominent national figure.

For a man who had hardly known politics before the Civil War, who had failed as a farmer and clerk and had been reduced in the late 1850s to peddling wood in the streets and even to pawning his watch, Grant had shown astonishing talents as a Washington politician following the war that had made him a national hero. He had walked the political tightrope both between Johnson and the congressional Republicans and between dutiful subordination to the commander-in-chief and accommodations with the Radicals. In contrast to his garrulous rivals on Capitol Hill, he had made silence into a political weapon, insisting when it suited him that a soldier must not intrude into politics. He had managed to move toward the winning side by keeping his lines into the congressional party, and he seems genuinely to have shifted toward a more militant posture on Reconstruction as the 1868 election neared. Following a rash of endorsements in the party press, the Republicans, meeting in Chicago, brushed aside such availables as Chase and Wade and chose Grant on the first ballot.

The old tradition that presidential candidates remain mute Grant found wholly to his liking; he remembered the summer and fall of 1868 as "the most quiet, pleasant time" since the start of the war. He let the Republican party platform speak for him; but on the paramount question of black suffrage that platform spoke with a delicately forked tongue: "the guaranty by Congress of equal suffrage to all loyal men at the South was demanded by every consideration of public safety, of gratitude, and of justice, and must be maintained; while the question of justice in all the loyal States properly belongs to the people of those States." In short, black suffrage for the South, but not necessarily for the North. The platform did uphold Reconstruction policy on "equal civil and political rights to all" and railed against Johnson for his "treachery" and "usurpation."

For President the Democrats nominated Horatio Seymour, a former governor of New York long active in national politics, and as his running mate Frank P. Blair, Jr., of Missouri, a former Union general and Republican party organizer who had turned violently against the Radicals. Soon the parties were locked in combat, the Democrats labeling Grant a drunkard, anti-Semite, military bungler, and potential despot, and the Republicans pillorying their foes as madmen and traitors and bigots. Black voting became a key issue as the Democrats taxed their opponents with favoring Negro equality and pursuing a balance-of-power role for blacks in the South. The Democracy (as Democrats called themselves) encountered such hostility in the North that Seymour and Blair offered to step down and be replaced—and leading Democrats seriously considered the idea in the final weeks of the campaign. But it was too late to switch the donkey's riders.

Grant swept the electoral college, 214 to 80, winning all the Northern states save for New York, New Jersey, and Oregon. The popular vote was closer: 3 million to 2.7 million, a majority of 52.7 percent for Grant. Although the Democrats achieved a net gain of eleven seats in the House, the Republicans retained their two-thirds supremacy in that chamber. The North remained loyal to the memory of Lincoln. The Republican party, hardly more than a dozen years old, had already developed a remarkably stable vote of about 55 percent above the Mason-Dixon Line. The Southern and Border states, which divided between the two sides, were more checkered and volatile. Overall, the Republicans had clearly established themselves as the majority party, just as an earlier Republican party had done. But that had been a different brand of republicanism.

"I'SE FREE. AIN'T WUF NUFFIN"

Some Radicals now were more optimistic than ever. Grant's election, they felt, provided a supreme and perhaps final opportunity to reconstruct the South. Now the Republicans had their own men in the White House; they still controlled both houses of Congress; they had established their supremacy over the Supreme Court; they had considerable influence over the federal military and civilian bureaucracy in the South. They still had the power to discipline the Southern states, by admitting them to the Union or expelling them. The Republicans had pushed through the Thirteenth and Fourteenth Amendments. They still possessed the ablest, most experienced political leadership in the nation. Stevens had died during the campaign, but Sumner had been handsomely reelected in Massachusetts. "So at last I have conquered; after a life of struggle," the senator said.

Other Radicals were less sanguine. They knew that far more than Andrew Johnson had thwarted Reconstruction. The national commitment to black equality was weak, the mechanisms of government faulty, and even with the best of intentions and machinery, the connecting line between a decision in Washington and an actual outcome affecting a black family in Virginia or Mississippi was long and fragile. Time and again, voters had opposed black wrongs without favoring black rights. Before the war, they had fought the extension of slavery but not slavery where it existed. During the war, they had come to approve emancipation only after Lincoln issued his proclamation. After the war, in a number of state elections—especially those of 1867—Northerners had shown that they favored black suffrage in the South but not at home.

Spurred by effective leaders, Americans were moving toward racial justice, but the journey was agonizingly slow and meandering. "It took America three-quarters of a century of agitation and four years of war to learn the meaning of the word 'Liberty,' " the *American Freedman* editorialized. "God grant to teach us by easier lessons the meaning of the words 'equal rights.' " How quickly and firmly Americans moved ahead on black rights could turn significantly on continuing moral and political leadership.

The crucial issue after Grant's election was the right of blacks to vote. Republican leaders in Congress quickly pushed ahead with the Fifteenth Amendment, which declared in its final form that the "right of the citizens of the United States to vote shall not be denied or abridged by the United States or by any State on account of race, color, or previous condition of servitude." It was a noble sentiment that had emerged out of a set of highly mixed motives. Democrats charged, with some reason, that the majority party was far less interested in legalizing the freedman's vote in the South than in winning the black vote in the North. But the Republican leadership, knowing that countless whites in the North opposed black voting there, were responding to the demands of morality as well as practicality. Senator Henry Wilson reminded his colleagues that the "whole struggle in this country to give equal rights and equal privileges to all citizens of the United States has been an unpopular one; that we have been forced to struggle against passions and prejudices engendered by generations of wrong and oppression." He estimated that that struggle had cost his party a quarter of a million votes. Another Republican senator, however, contended that in the long run adherence to "equality of rights among men" had been not a source of party weakness but of its strength and power. Most Republicans, the historian Michael Les Benedict has concluded, did not face a hard choice between expediency and morality, "for to a large extent the political fortunes of the Republican party were best served by fulfilling its liberal ideological commitments."

If political morality in the long run meant political practicality, the Fifteenth Amendment nevertheless bore all the markings of compromise. To gain the two-thirds support constitutionally required in each chamber, the sponsors were compelled to jettison clauses that would have outlawed property qualifications and literacy tests. The amendment provided only that Congress and the states could not deny the vote, rather than requiring them to take positive action to secure black suffrage; nor was there any provision against denial of vote by mobs or other private groups. And of course the amendment did not provide for female voting—and so the National Woman Suffrage Association opposed it.

Still, radicals in and out of Congress were elated when the Fifteenth cleared Congress, elated even more when the measure became part of the Constitution in March 1870, after Republican state parties helped drive it through the required number of legislatures. Some of the old-time abolitionists were euphoric too. Their prestige and influence now at a peak, they basked in the adulation they received in the press, their mail, and the hundreds of appearances they made every year in cities and towns throughout the country. Wendell Phillips was especially impressive on the lecture circuit. "Impracticable? Fanatical?" an Iowa editor wrote after hearing him. "Why, he is one of the most entirely plain, common-sense, practical and practicable men we ever heard." Henry Raymond's moderate *New York Times* had to admit that what the radicals "*propose* today may be *law* tomorrow." To the Democratic New York *World* the radicals were a marching army: "Mr. Weed lags in the rear; Mr. Raymond is only six months behind Mr. Greeley, and Mr. Greeley is only six weeks behind Thad Stevens, and Thad Stevens is only six days behind Wendell Phillips, and Wendell Phillips is not more than six inches from the tail and the shining pitchfork of the master of them all."

So euphoric were some abolitionists about the Fifteenth Amendment that they saw their task as done. The Fifteenth, resolved the American

Anti-Slavery Society, was the "capstone and completion of our movement; the fulfillment of our pledge to the Negro race; since it secures to them equal political rights with the white race, or, if any single right be still doubtful, places them in such circumstances that they can easily achieve it." Other radicals were more cautious, even cynical. Lydia Maria Child feared that the Fifteenth might "yet be so evaded, by some contrivance, that the colored population will in reality have no civil rights allowed them." Phillips converted his *Anti-Slavery Standard* into *The Standard,* dedicated to racial equality, labor reform, temperance, and women's rights.

The legal right of blacks to vote soon produced a phenomenon in Southern politics—black legislators, judges, superintendents of education, lieutenant governors and other state officials, members of Congress, and even two United States senators. These, however, made up only a fraction of Southern officeholders: in none of the legislatures did blacks hold a majority, except briefly in South Carolina's lower house. Usually black leaders shared power with "carpetbaggers"—white Northerners who came south and became active in politics as Republicans—and "scalawags"—white Southerners who cooperated with Republicans and blacks. While many black leaders were men of "ability and integrity," in Kenneth Stampp's view, the whites and blacks together comprised a mixed lot of the corrupt and the incorruptible, moderate and extreme, opportunistic and principled, competent and ignorant. The quality of state government under such leadership also was mixed, but on the whole probably no worse than that of many state and local governments of the time. The state governments in the South bore unusually heavy burdens, moreover—demoralization and poverty in the wake of a devastating war, the need to build or rebuild public services throughout the region, the corrupting influence of contractors, speculators, and promoters seeking subsidies, grants, contracts, franchises, and land.

Far more important than the reality of black-and-white rule in the South was the perverted image of it refracted through the distorted lenses of Southern eyes. It was not easy for the white leadership to see newly freed men, some of them illiterate, aggressive, and loutish, occupy positions of prestige and power; and it was perhaps inevitable that they would caricature the new rulers to the world. A picture emerged of insolent boors indulging in legislative license, lording it over downtrodden whites, looting the public treasury, bankrupting the state, threatening white traditions, womanhood, and purity. As sober an observer as Lord Bryce, writing almost a generation later, reported that such a "Saturnalia of robbery and jobbery has seldom been seen in any civilized country"; since "the legislatures were reckless and corrupt, the judges for the most part subservient, the Federal military officers bound to support what purported to be the constitutional authorities of the State, Congress distant and little inclined to listen to the complaints of those whom it distrusted as rebels, greed was unchecked and roguery unabashed."

The worst fear of the old white leadership—that black-and-white rule would produce a social revolution—turned out to be the least warranted of all. The mixed rule of blacks, scalawags, and carpetbaggers produced a few symbolic and actual changes: rhetoric drawn directly from the Declaration of Independence proclaiming liberty, "equality of all persons before the law," various civil and political rights; a mild effort in two or three states to integrate certain educational institutions; a feeble effort at land reform. Constitutions were made somewhat more democratic, legislative apportionment less discriminatory, more offices elective; "rights of women were enlarged, tax systems were made more equitable, penal codes were reformed, and the number of crimes punishable by death was reduced," in Stampp's summation. The constitution of South Carolina—the state that had served as the South's political and ideological heartland, and the state that now paradoxically had elevated the most blacks to leadership positions—was converted almost into a model state charter, with provisions for manhood suffrage, public education, extension of women's rights, and even the state's first divorce law. Shades of John C. Calhoun!

But what the black-and-white leadership failed to do was of far more profound consequence than what it did. Both radicals and moderates understood that education was a fundamental need for Southern blacks, but the obstacles were formidable and progress slow. Even the best educational system could hardly have compensated for decades of illiteracy and ignorance. "The children," James McPherson noted, "came from a cultural environment almost entirely devoid of intellectual stimulus. Many of them had never heard of the alphabet, geography, or arithmetic when they first came to school. Few of them knew their right hand from their left, or could tell the date of their birth. Most of them realized only vaguely that there was a world outside their own plantation or town." In the early years, teachers sponsored by "Freedmen's Aid" and missionary groups met the challenge, often finding to their surprise that black children had a passion to learn, could be taught to read as quickly as white children, and might be found laboriously teaching their own parents the alphabet and the multiplication table.

These private educational efforts were never adequate, however, to teach more than a fraction of the South's black children. The question was whether the reconstructed black-and-white state governments would take over the task in a comprehensive way, and here they failed. The difficulties were at least as great as ever: inadequate facilities, insufficient money, lack of teachers, inadequate student motivation, discipline problems (black teachers tended to be the harsher disciplinarians). But the biggest hurdle was the constant, pervasive, and continuing hostility of many Southern whites to schooling for blacks. "I have seen many an absurdity in my lifetime," said a Louisiana legislator on observing black pupils for the first time, "but this is the climax of absurdities." A Southern white woman warned a teacher that "you might as well try to teach your horse or mule to read, as to teach these niggers. They *can't* learn."

Behind these white Southern attitudes toward schooling for black children lay a host of fears. One was their old worry that blacks would be educated above their station and out of the labor supply. "To talk about educating this drudge," opined the Paducah (Kentucky) *Herald*, "is to talk without thinking. Either to 'educate,' or to teach him merely to read and write, is to ruin him as a laborer. Thousands of them have already been ruined by it." Even more pervasive was the white fear of integration, although most black leaders made it clear that their main interest was education, whether segregated or not. Southern fears often took the form of harassing and humiliating teachers or, more ingeniously, depriving them of white housing so that some teachers lived with blacks—and hence could be arrested as vagrants. Defending the arrest of a freedmen's teacher, the mayor of Enterprise, Mississippi, said that the teacher had been "living on terms of equality with negroes, living in their houses, boarding with them, and at one time gave a party at which there were no persons present (except himself) but negroes, all of which are offenses against the laws of the state and declared acts of vagrancy." Black-and-white governments could not overcome such deep-seated attitudes.

To many blacks, even more important than education was land—"forty acres and a mule." During the war, when workers on a South Carolina plantation had rejected a wage offer from their master, one of them had said, "I mean to own my own manhood, and I'm goin' on to my own land, just as soon as when I git dis crop in. . . ." Declared a black preacher in Florida to a group of field hands: "It's de white man's turn ter labor now. He ain't got nothin' lef' but his lan', an' de lan' won't be his'n long, fur de Guverment is gwine ter gie ter ev'ry Nigger forty acres of lan' an' a mule." Black hopes for their own plots had dwindled sharply after the war, when Johnson's amnesty proclamation restored property as well as civil rights to most former rebels who would take an oath of allegiance. His expectations dashed, a Virginia black said now that he would ask for only a single acre of land—"ef you make it de acre dat Marsa's house sets on."

Black hopes for land soared again after the congressional Republicans took control of Reconstruction in the late 1860s, only to collapse when Republican moderates—and even some radicals—refused to support a program of land confiscation. Black hopes rose still again when black-and-white regimes took over state governments; some freedmen heard rumors that they need only go to the polls and vote and they would return home with a mule and a deed to a forty-acre lot. But, curiously, "radical" rule in no state produced systematic effort at land redistribution. Some delegates to the Louisiana constitutional convention proposed that purchases of more than 150 acres be prohibited when planters sold their estates, and the South Carolina convention authorized the creation of a commission to buy land for sale to blacks, but little came of these efforts. One reason was clear: Southern whites who had resisted black voting and black education would have reacted with even greater fury to as radical a program as land redistribution, with all its implications for white pride, white property—and the white labor supply.

Black leaders themselves were wary of the freedmen's lust for "forty acres and a mule." In part, this caution may have been due to the class divisions between the black Southern masses and their leaders, many of whom had been artisans or ministers, had been free before the war, and had never experienced plantation life and closeness to the soil. Some of these leaders were, indeed, virtually middle-class in their attitudes toward property, frugality, "negative" liberty, and hard work, and in their fear that radical blacks might infuriate white power elites by talking "confiscation." Such leaders preferred to bargain with the white power structure rather than threaten its control over land and other property. Prizing liberal values of individual liberty, the need for schooling, and above all the right to vote, they played down the economic and social needs of the blacks. And they based their whole strategy on the suffrage, arguing that all the other rights that blacks claimed—land, education, homes—were dependent on their using the potential power inherent in their right to vote.

Would black voting make the crucial difference? Of the three prongs of black advance in the South—schools, land, and the vote—the limited success of the first and the essential failure of the second left black suffrage as the great battlefield of Southern reform. Certainly Southern whites realized this and, as the Republican commitment faltered during the Grant Administration, they stepped up their efforts to thwart black voting. They used a battery of stratagems: opening polling places late or closing them early or changing their location; gerrymandering districts in order to neutralize the black vote; requiring the payment of a poll tax to vote; "losing" or disregarding black ballots; counting Democratic ballots more than once; making local offices appointive rather than elective; plying blacks with liquor. These devices had long been used against white Americans, and by no means did all Southern whites use them now, but fraud and trickery were especially effective against inexperienced and unlettered blacks.

When nonviolent methods failed, many Southern whites turned to other weapons against voting: intimidation, harassment, and terror. Mobs drove blacks away from the polls. Whites blocked polling entrances or crowded around ballot boxes so blacks could not vote. Rowdies with guns or whips followed black voters away from the polling place. When a group of black voters in Gibson County, Tennessee, returned the fire of a band of masked men, the authorities put the blacks in jail, from which an armed mob took them by force to a nearby riverbank and shot them down. Fifty-three defendants were arrested by federal authorities and tried, none convicted.

Some of this violence erupted spontaneously as young firebrands, emboldened by liquor, rode into polling areas with their guns blazing. But as the stakes of voting rose, terrorists organized themselves. Most notable was the Ku Klux Klan, with its white robes and hoods, sheeted horses, and its weird hierarchies of wizards, genii, dragons, hydras, ghouls, and cyclopes. Proclaiming its devotion to "Chivalry, Humanity, Mercy, and Patriotism," the Klan proposed to protect the "weak, the innocent, and the defenseless"—and the "Constitution of the United States." The Klan had allies in the Knights of the White Camelia, the White Brotherhood, and other secret societies.

Incensed by mob violence, the Republicans in Washington tried to counter it with legislation. The Enforcement Act of May 1870 outlawed the use of force, bribery, or intimidation that hindered the right to vote because of race in state and local elections. Two more enforcement acts during the next twelve months extended and tightened enforcement machinery, and in April 1871 Congress in effect outlawed the Klan and similar groups. But actual enforcement in the thousands of far-flung polling places required an enormous number of marshals and soldiers. As army garrisons in the South thinned out, enforcement appropriations dwindled, and the number of both prosecutions by white prosecutors and convictions by white juries dropped, black voting was more and more choked off.

After his election to a second term Grant tried vigorously though spasmodically to support black rights for the sake of both Republican principle and Republican victories. In a final effort, the Republicans were able to push through the Civil Rights Act of 1875, designed to guarantee equal rights for blacks in public places, but the act was weak in coverage and enforcement, and later would be struck down by the Supreme Court.

By the mid-seventies Republicanism, Reconstruction, and reform were all running out of steam. Southern Democrats were extending their grip over political machinery; the Republican leadership was shaken by an economic panic in 1873, and the party lost badly in the 1874 midterm elections. The *coup de grâce* for Reconstruction came after Rutherford Hayes's razor-thin electoral-college victory in 1876 over Samuel J. Tilden. Awarded the office as a result of Republican control over three Southern states where voting returns were in doubt, and as a result too of a Republican majority on the Electoral Commission, Hayes bolstered his position by offering assurances about future treatment of the South. While these were in the soft political currency of veiled promises and delphic utterances, the currency was hard enough for the Democrats—and for Hayes as well. Within two months of his inauguration, he ordered the last federal troops out of the South and turned over political control of Louisiana, South Carolina, and Florida to the Southern Democracy.

*   *   *

And what of the objects of this long political struggle—the black people of the South? The vast majority were in the same socioeconomic situation as ten years before, at the end of the war. They had gained certain personal liberties, such as the right to marry, and a modicum of legal and civil and political rights, including the right to vote in certain areas; but their everyday lot was much the same as before. Most still lacked land, property, money, capital; they were still dependent on the planters, sometimes the same old "massa." It was not a black man but a prominent white Georgian who said of the freedman late in 1865: "The negro's first want is, not the ballot, but a chance to live,—yes, sir, *a chance to live.* Why, he can't even live without the consent of the white man! He has no land; he can make no crops except the white man gives him a chance. He hasn't any timber; he can't get a stick of wood without leave from a white man. We crowd him into the fewest possible employments, and then he can scarcely get work anywhere but in the rice-fields and cotton plantations of a white man who has owned him and given up slavery only at the point of the bayonet. . . . What sort of freedom is that?"

Many a freedman had exchanged bondage for a kind of bargaining relationship with employers, but his bargaining position was woefully weak. If he held out for better terms, he could be evicted; if he left, he might be denied work elsewhere and arrested for vagrancy; if he struck, he had no unions or money to sustain him. So the "bargains" were usually one-sided; contracts sometimes literally required "perfect obedience" from employees. Some blacks had had the worst of both worlds—they had left the security of old age and sickness in bondage, under masters who cared for them because they were valuable property, for a strange "free-market" world in which they developed new dependencies on old masters.

Could Reconstruction have turned out differently? Many have concluded that the impotence of the blacks was too deeply rooted, the white intransigence too powerful, the institutions of change too faulty, and the human mind too limited to begin to meet the requirements of a genuine Reconstruction. Yet the human mind had already conducted a stupendous social revolution with the blacks. For a hundred years and more, Southern planters, assisted by slave recruiters in Africa, masters of slaving ships, various middlemen, auctioneers, and drivers, had been uprooting blacks by the hundreds of thousands out of far-off tribal civilizations, bringing most of them safely across broad expanses of water, establishing them in a new and very different culture, and converting them into productive and profit-creating slaves. Somehow the human mind seemed wholly capable of malign "social engineering," incapable of benign.

Yet there were some Americans who did understand the kind of broad social planning and governmental action that was needed to reconstruct genuine democracy in the South and truly to liberate the freed people. Wendell Phillips understood the depth of the problem, the need for a "social revolution." He said: "You must plant at the South the elements which make a different society. You cannot enact four millions of slaves, ignorant, down-trodden, and despised, into personal equals of the old leaders of the South." He wanted to "give the negroes land, ballot and education and to hold the arm of the Federal government over the whole Southern Territory until these seeds have begun to bear fruit beyond any possibility of blighting." We must see to it, said Senator Henry Wilson, that "the man made free by the Constitution is a freeman indeed; that he can go where he pleases, work when and for whom he pleases; that he can sue and be sued; that he can lease and buy and sell and own property, real and personal; that he can go into the schools and educate himself and his children. . . ." Douglass and Stevens and Sumner took similar positions.

These men were not typical of Republicans or even of Radical Republicans, but many other radicals and moderates recognized that the freed people needed an array of economic, political, social, and legal supports, and that these were interrelated. Congressman George Hoar lamented that blacks had been given universal suffrage without universal education. Some radicals believed that voting was the black's first need and others that land or sustenance came first, but most recognized that no single "solution" was adequate. Antislavery men, said Phillips, "will believe the negro safe when we see him with 40 acres under his feet, a schoolhouse behind him, a ballot in his right hand, the sceptre of the Federal Government over his head, and no State Government to interfere with him, until more than one-half of the white men of the Southern States are in their graves."

Did the fault then lie with the political system? The checks and balances among President, Senate, and House; the curious nomination and election devices that brought in an "anti-nigger" Vice-President to succeed the Great Emancipator; the clumsy, fragmented federal system; the need for both houses to muster two-thirds votes on crucial issues; the underlying thinness and instability in the popular support for Reconstruction—all these testified to the inability of the national government to develop firm, comprehensive, consistent, and durable programs of reconstruction. On the other hand, the Republicans did get rid of Johnson; they enjoyed two-thirds majorities in Congress at intervals; they won popular support for Reconstruction programs in every national election for a decade; and federalism was largely suspended during Reconstruction. Never was the "system" so adaptable to high purposes as during Reconstruction.

The critical failure of Reconstruction probably lay far more in the realm of leadership—especially that of opinion-makers. Editors, ministers, and others preached liberty and equality without always comprehending the full dimensions of these values and the means necessary—in the South of the 1870s—to accomplish such ends. The radicals "seemed to have little conception," according to Stampp, "of what might be called the sociology of freedom, the ease with which mere laws can be flouted when they alone support an economically dependent class, especially a minority group against whom is directed an intense racial prejudice." Reconstruction could have succeeded only through use of a strategy employed in a number of successful postwar reconstructions of a comprehensive nature—a strategy of combining ideological, economic, political, educational, and institutional forces in such a firm and coordinated way as truly to transform the social environment in which Southerners, both black and white, were trying to remake their lives after the Civil War. And such a strategy, it should be noted, would have imposed heavy intellectual, economic, and psychological burdens on the North as well.

Not only would such a strategy have called for rare political leadership—especially for a leader, in William Gillette's words, able to "fashion a means and then persevere in it, bending men to his purpose by vigorous initiative, skillful influence, and masterful policy." Even more it called for a rare kind of *intellectual* leadership—political thinkers who could translate the component elements of values such as liberty and equality into policy priorities and operational guidelines. But aside from a few radicals such as Phillips, most of the liberals and many of the radicals had a stunted view of the necessary role of public authority in achieving libertarian and egalitarian purposes. *The Nation,* the most influential liberal weekly in the

postwar period, under Edwin L. Godkin shrank from using the only means
—government—that could have marshaled the resources necessary for
genuine reconstruction. "To Govern Well," *The Nation* proclaimed, "Govern Little." A decisive number of otherwise liberal-minded and generously
inclined intellectual leaders held similar views. Thus, leaders like Phillips
and like Sumner, who said that "whatever you enact for Human Rights is
Constitutional," were left politically isolated. There were many reasons for
the failure of Reconstruction, but the decisive one—because it occurred in
people's conceptualizing and analyzing processes and not merely in ineluctable social and economic circumstances—took place in the liberal
mind. Most of the liberals were effective transactional leaders, or brokers;
few displayed transforming leadership.

That liberal mind seemed to have closed itself off even to the results of
practical experimentation. During the war, General Sherman had set aside
for freedmen several hundred thousand acres on the Sea Islands south of
Charleston and on the abandoned rice lands inland for thirty miles along
the coast. Each black family was to receive its forty acres until Congress
should rule on their final disposition. Federal officials helped settle 40,000
blacks on these lands. When the whole enterprise was terminated by Johnson's pardon and amnesty program, and land turned back to former owners, the black farmers were incredulous. Some had to be driven off their
land by force. The program had lasted long enough, however, to demonstrate that freed people could make a success of independent farming, and
that "forty acres and a mule" could serve as the foundation of Reconstruction. But the lesson seemed lost on Northerners who shuddered at the
thought of "land confiscation."

Thus the great majority of black people were left in a condition of
dependency, a decade after war's end, that was not decisively different, in
terms of everyday existence, from their prewar status. They were still
landless farm laborers, lacking schooling, the suffrage, and self-respect.
They achieved certain civil and legal rights, but their expectations had
been greatly raised too, so the Golden Shore for many seemed more
distant than ever. Said a black woman: "De slaves, where I lived, knowed
after de war dat they had abundance of dat somethin' called freedom, what
they could not eat, wear, and sleep in. Yes, sir, they soon found out dat
freedom ain't nothin', 'less you is got somethin' to live on and a place to
call home. Dis livin' on liberty is lak young folks livin' on love after they
gits married. It just don't work."

Or as an Alabama freedman said more tersely when asked what price tag
he bore—and perhaps with two meanings of the word in mind:

"I'se free. Ain't wuf nuffin."

PART II
The Business
of Democracy

CHAPTER 3

The Forces of Production

H E must study politics and war, John Adams had said, so that his sons
might have liberty to study mathematics and philosophy, geography, natural history and naval architecture, in order to give *their* children
a right to study painting, poetry, music, architecture, statuary, tapestry,
and porcelain. But it did not quite work out that way. A son, John
Quincy, took up not philosophy but diplomacy, politics, and the presidency. A grandson, Charles Francis Adams, embraced not painting and
porcelain but law, diplomacy, and Republicanism. And a great-grandson,
Charles Francis Jr., took up not poetry and music but war, law, business
—and railroads.

"I endeavored to strike out a new path," Charles Francis Adams, Jr., said
later, "and fastened myself, not, as Mr. Emerson recommends, to a star but
to the locomotive-engine."

A locomotive engine! How could this young Adams, inheriting the
Adams disdain for money-grubbing, choose business over public service
and the professions? Because he was restless in that tradition; because as
a young Harvard graduate he felt hopelessly adrift and socially and politically inept, felt that he made the worst kind of "Adams impression"—of
hauteur and gracelessness—even when he wanted to be liked; because
railroads to him meant not only investments but the kind of railroad
regulation that would occupy him during the best years of his life. Above
all because, by the 1850s and 1860s, business and industry, with their
constant innovations, hair-raising speculation, huge losses and dizzying
profits, were coming into their own as respectable occupations for the
privileged—and even more, as a form of intellectual adventure and personal liberation.

The world into which Adams graduated from Harvard in the 1850s, and
the world to which he returned after war service in the 1860s, seemed to
beckon the free-enterprising spirit. The smell of individual opportunity,
the sense of boundless economic possibilities, the idea of unlimited progress seemed to pervade the very air men breathed. The well-established
mid-century businessmen had grown up in an earlier era of Jeffersonian
and Jacksonian individualism. Many had imbibed doctrines of personal and
political liberty, individual enterprise, laissez-faire, limited government.

73

The roaring prosperity of the flush 1840s and 1850s, the exploding technology, the cornucopia of farm and factory goods had whetted their appetites for more prosperity and profits.

Never mind that most Jeffersonians had been as suspicious of big business as of big government, that the federal government in fact built roads,
made grants for canals and railroads, improved rivers and harbors, passed
tariffs to help American exporters and shippers. No matter that some state
governments launched almost an orgy of public enterprise, subsidizing
banks and even establishing them, building and chartering turnpikes, canals, and railroads, providing bounties to farmers who grew certain crops,
experimenting with numerous social reforms. The ethic of individual responsibility, of personal progress, of economic self-fulfillment, prevailed.
Had not Emerson himself preached a need for the self-reliant man of
affairs?

Adams plunged into an economic arena in which technology paced the
growth of productive forces and production was the measure of all things
economic. As early as the 1820s American patents had averaged three
times those in Britain, the production center of the world; of course, as
Englishmen pointed out, Washington had far easier patent requirements
than London. "Machinery has taken almost entire possession of the manufacture of cloth," an observer noted in 1844; "it is making steady—we
might say rapid—advance upon all branches of iron manufacture; the
newly invented machine saws, working in curves as well as straight lines."
The planing and grooving machines, and the tenon and mortise machine,
were also impressive. In no field did technology move faster than in
Charles Adams's own, railroads. And not least of the forces for expanded
production was the collective talent of the young men in Adams's war
generation who had mobilized, organized, and transported armies of machines and men.

By the late 1860s the nation was poised for another huge economic
takeoff that would make it, within a quarter century, world leader in the
production of timber and steel, meat packing, the mining of coal, iron,
gold, silver. The only circumstances that seemed able to slow American
production were depression or panic. The fifty years before the Civil War
had seen periodic boom-and-bust: a small boom during the War of
1812–15 followed by speculation, a collapse in foreign market prices and
land values, amid numerous bank failures; a boom in railroad and canal
building in the mid-thirties followed by a drop in stock and commodity
prices and an acute bank crisis; a big expansion in business in the early
1850s followed once again by overspeculation in railroads and land and
then by a brief but sharp panic.

The remorseless sequence of boom-and-bust seemed to pick up again after the Civil War. In the wake of an overextension of railroad securities and the failure of the banking house of Jay Cooke and Co. in September 1873, banks failed, brokers went bankrupt, and prices dropped drastically. There followed two decades of steady rise in industrial investment, marred by downturns in the mid-eighties and at the end of that decade. The panics had their human cost, not least among the capitalists themselves. "Am going through a period of such stress—Bluest kind of a blue day—Stocks tumbling—I am caught and must bow my back to the burden—Took a cogitating sleigh ride—I'm trying to get sail in," young Adams jotted down in his diary day by day during the troubles of '83.

But Adams's woes could not compare with those of the masses of men thrown out of work in every depression or major panic—a fact well appreciated by Karl Marx and Friedrich Engels. And no capitalist was more concerned about the forces of production, and the failures of production, than the author of *Capital.* Not only was production an initial material test of the capacity of an economy to perform; even more, the *forces* of production—by which Marx meant workers, raw materials, technology, and organization—essentially determined the productive relations of classes, which in turn conditioned intellectual and political forces. His conception of history, he wrote in *The German Ideology,* started from "the material production of life itself" and the need to "comprehend the form of intercourse connected with this and created by this (i.e., civil society in its various stages), as the basis of all history; further, to show it in its action as State, to explain the whole mass of different theoretical products and forms of consciousness, religion, philosophy, ethics, etc., etc., and trace their origins and growth by which means, of course, the whole thing can be shown in its totality (and therefore, too, reciprocal action of these various sides on one another)." The mass of productive forces, not "idealistic humbug," was crucial.

"The bourgeoisie," he and Engels asserted in the *Communist Manifesto,* "cannot exist without constantly revolutionizing the instruments of production, and thereby the relations of production, and with them the whole relations of society."

Karl Marx. Twenty years after the Communist Manifesto of 1848, few Americans had heard of him or the blazing summons to the world proletariat, even fewer of his partner Friedrich Engels or of the recently published *Capital.* Some Americans had read his January 1865 letter to Lincoln, asserting that the "anti-slavery war" would bring the ascendancy of the working class just as the Revolutionary War had brought that of the middle class, and foreseeing the inexorable fate of the Emancipator—the "single-minded son of the working class"—to lead that struggle. Marx's views were doubtless better known to good bourgeois readers of the New York *Daily Tribune* than to American toilers, for Marx, with Engels's help, had written nearly five hundred articles on American, European, and Asian politics for the *Tribune* between 1852 and 1862, until Horace Greeley became disturbed by his views and dropped him.

Nor would most Americans have been impressed by the man himself, living and working in a grimy London flat among dense tobacco fumes, piles of newspapers and manuscripts, the heady talk of visiting revolutionaries. His family was blighted by illness and poverty; one child died, then another, and the father was afflicted with liver troubles, hepatitis, a facial ulcer, coughing spells, carbuncles. He spoke of the "wretchedness of existence." But, by sheer force of will and intellect, he and Engels were impressing their views on the quarreling, floundering revolutionaries of Europe.

Marx had long been fascinated by far-off America, by its economic dynamism, its vast frontier that could drain off steaming social pressures, its socioeconomic classes that seemed to him to "continually alter and mutually exchange their component parts," and above all by its "feverish and youthful movement of a material production" that "has to appropriate a new world [but] has left neither time nor opportunity for the abolition of the old spiritual world." The intensity of that production meant to Marx that—in contrast to his mentor Hegel's view of the United States as "outside history"—Americans had moved *within* history by the mid-nineteenth century. And production was crucial; he credited the bourgeoisie with freeing productive forces, accomplishing "wonders far surpassing the Egyptian pyramids, Roman aqueducts, and Gothic cathedrals." American railroads especially impressed Marx, for they would bring class unity.

For both communist and capitalist, in short, Production was king. And for both, technology was his sword.

INNOVATORS: THE INGENIOUS YANKEES

The Hoosac Mountains, northwest Massachusetts, the late 1860s:

Technology is a wholly practical matter to several hundred men slowly boring a tunnel through the Hoosac mountain range of northwest Massachusetts during the late 1860s. Knee-deep in muck, soaked to the skin, they have to attend to their drilling and blasting while staying on guard against falling rock, floods, suffocating dust and smoke, premature explosions. A hundred or more men have died in small accidents since the digging started; still more will die before the toilers glimpse their goal, the "pinprick of light." These are hardy men. Some have recently arrived from Canada, Ireland, and Italy; others are old Yankees whose forefathers might have included some of "Shays's rebels" who had stumbled over the Hoosac range through the bitter winter of 1787 as they fled from the state militia.

Over four miles in length, the most direct link between Boston and the busy Troy factories on the Hudson, the Hoosac would be the longest bore in the United States when completed. But when would this be? Originally proposed in 1819, actually started in 1851, the tunnel project had repeatedly run out of funds. The men had not faltered, only the machines. At the start, amidst much pomp and ceremony, "Wilson's Patented Stone-Cutting Machine," weighing seventy-five tons, had been hauled from South Boston and wheeled into the east portal of the bore. Its huge revolving iron cutters were expected to grind out a circle of rock; then black powder would blast out the center. While visiting legislators watched with delight, the monster crunched into the rock for about ten feet. Then it ground to a halt, never to run again, defeated by the Hoosac gneiss and schist.

Not for twenty-five years would the Hoosac barrier be pierced—and then only because of clever innovations. In the early years, the tunnelers used simple gunpowder to split the rock. One man held the star-pointed hand drill while his workmate whacked it three or four feet into the rock with a twenty-pound double-jack hammer. Next the powder—a mixture of saltpeter, sulfur, and charcoal—was tamped into the drill hole and ignited by a goose-quill fuse; then the igniter sprinted for safety while his mates cowered behind heavy wooden parapets. In later years a "safety fuse" made of powder thread spun in jute yarn and coated with coal tar was attached. Still later compressed-air rock drills, with holes in the center through which water was pumped to cool the bits and clear the dust, considerably quickened progress.

Even more important was the replacement of gunpowder with nitroglycerin. In a two-story factory in North Adams, at the west portal, glycerine was mixed, drop by drop, with nitric and sulfuric acids, in a solution bathed in ice and stirred continuously. Several times more powerful than black powder, nitro was also far more volatile. It had such a reputation for killing workers that its shipment was regulated abroad, and interstate in America, but it continued to take its toll among Hoosac men. One day, C. P. Granger was hauling a load of nitro to the bore when his sleigh skidded over a snowbank. Granger jumped into the snow and awaited the blast; hearing none, after a time he collected the now frozen cartridges, only to discover that they could not be detonated until thawed. Thereafter nitro was carried frozen.

Most of the technological progress, however, was due more to determined experimentation than to luck. New ideas and machines at first were imported from abroad, after Yankee engineers had scoured England and the Continent—especially Italy and France—for the latest tunneling techniques. In turn the Hoosac innovators, and others like them, fertilized inventions in other fields. In particular, the new drilling and detonating methods stimulated innovation in the coal and iron mines to the west. Coal production was soaring as more and more mines opened west of the Alleghenies and, as coal went, so went the flourishing iron industry, with its rolling mills and puddling furnaces. By the early 1870s, Henry Clay Frick was buying up extensive coal lands in southwest Pennsylvania, building thousands of beehive ovens, introducing machines for drawing coke from the ovens—a fuel that when fired produced far greater heat than raw coal—and shipping coke by the trainload to the Pittsburgh iron mills.

The American Iron Age had long before dawned as Missouri ore mountains were opened up and then the rich Marquette range in the 1840s. Transportation had been the bottleneck in the Lake Superior region—even sleds and sailboats had been used—until the federal government built a canal at the Sault Sainte Marie rapids in 1856 and steamboats and railroads took over the big hauling jobs. Civil War ironclads had dramatized the power of the dense metal. The reign of Iron really began as rock drills replaced the picks of earlier days, steam shovels scooped up the ore from the stockpiles and dumped it into the shipping cars, and the elongated ore ships, built of iron too, carried the huge loads on the long trip to the hungry furnaces. Just as Hoosac workers had been lowered through shafts to the bore below, the iron miners were let down in steel cages to the mining areas as these were tunneled ever deeper.

Technology paved the way for all this, and no technology was more pivotal than machine tools. Just as Hoosac tunnelers and Marquette drillers had to wait for their compressed-air drills and other equipment, manufacturers of a hundred products had to wait on the innovations of "ingenious Yankees" in the famous old firms of New England, New York, Pennsylvania, and Ohio. Gone were the earlier days when Americans had to borrow from the English engineer-entrepreneurs who had developed boring machines and planers mainly for the making of British steamships and locomotives; gone too were the days when American ingenuity seemed devoted primarily to the arms industry. Now, after the Civil War, "Yankee inventors" were brilliantly carrying forward their earlier progress in precisely formed, smoothly machined interchangeable parts.

Milling machines, developed intensively in national armories, served as the cutting edge of this cutting-edge industry. By 1880, thousands of these versatile machines had been built to fashion tools to make arms, clocks, sewing machines, and more machine tools. Turret lathes, which held a cluster of tools that performed a precise sequence of operations without needing resetting or removing of the workpiece, had virtually revolutionized the production of large quantities of small components such as screws; now the revolution was renewed through the automatic turret lathe, which "was eventually to make possible all modern automatic lathe operations." Other machinery had to be perfected—hard, durable, precise ball bearings, for one thing—as bigger and speedier machinery was put on the market.

By the late nineteenth century, celebrated American firms and their famous inventors were becoming the talk of the business world, even of industrial exhibitions abroad. At the old Brown and Sharp firm in Providence, J. R. Brown, son of the founder, produced the first micrometers to be manufactured commercially. Pratt and Whitney in Hartford perfected interchangeability of parts by developing a standard system of gauges, a comparator accurate to one fifty-thousandth of an inch, and finally a standard measuring machine. In Philadelphia, William Sellers developed a standardized system of screw threads, nuts, and boltheads that was to be adopted even in Europe. The most imaginative of the innovators was Frederick W. Taylor, who worked at a steel company headed by Sellers. A Harvard Law School graduate who climbed his way up from common laborer to chief engineer, Taylor became the genius-inventor of automatic grinders, forging and tool-feeding mechanisms and the biggest practical steam hammer ever built in the United States; later he introduced a steel alloy that vastly improved the efficiency of cutting tools at high temperatures.

Machines, like men, need one another. As drilling and cutting machines helped stimulate coal and metal production, innovations in iron and steel production made possible the development of tougher high-speed machinery. With the development of the Bessemer process, iron and steel technology moved a long way from the days of the blacksmith's forge or the puddler's mold. Into the Bessemer converter, which looked like a great pear-shaped egg, air was blasted from the bottom and molten pig iron poured from the top, with the effect of volatilizing the carbon, silicon, and other impurities in the iron ore. Slow to adopt the Bessemer process, American steel makers forged ahead rapidly after the Civil War as they built vaster—and vastly more efficient—blast furnaces.

Bursting into a volcano of sparks in the stygian gloom of the huge steel plants, the Bessemer converters became a symbol of the fiery age of iron and steel. Few could forget their first sight of the process: the seething pig iron in the converter—the flames flashing out of the pot as the air roared into the bottom—the dazzling explosion of sparks that rained down among the workers—the brawny steelmen, expressionless behind their heavy glass goggles, tilting the converter to pour out the molten steel, amid another shower of sparks. Almost as dramatic were the next steps, as the ingot castings were moved to the forge where enormous hammers molded them almost like butter, or to the rolling mills that flattened them into blooms and billets and then rolled them into rails, rods, bars, slabs, and strips.

Some of these rods and strips went into iron and steel's most conspicuous achievements—the bridges that spanned the nation's widest rivers. For some years American engineers, borrowing heavily from European experience, had been putting up suspension bridges which, aside from such brilliant achievements as John Roebling's Niagara span, had a tendency to collapse. Waiting to be bridged in the early 1870s was the mighty Mississippi—mighty in its width, in its depth, in its 200,000 cubic feet moving ten feet a second in high-water time, in the massive ice fields that drifted down from the north, in the deep mud that made abutments insecure. Waiting to bridge the Mississippi at St. Louis was a remarkable engineer, Captain James Eads. Little schooled except in the price of technological progress—he had arrived in St. Louis in 1833 at the age of thirteen in a steamboat that burst into flames as it docked, and he made his first fortune on the Mississippi salvaging wrecked steamboats with a diving bell—Eads had built ironclads during the Civil War, and now was responding to the pleas of St. Louis businessmen weary of having to ferry goods across the river.

Advised by experts to build either a suspension bridge or a standard multiple-span iron truss, Eads decided instead on the old arch form—but built of steel rather than stone or iron. He designed a center arch of 515 feet, attached to two piers resting in bedrock, with side arch spans of 497 feet running from the piers to shore abutments. These abutments had to be built down to a depth never before achieved. Borrowing from French experience, Eads devised a caisson down whose center spiral stairs diggers descended to the river floor. Emerging from work at the 76-foot depth, the crews began to complain of stomach pains caused by the change in pressure. From a depth of 93 feet, a man climbed to the top feeling fine, only to drop dead ten minutes later; five more men died of the bends in the next few days. Working with his personal physician, Eads hit on the solution— gradual decompression. With his deepest abutment solidly planted 103 feet below the surface, Eads then could turn to the task of cantilevering his arches out from the piers and joining the arch halves high over the river.

The bridge opened for vehicles and locomotives in June 1874—and still stands today.

Better steel and steel-making were already putting within reach the improved farm equipment that would in turn swell the farm produce that the long freight trains would now haul across the Mississippi. Steel would make possible a new harrow with long, curved spring teeth that could cope better than iron tines with hard roots and rocks. Another new harrow with discs of varying shapes and sizes, automatically scraped clean as they revolved, came into wide use. New American grain drills, with devices that fed seed into furrows opened up mechanically by fluted hoes, won praise abroad—even a gold medal at the Paris Exhibition of 1878.

One innovation, the twine binder, hardly looked imposing enough to revolutionize harvesting, but so it did. Men had for centuries walked behind reapers and rake, binding the straw into bundles—a slow and costly task. Then a new mechanical wire binder delighted farmers, until they discovered that bits of wire were showing up in cattle straw and even in flour. The twine binder, made of imported Manila jute and sisal rather than wire and employing an automatic knot-tying device, solved this problem so well that Cyrus McCormick sold over 15,000 of the new product in the single year of 1882.

Tunnels and mines—iron and steel—jute and sisal: still other fields would attract the innovators. During the first decade after the Civil War, Samuel Van Syckel installed an oil pipeline near Titusville, Pennsylvania; the Massachusetts Institute of Technology opened with fifteen students; Congress legalized the metric system (but did not require its use); Maria Mitchell became, at Vassar College, the nation's first woman professor of astronomy; America's first refrigerated railroad car was built in Detroit; the *American Naturalist* magazine was founded; George Westinghouse invented air brakes; the Federal Meteorological Service was established as part of the United States Army Signal Corps; Luther Burbank undertook experiments with plant breeding; *Popular Science Monthly* began publication; Louis Agassiz founded the first American school to concentrate on oceanography. During the following decade, James Sargent and Halbert Greenleaf patented a time lock for bank vaults; Josiah Willard Gibbs applied the laws of thermodynamics to physical chemistry in his *On the Equilibrium of Heterogeneous Substances;* the American Chemical Society was founded; Asaph Hall, astronomer, discovered two moons of Mars; America's first copper refinery was established in Connecticut; George Eastman patented a process for making dry photographic plates; the Archeological Institute of America was founded in Boston and the American Society of Mechanical Engineers in New York; Hiram Maxim invented a machine gun and a self-regulating electric generator; surgeons began to use silk sutures instead of catgut; Lewis E. Waterman patented a practical fountain pen; smokeless gunpowder was developed; and all through this decade Thomas Edison and others were patenting invention after invention in the field of electricity, culminating in the decking out of the Statue of Liberty with electric arc lamps as she waited to be dedicated in New York Harbor.

Americans seemed to be bursting with ideas, experiments, inventions, enterprises, projects. And why not? The nation offered an almost ideal setting for ambitious young men, inventive tinkerers, innovating leaders, risk-taking entrepreneurs. Its "relatively open and uncluttered scene," in economist John E. Sawyer's words, "the abundance of natural resources, the availability of labor and capital from abroad, the timing of 19th Century American expansion in relation to the long evolution of technology and of the institutions of market capitalism in the Western world—these constituted a set of conditions and objective possibilities without historical parallel. . . ." A fluid social structure, largely unorganized labor, and a generally noninterfering national government doubtless helped. And the fact that white Americans were perhaps the best-educated population in the world helped even more; the investment in popular schooling in the 1840s and 1850s was now paying off.

Marx, Engels & co. were not surprised by all this. They knew that the very heart of bourgeois rule was its technological dynamism, its incentives for higher productivity, its capacity to exploit scientific knowledge in manipulating the natural environment so as to satisfy human wants, whatever its colossal human cost in the end. There was a law, Marx said in *Wage-Labor and Capital,* a law of competition that gave capital no rest and continually whispered in its ears: "Go on! Go on!"

If capitalistic incentive was the mainspring of progress, experimentation was the method. The test of successful experimentation was simple: What worked? And the test of what worked was simple, on the face of it: that which satisfied economic demand reflecting human wants and needs. This practical, empirical, utilitarian test had long been familiar, going back to Benjamin Franklin and his contemporaries. While paying tribute to Franklin's earlier emphasis on things that were "useful," Jefferson had complimented Thomas Cooper on the practicality of Cooper's chemistry, in contrast to the chemists who had not, Jefferson felt, been attentive "to domestic objects, to malting, for instance, brewing, making cider . . . bread, butter, cheese, soap. . . ." He hoped Cooper would make his chemistry "intelligible to our good house-wives."

It was the old American tradition of practical experimentation—but it held possible dangers to longer-run progress. Technological development in America had typically consisted of experimental, step-by-step advances, conducted "by guess and by God," in specific, narrow fields calling for mechanical skill and ingenuity. The tinkerers and inventors had not conceptualized outside their fields because of the tradition of practicality, the immediate needs of hoped-for investors and customers, and the fact that their technical educations had been in the shop rather than in the science laboratory or lecture hall. "Our greatest thinkers," a practical man boasted, "are not in the library, nor the capitol, but in the machine shop." This view was understandable; before 1870 the nation had no journal wholly devoted to the subject of chemistry. But it meant that inventors might become imprisoned within specialities becoming obsolete, like mechanics improving the horse carriage while ignoring the advent of steam.

Alexis de Tocqueville had glimpsed the problem. Americans, he said, "always display a clear, free, original, and inventive power of mind." But hardly any of them, he went on, "devotes himself to the essentially theoretical and abstract portion of human knowledge," to the "loftier spheres of the intellect." Still, he granted, all the "energy and restless activity" could "bring forth wonders."

That Americans were developing a capacity both to bring forth wonders and to exploit broader scientific concepts began to be apparent, however, toward the end of the nineteenth century. It occurred in a world far beyond that of the horse, the steamboat, the locomotive; it occurred in the mysterious field of electricity. Early in the century, André Marie Ampère of France and Michael Faraday of England had pioneered with theories of electromagnetism. The main early work in the United States was carried on by men who came to be entranced by electricity and spent their lives studying and applying it. Thus Joseph Henry of Albany advanced the technology of the electromagnet as he increased the magnetic power of its core by means of thickened insulation. Thomas Davenport, a Vermont blacksmith, without training in electricity or any science, for "some unaccountable reason" saw in a new magnet a possible source of power, built a crude little machine with four battery-powered electromagnets, fixed two of the magnets in a wheel, and found that he could revolve the wheel as he applied current. This discovery made possible the first commercially successful electric motor.

Alexander Graham Bell had been following still another tune, and one that at the start had little to do with electricity. Son of an Edinburgh phonetician who specialized in acoustics and teaching speech to deaf children, Bell had emigrated with his family to Ontario in 1870 and soon moved on to Boston, where he began to conceive a way to transmit the actual sound of the human voice through an electric current. For many months Bell and an assistant, Thomas A. Watson, experimented with pairs of telegraph instruments until one day, when Bell was in one room, routinely tuning the receiving reeds, and Watson was in another, plucking the transmitting reeds to send the right pitch, Watson tapped a stuck transmitter to start it vibrating. Suddenly Bell heard a "twang" on his receiver that he knew instantly to be sound from the vibration induced by a current over the wire from Watson. Amid mounting excitement, Bell had Watson pluck the reed again and again while Bell held the variously tuned receiver reeds against his ear.

By the end of that afternoon, Bell knew that speech could be transmitted electrically. But nine more months of experimentation passed before the two men could transmit intelligible words at their true pitch and loudness. After many tests of more sensitive transmitters and receivers, Bell, one Friday in March 1876, made his last adjustment—adding a speaking-tube mouthpiece—and shouted into the mouthpiece to Watson two rooms away: "Mr. Watson—come here—I want to see you." When Watson burst into his room, Bell was delighted but still not sure. Repeat my words, he told his assistant. Watson: "You said, 'Mr. Watson—come here—I want to see you.'" Then Bell knew for sure.

By the late seventies, it appeared that the man who might eclipse Bell and all other Americans in the field of electricity was the practical experimenter par excellence: Thomas Alva Edison. Everything in Edison's early life had seemed to conspire to make him a mere tinkerer. He was born to a family so little concerned about his formal education that his parents let him leave school at about age twelve to do odd jobs around Port Huron, Michigan, and sell newspapers and candy on the local railroad. With his rumpled clothes, his cowlick, his rough speech (partly because of early deafness), and his tobacco chewing and spitting, he became a kind of Huck Finn of the railroads as he knocked about the Midwest. All the while, he showed a devouring interest in mechanics, saved his money to buy chemicals and batteries, developed an amazing facility both in mastering telegraphy and in turning an unused smoking compartment into his own personal laboratory, and patched up the crude machines of the day. Within a few years he devised improved telegraphy, a legislative vote recorder, a stock ticker, a carbon telephone transmitter, and—most originally—a phonograph.

Nowhere was Edison's empirical style of innovation more vividly illustrated than in his search for a practical incandescent lamp. In the 1870s, Americans were already lighting their city streets, department stores, hotels, and factories with arc lamps. Consisting essentially of two electromagnets between which an arc flared when voltage was applied, these lamps produced such an intense light that people came from miles around to watch them turned on, and even fell to their knees in fear and awe. Their intensity and size, however, along with a tendency to flicker, made arc lamps unsuitable for less public places; what was needed was a moderate, steady, easily controlled light. For years, inventors had been experimenting with incandescent lights, but they could not find a filament that would glow with a white heat and not be quickly consumed.

Edison's search for this filament became one of the great sagas of empirical investigation. "Somewhere in God Almighty's workshop," he is reported to have said, "there is a dense, woody growth with fibers almost geometrically parallel and with practically no pith, from which excellent strands can be cut." He and his associates tested thousands of plants and grasses—even hairs clipped from the beards of staff members—and sent investigators to the jungles of South America and Asia until a species of Japanese bamboo seemed to work. More successful was a carbonized cotton filament that burned for forty hours.

All through this and succeeding experiments—on electrical distribution, on a fluoroscope, on the magnetic separation of iron, on the storage battery, on a dictating machine and a mimeograph and a moving picture machine—Edison continued to pride himself on being the practical experimenter, to poke fun at theoretical scientists, to disdain the upper-class pretensions of the academic elite. Yet he had read deeply in Faraday and other scientists, he openly exploited scientific ideas, and he employed a mathematical scientist in his laboratory at Menlo Park, New Jersey. In effect he was an innovative and imaginative "man of science," if not a man of strikingly original theoretical ideas. Perhaps more than any other inventor of note, he personified the marriage of science and technology in late nineteenth-century America—a marriage that would spawn both benign and malignant progeny in the century ahead.

INVESTORS: EASTERN DOLLARS AND WESTERN RISKS

It was not easy to be an investor, even in the heyday of American capitalism and even when you inherited money. Charles Francis Adams, Jr., as he commuted between his idle and cheerless Boston law office and the ancestral home in Milton that could only remind him of his famous ancestors, alternated between periods of boring aimlessness and acute anxiety. His life was empty, "dull as ditchwater," he confided to his diary. At times he felt like "tearing things." Especially agonizing were the financial panics that periodically threatened his—and his wife's—small fortunes.

Adams felt too that he lacked courage, combativeness, the capacity to take risks and enjoy doing so. With sneaking admiration as well as disdain, he had written after visiting the New York Stock Exchange that he had seen "men as nature made them, with every affectation cast aside."

Investing called for more than available funds; it called also for a daring, an imagination, and an unquenchable confidence that were still remembered from the Boston of old and set the style for new entrepreneurs elsewhere. Men who had long sought their fortunes around the periphery of the Atlantic, in the Near East and the Far East, now turned to the uncharted resources of the American Midwest and West. And if the investors tended to define the West as anything the other side of the Connecticut River, or even of Dedham, they had overcome problems of terrain and technology, as in piercing the Hoosac barrier, that would anticipate greater challenges across the Appalachians and, later, the Rockies.

"A happy New Year to you, my beloved husband!" Susan Sedgwick of Stockbridge had written in the early days of 1828 to Theodore Sedgwick, who had just proposed the building of the Boston & Albany Railroad at state expense. "May it preserve to you all your blessings, multiply your strawberries, extend your grapes, & build your RAILROAD!" Amid failing health and jeering skepticism, Sedgwick had seen the line extended from Worcester to Springfield before he died.

Not even the trials and tribulations of railroading, however, could compare with the agonizing problems and dizzying profits of Boston's greatest feat—opening up the copper lodes of Michigan. Mined by Indians for arrowheads and ornaments long before Columbus, the copper deposits lay in a small peninsula jutting out into Lake Superior. Everything seemed to conspire against profitable investment: the isolation of the copper country; the cost of shipping copper by lighters and shallow vessels on Superior's waters, and then of unloading and reloading at Sault Sainte Marie; crude mining techniques that had miners digging by candlelight, hauling carts by their own labor, climbing up and down 100-foot ladders. But the Bostonians persevered, raising more capital and enlisting governmental aid. Their men on the peninsula installed steam hoists and pumps, modernized stamping and washing processes through "much trial-and-error fumbling" in William B. Gates's words, and eventually solved the "special problems of the native, low-content rock." Nevertheless, a host of old Bostonians lost their starched shirts as mines folded in the face of heavy costs and unstable world demand.

Then persistence paid off for some in the discovery of sensational lodes at the Calumet and Hecla properties, later combined. Louis Agassiz, already renowned as a Harvard naturalist, reported to his brother-in-law, Quincy Adams Shaw, that with some of the lodes yielding an incredible 15 percent of copper, the value of Calumet and Hecla was "beyond the wildest dreams of copper men." Between 1867 and 1872 the percentage of Michigan copper shipped by Calumet and Hecla rose from 8 to 65. About eight hundred predominantly Boston stockholders waxed for years on Calumet and Hecla dividends; owning C & H became a mark of financial perspicacity and a badge of social status. Some of the shareholders were far more equal than others in the huge fortunes they extracted from the mines; for decades the Shaws alone mined yearly dividends of almost $300,000 from the distant lodes on Superior.

Still, it was railroading that seemed most to arouse the avarice and passions of Boston investors. John Murray Forbes, who had returned home from China at the age of twenty-four after making a fortune in Canton representing a Boston countinghouse, came to exemplify the bold "general entrepreneur" defined by Thomas C. Cochran as owning a big share in many ventures but tying himself down to none. Reluctant at first to break away from the world of seafaring and trading, he eventually plunged into railroad investment, led a group of capitalists in buying the unfinished Michigan Central Railroad from that state for $2 million, pushed the Central to Lake Michigan and then to Chicago, and thereafter carried his little empire farther west to the Mississippi River and across Iowa.

Some of these railroad leaders were self-made men; Chester W. Chapin, with only a few years of schooling, owned an ox team, tended bar, and operated steamboats on the Connecticut, before making enough money to promote western New England railroads and head the Boston and Albany. Most of the railroaders, however, were "college men" knit by family membership or close friendship into the economic and social elite of Boston. Many did their investing through Lee, Higginson, which in itself united a host of old New England families. It was to Henry Lee Higginson, a fellow Union officer who proudly bore a Confederate saber cut on his face, that Charles F. Adams, Jr., would turn for solace and advice.

Within a decade or two of Appomattox, however, the old entrepreneurial spirit seemed to be dying out in Boston. Thomas Gold Appleton honored his father Nathan for building a vast fortune out of shipping and textiles, but he could not emulate him. Thomas, a Harvard man, had no interest in moneymaking and liked to spend his time abroad writing poetry, painting, and composing essays. His despairing father might well have wondered: Would John Adams have approved of *this* kind of third generation? Capital tied up in family trusts, according to Frederic Jaher, was often unavailable for new and bold business ventures. Men now concerned more with promoting education, religion, and the arts were increasingly distanced from the rough and grimy world of railroads, copper, and iron. Perhaps the most poignant symbol of all this was the fate of Daniel Waldo Lincoln, Chapin's successor at the Boston and Albany, who fell from the observation train while watching the Yale-Harvard boat race in 1880 and died.

Financial Boston seemed to be stagnating too, by the 1870s. The "hub" had long since lost out to New York and Philadelphia as a capital market. Manhattan's booming savings banks, insurance companies, and large and efficient investment banking and brokerage agencies had made it the real financial hub of the nation. The availability of ready "call money" in New York attracted millions of speculative dollars. Philadelphia, Baltimore, and Charleston, with their own ports and transportation facilities, shared in the expanding prosperity while Chicago, St. Louis, Cincinnati, and other "western" cities were racing ahead of the old New England centers.

It was A. Lawrence Lowell, himself a descendant of brilliant entrepreneurs, who had the last word, remarking to his fellow Brahmin George Cabot, "I'm getting rather worried about the Lowell Family, George. There's nobody in it making money any more."

Some persons seemed to have a special knack for making money—and also for losing it. These were the private bankers of New York and Philadelphia and other cities, an old-fashioned breed of men who were taking on new importance and becoming known as investment bankers. Private banking had long attracted entrepreneurs. Jacob Barker, a New York merchant and shipowner, at the age of thirty-six had founded the Exchange Bank on Wall Street with a capital investment of $250,000—a bank of which he was the sole owner—during the dying months of the War of 1812. During that war also, Stephen Girard of Philadelphia, another sea trader, became one of the nation's first investment bankers when he helped underwrite a government loan. Following in his footsteps, Nicholas Biddle undertook a full-fledged investment banking business by contracting and negotiating securities. Some of these and other ventures flourished, some failed, but by mid-century the investment banker—essentially a middleman between corporations and governments issuing securities and those corporations, banks, and insurance companies needing long-term capital funds—had become a vital part of the financial system.

War vastly swells the demand for big money quickly raised, and the Civil War was no exception. The need called forth the man—Jay Cooke. Son of an Ohio congressman, Cooke had left school at fourteen, probably more from ambition than need, to clerk in a general store in Sandusky, then in a wholesale house in St. Louis, a transportation company in Philadelphia, and a banking house in the same city. There, on New Year's Day in 1861, he opened his own banking house, Jay Cooke and Co. Through old Ohio and family connections with Secretary Chase, he gained an option to sell a $2 million bond issue in Pennsylvania. He did this so successfully that he was picked to peddle war bonds for the federal government.

Cooke soon proved to be a genius at the mass merchandising of these bonds. Immensely self-confident, still in his early forties, he used patriotic appeals, newspaper advertisements, and a large corps of field agents to sell "five-twenties"—a 6 percent loan payable between five and twenty years. He took the lead in raising half a billion dollars by 1864, and another $600 million in 1865. Perhaps a million Americans took shares in the public debt. A "creative entrepreneur," in Fritz Redlich's words, he vividly demonstrated the potential role in big government and business for multitudinous small pools of savings.

Private banking mushroomed after the war, enormously expanding the pool of investment money. By the early 1870s, over five hundred private banks were established in New York City, over a hundred more in Boston, Philadelphia, and Baltimore together, and hundreds more throughout the country, with a remarkably high number in the western states. Many of these were tiny local banks, but increasingly dominant were the big investment bankers, centered in Wall Street, who alone or with other houses could float whole issues of securities. Some of these firms bore "old" names, such as Morton, Bliss & Co., with roots in ancient mercantile establishments. Others sported new names; the field seemed open to anyone with money and daring. Then there were the "Jewish" houses, as they were viewed, such as J. and W. Seligman and Co. and Kuhn, Loeb, with major foreign contacts. Attracting more and more attention in Wall Street by the 1870s was "young" J. P. Morgan, scion of the famous Junius Morgan of London, the American banker who had won world fame when he coolly placed a $50 million loan for the French during their war with Prussia, in the face of thunderous warnings by Bismarck.

Far more typical of American firms was Morton, Bliss, which left extensive records of its week-to-week activities in the letters of junior partner George Bliss to his senior, Levi P. Morton, who liked to linger in London and Newport. Life at Morton, Bliss was one of constant vigilance—following the securities market, closely watching competitors, picking up rumors, mingling with the bigger financiers, keeping an eye cocked on Washington. The firm had major foreign connections through its English partner, Sir John Rose. Like many other financiers, Morton doubled as a politician; he ran three times for Congress and won twice, and established close ties to the Grant Administration. (He would later serve as Minister to France, Governor of New York, and Vice-President.) But Presidents were temporary conveniences, not permanent allies. When Hayes succeeded Grant,

Bliss wrote a friend that "our position with the new administration" would be "not less favorable (and it should be stronger) than with the last."

Financiers lived day and night in the heady world of Wall and Broad Streets. After feverish bidding in the exchange, men would repair to Delmonico's for more talk of finance, or they might thread their way through the long narrow alley that led to the plain but fashionable Dorlon's and its oysters. When the exchange closed at four, some would move uptown for decorous carriage-riding in the new Central Park, or for spirited trotting up in Harlem Lane. But, from fear and excitement and avarice, the financiers could not escape the market; many would return around six to the "Gold Room," a combination informal exchange and Republican party headquarters, where they kept on trading, sometimes around the clock.

These were enormously self-confident men. However watchful and even fearful they were from day to day in the market, they were also confident of the system that needed only their dynamic leadership. They could take pride, if they paid attention, in the tributes of old adversaries as well as new. "The bourgeoisie," the *Communist Manifesto* had proclaimed, "during its rule of scarce one hundred years, has created more massive and more colossal productive forces than have all preceding generations together. Subjection of nature's forces to man, machinery, application of chemistry to industry and agriculture, steam navigation, railways, electric telegraphs, clearing of whole continents for cultivation, canalization of rivers, whole populations conjured out of the ground—what earlier century had even a presentiment that such productive forces slumbered in the lap of social labour?"

From the perspective of a half-century later, Joseph Schumpeter would picture, as the true economic leaders, the entrepreneurs of this creative period of capitalism. They had to overcome environmental resistances ranging from simple refusal to finance a new thing to "physical attack" on the man who tried to produce it. "To act with confidence beyond the range of familiar beacons and to overcome that resistance requires aptitudes that are present in only a small fraction of the population and that define the entrepreneurial type as well as the entrepreneurial function," Schumpeter said. "This function does not essentially consist in either inventing anything or otherwise creating the conditions which the enterprise exploits. *It consists in getting things done.*"

The investors got things done. In particular, they largely financed the expanded "forces of production" that Marx celebrated. But did they innovate better products, or better ways to make products? Critics charged that the investors were reluctant to subsidize innovation, that they preferred the safe old ways. The trend toward bigger businesses, Thorstein Veblen

said later, and toward control by men with commercial rather than technical skills had led to a failure to innovate. Others disputed this view. But
what does seem clear is that investment in innovative industry was on the
whole safer than many of the entrepreneurs realized. The individual investor did run risks; but collectively the bankers and other investors could
hardly fail in late nineteenth-century America.

One reason for this was the tariff, which was designed particularly to
protect "infant industries." Another was the patent system. Hardly an
entrepreneur operated in this period save in a flurry of patent applications,
patent claims, and patent suits. Patents, to be sure, were also a source of
uncertainty, with some judges defining patents held without use as deserv-
ing little recognition in law and none in equity, and others defining them
as an inviolable property right whether the discovery was used or not. But
the patent system at least set up rules of the game that gave some protection to capitalists financing innovation. What primarily made risk-taking
safe in post–Civil War America, however, was the enterprise system itself
and the environment in which it operated. That system established multi-
ple channels for investors: if one venture failed, another would succeed.
And the environment minimized "interference risks" from a government
that largely kept hands off, a labor force that was largely passive, and
consumers who were largely unorganized.

*   *   *

Railroad issues continued to fuel the speculative market during this
period, and "western" railroads in particular called forth all that was best
and worst in the American entrepreneurial spirit—its daring, imagination,
ability to get things actually done, along with its greed, lack of scruples,
capacity to tarnish and corrupt everything it touched.

The extra-wide rails of the Erie, twisting and winding their way through
the southern tier of New York, epitomized Americans' bittersweet romance
with the railroad. Built with an unusual six-foot gauge in order to hinder
interchange of traffic with the rival Pennsylvania and Baltimore roads, the
Erie swallowed millions of dollars from American and foreign investors—
and from New York taxpayers—before reaching Dunkirk on Lake Erie,
then Buffalo, and finally Chicago, on the eve of the Civil War. During the
1850s, following one of the Erie's periodic money crises, Daniel Drew had
taken control of the railroad's finances. An old-time Hudson Valley cattle
driver and horse trader, Drew combined sharp wits and a lack of scruples
with a "sanctimonious devotion to Methodism." "Shrewd, unscrupulous,
and very illiterate," Charles Francis Adams, Jr., later described him—"a
strange combination of superstition and faithlessness, of daring and timid-

ity." Promptly living up to his reputation, Drew began to manipulate the Erie stock.

His competitive instincts had long before pitted Drew against an even more formidable figure, Cornelius Vanderbilt. As pleasure-loving and calculating as Drew was somber and bold, the "Commodore" had spent most of his sixty-odd years operating sailing ships, ferries, and steamboats on waterways ranging from New York Harbor and the Hudson to the Atlantic and Pacific routes to gold-feverish California. He first came into competition with Drew when the onetime horse trader ran "antimonopoly" boats against him on the Hudson and forced down the fares. The two men squared off again after Vanderbilt bought control of the Harlem Railroad in the late 1850s. In a famous "corner" in 1864, Drew "was outwitted," according to Allan Nevins, "went short on large commitments as the stock rose in five months from 90 to 285, and lost a half million dollars, an episode which left him eager for revenge."

Revenge was only a few years in coming, in what would be known as not merely another contest among capitalists but as the "Erie War." Both sides had prepared for combat. Using every political and financial resource he could muster, Vanderbilt had won control of the Hudson River Railroad and the New York Central; now, if he succeeded in adding the Erie to his rail network, he would monopolize the profitable grain freight from the west. His primary weapon was a long-tested one—the kind of vast financial resources he had used to buy out other lines.

Now, however, he faced not only the small but commanding figure of Daniel Drew but two lieutenant-generalissimos—and a most remarkable pair at that. Through skill, guile, and knavery Jay Gould had worked his way up from a blacksmith's forge and a country-store clerkship to the ownership of railroads and then of a Wall Street brokerage house. The other, James Fisk, onetime hotel waiter, circus ticket seller, traveling salesman, and dry-goods jobber, was a comic-opera figure in behavior and appearance—a plump, brassy, jovial voluptuary who wore the garish uniform of a purchased national guard colonelcy, sported diamond bosom pins and lavender gloves, and liked to parade around Manhattan in a four-in-hand flanked by footmen in livery. He had the "instincts of fourteen," Henry Adams wrote. Fisk was not a buffoon, though, but rather a canny and unscrupulous showman who believed it was a duty of the rich to provide entertainment to the poor.

The trio had one key weapon—possession of the Erie itself. Vanderbilt struck first, buying tens of thousands of shares of Erie stock. He knew his foes could not match his resources with money. But they could with chicanery. The trio issued to themselves $10 million of convertible bonds, changed them into stock, and dumped them on the market. After Vanderbilt replied with a New York contempt-of-court ruling against their issuing more watered stock, they made a retrograde movement across the Hudson to Newark, freed themselves from New York law, and then bribed the New Jersey legislature to legalize their stock issue. After this, Vanderbilt threw in his hand, and the Erie War ended tepidly in a division of the spoils.

Most of the railroad investing was conducted on a far higher plane than this, but often the issuance of rail securities reeked of collusion and fraud, with railroads despoiled and bankrupted in the process. The corruption of the railroads tainted the rest of the financial and political system. Soon it would be revealed that a group of railroad leaders had in effect bribed United States senators and representatives by giving them shares of stock, in a scandal that would come to be known as Crédit Mobilier.

Charles Francis Adams, Jr., observed all this; indeed, he wrote a searching and authoritative study, "A Chapter of Erie." He did not hesitate to call Fisk a "damned rascal" and Gould a "moral monstrosity." Yet Adams himself, as head of the Union Pacific, later was willing to pay $50,000 to a Kansas senator to gain his support of a Union Pacific funding bill. Feeling guilty, he blamed himself less for planning corruption than for ineptly failing to bring off the bribe. He justified his action as his duty to the stockholders; if he could not bribe the senator, he reflected, "it was questionable whether I had any right to retain my place as President."

The great-grandson of John Adams had indeed fastened himself not to a star but to a locomotive engine.

ENTREPRENEURS: THE CALIFORNIANS

It was a grand sight from the valley of Lake Donner, at eventide, a traveler reported, "to look up a thousand feet upon the overhanging cliffs where the workmen were discharging their glycerine blasts." In the dusk, great fiery blasts shook the mountainsides amid dense clouds of smoke. "Huge masses of rock and debris were rent and heaved up in the commotion; then anon came the thunders of the explosion like a lightning stroke, reverberating along the hills and canyons, as if the whole artillery of heaven were at play."

The time was 1868; the place, the east end of Summit Valley near Lake Donner; the occasion, the building of the Central Pacific Railroad east, through some of the most rugged mountainland in America, to meet the Union Pacific advancing west.

The men up on the cliffs earlier had brought the railroad across the Central Valley east from Sacramento, and were now blasting and digging their way through the high Sierras. Above, men were lowered down the sheer sides of cliffs, where they drilled holes, lighted the fuses, and tried to move out fast, with the American River raging more than a thousand feet below. It was even worse in the valleys, especially during the appalling winter of 1866–67, when snow lay fifteen feet deep by Christmas and one hundred feet or more later. Workers, living in deeply buried shacks, tunneled through the snow as much as two hundred feet to reach the railroad bore they were cutting. At day's end they dragged themselves back through their labyrinth of snow corridors to wash in powder kegs filled with hot water, dine on rice, dried fish, pork, pickled vegetables, and tea, and then perhaps to have a turn at fan-tan and a pipe of opium before throwing themselves down for sleep. But day after day, month after month, they pressed on, at best cutting through twenty-seven inches of granite in a whole day.

The men who were building the Central Pacific made up perhaps the most extraordinary work force in American history. They had fled from poverty, misery, and civil war in their homeland. They had traveled 8,000 miles to an American shore, but from the west, not the east. Their Taoist and Confucian beliefs were about as far from the Catholic faith and Puritan ethic of their fellow Californians as could be imagined. With their oriental appearance, costumes, language, and pigtails, they were the most harshly treated immigrant group in America. They were segregated both at work and at home, and thus formed one more caste in "classless" America.

The Chinese had not been wanted by either the railroad builders or the labor trades. They were considered too small for the heavy work, averaging hardly one hundred pounds, and were said to be addicted to gambling and opium; good enough to be laundrymen and farmhands . . . but railroad laborers? Moreover, the other workers—usually summed up as "the Irish" —hotly opposed the Chinese and their lower wages. But the "Irish," many of whom were miners of old, were prone to quit after payday, especially on news of a gold strike in the hills. At first taken on as potential strikebreakers—another red flag to union men—the Chinese proved such willing workers that several thousand were hired, many of them brought over directly from China.

And so here in the mountain passes and later on the burning sands of Nevada the dream of a transcontinental railroad was being carried out by a strange partnership of Sacramento capitalists and pigtailed "Celestials," as they were called. The dream was an old and grandiose one. A transcontinental railroad, it had been argued in the 1840s, would be a strategic as well as economic boon; it would place on the West Coast naval power that could dominate the Pacific and even the Chinese seas. Only the coming of the Civil War had broken the long deadlock over a northern versus a southern railroad, and it was during the war that Congress had passed the legislation, Lincoln had signed it, and the Sacramento group had laid the first rails.

In charge of the enormous undertaking was a quartet of capitalists who would come to be known as the Big Four. The acknowledged, though not unchallenged, leader was the president of the Central Pacific, Leland Stanford of Sacramento. A majestic figure with his burly frame, ramrod posture, and thick beard and hair, he had amassed a small fortune as a Placer County merchant and then served as Unionist governor of California before he reached forty. The CP's hard-driving construction boss was another big, burly young man with chin whiskers, Charles Crocker; two of its key capital raisers were the hardware merchant Mark Hopkins and a partner of Hopkins, Collis P. Huntington. Missing by now was the man who most of all had dreamed the great dream, Theodore Judah, a brilliant leader in conceiving the transcontinental route, lobbying the railroad bill through Congress, and raising money. He had died of yellow fever after crossing Panama.

As the Chinese threaded the railway through the mountain passes and over trestle bridges, Stanford's office in Sacramento became a kind of GHQ. The generalissimo recruited thousands of workers and horses and flung them into the battle, brought locomotives and other heavy weapons around the Horn and up the Sacramento River to the railhead, shipped quantities of food and other supplies to the front-line troops (but expected them to live off the land too), communicated with Crocker in code, fought the wretched weather, made visits to what he called "the Front." He had to deal with local nabobs commanding their territory, most notably with the imperious Mormon leader, Brigham Young. And he had to deal with labor shortages, to the point where the partners considered importing blacks from the East or even Confederate war prisoners.

Crocker was field commander. Spurred by messages from Stanford to "double his energy" or "move forward to north pass," he shuttled back and forth in his private car, or rode on his sorrel mare. "There was no need for sympathy for those men," he later told the historian H. H. Bancroft. "Why I used to go up and down that road in my car like a mad bull, stopping along the way wherever there was anything amiss and raising old Nick." When the Chinese workers finally lost patience and struck for a pay increase to $40 a month and an eight-hour day in the tunnels—"Eight hours a day good for white men, all the same good for Chinamen," their circular explained—Crocker put it down in a week. "I stopped the provisions on them," he said later, "stopped the butchers from butchering, and used such coercive measures." This was food the Chinese had already bought.

But the dread enemy was not strikers or slackers or Indians—it was the Union Pacific spearing its way west. Stanford and Crocker picked up rumors that the foe was stealing their supplies and even their men. Desperately they threw every reserve into the battle, hauling locomotives on sleighs and even on logs, working shifts of men through long days, goading their men to faster progress along the Nevada flats. When word arrived that the Union Pacific had laid 7.5 miles of track in a long, twenty-hour day, a Central Pacific crew put 10 miles down in thirteen hours. Seeking above all else the huge federal land grants, the two companies fought for exclusive rights-of-way and even graded 100 miles of parallel roadbed.

In the end, though, the two armies met peacefully at Promontory Point near Ogden, Utah. The CP's "Jupiter," wood-burning engine No. 60, proudly stood, cowcatcher to cowcatcher, facing the UP's coal-burner, No. 119. While the chief engineers of the rival roads shook hands, workers on the cowcatchers held out champagne bottles to each other. Stanford and his UP counterpart, Thomas C. Durant, used silver sledges to drive home the golden spikes. Both men missed the spike a few times, but no matter: America had its first transcontinental railroad.

The poet Bret Harte wondered what the engines said, head to head, each with half the world behind its back:

> You brag of your East! *You* do?
> Why, *I* bring the East to *you!*
> All the Orient, all Cathay,
> Find through me the shortest way;
> And the sun you follow here
> Rises in my hemisphere. . . .

After the ceremony of the golden spikes, the men who had built the Union Pacific, mostly Irish, could just keep "headed west," now traveling on the road their Chinese counterparts had built. The CP's Chinese workers (who are hardly evident in a photograph of the ceremony) drifted off to mining camps or headed back to California, some of them perhaps riding on the rails they had hauled into place. Newcomers and locals alike, they—and later a mellow philosopher from Concord, Ralph Waldo Emerson—could share in the glories of the trip: immense numbers of ducks settling in the northern shallows of the Great Salt Lake, purple mountains beyond, and snow-covered ranges in the distance. Emerson was fascinated by the constantly shifting tints and lights of this landscape.

For Easterners, the terrain seemed incredibly varied. At one moment the train would be steaming through irrigated fields where corn, wheat, potatoes, and diverse fruits grew luxuriantly. Then the engine would be chugging through the canyons of the Humboldt River—"torn, jagged, barren rocks and cliffs, that looked as if wasted by a hundred centuries of lightning and storm," a traveler with Emerson later remembered; "then through an alkaline region, where the surface of the ground was white like a city street that has been watered with salt water; but the alkali was thicker." All of this reminded Emerson of biblical lands. Then they were pounding through country without trees, nothing but sagebrush and a "prickly shrub, and a sort of Scotch broom," with small plumes of steam in the distance marking hot springs. Then finally the "grand stormy rush" down the Sierras and onto the Sacramento plain.

One sight above all electrified the passengers, causing some to get off and try their fortune—gold mining. They could see men spraying powerful jets of water against the gravel sides of mountains, washing away the earth so that the yellow ore might be exhumed. Long flumes carried the water, often for miles along the tracks. Almost the whole distance, indeed, mining towns were visible, perched on hills or straggling through canyons, and enveloped by once-barren hillsides covered with miners' tents and gear. Everything in these towns appeared to revolve around minerals, including quartz; everyone in town seemed to own a gold or quartz claim, almost the way Easterners owned gardens. A visitor in one of these towns, during much excitement about a coming circus, observed "little urchins going out to the fields beyond the town with their mothers' tin kitchen-pans" to "pan out enough to pay their entrance-fee to the circus."

Passengers riding the Central Pacific to Sacramento found a bustling little town, proud of its position as the state capital and the hub of Central Valley agriculture, at the head of the tidewater on the Sacramento River. Many passengers left the train here to take the riverboat west to San Francisco; others traveled south on the new Southern Pacific railway. Often these included Chinese and Irish who would find jobs on the railroad itself. Spearing south along the San Joaquin River, through the immense burning prairie between the Sierras and the coast, the Southern Pacific connected with lovely towns like Stockton, which seemed to one traveler aflutter with windmills which irrigated domestic gardens. At Merced, tourists could turn east to view the mountains, gorges, and waterfalls of Yosemite. It was in this spectacular area that Emerson in 1881 encountered a young botanist and sawmill worker who told him excitedly of the local flora and of his long rambles through the mountains he loved. This was the "father of the wilderness," John Muir.

Renewing their trip through the Central Valley as it widened out, travelers crossed a farmland of almost limitless expanse and diversity. At first, settlers from the east had found it hard to adjust their farming ways to the new seasonal rhythms of California. They had sown when the rains ended in May or June, only to see their crops turn brown in the long dry California summer. As time passed they found the grass on the plains to be abundant and nutritious, curing naturally in the summer sun and providing ample feed for sheep and market cattle. Only workhorses and oxen required grain. Plowing early in December and sowing and planting in March, farmers could grow six and even eight crops of alfalfa.

The rub was always water. Farmers often joined hands to build reservoirs and canals, windmills and artesian wells. Be more careful in buying water than land, old-timers advised.

It was a world of Spaniards and Indians. As travelers moved south, they could tell at a glance who lived in the houses along the way. "If the house is of reeds and straw, the owner is an Indian; if it is of adobe, it is a Spaniard who lives there; if it is of frame, be sure it is an 'American,'" noted a visitor from the East. It was a peaceful land. A traveler through the lonely southern counties reported he had "stopped to cook my dinner in the Indian huts, asked for a night's lodging at Spanish ranchos, slept sometimes on the green grass, with my horse staked out, my feet near a fire, and wrapped in overcoat and blanket; and journeying thus day after day, I had not even a revolver with me, and no arm larger than a pocket-knife."

It was also a land of big ranches. A Spanish *padrone* might own 40,000 acres, 1,500 or so young colts, several thousand sheep, and so many cattle he could not count them until after the annual rodeo. This was the big event of the year. After the stock in a large district had been driven onto one great plain, *vacqueros* would pick out each owner's cows, break them up into separate herds, brand the calves that innocently followed their mothers, and either turn the whole mass loose again or drive them home. The *señor* often lived in a house of adobe, perhaps with a store in front from which he sold dry goods and grape brandy to his Indian hands. Beyond the house might be a clay oven for baking bread, and beyond that the shanties for Indians and their roosting chickens. Many Spanish homes had earthen floors covered with expensive rugs, reflecting the new wealth of these landowners after the Gold Rush demand for beef made cattle owners rich.

The great Spanish landowners owned most of California, a traveler noted; the land, the cattle, the horses, the sheep were theirs. No-fence laws assured ranchers of almost unlimited range for their cattle. They had good relations with their hands, and in return "no vacquero addressed the master without either touching or taking off his hat." But they "were not business men; they liked to live free of care; and they found it easy to borrow money. . . . They knew nothing of interest" and they often squandered their money. This old, easy, bucolic life could not escape the currents surging through southern California in the 1870s.

In particular, the town of Los Angeles was just about to emerge from its drowsy, indolent past when one might, on driving into El Pueblo de la Reina de Los Angeles, encounter market wagons full of "oranges, pumpkins, a lamb, corn, green peas in their pods, sugar-cane, lemons and strawberries" and one-story, dilapidated houses whose inner courtyards were lovely gardens of flowers and fruit. The Southern Pacific came to the town in 1876, however, after the railroad exacted large subsidies from the city fathers. Los Angeles was not ready to be consigned to a backwater of progress, which was the fate of other cities that resisted the Southern Pacific's strong-arm tactics.

Soon the railroad began shipping to the east wine, paper-wrapped oranges packed in ice, lemons, walnuts, and other products of the area's new irrigated intensive farming. A growing emphasis on agriculture ended once and for all the cattle ranchers' rule over the range, for cattle now had to be fenced in to prevent their trampling freshly planted fields or ripening harvests.

Young entrepreneurs were helping transform the city. One of these was Phineas Banning, who had begun to make carriages at the port of Wilmington, south of Los Angeles, built a wharf and warehouses, and developed a stage connection with the city. Banning was said to be the first to use a wireless telegraph in the area, the first to dig an artesian well, and the first to have an oil well. But now a spectacular real estate boom was about to begin, one that would transform the city and its environs. The old Los Angeles of flowers and vineyards would no longer exist. After years of struggles with the Southern Pacific, Banning would sell out to it.

The most direct route from Los Angeles to northern Californian ports in the 1870s was still by steamer or packet. Beating their way north, passengers could watch the great Pacific rollers breaking on the sands, the wooded and craggy coastal ranges, and sometimes the snow-covered Sierra peaks in the distance. It was always a breathtaking moment when the ship entered the Golden Gate and turned starboard to the fabled city on the hills.

San Francisco! With its fog-shrouded mornings, steep dunelike hills, busy, picturesque harbor, and lusty yet cultivated style, the city was still a magnet for the richest rich and the poorest poor, for immigrants from west and east, for Chinese, Irish, Yankees, Italians, and more Spanish from the south. It was now the economic capital of the West, and a cultural and social center as well. The Big Four had not remained long in Sacramento after their Central Pacific was built and making money. In the mid-seventies Stanford, his wife, and his son moved into a $2 million mansion that was greeted in the local press as "Stanford's Palace, the Finest Private Residence in America." The place was a great pile with marble steps, bay windows, billiard room, picture gallery, "Pompeian reception room," ballroom, and forty or so other rooms, decorated in the Italian and other styles, and topped by a glass dome illuminating the entrance hall seventy feet below. Natives and visitors alike gawked at this and other ornate mansions built on Nob Hill.

While the Big Four ran their railroad empire out of their Southern Pacific offices, also long since removed from Sacramento, their wives and daughters dominated the social life of the city. For a wealthy young woman like Lucy S. Jones, niece of a high railroad executive, life in San Francisco in the 1870s was a weekly round of social calls, dress fittings, parties, cultural events, and church. Her brothers took singing lessons while she studied French. Her carefree life was shadowed only by the illnesses that coursed through San Francisco—influenza, consumption, scarlet fever. One young friend died, others were home in bed, the cook and Chinese servant were too ill to come to work, and Lucy and her aunt battled recurrent colds. "So many are going now," she wrote in her diary after one friend's death, and then crossed it out, as if it were bad luck.

Down in Chinatown, not many blocks north and east of Nob Hill, lived the people at the bottom of the social pyramid, in "dark and dingy garrets and cellars, steaming with air breathed over and over, and filled with the fumes of opium," according to a newspaper report. By the mid-eighties the Chinese quarter had become known as an inner city of brothels, opium dens, and gambling halls, described by the historian H. H. Bancroft as "closely packed with some 25,000 souls, nearly all males, with a sprinkling of loose females." This dense honeycomb was mostly owned by white absentee landlords. The Chinese experienced both discrimination and segregation, both legal and illegal harassment. "Negroes, Mongolians, and Indians" were excluded from the public schools. It was illegal to bring Chinese women into the country unless they were persons of "correct habits" and good character. In fact, estimated Bancroft, of 116,000 Chinese in California in 1876, 6,000—or 5 percent—may have been women, further arresting Chinese assimilation in California.

Feeling against the Chinese had mounted on the return of thousands of railroad workers from the Sierras. Whites reviled them for their willingness to accept low wages and harsh conditions, their alien ways, their pigtails, their Taoist stoicism, their habit of sending to the "old country" both their money and the bones of their dead. Labor leaders held mass meetings, formed "anti-coolie" clubs, organized mobs to climb Nob Hill and shout "the Chinese must go" outside the mansions of the magnates deemed responsible for bringing in Chinese labor. To win the labor vote, Democrats often passed planks against the Chinese.

The opposition of labor was especially telling, for San Francisco was already becoming a "labor town." Most of the trades had been organized since the fifties. Building trades were especially strong, in line with San Francisco's construction boom. In 1868 unions won the eight-hour day, but the following year labor faced its biggest challenge, the incoming flood of unorganized workers discharged from the Central Pacific Railroad.

Anti-Chinese sentiment became the binding force in the labor movement. Such organizations as the Knights of St. Crispin, shoemakers directly competing with a major Chinatown industry, and the Plumbers' and Carpenters' Eight-Hour League organized spectacular mass meetings throughout the 1870s, demonstrations that often exploded into riots and the burning and looting of Chinatown. Out of these meetings also erupted the meteoric Workingmen's Party, led by the fiery Denis Kearney and fueled by economic frustration—a drought, a decrease in mining returns, a depression, and railroad strikes in the East. In June 1878, Workingmen won one-third of the seats in the state's second constitutional convention, even against a coalition of Democrats and Republicans.

Fixed as it was on the issue of ending Chinese immigration, however, the Workingmen's Party's participation in the convention proved to be its undoing. Within a year of ratification of an anti-Chinese article of the new constitution, the United States Circuit Court declared that virtually all of its provisions violated the Fourteenth Amendment.

In the 1870s San Francisco was outliving its reputation as a frontier town full of saloons, opium dens, and gold seekers and other philistines. The city was becoming a place for thinkers like Henry George, poets like Bret Harte, historians like Bancroft, musicians, artists. The patronage of the rich was providing symphony orchestras, opera houses, museums, galleries. For years, Tivoli maintained a twelve-month opera season. Newspapers in seven languages offered a peculiarly western brand of humor, developed by Mark Twain and others. Edwin Booth broke all attendance records for American theater when he played for eight weeks in the city. Lillian Russell, appearing in *Babes in the Woods* wearing purple tights and high-buttoned shoes, delightfully shocked the city. Lucy Jones's cultural life included Shakespeare and Wagner.

Yellow and black and white, rich and poor, Yankee and Indian, Mexican and Spanish, Californians made up the most diverse population in the Union. They boasted of their extremes—the highest mountains and the

lowest deserts, the worst floods and the longest droughts, the biggest trees
and the fiercest forest fires. Californians grew silk—not very successfully
—and grain; the state ranked second in wheat production by 1890. By
century's end, San Francisco was a kind of experiment in good living, for
whites, at least, one of the most agreeable and bucolic cities in the world.
It seemed that this way of life, barring some act of God, might continue
forever.

Industrialists: Carnegie, Rockefeller, and the Two Capitalisms

American capitalism had its saints as well as its rascals. Its finest leader
and role model in the late nineteenth century was heroic in almost everything except appearance: five foot three, broad of face and nose, so youthful in features that even after he became a railroad superintendent and was
clearing up a train wreck, a burly Irishman in a busy work crew picked him
up and carried him to the side, saying, "Get out of my way, you brat of a
boy." In his career and achievements Andrew Carnegie was a Hero of
Capitalist Production.

That career read as though it had been contrived by a master scenarist
of Victorian dramas full of clichés and stereotypes. *Rags to riches:* he was
born in the attic of a Scottish weaver's cottage and died in his eighty-fourth
year the owner of one of Manhattan's finest mansions and one of Scotland's most ostentatious castles. *Poverty-stricken but determined mother:* Margaret Carnegie tried for a time to shore up the family earnings by binding
shoes and other cottage work, then bundled up her husband and sons and
belongings, borrowed twenty pounds, and took passage to America. *The
rungs of the ladder of success:* bobbin boy (at $1.20 a week) to engine tender,
to telegraph messenger boy, to telegraph operator, to personal secretary
to the superintendent of the western division of the Pennsylvania Railroad,
to superintendent himself, to Civil War head of transportation and communications, all by his early forties.

There was, however, a far more extraordinary side to Carnegie's life. He
came from a family of fiery Scottish Chartists who for years had been
agitating for political liberty, human rights, and religious toleration; his
uncle had been arrested for "seditious activity." When his father's linen
hand-loom weaving succumbed to the factory system, young Andrew
would never forget his coming home in despair, saying, "Andra, I can get
nae mair work." But the father and an uncle had time to educate the boy
in Scottish lore, the plebeian poetry of Robert Burns, and the evils of the

Monarchy and Established Church. As a boy in Allegheny, Pennsylvania, where the immigrant family settled, he became an ardent reader and a letter writer to the New York *Tribune,* especially on slavery. His whole early life—his roots in poverty and radicalism, his long trip to America across the Atlantic and then up the Hudson and along the Erie Canal and by lake and canal to Allegheny, his daily work in Pittsburgh among factory boys and railroad laborers—he had converted into a self-schooling in democracy.

None of this, however, seemed to slow Carnegie's determined rise through the capitalistic system. Observant, quick, steady, resourceful, everlastingly competent, he may not have rescued the boss's daughter from a runaway horse, but he was able on one occasion, when all the trains in his division were held up because of a wreck and his boss was late, to unscramble the whole mess on his own initiative and get the trains running. He was then not yet twenty. His passion was to make things work. When wrecked freight cars blocked service, he coolly ordered them burned —an act that astonished his colleagues but later became standard procedure with the Pennsylvania Railroad.

In 1865, at the age of thirty, Carnegie left the Pennsylvania to branch out into other fields. He invested his railroad income shrewdly in oil, sleeping cars, bridges, and other railroads, as steel became a kind of common denominator in his investments. In Europe, he came to know Sir Henry Bessemer and the Bessemer process. Already Carnegie was showing the daring and imagination that attracted attention from his rivals in Pittsburgh and abroad. Bridges especially challenged him; with Captain Eads he shared the agony and glory of building the first great bridge over the Mississippi. By 1872, staking his hopes on Bessemer and other improved technology, he was ready to make an irreversible commitment to steel.

The story of Carnegie's rise to czar of steel is the story of organization, cost-cutting, and competition. Take away his steel mills, his ores, his railroad lines, his coal, he liked to say, but leave him one thing and he would repeat his success. That one thing was *organization,* by which he meant picking skilled subordinates such as Captain "Bill" Jones, Henry Clay Frick, and Charles M. Schwab, and by which he also meant something that was still revolutionary in American industry—vertical integration. By such moves as acquiring massive iron deposits in the Mesabi range and buying railroads that linked Pittsburgh with the northwest water routes, Carnegie by the end of the century came to control raw materials, transportation, manufacturing, distribution, and finance. He stood astride the whole steel process, from mining ore to delivering railroad cars, boilers, nails, wires.

Cost-cutting was virtually an obsession at Carnegie Steel. The boss watched every nickel. "I cannot understand *Lime*," he complained; "13 tons of lime used to each ton of metal. It can't be lime, that is certain, half rock—I suspect." Or: "I am surprised at two items in cost. Coke 1/2 ton per ton rails—8 bushels should smelt the pig and certainly 4 bushels the Spiegel. How do you account for the remainder?" He fretted over labor costs. "Profits, for Carnegie, were always tangential to and a mere consequence of reduced costs of production," in Joseph Wall's estimate. "To reduce costs, he would quickly scrap a new machine, a new process, or an entire mill in favor of more efficient operations. Labor was simply another item of cost, but if wages were low, so also were salaries of management." Carnegie's salary, however, was not low.

All this made Carnegie a ferocious competitor. His attitude toward his rivals was, "Come, let's compete." He said this in absolute confidence that he would outcompete them, and so he did. He fought not only with rival steel makers but also with railroads. His old association with the Pennsylvania Railroad did not deter him from forcing down its ore, coke, and limestone rates. "What are you fighting the Pennsylvania Railroad for?" a Pennsylvania chief asked him. "You were brought up in its service. We were boys together." In answer, Carnegie handed him a list of his competitors' rates.

The growth of American steel-making was simply phenomenal. In just a few years, Carnegie and the others far outstripped Britain, long the heart of world iron- and steel-making. American steel production quadrupled in the last thirty years of the century. Benefiting from economies of scale, in 1870 the industry produced 60 pounds of metal for each dollar invested; in 1900, 112 pounds. Carnegie did far better than the rest, more than doubling his per-dollar production between 1880 and 1900. In those same twenty years he cut his cost per ton of rail from $28 to less than $12.

All through these years, however, the "other" Carnegie seemed to hover over the steel magnate, reminding him of youthful dreams and ideals. At the age of thirty-three, in the first flush of success, he had promised himself: "By this time two years I can so arrange all my business as to secure at least 50,000 per annum. Beyond this never earn." The reason? "No idol more debasing than the worship of money." Yet Carnegie continued to worship that idol, as he built a fortune of hundreds of millions of dollars even while preaching the "Gospel of Wealth"—the doctrine that making money was laudable, but only if the rich used their money to help the poor and benefit the whole community.

The most extraordinary manifestation of the "other Carnegie" appeared each spring when Carnegie returned to Scotland and England and reasserted his old Chartist faith. He had forgotten none of it during all the years of moneymaking. During the 1880s he bought out or into seven British dailies and ten weeklies and converted them into muckraking organs against the British monarchy, hereditary privileges, and limitations on the right to vote. He bored his radical friends and outraged his conservative foes with his fulsome tributes to American democracy. So stridently did Carnegie's newspapers attack the aristocracy that even Carnegie's liberal friends, including Prime Minister William Gladstone himself, felt embarrassed and heaved a sigh of relief when their American friend left for home every fall. Still, they could not help wondering at the man who supported radical political change, equality, and even striking coal workers on one side of the Atlantic, only to return to the Republican and capitalistic fold on the other.

Despite failures and frustrations, Carnegie never lost his Chartist faith —in the British Isles. Especially rewarding to him were the literary friendships he made among Britain's intellectual elite. Matthew Arnold, Herbert Spencer, and John Morley, among other littérateurs, befriended Carnegie intellectually in Britain and were entertained by him royally on their trips to America. Carnegie wrote articles for the *Fortnightly Review* and letters to *The Times.* He rarely resisted an opportunity to mount the platform, from which he excoriated special privilege, lauded America's form of democracy, and seemed far less the calculating capitalist than the arm-pumping radical—which in England he was.

*   *   *

By the end of the century, Andrew Carnegie was crowned in the press as the world's richest man, succeeding Jay Gould. But waiting to assume the golden throne was a man who differed from Carnegie in almost every way except in the ability to make—and to give away—hundreds of millions of dollars. John D. Rockefeller was the son not of a poor Scot but of a roving upstate New York salesman, speculator, spurious physician, and apparent bigamist. Sometimes absent for months, the father was home often enough to teach his son the importance of money, the sanctity of contracts, and how to make a profit. In his early boyhood, it is said, John bought candy by the pound and sold it piece by piece to his siblings at a profit.

After a good high school education and a business college stint, young Rockefeller drew up a list of sound Cleveland firms, made the rounds of all of them seeking a job, and was stolidly starting around the circuit a second time when he got a job in a commission house as a bookkeeper. A frugal, industrious, deeply religious young man, Rockefeller loved bookkeeping—meticulously checking and rechecking figures, handling thousand-dollar bills, and learning every aspect of the firm's business. Three months before his twentieth birthday, he and a young partner opened their own commission house. The firm prospered during the Civil War boom.

At the same time, Rockefeller and his associates became involved in the oil refineries that were springing up around Cleveland. Sensing that Cleveland could never outbid Chicago for the grain and meat trade, but that its railroad facilities would enable it to dominate oil-refining, he struck out boldly on his own. Slowly, methodically, he expanded his operation, taking advantage of the continuing oil boom. As his firm grew bigger, he found it easier to dictate terms to suppliers and railroads, and to profit from petroleum by-products. But Rockefeller came to fear and detest the chaos of the oil industry—the hundreds of tiny firms that sprang up in boom times and then folded, the ferocious competition of railroads and cities for business, the collapse of rates and prices to the point of bankruptcy for many firms. By 1870, when Rockefeller and his partners organized the Standard Oil Company (Ohio), the refining industry's capacity was three times the demand.

Rockefeller's answer to this problem was not Carnegie's kind of competition but his own brand of order and stability, achieved through alliances, "voluntary" associations, combinations, and ultimately trusts. Rockefeller did not talk much at the time—a kind of aggressive silence was one of his main weapons—but later he bluntly argued the case for combination over competition.

"We wanted a new idea to prevail," he said, "we wanted the old struggle to cease in the ugly forms it had assumed. . . . [We wanted] men to take their full share of the business, to be content with a fair share . . . and thus work together for the economies and enjoy together the success. . . . I think that it is fair to say that the strong men who were competitors in the oil refining business, the aggressive men . . . were the men who were most likely to take up the idea of cooperation. . . . The thing that caused the effort to be made to centralize the business was the exercise of this uncontrolled freedom for every man to have his own way in utter disregard of the rights of his neighbors."

How Rockefeller effected these combinations aroused as much controversy as the combinations themselves. His basic strategy was not to outcompete his rivals but to eliminate them, in the name of a higher cooperation. He denied using pressure tactics, but his critics said he did not need to—he had the power, and everyone knew it. Quiet, soft-spoken, even polite, he could suddenly intimidate his rivals with his "gunpowder eyes" and, even more, his ample funds. Through cost-cutting, favorable rebates, a big marketing organization, purchase of competitors, occasional price-cutting, Rockefeller and allied firms developed common ownership of refineries, lubricating oil plants, pipelines, cooperage companies. The Standard Oil combination of firms came to control about nine-tenths of the oil industry by 1881.

For all their differences—and their contrasting capitalisms—Carnegie and Rockefeller ended up with one great interest in common: philanthropy. Of the several hundred million dollars that Carnegie made, he gave $350 million for libraries, education, and world peace. Of Rockefeller's fortune of over $800 million, the oil tycoon gave over $550 million for medical research, education, religion, and, especially in the South, agricultural improvement. Neither man questioned the need for such giving; each considered it a duty. To radicals' charges that they had exploited the masses, skimmed off enormous profits, and kept much for themselves, they would have answered—if they condescended to answer—that they had given the public something it needed more than material improvement: they had given it education, health, more assurance of world peace, greater opportunity for spiritual and moral development.

As for the argument of Marxists and others that, while of course the masses did have higher needs than the economic, it was up to the people as a whole, not their economic overlords, to define those needs, probably neither Carnegie nor Rockefeller would have understood the argument, and certainly neither would have deigned to answer it.

*   *   *

Steel and oil were not the most important forces in the late-nineteenth-century production boom, only the most dramatic. Flour production, lumber production, and tobacco products roughly doubled between 1870 and 1890; paper almost tripled. American textile mills consumed 797,000 bales of cotton in 1870, over thrice that in 1891. "Using the year 1899 as a standard," according to John Garraty, "the output of manufactured goods increased from an index of 25 in 1870 to 30 in 1877, 42 in 1880, 71 in 1890, and 79 in 1892." By 1890 the billion-dollar textile industry led in capitalization, followed by iron and steel and by lumber; textiles also led in number of workers (824,000) followed by lumber and by iron and steel, while the latter, with its skilled workers, had the highest wage bill. Food processing had the highest "value of product"—a stupendous $1.6 billion.

Expansion was uneven. Industry continued to be heavily centered in the northeast and north-central regions, with 85 percent of the manufactured goods produced there in 1890. But the regional balance was slowly righting itself. California doubled the value of its manufactures during the eighties alone. Minnesota was specializing in flour milling, Michigan and

Wisconsin in lumbering, Illinois in meat packing and farm equipment. To a lesser but still marked degree, the South shared in the boom. Already, New England textile and textile-machinery firms were expanding south of the old Mason-Dixon Line.

If American production was the wonder of the world, success lay primarily in a combination both lucky and calculated, of seemingly inexhaustible raw materials, a fast-developing transportation system, a vigorous and talented labor force, massive foreign and domestic capital, an ethic of expansion, and brilliant innovators. Capitalism's power of "creative destruction" was already evident. America's rapidly expanding railroad system was pacing the booming economy and in the process supplanting many an expensive canal system—and supplanting countless canal workers too.

The third decade after the Civil War (1886–95) continued the diverse innovation of the first two. The new Westinghouse Electric Company built the nation's first commercially successful power plant in Buffalo. The United States Forest Service was established in the Agriculture Department. The Pennsylvania Railroad operated an electrically lighted train between Chicago and New York. William S. Burroughs patented a commercially successful adding machine. The National Geographic Society was founded, and the nation's first seismograph installed at the Lick Observatory in California. The Pullman Car Company built an electric locomotive for hauling freight; Singer marketed electric sewing machines; Otis Brothers installed an electric elevator in Manhattan. William Osler published *Principles and Practice of Medicine*. Westinghouse standardized alternating current at 60 cycles per second. A North Carolina chemist produced acetylene gas. The American Psychological Association was established, and the *Journal of Geology* first published. Chlorine was used to treat sewage in Brewster, New York, Boston schoolchildren began to receive medical examinations, and the world's first antitoxin clinic was opened in New York City. Pneumatic rubber tires were manufactured in Hartford, and pasteurized milk was produced commercially.

Not only was industry innovative—innovation was being industrialized. The benign figure of Thomas A. Edison, industrialist, loomed as a prime example. By the late eighties Edison was still the creative inventor, experimenting now with a Kinetoscopic camera. But he was more than this— while creating manufacturing establishments to market his inventions, he had become one of America's best-known small industrialists, employing between two and three thousand skilled and unskilled workers. He was an industrialist in an even more profound sense: in an era that recognized and rewarded systematically organized production, Edison was probably the first to found the "scientific" factory, one devoted to the production of scientific inventions rather than consumer or producer goods.

To a degree, Edison became a kind of "captive scientist"—captive to the entrepreneurs who could supply capital and to the marketplace. In creating Menlo Park as a scientific factory, he obtained funds before his next inventions were anything more than an idea or perhaps a quick sketch in his or one of his partners' lab books. As in a factory, work was subdivided among Edison's gifted inventors and technicians, a division of labor prevailed, and a bureaucratic organization evolved. And as in any other private enterprise, "practicality" ruled. Edison would not work on a project unless it would meet a present or future need and make money.

"A scientific man busies himself with theory," Edison said to a reporter. "He is absolutely impractical. An inventor is essentially practical. Anything that won't sell I don't want to invent. . . ."

Working around the clock in his rumpled clothes, taking catnaps on laboratory tables, smoking twenty cheap cigars a day, gouging chaws out of huge hunks of chewing tobacco he shared with his associates, leaving the floor around him covered with spittle, Edison hardly appeared a heroic figure. He was something more important. While winning a reputation as an independent and single-minded inventor—"my business is *thinking,*" he liked to say—he was in fact, as Norbert Wiener pointed out, a transitional figure who pointed the way toward the big, bureaucratically organized research of the technological age to come.

Philadelphia 1876: The Proud Exhibitors

The crowd gaped at the massive engine towering over it—at the gleaming cylinders pointed skyward, at the huge, delicately balanced walking beams above, responding at one end to the ten-foot stroke of the cylinders and from the other plunging down to the thirty-foot flywheel. Two diminutive figures down on a platform, Ulysses S. Grant and Emperor Pedro II of Brazil, on command gently turned some wheels and the walking beams began to rock majestically, the flywheel to turn, and now the engine's 1,500 horsepower was moving along leather belts to other mechanical showpieces—sewing machines, circular saws, presses, carpet looms, and thousands of other machines crowding the exhibition halls.

It was May 10, 1876, the opening day at the Philadelphia Centennial Exhibition. The rain seemed not to dampen the spirits of thousands pouring into Fairmount Park and jamming the pie stalls, lemonade stands, beer gardens, ice cream parlors, P. T. Barnum's "Wild Man of Borneo," and other attractions lining the approaches to the huge exhibition halls. But the keenest interest by far was in the exhibits. In the industrial exhibits: lathes, power looms, pumps, milling machines, a section of wire cable from John A. Roebling's Niagara suspension bridge, a model showing how the steel arches of Eads's St. Louis bridge had been formed, a 7,000-pound pendulum clock by Seth Thomas, Westinghouse's air brake, Philadelphia- and Hartford-made machine tools, "sober black iron monsters whose varied steel edges could cut, chip, stamp, mold, grind, and otherwise shape metal," in Joseph and Frances Gies's words. In the agricultural exhibits: reapers and mowers and horse rakes and fruit dryers and steam road rollers and gang plows.

Most exciting and baffling were the electrical exhibits, including "multiplex" telegraph devices. The Exhibition actually produced a historic event when Emperor Pedro II, who had met Alexander Graham Bell while visiting the Boston School for the Deaf, ran into the inventor at a Western Union exhibit and insisted on inspecting his "harmonic telegraph." The emperor electrified the crowd when he pressed his ear to Bell's receiver while the inventor declaimed Hamlet's soliloquy from some distance away.

"I hear, I hear!" the emperor cried. "To be or not to be!" The incident gave Bell the recognition he sorely needed. Other activities and exhibits at the exposition also portended a strange new future—most notably an internal combustion engine displayed by Langen & Otto of Germany. Perhaps many of the Exhibition's visitors felt as John Greenleaf Whittier did when he wrote in his "Centennial Hymn":

> Our fathers' God! from out whose hand
> The centuries fall like grains of sand,
> We meet to-day, united, free,
> And loyal to our land and Thee,
> To thank Thee for the era done,
> And trust Thee for the opening one.

CHAPTER 4

The Structure of Classes

S NORTING and bawling, their beady eyes glittering with fear, the cattle were driven out of the railroad cars by men with spiked poles and prodded down wooden ramps into the Chicago stockyards. Other men on horses herded the steers to pens that lay along alleys and streets, in blocks as regular as in the best-laid-out town. All was meticulously organized. Cowboys in the western ranges had rounded up their stock and driven them to towns like Abilene and Kansas City, Atchison and Hannibal, where they had been loaded into stockcars. Despite the length and frequent heat of the journey, stockmen usually delivered the cattle in good shape, since five dollars a head could be deducted for sick or damaged steers. Daily, the stockcars also disgorged thousands of hogs and sheep. They took their own places in pens that covered hundreds of acres on Chicago's west side.

After traders on horseback, trotting from pen to pen, bought and sold the stock, sealing their oral deals with quick handshakes, the beasts were driven into the nearby slaughterhouses. Here they were surveyed—"laid off like a map"—and delivered to the "chain." Workers hoisted them by nose or feet to an overhead belt, which moved them steadily and inexorably to other men with knives who slit their throats and sliced off their skin, men who bashed their brains in with hammers, men who cleaved backbones with axes, men who sometimes plunged a still palpitating carcass into a vat of boiling water. "Everything of the pig was used except the squeal," a meat packer boasted. A Chicago humorist noted, "A cow goes lowin' softly in to Armour's an' comes out glue, gelatine, fertylizer, celooloid, joolry, sofy cushions, hair restorer, washin' sody, littrachoor an' bed springs so quick that while aft she's still cow, for'ard she may be anything fr'm buttons to pannyma hats."

The workers—Poles, Germans, Slovaks, Irishmen—with their special tasks and chainlike organization were as regimented as the beasts. Signs in several languages enforced the rules. But this did not keep them from having fingers or hands sliced off as they grappled with carcasses and cutting machines on blood-soaked sawdust floors. Workers were often left with tubercular lungs, rheumatic bodies, hands scarred from the acid used to loosen wool from the skins of sheep.

111

This scene in the Chicago stockyards would not have surprised Karl Marx. In the late 1880s, the first English translations of the first volume of *Capital,* edited by Friedrich Engels, were reaching radical circles in the United States. Under capitalism, Marx had written, "all means for the development of production transform themselves into means of domination over, and exploitation of, the producers; they mutilate the labourer into a fragment of a man, degrade him to the level of an appendage of a machine, destroy any remnant of charm in his work and turn it into a hated toil; they estrange him from the intellectual potentials of the labour-process in the same proportion as science is incorporated in it as an independent power; they distort the conditions under which he works, subject him during the labour-process to a despotism the more hateful for its meanness; they transform his lifetime into working-time, and drag his wife and child beneath the wheels of the Juggernaut of capital. . . ."

"Capital is dead labour," Marx had written, "that vampire-like, only lives by sucking living labour, and lives the more, the more labour it sucks." Marx's passions seemed to rise as he wrote. "You rob me," he had the worker telling his boss, "every day of 2/3 of the value of my commodity. . . . You may be a model citizen, perhaps a member of the Society for the Prevention of Cruelty to Animals, and in the odour of sanctity to boot; but the thing that you represent face to face with me has no heart in its breast." Labor was hardly above the level of cattle, Marx implied; indeed, cattle had perhaps a higher status for, in its fattening, cattle was a raw material and at the same time a means of producing manure.

Industrial labor under capitalism, Marx contended, was degraded into the status of a commodity, transformed into the cog of a machine, converted into an urban proletariat. This was its tragedy, but in this also lay its great potential for liberation. Labor's common status at the bottom of the heap, its sharing of work experiences, its proletarianization, established a solid foundation for a common consciousness of its status, for united protest, for joint political action. Did American workers have such a potential? Marx lived in a city where in 1880, for example, "63 of every 100 Londoners were native to that city, 94 coming from England and Wales, and 98 from Great Britain and Ireland," according to Herbert Gutman, while in the same year the vast majority of the persons living in America's biggest cities were immigrants or the children of immigrants.

For that matter did the United States, with its capitalists concentrated not in one center like London but spread out in old and new industrial and financial centers across the country, possess even the potential for a "ruling class"?

Upper Classes: The New Rich and the Old

About three miles from the noisome stockyards, Philip D. Armour rose every morning at five in his home on fashionable Prairie Avenue, breakfasted at six, and soon, seated in his Goddard buggy drawn by two fast trotters and driven by a liveried coachman, he was on his way to his LaSalle Street office. He liked to get down to work, he would say, "before the boys with the polished nails show up." Soon the place was a beehive of activity, as Armour leaned back in his swivel chair summoning messenger boys, sending out telegraphic instructions to distant posts in his business empire, talking and moralizing at length to his associates. At six, no matter what business lay before him, he left for home and by nine was in bed.

One of six sons of New Englanders who had settled in the Mohawk Valley, Armour had traveled overland to California, panned gold and built sluices in the Sacramento River, returned home with several thousand dollars, and then had gone west again, plunging into the soap business in Cincinnati, selling hides in St. Paul, and moving on to grain dealing and meat packing in Milwaukee. During the Civil War, he made at least $2 million by agreeing to deliver, for $30 to $40 a barrel, pork that he was able to buy for $18 through a shrewd estimate of the likely fall of pork prices in the wake of Union victories. Soon he moved to Chicago, which had replaced Cincinnati as the pork-packing center of the nation. There, he pioneered in bringing live hogs to the city, slaughtering them, using the waste products, and refrigerating his shipments.

A big, thickset man with thinning sandy hair and reddish whiskers, Armour was a proudly "self-made" entrepreneur who did not pretend any interests except meat packing and moneymaking. Asked by a reporter, "You have made your pile; why not clear out?," he said, "I do not love the money. What I do love is the getting of it." He had no interest in art or music, and he was reputed to have read only one book in his life—*David Harum,* about the horse trader who liked to say, "Do unto others as they would like to do unto you, only do it fust." Armour enjoined his associates to "stick to facts" and avoid theory. But he liked to moralize about the value of hard work and rugged competition.

Despite his rough speech and appearance, and his occasional early-morning visits to the stockyards, Armour moved among a select circle. All of his five brothers worked for him. He sent his sons to private schools and made a place for them in his business. He had a paternalistic way with his subordinates, rewarding them with $100 handouts on the spot when they pleased him, bullying them when they did not. He had no stomach for labor unions and collective bargaining.

Even more select were the other notables on Prairie Avenue and environs: the millionaire merchant Marshall Field; his friend George M. Pullman, the sleeping car tycoon who lived in a palatial mansion down the street; the piano maker W. W. Kimball; and other meat packers, including Armour's arch-rival, Gustavus Swift, another self-made man and a specialist in beef. Such men as these often lunched together at the "Millionaires' Table" of the Chicago Club, or at the Palmer House, with its staircases of Carrara marble, its gigantic Egyptian chandelier over the reception desk, its "voluptuous Venetian mirrors" on the landings. Scattered around the North Side were other extraordinary edifices, with dining rooms sporting carved panels that portrayed rabbits, ducks, and prairie chickens; libraries of walnut and ebony set off with silver and curtained with raw silk lambrequins; music rooms with Gobelin tapestries and satinwood. In the sandstone mansion of Cyrus Hall McCormick, a fresco on the dining room ceiling pictured the emblem of the Legion of Honor, some sheaves of grain, and the McCormick reaper.

A thousand miles to the east, proper Bostonians liked to talk about the Chicago pork barons and their vulgar mansions, about the pork barons' wives in their silk hair nets with bangles of gold and silver braid and their frantic social rounds that seemed little short of stampedes. Chicago liked to talk about the Brahmins, too. A favorite story told of the Chicago banking house that asked Lee, Higginson in Boston about a certain Mr. Smith, a young Bostonian who had applied for a job in the banking house. The man at Lee, Higginson could hardly contain his enthusiasm for the young man. Mr. Smith, he wrote the banker, was a descendant of Peabodys, Cabots and Lowells, Saltonstalls, Appletons, and even Winthrops. Back came a brief letter from the Chicago banker. There seemed to have been a mistake, he wrote: "We were not contemplating using Mr. Smith for breeding purposes."

Bostonians called this story apocryphal, but they could not dispute the truth that lay behind it. As the old Brahmin elites faced intensifying economic competition from Chicago, New York, and myriad other centers, and as a flood of immigrants and outsiders overran Boston tenements and even Boston business offices, the Bostonians drew in among themselves economically, socially, culturally. What the new elites saw as an arrogant snobbishness, the old elites viewed as a discriminating exclusiveness. They retired into a bastion as many-walled as a feudal fortress. They tied their money up in trusts guarded by formidable attorneys. They sealed themselves off in organizations—the Massachusetts Society of Colonial Dames, the Society of Mayflower Descendants, genealogic societies—that no parvenu could crash. They sent their sons to select private schools and then to Harvard. Surrounded and besieged in the city, they retired to social citadels in the country. One family—the Forbeses—owned a good-sized island off Martha's Vineyard, all for themselves.

Above all, they protected their bloodlines through intermarriage. "In one Cabot family," according to Cleveland Amory, "out of seven children who married, four married Higginsons. In a Jackson family of five, three married Cabots. In a Peabody family of four boys and two girls, two of the boys and a girl married Lawrences. In one family of Boston Shaws, there were eleven children. Nine married members of other Boston First Families, one died at the age of seven months, and the eleventh became a Catholic priest." First Families had a penchant for marrying cousins, especially first cousins.

And then there was the fabled "Boston woman." Attired in sensible shoes and remarkable hats, often inherited, she spent her days in culture and good works, rushing from bookstore to church to symphony, from lecture to charity tea to indignation meeting. But she was not all this easily stereotyped, and she prided herself on her individuality. Most individualistic of all was Mrs. Jack Gardner, who publicly drank beer rather than tea, embraced Buddhism rather than Unitarianism, paraded down Tremont Street with a lion on a leash, told risqué stories in mixed company, had John Singer Sargent paint her in a costume that had all Boston talking, attired her coachman and two footmen in full livery—and left Boston an imported Florentine palace of pink marble with a fine art collection.

No wonder a Beacon Hill lady, questioned as to her disdain for travel, asked, "Why should I travel when I'm already here?" No wonder many a Boston man who did travel kept Boston time on his big Waltham watch. But the Boston elites that retreated into apartness did not descend into impotence. While they could no longer dominate Boston's electoral politics—before the Civil War seven mayors of Boston had held Brahmin status—men like Charles Francis Adams, Jr., chairman of the Massachusetts Board of Railway Commissioners and moderator of Quincy town meetings, held important posts in state and local government. In business, according to F. C. Jaher, "Brahmins maintained a vigorous entrepreneurial role and continued to control an appreciable segment of the great individual and corporate wealth in Boston." And the old Brahmin families—the Cabots, Higginsons, Lees, and the rest—maintained a firm grip on the city's cultural and charitable organizations, such as the Boston Symphony, the Public Library, the Museum of Fine Arts, the Somerset Club, the

Massachusetts General Hospital, the Board of Overseers of Harvard, the *North American Review*. For many with old wealth, these and family demands took most of their waking hours.

Other elites along the Atlantic seaboard displayed the same solidarity and exclusiveness as the proper Bostonians, but with local variations. Philadelphia society had long since moved from the old Independence Hall–Second Bank area a few blocks west of the Delaware to the Rittenhouse Square region a few blocks east of the Schuylkill. In this square and the blocks around it the banking, merchant, railroad, iron, coal, and—later —oil families built their mansions, held their balls, retreated to their clubs (Rittenhouse and Philadelphia), attended their Episcopalian churches (St. Mark's and the Church of the Holy Trinity), sponsored the arts (Academy of Music, Academy of the Fine Arts), discussed their Republican politics (Union League Club). Not only Biddles but Baldwins (locomotives), Distons (steel and saws), Bromleys (textiles), Wideners (traction and utilities), Cramps (ships), and Elkinses (traction and oil) who lived in the square and its environs "definitely felt themselves to be different, aloof and apart, from the rapidly developing heterogeneity of the rest of American society," according to E. Digby Baltzell. "Their wives and children lived in a money-insulated world of the great houses, private schools and fashionable churches surrounding the Square." Possibly, reflected Baltzell, this "privatization" went back to Andrew Jackson's triumph over Nicholas Biddle.

If Philadelphia First Families numbered fewer eccentrics than did Boston—Rittenhouse Square frowned on the idiosyncratic—Philadelphians were no less self-conscious and backward-looking. "To mention Walnut Street to an Old Philadelphian," wrote George Wharton Pepper, who was one, "is to awaken memories of a departed glory. On bright Sundays, after church, there was always an informal parade of fashion on the south side of this thoroughfare. There the city's Four Hundred could be seen to great advantage. They were the blended congregation of half a dozen mid-city churches. They made upon the onlooker an impression of urbanity, of social experience and of entire self-satisfaction. If, during church-time, they had confessed themselves miserable sinners, by the time they appeared on parade their restoration to divine favor was seemingly complete."

Woe to the family left out, especially the moneyed family who could not use poverty as the excuse for exclusion. A young Widener wrote a novel excoriating the snobs who had snubbed his mother for marrying across the tracks. A young Bullitt wrote a novel about the declining standards of the "Sacred Square." The Square was unmoved.

* * *

New York society was different—richer, brassier, more diverse, more volatile, less cohesive. And it was run by women.

The New York elites were attuned to a dynamic economy and a fast-changing city. Manhattan was now the unchallenged hub of the nation's finances, and itself challenged London as a center of world finance. The city was on the move. Arrivistes were crowding up against established wealth. Avenues were spearing far to the north in Manhattan, even into the Bronx. Looking north from Cortlandt Street and Maiden Lane in the early 1880s, one saw a forest of telegraph and telephone lines, a maze of shop signs, and a jumble of drays, streetcars, buggies, coaches, delivery wagons, all horse-drawn, in the streets. Walking up Fifth Avenue, one came upon the upthrust arm and torch of the Statue of Liberty—the great icon had not yet been put in place on Bedloe's Island—and the fashionable temple, Emanu-El. Farther north, Broadway was called the Boulevard. But Society, entrenched in its enclave on lower Fifth Avenue, hardly looked past 42nd Street to the "wasteland" beyond.

While this Society could boast of plenty of old families—Brevoorts, Fishes, Schermerhorns, Livingstons, Roosevelts, Rensselaers, and other "Knickerbockers"—new money and big money meant more in Manhattan than in any other metropolis in the East. Up to around the 1880s, said Ward McAllister, the deputy arbiter of New York society, "for one to be worth a million of dollars was to be rated as a man of fortune, but now . . . New York's ideas as to values, when fortune was named, leaped boldly up to ten millions, fifty millions, one hundred millions, and the necessities and luxuries followed suit. One was no longer content with a dinner of a dozen or more, to be served by a couple of servants. Fashion demanded that you be received in the hall of the house in which you were to dine, by from five to six servants, who, with the butler, were to serve the repast. . . . Soft strains of music were introduced between the courses, and in some houses gold replaced silver in the way of plate. . . ."

The center of action was the half-planned, half-mythical "Four Hundred," an attempt by the old rich to orchestrate wealth, birth, and style into a coherent social system that soon succumbed to the pecking order of big money. Anointed by Mrs. William Astor—*the* Mrs. Astor, born Caroline Schermerhorn—and with access guarded by her powerful court chamberlain Ward McAllister, the actual membership was found to consist of a combination of old and new family wealth when McAllister gave it out to the *New York Times*. Spurred by acute status anxiety, the new rich struggled desperately to make the sacred list and the even more select "Patriarchs," also monitored by Astor and McAllister. Bitter feuds broke out, as Fifth

Avenue hostesses fought for their own status, even while conciliating factions among their guests.

"I understand," said a character in William Dean Howells's *A Traveler from Altruria*, "that in America society is managed even more by women than it is in England." Entirely, he was told. "We have no other leisure class."

The ultimate confrontation, as "ambitious hostesses alternately laid siege, launched frontal assaults, or conducted flanking maneuvers against the bastions of higher respectability," occurred between Mrs. Astor, the acknowledged queen of the Four Hundred, and Mrs. William K. Vanderbilt. The Astors had looked down on the Vanderbilts as grandchildren of the self-styled "Commodore" Vanderbilt, who had been just a crude Staten Island ferryboat man, after all, and Mrs. Astor did not approve of railroad money. Vanderbilts in turn pointed to the Astors' opium smuggling into Canton, and their defrauding of East Side slum dwellers and of Indians. The climax approached as the Vanderbilts, after outbuilding the Astors' Newport "cottage," Beechwood, with The Breakers, decided to erect a $2 million palace at Fifth Avenue and 52nd Street. To the opening of this town house Mrs. Vanderbilt invited 1,200 persons—but not Mrs. Astor. A calling card bearing the legend "Mrs. Astor" had never been deposited on the salver of 66 Fifth Avenue, said Mrs. Vanderbilt, and how could she invite a perfect stranger? Intermediaries intervened, open hostilities were avoided, and a footman in the blue livery of the House of Astor duly presented a visiting card to a domestic in the maroon livery of the House of Vanderbilt. Mrs. Astor and her daughter attended the ball, in which dazzling young socialites with electric-lighted stars on their foreheads waltzed with men in baronial costumes.

If the Four Hundred felt beleaguered in their Fifth Avenue bastions, they could always retreat to mansions in Newport or the Berkshires or in the South or in Europe—or all of these—but here again the Vanderbilts seemed to gain the competitive edge, with their establishments in or near Asheville, North Carolina; Centerport, Long Island; Upper St. Regis Lake in the Adirondacks; and their endless yachting through the Caribbean and the Mediterranean. The Frederick W. Vanderbilts' mansion in Hyde Park was perhaps the finest monument to the era. Built at a cost of over $2 million, in a time when a construction worker might earn a dollar a day, the mansion was erected on such an accelerated schedule that carpenters worked shoulder-to-shoulder. The result was an Italian Renaissance–style edifice, packed with art and furnishings from abroad, surrounded by superb grounds, trees, and with a view up and down the Hudson.

Guests allowed into the family quarters marveled at the master's corner bedroom, with its single bed and no direct access to his wife's bed-room, and Mrs. Vanderbilt's boudoir, a reproduction of a French queen's bedroom of the Louis XV period. The headwall of the bed was covered with hand-embroidered silk; the heavily napped rug weighed over a ton; and Mrs. Vanderbilt's bed was separated from the rest of the room by a marble rail, like those behind which French courtiers had presented their petitions to the queen in olden times. Thus was symbolized the ultimate separation of the queens of society from the long hierarchy that stretched below them.

The class structures in other cities contrasted with that of New York and the other eastern metropolises. New Haven had lived for decades under a powerful patrician rule, which came to an end with the elevation of a long line of businessmen following the Civil War. The Richmond and Charles-ton elites were hardly altered in any fundamental way by the Civil War, while Springfield, Massachusetts, never developed an aristocratic leader-ship cohesive and powerful enough to hold back the young entrepreneurs.

Chicago of course accepted the rule of the arrivistes more readily than did even New York. But if Chicago scoffed at Boston, New York ignored Chicago. Mrs. Astor, an incessant traveler, had never even been there. To its balls each Patriarch might invite five gentlemen, four ladies, and two "distinguished strangers" from Boston, Philadelphia, Baltimore, or Charleston, or from London or the Continent—but not from Chicago or, for that matter, from any other city west of the Alleghenies.

THE MIDDLE CLASSES: A WOMAN'S WORK

She rose before dawn to dress in a high-collared, long-sleeved dress over flannel and muslin petticoats, bustle, and whalebone corset. After lighting the kerosene lamp in the kitchen and kindling the coals in the firebox, she kneaded the bread dough left to rise overnight in a warm place by the iron range. From part of the dough she baked a basket of rolls before preparing the rest of the heavy meal middle-class Americans ate upon rising—steak, fried potatoes, hotcakes, and coffee roasted and ground at home. Soon her husband, imposing in his waistcoat and "burnsides," would enter, fol-lowed by the children in sailor suits or frilly dresses, one child probably holding a baby brother or sister. After breakfast, she saw children and husband off to school and work, on horse-car or steam railroad.

Monday was always wash day: voluminous linen sheets, tablecloths, and napkins, yards of flannel or muslin petticoats, diapers, soaked in wooden tubs and then stretched across kitchen or backyard. "It was all the lifting that tired my back so," one woman remarked—water had to be carried in from the pump, heated on the stove, carried to the washtub, and then emptied outside after each rinse. Petticoats, shirts, cuffs, and collars would be starched, while all else—even diapers—required ironing with a heavy iron reheated on the stove every half-hour or so. In summer, the kitchen would be sweltering; in winter, women risked chilblains while hanging freezing wet garments on the line outside.

Housecleaning usually took a week in the summer and another in the fall. Each room in sequence was turned upside down, the horsehair and mahogany furniture moved aside, and the carpet lifted for a clean, a mend, a dye and then reinstallation. Mirrors, pictures, china, and bric-a-brac were scrubbed and polished, textured wallpaper and heavy ornate curtains brushed, soot cleaned out of fireplaces and lamps. Insects and vermin infested even wealthy homes as a result of inadequate drainage and outdoor privies.

The sewing machine, by the 1870s essential equipment in every home, helped turn the chore of sewing into a housewife's best chance for creativity. Many women took intense pride in the skill with which they remade old clothes, like "Hattie's 'opera cape' made out of Warrie's pink flannel baby cloak." The family's diverse activities stretched the housewife's ingenuity—one woman made two-tone graduation dresses for her sisters and later found out that wearing them had been "life's darkest hour" for the girls.

She might have time during the day to browse through her copy of *Harper's Weekly,* with its rich mixture of articles, stories, reviews, and George William Curtis's editorial comment, or through the *Atlantic* or the *Nation* or *Frank Leslie's Illustrated Newspaper.* If she had been brought up on *Godey's Lady's Book*—"The Only Magazine with Lady Editors"—she might now be reading *The Mother at Home.* Or if she had been brought up on *The Lady's Own,* "Devoted to the Advocacy of Working Females" and costing only three cents an issue, she might now be following one of the many suffragist organs. Her children might read *Home Companion: A Monthly for Young People* which, after going through many transformations, would become the *Home Companion,* "a journal suited to the entire family and read by all," and later the *Ladies' Home Companion.* In most of these journals she could scan a plenitude of mail-order advertising, patent-medicine claims, and premium offers.

Family members returned for a dinner of roast and Indian pudding, and then spent the evening hours together in the parlor, reading aloud or playing cards by lamplight. While the wife mended or embroidered, daughters played the piano or received gentlemen callers, always with the family or a chaperone present. At an early hour the family retired, the wife putting out the milk can and the husband banking the fire and barring the shutters.

Many middle-class housewives hired live-in "help," usually young women from small rural towns or newly arrived immigrants from Ireland, Sweden, or the Deep South. Housewives often proved exacting mistresses, grumbling audibly about newcomers' slow adjustment to service—"She seemed to have all the faults, and none of the virtues of help"—and vigilantly alert for signs of stealing or shirking. The maid, the complaints went, used "the weapon of degraded races pretty freely—Deceit," or "She is a *slouch* Poor white trash." Friction between mistress and servant masqueraded as "the servant problem" and made some women decide to "do their own work"—which often meant, in fact, supervising a cleaning woman several days a week.

*   *   *

To find guidance through the crises, large and small, of domestic life, most middle-class women read manuals of housekeeping or "domestic science," such as *The Mother at Home,* with recipes and tips on hygiene, physiology, nutrition, how to decorate, or how to get along with domestics. Educator Catharine Beecher explained how to have "Economical, Healthful, Beautiful and Christian homes." These guides, which poured forth from publishers in the latter half of the century, were especially important to a mobile society in which many women lost the benefit of their mothers' and grandmothers' knowledge. They also set higher standards of cleanliness, household skills, and child-rearing, standards that often consumed as much time as was gained from the new labor-saving devices.

Mothers also lightened their burdens by training daughters of the house from an early age in the skills of home management. One woman wrote proudly that her daughter, just turned three, "sweeps and dusts and bakes and enjoys it very much." At four, the little girl sewed a patchwork quilt for her dolls. All too often a young girl would have to leave school prematurely in order to take over management of the house—to substitute for a sick mother or to enable the family to concentrate all its resources on a son's education. "Mother explained very regretfully that she couldn't afford the lessons which would be needed to train me for a (music) teacher," one woman wrote. "She explained that she wanted David to have as much education as possible, so that if ever she, or father, couldn't take care of us adequately he'd be able to help." Much might depend on a daughter's ability to hold the home together.

One subject a mother did not discuss with her daughter was sex. Canons of modesty and purity kept some women from completely undressing throughout their adult lives and convinced others that sexuality was for men alone. Clergymen and politicians claimed that corresponding to the male sex drive was women's maternal instinct, a chaste tenderness never to be "tainted" with sex. "The full force of sexual desire is seldom known to a virtuous woman," announced one male authority.

At the same time, women's fashions were tending to maximize female-ness and limit freedom. "The poetry of dependence," feminist Elizabeth Cady Stanton called the combination of romance and restriction. The corset, a contraption of whalebone and steel tightly bound in back with laces in order to create a curvaceous form, was de rigueur, even for little girls, for almost a century. "It is no rare thing," wrote one English visitor, "to meet ladies so tightly laced that they cannot lean back in a chair or sofa; if they did so, they would suffocate." The tighter a woman's waist, the more ladylike she was, as hinted by her frequent swoons and headaches.

Young women and men entered marriage with little understanding of each other's sexual needs. Marriage often came as a shock to young brides who had only known their suitors through the formality of chaperoned courtship. "How many young hearts have revealed the fact," wrote Catharine Beecher after a tour, "that what they had been trained to imagine the highest earthly felicity, was but the beginning of care, and disappointment, and sorrow, and often led to the extremity of mental and physical suffering." "I am nearly wrecked and ruined by . . . nightly intercourse," one woman wrote. "This and nothing else was the cause of my miscarriage . . . he went to work like a man a-mowing, and instead of a pleasure as it might have been, it was most intense torture. . . ." Thinking their wives "unaccommodating and capricious," some men fled the house to visit prostitutes. And women turned to one another to find the intimacy and warmth they missed in marriage, developing a network of lifetime friends who exchanged diaries, sewed one another's trousseaux, supervised one another's pregnancies and childbirths, vacationed together, and shared chores, skills, and life's major events.

The fear of unending pregnancies and prolonged motherhood may have contributed more than any crusading clergyman or insensitive husband to the female aversion toward sex. "Confinement" indoors during and after pregnancy, lack of fresh air and exercise, and the physiological effects of the viselike corset often made childbirth all but unbearable. The intensifying shift to a money economy made smaller families more desirable, especially in the urban middle-class home where children's labor was less needed, and women were beginning to realize that by regulating their— and thereby, their husbands'—sexuality, they could augment their power within the family and also enjoy the autonomy that an endless parade of bawling infants denied them. The result of these developments was fewer, and healthier, babies.

Contraception was another unmentionable. After the passage of the "Comstock" law in 1873, it was illegal to advertise or distribute birth control material—"obscene literature and articles of immoral use"—through the mail. Male withdrawal, the most common method of birth control, was discreetly discouraged by male doctors as being unhealthy to the husband; the rhythm method, though popular, was ineffective due to ignorance of the female fertility cycle. Abortion was a last resort, often induced by patent medicines.

Defying all these obstacles, many women did enjoy happy sex lives. Elizabeth Cady Stanton wrote in 1883, "Walt Whitman seems to understand everything in nature but woman. In 'There is a Woman Waiting for me,' he speaks as if the female must be forced to the creative act, apparently ignorant of the great natural fact that a healthy woman has as much passion as a man, that she needs nothing stronger than the law of attraction to draw her to the male." Love and sex preoccupied young girls. "For such a person that I could so love, I would brave all—anything, I would give myself up soul and body," wrote Harriet Burton at age fifteen, with the passionate intensity that would characterize her later speeches for suffrage.

Three-quarters of the women questioned, in a remarkable survey taken by a female physician at the end of the century, wrote that they desired and enjoyed sex. Many said they needed it for spiritual, even more than physical, fulfillment, and resisted the idea that sex was for reproduction alone. "My husband and I believe in intercourse for its own sake," wrote one woman in 1893. "We wish it for ourselves and spiritually miss it, rather than physically, when it does not occur, because it is the highest, most sacred expression of our oneness." But with even a slight risk of pregnancy, "we deny ourselves the intercourse, feeling all the time that we are losing that which keeps us closest to each other."

Some middle-class women, including those of some affluence, found their prospects a source of despair. The feminist writer Charlotte Perkins Gilman, great-niece of Catharine, Harriet, and Henry Ward Beecher, suffered a crippling depression in 1885 at the age of twenty-five. "I went to bed crying; woke in the night crying, sat on the edge of the bed in the morning and cried—from sheer continuous pain," she wrote later. "Not physical—the doctors examined me and found nothing the matter." Still later she would write *The Yellow Wallpaper,* a fictionalized look at her illness which compared the confinement of a mental patient with that of a wife.

Other notable, talented women, including Jane Addams and Margaret Sanger, endured the same experience. Alice James, brilliant sister of Henry and William, suffered a mysterious disease from the age of nineteen until she died of breast cancer at forty-two. "I think the difficulty is my inability to assume the receptive attitude, that cardinal virtue in women, the absence of which has always made me so uncharming to & uncharmed by the male sex," she wrote, referring to her experiences with male doctors in particular. Countless other women, faced with a discrepancy between their potential, their dreams, and reality, took part in an epidemic of invalidism observed by Catharine Beecher as early as 1855. ". . . [T]he more I traveled, the more the conviction was pressed on my attention that there was a terrible decay of female health all over the land, and that this evil was bringing with it an incredible extent of individual, domestic, and social suffering, that was increasing in an alarming ratio."

At the same time the "idle wife" was becoming a status symbol for many an upwardly mobile man. In her vivid, lavish dress, the better-off middle-class woman had become the "chief ornament" of her husband's household, without the need—or ability—to work. An ideal of feminine beauty evolved in which the wife, pale and fragile, received visitors while languishing on a chaise longue. Charlotte Gilman for one considered a wife's only work in such a household to be sex, and could see no difference between that and prostitution. In direct opposition to her great-aunt, Gilman believed the household should be less, not more, central to a woman's life.

Doctors usually diagnosed the common complaints of these women as arising from disorders of the reproductive organs. Some even perceived a woman's body as a battleground between the brain and the uterus—generally, they concluded, it was healthier for the uterus to control. Cures abounded, from water cures to bleeding and purges. Toward the end of the century, symptoms of these "female diseases" increasingly included episodes of hysteria. A Viennese physician, Sigmund Freud, stated that these physical symptoms could have a mental source.

*   *   *

A sensational charge of adultery in the early seventies lifted issues of sexuality out of the whispered gossip of the social elite and plunged them into open courtrooms and the public prints, and hence into middle-class consciousness. These charges pitted the most celebrated preacher of the day, Henry Ward Beecher, against the most notorious woman leader, Victoria Claflin Woodhull.

Beecher had grown up with every advantage that Woodhull had lacked. He was one of thirteen children of the thrice-married Lyman Beecher, the famous Presbyterian clergyman. Educated at Amherst College, Henry had gone through years of inner turbulence and doubt until he decided to devote his life and love to Christ and man, a decision highlighted by a mystic revelation one May day in the Ohio woods. Throughout, he had the support of his father and two remarkable sisters, Catharine and Harriet. For all his religious devotion, Beecher was no stiff-necked, sanctimonious moralist. A big, genial, rumpled man, with sensual features and the head of a lion, he possessed a warmth and exuberance that endeared him to a multitude of friends, especially women. But he preached all the middle-class virtues to the huge middle-class congregation he drew to his Plymouth Church in Brooklyn.

Victoria Claflin grew up in a small Ohio town, one of ten children of a mother suspected of mania and a father of pyromania. After the neighbors gave a benefit to help the family out of town, Victoria and her sister Tennessee roamed through Ohio as itinerant spiritualists and vendors of such patent medicines as Elixir of Life, until one of Tennessee's "patients" died of cancer of the breast and the "healer" was indicted for manslaughter. Victoria, having married and divorced one Woodhull, and then one Colonel Blood, made her way to New York, with both men and her sister in tow. There the two sisters prospered. Tennessee, now plump and flirtatious, so entranced Commodore Vanderbilt with her "magnetic healing" that the aging tycoon wanted to marry her but settled for establishing the two sisters—with a check—as the "lady brokers" of Wall Street.

That was just the start. In April 1870, Victoria Woodhull announced her candidacy for President of the United States. Six weeks later she put out the first issue of *Woodhull & Claflin's Weekly*. Advertisements for bond issues and brokerage houses—including Jay Cooke & Co.—filled page one although, weekly, the masthead proclaimed, "Progress! Free Thought! Untrammeled Lives!" Inner pages advertised books on "The Physiology of Menstruation," "Impregnation," "Sexual Generation," "Monstrosities," "The Law of Sexual Intercourse." Woodhull set up and headed the Victoria League, which had nothing to do with the British queen, and she won a big following in labor and socialist circles. Viewed askance by some of the more respectable woman leaders, she made such an eloquent plea for woman's suffrage before the Judiciary Committee of the House of Representatives that she was invited to sit on the platform with Susan B. Anthony and other suffragists then meeting in convention in Washington. Endorsed by her own *Weekly* and by the Equal Rights party in 1872, she marched to the polls but was denied a ballot—and was unlisted on the ballot she was denied.

Woodhull's main concern, however, was always sexual freedom. Week after week her paper poured out pleadings, indignations, charges, and outrages. With the aid of Stephen P. Andrews, scholar, spelling reformer, spiritualist, and advocate of free love, she confronted the issues that middle-class Americans had ducked. Now that Negro slavery was overthrown, she said, "I intend to do all in my small power toward the overthrow of that other slavery, more deeply rooted, more subtle, more obscure and tenacious, and more demoralizing! than ever the slavery of the black man was." She went on: "Whether it be agreeable to people to hear these questions of marriage, divorce, abortion and prostitution discussed or not, the time is coming, nay, is upon them, when they will not only be compelled to *hear,* but to *decide.*"

More and more she veered toward open advocacy of Free Love. At a tumultuous meeting in New York's Steinway Hall, advertised by huge posters calling for "Freedom! Freedom! Freedom!" in the social as well as the political and religious sphere, she took her stand. Goaded by a heckler who shouted, "Are you a free lover?" she cried:

"YES! I AM A FREE LOVER! I HAVE AN INALIENABLE, CONSTITUTIONAL, AND NATURAL RIGHT TO LOVE WHOM I MAY, TO LOVE AS LONG OR AS SHORT A PERIOD AS I CAN, TO CHANGE THAT LOVE EVERY DAY IF I PLEASE!" The hall erupted in cheers, hisses, and catcalls, but Woodhull went on. Not only must no law interfere with this right, she declared, but "it is your duty" both to accord it and "see that I am protected in it." By free love she did not mean "sexual promiscuity," she explained that evening and thereafter, but "the highest kind of love" whose supreme "gratification comes from rendering its object the greatest amount of happiness."

But, more than sexual promiscuity, Woodhull despised sexual hypocrisy, and increasingly the man she saw as its chief embodiment—Henry Ward Beecher. Through mutual friends she learned that Beecher had carried on an affair with one of his parishioners, Mrs. Theodore Tilton; the wounded husband himself not only complained to Victoria but had an affair with *her* for six months. Goaded by the insinuations of Beecher's sister Harriet (long famous as author of *Uncle Tom's Cabin*), desperate over her weekly's loss of advertising and readers, she revealed the whole story in the November 2, 1872, issue, in a long, detailed article that she hoped would "burst like a bombshell into the ranks of the moralistic social camp." It did. In the same issue she told in most intimate detail how a prominent man-about-town—not related to the Beecher situation—had seduced two young virgins. This charge aroused to action Anthony Comstock, secretary of the Society for the Suppression of Vice, and shortly not the alleged seducer but the two Woodhull sisters were thrust into the Ludlow Street jail.

Victoria, bailed out after four weeks, spoke on "The Naked Truth" and was arrested again. She and her sister were acquitted of printing obscene matter, and the alleged seducer lost his suit against them for libel. Later, Tilton filed a charge against Beecher for adultery with Mrs. Tilton; after a long and sensational trial Beecher got off with a hung jury. First his congregation, and then 244 representatives of Congregational churches, backed him to the hilt. His popularity hardly dimmed, Beecher continued as "spokesman for a middle-class America," in the words of a biographer, though he was unquestionably an enlightened spokesman, defending women's and Negro rights, evolution, science, reform in general.

To the glee of her critics, Woodhull's *Weekly* failed; she was accused of using her lists of prostitutes' middle-class clients for blackmail purposes; she was denied lecture halls for her free-love talks. When Cornelius Vanderbilt died in 1877 and his family contested his will, "Mrs. Satan" and her sister sailed to England amid rumors that Vanderbilt money had paid their way. But in England the sisters had their final revenge. Victoria married into a rich banking family, Tennessee into a viscountcy. Thus virtue was rewarded, as the two sisters, captivating as ever, escaped the American middle class by bounding into the English upper.

The Farmer's Lot

Women migrating to the West would have scoffed at the "problems" of middle-class wives and mothers in eastern cities and suburbs. Often of middle-class status themselves, as they and their husbands had to possess some capital to strike out toward the prairie states and set up a new home, women pioneers and settlers were often reduced to a condition of labor that, by official finding, made them a vast and dispersed collection of sweated workers. "In plain language," concluded a Department of Agriculture study in 1862, "a farmer's wife, as a general rule, is a laboring drudge." On three farms out of four, "the wife works harder, endures more, than any other on the place; more than the husband, more than the 'farm hand,' more than the 'hired help' of the kitchen."

Once the settlers had finished camping out, usually under wretched conditions, while putting up their sod or frame house, farm women settled into their routine. For a time they might cook over an open hearth, bending low over the coals, until cast-iron, wood-burning stoves became available. In the postwar years, many farm women continued to spend hours at the spinning wheel, using flax and wool off the farm and buying a little cotton thread. They were still making soap by pouring boiling water into a hopper of hardwood ashes, collecting the lye in the trough below, stirring in kitchen fats and grease, and pouring the "come" soap into tubs or molds. On Mondays they heated water over hearth or stove, added the soap, pounded the clothes against a washboard, then rinsed them, wrung them out by hand, and hung them out on a line. Theirs was not only "inside" work. With the help of older children, women planted gardens, milked cows, cleaned out henhouses, helped the men butcher hogs and plant fields, along with cooking three big meals a day and bearing and nursing children. Rosie Ise, raising twelve children, not only had to wash clothes and cook meals for her Kansas family but care for frequent guests and churn butter to sell in town.

Conditions slowly improved in the homestead as farm women could buy factory goods and labor-saving devices. Yet, for many years, even a kitchen sink or a rotary egg beater were oddities. There was always a contrast between the husbands' huge machines in the field and the wives' primitive equipment in the home.

Somehow farm women coped—and some much preferred their rural way of life to that of the "old country" or the East. When E.B., a Missouri farm wife, complained in *The Household* in the late 1870s about a three-hour tussle with an "obstinate churn," cooking first for plowboys and then for harvesters and then for wheat stackers, and taking care of her twelfth baby, and entertaining "Mrs. Elite and her sister Miss Stylish," and "their nephew Bon Ton," and working often from 4:30 in the morning almost to midnight, other women wrote the journal to upbraid, advise, or reassure her. "When she wrote that," said one letter, "she must have had a fit of the blues, or her bread would not rise, or the cow had kicked over the milk pail."

Whatever the tales of hardship and woe, Americans continued to trek west by the hundreds of thousands. Most of the settlers who poured into the Plains came from nearby states like Illinois, Iowa, and Missouri, but a large number arrived from Canada, Germany, Sweden, England, and Ireland. The westward expansion accelerated in the 1880s and became an unprecedented boom. Kansas attracted the greatest number of settlers during this period—though it lost the most in the 1890s. The legislatures of Kansas and other prairie states carved out new counties by the dozens and new cities and towns by the hundreds.

Some settlers were lured west by advertising campaigns. Eager to sell portions of the vast landholdings given them by the federal government —a total area larger than the state of Texas, or one-tenth of the entire United States—railroads wanted a flood of settlers to build up their freight and passenger income. The Homestead Act of 1862 and follow-up legislation were not so great a boon to the new settlers as their proponents had hoped—except for Northern Civil War veterans, who were given a number of special advantages. The railroads, speculators, and vast "bonanza" farms—which hired migrant labor—took most of the best land, leaving homesteaders quarter sections that were often rocky and distant from railroad lines.

The more fortunate pioneers bought or laid claim to land that was by a river or creek. They constructed their homes and barns out of nearby timber, or out of sod made into bricks and dried in the sun. Solid and well insulated, sod houses could be kept fairly warm even in the coldest months, often with the help of buffalo chips and sunflower stalks as well as firewood. Weather was a constant concern. From the Dakota Territory down through Texas, rainfall came in mysterious cycles, and in the more westerly portions of this region, where rain was always sparse, droughts were especially long-lasting and severe. Drought or not, hot scorching summer winds sometimes seared the wheat and corn in their husks. Farm families had to cope as well with prairie fires, dust storms, tornadoes, buffalo herds, and devastating invasions of grasshoppers.

Human adversaries were often more threatening than natural ones. Banks and mortgage companies proliferated in the prairie regions, fueled by a surplus of eastern investment capital. Although farmers had to pay exorbitant interest rates of up to 25 percent or more, they tended to borrow more and more to build new barns and fences, buy the latest equipment, and expand their domains. The ubiquitous loan agents secured mortgages first on the land and then on farm equipment, working stock, and other chattel. The farmer's accelerating indebtedness soared over the years as the dollar appreciated, the currency contracted, and wheat and corn prices dropped.

The farmers might set out as did German immigrant Henry Ise in western Kansas, breaking up the sod with a hatchet in order to plant his corn, but new factories in the not-too-distant cities of Chicago, Rock Island, Moline, and Davenport mass-produced a cornucopia of newly developed farm machinery that alleviated the grueling toil. While some farmers in the Deep South continued to labor with hoes, shallow one-mule plows, and their bare hands, most farmers of the West cultivated the soil with disc gang plows and five-section disc harrows, planted wheat with grain drills and corn with "checkrowers," and harvested the crops with newfangled haymaking, harvesting, and threshing machines, many of which were driven by steam. American-style silos were first developed in 1875, starting out square or rectangular, then mushrooming everywhere in their circular shape. Much of this equipment was quite expensive—a wheat binder, for instance, cost $235—and thus put the farmer further into debt.

As the Plains states became the "granary of the world," the income of many farmers fell off. Despite an occasional good year, the prices for wheat and corn plummeted. Wheat which had gone for a dollar a bushel in 1870 sold for half that or less in the 1890s. Yet the markets for these grains kept growing steadily, particularly in Europe, which eventually consumed a third or more of the crop. With the shipping and marketing of their wheat, corn, and hogs to the East and across the Atlantic even more beyond their control than droughts and grasshopper plagues, farmers felt sorely exploited by railroads, trusts, "middlemen," and other capitalists big and small.

Farmers living far from the railroads carried their crops in wagons across the muddy and rut-filled roads called "loblollies" to grain elevators along the railroad tracks. There buyers paid as little as possible for the grain; often they downgraded the quality of the wheat to avoid paying the higher price for "number one" wheat that was "sound, plump, and well cleaned." Elevator companies, many of which were owned by the railroads, were notorious for discriminating against their smaller customers. And farmers who shipped directly found that the railroads charged them exorbitant rates—while giving rebates to their biggest customers—and regardless of the distance forced them to pay through rates to the train's last stop. For the ordinary farmer, shipping grain from the Dakota Territory to Minneapolis was more expensive than sending the same grain from Chicago to Liverpool.

Life was a perpetual struggle on the prairie frontier, but for the first two decades after the Civil War enough good years canceled out the bad for most farm families to eke out a subsistence living. Then a series of dry years starting in 1886 precipitated a radical change in the farmer's condition. Crops failed year after year, debts skyrocketed, loans went unpaid, eastern capital dried up, and credit tightened like a noose. Banks and mortgage companies foreclosed upon more and more farms, and more and more farm families became tenants on their own land, or gave up farming and moved back east. The percentage of tenant farmers in Kansas doubled between 1880 and 1890 to more than a third of all farmers, and tenancy in Kansas increased in the next two decades even more than in the South. Between 1888 and 1892, half the farm families of scorched western Kansas headed east, some of their covered wagons emblazoned with slogans like "In God we trusted, in Kansas we busted." In 1891 alone, 18,000 "prairie schooners" crossed the Missouri River from Nebraska back to Iowa.

But most farm families, particularly in the central and eastern parts of the Plains, stayed put and survived these hard times the best they could, with whatever ingenuity and resourcefulness they could muster. Susan Orcutt of western Kansas typified the plight of the worst-off. In 1894 she appealed for help from her Populist governor, Lorenzo Lewelling:

"I take my Pen In hand to let you know that we are Starving to death It is Pretty hard to do without any thing to Eat hear in this God for saken country we would of had Plenty to Eat if the hail hadent cut our rye down and ruined our corn and Potatoes I had the Prettiest Garden that you Ever seen and the hail ruined It and I have nothing to look at My Husband went a way to find work and came home last night and told me that we would have to Starve he has bin in ten countys and did not Get no work It is Pretty hard for a woman to do with out any thing to Eat when she dosent no what minute She will be confined to bed If I was In Iowa I would be all right I was born there and raised there I havent had nothing to Eat to day and It is three oclock."

If misery loved company, western farmers could look south. With farms and markets often devastated by the war, most southern farmers, black or white, were unable to achieve anything close to prosperity. The malaise was deep-seated and multifaceted: wartime pillage and destruction of farms, fences, crops, and livestock; antiquated farming that produced low yields and rapid soil exhaustion; a racism that removed incentives and crushed aspirations of black farmers and sharecroppers; overproduction and the sharply declining price of cotton; and probably most important, the constant pressure from rural furnishing merchants and northern capital to cling to the one-crop economy of cotton rather than diversifying. Southern farmers were not even able to remain self-sufficient in food production, which fell by nearly half after the war, and the South became an increasing net importer of corn and other foodstuffs from the North and West.

"Cotton planting has been a mania," one observer remarked. "The neglected corn field with all its consequences is a part of Southern history." "A planter reported that 'want and gaunt, haggard despair have prevailed everywhere in the Black Belt' of Alabama," according to C. Vann Woodward; "in Louisiana a farmer pointed to 'old fields abandoned in every direction' that he had seen cleared as a boy on the frontier as rich new land; in Mississippi, there was a poverty-driven exodus from the farm 'so strong and wide as to threaten whole sections of our country with desolation'. . . ." Politician Benjamin Tillman spoke bitterly in 1886 of a "fatal lethargy" among the farmers of South Carolina: "our minds become benumbed, deadened." Agrarian leader Tom Watson described Georgia farmers falling into peonage "like victims of some horrid nightmare . . . powerless—oppressed—shackled."

The emancipated black sharecroppers and tenants were by far the worst off of all Southerners—the most powerless, most oppressed, and still, though in new and different ways, most shackled. The defeated but

still powerful planter class made a concerted effort to revive the plantation system immediately after the Civil War, signing contracts with blacks
remaining on and near their lands to work much as they had before,
except now for meager wages. After an initial burst of success—cotton
prices were quite high for a couple of years after wartime shortages—the
experiment of wage slavery collapsed. Save in Louisiana and a few pockets elsewhere in the Deep South, the old-style plantation was virtually
dead by 1870.

Another experiment, sharecropping, was longer-lasting. Accepted by
blacks who aspired to greater autonomy and even future landownership,
or pushed by large planters who wanted to retain certain features of the
plantation system and gain more control over black labor and labor costs
than the wage contracts permitted, sharecropping often turned out a fraud
for those blacks who perceived it as the next and higher rung on the ladder
to liberation. Out of a variety of sharecropping arrangements, one form
became nearly universal: the white landlord divided his holding into shares
of up to fifty acres, each share usually to be farmed by one black family.
The landlord supplied everything except food and clothing: housing, fuel,
one or two mules or horses, feed, tools, seed, and fertilizer. Landlord and
sharecropper split the crop fifty-fifty; "working on halves," it was called.
Annual renewal of the contract strengthened the landlord's control over
the labor of his "croppers." Black sharecroppers thus achieved greater
autonomy in form but not in substance. Landlords generally supervised
them closely, in some cases even working them in gangs to cultivate the
soil. The sharecropper was a landless laborer, perhaps even less autonomous than European serfs in the Middle Ages. It was "slavery under a new
name."

Ned Cobb grew up in a black sharecropping family in Alabama in the
1880s and 1890s. He learned the sharecropper's trade at a very young age:
"My daddy put me to plowin the first time at nine years old, right after my
mother died. . . . And that country where we was livin was rough and rocky.
And he—my poor old daddy is dead and gone but I don't tell no lies on
him—he put me to plowin a regular shift at twelve, thirteen years old. And
I had to plow barefooted on that rocky country. . . ."

As a boy, Cobb saw his father "cleaned up" twice, first by a white
landlord who forced him to live and work on his land and then refused to
share the crop with him; later by a furnishing merchant who seized all of
his mortgaged belongings, including his horse, his new iron-axle wagon,
and his "fattenin hog," because the drought ruined his crop of corn and
cotton that year. Booker T. Washington, eating and sleeping with share-

croppers around Tuskegee, Alabama, in 1881, noted that in the plantation districts,

> as a rule the whole family slept in one room, and that in addition to the immediate family there sometimes were relatives, or others not related to the family, who slept in the same room. . . .
>
> The common diet of the people was fat pork and corn bread. At times I have eaten in cabins where they had only corn bread and "black-eye peas" cooked in plain water. The people seemed to have no other idea than to live on this fat meat and corn bread,—the meat, and the meal of which the bread was made, having been bought at a high price at a store in town, notwithstanding the fact that the land all about the cabin homes could easily have been made to produce nearly every kind of garden vegetable that is raised anywhere in the country. Their one object seemed to be to plant nothing but cotton; and in many cases cotton was planted up to the very door of the cabin. . . .
>
> The breakfast over, and with practically no attention given to the house, the whole family would, as a general thing, proceed to the cotton-field. Every child that was large enough to carry a hoe was put to work, and the baby—for usually there was at least one baby—would be laid down at the end of the cotton row, so that its mother could give it a certain amount of attention when she had finished chopping her row. . . .
>
> All the days of the family would be spent after much this same routine, except Saturday and Sunday. On Saturday the whole family would spend at least half a day, and often a whole day, in town. The idea in going to town was, I suppose, to do shopping, but all the shopping that the whole family had money for could have been attended to in ten minutes by one person. Still, the whole family remained in town for most of the day, spending the greater part of the time in standing on the streets, the women, too often, sitting about somewhere smoking or dipping snuff. Sunday was usually spent in going to some big meeting. . . .
>
> The state had not been able to build schoolhouses in the country districts, and, as a rule, the schools were taught in churches or in log cabins. More than once, while on my journeys, I found that there was no provision made in the house used for school purposes for heating the building during the winter. . . . With few exceptions, I found the teachers in these country schools to be miserably poor in preparation for their work, and poor in moral character. The schools were in session from three to five months.

Sometimes black schools had to close for lack of funds while the white schools stayed open. Most black sharecroppers and their children were illiterate.

Some black farmers managed to break the barriers to renting and owning their own land, and their numbers increased, though unevenly, throughout the South. Unlike sharecroppers, renters, or "real tenants," had considerable control over their labor, land, and crops, paying rent to the landlord either in cash or cotton at the end of the year. Like sharecropping, though, contracts were renewed annually. Neither renting nor owning by blacks was looked upon favorably by the white power structure, or by poor white tenant farmers and owners who competed with them. If black tenant farmers were always a minority of blacks on the land, black owners were even rarer. In the Black Belts of Georgia and Mississippi, the 1880 census reported, about one in a hundred black farmers owned their land; in other states the figures were a bit higher, especially in Virginia and South Carolina. By the turn of the century, a considerably higher percentage of blacks owned their farms, but they were still a small minority.

The obstacles to ownership were awesome. If blacks could scrape together enough cash to buy the land, tools, and working stock—no easy feat—they faced the active hostility of neighboring whites who often threatened violence against those offering land to blacks, or who engaged in "whitecapping"—terrorizing and forcibly expelling the blacks from their new property. Still, the aspirations of blacks for independence and dignity were powerful enough for some to realize their dream of ownership. Betty Powers, born a slave, recalled how her family felt when they finished building their cabin on land they had just bought: "Was we'uns proud? There t'was, our place to do as we pleases, after bein slaves. Dat sho' am de good feelin'. We work like beavers puttin' de crop in, and my folks stays dere till dey dies."

While the fortunes of some black farmers improved, those of many white farmers in the South often moved in the opposite direction, as they started out as owners of small or medium-sized plots, sank increasingly into debt, losing their land to the furnishing merchant, and ended up as tenant farmers or sharecroppers. From the 1880s on, farmland more and more fell into the hands of merchants, loan agents, and some of the financially stronger farmers, most of whom were absentee landlords. By 1900, most white farmers were tenants or sharecroppers, mostly sharecroppers.

The average farm family, according to agricultural historian Fred Shannon, tended only about seventeen acres of cotton. This meant "that a five-or-six-thousand-bale crop was all that could be expected. At the upper limit, and with the price at the rare ten cents, the three-hundred-dollar return allowed the worker's family a hundred dollars' credit for the year's living expenses, and this was spent at the weighted prices charged at the country store. On a cash basis the family, even when fairly large, probably got five dollars a month to spend for food, clothing, and incidental luxuries."

The most characteristic and most harmful feature of post–Civil War Southern farming was the "crop lien system" with its ubiquitous furnishing merchant—a system that in Woodward's view "came to be more widespread than slavery had been, for it was no respecter of race or class; and if it be judged objectively, by its economic results alone, the new evil may have worked more permanent injury to the South than the ancient evil." A contemporary observer, Charles Otken, described it as a "vast credit system whose tremendous evils and exorbitant exactions have brought poverty and bankruptcy to thousands of families, . . . crushed out all independence and reduced its victims to a coarse species of servile slavery."

As with sharecropping, the crop lien system was an invention of the postwar South, emerging out of the havoc of the war. Its prime causes were the lack of money and banks in rural areas of the South and the poor transportation facilities, especially the lack of good roads—all of which left farmers tied to purely local markets and suppliers. Originally serving black farmers mainly, particularly sharecroppers, the crop lien system spread throughout the South in tandem with the proliferation of cotton-growing, hooking in as many as 80 to 90 percent of all farmers, black and white, poor and middle class, without much distinction. Sometimes merchants became landlords to fifty or a hundred tenants as they gained title to more and more of their customers' land to settle debts. Sometimes landlords moved into town, opened stores, and sold goods to their own tenants and croppers.

All too often the result was a local rural monopoly of credit, supplies, and marketing. Typically a farmer would sign a contract with the merchant in January or February, when it was time for the soil to be prepared for cotton planting. The farmer would agree to give the merchant a lien on the entire crop for the coming year as payment for the purchase on credit of all provisions. These contracts were strictly enforced under lien laws that were enacted by most Southern states after the war. Every week or two for the rest of the year, from spring planting until harvesting in the late fall, the farmer would ride into town and "buy" various supplies—food, such as cornmeal, pork, flour, and lard, most of which the farm family could have provided for itself; farm supplies like fertilizer and a plow point; possibly some calico or other clothing material. The credit prices charged by the merchant were generally 40 to 100 percent higher than if the farmer had paid in cash.

The merchant would make a note in the ledger for each transaction; the farmer would leave the store each time a little deeper in debt, not knowing exactly how much since only the merchant kept records. At "settlin' up" time in November or December, the farmer brought the hard-earned cotton to the gin, where it would be ginned, bagged, tied, weighed, and handed over to the merchant, who would then deliver the verdict. Most often the farmer did not succeed in "paying out," meaning that he would have to sign a new contract, thus sinking even deeper in hock to the "furnishing man," one notch further into peonage.

Some Southerners defended the furnishing merchant as a pawn of Northern capital who had to pay exorbitant interest rates himself and took big risks in providing credit to farmers, especially in outlying areas; and though most merchants were moderately well off, few ever got rich. But the crop lien system must shoulder the blame for much of the South's ills. For the furnishing merchants, who demanded that more and more cotton be grown despite its falling price, were the major force preserving the one-crop economy and preventing diversification into grains and other foodstuffs that clearly would have improved the conditions of Southern farmers. "No cotton, no credit" was law everywhere the crop lien system had dominion, and this led to the depletion and wreckage of both the soil and the men and women who cultivated it. Though blacks were hit hardest by the merchants, who undoubtedly discriminated against them one way or another, the agricultural stagnation afflicted everyone in the South to varying degrees. The more cotton was sown, the more poverty was reaped.

There was always a final way out. Matt Brown, a poor black farmer in Mississippi, contracted for supplies from the Jones store in Black Hawk from 1884 to 1901. His accumulating debt was nearing $500 when a final entry appeared in the ledger—"marking it off" for a coffin and burial costs.

WORKING CLASSES: THE CONDITIONS OF EXISTENCE

Another escape was possible, especially for blacks: an overground move to the North and West. Blacks in Chicago numbered about 4,000 in 1870; within twenty years they multiplied over threefold. The newcomers came largely off the nation's farms, and especially the farms of the South—part of a mighty population movement that would continue for decades and store up social dynamite for the future.

For white or black to migrate from country to city during the 1870s was not always to plunge into dark tenements and crowded streets. For years, over half the families in the coal and iron regions around Pittsburgh had chickens, livestock, or vegetable gardens next to their homes, and pigs and goats could be seen in abundance in Brooklyn and on the streets of Manhattan as far south as the forties.

The relentless tide of industrialism, however, engulfed these little farms and backyards and other green places, leaving blocks of unpainted or grimy brick tenements in their place. Small cities as well as big were transformed. Lynn, an old Massachusetts seafaring and shoe-making town, was changed from a community of gardened cottages to a city of boarding-houses and triple deckers first clustered on Main Street and then spreading throughout the factory area. Living places could never escape the noise or stench of the mill, for workers had to live close enough to hear the shriek of the factory whistle. As early as 1880, according to John Cumbler, Lynn historians were penning "nostalgic works on how the city had changed."

As usual, the biggest city exhibited the most repulsive living conditions. We need not see these conditions only through late twentieth-century eyes; Jacob Riis saw at the time. Horrified as a thirteen-year-old in Copenhagen by a tenement built over a river and infested with rats, Riis had come in 1870 to a New York City in which those conditions were worsened tenfold. After knocking about for a few years mining coal, laying bricks, farming, and peddling, and after many a night in noisome lodging houses, he landed a job with the *Evening Sun* as an investigative journalist (then called police reporter). Later, he took up a free-lance career of writing books and articles and giving lectures. His knack for being both factual and graphic, both compassionate and unsentimental, gave great force to his reporting.

Suppose we look into a tenement on, say, Cherry Street? he asked his readers in his first and perhaps most famous work, *How the Other Half Lives*, published in 1890:

"Be a little careful, please! The hall is dark and you might stumble over the children pitching pennies back there. Not that it would hurt them; kicks and cuffs are their daily diet. They have little else. Here where the hall turns and dives into utter darkness is a step, and another, another. A flight of stairs. You can feel your way, if you cannot see it. Close? Yes! What would you have? All the fresh air that ever enters these stairs comes from the hall-door that is forever slamming, and from the windows of dark bedrooms. . . ."

Riis had a special sympathy for tenement children, as though he had given up hope for their parents. He investigated the death rate of infants. In one tenement some years back, he noted, of 138 children born during a three-year period, 61 had died, most of them before their first birthday.

"Listen! That short hacking cough, that tiny helpless wail—what do they mean?" It was a baby dying.

" 'It was took all of a suddint,' says the mother, smoothing the throbbing little body with trembling hands. There is no unkindness in the rough voice of the man in the jumper, who sits by the window grimly smoking a clay pipe, with the little life ebbing out in his sight, bitter as his words sound: 'Hush, Mary! If we cannot keep the baby, need we complain—such as we?' " "Such as we," Riis echoed.

He was sensitive to the city's endless variety, even while he shared some of the stereotypes of the time. The Irishman, he noted, was the true cosmopolitan immigrant, sharing his lodging impartially with Italian, Greek, and "Dutchman." A map of the city designating nationalities, he said, would show an extraordinary crazy quilt.

"The city on such a map would fall into two great halves, green for the Irish prevailing in the West Side tenement districts, and blue for the Germans on the East Side." But intermingled was an odd variety of tints.

From down in the Sixth Ward, upon the site of the old Collect Pond that in the days of the fathers drained the hills which are no more, the red of the Italian would be seen forcing its way northward along the line of Mulberry Street to the quarter of the French purple on Bleecker Street and South Fifth Avenue, to lose itself and reappear, after a lapse of miles, in the 'Little Italy' of Harlem, east of Second Avenue. Dashes of red, sharply defined, would be seen strung through the Annexed District, northward to the city line. On the West Side the red would be seen overrunning the old Africa of Thompson Street, pushing the black of the negro rapidly uptown, against querulous but unavailing protests, occupying his home, his church, his trade and all, with merciless impartiality.

For many immigrants, black or any other color, home life was work life and work life was home life; they toiled for "sweaters." A sweater's shop, according to a reporter for *Harper's Weekly*, "is generally one of the two larger rooms of a tenement flat, accommodating from six to fifteen or twenty 'sweating' employees—men, women, and children. In the other large room of the flat are his living, sleeping, and cooking arrangements, overflowing into the workroom. Employees whom he boards, who eat at their work, and who sleep on the goods, frequently complete the intimate connection of home and shop." Many a New England textile mill—including some located in pristine valleys near running streams—housed whole families in wings attached to the plant itself, so that employees moved from home to work without ever passing through the green.

The unholy wedlock of home and shop made it all the easier to sweat women and children. But the condition of children could be appalling whether at home or in a factory and, indeed, they often took their parents' jobs. Fannie Harris, thirteen, was interrogated in 1895 by a committee of the New York legislature. She had worked for six months in a necktie plant, earning $2 for a sixty-hour week.

What did she do with that two dollars? "Gave it to my mamma."

Did her mamma give her anything to spend? "Yes, sir . . . two cents every week. . . ."

Now, had she been to school in this country? "No."

Could she spell cat? "I forgot."

Did her mamma work? "Now she ain't working because I am working, but before, when I didn't work, she worked. . . ."

Her papa, she said, did not work because he was ill. When an "inspector" told her to quit work and go to school, her mother forbade it.

Dorothy Richardson, an orphan from rural Pennsylvania who had been a country schoolteacher and then sought a "genteel job" in New York City, finally gave up and decided to take almost any work she could get. She was turned away by two cigar factories for lack of experience; took a job as a learner in a book bindery at $3 a week but kept on looking; turned down a position in a small store at $3.50 for an eighty-seven-hour week; declined employment at $1.50 in an artificial flower sweatshop; and finally took a job at $3 in a paper box factory. Quitting this work, she went through the process all over again, ending up as a laundry "shaker" until the owner offered a promotion to the wrapping department, at the same time making "some joking remarks of insulting flattery," and pinching her bare arm. She left.

Few women had it worse than those who lived among wealth and display —household domestics. Their work was generally back-breaking, tedious, and lonely, with few minutes of their own in sixteen-hour workdays. At-tracted to the work by the promise of a comfortable home and good food, one found her room to be "a few hard chairs and two soiled quilts." The food might be inadequate, the master of the house sexually aggressive, the mistress's attitude demeaning. "You're never sure that your soul's your own except when you are out of the house," one domestic commented.

In the 1880s, a maid typically worked seven days a week, started at six and finished at her bedtime, around ten—unless her mistress was enter-taining, in which case she had to remain on call until the guests left, perhaps around midnight. She was allowed out one evening a week and every other Sunday afternoon and evening. "Thus she was," according to Robert Smuts, "usually on call for over 100 hours a week," with most of the labor a grinding, monotonous routine. The lack of privacy and auton-

omy was especially galling to the more spirited. Shops and factories like
the New England textile mills regularly drew off the more ambitious and
restless of these young women.

The city ghettos, the tenements, the sweatshops, the attics and the
basements of great houses—these were not mere misery. Many of these
sweated workers managed to cope, to endure, even to love and to laugh.
Yet the social data of the time, however inadequate in exactness and scope,
carry their own damning implications. Manufacturing wages, according to
Clarence Long, rose from slightly more than a dollar a day in 1860 to a
bit over a dollar and a half in 1890—a very gradual increase, considering
the economic expansion of this period. Real wages rose at the same rate,
since a steady decline in the cost of living made up for Civil War inflation.
Adult men on the average received three-quarters more wages than adult
women, and two and a half to three times as much as children and youths.
At the same time, Philip Armour had a yearly income in excess of $1
million, John D. Rockefeller could count on $3 million annually just in
Standard Oil dividends, and Andrew Carnegie—who once "couldn't imagine" what to do with the princely salary of $35 per month—made as much
as $25 million in a single year.

But even these statistics could hardly convey a sense of the enormous
class disparity in income, food, housing, hours of toil, leisure, self-esteem
—in happiness. Nowhere, perhaps, were the working and living conditions
of the poor more sharply etched than in Pittsburgh.

Merely to enter the steel works was a daunting experience—the electric
cranes moaning and rattling as they swept overhead; fiery tongues of
molten slag hissing out from the hearths; the steel emerging from the
blooming mill and moving to allotted places; and then the first encounter
with the pit itself, brimming with red-hot steel brighter than the day outside. Men clustered around furnaces, prodding the molten masses until
tiny streams of fire broke through, then jumped back in the nick of time
as great ladles tilted back and spouted out a torrent of incandescent steel.

In this inferno, men stood on platforms so hot their spit sizzled; every
so often they slapped their clothes to stop them from breaking into flames
from the sparks; they recoiled from the maddening screech of cold saws
biting into steel, leaving the air filled with particles that infested throat and
lungs; poured out sweat that immediately dried in front of a dozen ovens
each holding fifty or more tons of molten steel. They stood in recurrent
danger of dying from hot metal explosions, falling into the pit, or encounters with cranes or locomotives. And they did this for hours on end, though
with occasional rests as machines needed more time. Typically, steel mills
operated twenty-four hours a day, so that the men had to work in either

two shifts of twelve hours or three shifts of eight. Many men working twelve-hour days changed every two weeks from day work to night work or back, requiring them to work a terrible twenty-four hours straight at the "turnover." The twelve-hour day lasted until well after the turn of the century.

"Home is just the place where I eat and sleep," a steel worker said. "I live in the mills." Wives had to rise at five or so to prepare breakfast, perhaps go to work themselves, then serve supper fourteen hours later to an exhausted husband still deafened from the roar of the mills. Each of the mill towns in the Pittsburgh area came to have its splendid Carnegie library, with especially generous collections of books on metallurgy and mechanical arts. But few steel workers had the time or energy to visit the steel magnate's libraries.

Workers—particularly immigrants—lived in homes clustered around the mills along the rivers or hanging on the bluffs of the south side. Most of the steel hands, Stefan Lorant wrote, "lived in rickety shanties, ramshackle cottages, filthy, overcrowded tenements with primitive sanitation and toilet facilities." Wages, never unduly high, dropped sharply during the early 1890s. Workers, however, were allowed to gaze across ornate iron fences at the steel bosses' gingerbread mansions and other palaces, as expensive, ornate, and overstuffed as anywhere in America—homes such as Henry Clay Frick's "Clayton," four stories high with an enormous portico, Mrs. William Thaw's "Lyndhurst," the Phippses' "Grandview," the Westinghouses' "Solitude." Pittsburgh capitalists and workers had combined to make the city the steel capital of the world, outstripping Essen and Birmingham and all other American steel centers; but in the process the links between them, both on the job and in the community, were more and more frayed and broken.

In contemplating how the other half lived, Jacob Riis concluded that the source of most social evils lay in people's housing and city environment. In the tenements, he decided, "all the influences make for evil; because they are the hot-beds of the epidemics that carry death to rich and poor alike; the nurseries of pauperism and crime that fill our jails and police courts; that throw off a scum of forty thousand human wrecks to the insane asylums and workhouses year by year; that turned out in the last eight years a round half million beggars to prey upon our charities; that maintain a standing army of ten thousand tramps with all that that implies; because, above all, they touch the family life with deadly moral contagion. This is their worst crime, inseparable from the system. . . ." It was the *system* above all that challenged Riis's social imagination.

In Chicago, a very different sort of man came to somewhat the same

conclusion. By the 1880s, George M. Pullman had built the greatest railroad car-building organization in the world. Son of a general mechanic in
New York State, he had shown remarkable innovating and organizing
abilities even in his early years. After inventing a sleeping car in which back
and seat cushions could be joined to make a berth—a concept that has
hardly changed to this day—he had gone on to develop the combined
sleeping and restaurant car, the dining car, the chair car, the vestibule car.
Convinced that good housing was essential to people's well-being, he
decided on a great experiment in a vacant area nine miles south of Chicago
—a model city, centered on workshops, designed to refine and uplift his
workers' character. It was to be both a business and a community venture.
A self-respecting, well-mannered worker, he calculated, would be both a
happier person and a better employee.

Amid feverish activity the town was soon completed, adorned with lawns
and shrubs, spacious factories, wide streets, and even "imitation-bronze
street lamps with cone-shaped gloves and white porcelain shades." Visitors
came from near and far to admire; a French economist concluded that
"some brain of superior intelligence, backed by long technical experience,
has thought out every possible detail." Here, as in the sweatshop ghettos,
the distinction between work and home was blurred. Nothing in the town
seemed apart from the workshop or workplace. Had George Pullman
found the key to work-home integration, employer profit, employee happiness, and social progress?

Social Class and Social Outcast

"Now in all states," Aristotle said, "there are three elements: one class
is very rich, another very poor, and a third in a mean." A city, he added,
ought to be composed, as far as possible, "of equals and similars; and these
are generally the middle classes." A large middle class prevented the rich,
the strong, and the lucky from dominating the poor, and the envious poor
from plotting against the rich. "Great then is the good fortune of a state
in which the citizens have a moderate and sufficient property; for where
some possess much, and the others nothing, there may arise an extreme—either out of the most rampant democracy, or out of an oligar-
chy. . . ."

Americans in the late nineteenth century could boast of a burgeoning
middle class, but they could not deny gross disparities between the rich
and the poor. Jacob Riis and others who wrote of these extremes did not
exaggerate; sophisticated economic analysis many years later would demonstrate that the 1860s and early 1870s constituted one of the "highest

income inequalities in American history," comparable only to the 1913–1916 period and to the late 1920s, just before the collapse of stock prices. Combined regional and class disparities, as between Southern farm laborers and New York City craftsmen, were extreme indeed in the 1870s.

This glaring contrast between the lot of rich and of poor, a contrast that could be observed unforgettably within a mile's walk in almost any big city —what did it mean to the Americans of the day? To the great majority, not very much. Like the dying child's parents that Riis visited, they accepted their lot. Some harbored hopes: that they might still get a lucky break from the ever-turning roulette wheel of American capitalism; that their children would succeed if they did not; or that the virtuous poor would at least receive their reward in the Hereafter. Some of the poor also believed in the doctrine of rags to riches, the survival of the fittest; but the doctrine reflected more hope than reality. Even in Pittsburgh—reputedly the home of "shirtsleeve millionaires" like Carnegie—the iron and steel magnates "were largely the sons of businessmen, from upper-middle-class and upper-class backgrounds," according to John Ingham. Yet the myth persisted.

The condition and outlook of industrial labor posed the cardinal questions of the 1880s. The creation of new and immensely larger units of production, along with modernized technology and constantly expanding mechanization, tended to homogenize and flatten the "level of existence" for hundreds of thousands of workers. The common work experiences that resulted laid the basis for the class solidarity that Marxists predicted. But powerful forces were working in other directions. The dynamism of technology in itself was a disruptive force, constantly interrupting work routines. The spread of technology varied widely, as a result of the play of the market and the availability of capital, with the result that some workers might be operating eighteenth-century machines while others were, technologically, entering the twentieth century. Thus skilled craft workers, accustomed to "controlling production" on the shop floor, often had to yield to the impersonal dominion of the machine.

The main divisive forces, however, lay more in the workers than in their machines. The American working class, Gutman reminds us, was continually being "altered in its composition by infusions, from within and without the nation, of peasants, farmers, skilled artisans, and casual day laborers who brought into industrial society ways of work and other habits and values not associated with industrial necessities and the industrial ethos." These persons brought their own cultures into the factories and the factory towns. They lived in their own social and political worlds composed of churches, schools, unions, political "machines," baseball lots, even libraries, and—ubiquitously—saloons or "beer gardens." They were not suddenly divested of this world as they passed through the factory gate.

Amid this cultural diversity, immigrants and their offspring made up by far the most distinct and autonomous grouping. Of the 14,000 or so common laborers employed in the big Carnegie Pittsburgh plants, over 11,000 were Eastern Europeans. Underpaid, often given the meanest tasks, especially vulnerable to industrial accidents, these workers might have constituted a vast pool of militant opposition to the bosses. Sometimes they did—but more often they were the victims of illiteracy and misinformation, of intolerance and discrimination on the part of other employees as well as employers. Many, moreover, had no desire to stay in the United States. Often single, or married but with their wives left behind in the old country, they planned to save their money and return home. Their yearning for home was often sharpened by their work experiences. Wrote an Italian youth:

> Nothing job, nothing job,
> I return to Italy;
> Comrades, laborers, good-bye;
> Adieu, land of "Fourth of July."

Immigrant or not, a few American workers could establish their own work routines. Some were able to create their own "five-day week," for example, long before either legislators or employers established it. They did this through weekend celebrations so hearty that they would arrive at the shop on Monday in no condition for work. Employers sometimes responded by shifting payday from Saturday to midweek.

The impact of these many conflicting forces on working-class solidarity was inevitably a highly mixed one. In some cases, cultural influences reinforced solidarity—workers suffering discrimination in housing, for example, or sensing hostility to their religion, might well be reinforced in their class attitudes. But more typically in situations of "cross-pressures," the heterogeneous forces won out, especially where immigrants peopled the work force. Radicals charged—often correctly—that corporation heads deliberately sowed disunity among their employees. But the main source of working-class division was a constellation of cultural forces—including the tendency of many workers to dream that they too could rise to the top of the industrial heap.

The myth of rags to riches was a potent one, for it answered the questions of those who pointed to Americans' egalitarian creed, as set forth in the Declaration of Independence and other official scrolls, and asked: How come? The catechismal answer was, individual opportunity and reward.

Only money separated the lower class from the upper classes; to rise to the upper classes, one had only to make more money. Anyone could do this.

Such answers ignored the fact that far more than money cut the lower classes off from opportunity: poor health, inadequate education, low motivation, crude speech and clothes, damaged self-esteem, dire poverty. Indeed, by the late nineteenth century something insidious and ominous was taking place in the vaunted land of liberty and equality—the continuation or creation of sets of social outcasts who comprised virtually an array of castes, who could not break out of their castes, and hence could hardly hope to rise through the class hierarchy.

Few Americans of the day would have admitted that the land of the free had a caste system. Castes were alien, something one found and deplored in India. Black slaves had formed a kind of caste before the Civil War, it was granted, but had they not been liberated? It slowly became evident, however, that a black caste not only persisted in the South after Emancipation but that other castes endured or were developing in the United States, if a system of castes was defined as a closed and tenacious structure of social inequality, both in perceived status and in access to needed goods —a structure from which it was virtually impossible to escape, no matter what talents and virtues a person might possess.

Some caste systems might be founded almost entirely on possessions or income, with the poorest so marked by physical and psychological want that they could not break out of their low caste, as in India. This was true to a degree in America, as in the case of impoverished immigrants. But caste in this country was largely ethnic and racial. Money was the warm solvent of social class, given enough time, but money could not wash away caste walls.

The wealthy Jews who settled Manhattan's sixties and seventies, east of Fifth Avenue, could testify to this. These were the Seligmans, Loebs, Strauses, Lilienthals, Morgenthaus, Rosenwalds, and a score of other families of German origin. Such families, Stephen Birmingham judged, were the closest thing to "Aristocracy—Aristocracy in the best sense—that the city, and perhaps the country, had seen." They had fine houses, servants, carriages, country estates, and of course lots of money. With their leadership in New York finance and their close ties to Washington, they had a measure of economic and political power.

But they could not join Manhattan's Four Hundred or the exclusive men's clubs or other select circles; in this sense they were social outcasts. As in centuries past, they took refuge in their own community and solidarity—in "our crowd," with its active social life, in intermarriage among elite Jewish families, partnerships within the family, wills and trusts that tied generations together. They also took refuge in their own hierarchy. Sephardic Jews from Spain and Portugal had arrived in Manhattan as early as the mid-seventeenth century, some on a bark that came to be known as the "Jewish Mayflower." Numbering Baruchs, Nathans, Cardozos, Hendrixes, they stood for old wealth, fine manners, and established Judaism. The Sephardim tended to look down on the more recently arrived German Jews, with their "pushy" ways, show-off clothes and jewelry, loud speech, and status insecurities. In their turn the Germans, proud of their own background, education, and culture, clung to their own clubs and ran down the hordes of other Ashkenazic Jewish immigrants from Eastern Europe, with their coarse speech, dress, and manners.

Even the upthrust hand of the Statue of Liberty, in its temporary home at Fifth Avenue and 26th Street, seemed to separate Sephardic Jews from the Germans. The latter, according to Birmingham, were put off by Emma Lazarus's line, "the wretched refuse of your teeming shore." They may have arrived penniless, but they were not human litter. Raising Jewish money to put Miss Liberty on Bedloe's Island became largely a Sephardic effort.

Poor Jews in ghettos could not afford such fine airs. Fleeing the oppression and persecution in Eastern Europe—especially the pogroms that had erupted in Russia after the assassination of Alexander II in 1881—these immigrants had survived the adventurous crossing of Europe, the fetid Atlantic steerage, and the callous examination by immigration officials, only to land in a new ghetto in New York or other cities. Dumped ashore on the Battery, a youth of sixteen walked into the stench and noise of the Lower East Side, where dirty children played in the street and noisy, sweating Jews pushed peddlers' carts, and wondered, "Was this the America we had sought? Or was it only, after all, a circle that we had travelled, with a Jewish ghetto at its beginning and its end?"

For most such Jews the Lower East Side was indeed a ghetto, and they too were social outcasts, taunted even by other immigrants. By 1890 over five hundred persons lived there per acre, a density greater than in the worst sections of Bombay; living conditions, in Irving Howe's judgment, "were quite as ghastly as those of early-nineteenth-century London." At least half the employed Jews worked in the garment industry, notorious already for its sixty- to eighty-four-hour workweek and its wages (in 1885) of $7 to $10 a week for men, $3 to $6 for women, and $12 to $15 for whole families. Even more depressing was the Lower East Side environment: the squalor, filth, and disease, the pushing and shoving, and the feverish quest for money that so affronted Jews imbued with older and more spiritual traditions.

And the Jews were so conspicuous, at least to Jacob Riis. "No need of asking here where we are," he told his readers as he escorted them into "Jewtown." The signs along the sidewalk, the manners and dress of the people, "their unmistakable physiognomy," betrayed their race at every step, Riis said.

"Men with queer skull-caps, venerable beard, and the outlandish long-skirted kaftan of the Russian Jew, elbow the ugliest and the handsomest women in the land. The contrast is startling. The old women are hags; the young, houris. Wives and mothers at sixteen, at thirty they are old. So thoroughly has the chosen people crowded out the Gentiles in the Tenth Ward that, when the great Jewish holidays come around every year, the public schools in the district have practically to close up." "Hebrews" were not only overflowing Jewtown, Riis said, but buying up or rebuilding the tenements. He noted the taunts that greeted the invaders. "But abuse and ridicule are not weapons to fight the Israelite with. He pockets them quietly with the rent and bides his time."

In their living conditions, poor newly arrived Jews were probably no worse off than Irish and Italians. In a brotherhood of misery, all the "refuse" shared in the conditions of squalor, disease, overwork, and—above all—inescapable crowdedness. Immigration was rising to new peaks in the early 1880s—almost 3 million streamed in during the five years after 1880—and the vast majority settled in New York and other cities. From 1820 to 1900, 17 million arrived from Europe alone—6 million from Germany and Austria, almost 4 million from Ireland, over 3 million from Great Britain, a million and a half from Scandinavia, perhaps a million from Russia and Eastern Europe.

Invidious distinctions fragmented the fraternity of the poor newcomers. The British were mainly white Anglo-Saxon Protestants, and they spoke English, if not American. Northern Germans and northern Europeans were mainly Protestants, but did not speak English. Irish spoke English and Gaelic and were mainly Catholic. Most Italians were Catholic and did not speak any form of English. Eastern Europeans had compounded troubles. But no immigrant group was as segregated as the Jews, with their alien languages, customs, costumes, religion, and origins in the strange, far-off *shtetls* of Eastern Europe.

Still, all these ethnic groups were white. Whatever they had to overcome in the way of language, custom, low self-esteem, and bigotry, at least they did not have to overcome the color of their skin or a heritage of enslavement. At the bottom of the caste system lay, as usual, black workers and their families, although the conditions of their existence reflected the immense diversity of America.

Somewhat typical of American cities as a whole, but more harshly symbolic than any, were the work and life of blacks in the nation's capital. In Washington, D.C., in 1870 there were 133 black carpenters, 410 black waiters, and one black lawyer. Cheek by jowl with the big marble government buildings were the alleyways lined with brick hovels. Washington had its shantytowns too, such as "Murder Bay"—a "vile place, both physically and morally," an official reported. Poor blacks were sharply segregated: by century's end over 90 percent of all alley dwellers were black, making up more than one-fourth of the capital's Negro population.

Writing on the "color line" in Manhattan, Jacob Riis observed, "There is no more clean and orderly community in New York than the new settlement of colored people that is growing up on the East Side from Yorkville to Harlem." He noted particularly their "cleanliness"—in this respect, he said, the Negro was "immensely the superior of the lowest of the whites, the Italians and the Polish Jews, below whom he has been classed in the past in the tenant scale." Even the *Real Estate Record* reported agents agreeing that Negro tenants were clean, orderly, and "profitable." Why, then, did blacks have to pay higher rents for the "poorest and most stinted rooms"? Because whites would not live in the same house with blacks. "Once a colored house," said the agents, "always a colored house."

Race bias prevailed over objective facts. A Welshman traveling to the coal fields of West Virginia was warned that "the niggars were a most treacherous, devilish lot of people" who had to be kept down by being knocked down. On his way, however, he met two young black women of about eighteen, and they spoke to him so sweetly and melodiously that he said to himself, "By jove, if all the niggars are like these girls, I am jolly glad I came down here." He came to be extremely fond of the blacks who worked in the mines and lived in shacks round about, and came to hate the "contemptible" and "ignorant" whites who treated the blacks so abominably on and off the job.

Not that the "niggar" was without faults, the Welshman added. "By nature he is an awful thief," with chickens and turkeys his specialty, "but if you catch him in the act, he is not a vicious thief; he will only turn around and make up some cock-and-bull story to account for it." He was "outrageously lazy," and immoral to boot. "They eat, cook, and sleep all through and through—men, women, girls, and boys, makes no difference to them. Few of them go through the form of legal marriage but the greater number live in adultery and when they get tired of one another they change partners." Still, he liked them.

Perhaps the most integrated workers in America, during the late nineteenth century, were the cowhands in the western cattle ranges. About one-third of the 35,000 men who traveled up the trail from Texas during the "heroic age" of the cattle industry, according to the least unreliable estimates, were "Negroes and Mexicans," with the former outnumbering the latter perhaps two to one. Trailherd outfits often included a black cook, horse wrangler, and trail hand or two, out of a dozen or so men. Blacks were seen as having a special feel for horses and a knack for "singing" to the steers. Veteran black cowhands often showed the ropes to white greenhorns, as a black Cherokee did to a youngster named Will Rogers. In town, however, things were different. Black and white cowhands usually sat toward opposite ends of the bar; a black man might at best eat in the kitchen of a café; and a black would never, never enter a white house of prostitution. White cowhands, however, frequented black whorehouses.

Thus the color line wove its way through the complex fabric of human relationships. And that line deepened and hardened as the years passed. In New York, Riis noted that blacks were arriving from Southern cities bringing skills they could not use in the North, and even among native blacks the "colored barber" was disappearing. In the South, the caste system that had been shaken up by Civil War and Reconstruction was tightening toward the end of the century as a result of the rising Jim Crow system and attitudes of white supremacy. He doubted, said Senator James Vardaman of Mississippi, that the "coconut-headed, chocolate-colored, typical coon" who "blacks my shoes every morning" was fit for citizenship. Lynchings of blacks rose sharply after the early eighties.

Thousands of black workers moved into industrial cities, where they often took jobs as scabs and found themselves pitted against striking whites. Others moved west; the huge "Kansas Exodus" of 1879 brought thousands of Southern blacks to a state where, with mixed memories of "Bleeding Kansas," their new neighbors might or might not be friendly. A few blacks moved into the Plains states and points farther west, joining the waves of migration reaching across the western half of the nation. There they encountered a race that was being compressed into another segregated caste—the native Americans called Indians.

In the 1860s and 1870s the old, grim sequence—migration by white settlers, Indian resistance, violent confrontations, military suppression of the red people, continued migration—was asserting itself as remorselessly as before the Civil War. Only the nature of the migration had changed: whites—and blacks—might now come by train as well as by Conestoga wagon.

From a high ridge, Cheyennes somberly watched one of the first Union Pacific trains running along new track laid into the Platte forks. Riding down to "see what sort of trail" the train had left, they ingeniously figured how to derail the next "big wagon" with a heavy stick forced into the rails. The next wagon turned out to be a tiny handcar pumped by five maintenance men. As the car jumped high into the air, the men spilled out and fled, only to be hunted down and killed by the Cheyennes. Elated, the Indians bent a rail and derailed a whole train, which they plundered. Soon they were racing over the prairies with bolts of muslin and calico tied to their ponies' tails and unraveling behind them.

White men wanted the red people to "settle," just like themselves. But Ten Bears, of the Comanches, refused to lead his people into a reservation. "I don't want to settle," he told a big Indian gathering. "I love to roam over the prairies. There I feel free and happy, but when I settle down I feel pale and die. A long time ago this land belonged to our fathers; but when I go up the river"—the Arkansas—"I see camps of soldiers on its banks. These soldiers cut down my timber; they kill my buffalo; and when I see that it feels as if my heart would burst with sorrow."

The Sioux of the Great Plains fit the white stereotype, reflected in Hollywood Westerns and shown on Indian-head nickels, of the nomadic, warlike Indian, living off the open country and the buffalo. The Sioux, indeed, were the nouveaux riches among the western Indians, where wealth was measured not in money but in food and military prowess. They were a martial tribe, cultivating youthfulness, male strength, competitiveness, and individual achievement, as well as female beauty and purity. In their religious fervor, young men tortured themselves in exchange for supernatural power and social prestige. They danced to the point of exhaustion, and suspended themselves from cords and skewers which pierced their skin. A religiously inspired Ghost Dance was the last Sioux uprising. It ended in the infamous massacre at Wounded Knee.

The Sioux were true nomads. In their encampments the braves, wearing long buffalo skin robes, gathered in a circle at the center of the village. They clustered around a ring of buffalo skulls, over which the older men passed their weapons, prayed, and offered sacrifices. This ceremony prepared them for their imminent departure to seek buffalo for food and heavy winter furs. Then the camp broke. Baggage was loaded onto packhorses, called "mystery dogs," while the women walked. The women were responsible for everything but the kill itself and the spiritual rites of the kill—they butchered the downed animals, tanned the hides, dried the meat.

Other Indians were as settled as any white, though in their own traditions. The Pacific Indians of the Southwest—farmers, town-dwellers, weavers, potters—seemed almost the opposite of the Sioux. Related linguistically to the Aztecs of Mexico, the Zuni and Hopi shared many of their achievements. Dependent on the corn they grew and hence on water, they built elaborate irrigation systems—and organized religious ceremonies around the need for rain. The Hopis conducted their famed snake dance in the hope that the feted reptile would report to the gods such favorable treatment that rain would result.

These city-dwelling, or Pueblo, Indians lived in terraced apartment buildings made of adobe and supported by stones and wooden beams. The size and complexity of the pueblos reflected the engineering skills and social organization that were fixed in the Pueblo heritage. Some of these buildings were five hundred years old. Inheriting also a fine artistic tradition, the Pueblos fashioned marvelous pots and baskets and some of the finest rugs and blankets in the world. Since the men were not hunters—warriors were not honored and, indeed, were cursed by their victims—men as well as women spun, wove, potted, and farmed.

Not all the southwestern Indians were peaceful farmers. The Navajos and, to an even greater extent, the Apaches hunted and marauded as well as farmed. California Indians were generally agrarian, and the Kwakiutls, far up the Pacific coast, were ferociously competitive and even cannibalistic. The native Americans, indeed, were an extraordinarily diverse array of peoples. But this did not stop most Americans of the late nineteenth century from seeing them through dime-novel eyes, stereotyping all Indians as fierce, marauding, thieving aliens. This conception, coupled with the Indians' fear of white aggression and their distaste for most white ways, appeared to justify to whites their instinct to cast the Indians aside, to segregate them or to massacre them.

Thus was there developed not only one more caste in the American caste system, but a caste that was completely cut off from other Americans experiencing poverty, discrimination, oppression, and segregation. Before the war, it had seemed at least barely conceivable that the great numbers of Americans denied their moral claims to "liberty and equality" might join hands to some degree, if only because there were leaders like Frances Wright and certain abolitionists who could imagine a coalition of the deprived. But later in the century, any kind of political or even symbolic alliance among Jews, blacks, Indians, and the ghetto poor was not only impossible; it was inconceivable. Not only were these castes segregated from one another, each hardly knew the others existed. The concept of unity seemed to be fading out just when the conditions of work and life should, according to Marxist calculations, have promoted class solidarity. Instead the power of ideas seemed to be pulling in very different directions.

CHAPTER 5

The Power of Ideas

L IBERTY! A hundred Fourths of July broke loose yesterday to exalt her name, and despite the calendar rolled themselves into a delirious and glorious one," rhapsodized the usually dour *New York Times.* "At daybreak the city stirred nimbly and flung a million colors to the heavy air, for the cloud king had covered the heavens and moved upon the waters; but she plumed herself and showered scarlet, and snow, and azure, and gold, defying the skies to darken her festival."

Thus the *Times* pictured the dedication of the Statue of Liberty on a wet and foggy October 28, 1886. The massive icon represented a triumph of the human spirit as well as of the spirit of liberty. French intellectuals, struggling to establish a new republic out of the ruins of Napoleon III's Second Empire, had conceived the mad notion of a joint French-American project to erect a colossal statue of liberty as a stimulus to both peoples to cherish and safeguard freedom. They sought the common denominator between *"Liberté, Égalité, Fraternité"* and "Life, liberty, and the pursuit of happiness." Countless obstacles arose. Bartholdi, the sculptor, was noted more for his addiction to colossi than for his art. Viewing the project with suspicion, Congress granted funds for the dedication (but none for liquor) and for maintenance (as a lighthouse), and then cut off further aid. The public was importuned for funds, which the poor withheld because they viewed "Liberty" as a folly of the rich, but the rich did not give either. Still, some money was raised through auctions, benefit performances, and even a poetry contest, which attracted a reluctant contribution from one Emma Lazarus. And at a critical moment Joseph Pulitzer, an immigrant from Hungary, used his New York *World* and his St. Louis *Post-Dispatch* to pull in small gifts from over 100,000 donors, including countless schoolchildren.

So there the great figure stood, rising with her torch 152 feet above the pedestal on Bedloe's Island, 300 feet above sea level. Troops, bands, Templars, veterans, dignitaries disgorged onto the tiny island from ferry, tug, and yacht. The rich, now enthusiastic, were there, while the contributing public watched from the shores or excursion steamers. Count de Lesseps presented the gift. A senator—William Evarts—was celebrating Fran-co-American love of liberty when Bartholdi, perched far above on the head of the statue, acted on a false signal through the mists, unveiled the figure, and set off a cacophony of shouts, whistles, drums, horns, applause, and booming guns that drowned out the rest of the senator's remarks. A President—Grover Cleveland—accepted the gift, stating that "Liberty has here made her home" and would pierce the darkness of ignorance and oppression "until liberty shall enlighten the world."

Liberty. The idea had doubtless lost some of its enkindling power of old, but it was still the central and most compelling value in the American ideology. The pennies and nickels that jangled in newsboys' pockets still bore the magic word. Politicians still climaxed their declamations with appeals to the goddess of liberty, as did student orators evoking memories of the liberty of Patrick Henry, Thomas Jefferson, and above all Daniel Webster—"Liberty *and* Union, now and forever, one and inseparable."

In the post–Civil War years, the American idea of liberty was as complex, many-sided, and ambiguous as in the antebellum period, when diverse notions of freedom probably did more to divide than to unite Americans in dealing with the issue of slavery and its cure. Liberty still meant, most fundamentally, freedom of speech, religion, and assembly. It meant, even more powerfully, the right to own and use your "private" property as you wished. Property, John Adams had said, was "surely a right of mankind as really as liberty," and this idea flourished in a booming era of huge agglomerations of property. Liberty was still viewed in largely negative terms, as liberty *from* church and state and other establishments; the idea of achieving broader liberties, economic and social, *through* collective efforts, especially through government, was a matter more of philosophical debate than of practical consideration.

Ideas have consequences, but not merely because they exist as abstractions. They must be evoked and articulated and sounded forth, like music from a score. The social and intellectual context of the 1870s and '80s was such as to enhance the individualistic component of liberty—the emphasis on protection of individual rights, individual opportunity, private property as essential to a person's security and dignity, the curbing of external obstacles on individual development. But this kind of "individualistic liberty," or individualism, embraced a wide span of human thought and behavior—all the way, at least, from Emerson's spacious concepts of personal growth and fulfillment, spiritual and intellectual, to the narrowest kind of material self-seeking and success.

In a curious way, the Statue of Liberty itself seemed to symbolize both the power and the ambiguity of the idea of liberty in America. Bartholdi and his fellow republicans in France had conceived of the icon as Liberty facing away from *America* and "enlightening the world"—especially reactionary Europe. Emma Lazarus's noble words had Liberty turned toward arriving immigrants as persons seeking a new life away from the *old country.* Was Liberty more for export abroad or for internal use? And what did it mean, in this dedication year of 1886?

Across the Atlantic, in London, Karl Marx had viewed with scorn this kind of paean to liberty—bourgeois liberty. He had long since denounced bourgeois liberty as that "of man regarded as an isolated nomad, withdrawn into himself." The right of liberty under capitalism was simply the right of private property—"the right to enjoy one's fortune and to dispose of it as one will; without regard for other men and independently of society. It is the right of self-interest. . . . It leads every man to see in other men, not the *realization,* but rather the *limitation* of his own liberty. . . ."

DINNER AT DELMONICO'S

Americans had long been world-famous for their competitive spirit and enterprising ways. A century and a half before Carnegie and Swift made their millions, young Benjamin Franklin was selling thousands of copies of his *Poor Richard's Almanack,* which instructed that *God helps them that help themselves,* that *Keep thy shop, and thy shop will keep thee,* that *The used key is always bright,* that *Early to bed,* etc. In Franklin's time and after, however, overly bumptious entrepreneurial spirit had been checked and balanced by elitist public leadership, intellectual authority, legal due process, and civic virtue. Then the "victory" of the Northern economy in the Civil War and the long economic boom of the postwar decades brought a dynamic combination of a quickened spirit of individual enterprise—and a recharged doctrine of laissez-faire economics.

Central to the whole concept of aggressive economic individualism was this doctrine of "government let be"—a doctrine that had gripped the British and continental business mind at the turn of the century. The physiocrats of eighteenth-century France had contended not only that land was the basis of all wealth but that the "natural order of liberty" would flourish best in a setting of absolute freedom of trade, full rights of property, and abolition of restrictive laws. These ideas had profoundly influenced Adam Smith, who planned at one time to dedicate his *Wealth of Nations* to François Quesnay, the founder and leader of physiocracy. In publishing this quickly famous volume in the same year as the Declaration of Independence, Smith issued an economic declaration of individualism

—one that fell happily on the ears of businessmen frustrated by the old mercantilist regulations.

The brilliant (if by no means original) constellation of ideas—that the natural economic order tends to maximize individual well-being, that this order must not be interfered with, that collective as well as individual betterment results from that order, that if enterprisers were free to pursue self-interest, the "invisible hand" of commercial competition would be far more effective than the state as a regulator of economic behavior—closely influenced the practical policies of parties and politicians, especially in Britain. Smith's notions received powerful support from Thomas Malthus's contentions that population, especially among the lower classes, constantly tended "to increase beyond the means of subsistence," and that not poor laws but only the poor themselves could meet this problem. Another corollary to laissez-faire doctrine was David Ricardo's "iron" law of wages, decreeing that the total wage fund was fixed and hence any successful effort by workers to increase their wages simply robbed other workers of income.

These men were not scribblers in garrets but prestigious political and economic philosophers whose words carried enormous weight among ruling establishments. And they reached the minds of wellborn Americans at perhaps the most vulnerable stage of their lives—in their undergraduate years. Students at Brown University could listen to their president, Francis Wayland, defend the rights of property, proclaim that men should be allowed to use their capital as they wished, virtually equate the laws of laissez-faire economics with the laws of God; if the students missed Wayland's sermons and lectures, they could read any of eighteen editions of his *Elements of Political Economy.* The men of Bowdoin could read a volume of the same title by their great preacher and teacher Samuel Phillips Newman, based on the principles of classical economics, just as the men of Harvard could peruse a textbook on the principles of political economy by their young philosopher-economist Francis Bowen, with similar conclusions, and the men of Williams could learn the same doctrines from their young political economist, Arthur Latham Perry.

Through teachers like these—and countless others north, south, and west—college men drank in the thoughts of Smith, Malthus, Ricardo, of Jean Baptiste Say and Harriet Martineau, thinkers who themselves had absorbed the great individualistic and libertarian doctrines of Locke and his successors. If the American teachers were sometimes more Smithian than Smith, more Malthusian than Malthus, their students hardly cared. The young men embraced with fervor doctrines that seemed so well to fit the times. Practical politicians were often less ardent as they weaved their course between governmental hands-off and governmental intervention in the economy, but the practical men too, perhaps unknowingly, were the intellectual slaves of various economic theorists, alive or defunct.

Individualism could be a spacious and noble doctrine; it could be a crabbed and selfish one. In America it was both. It was the individualism of Jefferson, of free and responsible persons rationally and collectively seeking the good life and the just society; it was also the individualism of the market economists, of those competitors in the economic arena seeking to make money and attain personal success, on the theory that a good society would arise out of the struggle for individual reward. The individualism of Jefferson had been an enormously liberating and democratizing force, encouraging movements for more social equality, suffrage for poor men, and even freedom for slaves.

What happened after the Civil War in American elitist and popular thought alike was the steady divesting of individual liberty's broader, richer dimensions and their replacement by a narrow, egoistic individualism defined as competition, striving, and personal success. What Clinton Rossiter called the "Great Train Robbery of American intellectual history" became the means by which postbellum rugged individualists stole the word symbols of Jeffersonian liberalism, such as liberty, equality, progress, and opportunity, and glued them onto the platform planks of conservatism.

These refurbished planks would undergird American conservatism for at least a century. *The higher, immutable laws of economics:* anyone believing in a benevolent deity, said Edward Atkinson, must know that the operation of the higher law is "steadily, surely, and slowly working to the benefit of the great mass of the people." *Man as homo economicus:* persons were defined by their economic self-interest rather than by their social or aesthetic needs. "Political Economy," John Stuart Mill had written in 1844, "considers mankind as occupied solely in acquiring and consuming wealth." *The free market as regulator:* rents, profits, wages, prices were to be determined by the laws of competition. *Government as the enemy:* no matter how representative and democratic, government was meddlesome, incompetent, corrupt. "Men may vote as they please," said a theologian, "but the laws of production and of trade are as inexorable as the law of nature." *Liberty as economic individualism:* liberty, said the noted political scientist John W. Burgess, "is the absence of government in a given sphere of individual or social action."

*   *   *

Ben Franklin's Poor Richard reincarnated, the Jeffersonian belief in lean government revised and revived, the laissez-faire classicists revisited—the resurgence of all these currents of economic thought should have been enough to empower economic individualists with all the intellectual authority they needed in order to press for their marketplace version of liberty. And so it did. Following the war, however, two English thinkers immensely fortified the convictions of American individualists.

Charles Darwin's *On the Origin of Species* had burst upon the British scene in 1859. The first edition sold out within the day. Superbly explicated and massively supported, his thesis grounded the old theory of evolution on the propositions that a struggle for existence rages among the prodigal issue of organisms, that variations in the offspring helped certain plants or animals to survive and reproduce, and that these mutations spread to the whole species during succeeding generations. Popularly interpreted as a theory that man was descended from the apes, "Darwinism" promptly set off blazing disputes with "creationists" who believed in the fall of Adam and original sin. Darwin's theory was further popularized, and the argument extended, when Herbert Spencer dramatized the principle of natural selection as "the survival of the fittest." In a profusion of writings including ten weighty works of "synthetic philosophy," Spencer laid out an anti-statist doctrine that he had earlier embraced as a young editor at the London *Economist.*

Americans seemed cut off from these ideas by their absorption in the Civil War; then came the "Vogue of Spencer." His views that nature put all on trial and that the mentally as well as the physically weak perished; that true liberty consisted of every man having "freedom to do all that he wills, provided he infringes not on the equal freedom of any other man"; that state interference to protect the weak or deprived violated the process of natural selection; that public schools, state insane asylums, state poorhouses, state boards of health, even state post offices, were suspect; that, happily, government would decay as civilization progressed—these ideas, comprising the most radical defense of laissez-faire ever heard in America, fell with the tinkling melody of an intellectual aphrodisiac on the ears of the social and economic elites of America.

Why were they so incited by this far-off thinker—a man who had not even deigned to visit America—with his fastidious ways and intellectual arrogance, when they already had ample intellectual support in the "Manchester School" and other classic thought, in the laissez-faire view of some of their own Founding Fathers, in their own creed of individualism? In part because this was the Age of Science, and scientific discovery and thought had gripped the American mind as never before. Spencer, with his weighty treatises, seemed as scientific in applying the "survival of the fittest" to the social order as Darwin was in finding it in the natural.

There was a deeper reason. The great philosophical expounders of laissez-faire had often showed a deplorable tendency to "go soft" when it came to practical applications. Fundamentally humane and enlightened men, they ultimately balked at denying state aid to the poor and the helpless. John Stuart Mill, the great apostle of liberty, seemed to be turning almost socialistic in some of his thinking. But not Spencer—he supported the most rigorous application of laissez-faire not only as economically correct but as socially and morally valid, because the result would be the perfection of the human race and the eradication of social evils.

What a marvelous idea for the elites: to be individually selfish was to be socially sane and right! For these men, too, needed their ideas to be validated by some measure of higher morality, especially in this era when religious doctrine so often seemed old-fashioned and inadequate. Spencer, to boot, argued in strong dramatic terms understandable to every man, thus making him, as Hofstadter said, "the metaphysician of the homemade intellectual, and the prophet of the cracker-barrel agnostic." In the last three decades of the century, Spencer's American publisher, D. Appleton and Co., sold well over 300,000 copies of his writings. He was a philosopher, William James noted, who could be valued by those who had no other philosopher.

No wonder economic elites clutched Spencer to their austere bosoms. But the remarkable aspect of the Vogue of Spencer was the extent to which he was accepted and celebrated in the academic and religious worlds. A host of teachers of a variety of subjects preached Spencerism; indeed, the discipline of "political economy" was virtually equated with the doctrine of laissez-faire. While the scholars differed with one another on practical applications, as theorists, "free competition and denial of state interference was their dogma, economic liberty their slogan." They wrote books and pamphlets, testified before legislatures, pontificated in the press, lectured from their platforms. The message was simple: Social evolution meant social progress.

By far the most famous and effective of the laissez-faire academics was William Graham Sumner of Yale. Brought up by his English immigrant father to venerate the Protestant economic values, especially thrift, Sumner divided his life between writing a systematic science of society and crusading for economic individualism inside his classroom and outside. The "strong" and the "weak," he preached, were simply terms for "the industrious and the idle, the frugal and the extravagant." If we do not like the survival of the fittest, he said, we will have the survival of the unfittest. Millionaires were the "product of natural selection"; hereditary wealth guaranteed the enterpriser that he might continue in his children the qualities that had enabled him to benefit the community. But millionaires should not be artificially aided by the government, any more than should the poor.

Students flocked to Sumner's courses, looking for debate. One of them, William Lyon Phelps, later remembered Sumner's exchange with a dissenter:

"Professor, don't you believe in any government aid to industries?"

"No! it's root, hog, or die."

"Yes, but hasn't the hog got a right to root?"

"There are no rights. The world owes nobody a living."

"You believe, then, Professor, in only one system, the contract-competitive system?"

"That's the only sound economic system. All others are fallacies."

"Well, suppose some professor of political economy came along and took your job away from you. Wouldn't you be sore?"

"Any other professor is welcome to try. If he gets my job, it is my fault. My business is to teach the subject so well that no one can take the job away from me."

The most respectable men of God took up the tenets of Social Darwinism, though rarely did they utter the name of the controversial English biologist. No one, said Princeton's clergyman-president James McCosh, was at liberty to deprive us of our property or to interfere with it; attempts to do so were "theft." Love required the acquisition of property, said Williams's clergyman-president, Mark Hopkins, and those who had done the most for our institutions had been men with a "strong desire of property." In his renowned sermon *Acres of Diamonds,* Baptist clergyman Russell Conwell preached the gospel of success: "It is your duty to get rich. It is wrong to be poor."

Some of the most respectable journals preached laissez-faire. Occasionally, it was a laissez-faire that attacked business as well as the poor for demanding aid from government. "The Government must get out of the 'protective' business and the 'subsidy' business and the 'improvement' and the 'development' business," wrote Edwin Lawrence Godkin of the *Nation.* "It must let trade, and commerce, and manufactures, and steamboats, and railroads, and telegraphs alone. It cannot touch them without breeding corruption." The government had as much as it could do, he added, just to maintain order and administer justice. Words like these were repeated in hundreds of dailies and weeklies.

The dream of individual striving and success resonated most dramatically in the well-thumbed pages of boys' stories about "rags to riches." Perhaps the single most influential writer of the late nineteenth century

was a small, slight, diffident man, cursed by ill health and blighted romances, named Horatio Alger, Jr., who wrote about heroes—economic
heroes. Youngsters and oldsters totaling tens of millions devoured his 106
books and voluminous other writings. Rarely could it more properly be
said of an author that to read one of his works was to read them all.
Whether it was *Ragged Dick*—the first of Alger's famous works—or *Tony the
Hero* or *Dan the Detective* or *Tattered Tom,* whether the theme was *Luck and
Pluck* or *Strive and Succeed* or *Do and Dare* or *Brave and Bold* or *Paddle Your
Own Canoe,* Alger's novels followed a set format: the boy-hero is born poor,
leads an exemplary life, faces up to poverty, shows a lot of pluck, and ends
up rich, though usually not *very* rich. Yet Alger often departed from the
mythology of the self-made man. His heroes sometimes rise from the
middle class, not from poverty; they seem to depend as much on luck as
pluck; and his rich men are often not good people. More curiously, as
Richard Huber pointed out, his heroes are not self-made men but self-
made boys. And only one of his heroes, Tattered Tom, was a girl, and she
a tomboy—probably a reflection both of the sexism of the time and of the
near-certainty that Horatio Alger, Jr., was a homosexual.

Others besides Alger, most notably William Makepeace Thayer, wrote
success books, and rags-to-riches stories appeared in magazines as well as
paperbacks. The most notable of the success magazines was *Munsey's.*
Frank Munsey himself not only read and printed Alger's stories, wrote the
same kind himself, and put the Alger stamp on every issue, but, according
to Theodore Greene, "lived all his life in the fictional world" of Alger. He
spent his life in a feverish search for what he called "riches, power, the
world, the great big world," and after perilous ups and downs that matched
those of any Alger hero, he did indeed reach the top. There, however, he
bought, merged, killed, and trivialized so many newspapers as to earn the
obituary notice from a later editor, William Allen White: "Frank Munsey
contributed to the journalism of his day the talent of a meat packer, the
morals of a money changer and the manners of an undertaker. . . . May he
rest in trust."

Young would-be heroes did not even need to wait to read books and
magazines. Many of their schoolteachers shared the same ethic. And staring at them from the early pages of the *McGuffey Reader* were the lines:

> . . . If you find your task is hard,
> Try, Try Again!
> Time will bring you your reward,
> Try, Try Again;
> All that other folks can do,

Why, with patience, should not you:
Only keep this rule in view;
Try, Try Again.

No one in America exemplified Horatio Alger's type of hero better than
Andrew Carnegie. He rose from near-poverty to enormous riches; he was
industrious, neat, frugal, honest, lucky, and plucky; he was probably the
biggest individual success of the late nineteenth century. And, by a fitting-
ness all too rare in history, he was of all America's great men the leading
disciple of Herbert Spencer. "Before Spencer, all for me had been darkness," Carnegie liked to say; "after him, all had become light—and right."
To Carnegie and many others, Spencer was the "master."

People wondered when the master might visit the United States. A
hypochondriac, Spencer had an aversion both to travel and to noisy adulation. He finally responded to the entreaties less of Carnegie than of his
American publishers and his mass of American champions, who far surpassed his British devotees in both numbers and enthusiasm. He made the
crossing in August 1882 on one of the finest Cunarders. By the time
Spencer had been escorted by enthusiastic friends to Pittsburgh—where,
despite a personal tour by Carnegie, he found the steel works stifling and
the city repulsive—and then to a dozen other stops, he was physically
exhausted and emotionally in a funk about the planned climax of the trip,
a banquet at Delmonico's where he was to be main speaker and guest of
honor.

On the evening of November 9, 1882, a stream of broughams and
victorias and daumonts dropped their passengers in front of the wide
entrances of Delmonico's, the most fashionable restaurant in Manhattan,
at Fifth Avenue and 26th Street. In its banquet hall were gathering over
150 of the most distinguished men in America: political leaders like Carl
Schurz and ex-Secretary of State William M. Evarts, intellectual celebrities
such as Sumner and John Fiske, religious luminaries such as Lyman Abbott
and Henry Ward Beecher, publishers including the Appletons, university
presidents, a brace of business leaders. Carnegie himself escorted Spencer
to the dinner and delivered him over to the head table. Spencer made clear
that he was too exhausted for small talk.

When at 9:30 the bounteous meal was over, chairs pulled back, and
cigars lighted, the distinguished audience was in for some surprises. Spencer, pulling himself together, spoke not on Social Darwinism but, rather,
chided American businessmen that they worked *too* hard, passed their
"damaged constitutions" on to their children, even started to turn gray ten
years before their English counterparts did. Life was not for working but

working for life, he said. Nor did the other speakers follow the Social Darwinist script. As Joseph Wall pointed out, "Schurz stressed Spencer's moral and ethical probity, Carnegie stressed Spencer's detestation of the military, Fiske announced that Spencer had contributed as much to religion as he had to science, while Henry Ward Beecher, carried away with his own rolling oratory, told the startled Spencer that they would meet once again beyond the grave in that great banquet hall in Heaven." It was almost midnight and the air was dense with cigar smoke by the time Beecher rose to speak, but the world-famous pulpitarian spoke so brilliantly on the reconciliation of evolution and religion that men stood roaring their approval and waving their handkerchiefs at the conclusion.

Little had been said that clarified the tenets of Social Darwinism. Perhaps it was not necessary. The hardheaded businessmen there knew what they believed—in the gospel of rugged individualism in general but in countless exceptions in practice. Carnegie would go on venerating Spencer and favoring tariffs. Other industrialists would favor competition in general but not in their own fields of business. They believed in economic individualism but also in corporate, collective capitalism. Many a man of public affairs there wanted laissez-faire, except when it hurt the rich—or himself.

The delightful confusion of the evening was well expressed by Beecher during his remarks: "I had just as lief be descended from a monkey," said he, turning to Spencer, "if I have descended far enough."

THE BITCH-GODDESS SUCCESS

Hardly three weeks earlier, a quite different group of men had gathered at Delmonico's to honor a man who was neither a captain of industry nor a world-famous intellectual, but a journalist: Henry George. Compared to Spencer's hosts, the hundred or so men who lined up to greet George were a motley crowd, reflecting the vigorous and variegated mind of Gotham. Here were Perry Belmont, congressman and son of a longtime head of the national Democratic party; Felix Adler of the Ethical Culture Society; Thomas Kinsella, editor of the Brooklyn *Daily Eagle* and educational reformer; Roger Atkinson Pryor, Confederate soldier-politician turned Manhattan lawyer; David G. Croly, modernist editor who had actually spoken *for* miscegenation; Thomas G. Shearman, corporation lawyer, tax reformer, and defender of Henry Ward Beecher against charges of adultery; and the ubiquitous Beecher himself.

The apolitical Delmonico's did itself proud as usual, providing twenty-eight items of food and drink. The lion of the occasion hardly looked the part, with his slight build and scuffed shoes; but Henry George's editorial growls had sounded across the Western world. He had indeed shown the kind of spunk and competitive drive that Spencer and Alger alike would have admired. Young George had left his middle-class home and school at thirteen to serve as an errand boy in a Philadelphia importing firm, then shipped out on long sea voyages as foremast boy. Between trips, a typesetting job drew him into the world of publishers and journalists. He drank deeply of his travel experiences—the life of the common sailor before the mast, the scramble for land in California, the horrifying contrast of wealth and poverty in Calcutta and New York. A voracious reader, he ranged through the works of French physiocrats and English classicists, American Whigs and Jeffersonians, religious prophets and radical intellectuals. For years, he lived hand to mouth as a California newspaper writer, shifting restlessly from job to job while he pursued his own success ethic—even as, opinionated and cantankerous, he quarreled incessantly with bosses and fellow workers.

It was in the yeasty economic and journalistic milieus of California that George grappled with the problem of poverty. He himself was so down-and-out at one point, with a half-starved wife and child at home, that he accosted the first prosperous-looking man he saw on the street and asked him desperately for five dollars, which the stranger gave him; if he had not, George said later, he was ready to knock the man down. But soon in a series of newspaper articles and finally in *Progress and Poverty,* he propounded his long-fermenting ideas: that the ownership of land brings control over society; that every man has a natural "labor right" to land; that when he rents privately held land from others he is robbed of some of that labor right; that the solution is to regain the public right to rent through a single tax on land.

Man's right to himself, and to what he produced, George said, was accepted. "But man has also another right, declared by the fact of his existence—the right to the use of so much of the free gifts of nature as may be necessary to supply all the wants of that existence, and which he may use without interfering with the equal rights of anyone else; and to this he has a title as against all the world."

Recognition came to George only after he had moved back to New York and then traveled abroad. In England, he met the socialist H. M. Hyndman; Helen Taylor, the stepdaughter of the late John Stuart Mill; the political reformer John Bright; the rising radical Joseph Chamberlain. He did not meet Karl Marx. Highly sympathetic to the Irish cause, George hobnobbed with the leaders of the Irish Land League, who were in turn entranced by his views on land. His fame soared at home and abroad when he was arrested during a trip to Ireland; indeed, so many American Irish leaders attended the Delmonico's banquet that at least one of the diners thought they were welcoming a fiery rebel from Ireland.

George was perhaps the most arresting of a number of journalists whose ideas were agitating American opinion during the 1880s. Another inciter was Edward Bellamy, a struggling young editor who was beginning to taste success and fame during that decade of intellectual excitement. Raised in a western Massachusetts textile town, Bellamy attended Union College for a year, traveled abroad, studied law, worked for a time for the noted Springfield *Union* and the equally noted New York *Evening Post,* and then with his brother founded the Springfield *Daily News.* More and more drawn to social and political problems, Bellamy began publication in a country paper of *The Duke of Stockbridge,* a fictional treatment of Shays's Rebellion. He had several more works of historical fiction to his credit by the time, in 1888, he published *Looking Backward,* which embodied an effort, he said later, to "reason out a method of economic organization" by which the republic might guarantee its citizens' welfare "on a basis of equality corresponding to and supplementing their political equality."

The story of Julian West, a young Boston millionaire who fell asleep in 1887 and awoke in 2000, the novel pictured through his eyes an orderly, affluent, egalitarian, rational Boston of 2000, in contrast with the cruel, class-ridden, and altogether bleak city of the late nineteenth century. The novel gained in force from powerful metaphors—notably of capitalism as a prodigious coach pulled uphill by "masses of humanity" driven by hunger, and crowded on top by travelers who called down to the toilers, urging patience and hinting at possible compensation in the next world—and remarkable prophecies, including music piped into drawing rooms (by telephone) according to published programs. But mainly the book gained from its portrait of a new world in which equitable "credit cards"—Bellamy's term—had taken the place of money, a Boston without taxes or army or navy, without lawyers or law schools, a utopia of hierarchy and harmony and benign regimentation, in which women as well as men enjoyed liberty, equality, and fraternity.

Looking Backward was an instant hit. Not only did it sell by the tens of thousands, achieving finally a total sale of one million, but it produced a rash of Bellamy clubs formed to discuss the book and its implications. A decade later Bellamy wrote a sequel, *Equality.* Again the force of Bellamy's ideas overcame his heavy dialogue. At the start of *Equality,* Julian West's sweetheart Edith battered him with a cross-examination that Bellamy's hero could not bear.

She couldn't understand, said twenty-first-century Edith of nineteenth-century Boston, the gap between people's pretensions then and the "shockingly unequal conditions of the people, the contrasts of waste and want, the pride and power of the rich, the abjectness and servitude of the poor, and all the rest of the dreadful story."

"It is doubtful," Julian acknowledged, "if there was ever a greater disparity between the conditions of different classes than you would find in a half hour's walk in Boston, New York, Chicago, or any other great city of America in the last quarter of the nineteenth century."

"And yet," says Edith, "it appears from all the books that meanwhile the Americans' great boast was that they differed from all other and former nations in that they were free and equal. One is constantly coming across this phrase in the literature of the day. . . ."

They were supposedly equal before the law, Julian said, but he had to admit that in fact rich and poor were not. But they were equal in "opportunities." Edith leaped on this. It seemed, she said, that they all had an equal chance to make themselves unequal. Was there any way in which people were equal?

"Yes, there was," says Julian. "They were political equals. They all had one vote alike, and the majority was the supreme law-giver."

Then, asked Edith, why did not a majority of the poor put an end to their inequalities?

"Because," says Julian, "they were taught and believed that the regulation of industry and commerce and the production and distribution of wealth was something wholly outside of the proper province of government."

Then, asked Edith, "if the people did not think that they could trust themselves to regulate their own industry and the distribution of the product, to whom did they leave the responsibility?"

"To the capitalists."

"And did the people elect the capitalists?"

"Nobody elected them."

"By whom, then, were they appointed?"

"Nobody appointed them."

"What a singular system!" To whom then were the capitalists accountable?

They were accountable to nothing but their consciences, said Julian.

"Their consciences! Ah, I see!" In the end she forced Julian to grant that the people surrendered their power to capitalists in the name of "individual liberty," that they did not obtain such liberty, that capitalists used the government to quell the "quenchless blaze" of "greed and envy, fear, lust, hate, revenge, and every foul passion" of the poor and of the degraded "outcasts." And he admitted that the capitalists controlled the political as

well as the economic government by buying votes with money and with
"fireworks, oratory, processions, brass bands, barbecues," and the like.
And the worst thing, Julian admitted, was that the poor were kept in such
degradation as to be "not morally any better than the rich."

Rivaling George and Bellamy in the force of his protest against capitalism was still another journalist, Henry Demarest Lloyd. Brought up in a
New York City family of radical Democratic sympathies, young Lloyd had
plunged into the world of free traders, civil service reform, and anti-
monopoly on his graduation from Columbia College in 1869. Hired by the
Chicago *Tribune* as an editorialist, he moved steadily beyond political liberalism to a social radicalism that called for profound changes in the capitalistic system. In his writings, culminating in *Wealth Against Commonwealth* in
1894, he critically analyzed railroads and other corporations and championed small businessmen, consumers, and workers, including striking trade
unionists. His repeated calls for social justice and his attacks on monopoly
—especially the Standard Oil monopoly—brought him into virtually a
personal confrontation with John D. Rockefeller.

Lloyd's power lay less in his ideas, which were not especially original,
than in the analysis that supported them. Like a good journalist, he pored
through the records of court and legislative investigations of great corporations, and conducted on-the-spot investigations of conditions of coal
miners. An activist, he helped organize Milwaukee streetcar workers, and
he succeeded in gaining commutation of the death sentence of convicted
"anarchists." Unlike certain other radicals, Lloyd would not trade liberty
for equality. He "insisted that the rehabilitation of individual and economic liberty so essential to further democratic advances," according to
Chester Destler, "must result from the progressive, experimental harmon-
ization of individualism with social cooperation." For Lloyd, individual
liberty was both means and end.

Lloyd the social reformer, Bellamy the utopian, George the single-taxer
—these were men of highly diverse personalities but also of striking
similarities. Though men of ideas, they were not academic scholars; rather,
they were largely self-taught, drawing their learning from books, experiences, and travels, especially their journeys to a Britain itself undergoing
rapid social change. They came from deeply religious families. All three
rose to success in the fiercely competitive world of American journalism.
The lives of all three would become entangled in the climactic events of the
1890s. But what most typified them was what most divided them—their diverse solutions to the ills of capitalism and their largely separate followings.

Fundamentally, they disagreed with one another. George saw *Looking
Backward* as building a "castle in the air" but also tending toward govern-

mental paternalism. The youthful Lloyd called George a "quack" and dismissed Bellamy as too utopian. For his part, Bellamy felt that George's notion of nationalizing land first, rather than last, would antagonize so many interests at the start as to jeopardize any major reform. Bellamy must have known that Lloyd had little regard for *Looking Backward* and for Bellamy's creed of "Nationalism" and following of "Nationalists."

"Mr. George," Bellamy asked when the two happened to meet at a dinner, "why are you not a Nationalist?"

"Because I am an individualist," George replied.

"I am a Nationalist," said Bellamy, "because I am an individualist."

Each of these thinkers had his own following as well as ideas: George's single-taxers, Bellamy's nationalists, Lloyd's trade unionists. Each was a kind of politico of protest as well as entrepreneur of ideas. Each operated on his own success ethic. Nor did any of the three ground himself in doctrines of Marxist socialism that had a common foundation. Bellamy saw the word *socialist* as suggesting "the red flag with all manner of sexual novelties, and an abusive tone about God and religion." Marxists viewed Bellamy as a utopian, always a dangerous breed of reformer. To George, Marx was the "prince of muddleheads." Marx put down *Progress and Poverty* as an effort to save capitalism and George as "utterly backward" as a theorist. Lloyd rejected Marxist "determinism" and felt that the labor theory of value had too many exceptions.

Thus the social rebels argued and divided. Nor were other voices more united. Washington Gladden, Congregational pastor and shaper of the new "social gospel," favored trade unionism and public ownership of utilities but rejected socialism in favor of Christian compassion, love of justice, and social service. Ignatius Donnelly deserted conservative Republicanism to write a book proving the existence of a lost Atlantis, a second work contending that the earth had collided with a giant comet, a third demonstrating that Francis Bacon had written the works of Shakespeare, and a fourth—*Caesar's Column*—that rivaled *Looking Backward* in theme and popularity. Then there were the communitarians—especially the Shakers —who wanted local reform but feared the grand national experiments of Bellamy and the rest. Their intellectual godfather, the Englishman William Morris, called *Looking Backward* a "horrible Cockney dream."

*   *   *

Once upon a time, New England could have been depended on to focus the nation's intellectual concerns, to reinvigorate its founding ideas and ideals, to turn the needle of its moral compass to true north. And indeed, for a time after the Civil War, Boston at least opened up shop again for its old intellectual business. Emerson, Lowell, Longfellow, Whittier, and the literary giants of the past still adorned the drawing rooms of Beacon Hill and tramped the paths of Harvard Yard. Not only did Dr. Oliver Wendell Holmes once again preside as the "autocrat of the breakfast table," but he and the giants and lesser luminaries still might converse at length—sometimes for eight hours straight over a long dinner—at the Saturday Club, without any lag or lapse in the brilliance of the discourse.

Yet, if New England was not "in decay," it was clearly slipping into a long and languid Indian summer. Of Thoreauian Utopianism and Enlightenment vagaries and frontier bumptiousness it had had enough, Vernon Parrington wrote, "and so it turned back lovingly to the culture of earlier times and drew comfort from a dignified Federalism—enriched now by a mellow Harvard scholarship that was on intimate terms with Dante and Chaucer and Cervantes and Shakespeare—a Federalism that fitted the dignified Brahmin genius as comfortably as an old shoe." The years of its intellectual leadership were coming to an end. Boston, said Henry Adams, had stopped believing in itself.

Once supremely creative, New Englanders now concentrated on remembering, recording, observing—and criticizing. Mark Twain, as he was about to lecture before a Boston audience for the first time, described his prospective listeners as "4000 critics."

Above all, the spirit of reform seemed to be dying. Compared to the transcending and transforming issues of the past, the new ones—currency, tariffs, the debt, railroad land grants—seemed at once crass and complex. To the "terrible simplifiers" of New England, slavery had seemed a clear as well as a compelling issue; now, corruption and patronage offered less delectable indignation to the Puritan conscience. "Most of the old reformers were exhausted," Van Wyck Brooks concluded. "They had no energy left for fresh campaigns, although Boston, prolific in causes, swarmed with friends of progress and new reformers rose with other movements, the cause of peace, the cause of woman's suffrage, dietary reform and Darwinism, the cause of the short-skirts league and the short-haired woman who amused profane New York for a generation."

In some, nonetheless, the old flame of reform still burned. The magnificent Wendell Phillips, who had braved the mobs of old in his bitter attacks on slavery, now hurled his moral thunderbolts in support of penal reform, prohibition, woman's suffrage, the labor movement, justice to Indians. Elizabeth Peabody—onetime pupil of Emerson, longtime secretary and amanuensis of William Ellery Channing, sister-in-law of Nathaniel Hawthorne and of Horace Mann, a founder of the Brook Farm community—embraced a variety of reforms, from education to Indian rights. Nor could any cause be launched, from peace or suffrage to pure milk for babies, without Julia Ward Howe, of "Battle Hymn" fame, and her husband Samuel. Boston had its cynics, too. Charles A. Dana, once a devotee of the renowned utopian experiment Brook Farm, was becoming a foe of civil-service purification and everything else reformers seemed to believe in. And had Brook Farm itself not been used as a Union army camp during the war?

For a decade or so after that war, Boston served as a place where the older, moneyed "men of letters" lingered, passing on their intellectual heritage and political ideas to younger men who would spend most of their lives in retreat from New England. Perhaps the most noted of these was the young Harvard historian Henry Adams. As bald, high-domed, and stocky as his illustrious President-ancestors, Henry, like his brothers Charles and Brooks, had to adjust his eighteenth-century heritage of intellectual independence and rocklike integrity to the realities of late nineteenth-century capitalism. Unlike Charles, who had ventured into that world and retreated from it in bitterness against the moneymaking, "bargaining crowd," Henry had backed off from the start. At Harvard he taught medieval history, lecturing reluctantly to large classes that he tried to drive away, he boasted, with "foul and abusive" language. Leaving Cambridge for Washington in the late seventies, he retreated in his historical work to the Federalist-Jefferson era, while narrowly eyeing contemporary politicians in the nation's capital; and in later years, amid much travel abroad, he retreated again, and most creatively, to the world of the twelfth century and its great cathedrals.

All the while, he possessed an intense and morbid interest in politics, in power. Mrs. Lightfoot Lee, the heroine of his novel *Democracy,* wanted not merely an understanding of the source and mechanics of power; what "she wanted," Adams writes, "is POWER" itself. Adams himself wanted more than power—he wanted an intellectual comprehension, which of course might command power. He explored the great dualisms—morality and power, politics and statesmanship, the pastoral and the industrial, science and religion, the individual and the democratic mass, material progress and moral decline. Above all, he turned away from the multiplicity and volatility and materialism of the world in which he lived, for the harmony and stability, the maternal love and cathedral serenity of the glory days of Chartres and Mont-Saint-Michel. His choice was certain: the Virgin over the Dynamo.

Henry James did not reject the multiplicity of American types—indeed, he lived off it—but he too fled Cambridge after a dozen years, much interrupted by travel, of writing reviews and stories for the *North American*

Review and the *Atlantic Monthly*. Drawn to Europe since his boyhood journeys there, he was relieved to desert America—its excessive egalitarianism that diluted individuality, the "flatness" of its democracy, the vulgarities of the Gilded Age, the materialism of the rich, the "bitch-goddess success." Nor did he miss Boston, or, especially, its reformers; he caused a flap in the Athens of America when, in *The Bostonians,* he appeared to lampoon Elizabeth Peabody with a character, Miss Birdseye, whom he judged a humorless, confused, credulous, discursive old woman. Yet Parrington's later assessment has stood up: James "was concerned only with *nuances.* He lived in a world of fine gradations and imperceptible shades." At his best, he was "pragmatizing," as James later said, even before his brother William explained this "way of thinking." But neither from Boston nor London did Henry James discern the "figure in the carpet" of the American experiment.

The void left in New England by these writers—and by countless others of the "best and brightest," in John Hay's words, who left for Michigan copper lodes or California gold mines or Pittsburgh steel works—was not redressed in any other region. New England indeed continued to influence intellectual life across the nation because of the heritage of Emerson, Hawthorne, & co., and because of the migration of its sons and daughters to other parts. As a publishing center, Boston could still reach into the hinterlands. William Dean Howells had come to Cambridge from a poor boyhood in Ohio via journalism and a campaign biography of Lincoln that helped bring a consulate in Venice, where he absorbed history and culture. He arrived in New England adoring Cambridge and all it stood for and, improbably, Cambridge loved this young man from the heartland—for his open, ingenuous manner, for his limpid writing and developing "realism," and, not least, for his adoration of Cambridge. Adopted by the Brahmins and the whole *Atlantic* crowd, he quickly rose to its editorship.

Even so, Howells would leave Boston and the *Atlantic* after a decade and a half. Before doing so, however, he managed to open up the *Atlantic* to writers who otherwise might have been ignored by the Brahmins. One of these was Samuel L. Clemens, a former Mississippi pilot and California journalist who had first won note for a short story, "The Celebrated Jumping Frog of Calaveras County." Howells accepted his reminiscences, "Old Times on the Mississippi," the reception of which encouraged the narrator, Mark Twain, to go on to the exciting adventures of Tom Sawyer, Huckleberry Finn, and Jim on the river of American history.

For Twain, the great river was not history but life itself. She was indeed outside of history and of human control. She ran as she wished, changing course, moving villages from one side of the river to the other, following her natural freedom. Because the pilots were close to the river, Twain endowed them with mythical qualities: the pilots were childlike, brutish, spontaneous, and above all unfettered and independent.

The river was serene and beautiful, despite its occasional perils. "It was a monstrous big river down there—sometimes a mile and a half wide; we run nights, and laid up and hid daytimes; soon as night was most gone we stopped navigating and tied up. . . . The first thing to see, looking away over the water, was a kind of dull line—that was the woods on t'other side; you couldn't make nothing else out; then a pale place in the sky; then more paleness spreading around; then the river softened up way off, and warn't black any more, but gray; you could see little dark spots drifting along ever so far away—trading scows, and such things; and long black streaks—rafts; sometimes you could hear a sweep screaking. . . ."

Only man—especially his grasping, feuding, lynching representatives along the river—was vile: man and technology, whether guns or steamboats. Huck wishes to escape technology and regulation. He lights out for the Territory "because Aunt Sally she's going to adopt me and sivilize me, and I can't stand it. I been there before." For him and for Jim, who is fleeing slavery, the raft means freedom. When the raft is smashed apart by a riverboat and when Huck discovers that Jim has been recaptured, the image of the river as freedom collides with that of society as cruel and confining. But Huck lives *in* that society, and when he is tempted to return Jim to slavery because he, Huck, must live by local rules and mores, "I was a-trembling, because I'd got to decide, forever, betwixt two things, and I knowed it." His decision for Jim's liberty was a decision for his own—and for their equality and fraternity.

"N O T I C E," Twain proclaimed at the start of *Huck*, "Persons trying to find a motive, moral, or plot in this narrative would be, respectively, prosecuted, banished, or shot." Twain in fact offered a motive in the desire for freedom, a moral in the curse of "sivilization," a plot in the protection and eventual liberation of Jim. The book reflected Twain's own hope for people's liberation—a hope tempered by his realization that the currents of change, symbolized by Jim's freedom on the river even as the raft floats deeper and deeper into the slave lands, are remorseless. With the passing years, Twain's hopes for freedom and individuality dwindled as industrial "sivilization" advanced.

As the century neared its close, another novelist was exploring the external and internal forces that seemed to control human fate. Frank Norris's *McTeague* pictured ordinary men and women caught and dragged down by their instinctual drives. Money plays a central role in that downfall. One character, overcome by her instinct for hoarding money, "makes love" to her gold coins. A dentist, told he can no longer practice because he lacks a license, degenerates into an animal run amok and murders his penny-pinching wife with his bare fists before he himself is trapped and killed in Death Valley.

In a more ambitious novel, *The Octopus*—the first of a planned trilogy entitled *Epic of the Wheat*—Norris moved to a wider canvas and drew a harsher portrait of society. The railroad is the villain. Impersonal and cold, it destroys anyone in its way. Popular rage against the California railroad culminates in the deaths of protesting farmers. The novel contrasts a rich man's banquet and a starving mother and child. Wheat itself, though ample and life-giving, is impersonal and remorseless, literally engulfing and slaying a railroad functionary. Men are shot down, hearts broken, young girls "brought to a life of shame," old women starved to death. *"But the WHEAT remained,"* a mighty world force, untouched, unassailable, indifferent, resistless.

*   *   *

Henry George and his fellow social critics, Henry Adams and the other intellectual legatees of the Brahmins, Twain and his fellow realists—what did they have in common? Nothing very definite or explicit. They differed not only in their answers but in their questions. But what comes through their writings, expressed in a diversity of ways, is a common repugnance to the materialism, acquisitiveness, competitiveness, the success ethic of the time—the very reverse of the ideals of Carnegie and Alger.

At the heart of the rising industrial force was the machine, and the machine that continued to symbolize both the great hopes and intrinsic evil of industrialism and urbanism was the railroad. Henry Adams's brother Charles had been corrupted by it. The California wheat farmers were crushed by it. And Mark Twain's steamboat had the soul of a locomotive when Huck heard her "pounding along," not deviating an inch from her course, "looking like a black cloud with rows of glow-worms around it" and suddenly bulging out, "big and scary, with a long row of wide-open furnace doors shining like red-hot teeth, and her monstrous bows and guards hanging right over us."

And then "she come smashing straight through the raft."

"Toiling Millions Now Are Waking"

The voices of protest against mushrooming industrialism—the voices of reformers like George and Bellamy, of social critics like Adams and James, of radicals like Phillips and Peabody, of novelists like Twain and Norris—

were even more mixed and diverse than those of the defenders of capitalism. Most of the critics themselves were of middle-class or even upper-class origin. Could a more coherent and unified voice arise from the workers themselves—from a class that was experiencing the ills of industrialism firsthand? From a class that needed both liberty *and* equality—needed freedom from the boss and the foreman and long hours and wage labor, needed more economic and social equality as well as political, needed equality of women with men and of blacks with whites?

Had not the Declaration of Independence promised both liberty and equality? The Declaration, declared Daniel De Leon, was the product of its age's "experience and learning," promising a "future of freedom" requiring the "collective society in America" to assume the "duty of guaranteeing to the individual a free field—EQUALITY OF OPPORTUNITY." This kind of individual liberty—guaranteed to the individual *by* the state, rather than simply protected for the individual *against* the state—had a far more egalitarian and radical thrust than the individual liberty preached by the Social Darwinists.

Yet working-class unity of doctrine depended in large part on workers' class-consciousness, which Marx and others found lacking in the United States. The American labor market, Marx said, was repeatedly emptied "by the continuous conversion of wages laborers into independent, self-sustaining peasants. The function of a wages laborer is for a very large part of the American people but a probational state, which they are sure to leave in a longer or shorter term." Others observed that the workers, like other Americans, were "infected" by Social Darwinism and domestic Algerism. And by the late 1860s the American working class itself was fundamentally divided between socialists calling for radical economic and political efforts to transform or replace capitalism, and trade unionists trying to improve their economic conditions within the existing system.

Orthodox Marxists expected that American workers would go through a period of trade unionism; then, bamboozled or broken by the bosses, the trade unions would convert into a socialist movement. Rather, the reverse happened. Militant socialism had its heyday during the seventies and eighties and then gave way to a bread-and-butter "business unionism" that was the bane of all good Marxist socialists.

To many Americans in these years, socialism was not a new idea. The communitarianism of Robert Owen and the futuristic utopianism of Charles Fourier had excited the avant-garde in the East and had helped stimulate the founding of socialistic and egalitarian communities, especially in western rural areas. In the East, socialist ideas had taken root among sections of the working class. Germans and other Europeans fleeing from the repressions after the unrest of '48 had brought radical ideas across the Atlantic. By the 1870s, German socialists and trade unionists, swelled by arrivals now escaping from Bismarck's antisocialist laws, were organizing "Educational and Defensive" associations to protect themselves against police and employer repression.

European radicals brought a good deal of experience and sophistication to American socialism, but they tended to be hopelessly divided over philosophy and doctrine. Marx and Engels transferred the International Workingmen's Association from London to New York in 1872, not to find richer proletarian soil but to kill it off, for the first International had become, in their view, fatally infected with Bakuninist anarchism. Marxian socialists, under the leadership of Marx's American lieutenant, Friedrich Sorge, pursued two political strategies, forming the Socialist-Labor party in 1877 but also operating through sections of the trade union movement, notably Adolph Strasser's cigar-makers. Both Marxists and anarchists in turn jousted with Lasallean Socialists, followers of the great German revolutionary and romantic, who had been killed in a duel over a love affair in 1864 but whose belief in political action profoundly influenced his German-American followers.

In the tiny cauldrons of left-wing dispute, in the saloons and beer gardens and union halls of Chicago and St. Louis, of New York and Cincinnati and a dozen other cities, Marxist ideas collided and coalesced with these and other rival doctrines. Not only did Marxists compete with bread-and-butter trade unionists, with communitarians pursuing their dreams of brotherhood and sisterhood, with populists seeking relief for farmers, with native-grown socialists, with evangelical radicals, syndicalists, utopians of every hue, but these rival groups also divided among themselves over means if not ends—over political action versus economic, peaceful tactics versus violent, third-party tactics versus major-party collaboration, over internal organization and external propaganda, over questions of timing, leadership, money, secrecy, discipline.

Not only did many socialist battalions tend to be dominated by their talented German chieftains, thus alienating Irish, native Americans, and other groups, but they also attracted cranks, fanatics, charlatans, and polemicists. Doubtless the controversial Woodhull sisters were hardly socialism's greatest asset in the early seventies, though they had earned their salt by publishing in *Woodhull & Claflin's Weekly*, for the first time in the United States, the *Communist Manifesto*. But socialism at this point scarcely needed the nostrums spouting from their editorial page—Pantocracy (universal government), Universology (universal science), Alwatol (universal language), cooperation of the Spirit-World with the Mundane Sphere, and

"The Universal Formula of Universological Science—UNISM, DUISM and TRUISM."

* * *

During these years, thousands of American workers were pursuing a dream of their own—organization into one great national union that could face powerful corporations on its own terms. In the late 1860s, fearing both the concerted opposition of employers and the competition of immigrants, leaders of machinists, carpenters, and other national brotherhoods organized the National Labor Union, which focused on local producers' cooperatives and on national political action. The NLU helped win the eight-hour day in several states and for federal government laborers and mechanics. In 1872, the NLU had the audacity to convert itself into the National Labor Reform party and even to nominate Judge David Davis, Lincoln's old crony, for President; Davis's withdrawal doomed both the union and the party.

Labor organization, especially national, was still fixed in an old pattern: trade unionism—especially "business" unionism—seemed to thrive during good times, and then collapse in the face of depression as union members faded away along with their jobs. Many socialists, Marxists or otherwise, not only expected this but welcomed it, for workers must learn not to be so dependent on capitalism. Indeed, let "wage slavery" go on, they urged, let it expand so far as to leave wealth to "only two or three capitalists out of the millions of workers," and then a large and united workers' movement would take over. But most of the millions of workers preferred bread-and-butter unionism, step-by-step improvement.

The socialist strategy met a sharp testing in the mid-seventies. Only nine of thirty national unions survived the panic-induced depression of '73; union membership was decimated, reaching a low point of 50,000 members in 1878. The aftermath was not an enlarged and united socialist movement turning to political action in order to transform society, but despair, demoralization, unrest, protest, violence, and terrorism. In Pennsylvania the "Molly Maguires," an outgrowth of the anti-landlord Ancient Order of Hibernians in Ireland, terrorized the coalfields, systematically killing railroad bosses who ran the mines. Then, in 1877, wage cuts on the Baltimore & Ohio, the Pennsylvania, the New York Central, and other railroads brought a phenomenon few had expected in the United States— a "general strike" of railroad and other workers. As violence spread across the nation's railways, America for a time seemed on the brink of revolution. Railroad strikers and others seized junctions and depots, burned hundreds of freight cars, looted stores, exchanged fire with troops, even tried to stop a militia regiment in Baltimore from sallying forth from its armory.

The response was quick and harsh. Federal troops crushed the strike in Pittsburgh, after twenty-six persons had been killed. The army "restored order" in Martinsburg, West Virginia. State legislatures revived their old anti-strike laws. Found guilty of murder on the testimony of a secret Pinkerton infiltrator, ten Molly Maguires were hanged. Capitalists of diverse views seemed to unite against labor. Earlier, when railroad engineers had struck the Boston & Maine, Charles Francis Adams, Jr., had called for decent wages and conditions for railroad workers, but since the lines were public utilities, he wanted strikes to be outlawed and militant strikers fined and jailed.

Then, out of this suffering and violence, there developed perhaps the grandest effort American workers ever made to build a nationwide union, militant yet responsible. It was an organization that called itself noble—the Noble Order of the Knights of Labor. Founded as a clandestine society at a tailors' meeting in Philadelphia in 1871, the Knights shed their secrecy a decade later, opening their ranks to skilled and unskilled, men and women, immigrants and blacks—to all except saloon-keepers, gamblers, stockbrokers, bankers, lawyers, and doctors. Organized into local and district assemblies embracing workers of diverse crafts and skills, the Knights were a highly centralized but democratic organization, with their assemblies made responsible to the general executive board and to the Grand Master Workman. At last workers had "one big union."

The Knights, responding to a deep economic and psychological need among workers, rose like a meteor from about 100,000 members in 1885 to almost 700,000 a year later. Under its longtime Grand Master, Terence V. Powderly—"part idealist, part politician, part mountebank," in John Garraty's view—the Knights favored the eight-hour day, the graduated income tax, prohibition of imported contract labor, consumers' and producers' cooperatives, an end to the monopoly power of railroads and banks. Officially the Knights were opposed to labor violence, class conflict, and socialism. "I hate the word 'class,' " Powderly said, "and would drive it from the English language if I could." But their language was often radical and their songs militant:

> Toiling millions now are waking—
> See them marching on;
> All the tyrants now are shaking,
> Ere their power's gone.
> *Chorus:* Storm the fort, ye Knights of Labor.
> Battle for your cause;

> Equal rights for every neighbor—
> Down with tyrant laws!

While Powderly was still preaching cooperation, education, and reform, workers within the Knights of Labor and outside began striking in response to depression wage cuts and other ills. Thousands of unorganized workers walked off their jobs and joined the Knights. In the "great upheaval" of 1884, railroad union locals struck the whole southwestern system, controlled by Jay Gould. After the governors of both Missouri and Kansas backed up the strikers, Gould retreated. Wounding this capitalist dragon emboldened thousands more workers to join the noble order.

As the Knights of Labor burgeoned in numbers, however, it slackened in discipline. More strikes broke out, beyond the control of the Grand Worthies now running the organization. The Knights' decline seemed as fleet as a falling star. In the fateful year of 1886, the Knights again struck the "blood-sucking corporations" of Gould's southwestern system, only to give up the effort, amid violence and arrests, when the financier refused even to arbitrate. A general strike in Chicago for the eight-hour day collapsed. And the Knights suffered from the public hysteria following an incident in Chicago during the general strike.

This was the Haymarket Massacre. In origin it had nothing to do with the Knights, and involved a strike at the McCormick Harvester plant begun months before the general strike. After a violent clash at McCormick's, a small group of anarchist revolutionaries put out a flammable circular in English and German charging that "your masters sent out their blood-hounds—the police—they killed six of your brothers" (one had been killed) and calling for a protest meeting in Haymarket Square. The much-advertised "revenge" meeting was a flop: the crowd was disappointingly low, the speeches turgid, the weather rainy. The last speaker, his beard dripping, had just told the few hundred people still lingering that his was the last speech and "then we'll all go home," when a phalanx of 180 policemen swung into the square. Their captain ordered the crowd to "peaceably disperse." "Why, Captain," said the speaker, "we *are* peaceable."

There was a moment of tense silence, then a bomb burst among the police. Amid their dead and stricken comrades, the police re-formed ranks and opened fire on the crowd; workers fired back, then dragged their dead and wounded to friends' homes. Seven policemen died, seventy more were wounded, workers' casualties could never be calculated but doubtless were higher. Later, eight alleged anarchists were convicted on the charge of conspiracy and four were hanged.

1886 was a decisive year for American labor. Although the Chicago
Knights of Labor denied any sympathy or connection with the "cowardly
murderers" who had caused riot and bloodshed, the whole organization
was tainted and its decline began. The battle brought the first major "red
scare" in American history. It led some workers to abandon force, turned
others into ardent revolutionaries. It created, in Henry David's view,
"America's first revolutionary martyrs." Reactions to Haymarket brought
the drive for the eight-hour day temporarily to a halt.

*   *   *

1886 was also the year in which a whole new national labor organization
was founded, an old economic and political strategy revitalized and broadened, and the socialist and other radical trade unions outflanked.

The American Federation of Labor was founded in December 1886
in Columbus, Ohio, by twenty-five labor groups representing perhaps
150,000 members, mostly skilled workers. Its origin lay in a remarkable
craft union, the Cigarmakers' International, which numbered many Germans of the "old schools," both socialist and unionist. In part because the
cigar-makers had to face new technology, such as cigar molds and bunch-
breaking machines, that threatened their jobs, in part because they lived
amid philosophical debate and indeed liked to make their cigars while
someone read aloud from the classics, this union had to face all the urgent
questions of organization, discipline, centralization, political action, craft
exclusiveness that had challenged trade unionism from the start. Arguing
bitterly, some stuck to their craft union, some joined the Knights of Labor.
The cigar-makers were lucky to have leaders able intellectually to meet this
challenge.

One of them was Adolph Strasser, a Hungarian immigrant who had
proved a resourceful organizer of New York City cigar-makers. Strasser
was all practicality, which he defined as advancing the interests of cigar-
makers through patient negotiation, limited goals, and ample union benefits such as insurance. At a Senate committee hearing in 1883 on labor-
capital relations a senator asked him:

"Do you not contemplate, in the end, the participation of all labor and
of all men in the benefits of trades unions?"

"Our organization does not consist of idealists," Strasser answered.
"We do not control the production of the world. That is controlled by the
employers. I look first to cigars."

"I was only asking you in regard to your ultimate ends," the senator
persisted.

"We have no ultimate ends. We are going on from day to day. We are fighting only for immediate objects—objects that can be realized in a few years."

At first, Samuel Gompers too looked only to cigars. Born in a London tenement in 1850, the son of a Jewish cigar-maker, at thirteen he had emigrated with his family to New York's Lower East Side, where he and his father resumed cigar-making. Breathing in the heady New York atmosphere, he attended lectures at Cooper Union, read aloud, listened, and argued in the cigar-makers' workrooms. At first, Gompers spouted "wild plans for human betterment," as he recalled much later, but on the advice of a former Marxist who told him, "Study your union card, Sam, and if the idea doesn't square with that, it ain't true," he veered toward business unionism. Chosen head of his local, he, with Strasser, centralized control, boosted membership dues, and organized unemployment, strike, sickness, and accident benefits.

It was these ideas that Gompers carried into the organization of a new national federation. A sturdy, outspoken man of inexhaustible enthusiasm and energy, he articulated better than any of his comrades the philosophy of pragmatic labor organization and action. He wanted practical results: wages, hours, safety, benefits. From such advances, workers could progress further in economic and moral education and in their understanding of ultimate ends. The first step was to improve conditions of work and life. "The more the improved conditions prevail, the greater discontent prevails with any wrongs that may exist. It is only . . . the enlightenment begotten from material prosperity that makes it at all possible for mental advancement." This idea sharply separated Gompers's strategy from the Marxists'.

Gompers, indeed, was almost a neo-Social Darwinist in his ideology. He accepted industrialization and free enterprise. Capitalism was progress, and profits were necessary to capitalism. As corporations and trusts gained more power, labor must do the same—through solidly based organization. In the organization of business unions, Gompers believed that, in order to protect the adult male wage, unskilled as well as skilled, women as well as men, blacks as well as whites, ought to take part, though on a subordinate basis. These were "practical" views, for he believed not that blacks were equal to whites but that they could take over white jobs and hence must be organized. The same applied to women and immigrants. All this was crucial to the ability of organized labor to compete with organized capital.

He was far more cautious in regard to political action. He fought off any involvement of the AFL with socialist parties, preferring to deal with the major parties on the basis of expediency. He gave clear priority to economic action over political. Workers should expect little from the government. "The only desirable legislation for the workers," as a group of scholars later summarized Gompers's and the AFL's position, "is that which offers protection to their labor market by restriction of immigration, and which restrains government activities, such as the courts and police, from encroaching upon or hampering such union activities as strikes, picketing, and boycotts. The workers ought not to demand more positive legislation from the government. . . . Therefore such legislation as they need can be obtained more readily by opposing or supporting candidates of the two large parties rather than by organizing a separate labor party." Above all, no long-range, visionary programs or tactics should be used.

Government hands-off—broker politics—gradual betterment: this was Gompers's and Strasser's response to the Social Darwinism of the day; this was their own Social Darwinism. During the capitalist boom, it was an idea that seemed to work. While the Knights declined in leaps and bounds, the AFL moved ahead in numbers as slowly—and as steadily—as the tortoise. Its tests would come with hard times and in a political situation in which both "large parties" were conservative, and labor might have to look for allies on the left. By the late 1880s, such a potential ally seemed to be rising in America's South and West.

THE ALLIANCE: A DEMOCRACY OF LEADERS

Somewhere in central Texas, sometime in the late eighties: In the twilight splendor of the Plains, men and women march along dusty trails toward the glow of a campfire in the distance. Some walk; some ride horses or burros; some —whole families—jolt along on covered wagons or buckboards. With their creased, careworn faces, their poor gingham clothes, they might seem to be one more trek in the great western movement of American homesteaders. But not so. These people walk with hope and pride—even with exhilaration as they reach a hillcrest and see stretching for miles ahead and behind thousands of people marching with them, hundreds of wagons emblazoned with crude signs and banners. Soon they reach their encampment, not to settle down for the night but, in company with five or ten thousand comrades, to hear fiery speeches late into the evening.

These people will be part of an arresting venture in popular grass-roots democracy, part of the "flowering of the largest democratic mass movement in American history," in Lawrence Goodwyn's judgment. Ultimately they will fail—but not until they have given the nation an experiment in democratic ideas, creative leadership and followership, and comradely cooperation.

At first on the Texas frontier but soon in the South and Midwest, farmers in the mid-1880s collectively sensed that something was terribly wrong. In the South, farmers white and black were shackled by the crop lien system and the plummeting price of cotton. In the West, homesteaders were losing their mortgaged homes. Grain prices fell so low that Kansas farm families burned corn for heat. Everywhere farmers suffered from a contracting currency, heavy taxation, and gouging by railroads and other monopolies. As farmers perceived the "money power" buying elections and public officials in order to pass class legislation, some agrarian leaders and editors wondered if the farm areas trembled on the brink of revolution.

The crop lien system, tight money, and the rest of the farmers' ills—these seemed remote and impersonal to many an eastern city dweller. But for countless Southern cotton farmers "crop lien" set the conditions of their existence.

It meant walking into the store of the "furnishing merchant," approaching the counter with head down and perhaps hat in hand, and murmuring a list of needs. It meant paying "the man" no money but watching him list items and figures in a big ledger. It meant returning month after month for these mumbled exchanges, as the list of debts grew longer. It meant, as noted earlier, that the farmer brought in the produce from his long year's hard labor, watched his cotton weighed and sold, and then learned that the figures in the ledger, often with enormously inflated interest, added up to more than his crop was worth—but that the merchant would carry him into the next year if he signed a note mortgaging his next year's crop to the merchant. It meant returning home for another year's toil, knowing that he might lose his spread and join the army of landless tenant farmers. From start to finish it meant fear, self-abasing deference, hatred of self and others.

Above all, the system meant loss of liberty, as the farmer became shackled to one crop and one merchant—loss of liberty for men and women raised in the Jeffersonian tradition of individual freedom in a decentralized agrarian republic, in the Jacksonian tradition of equality of opportunity in a land free of usurious banks and grasping monopolies. Their forefathers had fought for independence; was a second American revolution needed to overthrow a new, an economic, monarchy? "Laboring men of America," proclaimed a tract, the voices of 1776 "ring down through the corridors of time and tell you to strike" against the "monopolies and combinations that are eating out the heart of the Nation." But strike how? "Not with glittering musket, flaming sword and deadly cannon," the pamphlet exhorted, "but with the silent, potent and all-powerful ballot, the only vestige of liberty left."

One course seemed clear—people must organize themselves as power-fully against the trusts as the trusts were organized against them. But organize how? Economically or politically? Experience did not make for easy answers. Farmers had plunged into politics with Greenbackers and laborites and ended up on the short end of the ballot counts. The answer of the recently founded Farmers' Alliance in Texas was to try both eco-nomic and political structures, but more intensively and comprehensively than ever before. Built firmly on a network of "suballiances"—neighbor-hood chapters of several dozen members meeting once or twice a month to pray, sing, conduct rituals, debate issues, and do organizational business —the state Alliance experimented with several types of grass-roots cooper-atives, including stores, county trade committees to bargain with mer-chants, and county-wide "bulking" of cotton.

The key to Alliance power was not organization, though, but leadership —and not the leadership merely of a few persons at the top but of dozens, then hundreds, of men and women who were specially hired and trained to journey across the state visiting suballiances, helping to form new ones, and above all teaching members graphically and in detail about the com-plex political and economic issues of the day, both national issues like money and finance and local ones like the building and expanding of co-ops. These were the famed "lecturers," who in turn were responsible to a state lecturer. The Alliance's first state lecturer was William Lamb, a rugged, red-haired, thirty-four-year-old farmer. Born in Tennessee, he had traveled alone at sixteen to the Texas frontier, where he lived in a log hut until he could build a house, raise children with his wife, and learn to read and write at night.

Lamb soon emerged as one of the most creative and radical of Alliance leaders. When the Great Southwest Strike erupted against Jay Gould's railroad early in 1886, Lamb defied the more conservative Alliance leaders by demanding that the Alliance back a Knights of Labor boycott. Though suballiances gave food and money to striking railroad workers, the strike collapsed. The Knights continued on their downward slide, but the Texas Alliance continued its phenomenal growth, with perhaps 2,000 subal-liances and 100,000 members by the summer of that year.

Lamb and other lecturers also took leadership on another critical issue facing the Alliance. Wracked by scorching drought, crop failures, and increasing tenancy, Texas farmers by 1886 were meeting in schoolhouses and clamoring for a new strategy—*political* action. They were impatient with the old shibboleth that the Alliance must steer clear of politics because politics would kill it. The decisive turning point in the agrarian revolt came at the Alliance state convention in Cleburne in early August 1886. A majority of the disgruntled, rustic-looking delegates from eighty-four counties "demanded" of the state and federal governments "such legislation as shall secure to our people freedom from the onerous and shameful abuses that the industrial classes are now suffering at the hands of arrogant capitalists and arrogant corporations"—legislation including an interstate commerce law and land reform measures. A conservative minority, opposing a proposal for greenbacks that defied the Democratic party, rejected the demands, absconded with the treasury, and formed a strictly "nonpartisan" Alliance.

At this critical moment Charles Macune, another leader fresh from the grass roots, stepped into the fray. Settled on the Texas frontier at nineteen after early years of poverty and wanderings, Macune had married, studied law and medicine, and practiced both. Developing into a skillful writer, compelling speaker, and innovative thinker, Macune had become well versed in farming matters and active in his county Alliance. And now this tall, magnetic physician-lawyer-farmer, buoyed by the rising militance of the delegates, proposed an ingenious compromise that was also a creative act of leadership.

Persuading the conservatives to give up their rival Alliance and the radicals to tone down their drive toward partisan politics, he proposed an expansion that was both geographic and functional. In his dazzling vision, a national network of state Alliance "Exchanges," starting in Texas, would collectively market cotton and buy supplies and farm equipment. This giant farmers' cooperative would not only achieve higher, more stable prices, but would provide the credit to free all farmers from the furnishing merchant and mortgage company. Thus, he proclaimed, mortgage-burdened farmers could "assert their freedom from the tyranny of organized capital." At a statewide meeting at Waco in January 1887 the farmer delegates enthusiastically adopted Macune's grand strategy, decided on merger with the Louisiana Farmers' Union, and chose Macune as first president of the National Farmers' Alliance and Cooperative Union. The state Alliance built a huge headquarters in Dallas even while doubling its membership and preparing a small army of lecturers to proselytize the South during mid-1887.

Even that army of enthusiasts seemed astonished by the response. "The farmers seemed like unto ripe fruit," one reported from North Carolina. "You can garner them by a gentle shake of the bush." He had held twenty-seven meetings in one county and left twenty-seven suballiances in his wake. With cotton down to eight cents a pound, farmers were desperate for relief. Together they and the lecturers set up trade committees, cotton yards, and warehouses in hundreds of counties, along with state exchanges. Georgia, with its big state exchange and its cooperative stores, gins, and warehouses, was the most successful. When manufacturers of the commonly used jute bagging organized a trust and doubled the price, the Georgia Alliance—and later other state groups—successfully boycotted the "jute trust," using cotton or pine straw instead, while protesting farmers donned cotton bagging and even witnessed a double wedding in which both brides and both grooms were decked out in that finery.

The idea of farm cooperation swept into the Midwest. The Alliance came to be most deeply rooted in the corn and wheat fields of Kansas, where a great boom had busted in 1887 amid mounting debts and foreclosures. When political efforts failed the next year, farm leaders visited Texas and returned full of missionary zeal. The formation of suballiances and the building of cooperatives proceeded feverishly until the entire state boasted of over 3,000 local units. When the "twine trust" hiked by 50 percent the price of the twine used to bind wheat, Alliance staged a boycott. The trust lowered its price.

As early as 1889, however, Alliance leaders in Kansas were concluding that education and cooperation were not enough, that electoral political action was necessary too. The question was not whether to engage in politics but how—independent political action versus third-party efforts versus working through a major party; lobbying and pressuring established parties versus direct action to take power. The existing political landscape was barren. The Republican and Democratic parties both were sectional entities, appealing to lingering Civil War hatreds to win elections. Farmers who actually shared common conditions and needs were polarized by politicians who waved the bloody shirt. Though most farm leaders in Kansas spurned "partisan politics" at every turn, what they actually rejected was the familiar brand of party politics animated by sectionalism and penetrated by railroad and other monopolies. Many envisioned not just an alternative party, but an alternative *kind* of party that would overcome racial and sectional hatred and respond to grass-roots needs.

A county "people's convention" that nominated—and elected—a "people's ticket" for county offices against the trusts inspired Alliance leaders in Kansas to raise their sights to state action. A convention of industrial organizations in Topeka, with delegates from the Knights of Labor and the "single tax" movement as well as from Alliance groups, assembled in Representative Hall in the statehouse, formally set up the People's Party of Kansas, and called a state convention to choose statewide candidates and adopt the first People's Party platform.

Once again new leaders emerged out of this agitation and conflict. In the "Big Seventh" congressional district in southwest Kansas, a Medicine

Lodge rancher and town marshal named Jerry Simpson quickly emerged as the most noted Kansas Populist. A sailor on the Great Lakes and later an Illinois soldier in the Civil War, Simpson had run a farm and sawmill in northeastern Kansas before turning to cattle-raising. After the harsh winter of 1887 killed his cattle and destroyed his life's savings, he turned to the Alliance and the new political insurgency.

Simpson won his imperishable title as "Sockless Jerry" during his campaign in 1890 against Colonel James Hallowell. "I tried to get hold of the crowd," Simpson recalled. "I referred to the fact that my opponent was known as a 'Prince.' Princes, I said, wear silk socks. I don't wear any." Hallowell, he went on, boasted that he had been to Topeka and had made laws. Picking up a book, Simpson recalled, he tapped on a page with his finger. "I said, here is one of Hal's laws. I find that it is a law to tax dogs, but I see that Hal proposes to charge two dollars for a bitch and only one dollar for a son of a bitch. Now the party I belong to believes in equal and exact justice to all."

Women leaders in Kansas attracted even more attention than the men. "Women who never dreamed of becoming public speakers," wrote Annie Diggs, "grew eloquent in their zeal and fervor. Josh Billings' saying that 'wimmin is everywhere,' was literally true in that wonderful picknicking, speech-making Alliance summer of 1890." While most Alliance women did rather mundane tasks, a good number of them emerged as compelling leaders and stump speakers. Diggs herself had worked actively in the Women's Christian Temperance Union in Kansas and as a lay preacher in the Unitarian Church when, in the mid-eighties, she journeyed east to become Boston correspondent for several Kansas papers. She returned to Kansas, worked with the Alliance, wrote on suffrage and temperance and Alliance issues despite a public disavowal by her Republican editor, and then joined Stephen McLallin, a leading Populist editor, as associate editor of the Topeka *Advocate.* Together they shaped it into the leading reform paper in the state.

There were other noted women leaders: Fanny McCormick, assistant state lecturer who ran for state superintendent of public instruction; Sarah Emery, author of the widely read *Seven Financial Conspiracies* and a spellbinding orator; Kansas-born Fanny Vickrey, another gifted orator. But attracting most attention of all was the indomitable Mary Lease.

Lease was born in Pennsylvania of parents who were Irish political exiles and grew up in a family devastated by the Civil War; her two brothers died in the fighting, her father in Andersonville prison. She moved to Kansas in the early 1870s, taught parochial school, raised a family, tried and failed at farming, studied law—"pinning sheets of notes above her wash tub"—

became one of the first woman lawyers of Kansas, and began a tempestu-
ous career as a speaker for Irish nationalism, temperance, woman's suffrage, union labor, and the Alliance. A tall, stately woman, she had "a
golden voice," in William Allen White's recollection, "a deep, rich con-
tralto, a singing voice that had hypnotic qualities." But she could also hurl
"sentences like Jove hurled thunderbolts," Diggs said, as she gave scores
of speeches, some over two hours long, throughout Kansas. Pointing to the
starving families of Chicago and the wasted corn piled along the railroad
tracks or burned for heat, she exclaimed, "What you farmers need to do
is to raise less corn and more Hell!"

Led by such women and men champions, propelled by acute needs and
high hopes, the Kansas Populists roared to a sensational victory in 1890.
They carried 96 of the 125 seats in the state's lower house and swept five
out of seven congressional districts, sending Sockless Jerry along with the
four others to Washington.

"THE PEOPLE ON TOP!" headlined the *Nonconformist*. But were they? The
Populists elected only one statewide official, their candidate for attorney
general. The Republicans still controlled the state administration, the
holdover Senate, and the judiciary. The House passed a woman's suffrage
bill but the Senate axed it. The Populists' one victory was to oust a conservative United States senator and send Populist editor William Peffer to
Washington in his place. And now they had a crucial issue—Republican
subversion of the will of the people. The Kansas Populists conducted a
repeat crusade in 1892 with massive parades and encampments. This time
they elected the entire state ticket and most of their congressional candidates again, including Simpson, and gained control of the Senate—but lost
their majority in the House, amid accusations of wholesale Republican
fraud.

The "first People's party government on earth" was inaugurated in
Topeka at the start of 1893. After a spectacular parade through downtown
Topeka the new governor, Lorenzo Lewelling, gave a stirring address—his
"incendiary Haymarket inaugural," a GOP editor called it—followed by
Lease and Simpson. But the gala was shortlived. When the new legislature
convened, the Populists organized the state Senate, but they and the
Republicans each claimed a majority in the House. There followed a tug-
of-war that would have been comic opera if the stakes had not been so high:
each "majority" organized its own "House" with speaker and officers;
neither side would vacate the hall, so they stayed put all night, with the two
speakers sleeping, gavels in hand, facing each other behind the podium;
finally Lewelling called up the militia—including a Gatling gun minus its
firing pin—while the Republicans mobilized an army of deputy sheriffs,

college students, and railroad workers. The GOP legislators smashed their way into the hall with a sledgehammer; and the militia commander, a loyal Republican like most of his troops, refused the governor's order to expel the invaders.

Bloodshed was narrowly averted when the Populists agreed to let the Republican-dominated Kansas Supreme Court rule on the issue, and predictably the court ruled against them. The Populists then paid the price. Their legislators fared worse than in 1891, passing two election reform measures and putting suffrage on the ballot, but not accomplishing much else. Their chief priority, railroad regulation with teeth, was a direct casualty of the conflict. Clearly, under the American and Kansan systems of checks and balances, a movement could win elections but still not win power.

Alliance cooperation and Populist politics spread through other Northern states, moving west into the mountain states toward the Pacific, north into Minnesota and the Dakotas, east into the big corn spreads. Everywhere the new movement mobilized people and encountered Republican party power and entrenched elites. Thus "in sundry ways, at different speeds, at varied levels of intensity, and at diverse stages of political consciousness, the farmers brought the People's Party of the United States into being," in Goodwyn's summarization. "In so doing, they placed on the nation's political stage the first multi-sectional democratic mass movement since the American Revolution."

*   *   *

It was in the South, however, that the Alliance continued to expand most dramatically and yet to encounter the biggest obstacles. The first of these obstacles was the Southern Democracy, which continued to live off its role as defender of the Lost Cause. The second, closely connected, was race—not *simply* race, as C. Vann Woodward has explained, but "the complexities of the class economy growing out of race, the heritage of manumitted slave psychology, and the demagogic uses to which the politician was able to put race prejudice." Southern Populists reluctantly concluded that they could not achieve the subtreasury plan for credit and currency and other reforms unless they forged a biracial coalition of small landowners, tenant farmers, and sharecroppers. This meant war with the Southern Democracy and potential division within Populism.

Georgia was an even more tumultuous battleground than Kansas. There one man, backed by the mass of poor farmers, personified the entire movement: Tom Watson. Descended from prosperous slaveholders, he had seen his father lose his forty-five slaves and 1,400 acres after Appomattox and end up as a tavern owner in Augusta. Young Watson managed to spend two years at Mercer University before running out of money. After years of poverty he turned to law, prospered, and won election to the Georgia lower house at twenty-six, but quit before his term ended.

"I did not lead the Alliance," Watson recalled. "I followed the Alliance, and I am proud that I did." After taking leadership in the "jute fight," he decided to run for Congress as a Democrat with Alliance backing. The white Georgia Alliance sought to field its own candidates within the Democratic party and back non-Alliance candidates only if they endorsed the Alliance program—the "Alliance yardstick," they called it. Alliance leaders took over the Democratic party state convention, wrote the party platform, won control of both houses of the "farmers' legislature," elected the governor and six of ten members of Congress. Watson trounced his Republican opponent almost ten to one in a fight as "hot as Nebuchadnezzar's furnace."

Coalitions embody conflicts. The lines were now drawn between Alliance members who were mainly Democrats and Democrats who were mainly Alliancers. The national Alliance had urged that its members of Congress not join any party caucus that did not endorse the Alliance platform. The whole Southern delegation but one stayed with the majority Democratic caucus and elected a Georgian, Charles Crisp, to the speakership. The exception was Watson. He and Sockless Jerry Simpson introduced the Alliance platform into Congress, fighting especially hard for the subtreasury proposal. Virtually none of the platform was even reported out of committee except the subtreasury item, which finally came to the floor after Watson used every maneuver to pry it out of committee; by then it was too late for action.

Beaten in Washington, Watson flourished politically at home. This was a time when many black tenants and sharecroppers were becoming alienated from the GOP and were turning to the new party. Watson called on blacks as well as whites to overthrow the plutocracy that had used race hatred to bolster its rule. "You are kept apart," he told black and white Georgians, "that you may be separately fleeced of your earnings." Campaigning for reelection in 1892, now as leader of the Georgia People's Party, Watson championed political equality for blacks, economic equality to a lesser extent—and social equality or "mixing" not at all. But despite both white and black Populist support, Watson was beaten for reelection in a campaign marked by massive election fraud and the killing of a score of Populists, most of them black.

Texas was having its own problems with the entrenched white Democracy and entrenched capital. The Texas Alliance Exchange, the linchpin of cooperative efforts, had gotten off to a flying start by selling vast amounts of cotton to eastern mills and abroad and buying supplies and equipment. Still, it could not break the enslavement of tenants and sharecroppers to the crop lien system, and increasingly it suffered from lack of capital. Banks in Dallas and elsewhere turned a cold face to requests for loans. Desperately the leadership turned to the suballiances themselves for money. In a remarkable popular mobilization, thousands of farmers marched to county courthouses to pledge help. It was not enough; a year later the Texas Exchange closed its doors for good.

The ever-resourceful Charles Macune now presented his subtreasury plan, providing treasury notes to farmers, as a means of financing cooperatives with public rather than private credit and thus enlisting the government in the struggle to raise agricultural prices. The indefatigable William Lamb fashioned this economic reform into a weapon of political revolt as he launched a full-scale lecturing campaign in each congressional district. The Texas Alliance won a stunning victory through the Democratic party in 1890, electing a governor and a legislature committed to most Alliance demands, but a host of Democratic "loyalists" opposed the subtreasury and bolted from the Alliance. Spurred by Lamb and other leaders, Alliance members decided to create the People's Party of Texas. At the founding convention in August 1891 white and black delegates forged a remarkable coalition, with a commitment to political and economic equality for blacks.

As the presidential election year of 1892 approached, Alliance leaders were concluding that a *national* People's Party was needed to consolidate the grand coalition of farmers and workers, strengthen the state parties, and seize control of the federal government. Plans were carefully laid. The Alliance organized a massive lecturing campaign, distributed vast quantities of books and pamphlets, including Bellamy's *Looking Backward,* and formed a National Reform Press Association to coordinate the propaganda efforts of the one-hundred-strong Populist newspapers. A St. Louis conference of farm, labor, and women delegates drew up a platform and heard the Minnesota Populist orator and novelist Ignatius Donnelly give an unforgettable speech in which he charged: "Corruption dominates the ballot box, the legislatures, the Congress, and touches even the ermine of the bench. . . . The fruits of the toil of millions are boldly stolen to build up colossal fortunes, unprecedented in the history of the world, while their possessors despise the republic and endanger liberty. From the same prolific womb of governmental injustice we breed two great classes—paupers and millionaires."

Then came the national founding convention of the People's Party, Omaha, July 4, 1892. The delegates adopted a platform that harked back

to the "Cleburne demands" six years earlier and indeed to decades of labor, farm, and socialist manifestos: a flexible "national currency" to be distributed by means of the subtreasury plan; free and unlimited coinage of silver and gold; a graduated income tax; government ownership and operation of the railroads, telegraph, and telephone; barring of alien land ownership and return of land held by railroads and other corporations "in excess of their actual needs"; political reforms such as the direct election of United States senators. But the platform ignored labor's most urgent needs and omitted mention of woman's suffrage. The convention also took a moderate course in nominating for president James B. Weaver of Iowa, the reform editor and ex-Union general who had led the Greenbackers in 1880, balancing him with an ex-Confederate general as his running mate.

Plunging into the election campaign, the Populists unsheathed their thousands of lecturers, their orators such as Lease and Donnelly, their tactics in some states of opportunistic coalition-building with Republicans in the South and especially with Democrats in the West. Weaver and his wife were rotten-egged in the South—Mrs. Weaver to the point that, according to Lease, she "was made a regular walking omelet by the southern chivalry of Georgia." The results were promising for a fledgling third party: Weaver polled over one million votes, actually carrying Kansas and four western states with twenty-two electoral votes. Populist governors were elected in Kansas, Colorado, and North Dakota. But in the Northeast, parts of the Midwest, and the South the party fared poorly. In Texas the Populists lost badly to the Democrats. It was with mingled hopes and an exhilarating sense of momentum that the Populists turned to the economic and political struggles ahead.

The idea of liberty had been the animating impulse behind the Alliance. But during the century soon to come to an end that idea had also guided organized capital and labor. Each group of course meant something different by "liberty"—businessmen meant freedom from interference with property, labor meant freedom from boss control of its working life, farmers meant freedom from furnishing merchants, banks, railroads, trusts. More than the other groups, however, the Alliance had made liberty into a positive idea—realizing and fulfilling oneself by gaining broader control of one's working environment through participation in Alliance cooperatives. Along with industrial workers, Populist farmers had also preached the idea of equality—a real equality of opportunity. But the cooperators, with their denunciations of "selfish individualism," had moved even more than labor toward the third great concept in the Enlightenment trinity—fraternity, or comradeship. The idea of cooperation had grown out of, and had sustained, the practices of sisterhood and brotherhood.

And if the Populists had realized all three values to a greater extent than any other large group, it was mainly because of a conscious effort toward the intensive use of massive numbers of second-cadre activists—35,000 or more "lecturers"—in rousing farmers to political self-consciousness. As in all deeply felt democratic movements, the great leaders were educators, and the great teachers were leaders.

CHAPTER 6

The Brokers of Politics

DEMOCRACY, rightly understood, is "government of the people, by the people, for the benefit of Senators," scoffed Henry Adams. He reflected a cynicism with American politics and government that was pervasive by the 1880s. The wretched poverty in city and country, the widening gap between rich and poor, the growth of an elaborate class system and an almost fixed array of castes, the suppression of blacks, women, Indians, and others, the violations of people's liberties and rights, the intensifying boom-and-bust, all seemed to blight the hopes and dreams of clement Americans. A democratic government, reflecting the needs—and the votes—of the great mass of citizens, was supposed to avert or alleviate such evils. But the situation seemed to be worsening, the cynicism deepening.

No one had embodied the aspirations of American democracy more exuberantly than a large, dreamy, sensuous, rustic-looking editor and writer in Brooklyn named Walt Whitman, who in 1855 had published at his own expense a volume of poetry that was tall and thin and a commercial failure. It was called *Leaves of Grass.* Looking at the world through his heavy-lidded eyes—eyes that Emerson had called "terrible" and John Burroughs "dumb, yearning, relentless"—Whitman seemed to miss nothing in the multihued world around him, or in his variegated, androgynous self. He wrote of ships, gardens, far-off places, children, trees, the Brooklyn ferry, nearby cities, stallions, women, beaches—everything and anything—and later of war and wounds and death.

He wrote of democracy. The very embodiment of the Enlightenment—"the poet and prophet of a democracy that the America of the Gilded Age was daily betraying," Vernon Parrington said of him—he evoked glowingly the revolutionary trinity of liberty, equality, fraternity. Whitman was familiar with Tocqueville's *Democracy in America* and its emphasis on freedom, and he had read John Stuart Mill's *On Liberty.* "There must be," the poet said, "continual additions to our great experiment of how much liberty society will bear." He preached liberty from external restraints, especially from government, and he practiced it to the point of license.

Even more, he embraced equality, even the kind of "leveling" equality that conservatives derided. "I chant," he wrote, "the common bulk, the

192

general average horde." He spoke of the "divine average." For him, according to Roger Asselineau, the mere fact of living conferred a divine character upon even the most despicable person. He would not look down on anyone:

> Walt Whitman, a kosmos, of Manhattan the son,
> Turbulent, fleshy, sensual, eating, drinking and breeding,
> No sentimentalist, no stander above men and women or apart from them,
> No more modest than immodest. . . .
>
> Whoever degrades another degrades me,
> And whatever is done or said returns at last to me. . . .
>
> I speak the pass-word primeval, I give the sign of democracy. . . .

Again and again in the pages of the Brooklyn *Eagle* he protested the plight of poverty-stricken women in the garment industry, of young clerks having to work sixteen hours a day.

"Great is Liberty! great is equality!" the poet exclaimed, but perhaps most of all he personified the idea of fraternity. He rarely used that term, or "brotherhood," preferring to call people—especially working people—"comrade." An ardent reader of George Sand and Frances Wright, he also preached feminism, proclaiming in *Leaves of Grass* "the perfect equality of the female with the male." Not that he idealized the virtues of men and women: he recognized that his "comrades" were mixtures of good and evil. But if the democratic promise was realized, the good in people would become dominant.

Perhaps it was inevitable that such exaggerated hopes would be dashed in the wake of the Civil War. Even Whitman rapidly succumbed to the postwar disillusionment. "Pride, competition, segregation, vicious wilfulness, and license beyond example, brood already upon us," he wrote in *Democratic Vistas.* Quoting Lincoln on "government by the people," he exclaimed, "The People! . . . Taste, intelligence, and culture, (so-called,)," he said, "have been against the masses, and remain so." He railed against "pervading flippancy and vulgarity, low cunning, infidelity . . . everywhere an abnormal libidinousness, unhealthy forms, male, female, painted, padded, dyed," etc. He still had a basic faith in the people, but now he saw the need for the natural leaders of the race to teach and uplift the people, in contrast to his earlier criticism of Carlyle for scorning the average man and glorifying heroes.

Whitman's ultimate hopes for American democracy lay in the future. Americans were perfectible; only materialism and repression had corrupted them. In London, Karl Marx had harbored the same expectation, though he had little regard for the American form of bourgeois republic. Classes in the United States had "not yet become fixed," he wrote in the early 1850s, "but continually change and interchange their elements in a constant state of flux, where the modern means of production, instead of coinciding with a stagnant surplus population, rather supply the relative deficiency of heads and hands," and where the "feverishly youthful movement of material production" had a "new world to make its own." But later, with the rise of monopolistic capitalism, much would depend on the militant organization of the working class.

Even crusty Henry Adams confessed a hope for the future. After sardonic old Baron Jacobi in *Democracy* called the United States the most corrupt society he had known, one Nathan Gore, Massachusetts historian, burst out:

"I believe in democracy. I accept it. I will faithfully serve and defend it." Democracy, he went on, "asserts the fact that the masses are now raised to higher intelligence than formerly." He granted it was an experiment, but "it was the only direction that society can take that is worth taking."

"And supposing your experiment fails," said Mrs. Lightfoot Lee, "suppose society destroys itself with universal suffrage, corruption, and communism."

"I have faith," Gore exclaimed, "not perhaps in the old dogmas, but in the new ones; faith in human nature; faith in science; faith in the survival of the fittest. . . ."

THE OHIOANS: LEADERS AS BROKERS

Crosby's Opera House, Chicago, May 21, 1868.
The President: "Is the convention ready? I await your pleasure."
A hush falls over the hall. The Republicans have gathered to choose Andrew Johnson's successor.
Mr. Logan of Illinois: "Is it the decision of the Chair that nominations are now in order?"
The President: "They are."
Mr. Logan: "Then, sir, in the name of the loyal citizens, soldiers and sailors of this great Republic of the United States of America; in the name of loyalty, of liberty, of humanity, of justice; in the name of the National Union Republican party; I nominate, as candidate for the Chief Magistracy of this nation, Ulysses S. Grant."
The hall erupts in a roar of cheers, shouts, whistles. Delegates flutter

handkerchiefs and wave standards; some weep as the band plays "Hail to the Chief."

The Secretary: "Alabama!"

The chairman of the Alabama delegation: "Mr. President, Alabama, through the chairman of her delegation, casts eighteen votes for U.S. Grant."

The Secretary: "The State of Connecticut!"

"Mr. President, Connecticut unconditionally surrenders her twelve votes for Ulysses S. Grant. . . ."

The Secretary: "The State of Ohio!"

"Mr. President, Ohio has the honor of being the mother of our great Captain. Ohio is in line, and on that line Ohio proposes following this great Captain, that never knew defeat; to fight it out through the summer, and in the autumn, at the end of the great contest, and to be first in storming the entrenchments, until victory shall be secured, and all the stars that glitter in the firmament of our glorious constellation shall again be restored to their proper order, and all the sons of freedom throughout the whole earth shall shout for joy. Ohio gives forty-two votes for U.S. Grant."

Amid the red, white, and blue bunting, the perfervid oratory, the heat and sweat of the Chicago convention hall, the Republicans nominated for President the "fittest" man of the time, their Civil War hero, Ulysses S. Grant. Five more times in the next three decades a stentorian orator would successfully offer an Ohioan for "the next President of the United States": Grant again in 1872, Rutherford B. Hayes in 1876, James A. Garfield in 1880, William McKinley in 1896 and again in 1900. Ohio would supply two more Presidents in the first two decades of the twentieth century, and during the whole period several Chief Justices and a host of second-cadre leaders—cabinet members, congressional leaders, military and civilian officers.

Thus rose the Ohio dynasty, successor to the Albany Regency earlier in the century and the brilliant Virginia leadership of the Founding period. How account for the dominance of the Ohioans? people wondered. Was it chance or—asked a journalist, tongue in cheek—a conspiracy? The explanation could be found less in smoke-filled rooms than in the nature of Ohio itself, in its history and makeup. Before the Civil War, Ohio, with its mix of militant abolitionists and Southern sympathizers, had been a microcosm of sectional politics. The great contrasts and divisions in the state mirrored the diversity of the Union. "The Ohioans," Rollin Hartt observed, "are the United States in vertical section."

Still the most striking division in Ohio after the Civil War was north

versus south. The Western Reserve, where the winters blew in cold off the
Great Lakes, had been settled largely by New Englanders, and the area still
retained a Yankee flavor. Elm trees, colleges, and blue laws flourished in
the northern tier of the state. Ohio's "south" lay along the Ohio River and
in the Appalachian counties of the southwest, where the southern counties
were populated by transplanted Kentuckians, Virginians, and Carolinians.
A river culture existed along the Ohio—life was warm, slow, agrarian.
Travelers noticed the drawling accents, the sprawling plantation houses
along the river, the crawling mosses on the cypress trees. In between lay
a broad plain of farmland having more in common with the rest of the
Midwest than with the rest of Ohio. The pace of the center counties was
set by Columbus, "a neighborly place . . . flat as a hayfield," whose quiet
seemed to be broken only by the rumble of farm wagons. North, South,
Midwest—Ohio "boxed the American compass."

Other divisions cut across and softened the old geographic boundaries.
Ohioans subscribed to a welter of religious persuasions—not just Congre-
gationalist, Presbyterian, Episcopal, but also Methodist, Baptist, Catholic,
Jewish, Campbellite, Dunkard, Mormon. More important was the diversity
of economic pursuits. "Northerners" were divided between farmers, merchants, gas drillers, the sailors and fishermen who lived off the Great Lakes.
The railroads invaded the central plains, bringing manufacturing, competition for markets, and new crop patterns. While "Southerners" along the
river farmed in much the same way as those along the Mississippi, their
brethren in the Appalachian counties mined coal and iron, or scraped a
meager living from the foothills.

Symbol and source of much of the change redrawing Ohio were the
growing cities—"inchoate, restless, surging." Walter Havighurst saw them
as becoming the essence of Ohio. Cleveland and Cincinnati were heading
toward populations of a quarter million people each by 1890, Columbus
and Toledo toward a hundred thousand, while another sixteen cities would
pass the 10,000 mark. The cities brought a new richness and variety to
Ohio life. Cincinnati, "the Paris of America," hosted an accomplished
music academy and nationally acclaimed music festival, and nourished the
writer Lafcadio Hearn, painter Frank Duveneck, sculptors Clement Barn-
horn and Charles Niehaus. More prosaic Cleveland was mother to artists,
but also to a baseball nine that won an invitation to the White House from
Ohio's own President Grant. The cities helped Ohio to sustain an educational system that was the envy of the nation—wide in variety, broad in
reach to the populace, and foremost in experiments with coeducation.

Industry was the signature of the cities—and each was unique, both
complementing and competing with her sisters. Sandusky on Lake Erie was

a shipping point for lumber, limestone, and fish, as well as a maker of oars and wheels. Youngstown produced steel; Toledo, glass, pig iron, machinery, and—as the century ended—motorcars; Dayton, rubber. Findlay, center of the northern natural gas fields, celebrated its new prosperity with a Gas Jubilee, where 30,000 flaming jets lighted the city from end to end. In the Appalachian coal mines of the Hocking Valley, technology marched on: first mechanical buckets replaced wheelbarrows for bringing coal up from the shafts, and then bulky car-dumping machines appeared to empty and refill railroad coal carriers. The railroads, with some 10,000 miles of track laid by 1890, brought welcome changes, doubling farmers' prices for flour, wheat, and corn during years when farmers in the South and West faced bankruptcy.

The growing industries brought hints of things to come. The winding Cuyahoga River was stained brown by the oil tanks, blast furnaces, sawmills, and coal bunkers that lined its marshy banks. Blazing oil slicks reached into Lake Erie, and a pall of smoke settled over Cleveland and other towns. But Hartt found Clevelanders willing to endure the outpouring of the smokestacks: "smoke means business, business means money, and money is the principal thing."

The thriving cities acted as a magnet for Ohio's blacks. By 1890, three-quarters of the state's Negro population of 87,000 were city dwellers, a proportion almost exactly the opposite of that for the rest of the country. Most of the black immigrants came from the Ohio countryside, where the increasing costs and mechanization of farming were eroding chances for land ownership or even tenant labor by blacks. But little of the prosperity of the cities trickled down to the new black residents. Excluded from many industrial jobs by employer hostility and union suspicion, the urban-dwelling blacks were largely confined to menial day labor, domestic service, and "Negro" trades like barbering.

Ohio's diversity made for change and conflict, which in turn made for a vigorous political leadership. The metamorphosis of the old Northwestern frontier—a "civilization resting on family, land and community"—to a society of feverish production and commerce threw up a new set of leaders closely in tune with the political and social flux of their state, and capable of dealing with change and conflict on the national level as well.

A number of common bonds drew these new Ohio leaders together. They were all young: the seven men who would dominate Republican politics on the state scene for a generation after the Civil War—Garfield, Hayes, Jacob Cox, Isaac Sherwood, Warren Keifer, Aaron Perry, and Edward Noyes—had averaged thirty-three years old in 1865. All of them had served as Union officers in the war, returning with habits of organization and command they could apply to the strife of commerce and politics. They were men on the make—college-educated, trained professionals in law or journalism, successful men attracted to the dynamism of Ohio's cities. The economic takeoff of the 1850s had first opened doors for them; then the chaos of Civil War had propelled them early to dizzying heights of power over other men. They had, in Felice Bonadio's view, a new faith "which was to be found in cities, in factories, in railroads." That faith would be translated into political doctrine—and into political power.

Ohio provided economic leadership too. Jay Cooke shook up the nation's finances; John D. Rockefeller reorganized industries; Thomas Edison transformed the world with his tinkering. But the attraction of politics proved too great for others. John Hay left a promising academic career to become a respected civil servant and, eventually, Secretary of State to an Ohio President. Whitelaw Reid evolved from historian to editor to party chieftain to diplomat over the course of thirty years. As in other states, politics and the law were intimately intertwined. Alphonso B. Taft won appointment as Attorney General while his son, William Howard, was becoming a popular young lawyer; William McKinley of Canton began dabbling in politics under the tutelage of Republican boss Mark Hanna; and, from a previous generation of leaders, Salmon P. Chase still sat as Chief Justice of the U.S. Supreme Court. And topping them all were three lawyer-politicians who dominated the councils of the GOP for nearly twenty years—Rutherford Hayes, James Garfield, and John Sherman.

With war and industrialization producing a set of new young leaders in every Northern state, perhaps it was only luck that the men from Ohio consistently came to the fore on the national scene. Perhaps it was the unique nature of the economic change in Ohio: the dynamic balance between agricultural boom and urban growth, the vast array of natural resources exploited and manufactures produced. Ohio was like none of her neighbors, yet she had tangible economic and social interests in common with all of them. Or perhaps the answer lay in Ohio's politics, "dynamic, complicated, and treacherous" as one historian found them to be. In a state so evenly divided between Republicans and Democrats, and with deep fissures weakening both parties from within, only the ablest political leaders could hope to survive. "It is utterly impossible to detect any nucleus of opinion," despaired Jacob Cox. "It is every man for himself." The men who climbed out of the thickets of Ohio politics were thus peculiarly suited to lead their colleagues through the jungles of Washington.

James Garfield exemplified the partisan skills of Ohioans. Although raised in straitened circumstances by his widowed mother, Garfield was able to earn enough money to get through the Western Reserve Eclectic

Institute and Williams College. The hefty, bearded schoolteacher studied law on the side, ran for the Ohio Senate in 1859, and did yeoman service in raising troops when the Civil War began. At the end of 1863 he left the army to represent Ohio's 19th District in Congress. He found Ohio Republicans, like those elsewhere in the North, still divided between ex-Whigs and ex-Democrats. The issue of slavery had brought them together to form the new party in the 1850s, but with slavery dead there was a very real danger that they would split again. Ohio Democrats, themselves badly factionalized, played skillfully on the former ties of the older Republicans.

Garfield and his younger colleagues, however, had no past loyalties to appeal to. Mobilized by the cause of preserving the Union, they had entered politics for the first time as Republicans, just before or during the war. Building on this base of support, Garfield moved quickly to check the disintegration of his party. If there was no "nucleus of opinion" among Ohio Republicans, he would replace it with a nucleus of organization. In the 19th District, Garfield built a tight hierarchy of local citizens' committees, campaign workers, and elected officials. Up the hierarchy flowed money and votes; down from the top flowed patronage jobs and favors for the district from Columbus and Washington. Binding the entire structure was a growing party loyalty. Garfield too bound himself to party loyalty, stumping for fellow Republicans at home and in Washington with such fervor that he soon won a national reputation for glib bombast. It was a military model of organization that Garfield applied to politics—rigid structure, firm command, and mutual loyalty—and it served him well.

For several years Garfield crossed political swords with John Sherman, Ohio's powerful Republican senator. Eventually, however, the two managed to work out an uneasy alliance, to the benefit of both themselves and the state party. While Garfield's influence in the House slowly increased, Sherman used his seat on the Senate's Committee on Finance to become the foremost representative of the Republican party's new orientation toward economic rather than racial issues. In the Finance Committee he grappled with vexing questions of currency and tariffs, working to balance the inflationary interests of his Ohio constituents with a more conservative policy suited to what he perceived as the nation's larger economic needs. Sherman strove to identify the Republicans in the public eye with business expansion and general prosperity; race relations he viewed as potentially fatal to party unity and public support.

The man whom Sherman and Garfield came to support for the governorship of their home state was of a somewhat different stamp. Rutherford B. Hayes tended not to become excited about partisan politics; he saved his passion for reform. A Harvard-trained lawyer and wounded veteran,

Hayes was sent by the Republicans to Columbus in 1867 for the first of an unprecedented three terms as governor. "Not too much hard work, plenty of time to read, good society, etc." was his self-effacing evaluation of the gubernatorial post, but in fact he pushed strenuously for asylum and prison reform, regulation of railroad abuses, lower taxes, and an end to "the appointment of unfit men on partisan or personal grounds." Election to a third term, with the solid support of the entire Ohio GOP leadership, opened to Hayes the dizzying prospect of ascending to the presidency.

The Republican party desperately needed a candidate with strong re-form credentials, for the mounting scandals of the Grant Administration threatened to swamp the GOP as 1876 drew near. "Grantism" had become synonymous with a degree of corruption and malfeasance unprecedented even by the relaxed standards of nineteenth-century American politics. Some of the scandals were mundane: the Secretary of War resigned when evidence surfaced that he had been involved in selling government con-tracts, and the Interior Secretary faced similar charges. Other gaffes were intercontinental: U.S. Minister to Paris Dan Sickles conducted an adulter-ous affair with the former Queen of Spain, Ambassador Robert Schenck lent his name to bogus western stocks being sold in London, and another political appointee enlivened his consulship in Egypt with duels, drunken-ness, and dancing girls. Still other scandals reached right into the White House, as a presidential aide was found to be involved in covering up the bribery of Treasury agents by whiskey manufacturers.

Grantism threatened to soil even the "ermine of the Supreme Court." When Chief Justice Chase died in 1873, Grant nominated his Attorney General to fill the center chair, only to see him charged with misusing Justice Department funds and selling immunity from prosecution. The President spent weeks seeking a more acceptable nominee. After several more missteps he settled on Morrison R. Waite, a relatively obscure Toledo attorney of limited political experience. Waite nonetheless won Senate approval, and, with scandals breaking all around him, ascended unscathed to the High Court. There he would preside, for fourteen years, over issues not of petty corruption but of fundamental rights for large groups of Americans.

*   *   *

The kind of leadership that Ohio produced in the late nineteenth cen-tury typified that of Northern Republicanism as a whole. It was a transac-tional leadership of barter and brokerage, both reflecting and shaping the competitive worlds of industry, finance, and commerce. As the political process was retooled following the war, the old ideological leaders, who

had brought about a military and then a constitutional transformation of
the nation, gave way to vigorous young politicos who operated within the
constraints of the federal check-and-balance system. The young attorney
Rutherford Hayes had written from Cincinnati: "Push, labor, shove—these
words are of great power in a city like this." The essence of politics indeed
was to push and shove in a giant game of King of the Rock—but always
in the end to compromise so that the game could go on another day. All
this was closer to Whitman's competition and "low cunning" than the
experiment in a higher intelligence and the faith in democracy that
Adams's Mr. Gore called for. It was the survival of the fittest—but who
were the fittest? And for what?

Only a leadership steeped in compromise and skilled at brokerage could
have brought off one of the most fateful transactions in American history,
in the wake of a political crisis that some feared might trigger another civil
war. When the 1876 presidential election gave Tilden a quarter-million
popular majority and a disputed electoral college majority, Ohioans and
other political brokers in both parties agreed on setting up an electoral
commission that would rule on the disputed election returns from Florida,
Louisiana, South Carolina, and Oregon. When the "swing vote" on the
commission, the "independent" Supreme Court Justice David Davis of
Illinois, suddenly—and with unexpected alacrity—resigned to accept election to the Senate, his place was taken by a most partisan Republican
justice, Joseph Bradley. The commission then proceeded by straight party
eight-to-seven votes to decide for Hayes in all the disputed returns.

Southerners cried foul amid rumors of a march on Washington by Confederate veterans. In fact the hands of the Southerners were tied because
the establishment of the electoral commission—and by implication the
acceptance of its verdict—was one part of a far-reaching compromise that
embraced much more than the presidency. The political crisis of the early
weeks of 1877, as Inauguration Day neared, has best been viewed not as
a straight power fight but as a mammoth game of poker played by shrewd
professionals, in which calculation, chance, bluffing, kibitzing, inside dealing, and miscalculation all had their role. The stakes were enormous—not
only selection of a President but control of the national government,
distribution of pork and patronage, the alignment of parties, and above all
political control of the South.

Southern Democrats appeared to hold some low cards—the power to
delay a final decision through filibustering and other congressional devices; the Democratic majority in the House of Representatives; vague
threats of violence; and claim to the moral high ground of having "won the
election." Hayes, House Republican leader Garfield, and the other North-

ern Republicans held the high cards: the electoral commission decision; control of the presidency, the Senate, and the Supreme Court; and President Grant, who commanded the army and knew how to use it. But the test, as always in political struggles, was not only power resources but political objectives. What did the two sides want? Southern Democrats wanted more federal patronage after sixteen years in the cold. They wanted federal money to shore up their roads and canals and their levees—especially those of the ever-flooding Mississippi—and federal grants for their railroads and particularly for their dream of a southern route to the Pacific. But above all—far above all—they wanted, bitterly and passionately, "home rule," an end to federal control of their region, the departure of the federal troops of "occupation."

The poker game itself was so complex, involving so many players with so many sets of cards, as to challenge historical analysis of precise cause and effect for years to come. But certain aspects stood out even at the time. It was a wide-open game, with legislators, party politicians, and lobbyists taking part by the hundreds. It was a most public game. Lobbyists saw no need to lurk in corridors and crannies; scores of them invaded the floor of the House itself, while the Speaker vainly urged them to be off. It was a most widely observed game. The press followed the key developments astutely, often quite accurately, and kept the public informed as to the key political plays and players.

And at the end of this marathon game there was a clear winner—the Southern Democrats. Not only did they gain the key patronage position in Hayes's Cabinet, the postmaster-generalship, and later their own railroad to the West; they also won their supreme goal of home rule, in whatever form this would eventually take. Winning the next biggest pot were the Ohioans and the other Republican party professionals. They saw their man Hayes securely into the White House and they could contemplate the possibility of re-creating the old Whig alliance of Northern and Southern property, as Southern entrepreneurs eagerly anticipated the uses of federal money and Northern investors saw new prospects in the South.

The losers, too, were painfully obvious. The Northern Democrats had had to stand by almost helplessly as their man Tilden was dealt out of the White House. Radical Republicans also stood by impotently as so much of what they had struggled for, on political and military battlefields for nearly a quarter century, was bargained away. But the main losers were never even close to the big poker game. These were the Southern blacks whose final hope of federal aid and protection for justice and dignity and jobs and land and life itself ebbed with the playing of the game. They had held no cards at all.

POLITICS: THE DANCE OF THE ROPEWALKERS

Radical caricaturists in the press pictured the poker players as in fact the puppets of the masters of industry and finance. It was not that simple. In fighting for home rule Southern Democrats acted more out of cultural heritage, regional pride, and psychological motivation than from narrowly economic considerations, just as Northern abolitionists once had put "conscience" before "cotton." Still, the force of capital, the subtle influence of class, and above all the pervasive power of ideology increasingly dominated the stakes and the cards in the political game. While politicos declaimed, denounced, debated, and digressed, the economic barons decided investment policy, built railroads and factories, deployed masses of workers, imported immigrants by the tens of thousands, set incomes, financed science and invention. If they could not work their way through government they could turn to direct action. When Huntington was thwarted politically by railroad rivals, the Californian speared his Southern Pacific rails eastward across Arizona, then talked a complaisant President Hayes into endorsing his fait accompli.

"The statesman and the captain of industry complement each other well," said Matthew Josephson of this era; "one talks, the other acts."

The power of the dominant economic players in the political game, and the impotence of the nonparticipants, were both sharply revealed in the conversion of the Fourteenth Amendment from a bulwark of Negro rights to a bastion of corporate property. Charles Sumner's Civil Rights Act of 1875, guaranteeing Negroes equal rights to public facilities, had represented the legislative high point of Reconstruction, at least after the law's legitimation by the Fourteenth Amendment. Much depended on judicial interpretation. During the 1870s era of compromise the Supreme Court pinched the Fourteenth into a narrow measure barring overt discrimination by states and not adding, in Chief Justice Waite's words, "anything to the rights which one citizen has under the Constitution against another." The Court struck down an anti–Ku Klux Klan act by labeling it an invalid interference in the activities of private individuals. Then in a series of cases the justices invalidated the Civil Rights Act of 1875 on the same grounds. With no constitutional mandate for federal protection against de facto discrimination, Southern blacks were on their own.

What was the purpose of the Fourteenth Amendment if not to protect black people? Despite universal understanding and categorical evidence that the Fourteenth had been passed to protect the freed slaves, attorneys for business interests argued that the "persons" protected by the amend-

ment were in fact *corporations*—that the amendment was designed to bar
governmental regulation of private enterprise. Roscoe Conkling, hired by
Huntington and Stanford to protect their railroads against California regulation, had the cheek to imply that Congress from the start sought to
benefit businessmen rather than blacks, thus giving rise to one of the
juiciest conspiracy theories in American history. Soon the High Court,
spurred by such politically partisan ideologues as Justices Joseph Bradley
(that swing man in the electoral commission) and Stephen J. Field, transformed the Court in case after case into a trumpet box for laissez-faire and
a mighty weapon for the protection of corporate property.

At least Negroes had the *legal* right to vote, some suffragists reflected
bitterly; women as a whole were dealt completely out of the political game.
Suffragists were indignant that the Fourteenth and Fifteenth Amendments
—granting rights to all "citizens," that is, "persons" born or naturalized
in the United States—should be construed to mean "men only." The
ambiguous wording invited a test.

Through a blinding snowstorm in 1870, the indomitable eighty-year-old
abolitionist Sarah Grimké led her sister Angelina and forty other women
on foot to the voting booth in Hyde Park, Massachusetts, only to place their
ballots in a separate box, where they were left uncounted. On November
5, 1872, Susan B. Anthony and some women friends voted in Rochester,
New York. Though her ballot was accepted, Anthony was arrested two
weeks later for "voting knowingly without having the lawful right to vote."
She wanted her case to go to the Supreme Court, but the trial court judge
allowed it to lapse. When a similar case—that of Virginia Minor—reached
the High Court in 1874, Chief Justice Waite found for the Court that if the
Framers had wanted women to vote, they would have said so and that the
rights of citizenship did not necessarily include suffrage.

White males North and South, holding the high economic, political, and
legal cards, seemed poised by the late 1870s to forge a new conservative
coalition uniting men of corporate and landed property in a North-South
party alliance rivaling the great Whig coalitions before the Civil War. "It
is quite the fashion," declared the Raleigh *Observer*, "to talk about reviving
the old Whig party, and to make appeals to the old Henry Clay Whigs once
more to come to the front." Men of substance excitedly discussed the
possibility of building a new party, of whatever name, that would draw
conservative, business-minded elements from both the Democratic and
Republican parties in order to protect property against the threats of
urban radicals, western populists, and the like.

But this hope was to fade away, and its demise indicated again the
difficulty of translating economic power directly into political, in the com-

plex politics and polyglot culture of 1870s America. The two old parties lived on in the hearts and minds of Americans. Since the early decades of the century they had responded to deep-seated needs and aspirations among the people, had transformed the political landscape as surely as a magnet shapes tracings on a laboratory table. Civil war and reconstruction had left these parties not only broadly intact but in a condition of interlock, unable to extricate each from the other's embrace. The Republicans, the party of the old Northwest, now had to compete with the Democrats for Ohio, Illinois, Indiana. The Republican "grand coalition" of business, labor, farmers, veterans, and blacks now had to cope with eastern financiers who gave money to the likes of Seymour and Tilden, farmers who shunned both parties, workers who were politically apathetic or alienated, and women and blacks who could not vote.

Above all the Republicans faced Democrats, and the Democracy had shown remarkable resilience and tenacity. Here was a party that had been on the "wrong side" of the Civil War, that emerged from the struggle with its Southern wing limp and shredded politically, that found no national leadership after Appomattox comparable with the great dynasty that had stretched from Jackson through Van Buren and Polk to Stephen Douglas, that had embraced much that was malodorous in American politics, whether Tammany in New York or lily-white county machines in the South. Yet even at the height of the war its presidential candidate, the somewhat discredited General George B. McClellan, had won 45 percent of the popular vote against Lincoln himself; four years later Horatio Seymour polled more than 47 percent of the popular vote; and in the disputed election of '76, Tilden won a popular majority. Clearly, a party dominant for at least forty years before Sumter would not die quickly, if ever.

And so, with blaring trumpets and ferocious war dances, the two great parties confronted each other on almost equal terms; but the result was often a sham battle. Each party stretched across such a wide spectrum of interests and attitudes that clean-cut conflict over policy, program, and ideology was impossible. "The major parties reflected the national policy cleavage on the issues arising from the slavery controversy, and a geographical cleavage between North and South," in James Sundquist's overview. "But they could not reflect these cleavages and at the same time express new ones that cut across the electorate in quite a different direction, dividing voters *within* the North, *within* the South, *within* groups supporting Negro suffrage, and *within* those opposing it." Inevitably the postwar parties "evaded and straddled and postponed" just as the prewar parties had done, especially on the big issues.

Instead of reflecting and intensifying a relatively clean-cut split between liberalism and conservatism or between left and right (whatever the actual labels) over the conditions and needs of workers or farmers or blacks or immigrants, each major party itself became the battleground in which such interests and ideologies skirmished. The result, in Keith Polakoff's words, was a "politics of inertia" in the post–Civil War period. "Not only was factionalism practically the central characteristic of both parties, but the precise balance between the various factions remained remarkably stable; and no wonder: each faction had its own little constituency on which it could always depend."

This almost static balance rested on both factions within the parties and interest groups and minor parties outside. Thus in policy or ideology Republicans split into ultra-radicals, "Stevens radicals," Independent Radicals, moderates, and conservatives, in David Donald's formulation. Geographically the Republicans were dominant in the northern tier running from most of New England across upstate New York into the "new" Northwest, while fighting close battles in more urban areas and in the "old" Northwest. Doctrinally the grand new party embraced the old abolitionist crowd, liberals preaching civil service and other reforms, and a rapidly expanding array of laissez-faire conservatives.

Ohio Republicans continued to boast of their leadership, organization, and principles. Older leaders recruited younger ones; in the 1880s Governor Joseph B. Foraker encouraged a blossoming young lawyer named William Howard Taft, who would flower in the next century. Civil War memories still inspirited the Ohio GOP, as its convention orators declaimed that the Grand Old Party would never "break up its battle formations" or "bury its wagon trains," no matter how deep the "scars of battle." The leaders still spoke for the black people, and some Negro politicians rose in its ranks. George A. Myers, the chief of barbers at Cleveland's grand political hotel, became one of the most astute and literate Republican leaders, in part because he was at the hub of a political network. But the great commitment to black rights was slowly waning, giving way to the defense of property rights.

The Democrats too were highly pluralistic, ranging from old moderate elements still voting the "politics of nostalgia" from the 1850s, through Douglas and McClellan Democrats, to elements of a strange new organization of "Night Hawks" and "Grand Dragons" and "Grand Wizards," calling itself the Ku Klux Klan and arising out of a Southland bent on "redemption." Like the GOP, the Democracy was increasingly tending toward its own brand of economic conservatism, especially under the impact of leaders like Grover Cleveland.

Given the narrow front on which the two major parties contended, it was inevitable that third parties would rise to press for cherished ideas. One of the first of these in the postwar years, the Liberal Republicans, was quite remarkable. Deeply alienated from the Grant Administration because of its corruption, its spoils, its cronyism with big business, its all-round mediocrity, independent-minded Republicans joined with defecting Democrats and others to rout the regulars. The movement attracted a diversity of followers—in the words of John Sproat, "free traders and protectionists, conservative New England patricians and agrarian radicals, civil service reformers and unvarnished spoilsmen, advocates of Negro rights and Southern redeemers," united only by their hatred of Grantism. The leaders were a diverse lot too—among them the Radical Republican and Missouri senator Carl Schurz, the Massachusetts blueblood and former diplomat Charles Francis Adams, the aged poet William Cullen Bryant, a host of editors, including notably Edwin Godkin of the *Nation* and Horace Greeley of the New York *Tribune*.

At an 1872 Cincinnati conclave sober in both speech and drink, the Liberal Republicans chose Greeley himself for President. Many reformers were as aghast as regulars were amused. With his big bald head and neck whiskers, his drooping spectacles and rumpled clothes, his high-pitched voice and awkward ways, the outspoken old editor was the delight of opposition cartoonists; even more, he had embraced so many causes, waxed hot and cold on so many issues, denounced so many leaders including Lincoln himself, that he was bound to antagonize more voters than he attracted. And so he did, dragging down not only the Liberal Republicans but the Democratic party, which, at the nadir of its own leadership, adopted him as its own candidate.

Still, the Liberal Republicans' main problem was not Greeley but liberalism itself. Skeptical if not contemptuous of the mass public, conservative in economic policy, compromising on Negro rights, moralistic but not always moral, amateurish and dilettantish in political mechanics, the movement virtually caricatured the liberal tendency toward disunity, as leaders divided over the tariff, Reconstruction, women's rights, and election strategy. With their narrow definition of liberty as economic and political individualism, their distaste in general for social egalitarianism or economic "leveling," their antipathy toward centralized government, their half-hidden disdain for the "masses," the Liberals both reflected and abetted the dominant ideology of Spencer and William Graham Sumner. Badly beaten by Grant in 1872, the Liberal Republicans' party faded away—though not their causes.

Other minor parties too were as impotent at the polls as they were vocal in protest. Rising out of wide grass-roots agitation over deflation, lack of capital, and the working conditions of labor, and galvanized by the panic of 1873 and resultant hardships, farm spokesmen, labor reformers, frustrated entrepreneurs, and assorted inflationists established the Greenback (or Greenback Labor) party. Its orators and platforms denounced hard-money policies and demanded that greenbacks be given full legal tender status and be issued freely. The party gained only a scattering of votes in 1876 with its candidate, the New York philanthropist Peter Cooper; won over a million votes in the off-year elections two years later; but fared badly at the polls in 1880 with General James B. Weaver at the head of the ticket, and faded away.

The Greenbackers' frustrations pointed up an endemic problem of third parties—disunity. Composed of diverse elements, the foes of hard money fought over reform issues and in particular over the age-old dilemma for issue movements: go it alone as a separate party or coalesce with the less unattractive of the two major parties. The Prohibitionists had less trouble with the "fission or fusion" problem, since they had long set their faces hard against the intemperate major parties, but the Prohibition leadership was often divided over which strategy to pursue—whether to concentrate only on liquor or to broaden their credo to appeal to woman suffragists and other reformers.

So the two big parties lumbered along, like two old stagecoaches, undaunted by guerrilla bands assailing them from right or left or threatening to cut them off at the pass. The net impact of third parties during this period may well have been to consolidate the major parties' shoulder-to-shoulder position in the center of the political spectrum, for the "single-issue" parties isolated activists who might otherwise have agitated *within* the major parties and pushed them toward more programmatic politics. If any of the parties had been able to reach out into the two great untapped sectors of the potential electorate, the stable party gridlock might have been upset. But those untapped sectors still lay beyond the electoral pale —women and blacks.

Proud of their vital Civil War roles both North and South, women had emerged from the War all the more prepared, they felt, for full participation in the American democracy. Hence they were all the more indignant that rights were extended to more men—blacks, of course, but also immigrants and others—but not women. Most woman suffragists strongly supported Negro enfranchisement—many had been ardent abolitionists—but even that veteran campaigner Elizabeth Cady Stanton was provoked into referring to "Sambo" and the enfranchisement of "Africans, Chinese, and all the ignorant foreigners the moment they touch our shores." Another veteran campaigner, Frederick Douglass, answered her a few weeks later at a meeting:

"When women, because they are women, are dragged from their homes and hung upon lamp-posts"—when their homes were burnt down over their heads, he went on, and their children torn from their arms—"then they will have an urgency to obtain the ballot."

"Is that not all true about black women?" came a cry from the audience.

"Yes, yes, yes," Douglass exclaimed, "it is true of the black woman, but not because she is a woman but because she is black."

Not only were many women rebels divided from blacks, but women suffragists were divided among themselves over priorities and tactics, and indeed split into the National Woman Suffrage Association, headed by such militants as Stanton and Susan B. Anthony, and the American Woman Suffrage Association, led by those old redoubtables, Lucy Stone and Julia Ward Howe. The former group concentrated on gaining a woman suffrage amendment to the United States Constitution, the latter on efforts in the states, whose legislatures controlled voting rights. Anthony et al. published *The Revolution* in New York, Stone et al. the *Woman's Journal* in Boston. Not for twenty years would this breach be healed.

Neither farmers nor workers upset the equilibrium of the two stately parties after the Civil War. In the early seventies midwestern farmers, burdened by mortgages and angered by discriminatory policies of railroads, grain elevators, moneylenders, and other instruments of "corporate power," converted the Patrons of Husbandry, founded in 1867 to improve agriculture, into a political movement. For a time the "Grangers" seemed irresistible, as they routed the Republicans in Illinois and won key elections in Kansas, Iowa, Wisconsin, Minnesota, and elsewhere under the banner of "Reform and Anti-Monopoly." The farmers proved themselves skillful and sophisticated in working with, against, or between the state Republican and Democratic parties, but they paid a price for their opportunism, for they neither built lasting strength within a major party nor built a party of their own. By 1876, the farmers' revolt had burned itself out and most of the activists were back in the major parties.

Nor did organized workers have a major disruptive influence on the major parties. Influenced by the Horatio Algerism of the era, splintered into crafts that stressed business unionism, disenchanted by their experience with separatist movements in earlier days, constantly tempted toward expedient coalitions with the major parties in state and local elections, workers on the whole bolstered either the Democracy or what was already becoming the "Grand Old Party." Labor scored a few striking victories over their major-party foes, only to see their gains washed away in the next recession or the next presidential election.

Still, the major parties were not mere shapeless collections of interests, sections, and attitudes. Often powerful at the state and local levels, they also showed continuities of leadership and strategy in national elections. By nominating a string of New Yorkers for President—Horatio Seymour in 1868, Greeley in 1872, Tilden in 1876, and Grover Cleveland three times in a row—the Democrats focused their campaign efforts on the Empire State as the big bellwether in the East; the only exception, Winfield Hancock, came from neighboring Pennsylvania. That Seymour and Tilden and a host of its other national leaders had their political roots in the Albany Regency attested to the long-run political impact of Martin Van Buren and the other creative party builders of the 1830s and 1840s. That the Democracy turned to the Midwest—usually Missouri or Indiana—for vice-presidential candidates reflected its desire to carry balance-of-power states rather than recognize its electoral bastion in the South. By the same token, the Republicans typically balanced their string of Ohioans with running mates from the East.

The more the parties played the politics of interest-group brokerage, sectional balance, issue compromise, and ideological rhetoric without substance, and the more political debate turned on secondary issues of financial corruption, patronage, personality, "honesty," the more outcomes were influenced by chance, luck, and trivia. The contest of 1884 between Cleveland and Blaine marked a low point in this tendency. As usual, the Republicans charged that the Democracy was controlled by Tammany, even though Cleveland had made his political reputation by opposing it; as usual, the Democrats taxed their foes with using federal troops to run state elections, even though the GOP had long since abandoned the South. The Democrats charged, correctly, that Blaine had been involved in dubious dealings with railroad promoters, epitomized by his instruction to one correspondent, "Burn this letter"; and the Republicans charged, also correctly, that Cleveland had fathered an illegitimate child, which the New Yorker admitted. The campaign was thus enlivened by two taunts at rival party meetings:

> Blaine, Blaine, James G. Blaine,
> The continental liar from the State of Maine,
> *Burn this letter!*
>
> Ma! Ma! Where's my pa?
> Gone to the White House,
> *Ha! Ha! Ha!*

Blaine had the worst of it. He managed to sit through a meeting of Protestant clergymen, all Republicans, at the Fifth Avenue Hotel in New

York City, and was too weary to notice and later too slow to repudiate a pastor's reference to "a party whose antecedents have been Rum, Romanism and Rebellion." The Democrats adroitly exploited this gaffe, bringing some offended Catholics into their fold. And that very evening, the "Plumed Knight" attended a millionaires' dinner at Delmonico's, in the company of Jay Gould, Chauncey Depew, Astors, Vanderbilts, and the inevitable Evarts—a dinner that promptly was caricatured in the New York *World* as the "Royal Feast of Belshazzar Blaine and the Money Kings," complete with a starving father, mother, and child begging for food.

Cleveland's razor-thin victory not only broke the Republicans' twenty-year hold on the White House; it signified the new power of independent voters, for many of the old liberal and reformist Republicans, now called "Mugwumps," had deserted the GOP, portending a future cleavage in that party. It put the Democracy, confined for twenty years to the hinterland but still essentially conservative, at the center of the nation's councils. Its return to power was symbolized by one small fact hardly commented on at the time: when Grover Cleveland took the oath of office on March 4, 1885, it was the first occasion that this former mayor of Buffalo and governor of New York had visited Washington.

THE POVERTY OF POLICY

Perhaps it was understandable that the New York governor had never visited his nation's capital, since Washington was neither a major tourist attraction nor a power center—and certainly not a dispenser of funds to desperate governors. Twenty years after the Civil War the city was more like a storm center without the storm. Compared to New York, wrote a correspondent, where everything throbbed "with the chase for the almighty dollar," Washington tended to "deaden, rather than quicken you into activity." Although full of energy, wrote an English visitor, "Washington . . . is a city of rest and peace." Virginia Grigsby, who had just taken a job in the dead-letter branch of the Post Office, wrote her brother, "We are fixed with every convenience, long desks, easy revolving chairs, footstools, plenty of servants and no specific work to be done.

"There are all ladies in this room," she added, "and therefore they do as they choose, most of them bring dressing sacques and put them on to work in. Some even take off their corsets. You know Mama *never* wears any at home, perhaps she may be able to do all this in the Land Office."

The White House in the mid-eighties was still a place where a job seeker could walk through the front door without being questioned, cross the big vestibule, climb a flight of winding stairs, present his card to a secretary, and expect to see the President. Lobbyists, cranks, deadbeats, pension lawyers, sightseers swarmed through the House of Representatives and crowded around the chamber itself, where members, their feet propped up on their desks and their pink-and-gold cuspidors at their side, conducted genial business in tobacco smoke so thick that ladies grew ill in the galleries above. Only a few elder senators took snuff, but they could still drink, even in the Capitol restaurant, where an order for tea, combined with a wink to the waiter, would produce a cup half filled with whiskey. Pennsylvania Avenue still connected—and separated—President and Congress. For years it was separated itself, by railroad tracks that cut across the Mall between the Capitol and the Treasury. Congress, which controlled the city government, time and again tried to compel the Pennsylvania Railroad to eliminate these grade crossings, without success. It seemed to Washington's leading historian that the railroad controlled the public domain in the very heart of the nation's capital.

What then did these legislators *do*? The most visible continuing struggle in the post–Civil War years was over the tariff, though this struggle more often resembled a giant game of kick-the-ball in which bands of players, now teaming with one group and then another, kicked a number of balls over a variety of goalposts, while the spectators tried vainly to keep score. Despite thunderous declarations in party platforms, there were no clear divisions between Democrats and Republicans over actual policy. Rather, the tariff was thrown into an arena of contending interests. Of foreign-policy interests: the need of western farmers for overseas markets and the national interest in friendly relations abroad, balanced against workers' fears of "pauper" competition, and such ethnic factors as Irish hatred of English "imperialists." Of regional interests: in general North versus South, save for contrary interests within each section; thus Louisiana sugar growers favored a protective tariff. Of economic interests: broadly, producers versus consumers, but many workers acted on the basis of their concrete palpable stake in a particular industry rather than their thin general interest as consumers and on balance favored protection, while some manufacturers and many merchants opposed it. Of ideological or intellectual divisions: protection seemed to challenge some of the hoariest ideas in the American pantheon—notably individual economic liberty, laissez-faire government, decentralization—but the power of protectionist interests easily overrode such ideas, in part because the ideas were ambiguous and ambivalent. Editorial lions roared: such organs as the New York *Evening Post* and the Louisville *Courier-Journal* favored lower tariffs; many others, like the Philadelphia *Press* and the New York *Tribune*, championed protection.

Amid the clash of rhetoric and the dust of battle the politicos of House and Senate calculated these contending interests almost with the accuracy of an apothecary's scale. This was what they were good at. The result was a series of compromises, now skewed in certain directions, now in others, as senators, congressmen, and Presidents came and went. Both parties, according to Tom Terrill, promised "prosperity and social harmony without fundamentally altering the nation politically or economically." The result was a series of "mongrel tariffs."

Some expected that Grover Cleveland would upset this equipoise following his presidential victory in 1884 on top of sweeping Democratic gains in Congress two years before. On the argument that "it is a *condition* which confronts us—not a theory," he demanded sweeping tariff reduction. But Cleveland faced a *political* condition—the fact that a band of Democratic congressmen had persistently opposed major tariff reduction. The President finally managed to corral almost all the House Democrats, but the measure ran afoul of the Republican majority in the Senate, the presidential race of 1888, and Benjamin Harrison's victory. This issue too would be projected into the turbulent nineties.

Struggles over silver and gold also aroused great sound and fury, usually signifying little more than a free-for-all among a jumble of interests. After 1873, when Congress demonetized silver and left gold as the sole monetary standard, silverites began to denounce this "crime of '73" as a gold conspiracy. Five years later agrarians opposed to deflation combined with silverites to pass over Hayes's veto the Bland-Allison Act, which required the Secretary of the Treasury every month to buy between $2 million and $4 million worth of silver at the market price. In 1890, the Sherman Silver Purchase Act raised the purchase to 4.5 million ounces per month and authorized the Treasury to issue in payment legal tender Treasury notes redeemable in gold or silver by Treasury decision, but it did not provide for free silver.

The rhetoric seemed to reflect a titanic struggle between rich and poor, easterner and westerner, upper class and lower class, debtor and creditor, farmer and financier, or some combination thereof. But the currency issue was not clear and sharp enough—or presented clearly or sharply enough —to pit mammoth interests against one another. Rather, the groups were divided among themselves—manufacturing interests against financial interests, big farmers against tenant farmers, hard-money businessmen against soft-money businessmen, New England textile interests against Pennsylvania iron and steel.

It was the job of party leaders to disentangle these webs of interests and to seek popular majorities for group coalitions, but for some years after the Civil War the crosscutting forces were too hard to master. Instead of grand electoral battles, with clear winners and losers in the congressional struggle over policy, currency battles dissolved into numberless obscure skirmishes, and policy into weak compromises and even vacuity. A government of "intricate partisan maneuver and token legislation," in Robert Wiebe's words, "elevated certain types of leadership," but the "apparent leaders were as much adrift as their followers. For lack of anything that made better sense of their world, people everywhere weighed, counted, and measured it." What kind of force was necessary to reshape parties, interests, coalitions, and leadership in a way that would make possible a transcending conflict between moral principles, grand policy, clearly polarized leaderships?

Certainly the railroad issue would not polarize party politicians, even though this issue sharpened in the seventies as farmers, workers, merchants, shippers, in varied ways and for varied reasons, attacked railroad monopolies, rate-making rebates and other discriminatory practices, corruption, and employment policies. By 1884, both national parties endorsed federal regulation. So did even a number of railroad men themselves, though most, including the likes of Jay Gould, opposed such governmental "interference." Having accepted huge public grants and subsidies from the start, railroad men could hardly escape the regulation that this would entail. Some railroad leaders welcomed moderate federal regulation in order to stave off "extremist" state controls. Their own efforts at self-policing—through rate agreements, pools, arbitration, and other forms of "cooperation"—had failed to work out practically and had aroused public hostility to boot.

Such a consensus for railroad regulation had developed by the 1880s that the House of Representatives, under the leadership of a Texas congressman expert in railroad transportation, John H. Reagan, was strongly supporting federal regulation. The national consensus for regulation had such frail and mixed foundations, however, as to diffuse the policy-making process itself. The Senate and House passed bills so diverse as to tie the measures up in conference committee for months. The outcome in 1887, the Interstate Commerce Act, was a compromise measure that did not set freight and passenger tariffs and was vague in key aspects, but it did prohibit the granting of rebates, higher rates for shorter distances over the same line, and pooling agreements, and it established a five-man commission to monitor the railroads and enforce the law through prosecutions in the federal courts.

The Interstate Commerce Commission itself soon fell victim to the diffusion of political and governmental power. Enjoying solid support neither in the government nor at the grass roots, it felt the shifting pressures of the various interests involved. The result was feeble enforcement of the law, considerable evasion of it, and a series of Supreme Court decisions that weakened federal regulation to the point of emasculation.

If federal regulation of railroads faltered, what about action by the states? Long before the Civil War the first efforts had indeed begun at this level, in the form of commissions that investigated and publicized conditions and later of state bodies that actually set maximum rates and prohibited exorbitant charges. But these bodies ran into the same difficulties that had long plagued state control of big enterprises: the impotence or incompetence of many railroad commissions, pro-railroad court decisions, the persuasiveness of railroad lobbyists clustered in state capitals, and above all the power of great railroad corporations operating across state lines combined with the competition of states and localities for railroad service. By century's end, in Morton Keller's summation, neither state nor federal supervision had "resolved the conflicts raised by the interplay of railroads, shippers, labor, and the public."

Some states, indeed, were arenas for railroad extravaganzas rather than regulation. California was perhaps the extreme case. Having conquered the Sierras, the Big Four—the big burly Stanford as politician-in-chief, the big burly Crocker as chief of construction, the big burly Huntington as chief financier and lobbyist, and the tall, thin Mark Hopkins as chief administrator—plunged into a twenty-year battle for economic and political power in the state. They propagandized in newspaper ads and in speeches to their employees, bought out opposition papers, handed out free railroad passes, lobbied and probably paid off legislators. These men were not hypocrites. "It is a question of might," Stanford told his stockholders, "and it is to your interest to have it determined where the power resides."

The Big Four confronted economic rivals as well as political assailants. Stanford and Huntington had to fight off railroad invasions from the east, "taking possession," Stewart Holbrook said, "of all the mountain passes." The Big Four were able to buy out or otherwise overcome a number of small railroad ventures on the West Coast, but they met their match in Thomas Scott, a veteran railroader who had first learned his trade with the famous Allegheny Portage Railroad and later as the man who advised President-elect Lincoln to proceed secretly from Harrisburg to Washington. Now president of the powerful Pennsylvania Railroad and of the Texas & Pacific, Scott speared his rail lines through the Southwest, but encountered stout resistance from the Big Four's Southern Pacific.

Huntington counterattacked his rivals in Congress and state legislatures as well as in the mountain passes. His comments and instructions to his agent minced few words: "I believe with $200,000 I can pass our bill." "I do not think we can get any legislation this session for land grants, or for changing line of road unless we pay more for it than it is worth." "Scott is prepared to pay, or promises to pay, a large amount of money to pass his bill." The Big Four poor-mouthed about their profits, complained of the risks of western railroading and the lack of investment money, and attacked any and all "government interference," but each amassed a fortune of several tens of millions of dollars.

This dramatic union of economic and political power—symbolized by Stanford's election as United States senator in 1885 by the state legislature —was not, however, typical of the nation's political economy as a whole. The American polity was dotted by numerous power centers, but far from a master power system in government or in business, there was a chaotic dispersion of influence. Even the Big Four had a serious falling-out among themselves over politics, and even the sprawling railroad baronies could not stop passage of the Interstate Commerce Act. Big business was powerful; it was by no means all-powerful.

Certainly big business was not powerful enough to bar legislative action against the acceleration of financial and industrial combinations, even if it had had a mind to. Rooted in hundreds of years of English and American common law, the antitrust movement was propelled by powerful forces: the early American belief in competition fortified by Social Darwinism; protests by small businessmen, farmers, and workers against big mergers that threatened their livelihood; regional feeling in the South and West against big eastern "monopolists." Liberal organs like the *New York Times* joined in the attack, as did an acute foreign observer.

"The power of groups of men organized by incorporation as joint-stock companies, or of small knots of rich men acting in combination," wrote Lord Bryce in 1888, "has developed with unexpected strength in unexpected ways, overshadowing individuals and even communities, and showing that the very freedom of association which men sought to secure by law when they were threatened by the violence of potentates may, under the shelter of the law, ripen into a new form of tyranny." The wave of mergers surged on. The upshot was the Sherman Antitrust Act, passed without opposition in the House and by a 52 to 1 vote in the Senate, and signed by President Harrison in July 1890. This unusual harmony was testimony less to universal enthusiasm over the measure than to wide acceptance of the need to slow combination. Big business hardly found the act very threatening. Instead of providing explicit legal prohibitions, the measure simply outlawed "every contract, combination in the form of trust or otherwise, or conspiracy, in restraint of trade or commerce among the several states, or with foreign nations." Instead of establishing an ICC type of commission charged with single-minded enforcement of the act, Congress left enforcement in the hands of federal prosecutors, private litigants seeking triple damages, and U.S. circuit courts. Competition itself, people hoped, would make the law virtually self-enforcing.

An enfeebled government enabled a few to amass colossal riches; it had only marginal impact on the lives of the mass of people. Almost obscured in the din of battle over "tariff-for-revenue-only" and silver, for example, was the ironic fact that the federal government ran a surplus during many of these years and was embarrassed as to how properly to get rid of it. Grover Cleveland had a penchant for vetoing as "fraudulent" tiny pensions begged by impoverished widows of Union men. Cleveland's successor, Benjamin Harrison, chose as Commissioner of Pensions a past commander of the Grand Army of the Republic, who took office with the war cry, "God help the surplus!" God didn't.

*   *   *

Far more tragically, God did not favor the American Indian in the decades after the Civil War. Following a near-century of land seizures and cessions, Congress in 1871 ordered an end to treaty-making with Indian tribes. By then the early Americans, their old space on the Great Plains shrunk to the Indian Territory that would later become Oklahoma, could no longer follow the old and desperate strategy of simply "moving west." In this vital human area too, federal action was marked by a volatility of policy operating through a weak and divided government, among a diffusion of interests. With no long-term program or principle behind it, policy shifted back and forth from treaty-making to subsidy to education to isolation to assimilation to relocation to force. The Interior and War Departments and the Board of Indian Commissioners fought for influence; President, Senate, and House differed; actual dealings with Indians were often controlled by settlers, traders, and local officials. For years the selection of Indian agents was left to the Catholic Church and various Protestant sects, until church officials fell to quarreling among themselves.

Reformers—among them old abolitionists like Lydia Maria Child, Harriet Beecher Stowe, and Wendell Phillips, and an eloquent new voice, Helen Hunt Jackson—criticized Indian policies, but western senators scoffed that the farther people lived from the Indians, the more they loved them. In 1887, however, Congress passed the Dawes Act, which dissolved Indian tribes as legal entities and allotted individual Indians portions of reservation land, in order to encourage both individual initiative and assimilation with the white culture. After twenty-five years Indians would have full ownership and the rights of United States citizenship. But however well intended, the act as administered substantially disrupted Indian tribal and communal organization and indeed virtually atomized Indian cultures.

Despite the severity of its policies, Congress never seemed to focus consistently on the Indian situation. Rather the legislators debated their future, in Wiebe's view, "as it might have discussed taxes." Almost none saw any connection between the plight of Indians and that of blacks. Congress treated Indians as the enemy with which to make treaties (for land cessions), to isolate, to "civilize," and finally, when all else failed, to fight, in a series of brutal encounters that preoccupied the United States Army during the late nineteenth century.

The Indian wars on the Plains curiously resembled the political fights in Washington: there were no clear battle lines or decisive clashes, just three decades of skirmishes between a constantly shifting array of small forces. The red warriors rallied behind a string of charismatic leaders: the Sioux nation's Sitting Bull, "of compelling countenance and commanding demeanor, quick of thought and emphatic in judgments"; wily Geronimo of the Apaches; the stoic Chief Joseph of the Nez Percé. Yet none of these tribal chieftains was able to reach across centuries-old clan rivalries to unite the 200,000 Plains Indians against the invaders from the east. Nor were the white generals successful in so maneuvering their disparate units of infantry, cavalry, and artillery as to pin the Indians down for a set-piece battle. Thus the "wars" were in fact a series of collisions, of regiment against tribe in hit-and-run raids, ambushes, and mounted clashes that usually ended in tactical draws—but ultimate strategic retreat for the native Americans.

As in the past, white settlers undercut federal efforts to contain the Indians on reservations. The army tried in vain to keep prospectors out of the Black Hills area assigned to Sitting Bull's Sioux, but the gold rush accelerated in 1875, and within a year the Indians were on the warpath. Unscrupulous white traders sold the warriors ammunition and guns—including repeating rifles that were superior to the Civil War Springfields still being used by the army. But Indians too turned coats; individual warriors and sometimes whole clans helped the army to hunt down rival tribesmen.

At first the soldiers, many of them Civil War veterans, held the Plains warriors in contempt. One captain boasted that he could ride through the Sioux nation with just eighty men; within weeks, he and his entire command were dead. In 1876, the flamboyant George Custer, after chasing Crazy Horse's warriors for six months, attacked the Sioux army at Little

Big Horn; he and his force were annihilated. The truth was that the Indians were skillful fighters. Their culture centered on the horse, the hunt, and the honor of combat. Lightly equipped, deftly led, increasingly armed with modern weapons, the red warriors were "a match for any man," as one cavalry general conceded.

But while the Indians could hold their own in battle, in defending their settlements and families they were at a disadvantage. Chief Joseph marched his entire tribe over 1,700 miles and outfought several columns of pursuers, only to be besieged in his camp and forced to surrender. In another camp, at Wounded Knee Creek in 1890, a brawl started between the surrounded Indians and soldiers of Custer's old 7th Cavalry; two hundred Indians of all ages, and twenty-five white soldiers, were gunned down, and the last halfhearted resistance of the Sioux nation ended in tragedy. For a time small groups of fighters, like Geronimo's Apache band, continued a guerrilla struggle, but the very foundations of the Indian way of life were disappearing. From on foot, horseback, and even train, whites slaughtered the vast buffalo herds upon which the Plains natives depended for food and shelter.

Meanwhile, settlers streamed into the Plains. By 1890, there were five times as many whites as Indians between the Missouri and the Rockies and the U.S. census reported that the western frontier had disappeared. Military stalemate had in fact spelled decisive defeat for the native Americans.

The army that held the Indians in check received little support and much criticism from Washington. The soldiers, thirty-six regiments of whites and four of blacks, were ill housed, ill clothed, ill fed; their discipline was harsh, their weapons mismatched and often shoddy, their tasks usually boring in the extreme. The drab life and grinding routine produced a hard set of men—"villins, loyars, teeves, scoundhrils and . . . dam murdhrers," they called themselves with perverse pride. Easterners sympathetic to the Indians and horrified by the cruelty of the frontier wars branded the soldiers as butchers and barbarians. Still, the small professional army kept alive in the West those lessons of leadership, tenacity, and improvisation that the volunteers had learned so painfully in the Civil War. The veterans of the Indian wars would be formidable opponents to any foreign foe.

Of foreign foes, however, there were very few in those years. Spain had reoccupied Santo Domingo during the war but prudently withdrew in 1865. French Emperor Napoleon III, under the pretext of collecting debts owed European investors, invaded Mexico in 1861 and set up a puppet government headed by the young Austrian Archduke Ferdinand Maximilian. But, by 1867, the continued resistance of Mexican patriots led by President Benito Juárez, as well as the specter of a victorious American army on the Rio Grande, convinced Napoleon to pull out of the venture; Maximilian's regime quickly collapsed, and the erstwhile emperor was executed by his subjects.

No leader had so few followers as Secretary of State William Seward, who met constant frustration in his attempts to revive the Manifest Destiny expansionism of antebellum days. Congress rejected his bids to acquire Hawaii, Cuba, the Virgin Islands, Puerto Rico, Iceland, Greenland, and parts of Canada. His treaty to buy Alaska from the Russians for just over $7 million was approved only after Seward undertook a massive campaign to educate the public as to the potential value of the territory—and after the Russian ambassador bribed key members of the House to appropriate money for the deal. Aside from this 1867 purchase of "Seward's Icebox," the only territory added to the United States after the Civil War was the tiny Pacific island of Midway.

But there was always John Bull. Britain still loomed as both friend and rival. English loans and English-built ships had buoyed the Confederates during the war; Yankee and Canadian fishermen clashed in northern waters; a border dispute in the Far West simmered on; Irish nationalists began raiding Canada from New York. Pressure for war built up in the Senate, where Chairman Charles Sumner of the Foreign Relations Committee rose to demand that Britain pay more than $2 billion in damages for its aid to the Confederacy—or else transfer Canada to the United States in lieu of payment. The British responded with disdain to the senator's claims, and war seemed imminent on several occasions; but President Grant and his able Secretary of State, Hamilton Fish, eventually defused the crisis and hammered out an agreement. Fish and Grant also succeeded in resisting pressure to go to war with Spain, whose colony of Cuba was in the throes of a bloody revolt. After preserving the peace for eight years, the warrior-president left office in 1877—and immediately embarked on a triumphant tour of the world.

Grant's two-year procession around the globe highlighted a subtle but important change at home. It was during this period that Americans began to look outward on the world with a new interest, a new understanding, and a new level of personal and economic involvement—all of which would help to reshape foreign policy in the 1890s and beyond. Sam Grant of Ohio, as he addressed crowds of English workers, discussed realpolitik with Germany's Prince Bismarck, and shook the hand of the Emperor of Japan, was not the only American taken up with a desire to see the world. Each year the State Department issued as many as 30,000 passports for travel abroad. It was the age of the Cook tour, when low-fare steamships made Europe accessible to middle-class families. Well-to-do families like the Astors and the Roosevelts sent their children abroad as a matter of course; immigrants sought to revisit their old homes; archeologists went to dig, engineers to build and measure, and the ordinary tourists—in Henry James's sour view—to "stare and gawk and smell, and crowd every street and shop." The most numerous Americans abroad were the students and scholars—such as young Professor Woodrow Wilson of Princeton—who brought home European ideas.

In the books of traveled authors like Henry James and William Dean Howells, Americans encountering Europe was a recurring theme. Henry James based half-a-dozen novels on the idea, while Mark Twain made his own sardonic contribution with *The Innocents Abroad*. Magazines and newspapers, most of which boasted at least one foreign correspondent, filled in those Americans who lacked the money or the inclination to see things for themselves, as did the new picture postcards introduced by the Eastman Company. America's new outward gaze was not fixed exclusively on Europe, however. For two decades, readers of the New York *Herald* could thrill to the adventures of the paper's African correspondent, explorer Henry M. Stanley. Congress briefly overcame its parsimony to vote funds for several expeditions to the Arctic.

The Far East became a subject of special fascination. Americans helped to finance Japan's first railroad and to modernize its education and farming methods. Lafcadio Hearn enlivened American literature with a dozen enthusiastic and sensitive books on oriental culture. The government became involved in this turn toward the East, sometimes in spite of itself. Commodore Robert Shufeldt was recalled from Korea after a political gaffe, but not before he opened that country to American merchants and diplomats. Congress ratified a series of reciprocal-trade agreements with Hawaii, and then strengthened ties with that island kingdom by leasing a naval station at Pearl Harbor in 1887. America's involvement in Samoa nearly resulted in a war with Germany in 1889, until a hurricane sank the rival German and American fleets off the islands, giving peace efforts time to succeed.

In looking toward America's nearest neighbors, however, the country's gaze seemed to lack focus altogether. Pan-Americanism, sponsored by Benjamin Harrison's Secretary of State, James G. Blaine, bore its first fruit in 1889 when delegates from eighteen North and South American states —including Andrew Carnegie for the U.S.—met in Washington. Yet Blaine came close to provoking war with Chile in late 1891 when a group of American sailors was assaulted in Valparaíso, and many Latin Americans were irked by the heavy-handedness of President Cleveland's intervention on behalf of Venezuela in its 1895 border dispute with Britain's colony of British Guiana. Nor could the various administrations in Washington make up their minds about the assorted schemes being discussed for a canal across Central America. Yankee investment in the southern nations— reaching several hundred million dollars by the end of the century— seemed the only consistent factor in U.S. policy toward Latin America.

The great corporations, however, had a most consistent foreign policy, as they reached out for new markets and new investments: Rockefeller's Standard Oil began selling its products abroad in 1879; J. P. Morgan floated loans for Peru; Cyrus McCormick introduced his wire binder to Russia in the 1880s, just as the Equitable Company began selling life insurance to the Czar's subjects. The impact of foreign sales reached down through the economy, to Pullman workers making railroad cars for England and to midwestern farmers raising wheat for Germany and hogs for Bulgaria.

"If all thim gr-great powers . . . was . . . to attack us," Mr. Dooley said, "I'd blockade the Armour an' Company an' th' wheat ilivators iv Minnysoty. I tell ye, th' hand that rocks th' scales in th' grocery store is th' hand that rules th' wurruld."

Neither commerce nor travel had much impact on the rhetoric of the age. Congressmen still courted votes with speeches that harked back to the isolationist dicta of Washington and Jefferson, while journalists sought to sell papers by calling for the abolition of the professional foreign service. "It is a costly humbug and a sham," said the New York Sun, that "spoils a few Americans every year, and does no good to anybody." But rather than disband the diplomatic corps, Congress and the State Department significantly strengthened it during the 1870s and 1880s. Businessmen in the burgeoning export trade—which grew from $13 million to $2 billion before the century ended—successfully pressured the government to upgrade the consular service, which in turn made available to merchants a wealth of detailed information on commercial opportunities abroad. The prestige and effectiveness of the professional diplomats were greatly enhanced when Congress created the rank of ambassador in 1893.

The government took one other step to put America on a par with its neighbors, after a long period of neglect. The Civil War had sparked revolutionary developments in naval warfare: ironclad warships; mines and torpedoes; revolving gun turrets and heavy rifled cannon; the central direction of fleets over long distances by telegraph. Yet, while the nations of Europe and South America rushed to apply and improve the new naval technology, the United States disbanded most of its wartime fleet and allowed its remaining ships slowly to rot. The steam-driven, armored warships of the other powers outclassed the wooden cruisers—many of which still relied on sails—and tiny ironclad monitors of the U.S. Navy. By the end of the 1870s, America was surpassed as a seapower by Chile, China, and ten other countries.

Studying the progress in ship design made by other navies, American officers struggled to train themselves in the use of weapons that they did not have. Pressure from the sailors—and from Republican politicians eager to get rid of the embarrassing budget surpluses generated by protective tariffs—finally bore fruit when President Chester Arthur agreed that "every condition of national safety, economy, and honor" demanded a "thorough rehabilitation of the Navy." The first bill to pass Congress called for building three armored cruisers; over the next decade, money was granted for a dozen more cruisers, as well as for five battleships to be the equal of any fielded by the Europeans.

The armored war fleet that slowly took shape was a monument to American industrial progress. In the yards of the Bethlehem Steel Company first one behemoth and then another grew and took form: the four-hundred-foot hull, reaching up forty or more feet over the heads of workmen; the twin propellers, projecting out the stern from steam engines larger than Americans had ever before installed in ships; the long plates of rolled steel stretching along the deck and waterline. After being launched, the ship was fitted out with heavily armored turrets mounting eight- or twelve-inch guns, torpedoes newly designed by inventor Arthur Whitehead, electric searchlights, modern signaling devices, and—after 1892—an internal telephone system.

As more and better ships came off the ways, some men in the naval establishment began to think in terms of a broader role than home defense for the navy. Benjamin Tracy, Secretary of the Navy during most of the period of expansion, consistently advocated an oceangoing fleet capable of attacking the shipping and coasts of any potential foe, and at the new Naval War College Captain Alfred Thayer Mahan conducted an influential series of lectures on seapower and the need for coaling stations abroad. But Congress remained committed to a smaller, defensive fleet. The very names of the battleships spoke of the nation's homeward-looking character: the *Texas,* the *Indiana,* the *Maine.*

Showdown 1896

Even as the nation's economy pounded toward new peaks of investment and production in the early 1890s, men of affairs were assailed by doubts about the future. Suddenly the days were gone when an Andrew Carnegie could write his *Triumphant Democracy* and, when asked "What had become of the shadows?," could answer that his book was "written at high noon,

when the blazing sun overhead casts no shadow." Now there were shadows
—produced by strains in the economy, a persistent agricultural depression, racial and religious tensions, and, above all, ferment among farmers
and workers. Editorialists worried about immigration, trusts, liquor, socialism, woman suffrage.

Though some feared a war between haves and have-nots, history would
be less simple but more decisive. Few at the start of the 1890s could predict
that the decade would produce social and political torrents that would
wash over old lines of conflict, precipitate an electoral showdown, and
leave in its wake a realigned and polarized party system that would dominate American politics for decades.

Still, a war between rich and poor seemed plausible as the rich in 1892
looked at the poor in farm and factory. In the West and South, the Populists were mobilizing for the 1894 elections with a militant campaign to
seek out black support, even while toning down their radicalism to win
urban and middle-class voters. In Georgia, Tom Watson ran again for
Congress in 1894, after winning nomination in a Populist convention that
was about one-third black—probably the peak of Southern black participation in the 1890s. The Populists increased their total vote in 1894 over the
previous presidential election, but both Watson and "Sockless Jerry"
Simpson were defeated, and widespread election fraud left the Populists
in a bitter mood as they planned for 1896.

The labor front appeared even more ominous to economic elites, especially after the bloody struggle at Andrew Carnegie's Homestead steel
works in July 1892. That summer Carnegie was reaching the height of his
economic power and world celebrity. His was now the biggest steel company on the globe, able to produce half as much as all the British steel
makers combined. A few years earlier, Carnegie had happily acquired the
most modern of rail mills in Homestead, Pennsylvania—but with it he
had less happily acquired several hundred members of the Amalgamated
Iron, Steel and Tin Workers, one of the best-organized unions of skilled
workers in the country. When Carnegie departed for Scotland in the
spring of 1892, he left in charge of Homestead his forty-three-year-old
managing partner, Henry Clay Frick. Named after his wealthy grandfather's political hero, Frick from his tenderest years had epitomized the
Horatio Alger ideal of pluck and luck. Through a fanatical commitment
to the making and selling of coke he had made his first million by the age
of thirty, and as the steel plants devoured more and more of the soft
black "coal cake," Frick had borrowed against his own future legacies,
borrowed from his uncles, borrowed from his father—who mortgaged
his small farm to raise the cash—to buy coal lands and build hundreds of

coke ovens. Soon the "coke king" was invited to join Carnegie's expanding empire.

Carnegie had defended unionism, especially in his preachings abroad,
but behind his rhetoric it was weak, local unions he favored, not national
organizations. Frick suffered no such ambivalence. Viewing the Amalgamated with implacable hostility, he sought a showdown that would break
this union which was resisting his demand for a lower sliding wage rate.
When their request for continued negotiations was denied, union workers
closed down the plant. Refusing concessions, Frick surrounded the mill
with a stockade of planks topped by barbed wire, ordered up three hundred Pinkerton guards as strikebreakers, and arranged for his hired private
army to be brought by barges to Homestead and landed inside the stockade in the dead of night.

The events of July 6, 1892, would become a grim saga of American labor:
the alarm sounded by sirens and factory whistles after union guards spot-
ted the Pinkertons; the frantic efforts of workers to beat off the barge
landings with hoes, guns, and fence staves; the Pinkerton strikebreakers,
drifting offshore in the infernal heat of the barges, finally running up a
white flag; the granting of safe-conduct to the Pinkertons so they could
march away; and then the gory climax as workers and their wives, now a
maddened horde bent on vengeance, fell on the Pinkertons, flailed at them
with clubs and iron-filled stockings, jabbed at their eyes with umbrellas,
tore off their bright-buttoned uniforms, and left three dead, a dozen injured, and the rest naked and bloodied.

In the end Frick and Carnegie won, of course, because they could summon superior force—in this case 8,000 state troops to open up the plant.
Both men paid a price. A "Nihilist" immigrant from Lithuania, Alexander
Berkman, burst into Frick's office, shot him twice in the neck, and stabbed
him repeatedly. Frick coolly wrote out telegrams to his mother and to
Carnegie about the event, informed the press that the company's antiunion policy would not be changed, and went home to recuperate. Carnegie, who had remained almost incommunicado in a Scottish retreat, was
ridiculed in the British and American press for his autocratic practices as
compared to his democratic preachings.

"Say what you will of Frick," the St. Louis *Post-Dispatch* trumpeted, "he
is a brave man. Say what you will of Carnegie, he is a coward, and gods
and men hate cowards."

The Homestead violence had embarrassed the Republican party, which
had an election to win against Grover Cleveland in 1892. A GOP emissary
visited the convalescing Frick with a proposal to recognize the union and
settle the strike. "I will never recognize the Union, never, never!" Frick

burst out. President Harrison—even Carnegie himself—could not make
him do this, he said. Later Harrison blamed Homestead for his defeat. But
if Harrison hoped to prick the industrialists' conscience, he did not know
these men. They considered Cleveland safer than Harrison.

"Cleveland! Landslide!" Carnegie wrote Frick on hearing the returns.
"Well we have nothing to fear and perhaps it is best. . . ." He was quite
right. Cleveland, in this his second White House stint, soon proved himself
sounder than ever on gold, civil service, federal spending—everything save
the tariff. He struck the theme of his Administration in his Inaugural
Address with a denunciation of "paternalism." The lesson must be
learned, he said, "that while the people should patriotically and cheerfully
support their Government its functions do not include the support of the
people." He would teach that lesson.

Hosts of farmers facing debts and declining prices, workers toiling sixty
hours a week, financiers skittish over bank failures abroad, and a President
who barred his government from "supporting the people"—the combusti-
bles were there for the igniting. The fuse was lighted in May 1893 when
converging financial pressures produced a detonation on Wall Street that
left prices sagging. By year's end, almost six hundred banks and perhaps
15,000 businesses had failed. Within a few months stocks lost several
hundred million dollars in value. At the depth of the depression, over a
quarter of the nation's railroad mileage was in receivership. Farm prices
dropped further. Two and a half million persons, it was estimated, were
left looking for work.

Cleveland's response to the crisis was to cling even more tightly to
orthodoxy. To stem the drain on the nation's gold reserve the President
forced repeal of the Sherman Silver Purchase Act through Congress, amid
the indignation of the silverites. He pressed for a lower tariff, then let a
moderate bill become law without his signature. He was in no mood to
make concessions to farmers desperate over mortgages or workers facing
wage cuts and layoffs. Soon he faced both these specters.

By the spring of 1894, masses of men who had been wandering the
countryside looking for work were beginning to cohere as leaders arose to
channel their desperate needs into a political force. The self-appointed
leader of the "Commonweal Army of Christ" was a thirty-nine-year-old
Ohio Populist and factory owner named Jacob Coxey. Soon Coxey was
leading his army, half-a-thousand strong, several hundred miles through
Ohio and Pennsylvania to Washington to offer a living petition, a "petition
in boots." Arrested in the capital amid much publicity for "walking on the
grass," the army was forcibly dispersed. Coxey's proposals for public
works jobs through the issuance of paper currency were introduced in

Congress—only to be ignored or jeered at by many of the lawmakers.

No one could laugh off the trouble that developed in Chicago in a conflict between a paternalistic employer and a militant union leader. By 1894, George Pullman had developed his Palace Car Company into a $36 million business employing 5,000 workers who built, serviced, and operated his plush and paneled sleepers. Pullman had also built a model town "bordered with bright beds of flowers and green velvety stretches of lawn," as the company proclaimed, which Pullman's men ruled with benevolent authority. "We are born in a Pullman house," one worker said, "fed from the Pullman shop, taught in the Pullman school, catechized in the Pullman church, and when we die we shall be buried in the Pullman cemetery and go to the Pullman hell."

When the company laid off men, cut wages, and yet maintained rents during the spreading depression, the workers turned to Eugene Debs's militant American Railway Union. Long active in the railroad brotherhoods, Debs had founded the ARU as a means of transcending craft rivalries and uniting the 150,000 railroad workers in the Midwest. When Pullman refused to negotiate with his workers, the ARU ordered a boycott of Pullman cars, the railroads began to fire any man who refused to switch Pullman cars, and soon 125,000 men on twenty railroads had quit.

Behind the issues of wages and rents was the central question of power —and the employers had far greater power resources. The General Managers Association, a militant organization of railroads, took command of the anti-strike effort. The ARU turned to the American Federation of Labor for support, but its president, Samuel Gompers, believed neither in industrial unionism nor in the prospects of an ARU victory. The AFL issued words of encouragement to the ARU but decided against a general strike. When some minor disturbances occurred along the tracks and an injunction was defied, Cleveland sent several thousand "special deputies" to restore order over the vociferous objections of Illinois Governor John P. Altgeld. Intensified violence followed, the strike was broken, and Debs was jailed.

The political pendulum oscillated wildly in response to the economic and social pressures of the early nineties. In the most volatile part of the country—the more heavily urban areas stretching from Wisconsin and Illinois through New England—the Republicans won 115 congressional seats to the Democrats' 54 in 1888, lost to the Democrats 63 to 106 two years later, split 88 to 89 in 1892, and overwhelmed their foes 168 to 9 two years later. The Democrats lost a total of 113 seats in the 1894 congressional elections, the largest pendulum sweep since the Civil War. Former Republican Speaker Thomas B. Reed—who now would return to the speakership—had predicted such Democratic losses that the dead would be buried in trenches and marked "unknown." He hardly exaggerated.

This midterm repudiation of Cleveland served mainly to harden the Administration in its economic policies. The Treasury now faced dwindling federal revenues, at the same time that gold reserves declined despite the repeal of the Sherman Silver Purchase Act. Desperately Cleveland turned to the big bankers for loans through bond issues, without much response; ultimately he was bailed out by a syndicate headed by J. Pierpont Morgan and August Belmont, Jr., which purchased 3.5 million ounces of gold.

With mounting indignation, silverites, Populists, and socialists watched Cleveland's failure to cope with the depression, his hard-money policies, his "sellouts" to the Morgans and the rest of the hard-eyed bankers. He was so unpopular personally by now—"I hate the ground that man walks on," declared an Alabama senator—as to have lost any hope for renomination in 1896, or even to have decisive influence in the convention. Richard ("Silver Dick") Bland and other leaders of the silver bloc in the House framed an "Appeal of the Silver Democrats" asking immediate restoration of free and unlimited coinage of silver at the ratio of 16 to 1, but the Administration was adamant. As a party the Democrats were in disarray, with Cleveland and the old "Bourbon" element almost impotent, except in their veto power, the silverites tied to one issue and lacking a compelling leader, and the whole party confronted on the left by a militant populist movement.

The Populists, however, were facing a severe internal crisis. Sobered by their election defeats in 1894 and pressured by the growing clamor for "free silver," Jerry Simpson and others resolved to make silver a magnet to draw the nation's reform forces into the People's party. Other Populist leaders held that narrowing their broad platform to free silver would mean dumping the rest of their reforms. "The scheme," roared Tom Watson, "is a trap, a pitfall, a snare, a menace, a fraud." It would mean "forever checking our advance toward government ownership of the railroads" and other key goals. Only as part of a broad set of measures could free coinage of silver do any good. A Populist party convention early in 1895 reaffirmed the whole sacred creed by a large majority, but it was clear that internal trouble lay ahead.

*   *   *

Times of heightened social pressures and political conflict often demand extraordinary leadership; the alternative may be chaos and worse. The mid-nineties produced not one but two remarkable leaders who were pitted against each other in one of the great dramas of American politics.

By this time, William McKinley had become an experienced and effective party politician and officeholder. Both political and personal setbacks had seasoned him. After six terms in the House, where he took leadership of tariff battles and served as chairman of Ways and Means, he was engulfed in the Democratic landslide of 1890, but he rebounded in 1891 by winning election as governor of Ohio. Then while governor he suddenly found himself nearly $130,000 in debt because an old friend who had once helped McKinley had failed in business and left notes countersigned by the governor. Wealthy friends bailed him out, with minimum publicity. One of the leaders in this effort was Mark Hanna, a Cleveland banker and traction magnate, who had consecrated himself to the mission of making McKinley President.

By 1896, as a leading spokesman for a Republican tariff, as a friend of Hanna and other men of money, and as a veteran legislator, executive, and party man coming from the most strategic of states, McKinley was the front runner for the Republican nomination. But his strength lay deeper than this. He had inherited, in H. Wayne Morgan's words, "the political tendencies of a whole generation. The ideals of party unity and loyalty, outlined when Rutherford B. Hayes sat in the White House, found a logical spokesman in the man who championed every aspect of Republican nationalism, and mastered the arts of political leadership in a confused and fragmented era. He was fatalistic about success; an air of predestination hung about his apparent victory. But he and Hanna insured that destiny with years of hard work, cultivation of mass opinion, and close attention to a new, widened industrial constituency."

As McKinley headed for a first-ballot nomination in the spring weeks of 1896, the press was anticipating a far more open convention for the Democracy. Increasingly, though, they were watching the rise of a young Nebraskan, William Jennings Bryan, who had taken vocal leadership of the silver Democrats. Like McKinley, he had been born and educated in the Midwest. Both men had started their professional careers as small-town lawyers and had turned to politics; and both, in Paul Glad's view, "were steeped in the moralistic tradition of American Protestantism." They had played congressional Box and Cox when Bryan had won appointment to the House Ways and Means Committee just after McKinley had left it. But there the resemblances ceased. Seventeen years younger than McKinley, Bryan had been only an infant during the Civil War. He differed sharply with the Ohioan on silver, tariff, and most other key issues. If both shared small-town moralities, Bryan was positively steeped in the rural virtues, in the agrarian myth of the independent, liberty-loving yeoman, in the Jeffer-

sonian concept of simple, grass-roots democracy. And if McKinley was a
good-looking, well-set-up man who fitted the image of a President, Bryan
was positively charismatic—"a tall, slender, handsome fellow," Robert La
Follette remembered, "who looked like a young divine."

Sure enough, the McKinley machine, well fueled by Hanna's energy and
ample funds, rolled to a smashing victory on the first ballot in the Republican convention in St. Louis. Assembling three weeks later in Chicago, the
Democratic convention in form followed the traditional pattern of the
great national enclaves: there was the usual crush of delegates, hangers-on,
and spectators in a big overdecorated hall; the usual stentorian speeches;
and the usual battle over the platform, with the silverites on this occasion
winning a plank calling for the free and unlimited coinage of silver at the
16 to 1 ratio. But it was one of those occasions when none of this mattered
very much, when a single event dominated the convention both at the time
and in retrospect. That event was merely a speech—but a speech that itself
became a mobilizer of people and a ganglion of history. Like most such
events, it was an act carefully contrived and long rehearsed, an act taken
boldly and at just the right moment.

Just the right moment was during the debate on the platform, when
William Jennings Bryan sprang from his seat and bounded up to the
rostrum, as a great wave of applause and exultation rolled across the floor
and into the galleries. He stood before them dressed in his black sack suit
of alpaca, a low-cut vest, trousers slightly baggy at the knees, his head
thrown back, left hand on the lectern, his right hand free for grand gestures. The address contained little new of substance, but few present on
that day would forget the magnificent sentences.

"I come to speak to you in defense of a cause as holy as the cause of
liberty—the cause of humanity.

"With a zeal approaching the zeal which inspired the crusaders who
followed Peter the Hermit, our silver Democrats went forth from victory
unto victory until they are now assembled, not to discuss, not to debate,
but to enter up the judgment already rendered by the plain people of this
country."

Bryan was speaking effortlessly, hardly raising his voice, yet reaching the
farthest seats in the convention hush.

"We have petitioned, and our petitions have been scorned; we have
entreated, and our entreaties have been disregarded; we have begged, and
they have mocked when our calamity came. We beg no longer; we entreat
no more; we petition no more. *We defy them.*"

The crowd was now rising and shouting as Bryan drove his points home.
When the gold men, he said, charged that the silver forces disturbed their

business interests, "we reply that you have disturbed our business interests"—workers, attorneys, merchants, farmers, all these were as much businessmen as the "man who goes upon the board of trade and bets upon the price of grain."

The crowd was in a near-frenzy as Bryan came to his peroration:

"Having behind us the producing masses of this nation and the world, supported by the commercial interests, the laboring interests, and the toilers everywhere, we will answer their demand for a gold standard by saying to them: *You shall not press down upon the brow of labor this crown of thorns, you shall not crucify mankind upon a cross of gold.*"

After a series of dramatic roll-call votes, Bryan bested Silver Dick Bland and went on to win the Democratic presidential nomination on the fifth ballot.

Bryan's nomination left the Populists in bitter disarray. Fusionists, expecting the Democrats to cling to gold, had insisted on holding their convention after the Democrats so that they could scoop up the droves of Democrats who would desert the party of Cleveland. Now, with their plans turned topsy-turvy, they decided that they must nominate Bryan—and the Maine banker and railroad man Arthur Sewall, who had been chosen for Vice-President. Anti-fusionists saw Bryan's nomination and the Democrats' plagiarizing of the Populist platform as a plot to cripple both the Populist movement and party. And they could not stomach the "anti-labor" Sewall.

"If we fuse we are sunk," Henry D. Lloyd summed up the dilemma: "If we don't fuse, all the silver men we have will leave us for the more powerful Democrats." At a convention racked with pandemonium and bitter debate, the fusionists won the nomination for Bryan, and—despite a telegram from the Commoner refusing the nomination unless he could run with Sewall —named Tom Watson for Vice-President. During the fall campaign both Bryan and the Populist hierarchy cold-shouldered Watson, who swallowed insult and ridicule as he barnstormed the country for Bryan and himself.

The other candidates followed their own strategy. McKinley remained in his hometown of Canton, receiving delegations as part of his front porch campaign. This was not a matter of sitting in a rocker and chatting with individual visitors. Rather, delegations poured into Canton by the hundreds, the thousands, the tens of thousands, marched to McKinley's home behind clamorous bands and huge banners, and received in turn a short, carefully phrased talk from the candidate. On one day, he gave speeches to a total of 80,000 persons. All the while Hanna & co. saturated the country with millions of leaflets and pamphlets, 1,400 orators, and arguments against free trade and free silver. The national committee reportedly spent the unprecedented sum of $4 million, probably much more.

Bryan went to the "plain people" he apotheosized. Covering over 18,-000 miles by train, speaking sometimes thirty or more times a day, he reached perhaps 5 million persons in twenty-seven states. He encountered an avalanche of criticism from the eastern press, which pictured him as an anarchist and revolutionist. For his part, Hanna was labeled "Dollar Mark," and this hurt him. But the Republican party, deeply bottomed organizationally and mobilized for action, appealed directly to all members of its grand coalition—labor, farmers, small businessmen, veterans, blacks.

On election night, Bryan sat imperturbably in his home as three telegraph operators brought in bulletin after bulletin spelling his defeat. In Canton, McKinley sat at his desk analyzing returns, smoking cigar after cigar, and then heard the first sounds of crowds nearing to cheer and serenade him amid dazzling fireworks. A telegram arrived from Bryan: "We have submitted the issues to the American people, and their word is law." At his home, Bryan told reporters: "The fight has just commenced." Watson, emotionally broken, mourned the death of the Populist party. Fusion, he said, had killed it.

TRIUMPHANT REPUBLICANISM

When the newspapers proclaimed a great Republican victory next day, the outcome at first seemed to be merely another party switch—the fourth in the presidency since 1884. As more returns were telegraphed in from the rural West and North, however, it became clear that not only was the White House to change occupants but a momentous shift had occurred in party fortunes and electoral patterns. Voting turnout, for example, had jumped from 12 million in 1892 to nearly 14 million four years later. And as the years passed, analysts realized that 1896 was one of the crucial elections in American history, leading to a "critical realigning era" that would reshape American politics and government for decades.

McKinley's majority over Bryan in the popular vote—7.1 million votes to 6.5 million—was the biggest presidential margin since Grant, but the significance of the vote lay less in its numbers than in its geographical distribution. Despite the Republican denunciations of Bryan for arousing the hatred of farmers and workers and "setting class against class," there was far less economic than regional polarization. The geography of the election results was indeed quite remarkable. As usual the Democrats had carried the South and the Republicans had swept the northern tier, but, in between, McKinley carried every state east of the Mississippi, including the border states of Maryland, Delaware, West Virginia, and Kentucky.

The great electoral heartland bordered by Illinois and Wisconsin on the west and New York and Pennsylvania on the east—the pivot of most presidential contests—had swung to McKinley by an enormous margin. Even across the Mississippi, Bryan had lost Iowa, Minnesota, North Dakota, Oregon, and California. As the head of the Democratic ticket failed in state after state, he dragged down with him hundreds of state and local Democratic candidates.

Bryan had simply failed to attract two of his great potential constituencies—eastern urban labor and midwestern farmers. Not a single county in Illinois, Indiana, Iowa, or Wisconsin, James Sundquist noted, showed a gain in its Democratic percentage over the combined Democratic-Populist strength of 1892. Cleveland's unpopularity, Bryan's inability to appeal to industrial labor, McKinley's coalition politics, and Hanna's massive propaganda campaign had left the grand old Democracy a shrunken remnant. Many voters had simply been scared away by Republican orators and editors. "To the image of the Democrats as the party of rum, Romanism, rebellion, and economic recession," in Sundquist's words, "was added another R—radicalism."

Not only did the GOP emerge as a grand new party combining its old business, farm, veterans, and black support with widened labor backing; it was emerging also as a powerful governing instrument in Washington and in many of the state capitals. Whether tested by the quality of the GOP's national leadership in McKinley, Hanna & co., its explicit platform speaking out forthrightly on major issues (save woman's suffrage!), its year-round organizational structure building up from town and precinct committees, its ability to mobilize electoral support, its high capacity for raising money and commanding publicity, its congressional leadership and cohesion, the "redeveloped" Republican party was in a position, according to Paul Kleppner, to control most of the nation's policy-making institutions after 1896.

It was easy for Bryan Democrats, silverites, and Populists to denounce the GOP as the party of plutocrats, tariff-mongers, monopolists, and gold bugs, because in part it was. But Republicanism was much more than this. The party not only reflected the interests of big capitalists; to a marked degree it disciplined those interests—in the party's own interest, of course. The party would limit immigration even though many big employers wanted to import cheap foreign labor; the party would restrict trusts to some degree; above all, the party would maintain its appeal to farmers and workers by returning to a "free homestead policy," restricting immigration, creating a National Board of Arbitration to mediate labor disputes. Furious at Frick and other industrialists who provoked fights with labor,

Republican party leaders would not let them dominate party councils.

So the McKinley Republicans prepared to govern in 1897 in a spirit of self-confidence and high expectations. Within four months of inauguration, McKinley signed the Dingell tariff bill raising rates higher than ever but also authorizing reciprocity negotiations with other countries. A year later, Congress passed the Erdman Act providing for limited mediation of railroad labor disputes—a belated response to the Pullman strike. But there was no rush of legislation—the Republicans had no interest in passing a lot of laws. Rather, McKinley and his congressional leaders ran a tight ship, at least in domestic policy. Especially notable was McKinley's firm but delicate touch—with assists from Hanna—in curbing the power of old-time Republican state bosses such as Thomas C. Platt of New York and Matthew Quay of Pennsylvania.

Not all the groups in McKinley's big coalition fared well during his presidential term. Lower-income labor, striking workers, and poor farmers received little help from the White House. As usual, the most forgotten group was blacks, North and South. Despite the GOP's "unqualified condemnation of the uncivilized and barbarous practice" of lynching in its 1896 platform, lynch law took more and more victims in the nineties. In 1896 the Supreme Court upheld segregation in railroad carriages, in *Plessy* v. *Ferguson;* two years later it sustained the poll tax and literacy tests in *Williams* v. *Mississippi.* Few were around to offer militant protest. Frederick Douglass had died in 1895, and Booker T. Washington accepted segregation. "In all things that are purely social," Washington liked to say, "we can be as separate as the fingers, yet one as the hand in all things essential to our mutual progress." Carnegie called him the most remarkable man alive, noting that Negro illiteracy had been almost cut in half in thirty years and that black land ownership had expanded.

Certainly Carnegie was satisfied with McKinleyism. "Triumphant Democracy is once more Triumphant," he had written a Scottish friend after McKinley's election. "All is well." Later he would break with the President on foreign policy, but domestically McKinley stood for the things the steel magnate believed in. They both believed in liberty, but a negative liberty to be achieved against government and not through it. "The Republic may not give wealth or happiness; she has not promised these," said Carnegie; "it is the freedom to pursue these, not their realization, which the Declaration of Independence claims. . . ." They both believed in Horatio Alger individualism, competitiveness, getting ahead, in the self-made man rising from rags to riches. They both believed in majority rule, perhaps in part because majorities had tended to vote the "right way."

Majority rule—that was the test. Populists, left-wing Democrats, socialists had long dreamed the dream of a coalition of the poor that would use
their only political resource, votes, to win control of government and
convert it into an instrument of social and economic justice. Third parties
had mobilized minorities, not majorities. Bryan had utterly failed to put
together a mighty coalition of the have-nots. And even if a truly popular
coalition had won control of government, checks and balances against the
majority within the government—the power of a money-dominated, unrepresentative Senate, for example—would have thwarted true majority rule.
Few of the have-nots would have found any triumphs in Carnegie's Triumphant Democracy. The have-nots were "ready to question whether, indeed, there was a democracy, when the courts could halt their strikes by
injunctions, jail their labor leaders, declare laws taxing men of wealth
unconstitutional, and smile indulgently on monopolistic trusts," in Joseph
Wall's view. "Congress seemed eager only to protect those who were
already secure, and the President looked to Wall Street, not Main Street,
for support and guidance."

Triumphant *Democracy?* McKinley, Carnegie, et al. seemed really to believe in a very Republican *Republic.* And soon people would charge that
McKinley, at least, seemed to believe in a most imperial Empire.

*　　*　　*

In Havana, late in January 1898, the *Maine* swung slowly at anchor in the
middle of the harbor, the increasingly tense crew confined on board.
Armed sentries were posted on deck, ammunition piled by the guns, steam
kept up. Still the men aboard waited week after week, as officials in Washington considered bringing the big battleship home.

The arrival of the *Maine* in Havana had been just one more step toward
American involvement in the Cubans' war for independence from Spain.
That struggle had resumed in 1895, after a truce of two decades, and by
1898, more than a hundred thousand men had fallen on both sides of the
conflict. Spain, with nearly 200,000 soldiers on the island, controlled
Havana and the other major cities; the revolutionaries, with only a fifth as
many men in the field at any one time, dominated most of the countryside.
The pleas of the revolutionaries received considerable support in the
United States. As meetings to support *Cuba Libre* mushroomed across the
nation, sympathy for the rebels was compounded by indignation at the
apparently heartless countermeasures of the Spanish.

Two flamboyant editors eyed the Cuban situation with avid interest:
William Randolph Hearst of the New York *Journal* and Joseph Pulitzer of
the New York *World.* Engaged in a no-holds-barred circulation war, they

largely ignored the gritty realities of the struggle, filling their columns with rumors, invective, fiction, and lurid atrocity stories designed to titillate rather than inform. By 1898, Hearst and Pulitzer were between them selling more than 1 1/2 million copies daily, and a host of papers across the country rushed to imitate them. Popular sympathy for the Cuban revolution, which predated the Hearst-Pulitzer war, surged to a new high. Grover Cleveland had resisted these pressures, being perhaps more concerned with the threat to U.S. commercial interests and by the possibility that the rebels, many of whose leaders were black, would establish a biracial republic just ninety miles from the United States.

William McKinley had come to office facing a welter of conflicting forces over Cuba. Spain still held the island, precariously, but it was tiring of the expensive conflict. The rebels continued to press for recognition in the United States and military victory in Cuba. A large portion of the American public and the Congress—and the Republican party platform—supported Cuban independence, but had no clear plan for bringing it about. Businessmen favored any peaceful means of bringing more stability and U.S. trade to the island. A small group of expansionists, including Senator Henry Cabot Lodge and McKinley's own Assistant Secretary of the Navy, Theodore Roosevelt, urged the annexation of Cuba as the first step in building an overseas U.S. empire. The yellow journalists continued to play up anything that would yield rousing headlines.

McKinley's deftness in shepherding domestic issues through Congress was matched by his careful handling of the Cuban crisis. He deflected congressional moves to recognize the Cubans, put increasing pressure on Spain to loosen its hold on the island, and continued to interdict arms shipments to the rebels. A new Madrid government seemed to respond favorably to McKinley's call for an end to the cruel and futile occupation policy when, in late 1897, it announced a number of reforms, including a plan for Cuban autonomy within the Spanish empire. The private messages from McKinley's minister to Spain make clear, however, that the President viewed autonomy as a step toward gradual United States absorption of Cuba, as either a commercial dependency or an outright colony. Thus McKinley carefully avoided any move that would help the rebels in Cuba to achieve independence on their own, Philip Foner has concluded.

McKinley's subtle intervention was hampered by the refusal of the rebels, and of many of the Spanish officers in Cuba, to accept autonomy. Late in January 1898, Havana was convulsed by riots protesting the new policy, and Secretary of the Navy John D. Long ordered the *Maine* to the city to protect American lives and act as a restraining influence. While the battleship kept its tense vigil in Havana harbor, Hearst's *Journal* published a letter, stolen from a friend of Spanish Ambassador Dupuy de Lôme, that called into question Spain's sincerity in granting the recent reforms—as well as containing some gratuitous insults to McKinley. Amidst great public outcry de Lôme was recalled, and the President was confronted with the knowledge that even the Madrid government doubted autonomy was feasible. Then, as pressure to recognize Cuba's independence again mounted, the *Maine* blew up, killing 266 of the men on board.

"THE WARSHIP MAINE WAS SPLIT IN TWO BY AN ENEMY'S SECRET INFERNAL MACHINE," headlined the *Journal,* while Assistant Secretary Roosevelt assured a friend that "the *Maine* was sunk by an act of dirty treachery on the part of the Spaniards"—but most of the public withheld judgment pending the findings of the official inquiry. Seventy-eight years after the sinking of the *Maine,* the U.S. Navy Department would publish a study, prepared by a senior officer and two experienced civilian engineers, attributing the disaster to spontaneous combustion in a coal bunker below decks, which ignited an adjacent ammunition store. But the four officers sent in 1898 to investigate for the U.S. government, pressured by press and public demand for a quick judgment, ruled that the battleship was sunk by "the explosion of a mine situated under the bottom of the ship." Who had put the alleged mine there, the four could not say.

The press jingoes had no doubt who put the mine there. The cry for war rose over the land. McKinley had already anticipated war by gaining a congressional appropriation for $50 million. Some in Congress, however, felt that America should enter the conflict as the ally of the Cubans. In an attempt to head off such a move, McKinley assured key legislators that he was negotiating with Spain for Cuba's independence. In fact, the Spanish did accede to most of the President's demands. They failed, however, to give independence to the island—which McKinley did not ask for—or to transfer it to the United States, which seems to have been the President's true aim. On April 11, just two days after Spain made further diplomatic concessions, McKinley sent his war message to Capitol Hill.

For more than a week a minority in Congress tried to force the President to recognize the Cuban rebels. Ohio's Senator Joseph Foraker charged that otherwise "this intervention" would be converted from an act of "humanity" into an "aggressive conquest of territory." On April 20, McKinley signed a joint resolution that did call for Cuba's independence and authorized American intervention to help achieve it, but withheld recognition of the revolutionaries. The resolution also incorporated the compromise Teller Amendment, which disclaimed any United States intention to annex Cuba. Congress rallied behind the President only after Madrid broke relations with Washington, and by overwhelming majorities

the House and Senate voted that a state of war existed with Spain. It was
April 25, 1898. For the first time in fifty years the United States faced a
foreign foe.

*   *   *

America had three assets in its war with Spain—a strong navy, a small
but professional army, and a well-thought-out strategy. It was the navy that
first made itself felt, striking a dramatic blow halfway around the world
from Cuba. On the morning of May 1, six U.S. cruisers and gunboats under
the command of Commodore George Dewey steamed into Manila Bay and
confronted Spain's larger but antiquated Asian fleet. For five hours, amidst
sweltering heat and drifting clouds of gunsmoke, Dewey's ships battered
the Spaniards; by noon, every Spanish ship had been wrecked, while the
American squadron was all but untouched. Dewey's telegram announcing
the victory—which took seven days to reach America from the Philippines
—electrified the country.

All eyes now turned to Cuba—and to the United States Army. Although
rearmed since the Indian wars, the 25,000-man Regular forces were inadequate to challenge Spain on the ground, so McKinley made the traditional
call for volunteers. Some 200,000 men, including Secretary Roosevelt and
William Jennings Bryan, joined the Volunteer regiments, while Congress
authorized the army to enlist another 36,000 Regulars. This tenfold increase over a matter of weeks swamped the peacetime bureaucracy of the
War Department. Conflicts between Washington and the states over who
would pay for what, the almost complete lack of trained officers and of
support personnel for the Volunteers, and the usual politicking in the state
capitals all multiplied confusion. Instead of waiting for the new recruits to
finish training, McKinley threw into action the Regular and national guard
units that were available.

On May 30, the President instructed General William Shafter to seize the
port of Santiago, where a Spanish squadron under Admiral Pascual Cervera was blockaded by the navy's battleships. After an unseemly rush for
the transports—where the Rough Riders saw their first action, against
other U.S. soldiers trying to get aboard the overcrowded boats—Shafter's
command sailed for Cuba. The fleet arrived off Santiago and began to
bombard the invasion beaches, much to the annoyance of the rebel force
waiting to run an iron pier out for the Americans. Once the seasick invaders were ashore, Shafter began a cautious advance toward the fortified city.
Ex-Confederate Joseph Wheeler, however, dashed ahead with his brigade
of dismounted cavalry and collided with a Spanish delaying force. Before
the Americans could work through the jungle on their flank, the blue-clad

Spaniards withdrew—prompting Wheeler to slip back thirty years and shout, "We've got the damned Yankees on the run!"

The main rebel army under Maximo Gomez, who had expected the Americans to land near Havana, was trapped by the Spanish in the center of the island, but one division was able to join Shafter, while other detachments worked to cut off Santiago. Thus reinforced, the American general pushed forward to San Juan Hill, where Spanish General Joaquin del Rey made a stand. Del Rey himself fell in the gallant defense, as the Spaniards shot down an American observation balloon, wrecked an artillery battery, and picked off scores of the attackers. Finally a brigade of Volunteers, stiffened with a black Regular unit led by John J. Pershing, pushed the Spanish off Kettle Hill and wheeled to charge the heights of San Juan. Sweating, holding their rifles across their chests as bullets clipped the waist-high grass around them, the Americans waded up San Juan Hill. The enemy broke, and Shafter advanced to the outskirts of Santiago.

After one assault on the city failed, the Americans and Cubans settled down to besiege it. Meanwhile General Nelson Miles, captor of Geronimo and Chief Joseph, landed virtually unopposed in Puerto Rico, and the American expeditionary force in the Philippines closed on the capital city of Manila. The last dramatic moment of the war came on July 3, when Admiral Cervera sortied from Santiago harbor, catching the American fleet by surprise. Once again the Spanish ships were outclassed; Cervera watched in despair as one by one his cruisers blew up or ran aground. Captain John Philip of the *Texas* was also moved, reportedly exhorting his crew, "Don't cheer, men—the poor fellows are dying."

With the defeat of Cervera, Spain had had enough. Representatives from the two powers met in Paris, and on August 12 the Spanish agreed to evacuate the Philippines and the Caribbean, pending a final peace treaty. After 113 days, the war was over.

America's striking success owed much to the astute strategy pursued by McKinley. Influenced in part by three years of staff discussions in the navy about the possible ways to fight Spain, the President from the first insisted on a limited war. The navy would defeat Spain's fleet in the Caribbean and isolate her colonies, which the army would then seize. There would be no need to attack Spain itself, and thus no need for a long conflict. McKinley held to this strategy through all the tactical shifts of the war, with outstanding results. At the price of 345 battle deaths, America had gained an empire.

But did the country want that empire? The treaty with Spain, signed just before 1898 ended, transferred the Philippines, Puerto Rico, and the Pacific island of Guam to the United States. The Spanish tried to convince the Americans to annex Cuba and thus assume the $400 million debt that Spain had run up on the island. But McKinley followed through with the Teller Amendment and insisted that Cuba be given its independence—under the supervision of an American army of occupation. The last imperial addition was Hawaii, taken as a stepping-stone to the Philippines. For five years, ever since a cabal of American seamen and sugar planters had deposed the native Hawaiian monarchy, the island's government had asked to join the United States. Signing the joint resolution to take the islands, McKinley declared: "Annexation is not change; it is consummation."

This empire-building delighted economic imperialists, who saw rosy possibilities for economic expansion abroad. Many disagreed. Andrew Carnegie, whose steel plants had armored the ships that won the war, viewed America's new empire with distaste. Hawaii was acceptable, and for keeping Cuba independent Carnegie had "nothing but praise for the President since he took his rightful place, that of Leadership." But the Philippines, in the eyes of the steel magnate and the New England Anti-Imperialist League that he helped finance, was a poisoned fruit: a distant, hostile, foreign province that never could be Americanized. The revolt of the Filipinos, who after years of guerrilla war against Spain found their country occupied by an American army, underscored the arguments made by the opponents of empire. Carnegie asked, "Are we to exchange Triumphant Democracy for Triumphant Despotism?" When the government turned down the industrialist's offer of $20 million to give up the islands, he resolved to oppose the peace treaty with Spain.

In the Senate debate on the treaty, both sides laid out strong cases. Administration supporters pointed out that the treaty would bring peace with Spain, secure the Philippines against other European colonial powers, and open the way for American commercial interests in all the new territories. Moreover, both Foraker and Lodge assured the Senate that America would keep the Philippines only briefly, until the islanders were ready for self-government. The anti-imperialists, led by George Hoar of Massachusetts, denounced as un-American the taking of any foreign territory. "The downfall of the American Republic," predicted Hoar, "will date from the administration of William McKinley." The defection of Bryan and several other Democrats to the pro-treaty side finally tipped the scales in favor of ratification; the treaty passed with one vote to spare. Lodge wrote proudly to Roosevelt, "Aldrich and I . . . were down in the engine room and we do not get the flowers, but we did make the ship move."

Having emerged victorious in Washington, McKinley could now turn his full attention to the struggle in Manila. Filipinos under the leadership of Emilio Aguinaldo had declared the establishment of a Philippines republic in January 1899; in February, Aguinaldo's forces clashed with the American occupying troops, and by the end of the month there was full-scale war. General Elwell Otis's troops broke up the Filipinos' semi-organized units in a series of bruising encounters, so that by November, Aguinaldo had to revert to guerrilla warfare. The revolt simmered on in the Philippines and American troops still occupied Cuba as the election of 1900 drew near.

Bryan, nominated again by the Democrats, announced his intention to make imperialism the "paramount" issue—and then campaigned mainly on monopolies and silver. The Republicans countered with a litany of their successes in "filling the lunchpails" of working Americans, but the nomination of Theodore Roosevelt as McKinley's running mate helped turn attention from economic progress back to foreign policy. Carnegie and other conservative anti-imperialists supported the President as the lesser of two evils. "McKinley stands for war and violence abroad," declared the industrialist, "but Mr. Bryan stands for these scourges at home." And Ignatius Donnelly, candidate of the radical Populists, viewed both with distaste: Democrats howled "about Republicans shooting negroes in the Philippines" and the Republicans denounced Democrats "for shooting negroes in the South. This may be good politics, but it is rough on the negroes."

Imperialism and the Full Dinner Pail won in November. McKinley bested Bryan by nearly a million votes and carried the electoral college by two to one. The success could not be attributed to any one set of issues either domestic or foreign, however; probably the election was more a personal triumph for William McKinley and the Republican philosophy that the Ohioan had come to represent. To a friend McKinley reflected, "I can no longer be called the President of a party; I am now the President of the whole people."

Of all the people save one. In September, McKinley journeyed to New York to speak at the Buffalo Exposition. On the 5th—Presidents' Day—he addressed a crowd of 50,000 on the theme that "expositions are the time-keepers of progress." The next day, after a trip to Niagara Falls, he stopped at the Temple of Music for a brief public reception. Waiting in line to shake the President's hand was Leon Czolgosz, a young anarchist. Czolgosz shot McKinley twice; one bullet pierced the President's stomach and lodged somewhere in his back. Guards knocked the assassin down as the stunned President sank slowly into a chair.

For a week McKinley lingered, and the nation hung on the confusing reports of his condition. The doctors tried in vain to locate the bullet; nobody suggested that the experimental X-ray machine, on display at the Exposition, be used. McKinley died on September 14; Vice-President Roosevelt took the oath of office the same day. In Canton, Ohio, as final rites were performed for the departed President, every factory fell silent.

PART III
Progressive Democracy?

CHAPTER 7

The Urban Progressives

IN the very last years of the nineteenth century, at the very height of McKinley Republicanism, a bracing weather change spread through urban America—a weather change that would peak during the first two decades of the new century, transform the nation's cultural climate, and then fade away. This profound metamorphosis, which came to be known as progressivism, was as puzzling as it was pervasive. Why did it arrive when it did—during an era of prosperity? What caused it? What composed it? What enduring effect did it have? For at least a century historians would debate the answers to these questions.

The timing of the rise of progressivism is not all that mysterious, and helps to explain the cause. During the 1890s, Western Europe was undergoing intellectual and social phases—Bismarckian "socialism," British social liberalism and Fabianism, French radicalism—to which Americans could not be immune. The incubation of American progressivism during prosperous times was not surprising, because it is not affluence but deprivation that causes people to "hunker down" in their homes and their ideas. For Americans, the nineties had been filled with tumult—the Populist revolt, the sharp and savage recession of '93, the searing Homestead and railroad strikes, Bryanism, Coxey's army, war with Spain. These crises made for conflict, the catalyst of new ideas.

But even more, progressivism was a response to the rise of the industrial city and its human wants and needs—most basically, for security. Much has been made of the status anxieties of members of "the old-family, college-educated class that had deep ancestral roots in local communities and often owned family businesses, that had traditions of political leadership," that had supplied leadership for civic improvement, and was now being pushed aside by "the agents of the new corporations, the corrupters of legislatures, the buyers of franchises, the allies of the political bosses," in Richard Hofstadter's words. But these threats to status paled next to the stark psychological and economic needs of masses of poor people in the big industrial cities.

These needs were manifold—needs of consumers seeking pure food and drugs at fair prices, of labor seeking higher wages and job protection, of women seeking employment without discrimination or harass-

ment, of businessmen weary of fierce competition and of the trend toward mergers, of railroad passengers and utility customers vulnerable to
the decisions of the monopolies. Businessmen made up a sizable segment of the urban progressives, in part because they shared many broad
needs as consumers. Businessmen in the middle corporate ranks also experienced at first hand the demanding and arbitrary ways of some of the
men at the corporate top.

Progressivism was as dynamic as the cities in which it flourished. "It
appeared first on the state and local level during the 1890s, where it
fused ideological, pragmatic, and political elements, most of which dated
to the earliest days of the republic," in Irwin and Debi Unger's summary.
"It became a national movement somewhere in the first years of the
twentieth century, when it pulled into its orbit all manner of reformers,
mavericks, opportunists, idealists, and malcontents. As time passed, its
mass grew and its qualities altered in response to new groups of adher-
ents and to new ideas, goals, and programs that emerged to meet new
circumstances."

The evolving nature of progressivism and its diversity of makeup—
including some business leaders who were not progressive in attitude but
saw progressivism as a means of staving off something worse, like socialism
—made for a marked tendency toward incoherence of program and policy.
This tendency was enhanced by the progressives' bent for "realism,"
which they viewed as experimentalism, opportunism, "immediacy." But
these "pragmatic" leanings were combined with a high moral fervor
against business and political corruption, a Christian socialist abhorrence
of gross materialism and inequality, a moralistic disdain for intemperance
of any sort. The harsh test of progressivism in America was whether the
pressing needs of masses of low-income workers in the great industrial
centers of the nation would make its program more coherent, its membership more united, its leadership more daring and purposeful.

The most compelling needs in turn-of-century America were those of
masses of newcomers. By 1900, the first great waves of immigrants, primarily from Britain, Ireland, Germany, and Scandinavia, had reached into
the American heartland, and now were yielding to another huge tide of
newcomers mainly from eastern and southern Europe. Pogroms and poverty in Russia were impelling Jews by the hundreds of thousands to begin
the long journey west toward the vaunted land of tolerance and freedom.
The stream of Italian immigrants broadened from about 1 million in the
entire nineteenth century to 2 million in the first decade of the twentieth;
and while the earlier immigrants had primarily been northerners, these
newcomers more often hailed from southern and rural Italy. French

Canadians were still moving off the poor farms of Nova Scotia and Quebec into the textile and shoe towns of New England. Chinese immigration, totaling over 300,000 by century's end, had slowed to a trickle in the wake of harsh exclusion acts in the promised land of liberty and equality.

Most of the immigrants headed toward where the jobs were, the cities. There they commingled with another vast migration of Americans from rural to urban areas. The desolate New England farms, with their sagging fences, broken windows, and overgrown pastures, hinted of earlier decisions to desert century-old homes for the rumored shorter hours and higher pay of factory life. Southerners, including blacks, were leaving for Northern cities; Chicago's Negro population of about 7,000 in 1880 doubled in the next ten years.

All told, in the sixty years after 1850 the population of the United States rose roughly fourfold—from 23 million to about 92 million—while world population rose by about one-half. The population explosion in American cities was phenomenal; between 1860 and 1900, New York City grew from 1 million to 3.5 million, Philadelphia from half a million to 1.3 million, Boston from 170,000 to over half a million, Chicago from a small city to almost 1.7 million. Equally spectacular was the rise in the number of cities with more than 100,000 persons—from nine to fifty between 1860 and 1910. People talked about the ever-growing midwestern and eastern metropolises, but smaller cities of the West also underwent rapid growth, as did some in the South—Birmingham, Louisville, Memphis, the bustling cities of Texas. In sum, the American people were becoming more numerous, more diversified ethnically, more urbanized, older, and a bit more "western."

Behind the big but impersonal figures lay countless life histories etched in fear, hope, expectation, and final reality. In the old days, many migrants to the city could bring their cows and pigs and chickens with them, but now newcomers experienced an almost total change of environment. Now they were crammed into buildings. One ward in Manhattan in 1890 had a density of 523 persons per acre, another 429. Cincinnati housed 25,000 families, numbering over 100,000 persons, in 5,600 tenements with a total of 54,000 rooms. The stench rising from open privies, garbage-strewn alleys, and stagnant water produced, someone said, a "stink enough to knock you down." It was worse than stench, the Chicago *Times* sniffed, for "stench means something finite. Stink reaches the infinite and becomes sublime in the magnitude of odiousness."

The crowding into urban America of migrants and immigrants coincided with decisions of financiers and industrialists in effect to industrialize the large American city. Most of these cities during the earlier years of the century had been primarily commercial centers serving rural hinterlands. Of the nine cities that had reached 100,000 in population by 1860, eight were ports on ocean, lake, or river. These commercial cities had taken on a special character with their mostly English-speaking merchants and clerks and bookkeepers, gathered in medium-sized populations that had a sense of coherence and community. Manufacturing establishments typically were located outside these trading centers, on power-generating streams or at transportation junctions or near the oil or coal or minerals they consumed.

The commercial centers were natural targets for industrialization. They already had sizable populations, work forces, transportation facilities, consumer markets. Of the fifteen leading cities enjoying natural trade advantages by 1910, Blake McKelvey notes, fourteen had become major industrial cities as well. "New York, the chief banker and printer, was even more busy manufacturing clothing and cigars. Chicago, which by 1870 had become the leading butcher and packer and the leading grain and lumber mart, was now taking the lead in steel fabrication. Philadelphia, which after 1905 lost top place to Lawrence in the production of woolen goods, stood second or third only to New York or Chicago in other important industries."

In effect these commercial centers added a whole new population of rural migrants and immigrants and a brand new economy of industrial production to their existing socioeconomic bases. By combining a variety of industries, they were able to take advantage of the "specialization and division of labor" much touted by economists. These forces stimulated one another in a relationship that was both dynamic and reciprocal, producing new industrial systems that were technically specialized, occupationally diverse, and yet economically integrated. Critical to this process, however, were investors' decisions on the location of plants—decisions influenced by the availability of cheap labor that could be trained and disciplined and deployed, and that would in turn serve as a growing market for goods produced. Capital was the catalyst, but human bodies provided the manual and brain power.

Thus urbanization meant industrialization—and the reverse. Some cities continued to specialize and became famous for their main product. Troy made shirt collars and cuffs, Waterbury brassware, Gloversville gloves, Providence silverware, Paterson silk goods, St. Louis tobacco products, Toledo glass, Springfield (Ohio) farm machinery, Youngstown iron and steel, South Omaha meat products, Tulsa oil, Houston railroad cars. But the big industrial city combined a variety of such enterprises into a dynamic whole. In the process, these cities were transformed, as were the rural populations that had come to stay. The ungainly, unplanned, and uneasy partnership of industrial elites at the top and masses of impoverished, non-English-speaking newcomers at the bottom unleashed a torrent of forces that produced the modern industrial city in its protean shape, its vitality, its ills, and its reformation.

THE SHAPE OF THE CITY

The grandest sight in most big cities was the railroad terminal. By century's turn, the modest old-time depot had become an imperial palace of extravagant gables, lofty towers, arched entrances, long colonnades, behind imposing Doric columns and pilasters. Cities vied with one another in terminal size and show. St. Louis boasted of the "largest depot in the world," with its enormous train shed and Grand Hall; Chicago of its clock tower rising 247 feet; Detroit of a shaft that was half tower, half skyscraper; Boston of an arched and columned entrance fit for the arrival of Hapsburgs. You had to look sharp, though, because "terminal madness" meant repeated tearing down of old depots and building anew. There were three Grand Centrals at 42nd and Vanderbilt in New York City. Borrowing heavily from European art and experience, depot styles in the United States shifted from the Romanesque to the Renaissance to the neo-Romanesque.

The main Chicago station was so elaborate and complex, with its various levels and a waiting room sporting a mosaic floor and marble wainscoting, that architect Louis Sullivan attacked its "public-be-damned" style. But for many Americans the depot was the common man's palace.

Into the wide-arching sheds inched the powerful new turn-of-the-century locomotives, snorting smoke, blowing off steam, and pulling dozens of cars. Down from the gleaming Pullmans stepped the magnates, the more successful traveling salesmen, the affluent professional men, and whole families with their maids and governesses and truckloads of luggage. The coaches disgorged also the plain people, carrying their valises and carpetbags. Arriving passengers paraded toward the cavernous terminals, amid flocks of porters and carters, then stepped outside into a hubbub of arriving passengers, besieging taximen, waiting trams, and drays piled high with barrels, boxes, bags of every size and shape.

It was usually a short distance from the terminal to the central business district; and here hubbub changed to bedlam. Crowds overflowed narrow sidewalks and fought with trams, hansom cabs, delivery wagons, and drays for passage space in the streets. People poured in and out of side streets packed with shoppers and lined with peddlers' carts. Messenger boys dashed in and out of office buildings; newsboys shouted out the day's headlines; deliverymen bent under cakes of ice, kegs of ale, piles of clothing. Overhead, telephone and tram wires were so dense as to shadow the streets. The tumult only increased at intersections, where streetcars, imprisoned on their rails, pushed aggressively ahead while drivers of smaller vehicles tried to thread their horses through to the opposite street and constables sought desperately to avert a hopeless standstill.

Huge and intimidating, piloted by imperious motormen, the trolleys were the lords of the street, and often so crowded that most riders had to stand, lurching and swaying as the cars made sharp turns over rough rails. A complaining youngster might hear from his father how the streetcars of old had been pulled by horses over even rougher rails, at a pace so slow that it was quicker to get out and walk. And that father might once have been reminded by *his* parents that in their earlier days they had ridden on horsecars over cobbled streets without rails, sometimes at a feverish pace as rival liverymen competed for business. And crowded? Mark Twain himself had mentioned horsecar platforms so packed you had to "hang on by your eyelashes and your toenails." Perhaps the grandparents remembered too the piles of horse manure left in the streets—several hundred tons a day in a medium-large city, according to measurers of such phenomena.

City transport was still the most dynamic element in urban change. Inventors had dreamed up alternatives to horsepower: compressed-air cars, propulsion by ammonia gas, steam engines on street rails, an endless underground cable powered by a stationary steam engine. Only the last of these worked. Tried out on the steep hills of San Francisco, the cable was used also in Chicago, Seattle, and a score of other cities in the 1880s. Steam-powered cables were also employed for elevated transit lines along Sixth and Ninth Avenues in New York and in the Chicago Loop. But none of these changes solved the intracity transit problem: steam engines were too big, noisy, and awkward for the streets; cables moved slowly at an unvarying speed, even during rush hours, and often broke down; the "els" deafened people in their second-story flats, blocked out light, and spewed dirt and oil on the streets below.

Electrified streetcars with overhead wires changed all this. First tried out in Alabama on Montgomery's Court Street line in 1886, electric railways came into wide use after Frank Sprague, a naval engineer who had worked for Edison, formed a company and built a successful line in Richmond. Sprague had to overcome so many technical problems, at such heavy expense, that he would not have signed the Richmond contract had he foreseen them, he said later. This remarkable inventor also designed a multiple-unit control system that enabled each trolley car to be independently powered, lighted, and braked, at the same time capable of being controlled by a master switch located in any one of them.

Soon the big rugged horses were disappearing from the city railways. Fifty cities had adopted trolley systems by 1890, another eighty-eight by 1895. Streetcars now sped along at twelve miles an hour, about twice as fast as the horses' pace. Sprague continued to pioneer and perfect, ultimately winning the title "father of electric traction." But Edison so dominated the popular imagination that he was often credited with inventing electric traction too, much to Sprague's chagrin. "Popular applause, commercial propaganda and sentimental gush have helped to build up a legend largely mythical, to the effect that if Mr. Edison ever had anything to do with anything electrical, no matter how remotely," Sprague complained, it "immediately became an Edison offspring." Hence it was all the more ironic that in 1890 his company was absorbed by the Edison General Electric Company.

Not until the 1890s did American cities adopt the most dramatic advance in city transportation, the subway. Some years after London had pioneered with travel through the "underground," Boston built a subway a mile long under Tremont Street, and New York in 1904 opened a longer line running from City Hall to 145th Street. Sprague's multiple-unit control system helped make the subway possible, for it eliminated the need of a steam locomotive, whose smoke and soot would have made tunnel traveling all but unbearable. This inventor-industrialist also helped perfect the most invisible but in the long run perhaps most consequential of improvements, the electric elevator. Lifts powered by horse, steam, and hydraulic power had long existed, but only when harnessed to electric power did they come into general use. Chicago, busily building skyscrapers, pioneered in the use of "express" elevators, which made "the passenger seem to feel his stomach pass into his shoes," a traveler wrote. Sprague, whose dependable, constant-speed motors were crucial to lifts, manufactured about six hundred of them before his business was turned over to the Otis Elevator Company.

Elevators made high-rise buildings possible even as the rising skyscrapers made elevators necessary. As the inner city grew more congested and its land more dear, one way out was the vertical. But the problem with building "up" had always been the enormously thick masonry needed to support sides and interiors. The solution, in the age of iron and steel, was first iron and then steel. Iron supports on buildings led to the first wholly cast-iron building in Manhattan at the corner of Centre and Duane. The strength, durability, and fire-resistance of cast iron brought a spate of office buildings, department stores, and warehouses built of this material, some of them surprisingly attractive and even elegant.

Within two decades, though, steel—tougher in both tension and compression—was replacing iron as the leading high-rise building material. William Le Baron Jenney erected the first steel-frame skyscraper, a ten-story insurance building in Chicago in 1885. A "Chicago School" of architects began designing skyscrapers for a host of cities. A maverick member of the school, Louis Sullivan, sensed that height was not just another dimension but a powerful means of combining form and function. "How shall we impart to this sterile pile, this crude, harsh, brutal agglomeration, this stark, staring exclamation of eternal strife," he asked, "the graciousness of those higher forms of sensibility and culture that rest on the lower and fiercer passions?" The skyscraper, he responded, "must be every inch a proud and soaring thing, rising in sheer exultation that from bottom to top it is a unit without a single dissenting line." Sullivan left notable structures in St. Louis, Buffalo, Chicago, and elsewhere.

Bursting out of its confined space, New York turned to the skyscraper as its solution if not salvation. The seventeen-story Manhattan Life Insurance Building was followed by rivals first of twenty stories, then of twenty-six, then of thirty, all by the end of the century. Then, in 1913, came the most sensational of all, the Woolworth Tower, sixty stories rising 792 feet from the street. Critics scoffed at its ornamentation and its cost—$7.5 million—but the public marveled at its majestic tower, incredible height, and 80,000 electric light bulbs. All agreed: it was the "Cathedral of Commerce."

*   *   *

Of course, cities expanded outward far more than upward, as streetcar rails spearheaded the deploying of urban population away from the commercial centers. The rich, using their private carriages, had long been able to live outside the city; now the middle class and even the poor could live miles from their work, at the price of two nickels a day. In most big cities, by century's end, a trip into the "suburbs" was a journey into monotony. Newer cities west of the Appalachians typically had been laid out on a grid pattern that led to long, straight, canyonlike streets disappearing over the horizon. "To the surveyor, the grid pattern produced a logical and orderly layout," according to two historians; "to the eye, it produced an eternity of unbroken squares and rectangles which made one town indistinguishable from another." Long after visiting American cities, Lord Bryce wrote that "their monotony haunts one like a nightmare."

Uniformity resulted in part from the common practice of cutting up land into small, easily sellable lots usually about twenty-five feet wide by one hundred feet deep. These property lines ran through hill and dale, pasture and woodland, with little logic except the realtors' interests. But the main cause of monotony in living areas was the almost universal adoption of the "balloon frame" in building residences. Early in the century most buildings had been constructed by skilled craftsmen using heavy beams and mortised and tenoned joints. The balloon frame used instead thin plates and studs, often the familiar "two-by-fours," running the entire height of the building and held together only by spikes and nails. "A man and a boy can now attain the same results with ease, that twenty men could on an old-fashioned frame," wrote an architectural expert in 1865. Soon the outlying city areas were dotted by thousands of balloon-frame skeletons soon to be clothed in whatever framing was handy and cheap.

The mass production of houses was part and parcel of the industrialization of the city. Such production required masses of timber, often brought long distances and processed by increasingly large and efficient woodworking machinery. Even more, mass frame housing depended on the simple nail in cheap and plentiful supply. The iron and steel industry had to provide ample metals for machines that cut and headed nails by the million. Hand-wrought nails had cost twenty-five cents a pound; by mid-century machine-made nails were selling for three cents a pound. Chicago was the ideal place to bring together masses of land, timber, nails, and carpenters, and the balloon frames came to be associated with that city; but this cheap housing was responsible for the "taming of the West" all the way to San Francisco and Los Angeles.

It was more profitable to erect houses than to provide for support services vitally needed in increasingly congested areas. Water was the vital need, for both comfort and sanitation. Toward the end of the century, the old sewerage arrangements were simply collapsing under pressure. In 1881 the mayor of Cleveland called the Cuyahoga River "an open sewer through the center of the city." Most families depended on local wells to obtain water and private cesspools to get rid of it. "Foul-smelling" privies often stood nearby. By the late 1870s, Washington still had 56,000 private sewer vaults and cesspools, and Philadelphia 82,000. Would sewerage be better in the West, where more land seemed available and cities could start from scratch? To keep their waste from pouring into Lake Michigan, Chicagoans ingeniously reversed the flow of the Chicago River away from the lake and into the Illinois River, with the aid of six pumping stations. But the waste now fouled the water of downstream towns and still backed up into the city and into Lake Michigan during heavy rains.

Some cities planned ahead. After completing its thirty-four-mile Croton aqueduct in 1842, New York found in three decades that it needed a second big Croton aqueduct, and not long after that, a huge new source of water in the Catskills. Los Angeles had to turn to Sierra mountain water 250 miles away. Often, however, it was not foresight that brought action but disaster. Just as Philadelphia had brilliantly experimented with ingenious water gathering and distribution methods after its yellow fever epidemic of 1793, Memphis built a new sewer system only after a similar plague in 1878. In this crisis, Memphis turned to George E. Waring, Jr., who argued that typhoid and other diseases could be traced to "the exhalations of decomposing matters in dungheaps, pigsties, privy vaults, cellars, cess-pools, drains, and sewers," and launched a campaign against filth. By 1910, over 10 million city people drank filtered water, cutting the death rate, it was estimated, by at least a fifth in New Orleans and several big eastern cities.

At least sewers were practical and useful, if expensive. What about green areas, recreation space? Few realtors trying to make a profit off land, few industrialists busy selling nails and construction machinery, had time to think much about parks, nor did workers intent on acquiring food, shelter, and clothing. Such green areas seemed the province of gentlemen-idealists like Frederick Law Olmsted, who helped conceive a magnificent plan for a central park in Manhattan, campaigned for its creation, and saw it completed in 1876 after twenty years' effort, in a manner that preserved the easy, undulating shape of the original land and related the park to the city. Henry W. S. Cleveland, a scientific farmer and engineer, designed parks and cemeteries in both North and South. He urged city leaders to think ahead to future needs and to acquire land before real estate interests did; Minneapolis, for example, must predict what would be the "wants" of its people when they became a million strong. But visitors from abroad were distressed to see, in the working-class sections of big industrial cities, street after street, block after block, without the green space of park, playground, or even cemetery.

The ultimate unit in the "rectangular street platting, the atom of mechanical design, was the individual rectangular plot into which each block was divided," wrote Lewis Mumford. He noted that the width of the plot was rarely greater than twenty feet; often, as in sections of Baltimore, it might be only fifteen or twelve. "As long as row houses were two rooms deep, this platting was tolerable; but as soon as the need for more dwelling space grew, the natural line of expansion was not laterally, to embrace a second costly plot, but backward, to eat up the back-yard areas and to increase thereby the sunless interior space. . . .

"The desire to utilize every square foot of rentable space possessed the owner, even when he was building for his own use, and not for sheer pecuniary exploitation; and in its search for profits it often over-reached itself, for an overcrowded plan does not necessarily bring the maximum financial return. Cumbrous, uneconomic plans, with a maximum amount of wasteful corridor space and dark ill-ventilated rooms, characterized the two-family houses, the three deckers, the higher tenements. And the habit of letting the shape of the individual lot determine the plan and layout of the house dominated the imagination of the architect: he lost the ability to design freely in more comprehensive units, built for common living and not for individual division, individual ownership, individual sale. . . ." This shotgun wedding of individualism and urbanization was a hallmark of the industrialization of the cities.

THE LIFE OF THE CITY

Into the balloon frames of Chicago and St. Louis, the four-storied "three-deckers" of Boston and Lowell, the "dumbbell" shaped tenements of Manhattan and Detroit, the shanties on the outskirts of Omaha, and the boardinghouses of the western cities flowed the gigantic tide of migrants and immigrants, with their extraordinary diversity of backgrounds, religions, customs, needs, perceptions, and expectations. Whatever the architecture, the new environment was essentially the same for all—urban, congested, noisy, stinking, treeless. Yet the newcomers for a time at least transformed their immediate environment far more than they were transformed by it. Consciously or not, ethnic groups adopted strategies for coping with their environment, converting it into something familiar and manageable, for a time making it a means of alleviating physical insecurity and uncertainty, a buffer against collisions with the volatile, kaleidoscopic new world into which they had plunged.

Walk west on East Houston Street in Manhattan's Lower East Side before the turn of the century and you can see how the Jewish newcomers are absorbing the shock of moving into a crowded and ugly urban environment. Look right, beyond Hamilton Fish Park—there, in an area of twenty or more blocks behind the docks and warehouses of the East River, live tens of thousands of Hungarian Jews. On your left, reaching down to Delancey Street, stretch a dozen blocks of Galician Jews. Turn left on Chrystie Street and you pass through an area of Romanian Jews on your right and Levantine and Romanian Jews on your left. Then take another left, off Chrystie onto Canal Street, and you enter the heart of the biggest Jewish district of all—Russian Jews from Poland, Lithuania, Byelorussia, the Ukraine. Don't try to hurry; the sidewalks and the streets are packed.

This is by far the most populated square mile in the city; in some acres here are packed more people than in the same square footage in Bombay.

The East Side Jews have moored themselves to the two most enduring foundations of social stability—race and nationality. Most of them act far more like Jews with a common culture, however, than Hungarians or Russians or Romanians with separate national identities. Here on the edge of the Russian district are the Hebrew Technical School for Girls, the Home for the Aged, the Jewish Maternity Hospital, the Hebrew Sheltering House. The Forward Building on Yiddish Newspaper Row, the Isaac Elchanan Yeshiva, and the Educational Alliance flank Henry Street. A dozen congregations meet in tenements or storefronts that serve as synagogues. Over toward lower Broadway lie the temples of entertainment—the Grand Theater, the Yiddish Rialto, the Thalia Theater.

The streets burst with life, action, clamor. People throng the narrow sidewalks, push through the streets with their carts, crowd onto fire escapes, call down from open windows. Even "the architecture seemed to sweat humanity at every window and door," the British novelist Arnold Bennett observed. In the Pig Market on Hester Street, peddlers sell fish and fruit from pushcarts, milk from big cans, cheap clothes off racks, secondhand eyeglasses and knickknacks from trays hanging on straps from the peddler's neck. Sharp-eyed housewives with large bags check pushcart goods and prices against those in the shops that occupy the ground floor of the tenements. Things are a bit grander over on Grand Street, with its department stores, restaurants, dancing halls (for proper dancing), and even a little park.

Still, no matter how successful East Side Jews were in reestablishing old social forms and institutions in the new world of the city, few could escape psychological stress and disorganization. For some, the repeated shocks had been almost too much to bear—being left in charge of the home in Vilna or Kiev or wherever, while the breadwinner took the long journey to America; then the family's own trip marked by fear, homesickness, illness, humiliations; the joyous reunion, followed often by shifts in the relationship of husband and wife, parents and children, parents and grandparents, as harsh new demands changed the roles of family members—especially mothers—and lowered immigrants' sense of competence in their new situations, altered their esteem for others, sapped their self-esteem. And now again the breadwinner might seem to be deserting his family—for twelve hours a day, perhaps, as he labored in a factory, or for weeks at a time when he carried his peddler's pack off into the wilds of Connecticut or western Pennsylvania.

For some, religion was a strengthening and stabilizing force. But, in

Irving Howe's words, "pressures of the city, the shop, the slum, all made it terribly hard to stay with the old religious ethic. The styles and rituals of traditional Judaism had been premised on a time scheme far more leisurely, a life far less harried than urban America imposed. As for the new ethic of materialist individualism, what could this mean to a garment worker who spent sixty hours a week in a sweatshop, physically present in America yet barely touched by its language, its traditions, its privileges? . . . Except for those who clung to faith or grappled toward ideology, the early immigrants consisted of people who were stranded—stranded socially, morally, psychologically." These especially were the ones who withdrew into their culture, their institutions, their families, themselves, as they tried to re-create the feeling of belonging they had once enjoyed in a town or village now distant.

In many respects, the experiences of Italian immigrants paralleled those of Jews and other newcomers, especially those from southern and Eastern Europe. The heaviest waves of Italians came from western Sicily and from rural provinces south of Rome—Aguila, Reggio, Bari, and others—that were almost as separated from one another in geography, history, and even language as were some of the nations of Europe. They brought with them powerful loyalties to native town and village, high expectations aroused by the advertisements of steamship lines and by agents shilling for cheap foreign labor, and the rural folkways of the "Italian shtetl."

Like the Jews and others, their goal in America was mainly economic betterment, but some Italians too left to find greater freedom—especially religious liberty—or to evade military service, or to break away from political oligarchies. Like other immigrants, but perhaps to an even greater extent, Italian immigrants settled into the dingiest tenements and took the most menial jobs in the stockyards of Kansas City and Chicago, the mines and steel mills of Pennsylvania, the construction gangs of Schenectady and Utica, in the "Little Italies" of Kansas City and Cleveland, in "Dago Hill" near the clay pits and brickyards of St. Louis. Even more than many other immigrants, Italians were slow to conquer the urban American language, as they converted street into "streetu," factory "fattoria," shop "shoppa," store "storu."

The most distinctive aspect of Italian immigration, however, was the manner in which the newcomers from southern Italy and Sicily coped with culture shock and economic need. This was to accept a leadership and authority system represented by the *padrone.* Italians arriving on the docks of American ports or in the terminals of great cities needed not sermons or patriotic speeches but *help*—help with officious immigration officials, help with the American language, help in finding jobs and housing. The *padrone,* or labor boss, was the man who met him when he arrived, took him and his family around to Little Italy, put him into some kind of flat, and knew where to find work. The *padrone* was essentially an agent for employers seeking low-paid labor, but in the process he often became an intermediary too; he "collected wages, wrote letters, acted as banker, supplied room and board, and handled dealings between workers and employers," in Humbert Nelli's description.

Because *padroni* recruited Italian labor not only for city jobs but for all parts of the country, Chicago as a railroad center became a stronghold for these bosses. And bosses they were, with their power to offer jobs or to withhold them, to overcharge for food, rent, and railroad tickets to construction centers, to collect fees for jobs that they then failed to produce. A United States government report in 1897 showed that prices charged by the *padroni* were often far greater than "those charged in Chicago markets for similar articles of food at the same quality"—almost twice as much for bread, over 50 percent extra for macaroni, two-thirds extra for tomatoes, sausages, bacon, and lard.

So Italian immigrants paid a steep price for help in acculturation at the hands of the labor bosses of Chicago. The price could be even steeper, for the *padroni* tied in with the criminal element that emigrated in large part from Sicily and would have a profound influence on Chicago's—and the nation's—urban life. But, above all, the *padroni,* performing their essential function of uniting labor and capital, testified to the desperate need of immigrants for help, understanding, communication, shelter, and jobs, in a nation that offered virtually no planned and comprehensive assistance or protection to the millions of newcomers flocking into its industrializing cities.

*   *   *

Would factory work serve as the great homogenizer? If the newcomers were bringing their cultures and subcultures with them, if they were implanting their old ways, their costumes, their pushcarts, their languages, their churches, and their family and ethnic loyalties into the heart of the industrializing city, could they carry their diverse ways of life past the factory gate? Man in all his diversity, Adam Smith had said, "is, of all sorts of luggage, the most difficult to be transported." But the factory had its own exactions, imperatives, disciplines.

Factories had power. Factories, whether second-floor sweatshop or huge steel works, commanded that workers arrive and leave at set times—usually many hours apart—and work in prescribed conditions. The capitalist work ethic and capitalist efficiency barred loitering, absenteeism, malingering, visiting around the floor, perhaps even talking on the job. "Modern industry has converted the little workshop of the patriarchal master into the great factory of the industrial capitalist," the *Communist Manifesto* had charged. "Masses of labourers, crowded into the factory, are organized like soldiers. As privates of the industrial army they are placed under the command of a perfect hierarchy of officers and sergeants. Not only are they slaves of the bourgeois class, and of the bourgeois State; they are daily and hourly enslaved by the machine, by the over-looker, and, above all, by the individual bourgeois manufacturer himself." Marx and Engels had looked to the future. With the development of industry, "the proletariat not only increases in number; it becomes concentrated in greater masses, its strength grows, and it feels that strength more. The various interests and conditions of life within the ranks of the proletariat are more and more equalised, in proportion as machinery obliterates all distinctions of labour, and nearly everywhere reduces wages to the same low level."

Yet immigrants and migrants found countless ways to thwart the discipline of the industrialists, the slavery of the machine. Used to their holidays in the "old country," Poles would spend several days celebrating a wedding in a far-off mill town. Accustomed to more than eighty festivals a year, Greeks were not prepared to give up these happy occasions in the New World. The Irish celebrated some of their old patriotic and religious days, such as St. Patrick's Day, *and* their new ones, like Independence Day. Nor could employers integrate holidays so that their plants would close only once, for all concerned; no one would dare synchronize Labor Day and Columbus Day. Even the nonreligious might follow the slower working-day tempo of their earlier peasant lives.

And one could seek to flee the machine. On the Lower East Side, Bernard Weinryb noted, a worker might open a candy store or grocery, or become a jobber and then a factory owner himself; the carpenter might become a builder or contractor; the peddler might become a storekeeper. A man or a woman might marry "up" and escape the factory. Others might lose themselves in radicalism or religion, or study evenings in order to take up a profession. Upward mobility often meant lateral motion as well. New York Jews were moving their stores from 14th Street to 23rd Street and then up to 34th, while some moved their families to the upper East Side. Italians, Poles, Slovaks, French Canadians often found the going harder, but they too pursued the American dream.

The Irish, after all, had long since shown that hod carriers and ditchdiggers—or at least their children or grandchildren—could rise from rags to riches. Particularly in less hierarchically structured societies, such as San Francisco during and after the gold strike, Irish immigrants like Peter

Donahue and James Phelan had founded businesses and banks, prospered, and ended up among the city's richest men. Tom Maguire built the Jenny Lind Theater, seating 2,000 persons—the biggest theater on the West Coast. There were countless success stories in other cities. To be sure, the "lace curtain Irish" were vulnerable to scornful remarks about their alleged social pretensions; a San Francisco weekly imagined the "Mac-Shinnegan coat of arms" as a "spalpeen rampant on a field of gold." The successful Irish, for their part, had a tendency to look down on later waves of immigrants—the Poles, the Jews, the Italians—almost as much as they despised blacks. But virtually all the nationality groups tended to decry the others, in large part because they were thrown into competition for jobs. Even co-religionists tended to divide: witness the separation of American Catholicism into Irish, French, Italian, and Polish churches that often kept their distance from one another on their local turfs.

For the few thousands who found room at the top, hundreds of thousands remained at the bottom of the social heap in the industrializing cities of America. Yet there remained a paradox. On the one hand, rarely in industrializing societies had the "objective" physical and economic nature of workers' existence seemed more conducive to proletarianization—the forcing of masses of men and women into a homogeneous and poverty-stricken collectivity. "Big industry," Marx and Engels asserted in *The German Ideology,* "destroyed as far as possible ideology, religion, morality, etc., . . . resolved all natural relationships into money relationships . . . in place of naturally grown towns created the modern, large industrial cities . . . created everywhere the same relations between the classes of society and thus destroyed the peculiar individuality of the various nationalities . . . makes labor itself, unbearable."

On the other hand, a proletariat in the social-psychological-political sense did not develop. For the American industrializing city seemed to inspire opposite tendencies—a huge and continuous flow of labor into and out of the cities; the recruitment of workers off farms, whether European or American, where pay and hours were far worse than even the factories would offer; tensions between native-born Americans and immigrants, and conflict among immigrants from diverse national and regional backgrounds; the relatively open access for some workers to middle-class occupations and status, if not to the top. Marx did not assume that class existence automatically meant class consciousness. But Marxist theory was drawn more from the European and British experience of relatively stable working-class populations, common language, lack of mobility—in Stephan Thernstrom's words, "some continuity of class membership *in one setting* so that workers come to know each other and to develop bonds of solidarity and common opposition to the ruling group above them." The Americans did not—at least, not yet—fit the Marxist model.

Nor were the lower strata of the middle class—"the small tradespeople, shopkeepers, and retired tradesmen generally, the handicraftsmen and peasants"—sinking into the proletariat, as the *Communist Manifesto* predicted. Most of the urban lower middle class, at least, changed its white-collar jobs rather than donning overalls. Many moved into the thousands of positions that were opening up in the towering new office buildings, banks, department stores, in the expanding corporate, educational, and government bureaucracies. The industrializing city required armies of technicians to staff the busy headquarters of communications and transport.

Middle-class women were finding more and more job opportunities in the industrial city, at the same time that industrialization was liberating them from some of their old household drudgery. Aluminum utensils were now taking the place of the old cast-iron pans, seasoned with beeswax and hard to clean. Refrigeration and faster shipping were bringing tomatoes into middle-class kitchens year-round, and oranges, lemons, plums, and grapes in season. Housewives were still baking bread at home, but now could more easily send out for baked goods. Still firmly entrenched as a housebound chore, however, was laundry, in part because of the intensive development and promotion of washing machines.

Some women found jobs teaching the home skills they had learned as daughters and mothers. The domestic science movement, led by Ellen Swallow Richards, gave birth to a host of training centers. Thus the Armour Institute in Chicago schooled Annie Thompson in sewing and nutrition, enabling her to clothe and feed her younger siblings after her mother's death; later, she became a dietitian and teacher of domestic science herself. A multitude of women found teaching jobs as school systems expanded to meet the spurt in city populations.

Other women, however, wanted to move out of home and classroom. Perhaps they remembered Louisa May Alcott writing to her father: "I can't do much with my hands, so I will make a battering-ram of my head and make a way through this rough-and-tumble world." Sometimes a battering ram seemed necessary. When Myra Bradwell, publisher of the Chicago *Legal News,* sought admission to the Illinois state bar in 1869, the Illinois supreme court rejected her because she was a married woman and not an independent agent. Her appeal to the United States Supreme Court failed. "The paramount destiny and mission of woman are to fulfill the noble and benign offices of wife and mother," a justice pontificated in a concurring opinion. "This is the law of the Creator." Bradwell was finally admitted to the bar in 1890.

In cities big and small, middle-class women were joining the swelling women's club movement. Although this movement brought cultural enlightenment and good works, perhaps even more it fostered solidarity among women otherwise isolated in separate households and attached to men competing in the business world. A dawning awareness of female identity and autonomy and a heightened sense of social effectiveness transformed some of these clubwomen's lives. Still, the movement was by no means radical: the clubs adhered to accepted views of "woman's sphere." Few openly supported woman's suffrage until after the turn of the century.

Indeed, the Federation of Women's Clubs, launched in 1890, soon became associated in the public mind with exclusive, fashionable society, for its membership included many of the wives of the nation's best-known business magnates—Phoebe Hearst in San Francisco, Mrs. George Pullman, Mrs. Cyrus McCormick, Mrs. Potter Palmer in Chicago. "The women were gowned to the Queen's taste," wrote a disconsolate delegate from Maine about the 1894 biennial convention in Philadelphia. "The president of the club was one blaze of diamonds. . . ."

The wealthy husbands—the Vanderbilts and Morgans and Rockefellers and the rest—continued to flourish and to prosper in the great economic boom after the turn of the century. Concentration and trustification brought them into closer collaboration, if not harmony. A powerful intercity class of business elites was intensifying in unity and purpose, communicating through the business press, Pullman car talk, rich men's clubs, corporate board meetings, and their increasing use of the telephone. All in all, the industrial cities were potent forces in fortifying the class system.

At the base of the pyramid lived and toiled the millions of industrial workers. "Assimilate" quickly or "face a quiet but sure extermination," the *Scientific American* had warned the "ruder" laborers of Europe in 1869. "Forget your past, your customs, and your ideals," a guidebook for immigrant Jews advised in the 1890s. "Do not take a moment's rest. Run, do, work." A Yiddish poet struck back at the "clock in the workshop" that urged him to labor and still labor on:

> The tick of the clock is the boss in his anger.
> The face of the clock has the eyes of the foe.
> The clock—I shudder—Dost hear how it draws me?
> It calls me "Machine" and it cries to me "Sew"!

THE LEADERS OF THE CITY

About two in the morning of a summer's day around the turn of the century, a Tammany district leader was awakened by the ringing of his doorbell: it was a bartender asking him to walk down to the police station and bail out a saloon-keeper who had run afoul of the law. The leader did so, got back to bed around three, only to be awakened again at six by fire engines. He followed the engines to the fire, met there with several of his district captains, took several burned-out tenants to a hotel, found them food, clothes, and temporary quarters.

After breakfast the leader repaired to the police court, where he found six of his people charged with drunkenness. He persuaded the judge to release four of them, and paid the fines of the other two. Half an hour later, at the municipal district court, he instructed one of his captains to represent a widow who was being dispossessed, and he paid the rent of a poor family also facing eviction, handing them a dollar for food. When he returned home at eleven A.M. he found three men who said they were looking for work. He found them jobs with the subway, the Consolidated Gas Company, and on the road, and he fixed things up for a fourth man who had been sacked by the Metropolitan Railway Company for neglect of duty.

The leader had only an hour for lunch before attending the funeral of an Italian constituent over by the ferry, and then rushing to the funeral of a Jewish voter. He made himself quietly conspicuous at both rites. Later he attended Hebrew confirmation ceremonies at a synagogue.

After dinner the leader presided over an hour-long meeting of his election district captains. Each reported on the political situation in his district, constituents in trouble and needing help, their attitude toward the party and its candidates. Then the leader visited a church fair, bought chances on everything, kissed the babies, jollied their mothers, and walked the fathers around the corner for a drink. Back at the clubhouse he bought tickets to a local baseball game, promised a subscription for a new church bell, and told a group of pushcart peddlers complaining about police persecution that he would go to the precinct station in the morning and see about it. Later in the evening he attended a Jewish wedding reception and dance, and got to bed by midnight.

The name of this Tammany Hall leader was George Washington Plunkitt and he would attain a special niche in American history not because his activities were unusual—on the contrary, this sort of thing was what he and scores of others did day after day—but because he was unusually candid about his activities, remarkably perceptive about the political world he lived in, and had a reporter friend, William L. Riordon, who carefully listened to him. To some, Plunkitt seemed almost a caricature, but allowing for a little blarney and a measure of exaggeration, the picture that emerged of him was true-to-life and important. Plunkitt was a leader in one of the most enduring power structures in American history.

Tammany as an organization was well over a century old by the time it reached its zenith in the 1890s. It had long since shed its old role as primarily a patriotic and philanthropic society. As political parties became more highly organized during the century, Tammany had turned into the power center of the Manhattan Democracy. Just as its sachems had championed the right to vote for the propertyless during earlier years, now the district leaders saw to it that immigrants and the rest of the poor had the practical right to vote. Tammany was unique in its longevity, not its organization. Similar "machines" existed in most of the big industrializing cities —some Republican, as in Philadelphia; some less centralized, as in Chicago; some less polyglot in membership, as in Detroit; but all with the same essential grass-roots structure and function.

That structure, in scores of cities across the nation, embraced a ward-and-precinct organization of party activists who might hold patronage or other jobs but made party business their main business. The party was organized in near-military fashion, with committeemen reporting to district captains, the captains to the district leader, and that leader to the boss or bosses of the whole organization. Typically the committeemen had deep and enduring roots in their neighborhoods. They formed a durable cadre that continued through the decades even while the top bosses came and went. Control at the top might be in the hands of one boss or a collectivity, but in either event the core of the organization was grass-roots leadership.

The formal function of the party machine was to help nominate and elect officeholders across the whole range of government, from the most local office to the President of the United States. Its informal functions included diverse activities all designed to ensure its continued influence. The burden of its business was dispensing the kind of assistance to constituents to which the Plunkitts devoted so much of their time. Not only were there turkeys at Christmas, and legal aid and help with authorities, but splendid treats—excursions up the river with bands playing, St. Patrick's Day parades, picnics, ball, sports events. Plunkitt had his own baseball team, and a glee club for the young folks. Catering to polyglot immigrant neighborhoods, the organization usually played no ethnic favorites, at least among whites. And the aid was usually specific, concrete, practical.

"I think that there's got to be in every ward somebody that any bloke can come to—no matter what he's done—and get help," Boston ward leader Martin Lomasney said to Lincoln Steffens. *"Help, you understand; none of your law and justice, but help."* Perhaps the party bosses' greatest achievement was to meet people's basic needs of food and shelter without robbing them of their equal need for self-esteem.

But the city parties were more than welfare-dispensing machines. "As part of the developing relationship between bosses and immigrants, the political machine became an avenue of advance—and, quite possibly, of 'Americanization'—for many citizens with foreign names," according to Charles Glaab and A. Theodore Brown. "The machine offered more than labor jobs in public or utility construction. For the brighter and more ambitious young men, there were clerical and other white collar positions in the machine itself; such positions represented for many the first step toward middle class respectability." The Horatio Alger ideal was not unknown in the precincts.

In the process of helping people, the bosses performed another function, even to a perverse degree—they united a fragmented governmental system and made it perform. The organizations turned the checks and balances upside down. If state constitutions, like the national, were ingeniously designed to divide local, county, and state power through separate electoral arrangements, the bosses with their grip on the nominating and electing mechanism at every level could make mayors and state legislators and county officials and governors work together. If city charters cleverly diked off executive and legislative and judicial power at the local level, the bosses often chose the aldermen, municipal judges, mayors, and—civil service laws to the contrary notwithstanding—administrative officials, and hence could make government perform.

This capacity to unite government was even more important for the organization's key role, in the big industrial cities, in helping businessmen gain contracts, franchises, and other grants from government, to avoid regulation, to get the right streets and bridges built, to subdue and stabilize the often anarchical world around them. The corporations, wrote Robert Merton, wanted the security of the "economic czar" who controlled, regulated, and organized competition, provided that his decisions were not subject to public scrutiny and control. Often the protected activities of business merged into the underworld of gambling, prostitution, liquor, outright crime. Operating in a political shadowland, the bosses often were able to provide business, legitimate or not, with the quiet help it needed.

*　　*　　*

Arrayed against the bosses in most of the big cities were the lords of reform. The conflict between these two sets of leaders provided most of the drama and much of the importance of political activity in the late nineteenth and early twentieth centuries. It was in many respects a conflict of ideologies—a clash between value systems, ethnic groups, class outlooks, power systems.

The reform movement in the big cities was essentially a bourgeois phenomenon, rooted in middle-class fears of urban disorder, immigrant ways, family disruption. A powerful rural myth of almost Jeffersonian dimensions persisted. Common to many of these reformers, according to Paul Boyer, "was the conviction—explicit or implicit—that the city, although obviously different from the village in its external, physical aspects, should nevertheless replicate the moral order of the village." Still responding to the old genteel, mugwump, independent thrust in the two major parties, as indignant as ever over the excesses of party spoils and patronage, still clinging to the *Nation* and *Harper's Weekly* and other journals of reformist tendencies, the reformers viewed the bosses as representing all they disliked in politics—corruption, manipulation, links with the underworld, and ties with monopolistic, favor-seeking businessmen.

Much earlier, a regiment of reformers had clashed with the most powerful and corrupt of bosses—and the reformers had won such a glorious battle that the victory colored their thoughts and tactics ever after. Their target and ultimate victim was William Magear Tweed, Jr. Of Scottish descent, son of a New York City chairmaker who invested in a small brush factory, Tweed by the age of twenty-one had learned bookkeeping, clerked in a mercantile office, become a member of the brush firm—and married the daughter of the principal owner. A good-natured, strapping young man of sober habits, he found his main recreation in running Americus Engine Company, Number 6, which with its emblem of a snarling red tiger became one of the best-known fire companies under the leadership of its dashing chief in his red flannel shirt and white firecoat.

New York City fire companies were intensely clannish, convivial, and political. With the loyal backing of his seventy-five fire-fighters, Tweed moved easily into Manhattan's political world, won election as alderman, and joined the common council that came to be known as "The Forty Thieves." It was also a school of practical politics and political moneymaking. Tireless and single-minded, Tweed broadened his influence in Tammany, occupied a variety of offices and controlled others, and made money out of every opportunity—kickbacks, city contracts, huge commissions from the Erie Railroad and other corporations, building a $12 million courthouse of which $8 million was graft. This was big business: the ultimate take of Tweed and his ring probably was measured in the upper eight figures.

It was the story of a young man's ambition, enterprise, rise to riches—and thorough corruption. As reformism rose during the Grant years, *Harper's Weekly* and the *New York Times* launched a long and tenacious campaign against the ring. Thomas Nast's merciless caricatures in *Harper's* converted the amiable, portly young man into a coarse, vicious-looking criminal, sinister of face and fat of belly. The cartoonists pictured him as William the Conqueror crushing the Constitution, as a crocodile, as a Roman emperor watching the Tammany tiger feasting on women's bodies in the Colosseum—and most typically, as a bloated dictator with the face of an Irish Fagin.

"What are you going to do about it?" Tweed liked to taunt his foes. A mass meeting of outraged citizens in Cooper Union, a committee of seventy reformers, revelations from dissident members of the ring itself, and prosecution brought Tweed and his cronies down in the short space of five months. He died in jail at the age of fifty-five. It was a glorious victory for reform, but it did not last long. Reformers found that the "tentacles of the octopus" remained intact even after the head was cut off, as the Plunkitts survived in the wards and precincts. Later Tammany leaders—the Crokers and Murphys and the rest—benefited from Tweed's downfall. They learned that they must discipline the organization, limit their greed, and share their take with their people in the old egalitarian spirit of Tammany.

Thus was set the pattern, in scores of cities, of boss control interrupted by bursts of reformism. Some of the machines were more honest and benign, some less so; the bosses were far more diverse in religion, ethnic background, civic virtue, education, appearance, and speech than the caricature of the Irish immigrant grafter would allow. But typically the organization persisted, and the reformers moved off to other interests. The perceptive Plunkitt observed this phenomenon:

"College professors and philosophers who go up in a balloon to think," he said from his pulpit, a bootblack stand, "are always discussin' the question: 'Why Reform Administrations Never Succeed Themselves.' . . . I can't tell just how many of these movements I've seen started in New York during my forty years in politics, but I can tell you how many have lasted more than a few years—none. There have been reform committees of fifty, of sixty, of seventy, of one hundred and all sorts of numbers that started out to do up the regular political organizations. They were mornin' glories—looked lovely in the mornin' and withered up in a short time, while the regular machines went on flourishin' forever, like fine old oaks."

The reason for the fading mornin' glories? Politics, Plunkitt explained, was a business—as much a "regular business as the grocery or dry-goods or the drug business." He had been learning it for forty-five years, ever since he had made himself useful around the Hall at age twelve. How could businessmen turn to politics all at once and make a success of it? "It is just as if I went up to Columbia University and started to teach Greek."

But the stakes were much deeper than merely between regular and reformer. In the industrial city, not only was politics a business; reform and bossism were so part and parcel of the corporate business world around them as to influence deeply the role of each. The more the bosses responded to business needs for franchises and other favors, the more they entered the business world—becoming in many respects brokers and businessmen themselves—and the more they tended to forfeit their old egalitarian role of giving to the poor. The commissions and bribes from business might trickle down to the needy poor, of course, thus fortifying the bosses' claims to be modern Robin Hoods, but much of the booty stuck to their own fingers.

The businessman, Steffens concluded, was the chief source of corruption. "I found him buying boodlers in St. Louis, defending grafters in Minneapolis, originating corruption in Pittsburgh, sharing with bosses in Philadelphia, deploring reform in Chicago, and beating good government with corruption funds in New York."

Nor could reformers escape the pervasive influence of corporate business. Many of them were businessmen themselves, and however much they might denounce the traction magnates and the like who dealt with the bosses, these reformers would not challenge the system of private property and corporate power that lay at the foundation of the industrial city. For some reformers, according to Wiebe, self-conscious businessmen alone among the progressive groups "had the inherent resources—the critical positions in the local economy, the money, and the prestige—to command some kind of response from the government. Weaker reformers, therefore, tried to attach their causes to these men's ambitions, relying upon their need for expert advice and their general sympathy for systematization and order." Ultimately, most reformers proved more interested in saving the lower class from liquor, gambling, and prostitutes—basic and necessary releases for those with few other means of diversion—than in reforming the socioeconomic system in which so many of the poor were trapped.

There was, indeed, a dangerously antidemocratic edge to the outlook of both regulars and reformers. That of the bosses was quite obvious: they perverted the ballot box, the cornerstone of democracy, by stuffing it, by hiring repeaters by the hundreds, voting names off gravestones, foiling the Australian ballot with the "Tasmanian dodge" (pre-marking ballots), intimidating voters, dumping ballots and whole ballot boxes into the river. Quite rightly did Joseph Choate cry out at Cooper Union: "This wholesale filching and slaughter of the suffrage is a deadly thrust at the very source and fountain of our liberties."

But some of the reformers, in reacting against what the *Times* called "the dangerous classes" who cared "nothing for our liberty and civilization," went much further in their quivering outrage and began to question the tenets of democracy itself. The curse of the city, wrote E. L. Godkin of the *Nation, is* the "people"—or the half of them that comprised the poor, "that huge body of ignorant and corrupt voters."

Noting how white Southerners had deprived Southern blacks of the vote through the "grandfather clause" and other devices, an "expert" predicted that once people became convinced that "universal suffrage inevitably must result in inefficient and corrupt government, it will be abandoned." From this vantage point it was but a step toward proposals to restrict the suffrage to the propertied class, to bar the poor immigrant, the unschooled, and the illiterate from the polls. And once that process got under way, where would it stop, as each class yearned to strengthen the morals and weaken the power of the class below?

THE REFORMATION OF THE CITIES

The answer of some to the plight of the poor and the blight of the city was to focus directly and intensely on what they saw as the heart of the problem—the lack of morality and character in the poor, especially the immigrant poor. This was peculiarly a strategy for preachers, lay and clerical, and many a church and forum resounded with thunderous appeals to the lower classes to shun vice and improve their ways. Some of the upright organized a Union for Concerted Moral Effort, and a leader of the National Union for Practical Progress proposed that a "new moral issue" be "presented to the people each month"—a kind of morality-of-the-month club.

The uplifters encountered a little problem, though—those to be uplifted were not in church. Most of the upright were middle-class in ideas, speech, dress, and geography; they were not speaking the same language as the immigrant poor. Recognizing this, many of the preachers made an enormous effort to bridge the gap by taking missions to the slums, turning churches into centers of social activity, sponsoring sports and theatricals. Under the creative leadership of a young native of Dublin, William S. Rainford, St. George's Episcopal Church, on East 16th Street, set up a boys' club, industrial training program, recreational activities, congregational singing. The Salvation Army, adapting adroitly to local conditions, helped meet needs for food and shelter and music and camaraderie so successfully that by century's end it directed seven hundred corps, staffed by 3,000 officers, across the nation.

The moral uplifters had to face a stark fact, however: even if they reached out to the fallen, poor immigrants would accept the tangible help, politely listen to the moral exhortation that might come with it, and then stick to their old ways. This was all the more reason, other reformers contended, to try a quite different strategy—improving the environment in which the poor grew up and lived. It was a problem of nurture and culture, not innate morality or heredity. Many of the upright recognized this in setting up recreational halls and trade schools, but the most direct and dramatic effort to reshape the environment was through settlement houses. The idea was to bring middle-class reformers into the very heartland of the industrial city, establish warm contacts with the poor, and attract some of the neighborhood people into these houses, which would serve as homes, schools, and social clubs.

The most famous of the settlement houses was Chicago's Hull-House, founded and run by Jane Addams and Ellen Gates Starr after they had visited Toynbee Hall, London's pioneering experiment in transforming the lives of the poor. As the settlement house movement spread to scores of other cities, Addams became its most eloquent promoter and defender. A powerful champion of environmentalism, she wanted transformed cities. "We are only beginning to understand," she asserted, "what might be done through the festival, the street procession, the band of marching musicians, orchestral music in public squares or parks." She mixed practicality with idealism: the "delicious sensation to be found in a swimming pool" would surely outweigh the temptation "to play craps in a foul and stuffy alley, even with the unnatural excitement which gambling offers."

The settlement movement had its critics. Some contended that the youthful volunteers tended to take on the outlook of those among whom they lived, rather than raising them up. They were "bowled over by the first labor leader, or anarchist, or socialist they met," said Mary Richmond of the Charity Organization Society. The settlement workers, however, were more likely to share the middle-class values of charity dispensers. The head of Boston's South End House, himself a prohibitionist, proposed to isolate tramps, alcoholics, and paupers; and Jane Addams, it was said, never doubted that the lower-class environment of saloons, dance halls, and street life needed to be made more like a middle- or upper-class neighborhood. Still, Addams emphasized—notably in her influential 1902 work

Democracy and Social Ethics—that the moral defects of the poor were the consequence, not the cause, of poverty.

Some environmentalists raised their sights far above charity and settlement houses. They would transform the entire city through creative and comprehensive planning, thus shaping a finer social and moral habitat. In part, this idea took the form of the City Beautiful movement, which in scores of industrial cities strove to replace filthy alleys, ugly billboards, overhead electrical wires, and littered vacant lots with trees, shrubbery, fountains, flower beds, even statuary and murals. This movement gained considerable impetus from the 1893 World's Columbian Exposition in Chicago, with its transformed lakefront, majestic fountains, broad walkways, wide lawns, and clean white buildings of monumental proportions.

But beautification was not enough, other environmentalists argued: the poor could not get to a world's fair or even to the parks in their own cities. What was needed was planning or replanning of the whole city. The city planners pointed to the transformation of Paris under Napoleon III, the exciting work in Prussian cities, the breathtaking concentric "rings" planned for fin de siècle Vienna. Could not Americans do better—at least in the nation's capital? Washington had been *planned,* after all, and Pierre L'Enfant's 1791 design for the city should now be completed. To do this Congress appointed a commission, which proposed a grand railroad station in the classical tradition, a triangle of neoclassical buildings, a memorial bridge to Arlington. A St. Louis committee rejected the monumental, centralized city in favor of clusters of neighborhood centers with comprehensive activities and programs catering specifically to the needs of the poor. The boldest plan of all, the 1909 *Plan of Chicago,* would expand the harbors and beaches, the parks and transportation, not only of the city but 3,000 square miles around it, from Michigan City, Indiana, to Kenosha, Wisconsin. Like its Exposition, Chicago would become a city of order, harmony, ennobling vistas, environmental delights, and hence of moral betterment.

Magnificent dreams—and almost wholly in vain. The city planners could not overcome the machinelike platting of city land into rectangular property lines and street grids; the fierce drive for profits of the real estate enterprisers and their allies in city politics; and the giant industries that ruled where people would reside, under what conditions they would work, and in effect how they would live. Most of the inspiring proposals were cut to pieces in the urban political meat grinders, or simply gathered dust on library shelves.

"Government must employ every resource in its power," one city planner's report asserted, and this was true in all the cities. But with its corrupted politicians, scattered authority, lack of sustained reform vigor, and state and local judges who defended private property to their last breath, government could not employ resources, for it had none. In an age that still respected private power and decried public, government was part of the problem, not its solution.

*   *   *

Was there, then, no hope for the industrializing cities—no hope that, with all their talent, vitality, and riches, they could be converted into communities that met the material and moral wants, the aesthetic and psychic needs of the citizens—and to do all this efficiently and within the law? The fate of most of the big cities indicated no, no such hope. Yet the experience of a number of cities hinted that, at least at intervals, they bore promise of becoming the kinds of community that the dreamers and utopians had envisaged. The realization of that promise in three cities turned on the quality of their leaders.

The most innovative and creative of these leaders, Hazen S. Pingree, ended up the least known. When this industrialist was elected mayor of Detroit in his fiftieth year, in 1889, his life had encapsulated a half-century of American history: raised on a poor Maine farm . . . mill hand in a Saco, Maine, cotton factory . . . apprentice leather-cutter in a Massachusetts shoe factory . . . raw recruit in the second Battle of Bull Run . . . prisoner of war in vile Andersonville . . . escapee and again a soldier . . . migrant to Detroit . . . shoe factory hand . . . shoe factory partner . . . shoe factory magnate . . . member of Detroit's economic and social elite. Angered by a corrupt city government, Republican leaders met to pick a candidate, but no one would run. Finally they turned to Pingree.

"Mayor?" he exclaimed. "Why that's political. What in hell do I know about politics? I'm too busy making shoes." He'd never even been in City Hall except to pay taxes, he said. But he finally gave in.

Politically, Detroit was enough to daunt any novice. As the old fur-trading town had grown from a commercial center to a big industrial city of steel foundries, machine products, and food processing, immigrants had crowded into the city and taken over the Democratic party. Republicans had run state politics for decades but could win in Detroit only when the Irish and the Germans fought each other for control of the city. The Germans, who by 1889 could boast of eight newspapers in their own language, including three dailies, were simmering over the reluctance of the Irish Democrats to slate them for office. A large Polish population felt even more ignored. Playing skillfully on these antagonisms, drinking red-eye whiskey at the bar to show that he was no prohibitionist, organizing his old shoe customers and shoemakers, Pingree won the election with a margin of 2,300 votes.

For a time Pingree was just the kind of mayor the GOP business leaders wanted—a cost-cutter and a corruption-fighter. But as he fought, in turn, the city bosses, a utility overcharging for street lighting, a monopolistic street railway company, and even more as he mixed informally with people in their neighborhoods and gained a better sense of their wants and needs, he broke with the business elite and moved toward progressive and even socialistic positions. By the end of his fourth term, when he left Detroit for Lansing and the governorship, Pingree had won lower utility rates, rebuilt the sewer system, built parks and public baths, exposed corruption in the school board and expanded the school system, modernized city transit, carried out equal-tax policies, made street railways and the telephone system more competitive, set up a city-owned light plant, and started a work-relief program that had as its goal, Melvin Holli noted, "both aid to the unfortunate and a change in the climate of public opinion toward 'paupers.' " A vocal foe of child labor, monopoly, and inequitable taxation, tolerant of Sunday drinking, opposed to required Bible readings in the schools, Pingree demonstrated over and again his commitment to both liberty and equality. He was deeply moral without being a self-righteous moralizer.

Judging by his nickname, preaching morality to other people might have been the avocation of "Golden Rule" Jones of Toledo, but he was a moralist of the Pingree stamp. As a manufacturer of oil well machinery, he posted the Golden Rule in his plant and instituted the eight-hour day, a minimum wage, vacations with full pay, Christmas bonuses; he forbade child labor, timekeepers, and piecework. As mayor of Toledo, he supported municipal ownership of utilities, free kindergartens, public playgrounds, free concerts; he made the police swap their police clubs for light canes and he disapproved arresting on suspicion and holding without charge. Jones too broke with the regular Republican organization and kept winning elections.

"Golden Rule" was an idealist, a utopian, a preacher who practiced what he preached. "In the ideal society that yet awaits us, in the co-operative commonwealth that is to be realized, in the kingdom of Heaven *that is to be set up here on this earth,*" he proclaimed, "there will be no patents, no railway passes, no reserved seats, no 'free list,' no franchises, or contracts or special privileges of any sort to enable a select few of the people to live off the toil of others."

In Cleveland, Tom L. Johnson, inventor, steel maker, street-railroad magnate, won election as mayor four times. During his eight years in office, he transformed the municipal government, but even more he transformed the people through a continuous educational campaign. In a circus tent big enough for 4,000 persons but small enough to be moved from neighborhood to neighborhood, he discussed public affairs and invited the audience to speak up and ask questions. Johnson too fought to limit utility franchises, urged city ownership of power and water, forced the trolley car fare down to three cents, expanded recreation areas and bathhouses, and protected prostitutes and madams against the police.

"Only through municipal ownership," Johnson said, "can the gulf which divides the community into a small dominant class on one side and the unorganized people on the other be bridged. . . . only by making men's ambitions and pecuniary interests identical with the welfare of the city can civil warfare be ended."

These three leaders—and a few others like them but with less success —achieved not merely the reform of their cities but their *reformation*—their restoration as places of harmony and dignity for all the people, their rebirth as moral communities, their revitalization as forces for liberty and equality and fraternity. Why these three men of wealth and status should have ended up as radicals and socialists has long been a conundrum of history. They grew up in impoverished circumstances—but many a man had done so, only to grind down the poor in his own turn at the top. Perhaps their most remarkable common quality was their capacity to learn not only from experience and human contact but from reflection and reading. Pingree read Washington Gladden, Henry Demarest Lloyd, Albert Shaw, Richard T. Ely; Jones was deeply influenced by Tolstoy, Bellamy, and Whitman; Johnson happened on a copy of Henry George's *Progress and Poverty* during a train trip and it launched him on his reform career. For these men, intellectual leadership and moral leadership were inseparable.

In the final assessment of the leadership and reformation of the industrial cities, though, these men stand as exceptions, almost as curiosities. Nothing—not leadership nor morality nor beautification nor technology nor governmental reorganization—nothing stemmed for long the overpowering force of industrialization. Neither the political machines nor the welfare agencies, neither philanthropy nor radical leaders, could cope with the tide of economic and social and psychological misery that enveloped tens of millions of migrants and immigrants. Neither the organized government of politicians nor the private government of capitalists could plan ahead, raise enough money, act comprehensively and persistently enough to overcome deeply rooted urban malaise and disarray.

The failure of the cities, however, dramatized the need for national action. And the ideas incubated in the city saloons and other forums, in universities and churches, in election contests and editorial chambers, would provide much of the content and controversy of the nationwide conflicts that would herald a new age of modernity in thought and progressivism in politics.

WOMEN: THE PROGRESSIVE CADRE

The brilliant political leaders who attracted national attention during the progressive era tended to obscure the remarkable array of women who emerged around the turn of the century, a group committed to an expansive view of women's social, economic, political, and sexual rights—and to action.

Julia Lathrop, descendant of Illinois pioneers and a graduate of Vassar, accepted Governor Altgeld's appointment in 1892 as the first woman member of the Illinois Board of Public Charities, and proceeded to visit the 102 county farms or almshouses to see the indigent, the epileptic, the insane, the delinquent children, and the rest of the unwanted, heaped together in those dreary and forlorn institutions. Florence Kelley, daughter of the famed William "Pig Iron" Kelley of Pennsylvania, graduated from Cornell, studied at the University of Zurich after being barred from pursuing law at the University of Pennsylvania because she was a woman, translated Engels's *Condition of the Working Class in England.* Returning home a socialist, she investigated tenement workshops as Altgeld's chief Illinois factory inspector—the first woman to hold that post. Emma Goldman emigrated from Konigsberg, worked in a Rochester clothing plant and a New Haven corset factory, embraced anarchism after the trial of the Haymarket Square workingmen, helped her lover Alexander Berkman plan the attack upon Henry Frick, and spent a year in prison for inciting a riot. These and a host of other indomitable women would soon be followed by a new generation with many causes: Grace and Edith Abbott, Alice Hamilton, Margaret Sanger, among many others.

Dazzling among even this galaxy of leaders was the incomparable Jane Addams. Daughter of a liberal-minded politician and businessman, she was broadly educated: Rockford Seminary, a term at the Women's Medical College in Philadelphia, lengthy European travels that included prowls through the slums of East London and Naples and a visit to Toynbee Hall, a community of young Englishmen seeking to uplift the poor through benevolence and culture. Returning home, she and her Rockford classmate Ellen Gates Starr established their own settlement house amid the tenements and factories, the immigrant Irish and Germans and Russians and Italians and Polish Jews, the nine churches and 250 saloons in the 19th Ward surrounding Chicago's South Halsted Street.

The old mansion on Halsted, with its big drawing room, high ceilings, and fancy cornices, soon was ministering to the needs of the poor it had long excluded, providing relief, food, medical care, community kitchen, an employment bureau, day nurseries. But Addams and her friends sensed that the poor wanted much more, that as their basic needs were satisfied, they increasingly craved comradeship, group activities, discussions, books, art, music, theater. Hull-House had its Women's Club, Community Kitchen, gymnasium, day nursery, Labor Museum, and the Hull-House Players, a pioneer in the Little Theatre movement. Upper and lower class were thrown intimately together. After the Women's Club heard a Christian Scientist urge her listeners to think of the smell of pine trees amid the setting sun rather than the stink of garbage at a nearby nauseous river, a German woman who had lived close to the stream rose to exclaim: "Vell, all I can say is if dot woman say dot river smell good den dere must be something de matter with dot woman's nose!"

Hull-House soon became a center of intellectual controversy and excitement. Arguments raged over politics, architecture, art, religion. To its Plato Club came John Dewey to lead sessions on Greek philosophy. Governor Altgeld and the rising young attorney Clarence Darrow dropped by. Beatrice Webb, visiting the house with her husband Sidney, persuaded Jane Addams to try a cigarette for the first time; it was also the last. Hull-House was also a training institution for hosts of women who would move out into other settlement houses, into government, academe, philanthropy. Julia Lathrop worked at Hull-House, as did Alice Hamilton. Florence Kelley would never forget arriving at the house on a snowy December morning, her children around her, to be greeted by Addams holding the cook's plump baby in her arms while keeping an eye on a lively Italian girl whose mother was working in a local sweatshop.

Addams seemed to serve in every role—as intellectual leader, project developer, fund raiser, morale booster, "community relations" manager. Her most ticklish outside relationship was with local ward boss Alderman Johnny Powers, who at election time liked to drive his bandwagon to the polling places, including the one at Hull-House, while the band played "Nearer, My God to Thee" and the boss tossed cigars to the men and nickels to the children. A smooth broker of jobs, favors, permits, ordinances, and money, Powers could not understand why Addams, whom he could not but admire, refused to work with him, even to accept his proffered favors. "Miss Addams is always O.K. with me," Powers would complain, "but I wish just once she'd ask me and not fight me all the time."

But Addams rivaled any boss in her readiness to help the desperate. When a young woman, ostracized by her neighbors because she was bearing a child out of wedlock, went into labor unattended as no one wanted to call a doctor and risk being stuck with the bill, Addams and Lathrop hurried to the tenement to serve as midwives.

As Hull-House expanded to thirteen buildings and a staff of sixty-five, Addams seemed to expand intellectually as well, broadening her activities to encompass virtually the whole gamut of social and political reform. She was active in the National Child Labor Committee, the National Society for the Promotion of Industrial Education, the National Playground Association, the National Consumers' League, the American Association for Labor Legislation, the National Tuberculosis Association, and, not least, the National Women's Trade Union League, as well as suffrage organizations and other reform efforts. Somehow she found time to write ten books and several hundred articles. She was a frequent and compelling public speaker, and although not an especially original thinker, she had, according to biographer Allen Davis, "the ability to see meaning and purpose in the confusing events of her day and to communicate that meaning to a wide audience."

In time, Addams became almost sanctified, evoking comparisons to Joan of Arc or the Virgin Mary, a humble woman serving the lowly and sharing their poverty. In fact, Addams remained an upper-middle-class woman who enjoyed good living, especially in her travels with her close companion Ellen Gates Starr, and happily accepted the lavish entertainment offered by her wealthy friends—though she usually took the opportunity to beg them for funds.

Still, Addams was only the brightest star in that large galaxy, and it was the social enterprise and imagination of thousands of women leaders in hundreds of reform efforts that produced betterment across the nation, rivaling that of Hull-House. This leadership cadre had its roots in the intense social needs arising out of the economic malaise of the 1880s and early 1900s—especially urban conditions of unemployment, crowded tenements, low wages, high infant mortality, and increasing numbers of working women with small children. The leadership was shaped and stimulated by the sharpening ideologies of the nineties, the rising populist and progressive protest movements, the general quickening of political excitement. But the direct source of that leadership was a cadre of middle- and upper-class women who were typically college-educated, well read and traveled, and from a secular reform background.

These women were often thwarted in their career aspirations, such as law—Julia Lathrop worked for ten years in her father's law office—or business, were often unmarried and wanted to remain so, and usually had access to wealthy benefactors, such as Julius Rosenwald in Chicago. Since professionally trained women were generally excluded from the upper ranks of university faculties, in Joan Zimmerman's view, they naturally turned to new areas where they could use their expertise. And many of these women shared middle-class feelings of morality and guilt about their privileged status compared to that of the urban masses. Hofstadter noted that as early as 1892 Jane Addams lectured on "The Subjective Necessity for Social Settlements," explaining how "the sheltered and well-brought-up young Americans of her generation, reared on the ideal of social justice and on Protestant moral imperatives," had become troubled over their own sincerity and usefulness.

These forces lent a certain tone and thrust to women's reform leadership. Settlement houses administered to a variety of human needs, not merely the economic, and they did so by seeking to satisfy them directly or "maternally," rather than depending on the needy to conduct their own struggle for realization of their own hopes, expectations, and demands. Workers' movements and organizations as such—especially trade unions—appealed directly to workers' economic interests and assumed that this motive power would accelerate "labor's demand for more." This is not to say that women leaders opposed unions—what good progressive could do that?—or that unions were not also concerned with comradeship, education, and summer camps. Indeed, leaders like Florence Kelley and Jane Addams also invaded the political arena to work for laws protecting women and children especially. But there was, on their part, a womanly caring for all the material, social, aesthetic, and self-fulfillment needs of their "charges" that went beyond the merely economic.

These broad concerns encouraged woman leaders to act in a diversity of fields. The settlement house idea itself spread to many cities. In the early nineties Lillian Wald, of an affluent Rochester family, moved to the Lower East Side of Manhattan with a determination to use her training in nursing to serve especially the needs of immigrants. With financial aid from the Schiffs and Loebs and other wealthy clans, she established the Henry Street Settlement, a large nursing facility that also offered classes in cooking and sewing, art and dancing. Appointed to the Mayor's Pushcart Commission, Wald extended her concerns to playgrounds, parks, housing, and the regulation of sweatshops as her social sympathies compelled her to embrace ever broader reform movements. But the central effort of the Henry Street Settlement remained nursing, in its broadest dimensions, as Wald and her colleagues pressed vigorously for the extension of public nursing into schools and homes.

Another woman's movement focused on a very specific threat to mothers and children—the saloon. Founded in 1874, the Women's Christian Temperance Union had grown rapidly during the next quarter century, reaching a membership of 300,000 by century's end. It was the largest woman's organization in the country, at least ten times larger than the suffrage organizations of the day, which were emerging from a political dry spell. The WCTU had not been concerned only with drunkards and their power to abuse their families and even grab the earnings of wife and children, without legal redress. Despite Carrie Nation's notoriety as a "saloon-wrecker," the women of the WCTU had studied and agitated on issues of labor reform, prostitution, health and hygiene, prison reform, needs of black women, drug use, international arbitration, and world peace. These broad interests were in part the product of the gifted leadership of Frances Willard, a onetime college president who moved into the temperance legions and governed with the inspired motto, "Do Everything." With her death in 1898, the movement drifted back to its original emphasis on drinking.

Margaret Sanger, the boldest of the women's leaders, confronted the most intimate and controversial question of all—sexuality and reproduction. A number of influences combined to convert this slight, mild-looking young woman into a dauntless crusader: a marriage at nineteen that ended in divorce; her friendship with Emma Goldman and militant radicals in the Industrial Workers of the World; her association with Malthus-oriented French syndicalists during a Paris visit in 1913. Returning to the United States the next year, she established a monthly called the *Woman Rebel,* advocated "birth control" (a term she coined), and aroused her foes even more by allying with anarchists, woman liberationists, and assorted radicals. After the federal government indicted her and her journal under the Comstock anti-obscenity act of 1873, she fled to England for almost a year, fearlessly returned to open the first birth control clinic in Brooklyn, and was arrested and jailed.

Sanger would not be silenced. "The basic freedom of the world is woman's freedom," she wrote in *Woman and the New Race.* "A free race cannot be born of slave mothers. A woman enchained cannot choose but give a measure of that bondage to her sons and daughters. No woman can call herself free who does not own and control her body."

*   *   *

As in the case of all strong leaders, these women divided potential followers as well as uniting them. Millions of low-income Americans, including hosts of women who desperately needed her counsels, feared and hated Margaret Sanger and all she stood for. Millions of American workers —including some women—who liked their beer and wine and the harder stuff, loathed the WCTU saloon closers. Many men—and a few women— opposed woman's suffrage. Few objected to the settlement houses, for they seemed caring and unthreatening, but some low-income women scorned the middle-class maternalists as members of what one woman trade unionist called the "mink brigade."

When would working women take matters into their own hands, build their own movement, choose their own leaders? At century's end, unionization of women, after many setbacks, seemed poised for a takeoff. They were moving by the tens of thousands out of farm labor and domestic service into occupations far easier to unionize. Women employed in non-agricultural pursuits had more than doubled, from 2 million to 4.3 million, between 1880 and 1900. But hardly 3 percent of those women were unionized by century's end. With populist and progressive winds blowing, surely women's trade unionism would escalate during the decade ahead.

It was not to be. Women's efforts to join men's unions or organize their own seemed to meet all the past furies, only redoubled. Trade unions themselves seemed weighted against women. Their leaders often held their meetings in saloons, amid the stench of cigar smoke and stale beer. They resented interference by women, suggesting they should stick to home and hearth. They charged high dues. They feared low-wage competition from women workers just off the farm or out of the kitchen. It seemed to some women workers that some unionists were organized as much against them as against the bosses.

For many women the only recourse was to form their own organizations, but this required able and militant leadership—and here above all women were disadvantaged. They could not find such leadership in the American Federation of Labor under Samuel Gompers, who was as conservative toward unionizing women as he was toward organizing blacks and the unskilled. The AFL did oppose discriminatory pay for women, in order to protect all workers from cheap labor, but this policy harmed the millions of unskilled women whose only hope of a job was one with low pay. The Federation had only one female organizer in the 1890s; when she left to be married, Gompers waited until 1908 before appointing another, Annie Fitzgerald. It was not until working women organized militantly in the Lawrence textile strike of 1912 that the AFL paid much attention to them.

Women workers had only the leadership they could mobilize from their own ranks; there was no Jane Addams or Frances Willard of female trade unionism. Brilliant leaders arose from the movement, especially in the conduct of strikes, as with the textile operatives of Chicopee and the clothing makers of Chicago. Twenty thousand New York shirtwaist makers walked out, over the opposition of their male leaders. Certain unions like the hat and cap makers generated their own activists, most notably in the person of the fiery organizer Rose Schneidermann. But typically women's leadership hardly rose above the level of "shop chairladies."

It was in this connection that the National Women's Trade Union League assumed special importance. Its goal was to enable women of social influence and progressive ideas to join hands with activist women in the trades. The former would supply creative ideas and leadership, the latter practical experience and information. Founded in 1903 at an AFL convention in Boston, the NWTUL became strong enough to help produce a peak organizing period for women between 1909 and 1915. Its platform called for organization of all workers into trade unions; equal pay for equal work, regardless of sex; the eight-hour day and forty-four-hour week; a "living wage"; full citizenship for women.

Effective though it was, the Women's Trade Union League could not wholly overcome the old class barriers. For "middle class feminists outside the WTUL," according to Robin Miller Jacoby, "class identity outweighed their rhetorical commitment to the ideal of cross-class female solidarity." It was the society women within the NWTUL whom Schneidermann had labeled the mink brigade. Women of all classes, however, could unite in the pursuit of two goals—woman's suffrage and social legislation—and the NWTUL plunged into both battles. Even so, suffrage leader Carrie Chapman Catt could not help observing, "I am a *good* democrat in theory, but my faith weakens when it meets bad air, dirt, horrid smells, the democratic odor diluted with perfumes of beer and uncleanliness."

Women could also unite as consumers, under the leadership of Florence Kelley, general secretary of the National Consumers' League. But Kelley was interested in far broader matters than consumer problems. Living at the Henry Street Settlement, she fought for the legal protection of women against long hours and unhealthful conditions; she was one of the founding members of the National Association for the Advancement of Colored People; she organized sixty or more local Consumers' Leagues pledged to boycott companies that employed child labor. She was so active and effective that years later a Supreme Court justice would call her "a woman who had probably the largest single share in shaping the social history of the United States during the first thirty years of the century." By expanding the concept of consumerism to cover the social price of making goods and not merely the money price in the stores, Kelley transcended some of the old conflict between low-income women factory workers and middle-class women consumers.

*   *   *

Whatever the differences among women leaders, they were minuscule compared to the conflicts that cut through the ranks of working people.

After vanquishing the remnants of the militant Knights of Labor in the late 1880s, the American Federation of Labor had come to hold a commanding place in the organization of skilled workers. By 1904, it was boasting a membership of over a million and a half. Under its founding leader, Samuel Gompers, now a burly, bespectacled gentleman usually attired in dignified clothes and carrying a cane, the Federation continued to practice business unionism—jealous guardian of the skilled crafts, protector of labor against injunctions and other hostile governmental action, critic of immigration. The AFL rejected socialism, radicalism, government welfarism, independent political action. While AFL unions often fought hard-line employers with strikes, boycotts, and other weapons, the AFL had become an essential buttress of the business system—conservative in outlook, restrictive and monopolistic in economic tactics, transactional in leadership, bargaining and competitive in its relationship with business. The Federation's membership rose and fell with the business cycle; it joined with business and government in the National Civic Federation founded in 1900 to "unite" labor and capital; President Gompers supped with the mighty, including magnates and Presidents.

As it fought off challenge after challenge to its power, the AFL left millions of workers unorganized, politically adrift, and ready to be led. The next threat to the Federation came less from the unorganized masses of the urban East than from the embattled workers in the West. There the pugnacious Western Federation of Miners had conducted a running and often bloody war with equally pugnacious mine and railroad owners. In the bloody Coeur d'Alene area of Idaho, mine workers thwarted by antiunion bosses had dynamited a company mill, leaving two men dead; the governor promptly obtained federal troops to round up strikers by the hundreds and throw them into bull pens. The WFM was everything the AFL was not—eager to organize the unorganized, including immigrants and even blacks, and totally opposed to capitalism and capitalists. And it had a new young leader, William D. Haywood, who was everything Gompers was not.

Son of a Pony Express rider who died when he was three, Big Bill had been raised in a mining camp, put to work at fifteen as a hardrock miner, and then drifted through the West as a prospector, cowboy, surveyor, and miner again, before joining the WFM. With his huge frame, a "dead eye" lost in a childhood mishap, and a "dead hand" crushed in a mining accident, Haywood intimidated bosses and union rivals alike.

But the western miners desperately needed allies. In 1905 Haywood and other WFM leaders, along with delegates from Daniel De Leon's Socialist Trade and Labor Alliance and individual socialists like Eugene Debs, gathered in Chicago to establish the Industrial Workers of the World, with the aim of uniting all workers, of all skills, races, and national origins, ready to use strikes, boycotts, and sabotage, if necessary, to realize their grand objectives of a socialist, classless, egalitarian society.

The "Wobblies" scored some organizing successes with western lumber workers and farm laborers and eastern textile workers. Haywood exercised brilliant leadership of a mass walkout against pay cuts in the Massachusetts textile town of Lawrence. As his picket lines held firm, he dramatized police brutality and won a great public-relations coup when striking parents sent their children to outlying towns to be fed. His strikers finally won in Lawrence in that year of 1912 and gave the union's organizing drives a big boost. But the IWW's victories—and Big Bill's—were ephemeral. The Wobblies fought among themselves, with the AFL, with their socialist and syndicalist friends. They purged De Leon's socialists, but they could not make a dent in the skilled ranks of the AFL. The WFM's metalworkers could not even establish unity with the AFL's coal miners. After a time the WFM pulled out of the IWW, leaving the Wobblies with a shrunken core.

It was a poignant state of affairs. Labor was producing its own luminaries in the progressive era—Gompers the labor "statesman" and executive, De Leon the doctrinaire syndicalist, Victor Berger the socialist politician, Eugene Debs the propagandist and election campaigner, Haywood the direct-actionist, and a host of others of almost equal talents. Yet these men could not work together for more than brief intervals. They preached unity above all else, but they could not practice it. They were not simply the victims of their own competing egos and ambitions. They were the victims too of conflicting ideologies, some imported and some homegrown, of nativist-immigrant tensions, of ethnic and racial rivalries, of an individualistic and competitive ethos that even penetrated radical labor, of capitalist opposition and divisiveness, of the sheer space and variety and regionalism of America.

And off to the side stood Emma Goldman, watching the radicals' Virginia reel with mingled concern and contempt. She believed in activism, not organization. Following McKinley's assassination, she was arrested, given the third degree, and then released for lack of evidence against her. Later she founded an anarchist monthly, *Mother Earth,* welcomed Berkman on his release after fourteen years in prison, became a friend and lover of Ben Reitman, the King of the Hobos. She scorned marriage as an institution that made wives the private property of their husbands. She scorned

woman's suffrage as tending to co-opt them into the political status quo.
She scorned unions as instruments of the capitalist system. Above all, she
came to oppose war. But, cut off as she was from parties and unions, she
could serve only as a gadfly, albeit one with a sharp sting.

The wide split between Gompers-style and Haywood-style unionism had
its counterpart in a deep political and philosophical chasm among black
Americans—and the opposing black leaders were as remarkable a set of
adversaries as the two unionists.

Booker T. Washington, born a slave on a Virginia plantation a few years
before the Civil War, emerged out of conditions that might have made a
white man either an Andrew Carnegie or a flaming radical. Washington
remembered growing up in a small log cabin with earthen floor and glass-
less windows, eating with hands and fingers out of the family pot of corn-
bread and pork, going to work after Emancipation in a salt-packing factory,
where he might labor seventeen hours straight. Illiterate and forbidden by
his stepfather to attend school, Booker developed a fierce desire to read,
prompted by his curiosity over figures on salt barrels and the gift of a
Webster's spelling book from his mother. He managed to take night lessons, then to attend day school, and finally to make the long trek to the
Hampton Institute, where he served as both student and janitor. Invited
to run the Tuskegee Institute, an industrial school, he set out with white
patronage to convert it into a major enterprise with 1,400 pupils and thirty
trades. From this base he fought his way to immense power and prestige.

The turning point for Washington came with a speech he gave in Atlanta
in 1895. At a time when almost half of American blacks were illiterate, he
urged schooling and more schooling. Speaking to a racially mixed audience, he in effect proposed a great transaction—that blacks acquiesce in
social subordination and political inequality in exchange for economic
opportunity and advancement; in time, the latter would end the former.
Agitating "questions of social equality," he said, was the "extremest folly."
His message—learn, work, earn, win respect—won a chorus of praise from
Southern whites and many blacks.

Washington himself rose to great social eminence, dining (once) with
the Roosevelts in the White House, receiving audiences with kings, con-
sorting with philanthropists like Carnegie and Rockefeller. He gained political power too, as he used his Tuskegee work as a base for the "Tuskegee
machine"—a personal political organization through which he placed hundreds of blacks in governmental and academic posts throughout the nation. He offered advice to Roosevelt and Taft, in exchange for which he
muted criticism of their treatment of blacks. But when Taft left office,
Washington's patronage power left with him.

William Edward Burghardt Du Bois seemed almost a polar opposite to Washington—born of an established mulatto family in western Massachusetts, graduate of Fisk University, student for two years at the University of Berlin, the first Negro to receive a doctoral degree from Harvard (for a notable thesis on the African slave trade). He moved on to an illustrious career as a sociologist, historian, and novelist. With success, however, Du Bois became more and more militant. He could not accept Washington's brokerage and accommodationism. On the death of his first son, Du Bois buried his anguish in anger: "Well sped, my boy, before the world had dubbed your ambition insolence, had held your ideals unattainable, and taught you to cringe and bow."

Du Bois came to oppose virtually everything Washington stood for. He chose militancy over cooperation, protest over patronage, black and trade-union resistance over endless deference. At a demonstration at Harpers Ferry, he and his fellow militants, in what Du Bois called some of the plainest English ever spoken by American blacks (Du Bois used the words Negro, black, and colored interchangeably, sometimes in the same sentence), demanded immediate full mankind suffrage, the end of segregation in railways and streetcars, the right "as freemen" for Negroes to walk, talk, and socialize with whites as well as blacks, and the enforcement of laws against rich as well as poor, capitalist as well as laborer, white as well as black. After two blacks were lynched and scores burned out of their homes and stores in Springfield, Illinois, forty-nine white progressives and socialists issued a "call" that gave birth to the National Association for the Advancement of Colored People; Du Bois was the only black among its first set of top officers.

Conflict intensified between the militants and accommodationists. Washington fought the NAACP and Du Bois with bribery and espionage, and Du Bois responded with burning attacks on the Tuskegee machine. Both sides sought to control black organizations, the Niagara Movement founded by Du Bois, the NAACP, the black press, access to white philanthropy. In place of Washington's transactional leadership—which ultimately might have served as a crucial transitional leadership—Du Bois proposed black struggle in the United States and in Asia and Africa and the "islands of the sea."

And off to the side stood the most extraordinary leader of all, Mary Harris Jones. Above all an individualist with a dislike for doctrine, Mother Jones had one simple strategy—to travel hundreds of miles to help whatever children, women, or men needed help, whether child laborers, persecuted Wobblies, jailed union leaders, women garment workers on the picket lines. This simply dressed, grandmotherly-looking woman symbolized the capacity of women leaders, to a far greater extent than men leaders of the time, to transcend small differences and unite behind humane, progressive goals. It was grimly ironic that the cadre of leaders best equipped for the struggle to broaden democracy in America were the very ones who, with their female constituencies, were denied the stoutest democratic weapon to extend democracy, the right to vote.

CHAPTER 8

The Modernizing Mind

"I know histhry isn't thrue, Hinissy, because it ain't what I see ivry day on Halsted Sthreet," said Mr. Dooley, the ruminative barkeep. Historians were like doctors, he went on, either making the wrong diagnosis or making postmortem examinations. The latter type "tells ye what a counthry died iv. But I'd like to know what it lived iv."

If life and action and excitement were what Finley Peter Dunne's favorite bartender was wanting, he could find them in turn-of-the-century Chicago, and in the nation during what came to be known as the progressive era stretching from the mid-nineties to World War I. And if these were retrogressive times as well as progressive, of "intriguing interplay" of old and new ideas, in Lewis Gould's words, it was also one of the most creative and innovative periods in the nation's history.

Nothing had symbolized the past and the future better than the Chicago World's Fair of 1893. On the lakeside, a dreary stretch of plain and swamp had been transformed into a site for gleaming white buildings of shimmering domes, lofty arches, and Greek columns. The Queen of Spain sent reproductions of the *Niña, Pinta,* and *Santa Maria.* Models of primitive ships and trains stood side by side with those of grand Pullmans and ocean liners. Alexander Graham Bell opened the New York–Chicago telephone circuit. For the 12 million visitors who entered the Court of Honor, the fair was "the first popular demonstration of the beauty of orderliness, of proper proportions, of classical lines"—a demonstration that would influence American architecture, furniture, and decoration for years to come. Even Henry Adams was impressed.

The fair, it was said, helped bring into vogue Charles Dana Gibson's black-and-white drawings of the tall, aristocratic, smartly dressed woman and the square-jawed, clean-shaven, well-groomed young man—drawings that put the Gibson girls up in rude mining cabins and helped take mustaches off men of fashion. Women's fashions were changing too. The turn of the century brought a "shirtwaist vogue" duly recorded by the *Ladies' Home Journal.* The new fashions, however, had to accommodate another vogue—bicycling. The dangerous early "wheels," consisting of a huge hoop topped by a saddle and connected by a curved backbone to a tiny rear wheel, had given way to two wheels of equal size, but skirts were raised and split a bit to prevent entanglement with gears and spokes.

Bicycles were but one phase in the ceaseless quest for ever new forms of transportation. The Sears, Roebuck catalogue of 1900 carried sixty-seven pages of ads for buggies, harnesses, saddles, and the like, but already hansoms, victorias, sulkies, phaetons, and buggies were giving way to electric "runabouts" and gasoline-fueled cars. And in December 1903 the Norfolk *Virginian-Pilot* ran a headline across the front page, FLYING MACHINE SOARS 3 MILES IN TEETH OF HIGH WIND OVER SAND HILLS, with a subhead explaining NO BALLOON ATTACHED TO AID IT. The Pennsylvania Railroad launched the "fastest long-distance train in the world," eighteen hours between New York and Chicago.

By 1900, Americans could boast that they produced more than half the world's cotton, corn, copper, and oil; more than a third of its steel, pig iron, and silver; and perhaps a third of its coal and gold. But Americans wanted to boast of their cultural progress too, and they were proud that their own authors like Winston Churchill (the *American* Churchill), Hamlin Garland, and Owen Wister were replacing Englishmen like Rudyard Kipling as best-selling authors. Most music was still imported, but black Americans were developing an indigenous musical culture with their "spirituals":

> O Lord, remember the rich an' remember the poor.
> Remember the bond an' the free.
> And when you done rememberin' all 'round,
> Then, O Lord, remember me.

Almost every bright promise of the progressive era seemed to have a darker side. The huge production was sweated out of men and women working sixty hours a week at subsistence wages in factory, farm, and home; out of children crawling through tunnels thick with coal dust. Blacks were coming to feel so hopeless about the "promise of American democracy" that the National Colored Immigration and Commercial Association in 1903 petitioned President Roosevelt and Congress for $100 million to carry American Negroes to Liberia. The same schoolchildren who were merrily playing Prisoner's Base, Follow My Leader, and King of the Rock on the school grounds were often subject to the leather strap and ruler not only for "misbehaving" but for failing to keep up with their lockstep lessons in McGuffey's readers.

Grown-ups also played their games. The annual report of the New York Society for the Suppression of Vice, Anthony Comstock, Secretary, offered a list of outrageous pleasures that, Comstock hinted darkly, were indulged in by the rich: indecent playing cards, roulette layouts, lottery tickets, pool scorecards, gaming tables, dream books, dice, slot machines, watches with obscene pictures, "Articles for immoral use, of Rubber, etc." Comstock reported that he had hired a horse and sleigh and driven through rural New England tracking down "devilish books" and "villainous" men.

Women, lacking the vote, jobs, and opportunity, were even imprisoned in their dress. Wrote Kathleen Norris of the conventionally dressed woman of turn of century:

"She wore a wide-brimmed hat that caught the breezes, a high choking collar of satin or linen, and a flaring gored skirt that swept the street on all sides. Her full-sleeved shirtwaist had cuffs that were eternally getting dirty, her stock was always crushed and rumpled at the end of the day, and her skirt was a bitter trial. Its heavy 'brush binding' had to be replaced every few weeks, for constant contact with the pavement reduced it to dirty fringe in no time at all. In wet weather the full skirt got soaked and icy. Even in fair weather its wearer had to bunch it in great folds and devote one hand to nothing else but the carrying of it."

The most pervasive and relentless change was still occurring in the industrializing cities, as work, work habits, and work environment responded to ceaseless innovation. Urbanization and innovation fortified each other. Hosts of inventors and experimenters of diverse talents and specialties cooperated and competed with one another on the industrial testing grounds in the big cities. The "ingenious Yankees"—now Irish and Italian and German and Jewish as well—endlessly tinkered on the job as they strove to lower costs and improve and speed production. Machines were becoming more dominant even as they became less visible—as pulleys and drive shafts gave way to covered wires and tubes, and as safety shields concealed the power apparatus.

At fin de siècle, however, more than ever before during the nineteenth century, industrial innovation was becoming dependent on advances in science and basic technology. Decades earlier Karl Marx had contended that only in particular times in human history was science enlisted in key ways in the productive processes, even as science itself was dependent on intensive development of such processes. The very late nineteenth century was such a time. Theoretical and practical developments in electricity exemplified change most dramatically, but new ideas burst forth in a variety of industrial fields.

And what enkindling ideas they were! At century's turn, Albert Michelson was working on the velocity of light, with the help of an "interferometer" he invented. Thomas L. Willson, a North Carolina chemist, was producing acetylene gas. Frank Austin Gooch was introducing the rotating cathode. Edward Acheson's carborundum was tough enough to polish diamonds. Edward W. Morley determined the atomic weight of oxygen. Ohio physicist Wallace Sabine devised a reverberation equation vital to the study of acoustics. Americans were closely studying—and exploiting—pioneering work abroad: Guglielmo Marconi's work on a wireless telegraph system; the discovery of X-rays by German chemist Wilhelm Roentgen; Lord Ernest Rutherford's discovery of alpha and beta waves; Marie Curie's identification of the elements polonium and radium; Max Planck's quantum theory; Niels Bohr's theory of atomic structure. Americans exported findings too: Michelson's and Morley's experiments served as a starting point for Einstein's special theory of relativity.

Inventors were doing the most outlandish things, especially up in the air and under the sea. Simon Lake in 1894 launched Argonaut I, a small, hand-powered submersible. Three years later, he created Argonaut II, a gasoline-powered submarine with wheels for rolling along the ocean floor; and a year after that, John Holland launched his cigar-shaped submarine, powered by gasoline on top of the water and by electricity below. After Hiram Maxim failed to conquer the air with a steam-powered flying machine and after astronomer Samuel Langley built the first successful engine-propelled model airplane, bicycle makers Orville and Wilbur Wright launched the world's first successful manned flight in a motorized airplane, at Kitty Hawk in 1903. Down on earth, after Charles and Frank Duryea had operated the nation's first successful gasoline-powered automobile, in Springfield, Massachusetts, in 1893, a host of inventors were feverishly perfecting improvements: sliding gear transmissions, steering wheels to replace the tiller, pneumatic tires, automatic lubrication.

Technology both stimulated and gained from advances in wide-ranging fields of science. Josiah Willard Gibbs at Yale and Charles Steinmetz at General Electric were working in sophisticated fields of mathematics. Geologists made key theoretical findings about glacial and other formations and practical ones about oil deposits. Astronomers were reaching farther out into the solar system, with the use of improved telescopes, photography, and a bolometer devised by Langley to detect extraterrestrial temperatures. Paleontologists—most notably Henry Fairfield Osborn at the American Museum of Natural History—were systematizing knowledge in the field through great finds of bones and fossil footprints. Anthropologists—especially Franz Boas and Clark Wissler—were taking sides between diffusionist theories stressing the geographical dispersion of Indian and other cultures, and "culture area" concepts focusing on interaction and integration within local cultures. In genetics, Thomas Hunt Morgan was doing notable work on heredity, embryology, and regeneration.

Medicine abounded in advances in anesthesia, radium and X-ray therapy, prevention, surgery, and a concentrated fight against a number of diseases, especially tuberculosis.

But the weather change of the late nineteenth century far transcended even these remarkable advances. In science, there was a shift from "normal," systematic reliance on step-by-step progress within established paradigms to imaginative leaps into the unknown, thus returning to the revolutionary pattern of great scientific breakthroughs of the past. In philosophy there was a revolt against the formal, "rational" metaphysics of the time, an exploration of new ways of understanding human motivation, of new perceptions of the relation between thought and action. These intellectual revolutions in turn stimulated new thought in law, history, political science, economics, and sociology.

The most transforming idea of the time was pragmatism, and it would become America's single great contribution to the study of principles underlying knowledge and being. Like other changes in the American intellectual climate, the pragmatic movement seemed to arrive extrarationally, almost mysteriously—seemed to "have suddenly precipitated itself out of the air." And no one so dominated and personified the pragmatic revolt as the author of these words, a most unrevolutionary-looking Harvard professor named William James.

The Pulse of the Machine

On a late January day in 1907, William James traveled by train from Boston to New York, took up his room at the Harvard Club on West 44th Street, and immediately plunged into the intellectual life of Gotham. He lunched, dined, and sometimes breakfasted out every day of his stay, with members of the Philosophical Club of New York and with eminent biologists, mathematicians, and literati. He capped his visit by dining with a company that included Norman Hapgood, Finley Peter Dunne, and Mark Twain. The last, he wrote to his brother Henry and his son William, "poor man, is only good for monologue, in his old age, or for dialogue at best, but he's a dear little genius all the same."

Once again, James was captured by the heady intellectual beat of Manhattan. He was hardly a stranger to the city, having been born in the Astor House sixty-five years before, but in later life he had never managed to stay there more than a day and a half, he said, so repelled had he been by the "clangor, disorder, and permanent earthquake conditions." Now, however, he seemed to find an *"entirely* new New York, in soul as well as in body, from the old one, which looks like a village in retrospect. The courage, the heaven-scaling audacity of it all, and the *lightness* withal" gave him a kind of *"drumming background* of life that I never felt before." On 44th Street, "in the centre of the cyclone, I caught the pulse of the machine, took up the rhythm, and . . . found it simply magnificent."

James even found the subways magnificent, "powerful and beautiful, space devouring," as he roared back and forth daily between the Harvard Club and Columbia University. There, at Teachers College, he was giving a series of lectures on pragmatism. Originally scheduled for Schermerhorn Hall, with its 250 seats, the lecture had to be moved to the chapel, where an audience of over a thousand greeted him.

James's listeners—many of them professional or amateur philosophers themselves—hardly expected anything new from their noted guest. He had given these lectures before, most recently at the Lowell Institute in Boston. They knew him to be the grandson of a multimillionaire businessman, the son of a well-known theologian, and the brother of the eminent novelist Henry James. They knew too that James had been heavily influenced by the half-legendary Charles Peirce of Cambridge, the amazingly versatile astronomer, physicist, mathematician, and logician who in 1878 had introduced something called "pragmatism" to the American lay public in an article in *Popular Science Monthly* called "How to Make Our Ideas Clear." After long bouts with bad health and deep depression, James himself had forged ahead, creating at Harvard the first American laboratory in psychology and helping gain recognition for the new science. Increasingly, he had immersed himself in philosophical study and was now the most celebrated philosophizer in America.

At Teachers College that night, James neither surprised nor disappointed his audience. He delighted them with his platform style—much moving about, gesticulating, and general animation—in contrast with the stereotype of the Harvard philosophers who, like Josiah Royce, sat immobile in a chair and rolled out their dogmas in sonorous periods. But, most of all, James impressed his listeners with his pithy comments.

"Philosophy is at once the most sublime and the most trivial of human pursuits. It works in the minutest crannies and it opens out the widest vistas. It 'bakes no bread,' as has been said, but it can inspire our souls with courage; and repugnant as its manners, its doubting and challenging, its quibbling and dialectics, often are to common people, no one of us can get along without the far-flashing beams of light it sends over the world's perspectives." And now a new dawn was breaking upon philosophy.

The lecturer drew a distinction between "rationalism" and "intellectualism" on one side and "sensationalism" and "empiricism" on the other. "Rationalism is always monistic. It starts from wholes and universals, and makes much of the unity of things. Empiricism starts from the parts, and makes of the whole a collection—is not averse therefore to calling itself pluralistic."

While the audience watched, fascinated, James chalked two columns on a blackboard, separating "rationalists" from "empiricists," but with a new and provocative heading:

THE TENDER-MINDED	THE TOUGH-MINDED
Rationalistic (going by "principles"),	Empiricist (going by "facts"),
Intellectualistic,	Sensationalistic,
Idealistic,	Materialistic,
Optimistic,	Pessimistic,
Religious,	Irreligious,
Free-willist,	Fatalistic,
Monistic,	Pluralistic,
Dogmatical.	Sceptical.

Most of you, James assured his listeners, were a mixture of both tendencies, had a "hankering" for both, but also were vexedly caught between "an empirical philosophy that is not religious enough, and a religious philosophy that is not empirical enough. . . ." The lecturer left no doubt where he stood. He rejected the world of philosophical absolutes, of the "transcendental idealism of the Anglo-Hegelian school," the philosophy of such men as Green, the Cairds, Bosanquet, Royce, of the absolutists who dwelt on "so high a level of abstraction that they never even try to come down." He welcomed his listeners into the world "of concrete personal experience to which the street belongs," multitudinous beyond imagination, "tangled, muddy, painful, and perplexed," contradictory, confused, gothic.

In succeeding lectures, to bigger and bigger audiences, James spelled out his views with never-failing gusto and pungency: that pragmatism "unstiffened" old, absolutist theories; that new truths were "go-betweens," "smoother-overs" of transitions from old theories to new facts; that when we say that this theory solves a problem more satisfactorily than that theory, this means more satisfactorily *to ourselves;* and—emphasized again and again—a theory must be tested by how it works in practice, as a practical matter; that "any idea upon which we can ride, so to speak; any idea that will carry us prosperously from any one part of our experience to any other part, linking things satisfactorily, working securely, simplifying, saving labor; is true for just so much, true in so far forth, true *instrumentally.*" And he limned the pragmatist in a few unforgettable phrases:

"He turns away from abstraction and insufficiency, from verbal solutions, from bad *a priori* reasons, from fixed principles, closed systems, and pretended absolutes and origins. He turns toward concreteness and adequacy, towards facts, towards action and towards power." Pragmatism meant *"looking away from first things, principles, 'categories,' supposed necessities; and of looking towards last things, fruits, consequences, facts."*

That James's ideas struck philosophical sparks had long been clear, and he did not need to wait long at Columbia. The New Yorkers, he wrote a friend, at the evening gatherings "compassed me about, they wagged their tongues at me"; neither side gave in. In particular, he provoked the theologians who preached the very absolutes—the Good, the Just, the Godly, the Pure, Beauty, Truth—that the tough-minded questioned. James was attacked as antireligious, though he had grown up in a religious family and had undergone a religious experience one evening alone in his dressing room when he suddenly was seized by a "horrible fear of my own existence"—an experience from which he had emerged "twice-born." He believed in God, but it was a less-than-absolute, a finite God, a position that enabled him to accept evil along with the goodness of God, and to urge men to rely on their own minds and wills and not merely divine intervention. So James—author of *The Varieties of Religious Experience*—could cope with theologians and metaphysicians.

But fellow philosophers and social theorists were a different matter. From Hugo Münsterberg, a onetime junior colleague and a German philosopher educated in the idealist tradition, came a polite but sharp comment: experience was not enough; he found reality in the fulfillment of will, as "transcendental power." "And that is really *my fundamental problem: why do I care for a moral deed or a true astronomical calculation if they do not bring any advantage to me?*" Münsterberg asked in good Kantian fashion. Others accused James of caricaturing absolutism, of making pragmatism itself into a catchall absolute, even of lacking in "academic dignity." James himself disliked the term "pragmatism" and all the baggage it had accumulated— he preferred the concept "humanism," but it was too late—and he knew that Peirce himself felt that James carried pragmatism too far. Peirce preferred *his* kind of pragmatism, which he labeled "pragmaticism."

If idealists, theological and lay, were repelled by aspects of pragmatism, the doctrine had special appeal to the practical men of law. Had not the very term, indeed, with its Greek root in *pragma*—"practical matter"— been extended by the Romans to mean "skilled in business, and especially experienced in matters of law"? Certainly it had a strong appeal to one lawyer who happened to be a Supreme Court justice. Oliver Wendell Holmes, Jr., hardly needed instruction from James on pragmatism; in the early 1870s, Holmes had met regularly in Cambridge with Peirce's Metaphysical Club, which also numbered such luminaries as Chauncey Wright and John Fiske, as well as James. He and James as young men had spent long evenings "twisting the tail of the Kosmos," and had remained in touch mainly by mail in later years.

"I heartily agree with much, but I am more sceptical than you are," Holmes wrote James in thanking him for a copy of *Pragmatism.* "You would say that I am too hard or tough-minded,—I think none of the philosophers sufficiently humble." Holmes had already responded to earlier writings of James on pragmatism. "For a good many years I have had a formula for truth which seems humbler than those you give . . . but I don't know whether it is pragmatic or not. I have been in the habit of saying that all I mean by truth is what I can't help thinking. . . . It seems to me that the only promising activity is to make *my* universe coherent and livable, not to babble about *the* universe. . . . To act affirms, for the moment at least, the worth of an end; idealizing seems to be simply the generalized and permanent affirmation of the worth of ends. . . . Man, like a tree in the cleft of a rock, gradually shapes his roots to his surroundings, and when the roots have grown to a certain size, can't be displaced without cutting at his life. . . ."

In his little masterpiece, *The Common Law,* Holmes—then forty years old—began with the flat announcement that the "life of the law has not been logic; it has been experience." His revolt against legal formalism and absolutism led to some stunning opinions—notably to his dissent in *Lochner* v. *New York,* in which the Supreme Court struck down an act limiting New York bakery workers to a ten-hour day and a sixty-hour week. Holmes protested that the word "liberty" in the Fourteenth Amendment had been perverted. That amendment, he said, "does not enact Mr. Herbert Spencer's *Social Statics.* " A "constitution is not intended to embody a particular economic theory, whether of paternalism and the organic relation of the citizen to the State or of laissez faire."

Asked once whether he had a general philosophy to help guide him as a judge, Holmes answered: "Yes. Long ago I decided that I was not God. When a state came in here and wanted to build a slaughter house, I looked at the Constitution and if I couldn't find anything in there that said a state couldn't build a slaughter house I said to myself, if they want to build a slaughter house, God-dammit, let them build it."

For all his ability to eviscerate dogma with the lance of skepticism, however, Holmes's pragmatism left him a divided thinker and judge. A conservative himself, he delighted in puncturing conservative shibboleths; but he was too much the skeptic and ironist to enlist in any liberal or humanitarian cause, nor did he make any pretense of doing so. His rejection of both conservative and radical ideology made it difficult for him to take a consistent position on the great economic and social issues coming before the High Court; but, then, he did not believe in consistency. Even in law itself, however, his judicial opinions, Eugene Rostow said, lost their power to lead; it was "rare to find in one of his opinions the germinal idea or the creative suggestion which starts a line of decisions and guides later judges on their quest."

Because Holmes and Louis Brandeis so often joined in dissent against their brethren's decisions, Holmes acquired good standing with the progressives. He and Brandeis shared a pragmatic concern with the facts of the case, with the reality of social and economic circumstances. But in fundamental philosophy the two sharply diverged. "I'm afraid Brandeis has the crusading spirit," Holmes said of his friend during the earlier Boston years. "He talks like one of those upward-and-onward fellows." Fueled by volumes of facts, Brandeis did indeed move upward and onward as he both analyzed and embraced the idea of a liberal society based on democratic institutions and ideals of social justice. Holmes acquired fame as both a legal philosopher and technician, but without a social creed firm enough to bind his ends and means together into a creative and lasting force.

Holmes's dualism—his stinging attacks on legal and social absolutes along with his cleansing and negative skepticism—reflected central ambivalences in the central doctrines of Peirce, James & co. The powerful emphasis in pragmatism on the inseparability of ideas from action, on the vital role of decision and choice, on ideas as plans of action, on the need to verify ideas by events, on the concept of ideas as instruments, on the mind as a crucial instrument of adaptation and survival, on ideas as changing and dynamic rather than fixed, and—always—on the knowledge that comes from immersion in experience and experiment—these notions, while by no means new, swept through the musty dogmas and received ideas of the fin de siècle like a clearing west wind. These ideas struck home in an America that was continually, feverishly experimenting, inventing, innovating.

Yet there were other tendencies in pragmatism that gravely impaired it as a tool for understanding the principles on which the nation had been founded and virtually crippled it as a means of understanding and solving the failure of Americans to make their democratic system respond to the transcending needs and aspirations of the people—in short, *really* to "work." In its attack on absolutes, pragmatism failed to grasp the power, not of dogmas, but of measured principles to provide practical guidelines for political activism and governmental action. Reality, yes—but the nature of reality was one of the oldest philosophical questions, and pragmatism threw little light on it. Practicality, yes—but what really was practicality, tested by what broader criteria? Experience, yes—but how did one evaluate experience? Experimentation, yes—but how did one know how to measure the results of the experiment? To a pragmatist it might seem foolish or utopian or "impractical" to measure practical results by old canons of liberty and equality, dignity and justice—but what were these canons if not the result of hundreds of years of human experience, tested in the most bitter intellectual, political, and physical struggles, out of which the great Enlightenment values had emerged?

It was because pragmatism could not answer such burning questions as these that it faltered as both a method of thought and a guide to action. On the one hand, the overextension of this antidogmatic creed converted it into something of a dogma itself, as the Williams College philosopher James B. Pratt protested to few listeners. And because it had no transcending central doctrine that would "stiffen" it as a theory, pragmatism was easily distorted in the public mind and perverted into a simple defense of the capitalist and Social Darwinian status quo. In his enthusiasm, James told his Columbia audience that "if you follow the pragmatic method, [you] must bring out of each word its practical cash-value. . . ." These words, torn out of their broader context, were used to flay pragmatism as a handmaiden of conservatism. This was unfair, but understandable. For the more that pragmatism emphasized practicality and realism and derogated principle and morality, the more the test of experience was short-run, tangible, quantifiable reward. And reward for whom? For the experimenter, the doer, the practitioner—and the devil take the rest. And in this sense pragmatism was a philosophy least needed in an America abounding with innovators and doers and experimenters, but short on wide moral vision, collective social organization, and long-range political action.

THE CRITICS: IDEAS VS. INTERESTS?

The most portentous change in the intellectual climate around the turn of the century came in the way Americans viewed their own history, under the guidance of the New Historians. Perhaps it was high time. A century and a quarter had passed since Americans had fought for their independence under the banner of liberty and equality, a century since they had organized themselves under a stronger national government, almost a century since they had bound themselves together more tightly through national political parties, and almost half a century since they had reaffirmed their commitment to liberty, equality, and nationhood in the Civil War, under the leadership of a man who proclaimed on a great battlefield that their government of the people, by the people, and for the people would not perish from the earth.

How well was the nation living up to its professed principles? For the past fifty years, journalists, theologians, intellectuals of many hues had been witnessing with deepening concern and revulsion the rise of an inegalitarian society in which some Americans lived in extravagant luxury and others in utter penury, in which Southern blacks still lacked meaningful freedom, women still lacked the right to vote, Indians lacked the right to live where they wished or even to live, Orientals lacked the right to welcome their kind from overseas, labor in most sectors lacked the right to organize. They were witnessing the rise of an increasingly concentrated corporate capitalism that wielded enormous political influence in national and state legislatures and before the bar. They were witnessing a saturnalia of vulgar display, party spoils, civic corruption, sordid materialism, in which the scramble for money, status, and power seemed to taint all that it touched.

Some New Historians reacted all the more sharply to all this because of their own feeling of vulnerability. They were part of a "status revolution" in which educated, middle-class professional persons and intellectuals had found themselves caught between the nouveaux riches and the rising claims of industrial workers, poor farmers, and immigrant masses. "The newly rich, the grandiosely or corruptly rich, the masters of great corporations," Richard Hofstadter wrote, "were bypassing the men of the Mugwump type—the old gentry, the merchants of long standing, the small manufacturers, the established professional men, the civic leaders of an earlier era." Alienated, the professional people were shifting in their own allegiances. Thus Protestant clergy, which had presented a "massive, almost unbroken front in its defense of the status quo," in the 1870s, and had denounced the railway strikers of 1877 as "wild beasts," had considerably softened in its attitudes; by the 1890s, the earlier social-gospel doctrines were coming to the fore among key sectors of the clergy. The legal profession, once dominated by small-town lawyers and partnerships, was becoming increasingly bureaucratized and commercialized. American lawyers seemed to the visiting Lord Bryce much less of a distinct professional class.

The historical profession was undergoing a transformation of its own. Not only had the New Historians emerged from the broadening, somewhat beleaguered middle classes. Not only had they witnessed the tumultuous economic and social changes of late-century, vast industrialization, swelling immigration, and sharp depressions like that of the 1890s. They represented a new breed of professional historians who, in the budding graduate schools of the nation, were replacing the literary gentlemen-amateurs —the Bancrofts and Parkmans and the like—who had written the great nineteenth-century histories. Now the trained, disciplined professionals, with their newly won Ph.D.s, were taking over.

While few of the professional historians were pragmatists in a philosophical sense, most of them shared the temper of pragmatism—its revolt against formalism, absolutes, abstractions, and patriotic pieties, in favor of economics, empiricism, and "realism." Frederick Jackson Turner, after presenting his famous paper on the significance of the frontier in American history to a meeting of the American Historical Association in 1893, had continued to argue that democracy had flourished on the frontier, which provided mobility and opportunity and an economic safety valve. Orin Grant Libby, one of Turner's students, analyzed the voting for the Constitution of 1787 on the basis of debtors and creditors. At the University of Washington, J. Allen Smith argued boldly that the Constitution of 1787, bluntly contradicting the democratic spirit embodied in the Declaration of Independence, was deliberately designed to block popular rule through its stultifying checks and balances, including judicial review.

By far the most conspicuous and controversial of the New Historians— at least by 1913, when he published his *An Economic Interpretation of the Constitution*—was a thirty-nine-year-old associate professor of politics at Columbia, Charles Austin Beard. Raised in a prosperous Indiana home where his father, a banker, businessman, and radical Republican, presided over vigorous family debate, young Beard had gone on to DePauw and then received an advanced education in Western industrial society. He had lived for a time in Jane Addams's Hull-House in Chicago, where he encountered urban immigrant life in the raw; studied at Oxford, where he plunged into Fabian socialism, Labour Party politics, and the writings of John Ruskin (which were already influencing a young Indian named Gandhi); helped establish Ruskin Hall at Oxford as a school for workingmen; spent two years lecturing to workers in and around Manchester, the heartland of British industrialism; and then returned home for graduate work at Columbia. There he joined a brilliant intellectual company including James Harvey Robinson in the New History and E. R. A. Seligman in economics. As he matured, his tall spare frame, bald eagle's nose, and piercing blue eyes gave him the appearance of a benign Uncle Sam.

Beard was a noted young historian when he published his *Economic*

Interpretation; suddenly he became notorious. To a nation still worshipping the Constitution and its framers, Beard calmly reported that the "first firm steps toward the formation of the Constitution were taken by a small and active group of men immediately interested through their personal possessions in the outcome of their labors"; that a "large propertyless mass" lacking the vote was excluded from participating in the convention through representatives; that almost all the members of the Philadelphia convention were "immediately, directly, and personally interested" in establishing the new system; and that the new constitution was ratified by one-sixth or less of the country's adult males.

Washington, Franklin, and the rest were simply lining their own pockets? A storm broke out over the head of the young professor. In Marion, Ohio, Warren G. Harding's *Star* headlined: "SCAVENGERS, HYENA-LIKE, DESECRATE THE GRAVES OF THE DEAD PATRIOTS WE REVERE." A recently retired Republican President, William Howard Taft, demanded to know whether Beard would have preferred a Constitution drafted by "dead bodies, out-at-the-elbows demagogues, and cranks who never had any money?" Asked if he had read "Beard's last book," Columbia's imperious president, Nicholas Murray Butler, exclaimed, "I hope so."

Why this furor at the time when many of the New Historians had been making much the same point about the influence of property on American politics and government? Partly because Beard had done an enormous amount of spadework, digging into the dust-covered records in the federal Treasury Department. Partly because the book bristled with lists of the Framers' holdings, but so starkly and dully presented that Max Lerner later would wonder if Beard had expected trouble and stripped the book of every adornment, "on the theory that a plain woman would be less suspected of being a wanton than an attractive one." Partly because the book offered, in sum, such a simple, understandable explanation of the almost exclusively economic motives that lay behind a great historic act—the framing of the Constitution.

This simple economic interpretation, which Beard later seemed to repudiate, told perhaps more about Beard and the New Historians than about the Framers. It dramatically posed the issue of whether ideas or interests had the greater—even the fundamental and ultimate—impact on the course of history. This was an ancient question, and might have been avoided by Beard himself except that he chose to pose it near the start of his *Economic Interpretation,* and in particular called to his cause James Madison as an economic determinist. Triumphantly he quoted Madison's famous dictum in the tenth *Federalist* that the "most common and durable source of factions has been the various and unequal distribution of property. Those who hold and those who are without property have ever formed distinct interests in society."

Was it significant that Beard, in quoting this noted paper, jumped over two cardinal passages: Madison's tribute to liberty as "essential to political life" and his listing of ideas—a "zeal for different opinions concerning religion, concerning Government and many other points, as well as of speculation as of practice"—at the very head of his causes of faction? Madison in any event spoke for a large number of Framers who studied ideas, took them seriously, and acted in response to them. Often these ideas expressed—and cloaked—crass self-interest or, more typically, group and regional interest, but more often their ideas—especially their profound and measured belief in liberty—expressed their Enlightenment values, their religious and secular education, their qualities of intellect and imagination. It was because Beard, despite his protestations to the contrary, virtually dismissed these forces in leaders and in history that Holmes could in turn dismiss Beard's "covert sneer" against the Framers and argue that "high-mindedness is not impossible in man."

The issue of ideas versus interests was far more important, during the progressive era, than an academic argument among historians or philosophers. The issue went to the heart of the progressive response to the rising economic and political power of concentrated industrial capitalism. If popular and democratic forces were to curb economic power, they must understand the capitalists—their interests, their motives, their ideas. If the capitalists were responding merely to naked economic interest, then indeed the democratic strategy would be clear: to "turn economic determinism upside down" and gain control of industry, capital, and perhaps the capitalists themselves. This might be done through the "socialization of the means of production," precisely what many Marxists, as confirmed economic determinists, were urging.

But if on the other hand *ideas* served as the crucial engines of history, a different strategy would be implied for the democratic control of economic power. That strategy must comprehend the infinite variety of noneconomic as well as economic interests, the pervasive influence of psychological forces rational and irrational, the power of ideology, the role of chance and contingency, and the daring leaps, the awful limitations, and the practical compromises of the human mind. It must understand why some persons' ideas were pinioned to their interests, others could not even calculate their own interests, and still others far transcended them. It must comprehend an Andrew Carnegie as well as a Jay Gould, a Theodore Roosevelt as well as a J. P. Morgan.

Such intellectual comprehension, such an economic and political strategy, called for grand theory, and the New Historians did not pretend to be philosophers of history. After demonstrating so brilliantly that the Constitution was designed to thwart popular rule, Beard had no comprehensive proposals for restructuring government in order to carry out the will of a popular majority. The New Historians generally supported such reforms as the initiative, referendum, and recall, as well as popular election of United States senators, but these reforms, however desirable in themselves, would not reverse the essential Madisonian strategy of pitting rulers against one another by making them representatives of conflicting constituencies and thus making "ambition counteract ambition." In the end the New Historians proved far more effective in demolishing old shibboleths and pieties rather than constructing new theories of history or conceiving new structures of power.

If the ablest, most progressive-minded historians failed to provide systematic theory for the control of concentrated economic power in a democratic polity, could economists fill this conceptual void? Generally not, for most established economists had no interest in radical reconstruction or change to begin with. Sympathetic interpreters of Marx's theory of history like E. R. A. Seligman of Columbia continued to work in their particular intellectual groove, but the Marxists were still finding it difficult to apply their dynamic creed to the loose-jointed American polity and the many-chambered American mind, with its intense commitment to individual liberty and economic individualism. A small band of labor and left economists were busy challenging the received economic wisdom but erecting little to take its place.

At the turn of the century, the most defiant of the icon-smashing economists was a scholar named Thorstein Veblen. Almost peasantlike in appearance, with his round face, hair parted in the middle, heavy brows and mustache, and rough country clothes, Veblen had seemed almost reclusive until he shocked academia with a series of writings culminating in *The Theory of the Leisure Class* in 1899 and *The Theory of Business Enterprise* five years later. Born on the Wisconsin frontier in 1857, Veblen had come easily by the burning scorn for pecuniary enterprise that marked most of his work. Both his grandfathers had run afoul of lawyers, government officials, and other "predators" in Norway and the United States. As a boy, Veblen had to cope with a dominant Yankee culture that regarded Norwegian immigrants as inferiors, and he grew up in a rural culture and national epoch filled with hatred and fear of merchants and lawyers and bankers, both in the country trading towns and in the nation's power centers. Although his family prospered as the years passed, Veblen himself underwent long stretches of poverty as a graduate student and more humiliating years of underemployment before he won academic positions—though never academic tenure, even after he gained fame. Among other accomplishments, he turned the Horatio Alger myth upside down.

No one had ever read a book quite like *The Theory of the Leisure Class*. In heavy, polysyllabic language that gave off a whiff of academic respectability, he struck out at the most sacred of idols.

The leisure class's addiction to sports: "Chicane, falsehood, brow-beating, hold a well-secured place in the method of procedure of any athletic contest and in games generally."

Upper-class dress: "Much of the charm that invests the patent-leather shoe, the stainless linen, the lustrous cylindrical hat, and the walking-stick . . . comes of their pointedly suggesting that the wearer cannot when so attired bear a hand in any employment that is directly and immediately of any human use. Elegant dress serves its purpose of elegance not only in that it is expensive, but also because it is the insignia of leisure."

Pets and other sacred cows: "The dog . . . is the filthiest of the domestic animals in his person and the nastiest in his habits. For this he makes up in a servile, fawning attitude toward his master, and a readiness to inflict damage and discomfort on all else." "The utility of the fast horse lies largely in his efficiency as a means of emulation; it gratifies the owner's sense of aggression and dominance to have his own horse outstrip his neighbor's." Cats: well, cats were "less wasteful" than dogs and horses and might "even serve a useful end."

Such wicked and scathing thoughts stimulated interest in Veblen's examination that became increasingly a vivisection and produced the titles of his major works—*The Instinct of Workmanship, The Higher Learning in America, The Vested Interests and the Common Man, The Engineers and the Price System, Absentee Ownership*. The overarching theme of these works was the subordination in capitalistic America of industry to business, of the industrial arts to pecuniary gain, of rational use to conspicuous waste, of genuine human values to money values, of function to ownership. In his turgid and repetitive treatment of this theme Veblen dealt with a host of other subjects, ranging from the subordination of women to the nature of science, the philosophical failings of pragmatism, the most subtle psychological and anthropological aspects of American culture.

But Veblen's writings always stopped short of presenting a system or program as an alternative to the pecuniary culture that he so despised. He had a lifelong interest in Marxism and delighted in picturing university presidents as captains of education modeled on captains of industry. Like Marx, he focused on the cultural incidence of industrialism and the machine process; like Marx, he held to an economic theory of history and a technological theory of economics; like Marx, he saw the alliance between vested interests and vested ideas. But he differed with Marxist thought in significant ways, and in any event refused to accept the glittering ideas and programs that socialists and communists were offering Americans during the progressive era.

What instead? Nothing. In later years, he proposed some kind of utopian technocracy under the leadership of rationalist engineers, but his power analysis was naïve, his political program quixotic, and some of his proposals almost authoritarian. On the cardinal issues of freedom and economic planning, Lev Dobriansky concluded, Veblen's power philosophy offered no enlightenment. Ultimately his devastating analyses would help clear the ground of much intellectual rubbish, but Veblen had few solutions for those American thinkers and actors who were struggling with the knotty problems of making economic means serve human ends.

If toward the close of the nineteenth century economists as well as historians were failing to grasp the relation of political democracy and economic power, who could master the problem? Some would have pointed to a man widely viewed as a historian—and who so viewed himself —but who was in fact far more. This was Henry Adams—social critic, political analyst, closet theologian, untitled cultural anthropologist.

It seemed that Clio herself had carefully prepared Adams for this exacting task. History was stitched into his very fiber. He could not forget that he was descended from two first families and if he happened to, he was reminded by an Irish gardener who said to him, when a child, "You'll be thinkin' you'll be President too!" He had known most of the intellectual and political leaders of the middle and late years of the century. Although he remarked that Harvard had provided him no education for leadership —only for moderation, restraint, *mesure*—he had a continuing close-up view of the foibles, frailties, and follies of men in office. And he had devoted himself to history, producing brilliant, massive studies of the United States and of particular leaders such as Albert Gallatin, whose democratic ideas and actions he admired as much as he disliked Jefferson's.

By turn of century, Henry Adams had long since ensconced himself in his Washington mansion, alongside a similar edifice built by his friend John Hay. There he entertained diplomats and politicians, counseled ambassadors and statesmen, and observed the rise and fall of politicos with a sardonic eye. He shared his writings with a small circle, corresponded with a few historians, even accepted the presidency of the American Historical Association. His brothers too were doing history—Charles Francis still into railroads, Brooks into such theories of history as the rhythmic oscillation of societies between barbarism and civilization.

Who better than Henry Adams—author of *Democracy,* analyst of the physics and psychology of power, perceptive observer of the role of women in history, morbid analyst of human nature—could solve the mysteries of the subtle interplay of political ambition and corruption, pecuniary motivation, sexual desire and jealousy, conflict of leaders, and lofty ideals? He was fascinated by political and economic power wielders without being in the least bedazzled by them—he considered himself superior to them. He was a student of the history of history, having studied his Marx and his Hegel and his Darwin. He swallowed none of the philosophical theories of history wholesale; indeed he was as critical of most of the established historians, conservative or radical, as he was of the political establishment. And he was a thoroughly modern historian, conscious of the power of the machine and the dynamics of the workshop. Surely Henry Adams could penetrate the citadels of power.

It was not to be. When Adams finally pulled together his notions of history, they emerged as a pretentious grand theory that sought to apply to the study of history the work of William Kelvin and other scientists on physical energy. Adams leaped at Kelvin's suggestion that modern biologists were "coming once more to a firm acceptance of something beyond mere gravitational, chemical, and physical forces; and that unknown thing is a vital principle." Adams saw "vitalism" as the social energy of history, subject to physical laws, and requiring a whole new approach to the study of social organization and evolution. It was a theory so dense and inchoate that even Adams's friend William James said privately to a friend, "If you can understand it all you can do much better than I."

A crucial test of the theory was its applicability to the understanding of men and events, and here it failed. Presidents, he said, illustrated the effect of unlimited power on limited minds. Theodore Roosevelt displayed such restless agitation and chronic excitement during the first year of his presidency as to make a friend tremble. Adams concluded that "power is poison" and its "effect on Presidents had been always tragic." Adams left the matter there. A long-term observer of "trusts," he wrote that they were unscrupulous and revolutionary, "troubling all the old conventions and values, as the screws of ocean steamers must trouble a school of herring," tearing society to pieces and trampling it underfoot. All he could see was a contest between the trusts, with their organized "schools, training, wealth and purpose," and the forces behind Roosevelt, their cohesion slight, their training irregular, their objects vague. Adams professed neutrality on the matter—and he offered no keys to solving the problems of either presidential or corporate power in a democracy.

How could the nation's foremost analyst of politics end up with such a bleak and constricted theory of society? Perhaps because of his own desire for power, magnified by his sense of lacking it, both the desire and the lack sharpened by his knowledge of the Presidents and power-wielders in his own family. Himself a small, balding, sensitive man, increasingly snobbish and even anti-Semitic as he grew older, he displayed a fascination with physical power, as he haunted the great industrial exhibitions of the time, standing transfixed before the huge dynamos at work. He was equally fascinated by political power, even as he despised the men who wielded it. Adams's impotence in his analysis of power symbolized the collective impotence of the fourth generation of Adamses, as Henry sat in his mansion staring out the window at the White House, Brooks Adams dallied with "laws" of civilization and decay, and Charles complained of New England winters and wrote Henry that "while I am not tired, I am bored." The three brothers were living on into the twentieth century amid the ghosts of the nineteenth.

Even more, Henry Adams's failure of analysis symbolized the intellectual tragedy of a nation unable to come to grips with the nature and implications of a powerful and expanding industrial machine challenging the pretensions of a "government by the people." But now different persons with different questions were offering differing sets of answers—and displays of artistic expression—in the many-chambered mansion of American democracy.

ART: "ALL THAT IS HOLY IS PROFANED"

In Greenwich Village—in the dingy rooming houses that had once been fashionable brownstones, in the dank art studios converted from stables, in the little cafés and tearooms dotting the crooked streets—rebellions in the arts and literature, in manners and morals, broke out during the first decade of the twentieth century. This tiny area in lower Manhattan had long seemed to hold a mystic attraction for free spirits: Tom Paine had lived here, and later Edgar Allan Poe, and still later Frank Norris and Henry James and Stephen Crane. In one of their ceaseless flights uptown from the huddling masses that occupied lower Manhattan, New York's social elites had abandoned this area, leaving their brownstones and their elegant Greek Revival houses and their shady little backyards. Now an exotic breed of artists, writers, bohemians, anarchists, and radical feminists moved in to take advantage of the low rents, while the Italian-American community looked on in wonderment.

The rebels and their causes *were* wondrous to onlookers. Artists were rebelling against the pastoral landscapes and sentimental domestic portraits favored by the established art institutes. Writers were repudiating the genteel tradition of *The Century,* the *Atlantic Monthly, Harper's Weekly.* Young intellectuals and aesthetes just out of college classrooms were turning against professors who promulgated old-fashioned morality, political conservatism, and Victorian values. Novelists were angry at established publishing houses that wanted sentimental writings lacking any sense of the grit and squalor of everyday city life. Cultural nationalists attacked the European grip on belles lettres. Behind these risings lay an intellectual revolution against bourgeois values and the corporate power of industrial capitalism.

The transcending ethic of Greenwich Village was liberation. "Everybody was freeing themselves and the world," a Village writer recalled, "and everybody was freeing the world faster than everybody else." Nowhere had the early ideas of Sigmund Freud been more happily, more greedily, embraced. Carl Jung even visited the Village in 1912 and lectured at the Liberal Club. Villagers endlessly discussed the meaning of their dreams, outdated morality, sexual permissiveness, and personal liberation, when they were not debating Marxism, socialism, trade unionism, bossism, pacifism, birth control, educational reform, abolition of prostitution, or Havelock Ellis's notions of sexual liberation.

The Village was, to be sure, far more a broker of ideas than a generator of them. Its rebellions drew from myriad intellectual and artistic sources. Villagers followed the writings of the European philosophers and social critics, visited the great men abroad, talked with Europeans who made the fabled Village their first stop on arrival. Nietzsche's assaults on Christian morality and middle-class culture, Henri Bergson's faith in relativity and intuition, Shaw's and Ibsen's acid portraits of bourgeois greed and hypocrisy fueled the Villagers' iconoclasm. James's and John Dewey's relativism and pragmatism gave sanction to their own skepticism and experimentation.

Everyone knew everyone else in the Village. On the street you might run into the long-arrived literary man William Dean Howells or the just-arriving Sinclair Lewis, the dancer Isadora Duncan, the ebullient young radicals John Reed and Max Eastman, the novelist Theodore Dreiser, the precocious young critic Randolph Bourne. If you stayed long enough, you saw everybody: one boardinghouse, on Washington Square South, was home at various times to Norris, Crane, O. Henry, Dreiser, Reed, Eugene O'Neill, Alan Seeger, Zona Gale. You came to know the eccentrics too, like the young man of respectable Chicago family who called himself a bastard and everyone he met a "bourgeois pig."

The best place to meet people in the Village, if you wanted hours of uninhibited talk, was the fabled salon of Mabel Dodge Luhan. A vibrant and imposing woman, with cool, dark gray eyes and a voice "like a viola, soft, caressing, mellow," Luhan threw herself into everything—art, politics, feminism, union struggles. In her salon you could meet Big Bill Haywood in from the labor wars, the anarchists Emma Goldman and Alexander Berkman, Lincoln Steffens, British socialists, visiting feminists. She boasted of her salon as a ferment of "Socialists, Trade-Unionists, Anarchists, Suffragists, Poets, Relations, Lawyers, Murderers, Old Friends, Psychoanalysts, I.W.W.s, Single Taxers, Birth Controlists, Newspapermen, Artists, Modern-Artists, Clubwomen, Women's-place-is-in-the-home Women"—and even clergymen.

Luhan and John Reed had a passionate love affair, after which he called her a "keen, cold, amorous" woman who demanded continuous change and excitement. Surely she wanted change; everyone in the Village seemed to want change, change for its own sake. Luhan wrote:

> Melt, You Women!
> Melt to August—grow ON and Ripen
> Give Yourselves Up!
> That is the only way to be Alive,
> That is what you want, isn't it?
> To be alive?
> Life lies in the Change,
> Try it and see.

"Constant revolutionizing of production," Marx had written sixty years earlier in the *Communist Manifesto*, "uninterrupted disturbance of all social relations, everlasting uncertainty and agitation, distinguish the bourgeois epoch from all earlier times. All fixed, fast-frozen relationships, with their train of venerable ideas and opinions, are swept away, all new-formed ones become obsolete before they can ossify. All that is solid melts into air, all that is holy is profaned." Villagers saw themselves as rebels against the system; Marxists saw them as a zany, fleeting expression of it.

Nothing seemed more volatile in the first decade than the visual arts. Nor was there a more obvious target for rebels. A small number of powerful institutions seemed to control the public outlets of artistic expression at century's end: the National Academy of Design and the Metropolitan Museum of Art in New York, the Boston Museum of Fine Arts, the Philadelphia Museum of Art, and the Art Institute of Chicago. These custodians of "high art" insisted upon the romantic landscape, the still life, the portrait of the celebrated, and best of all, the painting that told a moral story or epitomized a historical moment. "Organized by the urban elite, dominated by ladies of high society, staffed by professionally trained personnel, housing classic works of European art donated by wealthy private collectors," according to Alan Trachtenberg, the museums "established as a physical fact the notion that culture filtered downward from a distant past, from overseas, from the sacred founts of wealth and private power."

Now the establishment scented rebellion. Said the director of the Metropolitan, an appointee of J. P. Morgan, "There is a state of unrest all over the world in art as in all other things. It is the same in literature, as in music, in painting and in sculpture. And I dislike unrest." The chief source of "unrest" in American art was the movement toward a new realism. Its precursors were Winslow Homer and Thomas Eakins.

"When I select a thing," Homer once said, "I paint it exactly as it appears." Born in 1836 in Maine, Homer was retained by *Harper's Weekly* to record Civil War battlefield scenes, resulting in such graphic paintings as *Rainy Day in Camp* and *Sharpshooter on Picket Duty*. Years of painting lyrical pastoral scenes followed his war work, but when in 1883 Homer reestablished himself in his beloved Maine, he found in the violent power of the sea an enduring theme for his now-darkened temperament. Vigorous paintings in the 1880s and 1890s such as *The Life Line, The Herring Net, Undertow,* and *The Gulf Stream* depicted men and women pitted against boiling waters, at war with brooding and furious nature.

Thomas Eakins apprenticed under the genre painter Jean Léon Gérôme in Paris and analyzed the work of Goya in Spain, but perhaps more influential in the formation of his style was his study of anatomy at a medical college, fortified by his use of nude models in defiance of Philadelphia prudery. His work with Eadweard Muybridge, a pioneering photographer who with a series of cameras fixed staccato glimpses of men and animals in motion, supplemented Eakins's knowledge of "physiology from top to toe." Eakins's pictures of athletes—boxers, wrestlers, rowers—rendered in fine anatomical detail, and such daring portraits as that of Dr. Gross cutting open a living body, established him as Realism's foremost transitional figure.

By the turn of the century, the influence of Impressionism on American art was marked. Artists returned from France with reports of paintings that glowed with the reflected diffusion of light over yellows and greens and browns, and with news of painters named Monet and Pissarro and Cézanne who seemed less concerned with *what* they saw than with *how* they saw. In Greenwich Village, there emerged a group of artists who absorbed the lessons of Impressionism but united them to Eakins's faithfulness to detail, to the social satire of Goya and Hogarth and Daumier, and, finally, to a bent for common, homely subjects and indigenous American scenes. The result was the new Realism. Inevitably these artists were dubbed the "Ash-can School" and labeled socialists or anarchists for daring to "paint drunks and slatterns, pushcarts and coal mines, bedrooms and barrooms"—to "deliberately and conscientiously paint the ugly wherever it occurs." They were more fairly called "The Eight."

The finest artist of the Eight was doubtless John Sloan, who could paint with equal skill the wake of a ferry, a line of tenement dwellers' clothes drying in the bright sun, the Third Avenue elevated, or a couple of aging, sharp-eyed ladies in a coach on Fifth Avenue critically scrutinizing their passing rivals. But the most influential member was Robert Henri, for he was a brilliant teacher, if only a fair artist. Unlike Sloan, who had never left America, Henri had been rigorously schooled in France. He returned to America in the early 1890s with two convictions: that real people and real events should be the only subjects of painting and that these subjects had to be infused with the artist's own moral or religious point of view. Henri helped George Bellows, Edward Hopper, Rockwell Kent, and a host of other artists to see that life and art could not be separated, that the crucial thing was not the subject painted but the intention of the artist, that the idea of "art for art's sake" was morally bankrupt.

Henri's most important ally in storming the gates of the art establishment was the photographic genius Alfred Stieglitz. Still in his mid-thirties as the new century dawned, Stieglitz had grown up in an upper East Side brownstone full of good wines and books and presided over by an imperious German-Jewish father who had prospered as a wool merchant. Enrolled by his father in an engineering program in Germany, Stieglitz perceived photography as part of the accelerating industrialism of the early 1880s and spent the next quarter-century establishing it as an art form as valid as painting or poetry. Returning to America in 1890, he joined a camera club, quit it as too conservative, and established his own periodical, *Camera Work*, a term he used to include any faithful picturing of life's deepest experiences. He had to face the hostility of painters who, he noted wryly, wished they could reproduce effects as clearly as did his "machine-made" objects. Calling themselves "Photo-Secessionists," he and Edward Steichen established, in 1905, the Little Galleries of the Photo-Secession at 291 Fifth Avenue.

Seeing no incompatibility between fine photography and fine art, Stieglitz became a leading sponsor of advanced art. The work of unknown painters and sculptors at "291" seemed sometimes to eclipse even the brilliant photographs. His was the first gallery in New York to show, and *Camera Work* the first magazine in America to explain, the Postimpressionist art of Matisse, Cézanne, and Picasso. He was audacious enough to display Rodin's provocative drawings of nude women, which even admirers of the Frenchman's sculptures denounced as a "not very elevating" sight in a public gallery. He gave the first exhibit anywhere of Negro sculpture presented as art rather than as anthropological artifacts. By making available to the public art which might not otherwise have been seen, "291" and other small galleries gave artists institutional leverage against the establishment dealers, critics, art academies, and museums.

It took a group of independent artists, bursting with creativity and innovation, to bring off the most shattering public event in American art—the Armory Show of 1913. Renegades of the stature of Henri, Sloan, Bellows, Maurice Prendergast, and many others, representing diverse schools, raised money, hired the 69th Regiment Armory at Lexington and 25th, and scoured Europe and America for the best and most varied paintings, lithographs, and sculptures. Quarreling all the way—Henri even dropped out —they gathered 1,600 pictures and sculptures. The towering brick walls of the grim armory were hung with long green drapes, the huge drill floor divided into corridors and cubicles. Gossip floated about Manhattan that the organizers were planning to shock the public. And so they did, but less with the rumored erotic art than with a profusion of painting and sculpture the likes of which few of their visitors had seen.

The tens of thousands of visitors, Oliver Larkin wrote later, first encountered Barnard's monumental *Prodigal Son,* passed by naturalistic portrait heads by Jo Davidson, moved on to a stunning French display of Delacroix, Daumier, Corot, Monet, Manet, and Degas, climaxing with Cézanne's *The Poor House on the Hill,* Renoir's vibrant *Boating Party,* and a Gauguin frieze of tawny Samoans under vines heavy with exotic fruits. Next the Fauves, the wild men: Rouault's *Parade;* Derain's jug on a windowsill, framed by stiff and bare trees behind; Matisse's dancing nudes. And then the Cubists: the young Picasso's *Woman with a Mustard Pot* and—the talk of the town— Duchamp's *Nude Descending a Staircase,* an elegantly convulsive vision of an angulated, abstractive woman moving downward in a complex of geometric shapes and slashing lines.

And, not least, the "American room": "John Sloan's girls dried their hair on a roof top in the sun," Larkin wrote; Robert Henri's gypsy was "painted with as few broad strokes as possible"; George Bellows presented "prize fighters in rapid pencil notation, and constructed in solid, lively paint the snow-covered docks along the river, the stevedores working, the tugboats sending white puffs into a crisp blue sky."

The Establishment fought back through its reviews of the show. Cézanne was a smug ignoramus, the *Century* judged, Van Gogh a nutty incompetent, Picasso as cheeky as Barnum himself. Along with a nod to the show's enterprise, Theodore Roosevelt entered some reservations: he found little to recommend in the Cubists, the Futurists, and the "Near-Impressionists." The Cubists would interest those who liked the colored pictures in the Sunday papers—indeed, the nice Navajo rug in his bathroom he deemed a better example of "proper" Cubism; the Futurists should be called "past-ists" because their paintings resembled the "later work" of Paleolithic cave artists; and as for the *Nude Descending a Staircase*, it was simply a "naked man going down stairs."

Greenwich Village critics had their own reservations about the Armory Show, or at least about the new art forms. If the Romantics had ignored the impact of industrialism on American life with their bent for landscapes, still lifes, and sentimental vignettes, the "modernists" were ignoring it by their emphasis on abstraction, Cubism, Futurism, and other evasions. The world of Cézanne and Van Gogh, Larkin wrote later, "set a premium on the pseudo artist with his facile solution and his shallow grasp. The fruitful continuity between art and the normal experience of mankind had broken down." Why? "Henry Adams concluded it had happened when the Virgin ceased to be a power and became a picture; Tolstoy said it was when the artist forgot his fraternity with suffering men; Veblen, when art became a showy index of superfluous wealth."

A few of the critics, apprehensive about the disjunction between art and life, were suspicious of photography's "machine-made" objects; in this they reflected, perhaps not always knowingly, John Ruskin and William Morris, who detested machines and machinery because they served commercial greed and threatened the handicrafts of the "people."

But Stieglitz refused to equate machines with artistic or human degradation. Stieglitz, Lewis Mumford wrote, subordinated the machine to his human direction through understanding its potentialities and capacities. "When used thus, as part of man's organic equipment rather than as a substitute for a deficient organ, the machine becomes as integral as the original eyes or legs. Assimilating the machine in this fashion, Stieglitz was armed to reconquer the lost human provinces that had been forfeited by the one-sided triumph of the machine." Living in New York City and summering at Lake George in the Adirondacks, Stieglitz was closely attuned to both the industrial and the natural environments around him, and this, together with his understanding of the European artistic heritage, enabled him to avoid the ephemeral and disjunctive tendencies that afflicted so many of his fellow artists.

Though he worked in a quite different medium, Frank Lloyd Wright was no less aware than Stieglitz of the need to put mechanical and industrial power to the service of human aspirations. The young architect had long objected to the industrial uglification of America. "The buildings standing around there on the Chicago prairies were all tall and all tight," he complained. Chimneys were lean and taller still—"sooty fingers threatening the sky." Dormers were "cunning little buildings complete in themselves," stuck onto the main roofslopes "to let the help poke their heads out of the attic for air." Everything was overdecorated—walls "be-corniced or fancy-bracketed," roofs "ridged and tipped, swanked and gabled," the exterior "mixed to puzzle-pieces with cornerboards, panel-boards, window-frames, cornerblocks, plinth-blocks, rosettes, fantails, and jiggerwork in general."

If the home was to be a machine for living, Wright contended, this machine could and should help people live according to their "organic life" as well as in a democratic fashion. In a democracy especially, man must master the machine, not the reverse—and man *could* do so. The machine, Wright said, is "the tool which frees human labor, lengthens and broadens the life of the simplest man," and in doing so becomes the basis of the "Democracy upon which we insist."

WRITING: "VENERABLE IDEAS ARE SWEPT AWAY"

Fascinated by the big city—by its railroad yards, elevated trains, ferries, tenements, chimneys, skyscrapers—painters like John Sloan and George Bellows used more than their canvases to register their views. Often they turned to the radical or avant-garde magazines that were sprouting across urban America. In 1912 Sloan became art editor of *The Masses,* a struggling left-wing journal. Drawing with pen, charcoal, and crayon on thin paper laid over a pebbly surface, Sloan revolutionized the style and format of magazine illustration. He insisted that he was serving on the journal as an artist, not as a polemicist. Art Young, the leading *Masses* cartoonist, had no such inhibitions, even though he had been a fellow art student with Henri in Paris. Borrowing from the work of Hogarth and Daumier, he savagely caricatured plutocrats, imperialists, censors, and police as agents of a vicious and bloated capitalism.

The Masses had begun in 1911 as such a dull and doctrinaire sheet that it almost folded within a year. Then, in August 1912, Art Young read to the editorial board an article by an unknown young writer named Max Eastman. Impressed—and desperate—the group authorized a note to Eastman: "You are elected editor of the Masses, no pay." The new editor, who freely admitted he knew nothing about art, brought to the journal a beguiling mixture of "scientific socialism," applied logic, pragmatic experimentation, and Christian doctrines inherited from his parents, both of whom were Congregational ministers in upstate New York. But Eastman was no dogmatist. The pages of *The Masses* were soon open to a variety of radical philosophies and to a new and biting satirical tone.

The journal's editorial board boiled with squabbles, but Eastman was good-natured about it all. "We live on scraps," he said. "Twenty fellows can't get together to paste up a magazine without scrapping about it." Nevertheless, several illustrators quit the staff in 1916 after Art Young accused Sloan and other artists of wanting to "run pictures of ash cans and girls hitching up their skirts in Horatio Street—regardless of idea—and without title." *The Masses* never recovered from this secession.

In that same year of 1916, it happened that a wealthy New York socialite, Mrs. A. K. Rankine, and a young utopian socialist, James Oppenheim, were being treated by the same Jungian analyst. As a means of therapy, Rankine was urged to sponsor a magazine project of Oppenheim's. With her funding, Oppenheim began to realize his dream of "*the* magazine which should evoke and mobilize all our native talent, both creative and critical. . . ." For the new journal, *The Seven Arts*, Oppenheim gathered around him other writers in their twenties and thirties: Waldo Frank, whose association in Paris with the circle around *La Nouvelle Revue Française* had fired an interest in cultural nationalism; Van Wyck Brooks, who, under the influence of Santayana and other Harvard scholars, had written *The Wine of the Puritans*, a seminal critique of American fiction and poetry as sentimental, escapist, and imitative of English literature; and Randolph Bourne, who had fled to Greenwich Village via Columbia from his intellectually stifling middle-class home in New Jersey.

The most arresting of this quartet was Bourne. "I shall never forget," Oppenheim wrote, "how I had first to overcome my repugnance when I saw that child's body, the humped back, the longish, almost medieval face, with a sewed-up mouth, and an ear gone awry. But he wore a cape, carried himself with an air, and then you listened to marvelous speech, often brilliant, holding you spellbound, and looked into blue eyes as young as a Spring dawn." Bourne was even more arresting intellectually. Through those blue eyes he perceived Americans' "belittling" attitudes toward women, the need for equal economic chances for women and their right to divorce and birth control, the antiquated curriculum of American education, the need to develop an American "transnationality" that respected immigrants' old cultures instead of the "melting-pot" concept that was leaving Americans in "detached fragments."

A cosmopolitan and iconoclastic magazine of quite different cut was *The Smart Set*, founded in 1900. Far more amusing than *The Masses*, more irreverent than *The Seven Arts*, the monthly had a flair for presenting serious fiction by such authors as O. Henry, Zona Gale, Edith Wharton, and

Damon Runyon. But even with H. L. Mencken as literary critic and George Jean Nathan as drama critic, *The Smart Set* almost foundered in 1910, only to be rescued by fresh editorial talent daring enough to gather the work of D. H. Lawrence, Joseph Conrad, August Strindberg, and William Butler Yeats. After Mencken and Nathan took over the top editorship at *The Smart Set* in 1914, the monthly realized Mencken's aspirations for a magazine that was "lively without being nasty. . . . A magazine for civilized adults in their lighter moods. A sort of frivolous sister to the *Atlantic*."

It was Mencken who gave *The Smart Set* its distinctive style. Married to his beloved native Baltimore and to the Baltimore *Sun*, he kept his distance from the Greenwich Village dilettantes and bohemians, as he viewed them, by mailing material to Nathan and making only a tri-weekly trip to Manhattan, where he stayed at the Hotel Algonquin. But Mencken was as unorthodox as any Villager, working during long lunches at Luchow's or at the Beaux Arts, offering a "Poet's Free Lunch" of pretzels and smoked herring to visitors in his office, where his desk sported two large brass spittoons and the walls shrieked with posters of Follies girls. To Village radicals, however, he appeared a political and social Tory, and even though Mencken looked for fresh and unorthodox talent, he was cool toward some of the new poets, especially the Imagists and the experimenters in free verse.

The new poets found a warmer welcome at such New York journals as *Trend* and *Rogue*, but these havens were short-lived. *Others*, a more enduring monthly, provided young poets with a forum for the widest experimentation, occasionally devoting an entire issue to a movement or a theme. It was his connection with the *Others* crowd that brought Wallace Stevens to prominence in the New York literary world. *Others* published eighteen of his poems, including "Peter Quince at the Clavier" and "Thirteen Ways of Looking at a Blackbird."

But it was another journal, eight hundred miles to the west, that acted as midwife to the new era in poetry. In August 1912, after a season of fund-raising and hunts across library shelves for prospective poets, Harriet Monroe sent from Chicago a manifesto circular announcing *Poetry: A Magazine of Verse.* It would offer poets the chance, she wrote, "to be heard in their own place, without the limitations imposed by the popular magazine," and its readers would be those interested in poetry as "the highest, most complete expression of truth and beauty." Among the recipients of the circular was Ezra Pound, Idaho-born, living then in London. Monroe particularly wanted Pound's aid because of his place at the center of "the keenest young literary group in England," despite both his hostility toward most things American and doubts whether he would reply to the urgings of a Chicago spinster-poetess. To her surprise he did respond with a heartening letter enclosing poems for the first issue, pledges of further help, and the wish that *Poetry* would speed the advent of an American renaissance that would "make the Italian Renaissance look like a tempest in a teapot!" *Poetry* was launched.

With Pound, a tireless promoter of others as well as of himself, installed as "foreign correspondent," early numbers of *Poetry* included verses from across the Atlantic by the great Yeats, D. H. Lawrence, Padraic Colum, and Richard Aldington. Pound extracted contributions from his fellow expatriates, including his Imagist protégée "H.D." (Hilda Doolittle), and Robert Frost, who was establishing himself in England. The *Poetry* of June 1915 featured T. S. Eliot's "The Love Song of J. Alfred Prufrock." From Boston came the verses of Brahmin Imagist Amy Lowell, from New Jersey those of William Carlos Williams. Closer to home, *Poetry* published two of the Chicago Movement's seminal poems, Carl Sandburg's "Chicago" and Vachel Lindsay's "General William Booth Enters into Heaven." Pound himself was well represented, notably by his stunning "In a Station of the Metro." In the March 1913 number, Pound set out the principles of Imagism: "1. Direct treatment of the 'thing,' whether subjective or objective. 2. To use absolutely no word that did not contribute to the presentation. 3. As regarding rhythm: to compose in sequence of the musical phrase, not in sequence of a metronome." His "Image" he defined as "that which presents an intellectual and emotional complex in an instant of time."

Many of *Poetry*'s offerings were mediocre, some bad, a few next to unreadable. But at a time when poetry was in an unstable state of transition, Monroe's publication was supreme among literary journals. It maintained an unswerving seriousness of purpose; it was willing to take chances with untested poets and embryonic movements; above all, it resolutely "internationalized" American poetry, placing the work of domestic Americans in a context with the work of contemporary English and Irish poets and of American poets abroad, thus offering models and challenges to young poets groping for a voice.

*   *   *

In 1907 the editor of the *Delineator*, a woman's magazine, commissioned Mencken to ghostwrite a series of articles on the care and feeding of babies. The exchanges between the two men, both of whom were childless and fully intended to remain so, approached high comedy as the editor, Theodore Dreiser, instructed the cigar-chewing Baltimorean that babies informed their mothers of their various needs through subtly differing cries, and Mencken manfully responded with a piece on babies' diverse cries of habit, pain, hunger, and temper. When, a year later, Mencken visited Dreiser in New York, the latter's first impression was of a "spoiled and petted and possibly over-financed brewer's or wholesale grower's son who was out on a lark."

Doubtless Dreiser reflected on the difference between his own earlier life and that of the son of a rich Baltimore brewer. While Mencken's background had made him provokingly cocky, Dreiser's world could hardly have delivered more blows to his self-esteem. He was the son of German immigrants growing up in the nativist, provincial city of Terre Haute, Indiana. His parents were profoundly otherworldly, but in different ways —his father an obsessively puritanical Catholic, his mother a pagan who believed in fairies and sorcery. Misfortune racked the family. The father, once a self-confident businessman, had lost his woolen mill in a fire and was badly hurt by a falling beam while rebuilding it, after which he settled into despair and joblessness. Of thirteen children the three oldest boys died. His mother kept the conflict-ridden and poverty-stricken family together, but finally she took Theodore, then aged seven, and two of the other small children on what turned out to be a long search for a better life elsewhere. At sixteen Theodore headed off on his own for Chicago.

Catapulted into the seething Chicago cauldron of the mid-1880s, Theodore searched desperately for a job that might give him a modicum of self-esteem. He was sacked again and again for incompetence and inattention. As both his status and his sex needs rose to fever heat, as he saw men fighting for jobs in the raw industrial and commercial worlds of Chicago, Pittsburgh, and other cities, he lied, cheated, and stole in vain attempts to advance himself. It was only with the help of others—a prosperous brother who gave him money and jobs, a high school teacher who financed a year for him at Indiana University, the odd editor who was impressed by him, the large number of women, including his wife, who loved and cared for him—and by dint of his own prodigious production of hack writing—that Dreiser survived.

Later people marveled that a common hack could produce so ambitious, so moving, so "realistic" a story as *Sister Carrie*. It was no mystery to the few who knew his life. Many contemporary authors—especially the muckrakers—were writing of the havoc they had seen American industrial society wreak upon the vulnerable, but Dreiser had not merely seen it—he had lived it. He was the first important American writer, it was said, to come from a non-Anglo-Saxon, lower-class background. Many of his characters were not simply extensions of himself, they *were* himself, with all his psychological bruises, physical sufferings, degrading poverty, sexual frustrations, ferocious appetites, hopeless yearnings, fleeting successes. Later an

English writer, Ford Madox Ford, praised *Carrie* as few American critics had done. The "difference between a supremely unreadable writer like Zola and a completely readable one like Dreiser," he said, "is simply that if Zola had to write about a ride on a railway locomotive's tender or a night in a brothel, Zola had to get it all out of a book. Dreiser has only to call on his undimmed memories. . . ."

Dreiser was not merely a reporter, however; he embellished, dramatized, romanticized, philosophized, sentimentalized. But, hopelessly immersed in the turbulence of his existence, he lacked the distance necessary for a unitary vision. Rather, his fiction tended to display all his ambivalences— his irresistible sensual instincts versus the residue of his Catholic upbringing, the fatalist who saw life turning on luck and chance versus the individualist bound to determine his own fate; his compassionate feelings about humanity in general versus his selfish, mean treatment of rivals, friends, and lovers; his skepticism that often edged into cynicism versus a romanticism that often oozed into sentimentality; a Social Darwinian view of life as an industrial jungle versus his abject dependence on others for help at home and on the job.

Dreiser was frustrated to the point of acute depression by the reception of *Sister Carrie*, though he could have expected difficulties. Frank Norris, the reader for Doubleday, Page, had given the manuscript his warm endorsement, and Walter Page, acting head of the firm during Frank Doubleday's absence abroad, had told Dreiser they would publish *Carrie;* but when Doubleday returned to New York, he read the proofs, gave them to his wife to read, and together they agreed: *Carrie* was evil—sin had not been punished. After a stiff legal stand by Dreiser, Doubleday reluctantly published and even promoted the book, but with wan enthusiasm. Sales lagged badly compared to the author's wild hopes. Some of the early newspaper reviews were remarkably perceptive and fair-minded, but many of the established journals consigned it to the gutter for its sexual frankness and refusal to moralize. As an author Dreiser was in the most annoying position of all— *Carrie* was controversial enough to be kept off library shelves but not spectacularly controversial enough to cause a run on the bookstores.

A good part of the *Carrie* controversy centered on the simple question, Can he write? Of Dreiser's prose style, one critic wrote, "Mr. Dreiser can not punctuate. He knows nothing of sentence and paragraph structure. . . . He flouts [details] and lumbers over them, disdainful, with an uncouth grandeur. . . . The art of suggestion is unknown to him." *Carrie* was uneven, unsophisticated, in dire need of editing. Yet this critic and others found much to praise in Dreiser's vitality and suggestive treatment of reality. "Even if he is not a Balzac or a Dickens or a Dostoevsky," wrote Julian

Markels, "the whole of Dreiser's substance is frequently rich and moving and powerful." But those prepared to find *Carrie* morally reprehensible were quick to seize upon Dreiser's callow and cumbersome prose—"Evil and badly written"—as though bad writing were the handmaiden of evil intentions.

Against this controversy stands the book itself, with, as Dreiser wrote in another context, "a bitter, brutal insistence on [its] so-ness." In many ways, *Carrie* is a conventional story of a young woman who, coming—as Dreiser had—from a small town to Chicago, is animated by keen yearnings for money, fine clothes, pleasure. She graduates from an affair with a natty but socially limited traveling salesman to a bigamous marriage with Hurstwood, a well-to-do saloon manager. Smitten with Carrie, Hurstwood abandons his wife and children to escape—it is more an abduction—with her to New York. From this point Carrie's fortunes rise as Hurstwood's decline. He loses his money, resorts to begging, and ends a suicide, while Carrie meets with mounting success on the stage. And yet, at the height of her fame, she longs for more; she is still "the old, mournful Carrie— the desireful Carrie,—unsatisfied."

The novel is distinguished by the relentless detail of Carrie's rise and Hurstwood's fall, but above all by Dreiser's steady refusal to judge his characters, nor even to hold them fully responsible for their actions. Carrie is borne by ever-ascending ideals and yearnings, the source and meaning of which she has no comprehension. Dreiser's stance is that of an observer of a human field, in which external and impersonal pressures, accidental circumstances, indistinct impulses and desires play upon and often determine behavior and destiny and in which Christian categories of good and evil, sin and redemption, have no part. With one bold book, Dreiser knocked down and trampled those "rubber-stamp formulae," as Mencken called them, which had extorted from authors pieties and platitudes, decorum and parsable sentences. *Sister Carrie* brought American fiction within the gates of American industrial society and face to face with its realities.

In 1862, nine years before Dreiser was born, George Frederick and Lucretia Jones of Gramercy Park and Newport announced the birth of their daughter Edith. The child grew up in a world that was bounded geographically by Washington Square, lower Fifth Avenue, and the approaches to Central Park, socially by a circle of Schermerhorns, Rhinelanders, and other rich, mainly "old Dutch" families. Culturally it was a world that sponsored museums and libraries but had little interest in serious art or learning. Edith came to comprehend this world, through her imagination, family travel in Europe, and her father's library, full of Plutarch and Parkman, Dante and Milton and Pope, Scott and Irving and Thackeray.

At the age of eleven, Edith Jones produced her first literary effort, a novel. It began: " 'Oh, how do you do, Mrs. Brown?' said Mrs. Tompkins. 'If only I had known you were going to call I should have tidied up the drawing-room.' " Edith showed her work to her mother, who dismissed it. "Drawing-rooms," she said, "are always tidy."

By the time Dreiser was eleven, he had attended parochial and public schools, lived the meanest kind of peripatetic life with his family, gotten fired five times. By that age, Edith Jones had been schooled only by private tutors. At eighteen, Dreiser attended Indiana University for a year. Edith had hardly dreamed of going to college, knowing that it was the young men in her social set who would attend Harvard or Columbia, Oxford or Cambridge. In his twenties, Dreiser was drifting from job to job; Edith Jones was drifting from New York to Europe to Newport to Bar Harbor.

What Edith did come to learn—to see and touch and feel—was the richly upholstered and intellectually barren world of her set. First she learned about their houses: the huge brownstones, with their ballrooms that might be used one day a year; the drafty drawing rooms; the quiet libraries where the man of the house took refuge; the silk-stockinged footmen, the platoons of servants. About their cultural pursuits: the Academy of Music, where society gathered primarily to show itself; the Century Association, where young men—and men only, of course—took further refuge from their families; other clubs, where the waiting period for membership might be ten years. They traveled at home and abroad, always within the tight little cocoon of their social class.

Unblinkingly she observed the phenomenon that by the early 1880s dominated the talk of New York's old moneyed class day after day—the insidious infiltration into established society of the philistines; of the bumptious, even vulgar, capitalists whose industrial wealth vastly surpassed the landed capital of the old families. Ultimately the old class could not stop the new, for money in that environment eventually meant power. But they could slow it down by a rigid adherence to protocol—the proper manners, clothes, decoration, watering places, decorum, *taste*. Old wealth shunned ostentation, loud voices, innovation. It never discussed money; it simply assumed it. "Fortified as she was in her own class," Diana Trilling said of the struggling writer, "she knew the reality of class as no theoretical Marxist or social egalitarian can know it: not speculatively but in her bones."

Above all, Edith Jones observed the relations between the sexes. If gentility barred women from every function save the "cultivation of the home," as Alfred Kazin noted, the older married women were the arbiters of the protocol of established wealth. Guarding access to society's inner sanctum and policing its behavior, however, was a role that could turn some of these women inward and away from broader social responsibilities. This was still an era when the gentlemen, after dinner, stayed together to smoke their cigars and discuss weighty matters, while the ladies moved off for decorous, gossipy talk.

Such talk did not include the subject of sex. A formidable double standard prevailed here too: men learned about sex and pursued extramarital affairs with little penalty from the matriarchs except mild tut-tutting. Women were not supposed to talk or even think sex. The result was a profound ignorance, in which Edith Jones shared. Shortly before her wedding, as her biographer tells the story, she plucked up her courage, her heart beating wildly, to ask her mother "what marriage was really like." Her mother looked at her with icy disapproval, exclaiming, "I never heard such a ridiculous question!"

"I'm afraid, Mamma—I want to know what will happen to me," Edith persisted.

"You've seen enough pictures and statues in your life," her mother said impatiently. "Haven't you noticed that men are . . . made differently from women?" "Yes," said Edith falteringly.

"Well, then . . ." But her mother broke off as she observed Edith's blank, uncomprehending expression. "Then for heaven's sake don't ask me any more silly questions. You can't be as stupid as you pretend."

After her barely consummated marriage to Teddy Wharton, a Boston socialite, Edith Jones Wharton spent another dozen years making the social rounds and storing up impressions, recollections, reflections; then she burst forth in a small flood of stories, novels, travel articles, even a book on the decoration of houses. Her most important works dealt with high society's victims, especially women. In her 1905 novel *The House of Mirth* she portrayed a spirited young woman who lacks the one thing— money, or a husband who could provide it—that would secure her social status; Lily Bart gambles for success, but, lacking the necessary cards and caught between her head and her heart, she is inexorably drawn by society's conventions into poverty, social ostracism, suicide. Fifteen years later, Wharton's *The Age of Innocence* presented Ellen Olenska, who could have enjoyed status and riches if she had stayed with her unbearable husband, a Polish count; as it is, Countess Olenska flees to her relatives in New York, seeks to establish a foothold there despite her distaste for their culturally empty lives, and flees again to a lonely life in Europe after her family rejects her.

These were powerful portraits, as were other novels such as *Ethan Frome* and *The Custom of the Country*. Yet they rarely rose above the pathos of individuals caught in a social web to the level of real tragedy. Wharton herself seemed fixed in the social environment she knew so well. She seldom portrayed with much credibility the lives of the poor or lower middle class. She ignored the larger ideas that might have aroused old society, new plutocracy, or rising proletariat. Society put enormous constraints on people's liberties, but Wharton was not about to expand on the implications of this for a nation that extolled liberty (or freedom) at every opportunity. "There was no use in trying to emancipate a wife who had not the dimmest notion that she was not free," says Newland Archer, Countess Olenska's would-be lover, of his pliant mate. Wharton leaves Archer's wife caught in a benign web of restraints to which society allowed no alternative. A superb critic of manners, the author was content with this role.

Nor did Wharton pursue a political alternative. Her gentlemen had nothing but disdain for "risking their clean linen" in the politics of Manhattan. In *The Age of Innocence*, Governor Theodore Roosevelt, after dining with Archer in the latter's home, turns to his host and says, "banging his clenched fist on the table and gnashing his eye-glasses: 'Hang the professional politician! You're the kind of man the country wants, Archer. If the stable's ever to be cleaned out, men like you have got to lend a hand in the cleaning.' " Glowing over the phrase "men like you," Archer wins election as state assemblyman, serves a year, then fails of reelection—and Wharton leaves him back in obscure though useful municipal reform. Theodore Roosevelt, who became a personal friend of Wharton, went into "dirty politics" to stay. Why didn't Archer?

Along with the lack of noblesse oblige in high society, there was contempt for the tastes of popular democracy. By turn of century, the middle and even lower-income classes were devouring books from the best-seller lists: Alice Hegan Rice, *Mrs. Wiggs of the Cabbage Patch;* John Fox, Jr., *The Little Shepherd of Kingdom Come;* Kate Douglas Wiggin, *Rebecca of Sunnybrook Farm;* Gene Stratton Porter, *Freckles;* Zane Grey, *The Spirit of the Border;* Harold Bell Wright, *The Shepherd of the Hills;* Mary Roberts Rinehart, *The Circular Staircase;* and such robust tales as Owen Wister's *The Virginian* and Jack London's *The Call of the Wild* and *The Sea Wolf.*

Edith Wharton did not need to lower her literary standards for her novels and stories to achieve impressive sales; *The Age of Innocence* sold 66,000 copies in its first six months and was still selling steadily two years later. She emphasized the pathos of individuals while her own class was eroding away. Both Wharton and Dreiser kept their distance from the rising philistines—she by sticking ultimately with her own class, he by entering and exploiting the crass commercial world even as he hated and derided it. "It was wonderful to discover America," Dreiser said, "but it

would have been more wonderful to lose it." Cries Lawrence Selden in
The House of Mirth, "Why do we call our generous ideas illusions, and the
mean ones truths?" Readers were left with these haunting questions, but
with little understanding of their implications for culture in a democratic
republic and a capitalistic economy.

"ALL THAT IS SOLID MELTS INTO AIR"

One night in Greenwich Village in the spring of 1913, Big Bill Haywood
was telling his Village friends of the bitter strike of the silk workers in
nearby Paterson. Thousands of pickets had been arrested. Two strikers
had been killed by police. Whole families were starving. The IWW-run
strike needed money and publicity.

Mabel Dodge Luhan spoke up. Why not move the strike right out of New
Jersey and stage it in Manhattan as a pageant? Electrified, the group let its
imagination soar. Artists, actors, writers would work together. John Sloan
would paint a huge backdrop for the stage. The designer Robert Edward
Jones would lay out a graphic program for the show. John Reed, who had
written plays and songs for dramatic clubs, would draft a scenario and
stage the spectacle. Big Bill was enthusiastic. He liked to tell Villagers that
his workers were too busy fighting for decent wages to have time for
culture. But now the strikers themselves would be the actors.

Early on a June evening, over 1,000 silk workers ferried across the
Hudson and marched to the old Madison Square Garden on 26th Street.
Glowing red lights spelled out "IWW" as queues stretched twenty or more
blocks. On a huge stage inside, against a two-hundred-foot-long backdrop
reproducing the mill's grim façade, the Paterson workers acted out the
quiet start of the working day, sudden voices crying, "STRIKE! STRIKE!," the
hands pouring out of the factory, the shooting of a striker by the police,
his burial, the mournful spectacle of strikers' children being sent off to
other cities, the climactic strike meeting. Big Bill, Elizabeth Gurley Flynn,
and Carlo Tresca gave fiery speeches, as they actually had earlier at a
Paterson striker's graveside. John Reed, who had been a Harvard football
cheerleader, choreographed the huge cast and directed its singing of revolutionary words set to Harvard tunes. The pageant ended with actors and
spectators hymning "The Internationale" in one mighty voice.

"Who that saw the Paterson Strike Pageant in 1913 can ever forget that
thrilling evening when an entire labor community dramatized its wrongs
in one supreme outburst of group-emotion?" Randolph Bourne wrote. A
new collective social art was coming in America, he felt. Other memories
soon turned sour. A financial disaster, the pageant passed no money on

to the silk workers. The strike collapsed within a month. Suffering from ulcers, Haywood left with friends for Provincetown. An exhausted Reed sailed off with Luhan to Europe.

The spectacle had merely given the strikers a moment of pageantry, Flynn concluded bitterly, and left them back on the picket line. Doubtless he was expecting too much from art—which cannot resolve social problems—while understanding too little of art's power to sharpen people's awareness of these problems.

CHAPTER 9

The Reformation of Economic Power

N OT since the founding decades had Americans eyed a national leader of such prodigious versatility as the man who took the oath of office that September afternoon in 1901. From childhood, Theodore Roosevelt had seemed to reach out hungrily for experience and to lose himself in action. Like Washington and Adams and Jefferson and the others, he had come to know and embrace the natural world around him as well as the political flora and fauna. If he had the attention span of a golden retriever, as some critics said, he had at least emulated the Founding Fathers in recording his experiences in correspondence, articles, and books.

In his forty-three years, Roosevelt had already lived a half-dozen lives. The product of seven generations of Manhattan Roosevelts, he had fitted in with the Boston aristocracy as well, and had even married into it. As a Harvard student of mixed abilities but wide exposure—William James was one of his teachers—he had found time on the side to write scholarly studies on the birds of Oyster Bay and of the Adirondacks. He had come to know the West—the West of the Dakota Badlands—as few easterners had been able to. He had invaded the seamy Republican clubhouses of Manhattan and had courted or quelled their denizens.

Then he soared. At the age of twenty-three he won nomination and election as New York assemblyman and took on the legislative bosses in Albany. At twenty-six he was an influential delegate at the Republican convention that nominated Blaine. At twenty-eight he ran for mayor of New York City and finished third behind an old-line Democrat and Henry George, the single-taxer. At thirty-one he took office in Washington as a Civil Service commissioner; at thirty-seven he was New York City Police Commissioner; at thirty-nine Assistant Secretary of the Navy and Rough Rider; at forty governor of New York; at forty-two Vice-President of the United States. In between he raised a family, shot buffalo and grizzlies, published writings that ranged from serious works in western and naval history to appalling potboilers.

If Roosevelt embodied much of the history of late nineteenth-century America, he also reflected its contradictions and contrarieties. Like other upper-class fathers, he was a "devoted family man" who again and again deserted his family for weeks at a time as he pursued his ambitions. He adored his first wife, who died in childbirth, but in his grief exorcised her from his memory and from history by destroying their love letters and tearing her photographs out of their frames. He talked peace but carried a gun on any plausible occasion. He loved animals but slaughtered them, and when bothered by a neighbor's dog, he pulled out his revolver and shot it dead. He believed in liberty but of the "orderly" type. He believed in equality but only with people he respected—and never with those, including fellow legislators who were Irish, whom he termed "a stupid, sodden vicious lot, most of them being equally deficient in brains and virtue." He was a snob of the first water who made friends with cowboys and politicians once they were able to see past the side-whiskers, the monocle, the gold-headed cane, the silk hat, the cutaway coat—all of which accoutrements he brought with him in his first appearance in the New York Assembly.

His had been a life of almost continual conflict—fighting bosses in both parties, knocking down "muckers" who accosted him in saloon or club-house, hunting down western desperadoes, reprimanding constables asleep at their posts, charging up San Juan Hill, endlessly tangling with fellow commissioners, governmental superiors, pacifists, and members of the "wealthy criminal class." Life was strife. Not by nature a compassionate man, he had a contempt for "weak, spineless" men of inaction, effete intellectuals like Henry Adams and Henry James, milk-and-water reformers. This contempt stemmed in part from his own childhood weaknesses and insecurities—his small, frail body racked by asthma and other ills, his myopic eyes, his reedy voice that easily slipped into a falsetto. Through home exercises, days on end of horseback riding, and incredible feats of endurance in the Badlands he had built a bull neck and a protruding chest, over a slowly expanding waistline.

Inevitably, as an intensely competitive man, he was something of a Social Darwinist. Many industrial evils would disappear, he said, if there were more of that "capacity for steady individual self-help which is the glory of every true American." There were higher things than the "soft and easy enjoyment of material comfort," he told an audience. "It is through strife, or the readiness for strife, that a nation must win greatness." If the "best classes" did not reproduce themselves, he said, the "nation will of course go down; for the real question is encouraging the fit, and discouraging the unfit, to survive." Thus he favored sterilizing the criminal and the feebleminded. He viewed the yellow and black peoples as backward and ignorant. Yet he did not embrace Social Darwinist dogma consistently, and increasingly he saw the state as protecting people, without "paternalism."

Nor was he likely to read the turgid works of Spencer or Sumner. He devoured books in great gulps, even while riding horseback or boating down streams, and his reading reflected both his catholicity and his love of battle. If he admired Francis Parkman and James Fenimore Cooper and Frederick Jackson Turner and anyone else who wrote about the West, he positively adored epics of fighting men. Naturally he abhorred critics of America, whether Frank Norris ("preposterous") or Henry Adams and his *Democracy* ("mean and foolish"), and he cherished a particular contempt for Henry James as a "very despicable creature, no matter how well equipped with all the minor virtues and graces, literary, artistic, and social." Tolstoy he esteemed, as long as the Russian steered clear of unclean sex. Longfellow he found "simply sweet and wholesome" but Chaucer "needlessly filthy."

Still, it was difficult for Theodore Roosevelt to leave for long the subject of himself. If, as a family member remarked, "Uncle Ted" wanted to be the groom at every wedding and the corpse at every funeral, family friends also noted that he wrote a biography of Thomas Hart Benton that seemed mainly about Roosevelt, and a biography of Oliver Cromwell that was a "fine imaginative study of Cromwell's qualifications for the Governorship of New York." Henry Adams lampooned him as "pure act," but Adams and other writers were nearer the mark when they compared his career to an express locomotive, speeding to an inevitable destination.

The force of a locomotive, but to what end? Clearly, in Roosevelt's case, the capture of power, but for what purpose? To satisfy his own ego? So many of his friends suspected; hence their reluctance to give him office and authority. Or to realize some nobler purpose? The answer was not wholly clear, even to Roosevelt.

Like many other American leaders, he lusted for power but feared it. When two journalist friends asked him, during his days as police commissioner, whether he was working to be President, he jumped to his feet, ran around his desk, and with clenched fists and bared teeth advanced on the cowering men. "Don't you dare ask me that!" he shouted. Then he quieted down and explained: if a man in a political job was reminded that he might be President, he would "lose his nerve" and not do the great things, the hard things, that required "all the courage, ability, work that I am capable of. . . ."

The quality that distinguished the Founders from a man like Roosevelt was their capacity to ground their concept of power in a settled and sophisticated philosophy of majority rule and minority liberties, of democratic representation and republican checks and balances, whereas Roosevelt was at most an instant philosopher who looked on power as an all-purpose weapon for all seasons. In 1901, he held an enormous potential for either progress or regression; the tinder of popular hopes and expectations, fears and hatreds, lay around him, ready to be ignited by that spark of furious energy that burned within him.

Furious potential energy also glowed among the people. America was still a nation most sharply divided between the poor and the rich—a fact not lost on a Christian socialist poet, Edwin Markham, who for years had been haunted by a Millet painting, *The Man with the Hoe,* that he had seen reproduced in *Scribner's Magazine.* During Christmas week 1898, he had gazed transfixed at the original painting, temporarily on exhibition in San Francisco, and returned to his home on the heights back of Oakland to write the most quoted poem of the time. Over and over his stanzas asked by whose handiwork had the Man created by Lord God been reduced to this "stolid and stunned" brother to the ox. And he closed with a warning that for some would haunt the century ahead:

> O masters, lords and rulers in all lands,
> How will the Future reckon with this Man?
> How answer his brute question in that hour
> When whirlwinds and rebellion shake the world?
> How will it be with kingdoms and with kings—
> With those who shaped him to the thing he is—
> When this dumb Terror shall reply to God
> After the silence of the centuries?

THE PERSONAL USES OF POWER

"I was a sickly and timid boy," Theodore Roosevelt had written to an editor friend two weeks after the Governor's election as Vice-President. He was trying to explain a report from his friend's son at school that young Ted had "licked all the boys in his form." Roosevelt had to admit that he, the father, was responsible in some measure for some of Ted's "fighting proclivities." And he strove to explain why. His own father, the Governor wrote, had taken great and loving care of him "when I was a wretched mite suffering acutely with asthma." But he "most wisely refused to coddle me" and made him feel "that I was always to be both decent and manly, and that if I were manly nobody would long laugh at my being decent."

Nothing could have pleased Roosevelt more than to hear that his son, small and bespectacled as he himself had been, was a "fighter." Yet he had to write this long defense of Ted because he was defending himself, and he was doing so because of his own feelings of ambivalence and even guilt over physical conquest. He disclaimed ambition and the pursuit of power even as he feverishly pursued them, amid a loud self-righteousness, a high-minded moralizing, and a stubborn independence gained from the Roosevelts' social status, his Harvard education, and his background in independent Republicanism. And if any would deny that the ethic of the family and the playground could be applied to national or world politics, Roosevelt testified to the contrary.

"It is exactly the same thing with history," he continued in this same letter. "In most countries the 'Bourgeoisie'—the moral, respectable, commercial, middle class—is looked upon with a certain contempt which is justified by their timidity and unwarlikeness. But the minute a middle class produces men like Hawkins and Frobisher on the seas, or men such as the average Union soldier in the civil war, it acquires the hearty respect from others which it merits."

As Roosevelt assumed the powers of the presidency, his unquenchable blaze of energy not only would illuminate his own addiction to the elixir of power; it would spotlight the more portentous question of presidential power in a representative republic, and ultimately of popular rule in a democracy. Roosevelt possessed high office by virtue of an assassin's bullet, not of a majority vote. He held one position of power in a system of dispersed authority, in a society dominated by economic and social elites. The country waited and wondered. Would he keep McKinley's Cabinet and policies? Would he wait for Congress to act? Would he let the Senate dictate Supreme Court appointments? Could he deal with the economic barons whose influence pervaded the whole political system?

"The deep and damnable alliance between business and politics"—this challenge to public authority, and to his personal power, had increasingly preoccupied Theodore Roosevelt since his days in the legislature. During his navy days he had poured his "disgust" over this tie into the receptive ears of William Allen White, a young Kansas editor visiting Washington: so strong "was this young Roosevelt—hard-muscled, hard-voiced even when the voice cracked in falsetto, with hard, wriggling jaw muscles, and snapping teeth," that he swept away any doubts White had held. As governor, Roosevelt had forced through the legislature a franchise tax bill making corporations holding public franchises "pay their just share of the public burden." The actions of a single state, however, could hardly eliminate a national problem—the tightening concentration of economic control through pools, mergers, and holding companies—the "trust" problem.

And now, as President, Roosevelt was itching to attack this problem, indeed spoiling for a fight. At the start, nonetheless, he seemed to move slowly. His first message to Congress, in December 1901, presented a program of "moderately positive action," intended somehow to abolish abuses without abolishing combinations—a program so restrained and limited as to dishearten his more militant supporters and provoke the press, including Finley Peter Dunne, who spoke through his alter ego, Mr. Dooley, with his usual gentle but penetrating wit.

"Th' trusts are heejous monsthers built up be th' inlightened intherprise iv th' men that have done so much to advance progress in our beloved counthry," Mr. Dooley represented the new President as saying. "On wan hand I wud stamp thim undher fut; on th' other hand not so fast."

Roosevelt had reason to be cautious. If he confronted economic power in United States Steel, Standard Oil, and a host of other titanic corporations, he confronted only two miles away—at the opposite end of Pennsylvania Avenue—citadels of political power on Capitol Hill. Since the President tended to conceive of power in terms of persons rather than institutions, he saw his opposition not as Senate, House, and judiciary, but as friendly or hostile leaders holding pivotal positions. Senate influence was clear; what was less clear was its relationship to "big business."

Some senators *were* big business. Leland Stanford of California had died in 1893, but others in the upper house moved as easily between the business and political worlds as the railroad magnate had. Nelson Aldrich of Rhode Island, born of a poor farm family, had made a fortune in business, married wealth, and long acted in the Senate with aplomb for sugar, banking, and other enterprises in which he held investments. Suave, humorous, unflappable, he was the leader of a small coterie of Old Guard senators, of equal weight, who came to be known as the Big Four. Often allied with this group were men who held close ties to big business but were above all professional politicians and proud of it. Matthew Quay had fought his way to domination of Pennsylvania politics, masterminded Benjamin Harrison's presidential campaign in 1888, run the Republican party, and become his state's high-tariff man in the Senate, while amassing one of the finest private libraries in the nation. Thomas Platt, longtime Republican boss and businessman, continued to compete with Roosevelt for party influence in the Empire State. Also remaining in the Senate was old Mark Hanna, the "man who had made McKinley." He had disliked Roosevelt almost as much as he had loved and admired his fellow Ohioan. "Don't any of you realize that there's only one life between this madman and the Presidency?" he had raged when other Republican leaders balanced the ticket in 1900 and eased Teddy into vice-presidential impotence. When word had reached Hanna of McKinley's death he had cried, "Now look— that damned cowboy is President of the United States!"

Over in the House, power relationships converged in the Speaker and the men around him, especially those in the financial committees. Thomas Reed of Maine, the most powerful Speaker in memory, had quit both the Speakership and the House in 1899 in disgust over McKinley's expansionist foreign policies, but Joseph Cannon of Illinois, beaten in the Democratic sweep of 1890, would soon gain the office. And in its small Capitol chamber between the two houses, the Supreme Court continued to arbitrate key sectors of the nation's economic life. These gray eminences, appointed by a string of conservative Presidents, lay in potential ambush against antibusiness policy. Regarding the Court, the new President enjoyed one consolation: to the first vacancy that arose he would appoint a man he admired, Oliver Wendell Holmes, Jr.—though only after clearing his choice with his own good friend Senator Henry Cabot Lodge of Massachusetts, another baron of state and Capitol Hill politics.

"Go slow," the congressional Old Guard was urging Roosevelt, in Hanna's words, and the President knew what they meant. Wall Street, the conservative press, and even his brother-in-law, Douglas Robinson, were urging him to be kind to business. Even before McKinley died, a letter had reached Roosevelt in Buffalo by special messenger from Robinson: "I must frankly tell you that there is a feeling in financial circles here that in case you become President you may change matters so as to upset the confidence . . . of the business world." Later, two good friends of the new President, George Perkins and Robert Bacon, had come to the White House to urge caution. But they "were arguing like attorneys for a bad case," Roosevelt wrote Robinson. "I intend to be most conservative," he went on, yet he would pursue his course. He not only knew the cause Perkins and Bacon represented, but the man.

That man was J. Pierpont Morgan. Even Roosevelt had to grant that the financier's "strong and dominant" personality made him worthy of his steel. With his great flaming red nose, piercing eyes, and bristling brows, he radiated a sense of power as commanding in the business world as Roosevelt's would be in the political. He was indeed economic power incarnate. In the same year Roosevelt became President, Morgan had led a group of financiers in buying out Carnegie and other steel makers and forming the nation's first billion-dollar corporation, a congeries of iron and steel works, ore holdings, and shipping properties. And during Roosevelt's first weeks in the White House, the "First Lord of American Finance" had capped fifteen years of feverish railway acquisition by organizing the Northern Securities Company, combining the stock of the Union Pacific, the Northern Pacific, and the Burlington.

Roosevelt could hardly have felt more directly challenged. Well he knew, as did the Old Guard, that his predecessors in the White House had instituted remarkably few actions against business combinations under the Sherman Act; that the most vigorous prosecution under the law had been not against a businessman but a labor leader, Eugene Debs; that a federal action against the "Sugar Trust," which controlled 98 percent of the nation's sugar-refining, had been repudiated by a conservative Supreme Court in a decision notable for its tortured reasoning. Roosevelt vowed that *he* would not be a McKinley or a Cleveland or a Harrison. To him this was a question of power—the power of the people and of the President who represented them. Not trusting even his Cabinet, in great secrecy he instructed Philander Knox, his holdover Attorney General, to move against Morgan and the whole Northern Securities crowd, alleging conspiracy in restraint of trade.

Astonished by the move, Morgan seemed later to feel more hurt than intimidated. He had known Roosevelt for years. They were both gentlemen—New York gentlemen. Had not he, Morgan, endorsed young Roosevelt when he ran for the Assembly, contributed $10,000 through Platt when he ran for governor? To be sure, the young governor had sponsored a dubious corporation tax, but since then Theodore had seemed to be settling down. He had even as Vice-President-elect given a dinner for Morgan at the Union League Club—probably, Morgan may have (rightly) suspected, to show he was really a conservative in touch with the influential classes. And now this. There was only one way to settle such a difference between gentlemen. Morgan entrained for Washington and strode into the White House. After many handshakes the conversation reportedly went as follows:

Morgan: "If we have done anything wrong, send your man"—the Attorney General—"to my man and they can fix it up."

Roosevelt: "That can't be done."

Knox: "We don't want to fix it up, we want to stop it."

Morgan: "Are you going to attack my other interests, the Steel Trust and the others?"

Roosevelt: "Certainly not, unless we find out that in any case they have done something that we regard as wrong."

A most illuminating conversation, the President reflected after Morgan left. "Mr. Morgan could not help regarding me as a big rival operator, who either intended to ruin all his interests or else could be induced to come to an agreement to ruin none." While the President turned to his next target, the beef trust, the Morgan group appealed to the federal courts.

The President delivered an even sharper blow to the "arrogance" of the "big monied men" during an anthracite coal strike later in 1902. The coal operators, including the six railroad corporations that owned most of the mines, were balking at a wage increase, but even more they sought to break the power of the United Mine Workers union and its young president, John Mitchell. George F. Baer, head of a large Pennsylvania coal and iron company and the industry's main spokesman, typified the bland arrogance of the owners when he uttered his unforgettable pronunciamento, "The rights and interests of the laboring man will be protected and cared for not by the labor agitators, but by the Christian men to whom God in His infinite wisdom has given the control of the property interests of the country."

As the strike continued, coal prices skyrocketed. Mayors and congressmen called for a settlement to avert a coalless winter. The specter loomed of children shivering in icy schoolrooms. At a White House conference, Mitchell said that he would accept an arbitration tribunal if the other side would, but the operators indulged in such denunciations of union anarchists and criminals that Roosevelt said later that only one man behaved like a gentleman and "that man was not I," but Mitchell. Roosevelt was in a quandary. He would not call out federal troops, as Cleveland had done, but the operators still would not budge.

In desperation, the President let word filter into Wall Street that he was preparing to order federal seizure of the mines; and he put conciliatory feelers out to the House of Morgan through his friend Secretary of War Elihu Root. The financier and the Cabinet member worked out an arbitration proposal on Morgan's yacht. There was a last-minute hitch when the operators refused to accept a union man for the arbitration board, but the President adroitly solved this problem by placing the Grand Chief Conductor of the Order of Railway Conductors on the board under the title "sociologist." In the end, the arbitrators granted the workers a nine-hour day and a 10 percent pay increase—but not UMW recognition.

The President's business foes charged that he was "playing politics" with his eye constantly cocked on the 1904 election. They were quite correct. Roosevelt indeed had been running for President since virtually the day he entered politics. In his brief half-year as Vice-President, he had begun maneuvering for the job, and he had been the most likely man to succeed McKinley if only because he would have fought the hardest. McKinley's assassination simply speeded up the process.

Halfway through his term, with scalps from the Northern Securities case and the coal strike hanging from his belt, the President seemed to move toward the center of the GOP. He pulled back on his antitrust campaign, adopted a moderate position on the tariff and other simmering issues, placated the congressional Old Guard through word and deed, put out conciliatory feelings to Morgan and his people. He played ordinary old-fashioned presidential politics, courting blacks, labor, ethnic leaders, and other elements of the big Republican party coalition, exploiting patronage to the hilt, steering clear of state factional fights. He played his own brand of ruthless politics, as he coldly cut off Mark Hanna's patronage base in the South, falsely denied receiving large campaign contributions from Wall Street, and even helped delay the admission of Oklahoma, Arizona, and New Mexico because of the likelihood that they would vote Democratic in the 1904 election. When Hanna, already beaten, died from typhoid fever a few months before the convention, Roosevelt's nomination was guaranteed. And when the Democrats, returning to their old strategy of the Northeast-South axis, chose an upright but conservative and colorless New York judge, Alton B. Parker, for President, Roosevelt's reelection was guaranteed. He won in a sweep.

Roosevelt had camouflaged his campaign shenanigans in "boorishly self-righteous" protestations, in William Harbaugh's words. Perhaps it was because of some sense of "power guilt," some fear of power as an aphrodisiac, that on election night he made his fateful pronouncement, "Under no circumstances will I be a candidate for or accept another nomination."

But he would exercise power while he had it, especially against power in hands he considered irresponsible. Inevitably he returned to the challenge of big business. He felt, according to John Blum, "that the central issue of his time pivoted on the control of business because this control determined conduct. . . . He feared not the size but the policies of big business." And of all the sectors of big business, none concerned him more than the railroads. "The question of transportation," he stated in his annual message to Congress in December 1905, "lies at the root of all industrial success," and the revolution in transportation during the last half-century lay at the heart of the growth of industry. What was needed was "to develop an orderly system" through "the gradually increased exercise of the right of efficient Government control."

Now a seasoned political leader after eight years in high offices, Roosevelt followed the Machiavellian advice to combine the prudence of the fox with the might of the lion in attacking the citadels of railroad power. Within a few weeks of election he launched suits against railroads and other corporations for giving and receiving rebates. The most powerful roads—the Burlington, the Great Northern, the Chicago & Alton—were indicted. An official report, Roosevelt declared, demonstrated that the Standard Oil Company had profited "enormously" from secret rail rates. Roosevelt focused on the issue of rebates, which had been outlawed in the Elkins Act of 1903 but still remained endemic in the railroad industry.

Roosevelt also favored tariff revision, but he viewed this issue as so subordinate to curbing the railroad barons that he used tariff reform as a bogey to frighten the Republican Old Guard, then in effect withdrew his tariff card in order to gain more leverage on the railroad issue. Meantime he put steady pressure on Congress to grant the ICC authority to set maximum railroad rates. Greeted with enthusiasm by shippers, farmers, and travelers, especially in the West, rate regulation passed through the House easily but ran head-on into the Republican Old Guard in the Senate. Most of the conservative senators, not willing to defy public opinion, favored the Hepburn regulatory bill but argued for proposals to broaden the power of the judiciary to review the ICC's rate-making and thus in effect cripple the commission's effectiveness.

This notion of broad court review touched a most sensitive nerve in Theodore Roosevelt, for it revived a painful memory. When, in 1902, he was considering Oliver Wendell Holmes as his first and stellar appointee to the Supreme Court, the President had written Lodge that he liked Holmes's personality, his Americanism, his record as a gallant Civil War soldier, his earlier pro-labor decisions as a Massachusetts judge. In the low and ordinary sense of "partisan" and "politician," Roosevelt went on to Lodge, a justice should be neither. "But in the higher sense, in the proper sense, he is not in my judgment fitted for the position unless he is a party man, a constructive statesman," who could work with "his fellow statesmen" in the other branches of government. Chief Justice Marshall had been that sort of man, Chief Justice Taney a "curse to our national life" because of his narrow view of federal power. "Now I should like to know that Judge Holmes was in entire sympathy with your views and mine. . . ."

He would not put on the Court someone who was not "sane and sound" on such matters. Lodge had evidently reassured the President. But when the Court passed on Northern Securities in 1904 and supported the Administration's trust-busting by a margin of one vote, Holmes had dissented. Roosevelt greeted the news with indignation: "I could carve out of a banana a judge with more backbone than that," he was reported to have exclaimed—the same judgment he had made of McKinley on an earlier "backbone" issue.

Now, in 1906, to push the railroad rate bill through the Senate, Roosevelt had to thread his way between Aldrich's group demanding broad review—even Lodge came out against federal rate-making—and a band of senators, headed by Robert La Follette of Wisconsin, demanding the addition to the bill of a most controversial provision for the evaluation of railroad properties. In a desperation effort, Aldrich turned over floor leadership on the bill to one of Roosevelt's mortal enemies, Democrat Benjamin R. Tillman of South Carolina, the old populist and outspoken racist. In a virtuoso display of personal politics Roosevelt flirted with Tillman, but pulled back when Pitchfork Ben could not carry the Democratic caucus; then TR returned to a formula of ambiguous language on the issue of court review; and finally accepted a bill without provisions for physical valuation of the railroads, to La Follette's chagrin.

The final version of the bill, however compromised, was a notable victory for the President. The Hepburn Act empowered an enlarged Interstate Commerce Commission to fix maximum railroad rates; extended the commission's jurisdiction to include sleeping-car companies, ferries, bridges, and terminal facilities; and made its orders binding on carriers pending a court decision, thereby placing the burden of proof on the carrier. Nestled in the bill also was a provision for ICC control of interstate oil pipelines—a provision that could only have been aimed at the Standard Oil Company and its old master, John D. Rockefeller.

FOREIGN POLICY WITH THE TR BRAND

With teeth clenched and pince-nez flashing, Roosevelt would stride round his office, dictating letters: "The Colombia people proved absolutely impossible to deal with. They are not merely corrupt. They are governmentally utterly incompetent. They wanted to blackmail us and blackmail the French company . . . in spite of the plainest warnings they persisted in slitting their own throats from ear to ear."

The President often shouted out paragraphs, punctuating them with fierce gestures as though he were haranguing a crowd. But, in the next moment, he might sit on the edge of his desk, feet dangling idly, and continue in a casual or ironic tone: "I am not as sure as you are that the only virtue we need exercise is patience. I think it is well worth considering whether we had better warn those cat-rabbits that great though our patience has been, it can be exhausted." Sometimes he intermixed cool reason and savage denunciation, causing his secretaries alternately to marvel and to quail: "At present I feel that there are two alternatives. (1) To take up Nicaragua; (2) in some shape or way to interfere when it becomes necessary so as to secure the Panama route without further dealing with the foolish and homicidal corruptionists in Bogotá. I am not inclined to have any further dealings whatever with those Bogotá people."

Not since the days of Andrew Jackson, it seemed, had an American

President so strongly put his personal mark on the nation's foreign policy. Teddy Roosevelt brought to diplomacy a quick temper, unquenchable energy, a rigid moral code, and a vocabulary of curses that Old Hickory would have admired. Yet at the same time Roosevelt could be charming, humorous, and a patient negotiator. His intensely personal style surprised and occasionally flustered members of the staid diplomatic establishment. "We drove out to the Rock Creek," wrote British Ambassador Sir Mortimer Durand of one interview with the President; "he then plunged down . . . and made me struggle through bushes and over rocks for two hours and a half, at an impossible speed, till I was so done that I could hardly stand." Roosevelt talked nonstop, much to the relief of the winded Englishman.

In an age when diplomacy was still a leisurely ritual practiced by gentlemanly initiates, Roosevelt was eager to charge straight toward his goals with all the force of a locomotive. His barrages of letters, disregard of proper form, public gestures of friendship and defiance, all strained tempers from Caracas to St. Petersburg—and occasionally produced results.

The goal that Roosevelt eyed most impatiently was the building of a canal to link the Atlantic and Pacific. Schemes for digging a waterway across Central America had been a fixture in U.S. diplomacy since the 1840s, when the United States acquired California and Oregon, thus becoming a two-ocean power. The need for a canal was underlined during the war with Spain, when warships from the Pacific coast had to steam 14,700 miles, all the way around South America, to join in the fighting off Cuba.

During McKinley's Administration, Secretary of State John Hay had already begun trying to clear away obstacles to the project. The first barrier was the Clayton-Bulwer Treaty, a fifty-year-old agreement that bound America not to construct a Central American canal without the consent and participation of Britain. Hay persuaded the British to grant the United States exclusive control in exchange for a pledge not to fortify the waterway. But the Senate, inflamed by anti-British rhetoric in the election campaign of 1900, rejected the proposed pact. Hay was livid. "I felt sure that no one out of a mad house could fail to see that the advantages were all on our side," he wrote. "But I underrated the power of ignorance and spite acting upon cowardice." The negotiations collapsed; then McKinley died and TR became President.

The scholarly Secretary of State had been an aide to Abraham Lincoln when Roosevelt was still a toddler. Of frail health and a morbid cast of mind, Hay presented a sharp contrast to the new President, but the two men became good friends and made a working team. Under Roosevelt's prodding and Hay's gentle suasions, the British made further concessions. By the end of 1901, the two sides concluded a second Hay-Pauncefote Treaty, which this time did survive the Senate.

The next step was to choose a site for the canal. Most congressmen—including Alabama's Senator John T. Morgan, longtime leader of the pro-canal forces—favored a route through Nicaragua. But Roosevelt, at the advice of engineers and naval officers sent to inspect the possibilities, leaned toward the Isthmus of Panama, where a French company had dug about a third of a canal before collapsing in bankruptcy. Two members of the successor of the defunct company, lobbyist William Cromwell and engineer Philippe Bunau-Varilla, joined the President in trying to bring Congress around to the Panama route. Cromwell's sizable cash contributions to GOP war chests won him a favorable hearing from Mark Hanna and other Republican leaders, but it was Bunau-Varilla who pulled off the flashiest coup of the campaign. When a volcano erupted in the West Indies, destroying a city of 30,000 people, the Frenchman bought ninety sets of Nicaraguan postage stamps that pictured one of that country's volcanoes and sent one to each senator with the inscription, "An official witness of the volcanic activity of Nicaragua." In June of 1902, after a long but futile fight by Morgan, Congress authorized Roosevelt to explore the Panamanian alternative.

Bunau-Varilla's company avidly agreed to sell its assets in Panama to the United States for $40 million. Now all Roosevelt needed to do was to persuade Colombia, which after all owned the isthmus, to let the United States begin construction. The President offered the Colombians a cash payment of $10 million and a rent of $250,000 per year in exchange for control of the canal and a zone six miles around it. The Colombian government resisted, hoping to gain more money and a firmer guarantee of its sovereignty over the canal zone. Despite warnings from the U.S. envoy in Bogotá that his terms were unacceptable, TR kept up the pressure through the fall and winter of 1902. One Colombian ambassador resigned in disgust. The next, Tomás Herrán, fearing that the "impetuous and violent" President might seize Panama by force, signed the treaty despite instructions from Bogotá.

By unanimous vote, the Colombian Senate rejected the Hay-Herrán pact on August 12, 1903. Roosevelt fulminated, sending letters and expletives flying in every direction. Evidently the Colombians hoped to wait until October of 1904, when the lease of the French company would expire and the $40 million could be paid to Colombia instead. The obvious difficulty with waiting, for Roosevelt, was the approach of the 1904 election. If he was to get the canal started before he faced the voters, the President would either have to make a much better offer to Bogotá, open an entirely new set of negotiations with Nicaragua—or hope for some change in Panama itself. The Panamanians had revolted against Colombia a number of times in the past; would they do so again when faced with the prospect of losing the canal project forever?

"Privately," Roosevelt wrote to a friend, ". . . I should be delighted if Panama were an independent State, or if it made itself so at this moment; but for me to say so publicly would amount to an instigation of a revolt, and therefore I cannot say it."

The President's reticence about encouraging the Panamanians was not shared by other Americans, however. In Panama City, a group of U.S. Army engineers, railroad employees, and even the American consul general became involved in the incipient plan for a revolt. In New York, in Room 1162 of the Waldorf, an emissary from the would-be insurgents, Dr. Manuel Amador, met with Cromwell—who promised $100,000 to speed up the revolt—and Bunau-Varilla. It was Bunau-Varilla who sounded out Roosevelt and the State Department as to the government's attitude toward a revolt. Apparently satisfied with their responses, and with the news that a U.S. cruiser was on its way to the isthmus, the Frenchman urged the plotters to proceed.

Amador returned to Panama with a flag, a constitution, and a battle plan —all thoughtfully provided by Bunau-Varilla—and on November 3, 1903, the Republic of Panama was proclaimed. Acting on secret orders wired from Washington the day before, the captain of the U.S.S. *Nashville* prevented the Colombians from landing troops to stamp out the revolt. After more American naval forces arrived, the United States formally recognized the new nation.

Bunau-Varilla had stayed in New York to act as "Envoy Extraordinary" for the revolution. The French engineer opened negotiations with Hay and quickly struck a deal: Panama would receive the $10 million and $250,000 rent originally offered to Colombia, plus an explicit American guarantee of its independence. In return, the United States was granted absolute sovereignty over an enlarged canal zone. Bunau-Varilla signed the agreement for Panama on the evening of November 18. Just hours later, Acting President Amador arrived in Washington, only to find his new nation committed to a treaty that he had never seen. Realizing that Panama was totally dependent on the protection of the U.S. fleet, Amador and his government had little choice but to accept the deal.

The agreement was not greeted by universal acclaim in the United States. The head of the American Bar Association denounced America's role in the insurrection as a "crime"; the *New York Times* termed it an "act of sordid conquest." In the Senate, John Morgan led a concerted assault on the treaty, calling it a "caesarian operation" midwived by Roosevelt. But the country at large rallied behind the President; Morgan's forces went down to defeat, and the senator himself reluctantly voted for the treaty in the end. Better a stolen canal than no canal at all, he and others reasoned.

The 1904 Republican platform, however, expressed no shame at the outcome: "The great work of connecting the Pacific and Atlantic by a canal is at last begun, and it is due to the Republican Party." Touting Roosevelt for a presidential term in his own right, it proclaimed that "foreign policy under his administration has not only been able, vigorous, and dignified, but in the highest degree successful."

*   *   *

Roosevelt's own account of the Panama Canal's beginnings harked back to his days in the Badlands. Colombia was a "road agent" who had tried to hold the President up, but Roosevelt had been "quick enough" and had "nerve enough to wrest his gun from him." In his analogy the Colombians' gun was Panama, and TR refused to heed the protests of any "hysterical sentimentalist" who wanted him to return it.

Other observers, then and since, have also seen Panama as highway robbery—but with Roosevelt as the bandit. Nor was Roosevelt's willingness to risk conflict confined to this one affair. He convinced Britain that he would use force to settle Alaska's disputed boundary, thus causing the British to accept the line claimed by America. He sent gunboats to Morocco to secure the release of a person who turned out not to be a U.S. citizen. In the Caribbean, the President pressured the Germans over Venezuela, took control of the Dominican Republic's customhouses, and sent troops to occupy revolution-torn Cuba. To the Monroe Doctrine he added the so-called Roosevelt Corollary, a warning that "flagrant cases of . . . wrongdoing or impotence" in the Western Hemisphere would be checked by the United States acting as an "international police power." Once again TR painted himself as fighting outlaws as well as European powers who might take over weak Latin American states unable to pay debts or protect foreign nationals.

Roosevelt quite clearly relished conflict, confrontation, even the risk of war. "No merchant," he declared, "no banker, no railroad magnate, no inventor of improved industrial processes, can do for any nation what can be done for it by its great fighting men. No triumph of peace can equal the armed triumph over malice domestic or foreign levy." He was much influenced by the idea of the "competition of races," preached by Josiah Strong and others who saw America as engaged in a tremendous struggle for the dominance of the fittest among nations. In effect, Strong's doctrine was Social Darwinism applied to international relations—and Roosevelt subscribed to it heartily.

In the hands of Strong, Roosevelt, and other expansionists, Manifest Destiny became practically indistinguishable, as a concept, from the imperialism being practiced by the nations of Europe. The contrast with the dominant ideas of a century earlier was striking. In the early days of the American republic, with France setting all Europe aflame with revolution, men like Tom Paine and Thomas Jefferson could well hope that democracy was destined to spread throughout the world. Theirs was a belief in the power of ideas—particularly in the idea of liberty. Theodore Roosevelt, President in an era when Europeans were using force to subjugate much of the globe, was wedded instead to the idea of power.

If Roosevelt, in his self-proclaimed role as policeman among nations, was open to the charge of imperialism, then other actions of his require a very different explanation. One strand in Rooseveltian diplomacy was composed of force and conflict, yet an opposing strand consisted of conciliation and quiet diplomacy. Behind the scenes, the blustering Rough Rider often acted as a force for moderation.

The most dramatic display of the "other" Roosevelt came in 1905, when he moved to end the Russo-Japanese War. Fighting had broken out a year earlier, when the two powers clashed over their rival interests in Manchuria and Korea. Japan won a series of naval victories and most of the land battles, only to find her economy in critical condition as the war dragged on. The Russians, meanwhile, were bedeviled with internal turmoil, terrible incompetence in their army, and the disastrous loss of their Baltic fleet at Tsushima Straits, after its epic voyage around the world. Neither side could afford to continue the struggle, yet neither would sue for peace. In desperation over the stalemate, Japan turned to Roosevelt in April of 1905.

Initially TR had favored Japan. "You must not breathe it to anyone," he wrote TR, Jr., after the battle of Port Arthur; "I was thoroughly well pleased with the Japanese victory." The Japanese seemed able and intelligent, while the Russians annoyed him with their "supine carelessness" and "contemptuous effrontery." Throughout the war, Japan's diplomats courted Roosevelt's further goodwill by joining him for hikes and tennis games, arranging wrestling lessons for him, and deluging him with books on the island kingdom. Roosevelt was responsive to this kind of personal approach. He tended to draw advice from his "Tennis Cabinet," a loose group of friends and sports cronies that already included several foreign diplomats. But apparently the Japanese miscalculated the effect of their efforts. Educated by his crash course of readings—and by the string of

Japanese military successes—Roosevelt began to wonder aloud whether the Japanese "did not lump Russians, English, Americans, Germans, all of us, simply as white devils inferior to themselves" and were planning to "beat us in turn."

Aware of the big stakes involved, Roosevelt brought to the peace-making process both his vigor and his finesse. While bombarding Czar Nicholas with plans and suggestions for a peace conference, he worked on the Japanese diplomats, urging them to moderate their terms. Notes and telegrams flowed between the President and officials in London, Paris, and Berlin as Roosevelt sought for every opening to influence the belligerents. In June, convinced that at last he would receive a favorable response, he formally invited Japan and Russia to come together for direct negotiations. The two powers consented, designating the United States as the site of their conference.

At the U.S. naval base in Kittery, Maine, just across the river from Portsmouth, the two sides confronted each other. From Sagamore Hill, Roosevelt followed every nuance of the negotiations. It soon became clear that the talks would deadlock; Russia refused to concede defeat or pay an indemnity, while Japan would give up none of its military gains. "I am having my hair turned gray by dealing with the Russian and Japanese peace negotiators," TR fumed to his son Kermit. "The Japanese ask too much, but the Russians . . . are so stupid and won't tell the truth." Again the telegraph wires to St. Petersburg burned with new arguments and proposals. First the Japanese and then the Russians were invited down to Oyster Bay for a private talk with the President. From Japan's representative, he secured a compromise on two of the four points still at issue. Then, returning from a cruise beneath Long Island Sound in an experimental submarine, Roosevelt offered the Russians a change of wording that helped put a better face on their concessions. His skillful interventions helped to produce a treaty of peace.

Roosevelt displayed the same firm but gentle touch that made the Treaty of Portsmouth possible in other controversies between the major powers. When war threatened to break out between France and Germany over Morocco in 1905, the President again provided his good offices for settling the dispute. America's participation in the ensuing Algeciras Conference was greeted with skepticism in Congress, but Roosevelt took considerable pride in the peaceful outcome. He also was the moving force behind the 1907 Hague Conference, which denounced the use of military force to collect foreign debts and tried to establish limits of civilized conduct in war. Watching the emergence of Roosevelt as a "diplomatist of high rank," the London *Morning Post* professed to be amazed. "He has displayed . . . great tact, great foresight, and finesse really extraordinary. Alone . . . he met every situation as it arose, shaped events to suit his purpose, and showed remarkable patience, caution, and moderation."

* * *

Roosevelt, notes biographer Elting Morison, had a "horror of anarchy, disorder, and . . . wanton bloodshed." His experiences with the chaos of modern life were intensely personal: he lost a cherished wife in childbirth and a beloved younger brother to alcoholism, witnessed frontier violence, ascended to the presidency through the whim of an assassin, and watched his friend John Hay die as the Portsmouth negotiations commenced. Roosevelt courted strife because he could not seem to avoid it, yet he also was able to rise above the battle, to convert struggle into a personal and political source of power. "TR's supporters focused on his ability to master seemingly uncontrollable forces and, in so doing, advance the cause of moral order," according to Robert Dallek. The need to control events underlay Roosevelt's words and beliefs as well as his actions; it was the thread that united TR the imperialist with TR the peacemaker.

Solid accomplishments were the only adequate response to life's natural disorder. "The chief pleasure really worth having," Roosevelt confided to a friend, ". . . is the doing well of some work that ought to be done." Thus no prospect delighted him more than the actual construction of the isthmian canal. Although no President had ever before left the country while in office, Roosevelt could not keep away from Panama.

The President sailed to the Canal Zone on a battleship, purposely timing his arrival to coincide with the height of the rainy season so as to see the site at its most daunting. The weather pelted him as he rode through the streets of Panama City with Amador, wilted his white suit as he climbed aboard a huge steam shovel to do a little digging on his own, and threatened to derail his train as he inspected the locks. Everything had to be explained to him: engineers' salaries, the crews' kitchens, the controls of the various equipment.

"This is one of the great works of the world," he assured the assembled diggers. "It is a greater work than you, yourselves, at the moment realize."

On his return from Panama, Roosevelt had to take hold of a more prickly situation. The San Francisco Board of Education, under pressure to stem the flow of Japanese immigrants to California, had passed in 1906 an order that segregated all oriental students in the city's public schools. Labeling the segregation order a "wicked absurdity," the President tried to bring pressure to bear on the westerners, only to find himself stymied by the constraints of federalism. As Japanese indignation and Californian defiance mounted, TR turned on the charm instead. The mayor of San Francisco and seven school board members accepted his invitation to come to the White House, and in a series of meetings refereed by Hay's successor, Elihu Root, Roosevelt and the local officials reached an understanding. San Francisco repealed the segregation order, and the President undertook to persuade the Japanese to limit their immigration to America.

The same mix of finesse and force was evident in Roosevelt's negotiations with Japan. To fulfill his promise to the San Franciscans, Roosevelt sent another friend, Secretary of War William Howard Taft, to Tokyo. The genial Taft quickly found a face-saving formula for the Japanese: both sides would enter into a Gentlemen's Agreement to reduce immigration to the other's country. Roosevelt continued his efforts to assuage the Japanese and, in 1908, Root and Japan's ambassador, Baron Kogoro Takahira, reached an agreement to maintain the status quo in the Pacific and uphold the continued independence of China. Both Taft's and Root's understandings were embodied in executive agreements rather than formal treaties; Roosevelt was not going to stake the fragile détente he had built in the Pacific on the uncertain outcome of a Senate ratification fight.

Yet while TR wooed Japan, he also sought to show the Tokyo government that he was not negotiating out of fear. In the summer of 1907, he conceived of a grand gesture of American might—a triumphant procession of the U.S. fleet around the world, with its first stops to include Japan. The sixteen sleek white battleships, many of them launched during his term, were other tangible proofs to TR of his success in wielding the power of the United States. In sending them to what the fleet commander thought might be a "feast, a frolic, or a fight," Roosevelt was putting to the test the prestige of his personal leadership.

In its fourteen-month tour the fleet encountered much feasting, in Tokyo and elsewhere, some frolic—and a number of disturbing technical failures. The tremendous diplomatic success of the cruise tended to hide the fact that America could not fuel or repair a globe-circling navy, and that the ships themselves had distinct mechanical problems—ruptured boiler tubes, cracked armor plates, defective shell hoists. Nor did Roosevelt anticipate that his show of force would encourage navalists in Tokyo to speed up the expansion of the Japanese fleet, undermining the balance of power in the Orient.

Ironically, the cruise of the "Great White Fleet" pointed out the limits to Roosevelt's reliance on the force of personality. Even as vigorous an executive as TR was unable to control all the factors at work on the disorderly world scene, or to judge correctly the consequences of all his actions. At home, too, there were forces for change at work, forces that also threatened to evade Roosevelt's controlling hand.

REFORM: LEADERSHIP AND POWER

At the time Roosevelt entered the White House, a new and intoxicating feeling of reform and change was pervading the nation. People were still reading George and Bellamy and Norris and the rest; an older generation could remember the exhortations of Phillips, Garrison, and Douglass, of Anthony, Stanton, and the Grimké sisters. But a different breed of reform leaders was now pushing forward and gaining public attention. The single-taxer Tom L. Johnson gained election as mayor of Cleveland, and the reform mayor of Toledo was winning reelection as "Golden Rule" Jones. A young reporter named Josiah Flynt, who had lived with tramps and pictured tramping as just another way of living, was starting a series on graft for *McClure's*. The same journal was publishing Lincoln Steffens on bossism in St. Louis and Ida Tarbell on the Standard Oil Company.

Time was, Mr. Dooley opined to Mr. Hennessey, when magazines were very calming to the mind. "But now whin I pick me fav'rite magazine off th' flure, what do I find? Ivrything has gone wrong. . . . All th' pomes be th' lady authoressesses that used to begin: 'Oh, moon, how fair!' now begin: 'Oh, Ogden Armour, how awful!' . . . Graft ivrywhere. 'Graft in th' Insurance Comp'nies,' 'Graft in Congress,' . . . 'Graft be an Old Grafter,' . . . 'Graft in Its Relations to th' Higher Life'. . . ."

Others shared Mr. Dooley's perplexity. How could reform become so popular, so fashionable, in a land that had been enjoying McKinley's Full Dinner Pail, a nation that had easily bested an ancient European power, a society on the whole quite satisfied with itself? Time would bring some clues. People enjoying material well-being are more likely to move to higher needs and aspirations—such as the pursuit of liberty, equality, and happiness—than those desperately scrabbling for food and shelter. But to move people to higher levels of moral behavior, leadership is required, and not only was Roosevelt all too ready to provide moral leadership, but a "second cadre" consisting of hundreds of zealous young publishers, editors, and writers was now taking the lead.

The striking aspect of these two levels of leadership was the engagement between them. Roosevelt knew many of the reformers personally—he knew Jacob Riis, Lincoln Steffens, Finley Peter Dunne, Norman Hapgood, William Allen White, Ray Stannard Baker. He read them, wrote to them, scolded them, praised them, inspired them. They read *him*, talked with him, corresponded with him, alternately loved him and hated him, sometimes at the same time. It was this mutually stimulating relationship that, in large part, pushed the President toward increasingly radical positions. The reformers liked his style, his gusto, his personality. "Teddy was reform in a derby," William Allen White said, "the gayest, cockiest, most fashionable derby you ever saw."

Perhaps even more important, however, in the rise of reform were other types of leaders—the inventors, printers, investors, and publishers who were developing new types of magazines that became the vehicles for disseminating reform ideas. The 1890s had seen the rise of the "cheap magazine," selling for only ten cents but offering excellent illustrations with the help of improved engraving, lively and varied editorial fare, graphic descriptions of science and invention, and articles with broad popular appeal. The fine old journals—*Harper's*, the *Atlantic*, *Scribner's*, and the like—continued to flourish editorially and financially on the whole, but the ten-centers were stealing the show.

Their rise—and indeed the explosion of the whole magazine population—was as sensational as some of their feature articles. The number of periodicals in the United States rose from about 3,300 in 1885 to about 6,000 in 1905, thus almost doubling in one generation. Perhaps 7,500 magazines were actually founded in this twenty-year period, but many failed. The variety was also astonishing. "There is scarcely a province in the entire realm of science and scholarship which is now without an official organ in America," the *Philosophical Review* stated as it added itself to the number. "Magazines, magazines, magazines!" exclaimed one of them. "The news-stands are already groaning under the heavy load, and there are still more coming."

One of the earliest and most impressive of the ten-centers was *McClure's*. Founded by young Samuel S. McClure and a college classmate, the journal almost collapsed when its first issue appeared during the slump of 1893 and 12,000 of the 20,000 copies were returned. But with the conviction that "if I like a thing," then "millions will like it," McClure found a winning editorial formula in articles about Napoleon, Lincoln, and other heroes. He also pridefully published Robert Louis Stevenson, Rudyard Kipling, Thomas Hardy, Stephen Crane, and, unknowingly, a convict named O. Henry who sent a Christmas story to McClure through an intermediary. Part genius, part madman, and part inexplicable, in Eric Goldman's profile, McClure was less a great reformer than a superb editor, but he became more and more engulfed in the reform wave as his investigating reporters helped boost his circulation to 370,000.

And what a remarkable stable of reporters they were—not only Flynt and

Steffens and Tarbell but Ray Stannard Baker, Burton J. Hendrick, Samuel Hopkins Adams, and—later—Jane Addams. And as *McClure's* circulation swelled, competing journals looked for crusading journalists. The *Ladies' Home Journal* published Edward Bok on patent medicine evils; *Everybody's,* Thomas W. Lawson on crooked finance and Charles Edward Russell on the beef trust; *Cosmopolitan,* David Graham Phillips on "The Treason of the Senate." When McClure seemed to succumb to grandiose visions of out-combining the combines against which his reporters wrote, Baker, Steffens, and Tarbell left him, enlisted White and Dunne, and bought the *American Magazine* for more crusading.

To many, Steffens seemed the most gifted of the lot. Reared in an affluent home, in the half-commercial, half-rural hubbub of Sacramento, educated in philosophy and ethics at Berkeley, Heidelberg, Munich, Leipzig, London, and Paris, he found newspaper jobs in New York City in the mid-1890s before joining *McClure's.* There he began a long career of exposing bossism, traction magnates, municipal corruption, timber frauds, and other perversions of democracy. Published under eye-catching titles —"The Shamelessness of St. Louis," "Pittsburgh: Hell with the Lid Lifted," "Philadelphia: A Defeated People"—his exposés won enormous interest in high places and low. Steffens had a knack for gaining the confidence of bosses and magnates, getting them to converse with amazing candor, and printing the exchanges with apparent line-by-line accuracy. But even more, he presented his subjects, their views, and their failings with such humorous tolerance and philosophical understanding as to raise his work far above the level of mere reportage.

In the long run, however, Ida Tarbell may have had more influence on reform, if only because at the start she penetrated to the heart of economic power in the form of the Standard Oil Company and stayed with it. She had reason to dislike Rockefeller and his ilk: her father, a stalwart Republican, had been forced out of business by the oil tycoon, and her mother, reduced to peddling milk while her husband labored in the oil fields, poured out her feelings to Ida about the twin evils of whiskey and monopoly. After winning some fame for her series on Napoleon for *McClure's,* she won an assignment from McClure to write a detailed study of Standard Oil and of Rockefeller, the "Napoleon among businessmen," as the press dubbed him. On the basis of five years of intensive research in archives and corporation records, including some of Henry Demarest Lloyd's collection of documents, Tarbell produced a series of accounts "so heavily laden with questionable business maneuvers, so bound up with bribery, fraud, coercion, double-dealing and outright violence," in Louis Filler's summary, "that the fact of efficiency and organization inevitably gave place to the question of whether such a concern had the right to exist."

Few could doubt the combustibility of reform, reformer, and Roosevelt after passage of the Pure Food and Drug Act and the Meat Inspection Act of 1906. For years, Department of Agriculture reformers headed by Harvey Wiley had been pressing for federal legislation to require accurate labeling of foods and drugs. A bill had twice passed the House, but Senate approval had been held up by an alliance of conservative Republicans and Southern Democrats. Aldrich, deriding the "chemists" in the Agriculture Department, claimed that the people's "liberty" was at stake. Then exposés of the patent medicine industry in *Collier's* by Samuel Hopkins Adams and a horrifying portrait of the meat-packing industry by Upton Sinclair in *The Jungle* aroused middle-class public anger to its peak.

Upton Sinclair—a new face on the reform scene. A product of City College of New York and Columbia, Sinclair had been a failed novelist until he produced a novel in which a failed novelist committed suicide. He won more attention with *Manassas,* a Civil War novel, and then took a $500 retainer to visit Chicago's packing industry and write a novel about it. Sick at heart after seven weeks in Packingtown, Sinclair returned to his New Jersey home and poured into *The Jungle* all that he had seen of workers' misery and the industry's nauseating conditions.

Naturally Roosevelt read *The Jungle.* And after a long lecture to the young author in a letter that warned of the perils of socialism and "men of hysterical temperament," he concluded with a handwritten postscript: "But all this has nothing to do with the fact that the specific evils you point out shall, if their existence be proved, and if I have power, be eradicated." Roosevelt's investigations soon proved that existence, and he gained power by threatening to publicize the investigations, pressing key congressmen unmercifully, and after some strenuous give-and-take, settling for essentially the measures he wanted. The food bill made illegal the manufacture, sale, or transportation of adulterated or falsely labeled food and drugs in interstate commerce; the Meat Inspection Act, passed the same day (June 30, 1906), provided for federal inspection of companies selling meats in interstate commerce.

* * *

Buoyed by the winds of reform, propelled by Old Guard opposition and his own reaction to it, Theodore Roosevelt during his last two years in office veered tempestuously to the left. This shift was partly rhetorical, but much of it embraced a series of most explicit proposals to Congress and the public. In December 1906, not content with passage of the Hepburn

bill, he declared that all big business should be subject to federal inspection of its books, publicity of its accounts, and—to the satisfaction of La
Follette—physical valuation of its railroad properties. He called again for
a federal inheritance tax. He urged "compulsory investigation" of major
labor disputes. After having long contended that he was an umpire and
balance wheel between radicalism and conservatism, by 1907 he was, in
George Mowry's words, "trying to keep the left center together."

Left center was far too left for the Republican party of McKinley, Aldrich, and Cannon. Roosevelt's long struggle for conservation sharpened
the divisions between "presidential" and "congressional" Republicans.
Within a year of taking office he was pressing for passage of the Newlands
bill, which would set aside proceeds of public-land sales in states in the
South and West to pay for building and maintaining irrigation projects.
This measure passed despite the noncooperation of Cannon, whose environmental views were summed up in his remark, "Not one cent for scenery." While Congress also passed other conservation measures, Roosevelt relied more on his ample executive power, granted in previous
legislation, to protect the nation's resources by withdrawing lands from
private exploitation, preventing lands from overgrazing, safeguarding forest lands, and curbing the depredations of cattle ranchers, sheepmen,
mining companies, and timber cutters. When, in 1907, Congress amended
an agriculture appropriations bill to ban the creation of new forest reserves
in several western states, Roosevelt, rather than vainly fight the amendment, and with the help of his Chief Forester, Gifford Pinchot, in a series
of "midnight" proclamations added twenty-one more forest reserves just
before signing the amended bill—a foiling of Congress that gave the President immense satisfaction.

Roosevelt could not forget, however, that the main challenge to presidential and popular power came not from the congressional Old Guard or
the parochial interests it represented but from big business. He knew too
that corporate power did not speak with a single voice. Since Roosevelt
tended to personalize that power—indeed, all power—he tended to divide
his business foes into "good guys" and "bad guys," or at least into bad
guys and not-so-bad guys. What he was dealing with, in reality, was the
continuing thrusts of the two capitalisms and their impact on politics.

One man personified Roosevelt's bad capitalism—John D. Rockefeller.
Not only had the oil magnate hired a substitute to serve for him during the
Civil War, he was not a "gentleman" of old family wealth, eastern society,
or college education. More fundamentally, Standard Oil, with its competitive methods and its power over transportation—railroads, pipelines, ships
—was the biggest and most powerful combination of them all. Roosevelt

knew of its reputation for "buying" senators and congressmen; during his 1904 campaign, he piously ordered the return of contributions from officials of Standard Oil. On the basis of investigations by the Bureau of Corporations, which he had persuaded Congress to establish, the President in 1905 reported that Standard Oil had wrung enormous profits from secret rail rates. By 1907, the federal government had seven suits pending against the corporation and its subsidiaries.

Even these challenges to Standard Oil hardly reflected Roosevelt's bitter hostility to Rockefeller and the men he associated with him, such as Edward H. Harriman. Time and again during Roosevelt's full term, his letters and conversations turned into diatribes against their "trickery," "scoundrelism," and sheer evil. He was convinced, moreover, that powerful corporate heads—often vulgar nouveaux riches, to boot—were plotting with their tools in press and bar and pulpit and classroom to gang up on him, discredit him, block his programs. He welcomed the news that Judge Kenesaw Mountain Landis had fined Standard Oil over $29 million for violating the Elkins Act—and doubtless welcomed the ensuing fury in the business world against both the judge and himself.

But he still had to contend with the mighty Morgan, a capitalist of a different color. The banker was, of course, a gentleman with whom one could make arrangements. But he was a gentleman of power—of pervasive national influence and, with his wide international investments, of world stature. And Roosevelt needed such a banker friend in 1907. Worldwide credit expansion and price inflation amid the general prosperity of the time produced strained conditions in money markets in the United States as well as abroad. Rockefeller and other business leaders were already admonishing Roosevelt that the "political adventurer's" attacks on capital were undermining business and risking a slump. After warning signals mounted in the summer, Roosevelt directed his Secretary of the Treasury, George Cortelyou, to work with the House of Morgan to shore up the securities market. When the Knickerbocker Trust Company closed its doors and a run threatened other banks and brokerages, the Morgan people proposed that the United States Steel Corporation be allowed to purchase controlling assets in the Tennessee Coal and Iron Company to prevent a collapse of the whole banking structure.

But there was a hitch: Would such an action violate the antitrust laws? After a hurried trip to Washington through the night, Morgan's men Judge Elbert H. Gary and Henry C. Frick called on the President and gained what they wanted—a statement by Roosevelt "that while of course I could not advise them to take the action proposed, I felt it no public duty of mine to interpose any objection." Thus reassured, the House of Morgan did help rally the market and avert further panic—and then proceeded to add the rich Tennessee coal and iron properties to the vast holdings of Morgan's U.S. Steel.

Roosevelt publicly congratulated "those conservative and substantial businessmen who in this crisis have acted with such wisdom and public spirit," as compared with the bad capitalists' "dishonest dealing and speculative enterprise." Yet to share power on such equal terms even with the Morgans and the other "good" capitalists cost Roosevelt self-esteem, for his esteem for himself was closely allied to his feeling of possessing power to do good. More than ever, now, the issue for him was stronger federal supervision and regulation of big business and big money. In his annual message to Congress in December 1907, he called for an income as well as an inheritance tax, national regulation of interstate business, postal savings banks, and extension of the eight-hour workday to all employees of the federal government and of its contractors. Then, the next month, his sense of desperation and frustration overflowed in what Harbaugh called "one of the most bitter and radical special messages on record."

He struck out at the "representatives of predatory wealth—of the wealth accumulated on a giant scale by all forms of iniquity, ranging from the oppression of wage workers to unfair and unwholesome methods of crushing out competition, and to defrauding the public by stock jobbing and the manipulation of securities." Last year's panic, he said, had been caused not by the Administration but by the "speculative folly and the flagrant dishonesty of a few men of great wealth." He then even named the heads of the Standard Oil Company and the Santa Fe Railroad as examples of men who had fought with unlimited money and unscrupulous craft every measure for honesty in business that had been passed during his Administration.

To Roosevelt, the cure for all this was not to break big business down into small, inefficient units through trust-busting, but strong, steady, central federal control, with big business serving at best as junior partner. But there was a fateful contradiction in his views. How could a political and governmental system as deeply corrupted as the American exert effective and responsible control over the corporations whose influence reached into every sector of American life? No one had excoriated that system more sharply than Roosevelt. In this very special message, he had denounced politicians as well as editors and lawyers who were "purchased" by big business and were "but puppets who move as the strings are pulled." How could he propose putting corporations under the control of legislators who tended to be either radical extremists or corporate pawns, under judges who, on the one hand, "truckled" to the mob or, on the other, failed to "stop the abuses of the criminal rich"? If neither legislature nor judiciary could do the job, who could?

Roosevelt's answer to this question was of course the executive branch, the presidency, or really himself. He had been vigilant in fighting off what he viewed as excessive judicial or congressional control of policy-making bureaucrats. Yet he could hardly contend that the small, patronage-ridden, graft-tainted executive branch could handle the enormous task of corporate control. The most potentially powerful national organization that might deal with collective corporate power on at least equal terms was the Republican party, with its own roots in virtually every locality outside the South. But the GOP, with its hundreds of competing leaders in Congress, the executive, and the states, represented inchoate strength at best, and Roosevelt had done little with it other than use it to protect and enhance his personal authority.

This left the presidency as the only feasible means of corporate control, and no one had greater confidence in the integrity, wisdom, and determination of Theodore Roosevelt than Theodore Roosevelt. Yet he knew that "one-man" presidential power was anathema to most Americans. The Revolutionists of 1775–83 had revolted in large part against executive "tyranny"; the constitution makers of 1787–89 had hemmed in the chief executive with a host of checks and balances; some of the great moments of American history had seen "liberty-loving" legislators and citizens pitted against governors and Presidents. Not since Lincoln had a President exploited his constitutional and extraconstitutional authority as intensively as had Roosevelt, or made fuller use of his presidential powers of publicity—"the bully pulpit"—and the arts of bargaining, rewarding, punishing, conniving, co-opting, persuading, threatening, manipulating, cooperating, of the strategy of almost indiscriminate use of the carrot and the stick.

Lincoln had civil war as an excuse; Roosevelt had no war. But he had a temperament, and this was the problem. Increasingly, during his years in the White House, he exhibited the kind of volatility, emotionalism, anger, and overreactiveness, and indulged in the type of self-aggrandizement through personal politicking and policy-making, that had always worried prudent republicans about executive excess. At a Gridiron Club dinner in April 1906, he had suddenly and unaccountably turned on his journalistic reform friends and foes by branding them as "muckrakers," meaning the person who "never thinks or speaks or writes, save of his feats with the muck-rake" and hence became "not an incitement to good" but "one of the most potent forces for evil." At a later Gridiron Club affair, Roosevelt castigated senators to their faces on their lack of respect for the presidential office, only to be handed a senatorial lecture in return on presidential respect for the Senate; then he stalked out.

Some of his aberrations seemed more quixotic than dangerous. He campaigned for "simplified spelling" and even ordered the government printer to use "nite" and "thoro" until the House of Representatives instructed the printer otherwise. He lashed out at "nature-fakirs" who imputed human qualities to animals; it was not the sort of thing a President should do, he admitted, but "I . . . proved unable to contain myself." Neither did one of the "fakirs," who denied that Roosevelt was a naturalist: "Every time Mr. Roosevelt gets near the heart of a wild thing he invariably puts a bullet through it."

But the most poignant and significant of Roosevelt's aberrations was the "Brownsville affair." A gang of black soldiers quartered near this Texas town conducted a wild midnight raid in which a white bartender was killed. The President ordered the incident investigated, but when no one in the whole black regiment would talk, he directed that the entire complement be "discharged without honor" and "forever barred from enlistment." This punishment of 160 men—including six Medal of Honor winners— without a trial, military or civil, left a stain on the record of a man who had brooked Southern fury by having Booker T. Washington to dinner at the White House, appointed or reappointed worthy blacks to federal positions over much white opposition, and in general tried to accord blacks as much recognition and status as the political situation allowed. All was forgotten during the furor over Brownsville.

To the critics of Roosevelt's abuse of executive power, he had one compelling answer: a President did not govern for life, he had only three or four years to do his work, and then had to yield. And Roosevelt's term was to end March 4, 1909. The President had long since selected William Howard Taft as the best candidate to succeed him, and now he stuck to that commitment despite his conviction—which he did not conceal—that he himself could have the nomination by merely lifting his finger. Taft would indeed serve as a check on Rooseveltian power, for he dropped many of Roosevelt's people, pursued an intensive trust-busting policy in which Roosevelt had little faith, and allied himself with the conservative elements of the Republican party in Congress and country that Roosevelt had battled.

All this lay in the future. For the moment, Roosevelt could leave office knowing that he had been a vigorous and effective leader. If he had not solved the enigma of how a representative republic deals with concentrated economic power, at least he had sharply posed the issue and offered some answers. If he had not solved the questions of the role of strong leadership in a democracy, of the role of party in stabilizing and empowering leadership, of the powerful veto power left in the hands of the Congress and of the judiciary, at least he had made people think about these questions.

And possibly he had helped avert tumult and rebellion. After Mr. Dooley had told his friend Hennessey that he was reading so much about graft that he had to lock "th' cash dhrawer" at night, Hennessey claimed to have even sniffed a revolution. Mr. Dooley hastened to reassure him:

"Th' noise ye hear is not th' first gun iv a rivolution. It's on'y th' people iv th' United States batin' a carpet."

CHAPTER 10

The Cauldron of Leadership

T HE rising winter storm outside seemed hardly to chill the spirits of a small group gathered in the White House on the eve of March 4, 1909. The next day William Howard Taft would be inaugurated as twenty-seventh President of the United States, and President Roosevelt had invited the President-elect and Mrs. Taft to stay overnight in the home they would occupy for at least four years. Around the table in the State Dining Room the talk ran fast and free, punctuated by Roosevelt's high-pitched chortling and Taft's huge booming laughter.

The two Republican leaders had much to celebrate. Their party had won all but two presidential elections since the Civil War. It had turned back the spellbinding Bryan three times. Republicans utterly dominated the legislatures of a swath of Northern states. The party had produced a series of leaders ranging from the safe and solid to the statesmanlike and even innovative. Symbolizing the power and continuity of the Grand Old Party on this very evening was the presence of Elihu Root, McKinley's Secretary of War, Roosevelt's Secretary of State, now with six years ahead as senator from New York.

Yet all was not well that March evening under the bright chandeliers of the dining room. Taft was apprehensive about being President; he had wanted an administrative and especially a judicial career. He admired Roosevelt's political skill and sheer energy but had neither the desire nor the ability to become a strenuous President in the Teddy Roosevelt mold. He agreed with virtually all of Roosevelt's policies, but not always with the rambunctious way the President had pursued them; and, like other party leaders, he had been worried by Roosevelt's sharp turn to the left in the year or two just past. As for Roosevelt, he liked "Will," this big hearty jovial fellow who had served him so well in the Cabinet and provided warm personal encouragement. In endorsing Taft, he had said that rarely had two public men "ever been so much at one in all the essentials of their beliefs and practices." He expected that his chosen heir would carry on his policies. But he had doubts about Taft's resolution and commitment.

"He's all right," the President said to Mark Sullivan when the reporter had stopped in earlier that day. "He means well and he'll do his best. But he's weak. They'll get around him. They'll"—the President put his shoulder against Sullivan's and pushed—"they'll lean against him." But neither the new nor the retiring President expressed his misgivings to the other. In the morning, as they sat down to breakfast, a heavy snow was falling outside, and Roosevelt exclaimed to Taft that he had known there would be a blizzard when he went out, but it would be over as soon as "I can do no further harm to the Constitution." Taft said: "It is my storm. I always knew it would be a cold day when I became President of the United States."

Within a year, friends of the two men were drawing them apart. Within two years, they would become mortal political enemies, and within three, each would have killed the other politically. Neither man had expected such a fight. Neither man wanted it. Their gunplay at the high noon of Republicanism emerged from conflicts of personality, economic interests, political institutions, and—above all—ideology.

TAFT, TR, AND THE TWO REPUBLICAN PARTIES

Taft proposed to be a party unifier and moderate. He was well aware that the Grand Old Party embraced two sets of traditions, leaderships, loyalties, and doctrines. But even Taft, a shrewd appraiser, could not fully comprehend how wide was the gulf between the party regulars, under their conservative Old Guard leadership, and the progressives or reformers or insurgents, as they were variously called, carrying on the great mugwump tradition of part of the party. Nor could he see that this gulf was deepening when he entered the White House, even apart from any threat from Theodore Roosevelt, who was leaving for a long trip to stalk lions in Africa and potentates in Europe.

For a time, Taft followed a wavering middle course between the party regulars and progressives. He planned to continue the Square Deal policies, to ask Congress for tariff revision downward, to administer existing reform legislation, such as antitrust, more tenaciously—though less flamboyantly—than Roosevelt had. On the other hand, he kept some distance from the progressive leadership; he cramped his exercise of authority because of his deeply held views as to constitutional limitations on presidential power; and he filled his Cabinet with corporation lawyers, conspicuously replacing the Roosevelt men. And all the while, he sought to propitiate the absent Teddy and his present friends.

Taft's middle way was doomed from the start. He was dealing not simply with two wings of the party, which could be kept in harness through long accepted ways of distributing patronage and moderating policy; he was confronting two diverging structures—leadership-followership structures.

The Old Guard leadership was rooted in the regular party organizations stretching across the North, in the federal and state officials who lived off patronage, in the malapportioned and gerrymandered state legislatures that overrepresented conservative rural areas and elected standpatters to the United States Senate, in the party offices and committee chairmanships in Congress. The Old Guard regulars had consolidated their power year after year because of the huge majorities they had rolled up over Democratic candidates, and during the first years of the new century they were still at the apogee of their power.

The progressive leadership spoke for a new breed of mugwumps, entrenched in some states and districts, especially in the West, but emerging mainly from the nation's growing professional and business elements both East and West. Most of them born and bred Republicans, they had often kept their distance from country populists, silverites, and labor groups, but many still passionately embraced the old causes of political purity and mugwump reform. By 1909, this was the party of the Square Deal, headed by Roosevelt and his reform leaders in Washington and the states.

The stiffest challenge to Taft's middle way was posed by the progressives' attack on Cannonism and Aldrichism. In the House, Joe Cannon, after six years in the speakership, had established an autocratic leadership that rivaled Czar Reed's of old. A bantam rooster of a man, as coarse in manner as he was reactionary in doctrine, Cannon controlled the committee system through his power to hand out choice committee memberships. Taft disliked both Cannon and Cannonism, and might have heeded the rumblings of George Norris and other progressives who planned to strip the Speaker of his appointing powers. But the President crumbled when Cannon and Senator Nelson Aldrich warned him to his face that a defeat for Cannon would jeopardize the President's program, especially tariff revision.

Rather, they offered him a deal: if the President stood by Cannon, the Speaker would help carry out the Republican platform. Taft agreed, to the consternation of the insurgents; soon he was out on the hustings, embracing Aldrich politically and Cannon literally. Then he had to stand by helplessly as the Speaker stripped rebel congressmen of choice committee assignments and continued to promote his own brand of Republicanism.

Later Roosevelt would attack Taft for his "bungling leadership," which Roosevelt blamed for splitting the party. Taft was indeed inept in dealing with other politicians, especially progressive leaders. But he was no fool. He simply lacked the personal qualities necessary to carry out his strategy of "party unity." To maintain links with both wings, to play one group against the other, to avoid alienating either side for good, called for rocklike self-confidence, unflagging energy, a firm direction, and a willingness to exploit and even expand presidential power. These strengths were not Taft's. He lacked the steady willpower and purpose that enables strong leaders, with all their twists and turns, to move toward their goals; rather, as Secretary of Commerce and Labor Charles Nagel remarked, Taft had only the stubbornness of the uncertain man.

He was indolent, too; his personal political voltage was not high and steady enough to energize the circuits of power leading out of the White House. Doubtless, part of the problem was his sheer corpulence, though by a mighty effort he had reduced his weight from 326 to 250 pounds. He believed that the Constitution restricted presidential power, and this inhibited him from "interfering" in the bill-making process during the early crucial stages on the Hill. He was too high-minded to use some of Roosevelt's blustering, bullying methods; and he lacked what Mowry called Roosevelt's catlike political touch.

The more Taft succumbed to the Old Guard embrace, the more he was caught in the network of obligations and pressures surrounding the congressional party. He became more psychologically dependent on the Old Guard too. "When you and Senator Aldrich are both absent from the Senate," the President wrote to the extreme right-wing Senator Hale of Maine in June 1910, "I yearn for the presence of an old parliamentary hand." To Aldrich he wrote: "I long for your presence." He was on such good terms with the Old Guard leadership that when Chauncey Depew in a jocular mood put his hand on the President's huge stomach and asked, "What are you going to name it when it comes?" Taft shot back, "Well, if it is a boy, I'll call it William; if it's a girl, I'll call it Theodora; but if it turns out to be just wind, I'll call it Chauncey!"

Taft's marriage of convenience with the Old Guard helped bring him some major legislative victories during his first two years in the White House. Congress passed a controversial tariff act which Taft absurdly termed the best bill ever passed by the Republican party; the Mann-Elkins Act placing telephone and telegraph companies under the Interstate Commerce Commission; a postal savings bank law; and the Mann Act prohibiting interstate transportation of women for immoral purposes. But the more Taft compromised with the regulars to pass his bills, the more he frayed the frail cords still connecting him with the progressives.

*   *   *

Theodore Roosevelt returned home in June 1910. He was fifty-one, restless, and jobless. He was apprehensive about Taft and the political situation, about himself and his ability to resist the siren call of ambition and power. His reception in New York—a welcome by the battleship *South Carolina,* a twenty-one gun salute followed by bugle calls, a reunion with his kinsfolk, including his young niece Eleanor and her husband Franklin, and a monster parade up Broadway headed by Rough Riders—boosted his self-esteem without slaking his ambition. And as he settled back into Oyster Bay life and met with old political cronies, his moral indignation began to accelerate.

Even while in Africa, runners had brought him news of Taft's dalliance with the Old Guard. Roosevelt's United States Forester, Gifford Pinchot, had intercepted the former President in Paris with a long bill of complaints from outraged progressives. In particular, Pinchot had filled his ears about the most sensational political issue that had boiled up during Roosevelt's absence—Taft's sacking of Pinchot after the forester publicly attacked Taft's Interior Secretary, Richard A. Ballinger, for harming conservation in order to aid corporate interests. Republican regulars, including Roosevelt's old and close friend Senator Henry Cabot Lodge of Massachusetts, urged on him that any man who publicly attacked his superior was asking to be fired, but to Roosevelt it was a moral issue.

For a time, Roosevelt, despite his rising feeling, tried to follow a moderate and middle way. He could not forget his longtime friendship with good old Will, and he preferred not to antagonize the rank-and-file Republican regulars; yet progressive leaders were pressing him to move against the Old Guard. He tried to be a "regular with a conscience," staying in touch with regulars like Lodge and with Taft, whom he placed in that category, while pouring out his progressive views in speeches and correspondence. But his heart was no longer in moderation or centrism. He had never had a more unpleasant summer, he told Root.

Roosevelt could no more keep to his middle course than Taft had been able to a year earlier. His indignation soared as Taft moved into closer embrace with the Old Guard. He now dismissed his successor as a man who had been a good first lieutenant but was not fit to be captain. Taft's shift toward the right had left a leadership vacuum and progressives were now turning to Roosevelt to supply it. A "Roosevelt party" indeed stretched across the country, founded in the moralistic mugwump tradition, rooted in the nation's social and political fabric, and fully equipped with its own ideology and platform, zealous troops, and an unemployed hero.

From the grass roots of this Roosevelt party came seductive words of praise and even more seductive calls of moral duty. In January 1911: "On the trains and in the hotels, you are the main subject under discussion"—people now "awaken to a realization of what you were trying to do for the people." "Don't attempt to thwart the spontaneous movement for you."

"I trust and admire you more every year"—this from editor William Allen White. "Will you lead in the formation of a new party [that will] break the solid South?" By 1912, the appeals—and invitations to speak—had risen from a trickle to a torrent. Even a former President "is not big *enough*" to decline a nomination which comes to him "unsought." He should brush aside the "third term phantom—you were only elected once and you did not serve two full terms." "It is God's will that you be our next President."

All that was needed now was the spark to bring this movement to life. That spark was struck from Roosevelt's smoldering ambition. Into his letters during 1911 crept a note that betrayed his appetite for leadership and power even as he tried to contain it. "I very emphatically feel that to me personally to be nominated in 1912 would be a calamity," he wrote in a typical letter of 1911. But then came the giveaway sentence: "Moreover I am absolutely certain that it would be criminal folly under any circumstances to nominate me unless it could be made clear as day that the nomination came not through intrigue or political work, not in the least to gratify any kind of wish or ambition on my part, but simply and solely because the bulk of the people wanted a given job done, and for their own sakes, and not for mine, wanted me to do that job." Elihu Root astutely compared his old chief to a "thirsty sinner."

While Roosevelt invited the call that was sure to come, opposition was looming on the left. By 1910, Robert La Follette had become the acknowledged leader of western progressives in the Senate. La Follette met the Alger image in politics: born in a two-room cabin in Wisconsin pioneer country, he had worked his way through the University of Wisconsin, served as a horseback district attorney, and was making his way through the power system of the House of Representatives as a run-of-the-mill congressman when he rebelled against the reactionary Republican establishment in Congress and back home and struck out on his own progressive course. As perhaps the most effective governor of his time, he had forced through an opposition legislature measures for an industrial commission to protect the health and safety of labor in his state, a railroad commission that slashed rates, a direct primary, and ample money and recognition for the university.

La Follette had created his personal organ, *La Follette's Weekly*, in January 1909; he created his personal organization two years later when he convened a meeting of progressives in his Washington home. The cream of the progressive leadership was present: Norris of Nebraska, Senator Jonathan Bourne of Oregon, Governor Chase S. Osborn of Michigan, bathtub tycoon Charles R. Crane of Chicago, and reformer Frederic C. Howe of New York. These men and Senators Joseph L. Bristow of Kansas and

Moses E. Clapp of Minnesota, and such redoubtables as Congressman Irvine L. Lenroot of Wisconsin and Gifford Pinchot of Pennsylvania, were elected to the leadership of a new organization, the National Progressive Republican League. The aim of the League was announced as the promotion of democratic government and progressive legislation, but politicos and press suspected that it was a vehicle to promote La Follette for President.

Certainly Roosevelt so suspected. He had long been personally friendly with the Wisconsin senator, but had kept a political distance from him. Now he could hardly ignore "Battling Bob," who was the very image of progressive militancy with his eloquent speeches, quick and savage thrusts in debate, and shock of bristling hair crowning photogenic features and a sturdy frame. Roosevelt moved warily, not wanting to alienate rank-and-file progressive leaders in the West. Some of these leaders had supported La Follette on the premise that Roosevelt was unavailable; as the former President inched toward availability, La Follette suffered serious defections.

In vain the La Follette forces sought to stem the Roosevelt tide. Warning the former President that Taft delegates would carry Nebraska because of division in progressive ranks, Norris asked Roosevelt to support La Follette delegates—or at least not oppose them. If later La Follette failed of nomination, the Wisconsin's delegates would shift toward Roosevelt. Would Roosevelt announce categorically his noncandidacy? Roosevelt would not.

The denouement came unexpectedly in early February 1912, when La Follette, himself ill and exhausted, and with his daughter facing a serious operation, gave a speech in Philadelphia to a dinner audience of publishers and politicians that included such luminaries as Alexander Graham Bell, Lincoln Steffens, and Governor Woodrow Wilson of New Jersey. As the six hundred banqueters watched first indignant, then astonished, and finally embarrassed, La Follette, after vitriolically attacking the press, the bankers, and the interests, lost control of himself and simply ranted for over two hours. After the press caricatured La Follette as having had a mental breakdown, a number of progressive leaders found the episode a good reason—or excuse—for shifting to their true love, their "colonel."

And by now their true love was ready. For Roosevelt, the decision to run had not been as easy as the press suspected. Certainly he wanted to beat Taft and the Old Guard. But he did not wish to do so at the risk of sending La Follette or even Bryan to the White House. And he could not forget the prospect of 1916. If he supported Taft and in the end the President lost, as Roosevelt expected he would, TR would stand well with the regulars, and, backed by his progressive followers, he could take over the GOP after some incompetent Democrat served one term. If Taft won in 1912, Roosevelt could still succeed him after the President's second term.

Oddly, it was Taft who forced the issue, as much as Roosevelt. During 1911, he mobilized the congressional Old Guard and the rank-and-file regulars with promises, patronage, and portents. With its usual lack of skill, the Taft White House took a number of steps bound to infuriate the thin-skinned Roosevelt. A few days before Roosevelt announced, Taft wrote his brother that the former President was "surrounded by so many sycophants and neurotics who feed his vanity and influence his judgment that his usual good political sense is at fault in respect of the election." Such provocations from Taft were not slow to reach the ears of his predecessor.

Rising differences over issues, bolstered by each man's followers and sharpened by ambition and self-esteem, lay at the center of the escalating conflict between the two old comrades. Of all Roosevelt's heresies, the one that Taft found most incomprehensible and unforgivable was his proposal for the people's power to recall judicial decisions. For Taft, judicial power and independence were almost sacrosanct. He had vetoed the admission of Arizona because of a provision in its constitution authorizing the recall of judges. (The astute Arizonans removed the offending clause, gained admission to statehood in February 1912, and later restored the provision.) Roosevelt's call, in a Columbus speech, for recall of state—but not federal—judicial decisions roused Taft to hyperbole. Such extremists, he said, were "political emotionalists or neurotics" who would cause "bubbling anarchy." Since calling his enemies lunatics or neurotics had long been one of Roosevelt's own specialties, he could not help being infuriated by the charge.

Each man worked from his political base. For Taft, this was the great pyramid of local and state parties, fueled by corporate money, secured by patronage, and long accustomed to the business of choosing the right delegates to state and national conventions. Early, and as quietly as they could, the Taft managers picked loyalists as delegates to the 1912 Republican convention, while Roosevelt men vainly howled in protest against the shenanigans in smoke-filled rooms. Roosevelt's strength lay—as he was not slow to point out—in the hundreds of thousands of "plain Republicans" who had embraced the party's progressive tradition. In this, the first election in which the direct primary was extensively used, Roosevelt after some initial setbacks rolled up 1.2 million votes against 760,000 for Taft and 350,000 for La Follette.

But delegates counted in the convention, not primary votes, and it

seemed likely weeks before the conclave that Taft had it sewed up. Characteristically, Roosevelt resolved to carry his fight into the convention. By
now, the two sides were excelling mainly in invective. Roosevelt men called
Taft men crooks and robbers, apaches and garroters, for issuing credentials to bogus delegates risen from the "cesspools of Southern corruption," while Taft men responded in kind, and Taft and Roosevelt labeled
each other demagogue and fathead, respectively. When the Taft forces
selected Elihu Root as their man for convention chairman, Roosevelt forgot the old days when he had singled out Root as the very model of an
American statesman. Now he was a "representative of reaction" and had
to be rejected.

Mr. Dooley forewarned that the convention would be a "combynation
iv th' Chicago fire, Saint Bartholomew's massacres, the battle iv th' Boyne,
th' life iv Jessie James, an' th' night iv th' big wind," but he was going
anyway, because he hadn't "missed a riot in this neighborhood for forty
years." The convention opened amid fisticuffs, charges of "liar" and
"thief," and tumult so noisy that even the shrillest speechifiers were
drowned out. Amid the pandemonium, the Taft steamroller did its work,
producing a 558 to 502 win for Root that meant the President's men would
control the convention. While Roosevelt men walked out or sat on their
hands, the convention proceeded to nominate William Howard Taft,
whose name was put forward by a small-town Ohio editor, Warren
Gamaliel Harding.

Roosevelt was prepared for his defeat and for a bolt. He had already
given his nomination speech the night before the convention, to a hysterical crowd of thousands that overflowed a hall and into the street, ending
with a prophecy: "We stand at Armageddon," he trumpeted, "and we
battle for the Lord."

WILSON AND THE THREE DEMOCRATIC PARTIES

Delegates were starting to leave their convention hall, an opera house
in Trenton, late on a September afternoon in 1910, when they heard an
unexpected announcement from the rostrum: Mr. Wilson, "candidate for
the governorship, *and the next President of the United States,* has received word
of his nomination; has left Princeton, and is now on his way to the Convention." Soon a tall bespectacled man in a dark gray sack suit was making his
way to the stage through cheering ranks of New Jersey Democrats. "God,
look at that jaw!" a ward politician exclaimed. Not all the Democrats
cheered; a group of reform Democrats sat glumly on their hands as they
reflected that the bosses had beaten them once again, this time with a

college professor. Most of the delegates were simply curious, never having seen Wilson before or perhaps even heard of him.

Within a few minutes the man from Princeton was transporting the crowd into a fever of enthusiasm. He electrified the reformers at the start by declaiming, "As you know, I did not seek this nomination. It has come to me absolutely unsolicited. With the consequence that I shall enter upon the duties of the office of Governor, if elected, with absolutely no pledge of any kind to prevent me from serving the people of the State with singleness of purpose." Scenting victory in November, the regulars too kept applauding. Wilson placed himself squarely behind the progressive platform the delegates had adopted, save for the direct primary, which he did not mention. Out of the ranks of the reformers came the cry, "Thank God, at last, a leader has come!"

"Go on, go on," delegates shouted when Wilson halted, and the orator did. Americans must reconstruct their economic order, he said, and in doing so would reconstruct their political structure. Then delegates rushed up to the platform to greet him, to lift him to their shoulders—but even the exultant speaker would not go this far. Next day the press across the country was hailing a new star in the political firmament.

It was Woodrow Wilson's first political speech—and a moment he had been anticipating for decades. As a young man, he had devoured Houghton Mifflin's *American Statesmen* series and its tales of the great orators. As a young professor at Wesleyan, he had tried to convert the debating society into a House of Commons. In his first academic writings, he had called for better parliamentary debates. He had indeed become one of the most accomplished and renowned college lecturers of his time.

And now he had held spellbound the political folk he was so eager to recruit. Still, for Wilson, oratory was a vehicle of leadership, not the heart of it. And leadership was the essence of true statesmanship. These were not pieties. By now, he had become the nation's leading student of the complex phenomenon of leadership. Public opinion, he felt, had to be educated and persuaded by a forceful leader who, in John Blum's summary, could perceive the inchoate desires of the community and formulate them in broad, clear, convincing arguments, and such leaders would possess poetic insights and talents. But for Wilson this was by no means a one-way process. Leaders led followers in order to mobilize and empower them. "All the renewal of a nation," he said, "comes out of the general mass of its people."

"The ear of the leader must ring with the voices of the people," Wilson had told a Tennessee audience twenty years before this triumphant evening in Trenton. "The forces of the public thought may be blind: he must lend them sight; they may blunder; he must set them right." Twelve years later, he wrote a memorandum on leadership that anticipated theory about and analysis of the subject over the next sixty years. Leadership, he said, "is the practicable formulation of action, and the successful arousal and guidance of motive in social development." Only by the action of leading minds was the organic will of a community stirred to a guiding control of affairs.

Leadership was not an end in itself. It was a means of realizing a people's elevated values, a nation's noblest goals. Nor was leadership a one-man show. The most effective leadership in the long run was collective—and this was one reason Wilson, in contrast to many of the educated persons he knew, believed in the indispensable role of strong parties in a democracy. He had long admired the superb debates, the orderly conflict, and the collective cabinet leadership of the two big British parties.

Who was this practitioner and theorist of leadership? some were asking after the triumph in Trenton. The man who had come to embrace an almost philosophical view of purposeful, high-minded leadership had spent his first twenty-five years in a condition of outward serenity and inner turbulence. Born in Virginia in 1856 into a religious and intellectual family, he did not learn his alphabet until he was nine or read well until he was eleven, probably as a result of a form of dyslexia. Undoubtedly this aroused considerable anxiety in his most literate and formidable father, a theologian and minister of the Presbyterian gospel, and a perfectionist as to the use of words. Sigmund Freud, with William Bullitt, theorized that Wilson's "alienation from the world of reality" related to his religious feelings, that a passionate love of his father was at the core of his emotional life, that he probably exhibited extensive narcissism as a child, that he developed a hostility to his father which he repressed, but which broke out against father substitutes—rival leaders. Much later, Alexander and Juliette George hypothesized that power for Wilson was a means of compensation for self-esteem damaged in childhood. He could indulge his secret desire to dominate only by purifying his leadership, "by committing it to political projects which articulated the highest moral and idealistic aspirations of the people." He had to feel virtuous.

The presidency of Princeton gave Wilson the opportunity to lead, and he seized it greedily. He promptly recruited fifty top-notch young teachers and some older and most distinguished ones. In 1905, he appointed the first Jew to the faculty and four years later the first Catholic. He instituted the preceptorial system. He immensely expanded Princeton's physical plant. He raised an institution that was essentially at the level of excellent small colleges like Dartmouth and Williams to that of excellent universities like Harvard, Yale, and Chicago, John Cooper has noted. He did these things not alone but in close cooperation with trustees and faculty. He failed in two efforts: to convert the Princeton eating clubs into a more democratic and educationally effective system, and to locate a proposed graduate college in close proximity to undergraduates and teachers.

Wilson was later accused of inviting these two failures by being rigid and dogmatic. Yet these qualities—renamed consistency, determination, persistence, and principled leadership—helped make him a transforming leader at Princeton. And all these qualities reappeared in Wilson's governorship of New Jersey during 1911, his first year in the post. He won the governorship by a most skillful mobilization of progressive and reform Democratic support without alienating the big-city bosses who had arranged his nomination in the first place. He then proceeded, by a careful combination of high principle and low expediency, to put through the program that he and his party had promised. During 1912, his legislative leadership faltered, in part because the Republicans had won control of the legislature, in part because Wilson was turning to the national political battle—but not because there was any discernible falling off of his ability to combine doggedness and flexibility.

*   *   *

The national arena—and especially the national Democracy—confronted Wilson with far severer challenges than Princeton or New Jersey. Not only was he plunging into a battle zone dominated by formidable leaders such as Roosevelt, La Follette, Bryan, and Taft; he was seeking the presidential nomination of a party that was really three parties.

The dominant wing of the Democracy was the party of Bryan and his fellow silverites and agrarians. The former "boy orator of the Platte," now entering his fifties, was still the peerless leader of those who had fought the battle against McKinleyism in 1896 and who had nominated their man for President twice after that. He continued to appeal to the old prohibitionist and moralistic vote, to the western silverites and other insurgents, and to much of the South. Responding to the urban reformism of the decade, he was by 1910 moving toward the left, as he urged adoption of a graduated income tax, governmental ownership of the railroads, woman's suffrage, direct primaries, the initiative, referendum, and recall. He reached out to labor with his denunciation of labor injunction abuses. But while the Nebraskan was still a formidable party leader, few expected that he could bring his personal following over to a true progressive-labor-farmer coalition.

The electoral base of the Democracy still lay in the solid South. The South—even the Southern bourbons—had stuck with Bryanism in 1896;

above all, they offered loyalty, if only because they had no other place to go. The Southern Democracy had recovered with remarkable speed after the Civil War and by 1880 had crowded out the Republicans in most areas except for GOP patronage holders. Later Southern Democrats had taken a far more portentous step. Fearful of the threat to white supremacy and one-party politics that briefly loomed during the Populist years, Southern party leaders, governors, and legislatures destroyed the black political potential by systematically adopting a battery of devices to keep blacks from voting: literacy tests, poll taxes, property requirements, the "grandfather" clause. Southern elites had never been able to place their own man at the head of a presidential ticket, but they still could play a pivotal role in the choice among Northerners.

The heart of the oldest Democratic party—the "party of Jefferson and Jackson"—still beat steadily, if a bit feebly, in the new century. This was the party of presidential nominees Seymour, Tilden, and Cleveland, and a host of Northern governors, senators, and congressmen, largely faithful to sound money, lowered tariffs, and states' rights, to economic individualism, Bill of Rights liberties, laissez-faire, and governmental economy. They made bold bids for the presidency, sometimes carrying the popular vote but less often the electoral college because of the concentration of their vote in the one-party South. The election of 1896 had left this party shattered across the North; only the pride of vindication had survived, as the Clevelandites witnessed the drubbing of the Bryanites. Cleveland himself had died in 1908, a few months before Bryan was beaten for the third time, but he had fought to the end for a conservative Democracy, with unabated attacks on silver Democrats as "confidencemen, sharpers and swindlers."

Buffeted by these divergent party impulses, the Democracy had teetered between acquiescence in the power of the burgeoning industrial and financial elites, and challenging that power, and ended up doing neither. If the Republicans were now "firmly established as the party of rapid industrialization," as Everett Carll Ladd concludes, the Democrats failed to take clear leadership of the loyal opposition. The Populists of 1892 could condemn both parties for drowning "the outcries of a plundered people" with a "sham battle" over the tariff. But even on the issue of protectionism—the ancient rallying ground of the Democracy—the party of Jefferson and Cleveland failed to offer a strong and united opposition. When Taft called for tariff revision in 1909, House and Senate Democrats defected from their party's 1908 antitariff pledges and backed protection for lumber, hides, pelts, barley, and other products of rural counties. In the struggle over the Payne-Aldrich tariff, the press labeled the

Democracy as leaderless in the House, utterly factionalized in the Senate.

It was this party that Woodrow Wilson confronted in 1912—a party that he quite consciously planned to win over to his support, then to use first to win the presidency, then to govern the nation. To a degree, he embodied both the strengths and weaknesses of the divided Democracy. A native Virginian who could remind Southerners about his upbringing in Georgia and South Carolina, he had never established a clear identity with that section. An antimachine reformer of the old *Nation* school, he had smoothly accepted the backing of some of New Jersey's most notorious bosses in order to win the governorship, just as Cleveland and the rest had welcomed machine support in earlier days. Increasingly progressive during the muckraking decade, he had established few ties with organized labor, Bryanites, or urban reformers.

Nor was Wilson fully aware of the political forces heating up on the socialist left. Out of their fiery and fractious movements the socialists had forged a political party that was still rent with ideological and personal divisions but strong enough to arouse leftist hopes of eventual victory. For years, socialist parties had been nominating presidential candidates, receiving a scattering of votes, but the Socialist Party of the United States, founded in 1901, appeared to be better led, organized, and financed. And it had a candidate with wide appeal to labor in Eugene Debs. In 1904, the homegrown Indiana radical had won 400,000 votes for President. Four years later, he had crisscrossed the nation in his own railroad train, equipped with his portrait on the front of the boiler, a brass band, and a baggage car filled with campaign propaganda—a train soon dubbed the "Red Special." He had won only a few thousand more votes than in 1904, but socialists vowed that 1912 would be their big election year.

And now it was 1912, and the Socialist party had never appeared so popular and promising. In eight years, the dues-paying membership had soared from 20,000 to a peak of 135,000; the national office budget was almost $100,000, and the party planned to spend another $60,000 or so on the campaign. At its May 1912 convention in Indianapolis, the party once again chose Debs as its standard-bearer, over the opposition of the moderates. Good socialists were now united behind their spellbinding candidate and behind a radical, hard-hitting party platform full of biting attacks on the two "capitalistic" parties and glowing promises to the nation's toilers.

*   *   *

Governor Wilson's moral and political leadership in New Jersey had brought him national press attention, but he needed far more than this to win the nomination of the tripartite Democracy. And he faced formidable rivals in each wing—Alabama's Oscar Underwood, eager to prove that a true-blue Southerner could at last become President; Missouri's Champ Clark, Speaker of the House, strict party man, and longtime Bryanite who even in his country attire and rustic ways seemed to resemble the Commoner; and a host of Northern favorite sons. Moral standing hardly helped in winning the backing of countless bosses and delegates who viewed the convention as a trading house for future patronage and other favors. Nor did morality help in dealing with Polish, Hungarian, and other groups who denounced Wilson for slurs against immigrants in his *History of the American People.* Wilson not only apologized to the ethnic leaders but promised to instruct his publisher to change the offending passages in the next printing. The governor writhed under the hatchet blows of William Randolph Hearst—himself an expert at political acrobatics—who labeled the "Professor" a "perfect jackrabbit of politics, perched upon his little hillock of expediency," keenly alert to every scent or sound, "and ready to run and double in any direction."

Expediency was the order of the day at the Democratic convention that met in Baltimore late in June 1912, with hopes whetted by Roosevelt's defiance of the GOP a few days before. While Wilson in New Jersey announced that he would not honor any trading done in his name—the same announcement Lincoln had made fifty-two years earlier during his party's convention in Chicago—the governor's lieutenants in Baltimore went about the time-honored task of wheeling and dealing. It took the Peerless Leader himself to rouse the convention from pragmatics to principle. Renewing his crusade against capitalists allied with Tammany and other machines in the old Cleveland party, Bryan at a tumultuous moment in the proceedings suddenly introduced his motion:

"*Resolved* . . . As proof of our fidelity to the people, we hereby declare ourselves opposed to the nomination of any candidate for president who is the representative of or under obligation to J. Pierpont Morgan, Thomas F. Ryan, August Belmont, or any other member of the privilege-hunting and favor-seeking class."

In the tumult that followed, as Bryan stood immobile before the howling mob, his long slab mouth resolutely closed, some delegates remembered the triumphant moment of '96. But now the roar from the audience contained hate as well, and even Bryan's friends wondered if he was trying to smash the party. After police restored order, Bryan went on to charge that "an effort is being made right now to sell the Democratic party into bondage to the predatory interests of this nation." With one stroke, the Commoner had catalyzed his party.

The balloting of the delegates was almost dull compared to the oratory, as roll call followed roll call without decision. But behind the scenes, in the fabled smoke-filled rooms, a thousand dramas were enacted as the candidates' men baited their hooks with promises of future recognition and influence, state factions traded convention votes to achieve local gains far removed from the contest in Baltimore, charges and countercharges cannonaded out of the several camps, favorite sons tried their luck and failed, all in a smoky atmosphere of hostility and paranoia. Much of the time, chance and contingency had their sway. When Clark gained a majority, Wilson suddenly lost his nerve and wired his manager, William F. McCombs, to release his delegates; McCombs stood fast. Later McCombs lost *his* nerve and gained Wilson's agreement to pull out, but another Wilson man, William G. McAdoo, countermanded the order.

For four days, the convention lay in gridlock as the ballot totals, with glacial slowness, edged toward Wilson. Underwood's men would not give Clark the necessary votes to win because the Southerners hoped that after Clark and Wilson in turn rose and fell, the South would have its chance. Bryan seemed to shift to Wilson when the New York delegation, controlled by Tammany, moved toward Clark, but he made clear he would shift back if New York shifted back; all the while delegates suspected that the Commoner was angling for his own nomination.

When the convention finally broke toward Wilson on the forty-sixth ballot, it was the immediate result of expedient trading by the Wilson men, notably with the boss-controlled Illinois delegation. But the main cause transcended the vast brokerage on and off the convention floor. Powerfully working for Wilson was his fresh image as reformist and progressive. A Democratic convention was not going to choose a reactionary or a machine candidate after a solid decade of ferment and reform. At a crucial moment, Bryan had thrown the convention into a right-left alignment. He had also thrown himself into an alignment with Woodrow Wilson, with major consequences in the days to come.

ARMAGEDDON

Not since the founding years had the nation produced such a galaxy of leaders as those who confronted one another on the hustings of America in the fall of 1912. Not since the Civil War era had the nation found leaders so passionately committed to their causes, so willing to risk the politician's ultimate sacrifice—defeat—in fighting for their goals. Not for many years would Americans forget their glimpses of the men on the stump: Debs, his thin body coiled like a spring, the veins swelling in his forehead, as he reached out to his listeners with moving, imploring hands; Roosevelt, pulsating with energy, grimacing, gesturing, snapping his jaws open and shut, screeching out his denunciations of the two old parties; Wilson, warming to the task as he spoke, vibrant, even impassioned, but disdaining the demagogic or theatrical; Taft, seemingly calm and resolute as he looked out on the crowd from behind his thick white mustache, inwardly despairing of victory and hoping that at least he would place ahead of the man he had come to hate, Theodore Roosevelt.

Nor had Americans ever quite witnessed such a convention as founded the Progressive party and nominated Roosevelt in Chicago in August. Youthful idealists, political opportunists, social reformers, urban planners, patronage seekers, cranks, suffragists, muckrakers were among the 10,000 or more persons, including 1,200 delegates and alternates, who converted the convention hall into an evangelical camp meeting. They gave their hero a rapturous welcome as he strode to the platform to offer his "Confession of Faith." As he stood on the platform in his old familiar style, his body rocked back and forth to the rhythm of the applause.

"Fifteen thousand people roared their welcome," in Mowry's words. "For fifty-two minutes, wildly waving red bandannas, they cheered him as they had never cheered anyone else." When Roosevelt tried to stop them, they broke into song:

> Thou wilt not cower in the dust,
> Roosevelt, O Roosevelt!
> Thy gleaming sword shall never rust,
> Roosevelt, O Roosevelt!

Out of this convention rose the authentic voice of the old Republican conscience—the conscience of the abolitionists, of the crusaders against spoils, of the middle-class respectables who despised the vulgar new rich, of the urban reformers who glimpsed the heightening needs of twentieth-century urban America. Taft had been left with a party of regulars who knew how to use the power of the Republican party for their own purposes. The party conscience had bolted with Roosevelt. But now the Progressives were a party without regulars, a conscience without power. The "old Colonel" who had united the two so brilliantly now found himself commanding cavalry without foot soldiers. No wonder a reporter at the convention noted that he seemed bewildered at the wild welcome of the crowd: "They were crusaders; he was not."

The supporting cast in the campaign that followed was almost as illustrious as the principals. After Jane Addams seconded Roosevelt's nomination, he wrote a friend that he deeply prized her support, though there were "points where I had to drag her forward, notably as regards our battleship program, for she is a disciple of Tolstoi." William Jennings Bryan, old grudges handsomely forgotten, threw himself into Wilson's campaign and ranged the West trailing Roosevelt. Hiram Johnson, chosen Roosevelt's running mate, sought to hold the progressive spotlight in his own California. La Follette came to Wilson's support even while remaining a Republican. The aging Elihu Root, sick at heart over the Republican disruption, spoke for Taft to the degree his failing energies allowed. Norris backed Roosevelt while remaining both a Progressive and a Republican. But seven governors who had supported Roosevelt failed to join the new party because they feared losing the backing of the Republican rank-and-file in their states.

The campaign of 1912 was a confrontation of leadership; even more it was a conflict of ideas. "I have no part to play but that of a conservative," Taft wrote a friend, and he faithfully played that part to the end. He charged the Progressives with planning "dangerous changes in our present constitutional form of representative government and our independent judiciary"—changes that would threaten individual liberty. He inveighed against the pledges of both Democrats and Progressives to direct democracy. "These gentlemen," he said, would cure defects caused by the failure of the public to attend to its political duties by asking that same public to assume three times the burden they had failed to assume. Deserted by most of his Cabinet, who pleaded illness or sat on their hands, Taft stolidly awaited his defeat.

Debs preached a very different kind of liberty and democracy, as he summoned socialists to wrest control of government and industry from the capitalists and make "the working class the ruling class of the nation and the world." But Debs too was plagued by division within his ranks, especially the old split between moderates who pressed immediate demands and revolutionaries who had set their hopes on ultimate goals. Debs preached unity and gained some, but even the great socialist leader could not control his irrepressible followers. Touring the Midwest he encountered the "Ohio yell":

> Ripsaw, ripsaw, ripsaw, bang!
> We belong to the Gene Debs gang.
> Are we Socialists? I should smile!
> We're Revolutionists all the while.

With Debs pounding away on the left and Taft still finding time to play golf, it was Wilson and Roosevelt who fully confronted each other on the most vital questions of liberty and democracy. The debate started abruptly when Wilson, during a long talk at the New York Press Club, said, "Liberty has never come from the government. Liberty has always come from the subjects of government. The history of liberty is a history of the limitation of governmental power, not the increase of it. Do these gentlemen dream that in the year 1912 we have discovered a unique exception to the movement of human history?"

Roosevelt pounced on this statement when he read it in the New York *Tribune* the next day. Calling it the "key to Mr. Wilson's position," he labeled it "professorial rhetoric" without "a particle of foundation in facts," a statement of a "laissez-faire doctrine of the English political economists" of seventy years earlier. It meant that "every law for the promotion of social and industrial justice which has been put upon the statute books ought to be repealed, and every law proposed should be abandoned." Would Wilson propose abolishing the Interstate Commerce Commission?

A cartoon in the Boston *Journal* showed Professor Wilson didactically lecturing to an Uncle Sam trussed up in a straitjacket marked "Limitation on Governmental Power," while the interests and trusts applauded the professor from the sidelines. Wilson struggled to gain the initiative. He favored governmental exercise of power to the utmost, he explained, as long as this meant government "by the power of laws, and not by the power of men." The Democratic party, he began to emphasize, did not stand for limiting either state or national power. "There is not a Democrat that I know who is afraid to have the powers of the government exercised to the utmost."

The candidates' debate over liberty became part of a broader discussion of democracy. Both Wilson and Roosevelt stood on their party platforms, but the Democratic definition of democracy had been woefully weak compared to the Progressives'. Calling for "rule of the people," the Democrats stood only on reforms already achieved—and achieved primarily by others: the overthrow of "Cannonism" and direct election of senators. The Progressives declared also for extension of the direct primary, easier amendment of the Constitution, "equal suffrage to men and women alike," and urged on the states "the short ballot, with responsibility to the people secured by the initiative, referendum and recall." And the Bull Moosers, boldly picking up on Roosevelt's earlier speeches, demanded "such restriction of the power of the courts as shall leave the people the ultimate authority to determine fundamental questions of social welfare and public policy."

Wilson did little to spell out the Democratic plank on democracy. Interrupted during a speech with a question from the floor, "What about the referendum?" he shot back, "The referendum you can take care of in Pennsylvania. It is not a national question." Throughout the campaign, Wilson offered homilies about democracy without clarifying what he meant. An observer remarked on his "vagueness and reiteration, symbolism and incantation," as the chief secrets of his "verbal power." He had mastered the technique of oratory, Alexander and Juliette George noted, he "knew the value of repetition, of catch phrases, of pleasing combinations of sounds." Five or ten thousand people would stand or sit for an hour or so in mainly rapt attention while Wilson elegantly skated over the surface of explicit ideas and specific policy.

Wilson's ideas were much clearer on the most central issue of the campaign—economic policy. He campaigned proudly on the Democratic platform declaration that a "private monopoly is indefensible and intolerable," on its promise to enforce vigorously the criminal as well as the civil law against trusts and trust officials, and on its support of the regulation and possible "prevention of holding companies, of interlocking directors, of stock watering, of discrimination in price, and the control by any one corporation of so large a proportion of any industry as to make it a menace to competitive conditions." The Democrats would also restore the Sherman Antitrust Act to the full power it had had before its evisceration in the courts.

The Progressive party platform was even more positive and forthright, but still lacking in precision. It demanded "a strong National regulation of inter-State corporations." Admitting that business concentration was to some degree necessary and inevitable, it went on: "But the existing concentration of vast wealth under a corporate system . . . has placed in the hands of a few men enormous, secret, irresponsible power over the daily life of the citizen—a power insufferable in a free Government. . . ." The Progressives promised the establishment of a "strong Federal administrative commission" that would use publicity, supervision, and regulation in curbing the power of monopoly. Taft's plank promised to continue his Sherman Act policy toward the trusts, and Debs proposed simply to nationalize them.

With such forthright party positions, the stage seemed set for a four-sided debate over monopoly; but the candidates, in the time-honored way of vote seekers, tended to blur the differences. What had seemed to be a yawning gap between Wilson and Roosevelt—the former's emphasis on breaking down the big trusts into more efficient and responsible small units, versus the latter's on better supervision and regulation of bigness —turned into a vague consensus as Wilson disclaimed any attack on big business as such and Roosevelt indicated he would still use the antitrust weapon.

"You recall Mr. Pierpont Morgan said 'You can't unscramble the eggs in an omelet,' " Roosevelt explained. He overrode the attacks of those who charged—correctly—that one of his key economic advisers and contributors, George Perkins, had deleted a strong antitrust plank from the Progressive platform, and that when the original antitrust plank was inadvertently read to the convention, Perkins got it deleted all over again, and for good. Wilson was now taking the economic advice of the brilliant Boston lawyer Louis Brandeis, who had never met or seen Wilson before the governor was nominated, but found him so promising he even fantasized that Roosevelt might throw his Progressive support to Wilson. It was almost September before Brandeis met the Democratic candidate. They talked for three hours.

"Was very favorably impressed with Wilson," Brandeis wrote his brother Alfred. "He is strong, simple, serious, open-minded, eager to learn." But the lawyer did not yet have a major impact on the candidate's utterances. Wilson was eager to reassure big business that he was not against big business as such, but only irresponsible big business, while for Brandeis the central problem was bigness itself. Still, Brandeis helped Wilson sharpen his ideas and liven up his debate with Roosevelt.

*   *   *

As campaign fever mounted, five, ten, fifteen thousand persons flocked into the political gathering places or watched the candidates parade through town. Racked by fatigue, their voices worn down to a whisper, the candidates pleaded for quiet so that they could reach the outer fringes of the crowds. It seemed as if all America was now part of the campaign. But two large groups had to stand aside—blacks in the South, and women North and South.

Whether to involve Southern blacks had posed the harshest of moral and political dilemmas for Roosevelt. Deeply ambivalent in his attitude toward blacks, he hardly knew what to do about contested Negro delegations that had come to the Progressive party convention because they too had been inspired by the Colonel's commitment to moral leadership and social reform. He tried to solve the problem by approving mixed delegations from border states and lily-white delegations from the South. Thus the Progressives no less than the Republicans would repudiate the legacy of Abolition and Reconstruction. Taft Republicans could sit tight: they controlled most of the anti-Democratic leadership in the South. So could

Wilson, who depended on solid support from Southern segregationists. But militant women suffragists *were* a problem for the governor—especially when a woman named Maude Malone suddenly rose in the audience while he was speaking on monopoly at the Brooklyn Academy of Music.

"Mr. Wilson, you just said you were trying to destroy a monopoly, and I ask you what about woman suffrage. The men have a monopoly on that."

"Woman suffrage, madam, is not a question that is dealt with by the national government at all, and I am here only as a representative of the national party."

"I appeal to you as an American, Mr. Wilson."

"I hope you will not consider it a discourtesy if I decline to answer this question on this occasion. . . ." By now a hubbub was rising in the hall.

"Why do you decline?" Maude Malone persisted. As Wilson answered again, a large detective swooped down on Maude Malone and carried her out. Wilson protested immediately that he did not "wish that the lady should be ejected," and he kept his composure. Maude Malone was hardly in a position to do so.

By mid-October Roosevelt's throat was so raw that he had to cancel some appearances, but he insisted on making a major speech in Milwaukee. As he stepped out of the Gilpatrick Hotel, he waved to admirers and turned to sit down in an open car. At that moment, a man sprang from the darkness, screamed something like "No third term!" and fired a shot at the Colonel. The bullet tore through his overcoat, a metal glasses case, pages of a long speech, and sliced along four inches of his chest wall. As onlookers began to pummel his assailant, Roosevelt called out, "Don't hurt the poor creature." Then he insisted on proceeding to the auditorium.

Unaware of the incident, people there applauded wildly as Roosevelt strode to the platform, then sat back horrified when the chairman announced that the Colonel had been shot. Roosevelt moved up to the rostrum. "There is a bullet in my body," he said in a low, tense tone. "But it is nothing. I'm not hurt badly." He pulled the mangled manuscript from his pocket, lifted it over his head, and proclaimed, "It takes more than that to kill a Bull Moose!"

For over an hour he spoke, faltering at times, pushing away efforts to aid him. Finally taken to a hospital, he announced that he was willing to go down in the cause. "If one soldier who carries the flag is stricken, another will take it from his hands. . . ." It was Roosevelt's most glorious hour. He evoked such a wave of sympathy that pundits hitherto forecasting a Democratic landslide now hedged. Wilson announced that he would suspend talk on national issues until Roosevelt recovered. Wilson himself had tasted the perils of campaigning when a runaway freight train had smashed the observation platform of his Pullman while he slept, and later when the campaign car in which he was speeding hit a deep pothole and he smashed his head against the car roof.

Both candidates were ready for their climactic speeches. In Madison Square Garden, before a roaring crowd, Roosevelt urged his followers not to allow "the brutal selfishness of arrogance and the brutal selfishness of envy, each to run unchecked its evil course. If we do so, then some day smoldering hatred will suddenly kindle into a consuming flame." Proposing to cast out "dead dogmas of a vanished past," he promised to "lift the burdens from the lowly and weary, from the poor and oppressed." He appealed to "the sons of the men who followed Lee no less than to the sons of the men who followed Grant." It was a grand performance.

In the Garden next evening, to an equally fervent crowd, Wilson proclaimed, "We are proposing nothing for these people except what is their due as human beings." He would go about "with the strong hand of government" to see that "nobody imposes on the weak, to see that nobody lowers the levels of American vitality by putting on the working people of this country more than flesh and blood and nerves and heart can bear."

On election day, the voters seemed to suspend their sense of excitement and to settle back into familiar voting patterns. Wilson won 6.3 million votes, less than Bryan had totaled three times, but Bryan had faced only one opponent. Roosevelt with 4.1 million votes and Taft with 3.5 million sliced in two the Republican constituency. Because of the peculiar workings of the electoral college Wilson won 435 electoral votes, Roosevelt 88, mainly from Pennsylvania and the West Coast, and Taft 8—Utah and Vermont. Debs gained an amazing 900,000 votes, but carried no states. The total vote of Democrats, Republicans, and Progressives had hardly increased over the major-party vote of 1908. No fundamental voting shifts had occurred that would be lasting; no major party realignment had occurred. After the smoke of conflict cleared, the political battlefield appeared unchanged.

Roosevelt felt overwhelmed by his defeat. He had expected to lose, he wrote a friend, but not so badly. "We had all the money, all the newspapers and all the political machinery against us and, above all, we had the habit of thought of the immense mass of dull unimaginative men who simply vote according to the party symbol. Whether the Progressive Party itself will disappear or not, I do not know; but the Progressive movement must and will go forward even though its progress is fitful."

To another friend he wrote, "We have fought the good fight, we have kept the faith, and we have nothing to regret."

PART IV
Democracy
on Trial

CHAPTER 11

The New Freedom

T*he Gary Steel Works, Gary, Indiana:* A huge charging machine rumbles past a quarter mile of the new open hearths. The machine pauses by a hearth, the furnace door opens, red and white flames spew out; unperturbed, the charging machine thrusts a carload of pig and scrap metal into the maw as the furnace erupts in a new crescendo of flame and smoke. Behind the pit, a ladle slides into place and 150 tons of molten steel pour into it as the flame now billows into a whirlwind of blue and purple heat.

At the end of a narrow tunnel under Appalachian hills, coal miners slowly drill a hole in the black face with a six-foot auger and pack the hole with dynamite. Crouching in the heading, they set off the blast, then move back to shovel coal into the cars. As they drill and blast and shovel, they push the tunnel forward, shoring up the roof with short pieces of timber they call sprags. The pick mining of old is giving way to cutting machines, and the hand shoveling is yielding to loading machines that, like prehistoric monsters, reach their long thin snouts into the slack. A thousand feet above, managers are lamenting the passing of the "wonderful craftsmen" of old; today, they say, miners need no "great brains" but merely a strong back.

In the spinning room of the Amoskeag Company in Manchester, New Hampshire, long lines of men, women, and children tend more than a hundred thousand spindles. Opened in 1909, the huge spinning room, with its solid banks of milling machines stretching hundreds of yards, looks little different from the Lowell and Lawrence manufactories of six or seven decades earlier. Life in the textile factory has not changed much either—the noise, the heat, the dirty fuzz from the cotton, the long hours and days. But there are more specialized machines now: bale breakers that pick apart the compressed cotton that has been brought to Manchester by railroad; openers that break apart the tufts of cotton more thoroughly; pickers that beat out the coarser impurities in the cotton, until the cotton is ready for carding, combing, roving, spinning, weaving, burling, bleaching, and finishing.

At the big Firestone Tire and Rubber plant in Akron, workers no longer have to pull plies of fabric by hand over the iron forming-core and smooth them down with stiff fingers, layer after layer. Machines feed the fabric into a rotating core, with little wheels on each side precisely stitching the ply. Then men take over, smoothing on a chafer strip of rubberized fabric, applying sidewalls of specially strengthened rubber, laying down a cushion of rubber to bind tread and body. With the new machines, the workers' functions are more specialized and routine now, and the direct labor cost of building a tire is cut in half.

During the progressive era, Americans underwent one of the longest and most expansive periods of prosperity in their history, interrupted only by short recessions in 1903 and 1907. Gold flowed into the capital markets from Alaska, South Africa, and the Rockies; immigrants flowed in from Europe, sometimes more than a million in a year. A steady rise in wholesale prices between 1897 and 1914 helped fuel heavy industrial growth and agricultural output. The prophets of capitalism were exultant. Yet during the same years the currents of progressive thought and action ran strong, perhaps because the fulfillment of some people's basic needs—especially those of the burgeoning middle class—aroused "higher" needs of self-esteem, including the sense of moral self-fulfillment involved in "doing good."

To American Marxists, applying the Master's teachings in their own way and for their own purposes, the mighty economic and social forces rolling in America were predictable and inescapable. Evolving technology—the new inventions, mass production, industrial integration—inevitably forced wider and deeper economic combination. Corporate capitalism, crushing the workers in its industrial and financial grinders, was producing an unintended product—socialism. As the capitalists triggered imperialist wars in their global struggles for markets, as they aroused proletarian consciousness in workers in all lands, they would incubate a militant worldwide proletariat poised for revolution. At last, workers of the world would unite.

Everything depended on the crucial nexus between workers' blighted needs and hopes and their rising revolutionary consciousness. And here something seemed to be going wrong in the New World. American capitalism had burgeoned and exploited, the proletariat had swollen and suffered —but then something had cut into the logical flow from economic misery to class consciousness to proletarian militancy. American workers seemed conscious enough of their low wages and long hours and atrocious working and living conditions, but they seemed conscious of much more—of their religious feelings, their ethnic affiliations, their roots in the old national rivalries of Europe, their special little statuses in factory and office, their faith in individualism, their hopes for improving their lot.

Something clearly had gone wrong with the socialist scenario, something had gone askew in the world of ideas. Eugene Debs had gained almost a million votes in 1912, but many more millions of workers had voted for the old party of Wilson or the new party of Roosevelt. Progressive Republicans had found a new political vehicle that would continue under TR; progressive Democrats could hope for a liberalized party under this new man from academe. Only the Old Guard Republicans under Taft seemed to follow the scenario of the left—and even Taft had busted trusts and backed the income tax.

A new leader had arisen to champion democracy and challenge corporate power. His was a fresh face on the national scene, a rather stern, composed face, bespeaking a man utterly committed to the task ahead and remarkably clear as to how to undertake it. Everything seemed to conspire to Woodrow Wilson's advantage as his inauguration neared early in 1913. He appeared to hold a firm mandate from the electorate, after an election campaign that had posed central issues of trusts and monopoly as sharply as any party battle in memory. He led a party that after decades of Bryanite division had squarely confronted the issue of concentrated economic power in a democracy. He presided over a citizenry eager for action.

Wilson was ready. He had lived his life for this moment. He had studied and preached the vocation of leadership. "This vast and miscellaneous democracy of ours must be led," he had said; "its giant faculties must be schooled and directed. Leadership cannot belong to the multitude; masses of men cannot be self-directed, neither can groups of communities." He would lead. But he stuck to his old belief that great leaders must truly engage with their followers. The nation could not move forward, he said a few weeks before taking office, "by anything except concert of purpose and of judgment. You cannot whip a nation into line. You cannot drive your leaders before you." He would concert his party, his government, his people.

THE ENGINE OF DEMOCRACY

Woodrow Wilson looked down at the 50,000 persons massed in front of the Inaugural stand. It was March 4, 1913, a cold day but sunny. Shortly before, he had descended the east Capitol steps with William Howard Taft, followed by Vice-President Thomas Marshall and members of the new Cabinet. He had taken the oath of office before Chief Justice Edward D. White, and had kissed the Bible, his lips touching the 119th Psalm: "And I will walk at liberty: for I seek thy precepts. . . . And I will delight myself in thy commandments, which I have loved." Turning to the crowd, he had observed a large cleared area just in front of the stand. "Let the people come forward," he had commanded, and they did.

"There has been a change of government," Wilson began abruptly. "It began two years ago, when the House of Representatives became Democratic by a decisive majority." The Senate also would be Democratic. "What does the change mean?

"It means much more than the mere success of a party. The success of a party means little except when the nation is using that party for a large and definite purpose. No one can mistake the purpose for which the nation now seeks to use the Democratic party. It seeks to use it to interpret a change in its own plans and point of view. . . .

"We have been proud of our industrial achievements, but we have not hitherto stopped thoughtfully enough to count the human cost, the cost of lives snuffed out, of energies overtaxed and broken, the fearful physical and spiritual cost to the men and women and children upon whom the dead weight and burden of it all has fallen pitilessly the years through. The groans and agony of it all had not yet reached our ears, the solemn, moving undertone of our life, coming up out of the mines and factories and out of every home where the struggle had its intimate and familiar seat. . . .

"There has been something crude and heartless and unfeeling in our haste to succeed and be great. Our thought has been 'Let every man look out for himself, let every generation look out for itself,' while we reared giant machinery which made it impossible that any but those who stood at the levers of control should have a chance to look out for themselves. . . . There can be no equality or opportunity, the first essential of justice in the body politic, if men and women and children be not shielded in their lives, their very vitality, from the consequences of great industrial and social processes which they can not alter, control, or singly cope with. . . .

"The nation has been deeply stirred, stirred by a solemn passion, stirred by the knowledge of wrong, of ideals lost, of government too often debauched and made an instrument of evil. . . .

"This is not a day of triumph; it is a day of dedication. Here muster, not the forces of party, but the forces of humanity. Men's hearts wait upon us; men's lives hang in the balance; men's hopes call upon us to say what we will do. Who shall live up to the great trust? Who dares fail to try? I summon all honest men, all patriotic, all forward-looking men, to my side. God helping me, I will not fail them, if they will but counsel and sustain me!"

*   *   *

There began, during the next few days, a government that would become a textbook example of presidential leadership of party and Congress. Building both on his theory of governing and his practical experience in New Jersey, Wilson appeared in person before Congress to propose measures; conferred often with party and committee leaders in the White House and on the Hill; exploited the caucus to unify the congressional party behind his program; threatened to wield the veto power against obnoxious bills; mobilized the influence of Bryan and other party leaders against wavering Democrats. The President, he had said a few weeks before his inauguration, must act and serve as "prime minister," directing and uniting party, legislative, and executive leadership. And that was how he governed.

Wilson was not one to ignore the role of President as moral leader, however, especially when a swarm of Washington lobbyists opposing tariff revision gave him the perfect opportunity. A "brick couldn't be thrown without hitting one of them," he told the press at his semiweekly press conference. Then he made a public statement: "I think that the public ought to know the extraordinary exertions being made by the lobby in Washington" on the tariff bill. "Washington has seldom seen so numerous, so industrious, or so insidious a lobby. The newspapers are being filled with paid advertisements calculated to mislead the judgment of public men not only, but also the public opinion of the country itself. . . ." The public at large had no lobby, he added.

Above all, Wilson demonstrated a remarkable flair for executive leadership. He chose able subordinates for his Cabinet: the now-veteran Bryan for Secretary of State; William Gibbs McAdoo, a Southerner turned Northerner like Wilson, and a master of the politics of economics, for the Treasury; Josephus Daniels, editor of the Raleigh *News and Observer,* for Navy; Lindley M. Garrison, a New Jersey attorney, for War. "I've got to have men in the cabinet who have passed the acid test of honesty," he told his confidant, Colonel House. "Men who are brave. Men who are efficient. Men who have imagination." There was a limit to Wilson's own courage, however. Louis Brandeis of Boston fit all those criteria, and the President wanted him at his side as Attorney General. But Brandeis had fought the railroad interests of the Northeast, which, with the help of influential Wall Streeters, the conservative Massachusetts bar, and such bluebloods as President A. Lawrence Lowell of Harvard and Henry L. Higginson, warned Wilson off. House also opposed him. And when Wilson leaned instead toward picking Brandeis for Secretary of Commerce and Labor—then still one department—the united Democracy of Massachusetts, including Mayor John "Honey Fitz" Fitzgerald of Boston, and a number of other

Irish Democrats, dissuaded the President. The rejection of Brandeis, said La Follette, "breaks all our hearts."

It was as commander of his party that Wilson proposed to exert central leadership, and this was an imposing task. Most of the important Senate committees, and fifteen of the seventeen key House committees, were chaired by Southerners, who also in sheer numbers dominated both houses and both Democratic caucuses. It was not surprising that Wilson chose half his Cabinet from the South, and it helped that Colonel House was a Texan. During Wilson's early presidency, he "established a degree of personal control over his party rare in American presidential history," in John Broesamle's estimate. He took such a firm grip of the congressional party that he organized the whole legislative package. "He personally delivered messages to both houses, employed careful timing and constant pressure, haunted the president's room in the Capitol, working continuously with members and advisers, wielded the patronage and the influence of powerful figures like Bryan, threatened vetoes, and, when the time came and other resources had failed, appealed to the public over the heads of Congress." The man who thirty years before had warned of disintegrated rule in *Congressional Government* now enjoyed the heady experience of uniting it.

Policy was the payoff. Even before he entered office, Wilson was helping to marshal the forces of the Democracy for a counterattack on the high-tariff legislation of the Grand Old Party. In his personal appearance before Congress—the first by any President since Jefferson—Wilson declared, "We must abolish everything that bears even the semblance of privilege or of any kind of artificial advantage, and put our business men and producers under the stimulation of a constant necessity to be efficient, economical, and enterprising, masters of competitive supremacy, better workers and merchants than any in the world." Andrew Carnegie himself could not have said it better. The House enacted a moderate downward revision by a two-to-one vote early in May; the big test would come in the Senate, long the burying ground of tariff reduction. There the western sheep farming and beet sugar interests were overrepresented, and it took all Wilson's leadership skills to persuade western Democrats in the Senate to accept his argument that sheep raisers and sugar growers could compete with foreign imports. Major tariff revision downward emerged from Congress by September—along with a hotly debated and momentous graduated federal income tax designed to compensate for anticipated revenue losses under the reduced tariff.

"Think of it—a tariff revision downwards after all—not dictated by the mfgs," wrote Agriculture Secretary David Houston, "lower in the Senate than in the House! . . . A progressive income tax! I did not much think we should live to see these things."

More challenging even than the tariff was the other key issue that dominated presidential-congressional politics during Wilson's first year—the nation's monetary system. Embracing the intertwined problems of currency, banking, the money supply, inflation, and the scope of corporate power over the economy, this issue had roiled the nation's politics for almost a century and had come to a head during the later progressive years. "It is not like the tariff, about which opinion has been definitely forming long years through," Wilson remarked in June 1913. "There are almost as many judgments as there are men. To form a single plan and a single intention about it seems at times a task so various and so elusive that it is hard to keep one's heart from failing." But forming a single plan and intention is precisely what Wilson accomplished.

The way had been prepared by years of debate and, more recently, by the Pujo committee's investigation of the "money trust," by now viewed as a "spider web of interlocking Wall Street directorates," in Arthur Ekirch's words. The probe predictably found an intensive concentration of control over the nation's credit supply by J. P. Morgan & Co. and associated investment firms. Two sharp issues reemerged in the ensuing debate: whether to maintain a centralized or decentralized monetary system, and whether it should be privately or publicly controlled. Unfortunately for Wilson, these sets of issues crosscut each other, producing a parallelogram of pressure. The old inflationist wing of the Democracy was exemplified particularly by Congressman Carter Glass of Virginia, head of the House Banking Committee, who favored a decentralized and privately controlled system. Populists and progressives, including Bryan, La Follette, and Brandeis, wanted public control.

The President took the latter stand. "The control of the system of banking and of issue which our new laws are to set up," he said in his second appearance before Congress, "must be public, not private, must be vested in the Government itself, so that the banks may be the instruments, not the masters, of business and of individual enterprise and initiative." But how master Glass? Wilson won him over to a creative compromise through sheer patience and persuasiveness, while fending off Wall Street pressure for a central bank, European style. The compromise blossomed in the Owen-Glass Act, passed in December 1913, which combined centralization *and* decentralization, governmental *and* private control. A Federal Reserve Board in Washington, composed of public officials, had authority to raise or lower the rediscount rate, thus wielding direct control over the credit supply. Federal Reserve regions were established; in each a Federal Reserve bank, six of whose nine directors would be appointed by the Federal Reserve Board, served as depositories for the cash reserves of the national banks—which were required to join the system—and of state banks. But the regional reserve banks would remain in the ownership of private bankers, and hence in their control too—to the extent that La Follette and Representative Charles A. Lindbergh of Minnesota charged that the act legalized the "Money Trust." The act, in Arthur Link's view, was the greatest single piece of constructive legislation of the Wilson era.

Once again Wilson had demonstrated his uncommon ability both to lead and to follow, to stand firm and to give way. This was the hallmark of his early years in the White House, in the teeth of expectations that he would be professorially rigid and dogmatic. He made a point of treating legislators with respect, as partners in a common cause. And he learned from them. When, shortly after his inauguration, he piously told his Postmaster General and chief patronage dispenser, Albert S. Burleson, that on appointments "I am not going to advise with reactionary or standpat Senators or Representatives," Burleson reacted like the seasoned old party pro that he was.

"Mr. President," he exclaimed, "if you pursue this policy, it means that your administration is going to be a failure. . . . It doesn't amount to a damn who is postmaster at Paducah, Kentucky. But these little offices mean a great deal to the Senators and Representatives in Congress." He knew these congressmen and senators. "If they are turned down, they will hate you and will not vote for anything you want. It is human nature. . . ." Wilson gave way.

The President also gave way on a far more vital question of strategy. He had not only wanted to lead the Democratic party; he had planned to transform it into a more progressive party—indeed, to reconstruct the Democracy and align it with liberal-minded independents and Republicans. Patronage for progressives in Congress was to be only one element of this strategy; he planned to reconstruct the New York and other state and local political parties by granting or withholding White House recognition. He quickly encountered the powerful defenses of political gridlock. When McAdoo and others, with Wilson's blessing, sought to revamp the New York Democracy, its man in the Senate, James A. O'Gorman, warned that he would invoke his personal privilege as a senator to hold up appointments of anti-Tammany Democrats and independents. Wilson backed off. He discovered, though, that if he traded with the regulars, they supported him more dependably than many progressive lawmakers.

"What you told me about the old standpatters is true," he told Burleson. "They will at least stand by the party and the administration."

The President's flexibility helped him immeasurably in getting his big bills through Congress. But this was short-run politics against longer-run, pragmatic politics against principled. In the long run, he might need a more progressive vehicle than the boss-ridden, disorganized, rurally oriented, fractionated Democracy; he might need liberal-minded Democrats, independents, and internationalist Republicans. In the short run, he was pushing his bills through Congress. But there would be a price to pay for pragmatism.

THE ANATOMY OF PROTEST

The commanding intellectual issue in Woodrow Wilson's first term was not the tariff or even banking and currency. It was the issue of economic monopoly in a representative democracy. For almost a century Jeffersonians, Jacksonians, farmers' and workers' parties, Locofocos, Grangers, Populists, and reformist Democrats and Republicans had been calling for the curbing, in various ways, of the monopolistic tendencies of big business. For half a century—ever since the Civil War—trusts had come more and more to dominate the economic landscape. In the eyes of antimonopolists, nothing seemed to stop these behemoths. The Sherman Antitrust law had been fitfully enforced and judicially eroded. At century's turn, ten years after the act was passed, business underwent "a burst of merger activity never exceeded in importance in our history." Left holding the economic high ground were the new giants: U.S. Steel—the first billion-dollar company—American Tobacco, International Harvester, Du Pont, American Smelting & Refining, and scores of others.

Now at last it seemed that the monsters could be tamed. Not only had business concentration been a dramatic and central issue in the 1912 campaigns; not only had all the four leading presidential candidates taken some kind of position "agin the trusts"; they had divided so contentiously over proposed solutions as to offer at least a rough guide to the voters' minds and the new Administration's mandate. During 1914, his second year in office, Wilson won from Congress the Federal Trade Commission Act as part of his trust regulation program. A new bipartisan commission was empowered to investigate and police corporations in order to prevent unfair business practices such as adulteration of goods, combinations for maintaining resale prices, and mislabeling. Congress also passed the Clayton Antitrust Act, which prohibited price-cutting that aimed at the destruction of competition, interlocking directorates in industrial entities capitalized at $1 million or more, and stock purchases by corporations of other corporations when these tended to lessen competition.

The passage of these acts, however, seemed less to satisfy concern over monopoly than to intensify it. This apparent paradox was due in part to widespread doubt that any legislation, federal or state, could actually master private economic power. Even more, the skepticism stemmed from the view that the problem was a much broader one than mere monopoly, that the great popular and progressive mandates of 1904 and 1912 were in jeopardy, that American democracy itself was at stake.

Fear of economic—and political—power in a few hands lay deep in the American psyche. During the progressive era, Hofstadter noted, the entire structure of business "became the object of a widespread hostility" as a result of belief that business was becoming "a closed system of authoritative action." Wilson had touched the people's nerve in 1912. He was engaged, he proclaimed in Denver at the height of the 1912 campaign, in a "crusade against powers that have governed us—that have limited our development—that have determined our lives—that have set us in a straitjacket to do as they please." Raising the stakes, he went on to call the fight a "second struggle for emancipation."

Yet Americans seemed to be as ambivalent about the "second emancipation" as they had been about the first one. For one thing, defenders of big business were putting up powerful arguments. Consolidation, they claimed, lowered prices. "We think our American petroleum" is "very cheap," said John D. Rockefeller smoothly. "It is our pleasure to make it so." Big business, the argument continued, was more efficient and economical because it could buy and sell in large quantities, hire the ablest people, experiment and innovate without undue risk, use the latest labor-saving machinery. Nor was big business undemocratic, because it was controlled by shareholders with voting power. Critics of business disputed all these points, especially the last. It was already becoming clear to perceptive observers that stockholders, if they had ever really had control, were yielding it to managers, executives, and insiders.

People argued the case in terms also of their basic values, but values were not clear guides to action. Almost everyone believed in Individualism, Democracy, and of course Liberty or Freedom, but how did these terms translate into economic or governmental policy? Individualism was a case in point. It was in the name of Individualism or individual liberty that the businessmen of the late nineteenth century had fought off governmental interference and apotheosized the Horatio Alger man who rose to the top through the untrammeled exercise of ambition, competition, and talent. Then Wilson, La Follette, et al. had turned Algerism upside down by proclaiming that monopolies had blighted individual liberty, opportunity, competition.

Or consider democracy. Economic? Political? Social? In both the private and public sphere? Exercised through the majority will? Stockholders' meetings? Party politics? Coalitions of minorities? Or through a scramble for power and pelf, open to all on an equal basis, favoring none? For most Americans, for most of their leaders, these questions were still open.

Then, the thorniest question of all: If economic concentration did indeed threaten American democracy, what should be done about it? Those who favored some kind of governmental action had divided most clearly in 1912 between Wilson's promise to break up economic bigness and Roosevelt's proposal to regulate it. It turned out, though, that these differences were not as polar—or as profound—as the two sides believed. In practice, policy crept out of these narrow categories and found its own crisscrossing paths. Then too, Wilson showed considerable flexibility in carrying out his programs. Thus, after having flayed Roosevelt's proposal to regulate big business through a strong Federal Trade Commission, Wilson himself moved around to this position.

*   *   *

However much he might have altered course, President Wilson's forceful leadership stimulated and catalyzed thought throughout the ranks of progressive thinkers. Out of the clash of ideas during the Roosevelt and Taft years arose an intellectual leadership that was centrally concerned over the sharpening conflict between the ideological defense of big business and the claims of democratic progressives. Four men took the lead in rethinking the role of democracy in the booming American workshop, the whole question of "industrial democracy."

By far the most influential of these—measured both by access to power and by influence on policy—was Louis Brandeis. Unperturbed by Wilson's failure to offer the "people's lawyer" a major post in the face of conservative opposition, the Boston attorney continued to advise the President on major economic policy. "Brandeis and Wilson initially used Wilson's presidency, and the potential power it gave him, to teach the nation about the ideals of Brandeis and the progressives and to enact some of them into law," according to Philippa Strum. Brandeis successfully backed James McReynolds for Attorney General; met often with Cabinet and other Administration officials; worked with Secretary of State Bryan to influence Wilson against allowing the "money trust" too much control over the new Federal Reserve system; and, changing his own mind, helped change Wilson's mind as to the desirability of a regulatory, rather than merely investigative, Federal Trade Commission. Though disappointed by Wilson's conservative appointments to both the commission and the Federal Reserve Board, Brandeis remained on cordial terms with the President.

Still, Brandeis from the start took a stronger line against big business, the trusts, and especially the money trust than Wilson did. The theme that "never varied in Louis Brandeis's thought," according to Melvin Urofsky, was that "too great a concentration of economic power constituted a social, economic and political menace to a free society; a business could be efficient only up to a certain size beyond which bigness caused inefficiency; trusts could never stand up to smaller units in a freely and truly competitive market place; proper rules regulating competition could insure such conditions; competition is the atmosphere which a free society breathes."

For Brandeis the paramount issue was not efficiency but democracy—industrial, political, governmental democracy. In "striving for democracy," he told the Commission on Industrial Relations in 1915, "we are striving for the development of men." Industrial democracy would not come by gift; it "has got to be by those who desire it." Brandeis's great hope was that industrial workers would want it, for they had the most to gain from it. Individual employees had no effective voice or vote, but collectively workers should exercise more control through their unions, just as stockholders should be held responsible for decisions made by their companies. Brandeis pointed to the garment industry, where an agreement had created a system of government for both employers and unions, including even "administrative officers, courts, and a legislature always ready to take up questions arising in the trade." The smaller the business, Brandeis suggested, the more likely such industrial democracy could grow.

Second only to Brandeis in influence over presidential leadership was Herbert Croly, friend of Theodore Roosevelt. Raised by activist parents—his father the editor of the crusading New York *Daily Graphic,* his mother a journalist and pioneering feminist—Croly left for Harvard in 1886 imbued with his family's Comtean positivism and dedicated to the welfare of mankind, and after intermittent years of study under James and Santayana, and as editor of the *Architectural Record,* he became even more dedicated to the welfare of mankind. He produced in 1909 his masterwork, *The Promise of American Life,* a 468-page tome as relevant and powerful as it was long and prolix. It was Roosevelt's reading of this book, shortly after his return from Africa, that mightily strengthened the radical thrust of the former President's progressivism and brought the two men together.

Two progressives could hardly have been more philosophically divided than Croly and Brandeis. Brandeis looked back nostalgically to Jeffersonian ideas of local democracy, individual liberty, rural culture, and small-scale economic competition. Croly called for a strong national government, under vigorous executive leadership, prepared to carry out progressive and humane policies at home and pursue nationalistic policies abroad. To him, individual liberty was important, but no less was liberty of the whole people to shape their own destiny. Only the centralized power of the people could deal with the centralized power of big business. Croly, it was said, would use Hamiltonian means to achieve Jeffersonian ends, though he complained that Hamilton perverted the "national idea" with his upperclass bias almost as much as Jefferson perverted the democratic idea with his extreme individualism and egalitarianism.

Croly was in fact calling for rare national leadership. He was man enough to chide his friend the Colonel for trying to make the American citizen into a "sixty-horse-power moral motor-car," for doing little to encourage "candid and consistent thinking," for his "sheer exuberance of moral energy," and TR was man enough to accept the soft impeachment. The two worked together, each hardening the other's convictions, through the 1912 campaign, and then collaborated while Roosevelt debated whether to stick with the Progressives or return to Republicanism. But as the Colonel's 1916 election prospects dwindled, Croly turned increasingly to the Democrat in the White House who was practicing leadership, no longer merely preaching it.

When Croly began to plan a new weekly of progressive opinion in 1913, it was only natural that he would turn to his recent acquaintance Walter Weyl. A product of the Wharton School in his native Philadelphia and of the University of Halle in Germany, Weyl in 1912 published *The New Democracy*. "America today is in a somber, soul-questioning mood," were Weyl's opening words. "We are in a period of clamor, of bewilderment, of an almost tremulous unrest. We are hastily revising all our social conceptions. We are hastily testing all our political ideals." He was happy to help with both conceptions and ideals. In the next 356 pages, he listed the nation's gains but also its failures—"sensational inequalities of wealth, insane extravagances, strident ostentations," along with boss-ridden cities, wretched slums, pauperism, vice, crime, insanity, dangerous factories, unemployment, premature deaths of babies, the scrapping of aged workmen, rising class conflict, hunger, "social vice," the breakdown of government.

What would Weyl do about all these evils? First, measure them; he was an avid statistician. Second, work with consumer and labor groups, as he did in several years of involvement with the labor leader John Mitchell and his coal miners. Third, find a solution midway between Manchester liberalism and Marxist socialism. Finally, in all this be practical, "pragmatist." Marx was wrong, Weyl contended, in teaching that progress would come through the poverty and proletarianization of the working class. Weyl proposed the doctrine of "progress through prosperity." Reformers should use democracy—the right to vote, the initiative and referendum, the party primary—as both means and end. A sweet and easygoing man, considered almost saintly by his friends, Weyl believed in progress without pain.

Weyl was forty when tapped for the new weekly; Croly also recruited another thinker fifteen years younger than Weyl, and the most remarkable of the future editors. Like Weyl, Walter Lippmann was born of German-Jewish parents. Growing up on Manhattan's upper East Side, he was indulged as a child and later granted independence and the money to sustain it. During his first three years at Harvard, he took one course each in history and government, three in economics, five in language, and seven in philosophy. He studied under Harvard greats—Hugo Münsterberg in psychology, George Lyman Kittredge in English, Irving Babbitt in French literature, and in philosophy, George Santayana and, above all, William James, who profoundly influenced the eager young scholar. Lippmann also learned something about political psychology and human motivation from a visiting British professor, Graham Wallas, one of the original Fabian socialists. By the time Lippmann left Harvard, he had headed the student socialist club.

By twenty-five, Lippmann had lived the average man's lifetime: assistant to Santayana, reporter for the Boston *Common*, research aide to Lincoln Steffens, secretary to the socialist mayor of Schenectady, and author of two important books, *A Preface to Politics* and *Drift and Mastery*. Through luck and design, he had come to know scores of persons of political or literary note on both sides of the Atlantic—Beatrice and Sidney Webb, George Bernard Shaw, H. G. Wells, Arnold Bennett, G. K. Chesterton in England, and at home such unlikely persons as W. E. B. Du Bois, whom he put up unsuccessfully for Manhattan's Liberal Club. When, in October 1913, Croly invited him to lunch at the fashionable Players Club and offered him sixty dollars a week to work for the new weekly, Lippmann accepted on the spot.

"Lippmann, as you say, is an interesting mixture of maturity and innocence," Croly happily wrote his close friend Judge Learned Hand. No matter how Lippmann turned out as a political philosopher, "he certainly has great possibilities as a political journalist." He did not know as much as he thought he did, "but he does know a lot, and his general sense of values is excellent." He was a bit impertinent, but it would be an impertinent journal. Croly added roguishly, "We'll throw a few firecrackers under the skirts of the old women on the bench and in other high places."

The weekly—it would be called the *New Republic*—did toss a few fire-crackers, some of which exploded, but it became primarily a journal that reflected the eclectic and limber attitudes of its several editors. Lippmann's political philosophy was changing even as he joined the weekly. Already he had given up his socialist beliefs, especially after his experience with the socialist mayor, who moderated his program to pander to the sluggish masses. His *Preface to Politics* was an "intellectual potpourri," in Ronald Steel's words, filled with Lippmann's student collocation—James's tribute to practical results, Henri Bergson's creative intuition, Nietzsche's will to power, H. G. Wells's scientific utopianism, a chunk of Freud, and John Dewey's master plan for social change. He attacked majority rule, the two-party system, trust-busting, electoral reform, and other products of "uptown" reformers or the mass mind. He called for national leadership, scientific management, and, in Freudian style, a new morality based on directing instead of "tabooing our impulses." *Drift and Mastery* was a more intellectually focused and limited book that seemed to abandon Lippmann's earlier emphasis on irrationality in politics, fretted over the "chaos of a new freedom," but still contained a dash of youthful iconoclasm.

Still, it was the old story of progressives and reformers having a far better grasp of what they opposed than what they wished to substitute. The *New Republic* crowd, and their friends and friendly critics like Brandeis and Dewey, brilliantly dissected problems of economics, religion, politics, morals, psychology; they made many a sensible proposal for specific reforms in government, industry, education, law, crime prevention, social welfare, civic life. But they did not come to grips with the central issue that for many intellectuals lay behind all the specific issues—the threat of corporate power to American pluralistic democracy. This failure stemmed from a number of sources—the lack of adequate economic and social data, the limited tools of economic analysis, the power of reform shibboleths like "direct democracy," the pleasures of iconoclasm as compared to the drudgery of policy analysis. But, above all, the failure lay in habits of thinking, especially in the pragmatism that dominated social thought in the progressive era. Rebelling against the windy, absolutist doctrines of left and right, such as Marxism and Social Darwinism, the progressive thinkers made a fetish of practicality, immediate results, manageable reforms. They did so at the expense of hard and creative thought about the economic and political changes that would be necessary to curb the economic behemoths and, through transforming leadership and creative popular action, bring about the reconstruction of society.

*   *   *

The reconstruction of American society—this was the cardinal goal of American socialists of almost all hues and tints, but they wrangled year after year as to how to define this goal and how to realize it.

Of the socialist parties still existing in 1913, however feebly, the Socialist Labor Party had taken the most consistently radical position for revolutionary action leading to the abolition of the wage system, the destruction of capitalism, and the collective ownership by the people of the means of production and distribution. Drawing its strength from Marxists—both European and homegrown—and from militants in the workingmen's parties of the 1870s, the SLP had preached a vaguely defined revolutionary strategy, and had denounced bread-and-butter unionism even while making concessions to short-run trade union tactics. By the mid-nineties, the party had established itself especially in German-American unions and virtually controlled the Central Labor Federation of New York.

A type of leader hardly known in the United States but familiar to radicals abroad supplied powerful leadership to the SLP. He was Daniel De Leon, brilliant theoretician, doctrinaire socialist, ideological purist. His early years would hardly have seemed likely to produce such a sectarian: son of a Curaçao surgeon, De Leon studied in Germany, then in 1874 settled in New York City, where he taught Greek and Latin, edited a paper supporting independence for Cuba, won a law degree from Columbia, and became a lecturer on international law at that university, meanwhile carrying political lances for Henry George and Edward Bellamy. Winning the editorship of the SLP party organ, De Leon dominated the organization for almost a quarter-century. He fought to convert trade unionists to socialism without being converted *by* them, launched ferocious personal attacks on his rivals from left to right, sought to create through the SLP a revolutionary industrial union, and tried to drive the AFL out of business —all with the goal of demanding the "unconditional surrender of the capitalist system." By 1912, after years of secessions, expulsions, and schismatic infighting, capitalism reigned triumphant and the SLP was reduced to a tiny band of militants, but De Leon had posed the question that no leader now could duck: Should industrial workers try to reform and shore up capitalism from within, or replace it with some kind of socialism?

The Socialist Party, launched in 1901, never seemed to make up its collective mind on this central question, in part because its origins were even more diverse than those of the SLP. Its early members, according to Milton Cantor, included veterans from the Populist movement, from Eugene Debs's American Railway Union, from Christian socialism, leavened by settlement workers, millionaire socialists, scions of German Forty-eighters, "and the cultural radicals—bohemian writers and artists—who fought for birth control, women's suffrage, and uninhibited social-sexual behavior." The party included New York intellectuals, hard-boiled union bosses, practical-minded candidates for mayor and governor, hundreds of socialists who actually won local office.

The Socialists evolved an ingenious device for preaching both the reform of capitalism and its abolition. In the preambles, their party platforms proclaimed lofty and even revolutionary goals, such as the abolition of wage slavery or the building of a cooperative commonwealth, and then the platforms settled down to the nuts and bolts of reforming the capitalistic system: welfare measures, state and municipal reforms, protection of labor, conservation, public works for the unemployed, and the like. This device seemed to satisfy both "immediatists" and "impossibilists." As the years passed, the party became increasingly meliorist, but the rhetoric of revolution hung evocatively over convention orators and county stump speakers.

The Socialists could boast of seasoned leadership at every party level. During the decade leading up to his 900,000-vote triumph in 1912, Eugene Debs won worldwide fame. He ran for the presidency, he told Lincoln Steffens, to raise "social consciousness." When socialism came to the verge of success, he continued, the party would choose "an able executive and a clear-minded administrator; not—not Debs." Debs was party candidate and spokesman, not manager. The task of running the organization fell on men like Morris Hillquit and Victor Berger, who also heavily influenced the adoption of party policies for "gas and water" socialism. In particular Berger, leader of the Milwaukee party, fought for constructive, "safe and sane" socialism—a position that helped him win congressional office.

The Industrial Workers of the World continued to roil socialist politics during these years, but its brand of socialism was even less coherent than that of the SLP or the Socialist party. The organization was rent by factions variously supporting syndicalist and even anarchist policies, straight industrial action, and vigorous political activism. In the wide-open brawls of the Wobblies, leaders fought to be "king of the rock." In a showdown battle IWW's pugnacious leader, Big Bill Haywood, not only vanquished De Leon but, in the noncomradely fashion of the day, helped expel him from the organization. At the core of the IWW, Aileen Kraditor concluded, "were extreme individualists who rejected not just the content of the conventional community relationships but the social bonds themselves." Though the Wobblies proclaimed lofty socialist and syndicalist goals, Haywood and other leaders stressed the need to win labor's immediate battles, and Big Bill sounded off against the "scum proletariat" of lawyers, preach-

ers, authors, lecturers, and "intellectual non-producers generally," whom
he called even more dangerous than the "lumpen proletariat."

Just after the height of its electoral success in 1912, the Socialist party
and movement underwent a decline that, with occasional interruptions,
continued for decades. The reason was partly organizational and "practical." The movement was never able to build an all-encompassing organization or party; on the contrary, relations within and among socialist groups
were marked by hostility, recrimination, schisms, expulsions, and searing
invective. Radicals reserved their choicest epithets for socialist heretics
rather than capitalist infidels. De Leon castigated an opposing faction of
Debsites and others as a "vocal collection of freaks, frauds, and incompetents," consisting not of "the raw material that a new social system is to
be woven out of, but of the garbage-barrel material, the offal and refuse
of society. . . ."

Still, intolerant conviction came with the radical territory; most socialists
felt more deeply about social ills than did most centrist party brokers. The
organizational problem lay much deeper. As a whole, and despite the
activism of such socialists as Kate Richards O'Hare, Ella Reeve Bloor, and
Rose Pastor Stokes, socialist leaders were not sensitive to the needs of
women. Some leaders were overtly sexist; most assumed that the abolition
of capitalism automatically meant the liberation of female workers as well
as male. In short, they invited women into their ranks on socialist terms,
not on women's terms. These leaders on the whole were even more cul-
ture-bound in dealing with Negro workers. At the height of segregationism
it seemed impossible to confront the problem of class *and* race, especially
in the South, where radical workers would not sit next to blacks in union
halls or let them into their locals. So blacks too had to wait for the socialist
tide that would raise all boats. If, as Vann Woodward said, it was "Progressivism—for Whites Only" in the post-Populist South, it was also "Socialism for Whites Only" in that region and in certain enclaves of the
North.

Even with "their own people"—immigrants, ethnics, workers settled in
communities—socialist leaders were often unable to penetrate the family,
neighborhood, religious, linguistic, recreational, and political party worlds
in which the workers actually lived most of their lives. These persons were
not blank pages for radicals to write on. Among the workers' worlds might
be a trade union that ignored talk of class war and concentrated on immediate benefits. Class consciousness, Lenin was saying, could only be
brought to workers from without; left to themselves, the working class
would "develop only trade-union consciousness." To transform all those
workers' "consciousnesses"—union, family, religious, and the like—would

have taken a far more powerful organizational effort and psychological understanding than the socialists were able to achieve.

Ultimately, the towering problem for American socialists was more intellectual even than organizational. Their leaders failed to establish a clear and convincing case for reconstruction rather than mere reform, for some kind of revolution rather than the usual gradualism, for a central and disciplined political strategy rather than the familiar trial-and-error, one-step-at-a-time, by-guess-and-by-God tactics. Not only were the political means unclear; even more so were the goals. The socialists collectively were not agreed as to what the grand new commonwealth would be like —whether more socialist or syndicalist, how governed, how heavily egalitarian, committed to what values and to what priorities among those values. In the absence of clear guidelines, these questions of both means and ends were left to criteria of practicality—what might work today or tomorrow for narrow and specific ends. Thus inarticulate premises of common sense, pragmatism, and practicality hung over the thought and actions of socialist leaders who might never have read William James or John Dewey.

The socialists offered the workers pie in the sky, and that was all right: it was an old American custom. But just as American thinkers had so often propounded specific short-term steps on the one hand and vague long-term goals on the other, skipping over the vital linkages of interrelated ends and means, so did the radicals. They offered pie, and a future of lots of pie, but they rarely told the worker what she wanted to know—how baked, with what ingredients, how to be distributed—and whether it would really be Mom's apple pie or a confection with a strange and alien flavor.

MARKETS, MORALITY, AND THE "STAR OF EMPIRE"

Woodrow Wilson's early efforts to translate into policy the ideology of the New Freedom took place against a background of turmoil and conflict on the international scene. Foreign affairs had figured little in the three-way debate of the 1912 campaign; at most it was a tangential issue, raised by Pujo Committee charges that the Taft Administration had favored bankers and investors in its diplomatic dealings. Aside from echoing these attacks on the "Money Trust," Wilson shied away from any debate on America's role in the world. "It would be the irony of fate," he noted after his election, "if my administration had to deal chiefly with foreign affairs."

Wilson had very firm ideas about America's interests abroad, however. Like most of his thinking, these ideas grew out of his deep moral commitment to justice, democracy, and Christian values. Wilson revived the Jeffersonian theme of America as a beacon star of democracy for the world, an exemplar and—with its newfound power in the twentieth century—promoter of human rights and social development. "We are chosen," he declared in 1910, "to show the way to the nations of the world how they shall walk in the paths of liberty." Yet this moral thrust had a practical self-interested side. Wilson's graduate study under Frederick Jackson Turner had left him convinced that America must seek new frontiers abroad to replace the western frontier that had disappeared. One form that moral duty could take was the responsibility of empire, in the Caribbean and the Far East—for empire, notes Sidney Bell, was in Wilson's eyes "an engine of liberty."

That engine was to be economic as well as ideological. Wilson, as much as Taft or Roosevelt, believed that America's foreign trade and investment should be encouraged to grow. In his official acceptance address, delivered more than a month after the Baltimore convention, Wilson declared that "our industries have expanded to such a point that they will burst their jackets if they cannot find a free outlet to the markets of the world." On the one hand, he and the Secretary of State–designate, William Jennings Bryan, denounced the alleged machinations of investment bankers and called for a "war for emancipation from . . . the concentrated and organized power of money." Yet, on the other hand, Wilson viewed the pursuit of what he called the economic "Star of Empire" as being vital to both prosperity at home and efficacy abroad.

China posed the first test of Wilson's faith that he could reconcile these two conflicting tenets. Economics had long played a key role in shaping America's policy toward the Celestial Kingdom. As the European powers and Japan proceeded to extract concessions and spheres of influence from the Chinese at the end of the nineteenth century, Secretary Hay had responded with a series of diplomatic notes calling for an "open door": America's desire, Hay asserted, was to "safeguard for the world the principle of equal and impartial trade with all parts of the Chinese Empire."

The powers paid lip service to Hay's Open Door doctrine while continuing to undermine the independence of China. When the Emperor's government was forced to pay the Europeans—and the United States—a large indemnity after Chinese mobs attacked foreigners in the abortive Boxer Rebellion, Western bankers agreed to fund the debt in return for further concessions. Foreign control in the various spheres of influence grew; the Japanese in Manchuria, for example, collected taxes, appointed police, and supervised the population all along the railroads they operated. Meanwhile America's share of China's imports dwindled from 10.4 to 7.5 percent.

Rather than selling vast quantities of American manufactured goods, merchants found a market for only modest amounts of U.S. lumber, tobacco, unbleached cloth, and Standard Oil kerosene.

President Taft had endeavored to reverse, with vigorous diplomacy, the decline of American commerce and influence in China. Drawing upon his own experiences in Manila and Shanghai, he wanted a Peking embassy that would employ "force and pluck" to counter the other powers and promote U.S. interests. His plan was to expand substantially American investment in China, on the theory that increased trade would follow. To Prince-Regent Chun, Taft wrote of his "intense personal interest in making the use of American capital . . . an instrument for the promotion of the welfare of China." The United States would join the Europeans in their game of economic imperialism and try to beat them at it, to the alleged benefit of both America and China.

The Taft Administration launched a series of investment projects, offering funds for railroad construction, currency reform, and reorganization of Peking's finances. Edward H. Harriman, the great magnate of western railroads, was enlisted to incorporate Manchuria into his scheme for a global network of railways and steamships. But Harriman died in the first year of Taft's presidency. Secretary of State Philander Knox undermined several loan proposals by making unacceptable political demands on the Chinese, while other ventures were hamstrung by disputes with and among the European co-investors. Overall, American bankers were reluctant to risk their capital to promote the schemes of Taft and Knox; only persistent pressure from Washington kept "dollar diplomacy" moving at all.

The Chinese people, however, were also on the move. Reacting to increasing foreign influence, the population of the southern provinces rose in protest and toppled the Peking monarchy in 1911. Secretary Knox would neither recognize the rebel forces of Sun Yat-sen nor continue loans to Yuan Shih-kai's self-styled republic newly organized in the capital; the entire question was left as the first foreign crisis for the Wilson Administration.

From the very beginning the incoming Democrat took a longer view of American interests in China. Political development, he concluded, was essential to economic growth; thus the United States should make its first goal the advancement of a free, democratic China. To Sun Yat-sen Wilson cabled his "strongest sympathy with every movement which looks towards giving the people . . . of China the liberty for which they have so long been yearning and preparing themselves." Bryan, meanwhile, sent congratulations to Yuan—along with a copy of the works of Thomas Jefferson. When the two Chinese leaders reached a precarious compromise and formed a united government, Wilson made America the first major power to recognize the new republic.

For Wilson the "awakening of the people of China" was the "most significant . . . event of our generation." The Peking embassy, Wilson and Bryan believed, should go to an ambassador who would work closely with the American missionaries and Young Men's Christian Association activists who were penetrating the country in increasing numbers. When Henry Morgenthau asked for the appointment, Wilson demurred, replying that the post had to go to an "evangelical Christian." The choice fell on Professor Paul Reinsch, a former editor of La Follette's journal. To Reinsch, Wilson emphasized that education and political example should take precedence over economic involvement. Indeed, the President noted in a letter to Harvard's Charles Eliot, American diplomacy had to be reordered across the board to put "moral and public considerations" ahead of the "material interests of individuals."

Early on, Wilson was presented with an opportunity to put those principles into practice, when a group of American bankers applied for government permission to continue in an international loan to Yuan's regime. Noting that the terms of the loan called for foreign control of tax collection and of expenditures, Wilson pulled the American firms out of the consortium. The United States, he declared, would take an independent course to aid China without undermining her national sovereignty.

The public greeted the rejection of the bankers' consortium with applause. Henry George (Jr.) declared that Wilson had prevented the "prostitution of our State Department by our princes of privilege." *Outlook* foresaw the triumph of progressive reform, with American guidance and trade helping to build a "New China" of "parks, and sewers, and filtered water, and war on rats and mosquitoes." The New York *World* ran a cartoon entitled "Leaving the Firm," that showed Uncle Sam turning his back on J. P. Morgan & Company. Wilson himself, however, was aware that the Taft Administration had dragooned the bankers into their Chinese loans in the first place. Now that the new President had reversed the government's policy, freeing Morgan and his associates from an imbroglio of which they were "dead sick," the bankers were glad to see meddling Uncle Sam take his leave.

*   *   *

How apply "moral considerations" much closer to home—to Mexico and other restless, poverty-racked nations of Latin America? The approach of Wall Street and Washington was mainly financial. In 1912, Americans sold more than $130 million worth of manufactured goods south of the Rio

Grande and bought $250 million in foodstuffs and raw materials. Long-term investments in the region passed the $1 billion mark. In Mexico alone, Americans were estimated to own 43 percent of the invested property.

Alongside American trade, exploitation and tyranny still flourished too; could Wilson, in the spirit of the New Freedom, promote the former while combating the latter? He had little enough freedom himself, for the actions of previous Administrations narrowed his choices in dealing with the southern nations. Taft's Latin American policy, modeled on the quasi-protectorate that TR had established over the Dominican Republic, put American experts in charge of the finances of various Caribbean republics. The system had seemed to work splendidly in Santo Domingo, where U.S. control of the customs revenues ushered in a period of political calm and economic growth. But elsewhere Taft had encountered obstacles to his paternalistic policies. The prickly Philander Knox alienated many of the Latin American diplomats who tried to work with him; Taft himself failed to get several key treaties through the Senate; and revolutionary upheavals on the scene threatened to sweep away fiscal solutions that seemed promising in Washington. Taft had characterized his policy as one of "substituting dollars for bullets," but in Nicaragua he had to rely on both, sending in U.S. troops to prop up an unpopular government friendly to American investment.

Thus Wilson entered office bound by a series of commitments in Latin America: a historical commitment to the Monroe Doctrine; a strategic one to the defense of the Panama Canal, just now being completed after a decade of work; a military one to the American soldiers already stationed in Nicaragua, Santo Domingo, Puerto Rico, and Guantánamo. And finally there was a financial commitment: fully one-half of America's investments abroad were in Latin America. Old foreign policy hands wondered how these practical considerations would interact with Wilson's underlying moral precepts.

Wilson did not hesitate to protect American interests with vigorous action. August 1914: Nicaragua yields control of a naval base and the alternate isthmian canal route to the United States. July 1915: American Marines land in Haiti to quell bloody disorders. November 1916: the United States establishes military control over the Dominican Republic. January 1917: Wilson purchases the Danish Virgin Islands in order to secure the approaches to the Panama Canal. February 1917: more U.S. troops land in Cuba to block a revolt against the Menocal government.

Morality had its place too in a lingering crisis in American relations with Mexico. Two years of political turmoil in that country had climaxed on

February 22, 1913, when President Francisco Madero was killed, allegedly by the forces of his opponent, General Victoriano Huerta. Taft's ambassador in Mexico City advised the newly inaugurated Wilson to accept Huerta's coup, for the general had disavowed the murder of Madero, ended the fighting that had gripped the capital, and won the support of key European envoys. The American President, however, was unmoved. To his Cabinet, Wilson exclaimed that he would not deal with "a government of butchers"; publicly he announced that "morality and not expediency" would guide American policy.

Rather than recognize Huerta, Wilson recalled the U.S. ambassador, froze Mexican government funds in the United States, and instituted a policy of "watchful waiting" toward the dictator's regime. To the traditional tests for recognizing a foreign power, Wilson added a new formula: its government must be "constitutionally legitimate." American friendship, he postulated in a "Declaration of Policy in Regard to Latin America," must be predicated on "the orderly processes of just government based upon law, not upon arbitrary or irregular force."

Wilson's ideological approach to the Mexican crisis came under a storm of fire. The European powers regarded his new doctrine of legitimacy as an insufferable affront to accepted diplomatic practice. At home, Roosevelt and others took a different tack, charging that the President was not acting strongly enough, and calling for war with Mexico. For Wilson, the conflict soon assumed the aspect of a personal vendetta with the Mexican dictator. "There can be no certain prospect of peace in America," he warned Congress, "until General Huerta has surrendered his usurped power." In private Wilson also railed against his critics, charging them with base motives of gain. "I have to pause and remind myself," he told his secretary, "that I am President of the United States and not of a small group of Americans with vested interests in Mexico."

Wilson hoped that the United States could continue to exercise "the self-restraint of a really great nation, which realizes its own strength and scorns to misuse it." Slowly, however, the country edged toward war. In February 1914 the President allowed arms to be shipped to the rebel Constitutionalists in Mexico. Still, Huerta seemed to be growing stronger; only military intervention, wrote Wilson's personal envoy in Mexico City, could bring to an end the dictator's "saturnalia of crime and oppression." When U.S. sailors and Mexican police clashed in Tampico, Wilson went before Congress and requested authority to use force. The next day, April 21, American troops seized the port of Veracruz after overcoming stiff Mexican resistance.

The occupation of Veracruz helped bring about the downfall of Huerta and the elevation of Venustiano Carranza, chief among the Constitutionalist rebels. But Carranza was no more legitimate a ruler than Huerta; Francisco "Pancho" Villa and others kept revolt brewing in the northern provinces, while Carranza took a harshly anti-American position. Wilson was rescued from this embarrassing impasse by the diplomats of Argentina, Brazil, and Chile, who offered to mediate between Washington and Mexico City. With the help of the ABC powers, Wilson was able to evacuate Veracruz in November, and a year later he grudgingly extended recognition to Carranza.

Were Wilson's moral pronouncements merely a smokescreen for a policy of economic imperialism? Holding up Veracruz and the Caribbean interventions as examples, some observers—and some historians later—charged that Wilson "outraged the sovereignty of unwilling nations" in the interests of American business, and that his actions were indistinguishable from those of his Republican predecessors. Actually, Wilson displayed considerable restraint in dealing with Mexico. American property, and even American lives, continued to be lost in that country, yet Wilson resisted pressures to launch an all-out war. Presented with a stark choice between economic and ideological interests, Wilson used limited means and pursued democratic ends.

When he could, Wilson did try to reconcile material interests with morality, and he achieved some success. The Philippines gained limited self-government under his Administration, and the inhabitants of Puerto Rico were granted the rights of American citizenship. In the Caribbean, intervention by the United States brought democratic reforms to several states, at least on paper. Yet it is questionable whether Wilson achieved his stated goal, to "teach the South American republics to elect good men." Certainly in China, where there were no U.S. Marines to back up his edicts, Wilson's policy drifted toward failure as Yuan's regime degenerated into despotism and Sun Yat-sen was forced to flee the country. The practical question, of how ideas and force should be mixed in a single consistent approach to foreign affairs, remained unresolved. At the very least for Wilson—and for all twentieth-century Presidents—Latin America was an early schooling in the complex and powerful autonomous forces operating in what would come to be known as the Third World.

Events in Mexico continued to frustrate Wilson. There Pancho Villa, the illiterate but wily peasant leader, had emerged as an even greater threat than the hostility of Carranza. Villa's men lent a nationalist tincture to their banditry by killing Americans, blackmailing U.S. firms, and even raiding into the United States. Henry Cabot Lodge rose in the Senate to denounce Villa as a murderous peon, although to other Americans he seemed a Latin Robin Hood on horseback.

Wilson finally was forced to act when Villa shot up the border town of Columbus, New Mexico, in February 1916. The President dispatched a cavalry force under General John Pershing across the border to track down the bandit chief. Pershing's men crisscrossed northern Mexico on horseback, in automobiles, and with airplanes; they had a few colorful gunfights with the Mexicans, but Villa and his main force eluded a showdown. The main effect of the expedition was further to poison relations with Carranza. At last, in early 1917, Wilson was forced to withdraw his men—they were needed elsewhere.

CHAPTER 12

Over There

L*iège, Belgium, August 12, 1914:* From concealed bunkers cut into the hillside, machine-gun bullets spray out at the advancing German soldiers. The attackers hit the dirt, their freshly issued uniforms soiled with blood and grime. The Germans continue to crawl forward, only to be checked by a Belgian counterattack. Suddenly the attack halts; the battlefield is gripped by silence. Then the German siege guns, the largest in the world, come into play. Shrilling like speeding express trains, their shells arch over the crouched men in *feldgrau* and smash into the Belgian forts. The cannon, with their yard-long shells and barrels the length of a freight car, easily dwarf the two hundred men that service each of them. They are the "guns of August," the heralds of Europe's twentieth-century holocaust of total war.

The German emperor, Kaiser Wilhelm II, had inspected the guns in their Krupp factories and approved their destructive purpose. But back in his palace outside Berlin, as the assassination of Austria's Archduke Franz Ferdinand pushed Europe toward the continental war that Wilhelm had often blustered about fighting, the Kaiser's nerve failed. Although Austria had already attacked Serbia, and Russia was mobilizing, Wilhelm summoned his army chief of staff to the royal chambers. Tall, gloomy Helmuth von Moltke informed the agitated monarch that there was no alternative: Germany's Schlieffen Plan, for a two-front war against Russia and France, was under way and could not be stopped. Eleven thousand trains, half a million railroad cars, and nearly 2 million men were moving with meticulous precision across Central Europe. Five German columns thrust into neutral Belgium, aiming to reach Paris and destroy the French army before Russia could act. Chancellor Theobald von Bethmann-Hollweg announced to the German people that their fate now rested on the "iron dice" of war.

In Paris, the leaders of the French government also met in a palace—the beautiful gilded Elysée, which seemed to embrace the diverse glories of France's democrats, kings, and despots. Here too the political leaders found themselves at the mercy of the soldiers' long-drafted plans. General Joseph Joffre, the stolid commander of the French army, brushed aside President Raymond Poincaré's suggestion that a force be detached to help

407

the Belgians. Instead, the entire army was launched against Alsace-Lorraine with the aim of wresting those two provinces back from Germany. But within days—hours in some places—the spirited French attack was bloodily repulsed. Gallic *élan* proved no match for German barbed wire and machine guns.

As the French army recoiled in defeat from the German frontier, Britain's Cabinet met in the modest row house at 10 Downing Street. Prime Minister Herbert Asquith and Foreign Secretary Sir Edward Grey had led their country into the war over Germany's attack on Belgium, despite the opposition of much of their own party. Now they watched in consternation as staff officers sketched out on a large-scale map how the Germans were sweeping with unexpected strength and strategic effectiveness across the Belgian plain, heading straight for France's unguarded northern frontier and Channel ports. Britain itself seemed suddenly in danger.

Only one minister appeared undaunted by the Germans' quick success. Winston Churchill, First Lord of the Admiralty, at thirty-nine was regarded as a reckless soldier, a melodramatic author, and a political jackanapes of considerable flair but little reliability. Less obvious was his passion for the fleet that he had built under the tutelage of crusty Admiral Lord John Fisher, and his cool efficiency in directing it. When the Cabinet voted for war, it found that Churchill already had the navy assembled and at battle stations, ready to block any further German surprises. In Churchill's fleet —their answer to the Germans' cannon—the British possessed the second-strongest piece on the European chessboard.

The most awesome piece, the 6-million-man Russian army, was commanded by the weakest player. Nicholas II, "Czar of All the Russias," was not even master in his dreary palace on the gray Baltic seashore. Dominated by a jealous and superstitious wife; manipulated by fawning, reactionary ministers; gulled by the vicious yet mesmerizing monk Rasputin— still Nicholas himself believed the myth of his own absolute power. Honoring a pledge to come to France's aid at the earliest possible moment, the Czar ordered the first mobilized units of his ponderous force to make an immediate attack on Germany.

As two hastily assembled armies of white-uniformed peasants advanced slowly over sandy roads into East Prussia, the limitations of czarist fiat became clear. Nicholas could not will into being the supplies of telegraph wire, shells, horses—even the black bread and tea of the men's rations— that ran short in the very first days of the offensive. Nor could he overcome the years of neglect by a war minister who denounced machine guns and rifled cannon as "vicious innovations" and insisted that the Russian army continue its reliance on the bayonet. Most of all, there was an unfillable void of leadership. Men of ability—including the Czar's own cousin—had been systematically barred from power as threats to the regime's sclerotic stability. Even the cunning Rasputin was incapacitated at this crucial moment, hospitalized with a knife wound inflicted by an outraged woman. And Russia's finest strategic mind was a thousand miles away, in exile and bitter opposition.

In neutral Switzerland, a small group of Russian émigrés watched with a wild surmise as Europe disintegrated around them. Most of these assorted literati and revolutionaries had their eyes fixed on Russia, where the czarist regime began to crumble beneath the hammer blows of 1914 and 1915. A few, however, looked farther, and among these was a balding, Tatar-eyed Marxist named Vladimir Ilyich Ulyanov.

Ulyanov, a brilliant lawyer turned revolutionary, had for more than two decades cut a swath through Russia's underground politics. Under the *nom de révolution* of Lenin he had led the Bolsheviks, the most extreme faction of the Marxist Social Democratic Party. Now exiled in Zurich, Lenin was at low ebb politically. He was cut off from Russia, bereft of all but a few diehard supporters, earning a meager living with occasional library work. Sharing an apartment with the family of a shoemaker, he and his wife Krupskaya took their meals at a dilapidated boardinghouse that Krupskaya suspected of being frequented by criminals.

Yet if Lenin was almost barren of political resources, he was powerful in intellectual ones. In his Zurich rooms, he drafted his most devastating attack on the international political-economic order, in a pamphlet entitled *Imperialism: The Highest Stage of Capitalism,* which laid the blame for the holocaust of World War I squarely on the system of industrial monopolies that had transformed Europe and America over the preceding decades. The war was caused not by faulty leadership or rising nationalism or uncontrolled militarism; rather it was "an annexationist, predatory, plunderous war" being fought "for the division of the world, for the partition and reparation of colonies, 'spheres of influence' of finance capital." The strains and contradictions of monopoly capitalism had reached out to engulf the entire world, and now they were grinding to their inevitable bloody conclusion in the trenches of Europe.

Drawing on the work of J. A. Hobson, Lenin documented the growth of industrial capitalism into a global system of investment and control, especially the concentration of industrial holdings into giant monopolistic holdings throughout Europe and America. In the United States, for example, 1 percent of the firms in the country employed 30 percent of the workers, used more than 75 percent of the electric and steam power generated, and produced 43 percent of all output. These huge combines, Lenin concluded, were forced to look abroad for further growth. Thus Rockefeller's Standard Oil Company, the Anglo-Dutch Shell trust, and a consortium of German banks divided up control of wells in Russia, Romania, and the East Indies, as did the House of Morgan and German shipping cartels of world steamship lines. "Today," he summarized the world situation, "monopoly has become a fact."

Railroads in particular seemed to fascinate Lenin. Railroad construction, he claimed, seemed a "simple, natural, democratic, cultural and civilising enterprise. . . . But as a matter of fact the capitalist threads, which in thousands of different intercrossings bind these enterprises with private property in the means of production in general, have converted this work of construction into an instrument for oppressing *a thousand million* people (in the colonies and semi-colonies), that is, more than half the population of the globe."

As the economic struggle for division of the world continued, Lenin claimed, it increasingly took the form of violence and political domination. By the early 1900s, the world was completely divided; only a redivision was possible. Since the industrial nations, in Lenin's analysis, were buying off their working classes with the profits squeezed from colonies, that redivision was imperative. Since each of those nations had built great military machines, the redivision would be by force. The result, he concluded, was the World War.

In 1914 events appeared to be marching to Lenin's arguments. One by one, the nations touched by the industrial revolution were drawn into the European war: Japan, Turkey, Italy, Bulgaria, Romania, Greece. Armies clashed in eastern Africa and the Arabian deserts; fleets battled off South America; men came from Saskatoon, Pretoria, and Auckland to fight in Flanders. Only one industrial power was still uninvolved—and for it too time might run out.

WILSON AND THE ROAD TO WAR

The outbreak of fighting in Europe came as a sudden shock to most Americans—"like lightning out of a clear sky," one congressman wrote. Even Edward House, who from Berlin had warned Wilson in May that "an awful cataclysm" was in store, returned to the United States on July 21 confident that the situation in Europe was improving. Seven days later, Austria attacked Serbia; within another week eight countries were in the war.

In contrast to the galvanized chancelleries of Europe, the military and diplomatic establishments in Washington hardly stirred in the August heat. The State, Navy, and War departments—all housed in a massive granite and iron pile that Henry Adams had dubbed the "architectural infant asylum"—responded but feebly to the distant crisis. Assistant Secretary of the Navy Franklin D. Roosevelt, after rushing back to his office from Cape Cod on July 30, was appalled to find that "nobody seemed the least bit excited" about the war. In Theodore Roosevelt style, the young Roosevelt struggled for several days to get the American fleet mobilized and concentrated for possible action, but he sparked little response from the officers and bureaucrats around him. The War Department, meanwhile—with its bare rudiments of a general staff and a peacetime army of just 100,000 men —was even more somnolent.

Over in the State wing of the building, Secretary Bryan tried to intervene on the side of peace. Roosevelt thought him hopelessly naïve. "These dear good people like W.J.B.," FDR wrote to his wife Eleanor, ". . . have as much conception of what a general European war means" as his four-year-old son had of higher mathematics. But it was neither naïveté nor unpreparedness that was frustrating Bryan; rather, it was the lack of direction from across the street, at the White House.

Wilson, who had never shown a strong interest in European affairs, now seemed to turn his back on the Continent. When reporters asked whether he would tender his good offices to the warring powers, Wilson snapped that tradition forbade America to "take part" in Europe's quarrels. Likewise he spurned repeated suggestions from Bryan that the President offer himself as a mediator. Wilson met with the Cabinet on August 4, approved a plan to evacuate Americans stranded in Europe by the war, and agreed to an immediate declaration of neutrality accompanied by a statement urging Americans to remain "neutral in fact as well as in name, impartial in thought as well as in action." Then he hurried back to the sickbed of his wife, whose worsening health had preoccupied him throughout the crisis. Later that night he wrote to a friend, "The more I read about the conflict across the seas, the more open it seems to me to utter condemnation. The outcome no man can even conjecture." Two days later Mrs. Wilson died, and the President briefly seemed on the verge of collapse.

Emotion shaped Wilson's initial response to the war: contempt toward the Europeans for allowing it to occur, outrage at the German violation of Belgium, and most of all his personal sorrow. But underlying his emotional rejection of the war was a moral vision, and as the months passed and Wilson more dispassionately studied the deadlock in Europe, that vision came to dominate his thinking. America would redeem warring Europe (just as she sought to uplift Asia and Latin America) by holding aloft the beacon of liberty and peace. By January 1915, he was calling on his countrymen to exult in their neutral stance. "Look abroad upon the troubled world. Only America at peace!

"Think of the deep-wrought destruction of economic resources, of life and of hope that is taking place in some parts of the world, and think of the reservoir of hope, the reservoir of energy, the reservoir of sustenance that there is in this great land of plenty. May we not look forward to the time when we shall be called blessed among the nations because we succored the nations of the world in their time of distress and dismay?"

For Woodrow Wilson the World War offered both horror and hope. Like Lenin, Wilson believed that a radically different world order could be built from the international system that the war was smashing to pieces. Both men, from their neutral sanctuaries, saw the holocaust engulfing Europe as the product of fundamental flaws in the old order. Beyond that, however, their agreement ended. For Lenin, Europe's crime was capitalism; for Wilson it was selfish power politics. Lenin took his blueprint for change from *Das Kapital,* Wilson from the New Testament and his father's Presbyterian sermons. And while Lenin commanded only a dispirited handful of revolutionaries, Wilson led one of the most powerful nations on earth.

Wilson's conception of America's potential role in the war was a positive and activist one. He sought to keep his nation neutral, Barbara Tuchman suggests, in order to "make America a larger, rather than a lesser, force in the world." The British historian Lord Devlin concluded that Wilson was from nearly the beginning animated by the desire to use the neutral power of the United States for "restoring the peace of the world." From that desire would flow three years of tortuous diplomacy that would end, in seeming failure, in April of 1917.

Wilson tried to take the long view. "I have tried to look at this war ten years ahead," he told Ida Tarbell, "to be a historian at the same time I was an actor. A hundred years from now it will not be the bloody details that the world will think of in this war: it will be the causes behind it, the readjustments which it will force." Since he saw those causes as lying in the actions of both sides, he felt qualified to act as an impartial mediator.

Several obstacles stood in the way of Wilson's attempts to mediate the conflict and in so doing to guide the peace talks to the higher goal of fashioning a new world order. One was the propaganda efforts of the belligerents, by which they tried to draw America into the war or at least to bend her neutrality to serve their own purposes. Another was the domestic agitation, both for and against America's entering the war, led by such figures as Theodore Roosevelt for intervention and Jane Addams for pacifism. Indeed, the controversy reached even into Wilson's inner councils, dividing the isolationist Secretary of State Bryan from Wilson's more belligerent advisors, Robert Lansing and Edward House.

The greatest barrier to Wilson's goal of a negotiated peace, however, was the European powers' imprisonment within the military juggernaut they had unleashed. Only a total victory would seem to justify the tremendous sacrifices of lives and wealth that they were making. Every new weapon—the submarine, the tank, poison gas—and every new ally tempted the side possessing it to believe that one more great push would bring complete military success.

These delusions of victory were never stronger than in the first months of the war. With German armies nearing the outskirts of Paris, and a Russian force thrusting deep into East Prussia, Wilson despaired of being able to put his principles into effect. To House he wrote that "there is nothing that we can as yet do or even attempt. What a pathetic thing to have this come." The German advance finally was halted in the Battle of the Marne, and an entire Russian army was destroyed at Tannenberg; still it took several more months for the two sides to exhaust their first efforts. Only at the end of 1914 could the first moves toward peace be made.

*   *   *

Wilson's Secretary of State was to play a key role in shaping America's first peace initiatives. William Jennings Bryan was no longer the stentorian "Boy Orator" who had shocked and aroused the country in 1896. Four Democratic conventions, and two more runs for the presidency, lay in between. The onetime "demagogue" from the West had made his share of partisan compromises in the intervening two decades: seeking a commission in the Spanish war and then campaigning against imperialism in 1900; supporting free silver but not disavowing the conservative, Alton Parker, whom his party nominated in 1904. Bryan's receding hair and expanding paunch seemed to confirm his evolution into a conventional, albeit progressive, politician.

But Bryan the moral visionary was in fact far from dead. Indeed, he often outstripped Wilson in applying idealistic principles to foreign policy. Bryan was the guiding force behind the negotiation of conciliation treaties between the United States and thirty other nations. He also was Wilson's chief prop in the struggle to avoid war with Mexico. For the Secretary as much as the President, World War I represented a crowning opportunity to bring to life his most cherished visions of a new world order based upon the tenets of Christian charity and fellowship.

Like Wilson, Bryan was committed to the belief that "war could be exorcised by making moral principles as binding upon nations as upon individuals," Paolo Coletta noted. But he conceived America's neutral role in the war differently from Wilson. While the President searched with increasing desperation for some form of diplomatic leverage that would enable him to force the belligerents to the peace table, Bryan advocated what he called a "Real Neutrality" where America would remain even-handed, uninvolved, and thus free to influence Europe by its moral example. Wilson's principles led eventually to the internationalist ideas embodied in the League of Nations and the United Nations; Bryan's evolved into the isolationism of the 1930s.

In 1914, the two men were still working in harmony. At first, they had to grapple with foreign actions that threatened both American leverage and American neutrality. Early in the war, the British government took decisive steps to cut off all commerce with Germany, steps that severely infringed upon the previously accepted rights of neutrals to trade with belligerents. Through their Orders in Council, the British extended the category of contraband to include foodstuffs and most other materials and used the doctrine of the continuous voyage to limit the trade not only of Germany but also of her neutral neighbors. Additional British actions particularly aroused resentment in America: the opening of U.S. mail to Europe; the blacklisting of American firms that did business with the Central Powers; the flying of neutral flags by British ships.

Bryan drafted a series of protests against Britain's infringements of America's neutral rights, but he had his misgivings about the use of force. The Secretary would countenance no implied threat of retaliation against Britain, nor any American military buildup that might alarm the European powers. An arms embargo would have been perhaps the best means of forcing the Allies to change their maritime practices; yet Bryan actively opposed legislation that would have cut off arms shipments the combatants needed.

Instead he sought a humanitarian solution to the impasse over neutral trade. In February 1915, at Bryan's urging, Wilson proposed to the belligerents a plan for reopening trade, at least in foodstuffs, to the Central Powers. Only food for Germany's and Austria's civilian population would be admitted through the British blockade, and the United States would undertake to monitor German compliance with those conditions. Britain and Germany were quick to see the tremendous power that control over food shipments to Europe would give Wilson; both sides rejected the offer. Thus the closest collaboration between Bryan and Wilson ended in failure.

The two men were increasingly forced apart as Germany radically changed the stakes in the debate over neutral rights. In the same month that Wilson made his offer to supervise food imports, the German navy unleashed its U-boats against shipping around the British Isles. This initial submarine campaign, undertaken with only a handful of boats, was aimed more at forcing the British to negotiate than seriously challenging their command of the seas. Still, the Germans were sinking ships and killing people—including, on March 28, 1915, an American named Leon Thrasher, who was traveling on the unarmed British liner *Falaba*.

The death of Thrasher divided the American government. Bryan urged that the President bar Americans from traveling on the ships of belligerents, even circumscribe U.S. trade with Europe if necessary, in order to preserve the impartial position of the United States. Lansing, on the other hand, termed the sinking of the *Falaba* a "wanton act . . . in direct violation of the principles of humanity as well as the law of nations." He called for a strong protest against Germany's U-boat campaign. Wilson temporized between the opinions of his two advisors, and meanwhile had warned the Germans that he would hold them to "strict accountability" for any further American deaths. The debate within the Administration continued for another five weeks, until a U-boat commander dramatically forced the issue.

On May 7, 1915, the British passenger steamer *Lusitania* was torpedoed and sunk off the Irish coast. Nearly 1,200 people died in the sinking, including 128 Americans. Bryan immediately suggested—and historians have subsequently confirmed—that the *Lusitania* was secretly carrying munitions and thus was a legitimate target of war. He used the public outcry over the sinking to reiterate his case: that Americans be warned off traveling on belligerent ships, that any apology or compensation for the incident could be postponed until the war in Europe ended, and that in the meantime an evenhanded protest to both Germany and Britain be sent. The alternative, Bryan feared, was war.

Wilson disagreed. A retreat into isolation, he told Bryan, might save lives, but in the long run it would only diminish the chances of finding a way to lasting peace. "To show this sort of yielding to threat and danger would only make matters worse." When the German government quibbled over Wilson's first note protesting the *Lusitania* incident, the President drafted a second in which he demanded that the Germans give specific guarantees not to attack unarmed ships. Unwilling to sign the note, Bryan resigned on June 7, and Lansing replaced him as Secretary of State.

Ironically, the submarine threat gradually receded after Bryan's resignation. When, in August, two Americans died in the torpedoing of the British steamer *Arabic*, the Germans offered an apology and indemnity. More important, Wilson extracted from German Ambassador Johann von Bernstorff the so-called *Arabic* pledge that no more passenger ships would be

attacked, a pledge that Berlin finally confirmed nine months—and another
torpedoed passenger ship—later with the *Sussex* pledge. The German submarine skippers, meanwhile, turned their attention back to sinking Allied
warships and freighters.

*   *   *

The threat of war between Germany and America really had never been
serious. The phlegmatic Colonel House may briefly have lost control,
warning the President that Americans "can no longer remain neutral spectators" after the *Lusitania* sinking, but the overwhelming majority of the
public seemed opposed to an outright break with Germany. The editors
of the Chicago *Standard,* echoing the sentiments of publicists and politicians across the country, urged its readers to view the incident with calm-
ness and deliberation: "We must protect our citizens, but we must find
some other way than war." Thus, when Wilson spoke of America being
"too proud to fight" over the submarine sinkings, too sure of its own
righteousness to descend into the morass of war with Germany, he struck
a responsive chord.

Some of Wilson's critics, however, responded with anger rather than
applause. Theodore Roosevelt characterized the President's course in the
submarine controversy as "supine inaction," mere "milk and water" diplomacy. Wilson, the old Rough Rider growled, spoke for "all the hyphenated
Americans . . . the solid flubdub and pacifist vote . . . every soft creature,
every coward and weakling, every man who can't look more than six inches
ahead." The *Lusitania* galvanized partisan opposition to the President in
Congress, and guaranteed him the enmity of the small but influential band
still clustered around Roosevelt. Foremost among its members was Senator Henry Cabot Lodge, senior Republican on the Foreign Relations Committee.

The British were quick to capitalize on American revulsion at the submarine attacks. British spokesmen linked the *Lusitania* to other alleged
German atrocities in France and Belgium, played up the theme of Prussian
autocracy and militarism, and sought to persuade Americans that a victory
by the Central Powers would endanger the safety of the United States. The
Germans, however, countered with an extremely effective propaganda
campaign of their own, playing in part on the sentiments of German-
Americans and the anti-British feelings of Irish-Americans. The latter received a particular boost in mid-1916, when the British bloodily sup-
pressed an uprising in Ireland and, over the formal protest of the U.S.
Senate, executed several Irish leaders. In the end, scholars have concluded, the propaganda efforts of the two sides largely canceled each other

out, and in the process left the American public with a better grasp of the war situation than the populations of the belligerent countries.

Wilson thus faced challenges to his policies from his political opponents, from abroad—and also from within his own party. William Jennings Bryan had not renounced his belief that the Administration's hard line toward Germany was leading to war, nor had he stopped trying to change it. While Wilson was struggling in early 1916 to get the German government to confirm von Bernstorff's *Arabic* pledge, two Bryan supporters—Thomas Gore of Oklahoma and A. Jefferson McLemore of Texas—introduced legislation in Congress to bar Americans from traveling on armed ships of the warring powers. Bryan and others hoped by this means to induce the British to disarm their commercial steamers, thus allowing German submarines to stop the ships and search them as per the old rules of cruiser warfare. Failing that, at least U.S. citizens would be kept out of the way of German torpedoes. Wilson handily defeated these Gore-McLemore resolutions, but the price in lost congressional goodwill was high.

The President further alienated the peace wing of the Democratic party when he pushed through Congress, with considerable Republican support, a "preparedness" program involving major increases in land and naval forces. Taking these defeats in good grace, Bryan continued to pledge his personal support to the President. However, the Nebraskan also kept up his public warnings against the "Jingoes" within the Administration who would "drive us into war."

*   *   *

In Europe, 1916 was another year of bloody stalemate. The German attack on Verdun and Britain's counteroffensive along the Somme both ended in defeat. In the east, the Central Powers and Russia traded staggering blows without altering the strategic balance. The British and German fleets clashed off Jutland in the North Sea, to no avail. Likewise, Italy's armies were checked on the southern front by the Austrians.

Amid the whirl of events during late 1915 and early 1916, as Wilson was spun about in the European maelstrom, the President moved at home and abroad toward new strategies that would mark one of the transcendent acts of political leadership in American history—an act rivaling Jefferson's assuming command of the republican movement in the 1790s and Lincoln's decision for Emancipation during the Civil War. In all these transforming acts, the leader sensed profound human needs on the part of followers, took action, raised supporters' hopes and expectations, and worked with followers-turned-leaders in a supreme enterprise in collective leadership.

Wilson had followed a wavering middle-of-the-road course since the

New Freedom's glory days of 1913–14. His tariff, banking, and other reforms stood proudly on the legislative books, but he appeared to compromise them by some of his appointments—notably of conservatives to the new Federal Reserve Board and Federal Trade Commission. He supported trade unionism but straddled the issue of labor's immunity to the antitrust laws. He favored the curbing of child labor—but not a *federal* child labor law because he deemed it unconstitutional; he favored woman suffrage, but preferred to leave the matter to the states, and hence to the reactionary state legislatures; he had promised that Negroes too would share in the New Freedom, but tolerated increased segregation in federal employment. For a time, he welcomed controversial business leaders like Henry Ford and even J. P. Morgan to the White House.

In foreign policy, the man who had denounced Republican imperialism in 1912 put American troops into Veracruz in 1914, established a *de facto* United States protectorate over Haiti in 1915, and perpetuated American intervention in Nicaragua and Santo Domingo. The Administration that ruled against loans by American bankers to European belligerents in August 1914 allowed American investors to buy over $2 billion in bonds from the Allies within the next two and a half years. The President who urged Americans to remain neutral in thought as well as in deed kept in London a U.S. ambassador more rabidly anti-German than many Englishmen. As the Central and Allied powers grappled and tottered, at times Wilson seemed bound for war, at other times bound to peace.

Like most changes in grand strategy, Wilson's did not result from a sudden revelation but from his and his party's close watch of the shifting balance of political forces at home and military forces abroad. Like most acts of creative leadership, Wilson's was compounded of commitment, opportunism, and chance. His shift in strategy was signaled at the end of January 1916 in a decision of calculated audacity—his nomination of Louis Brandeis as associate justice of the Supreme Court.

"I tell Louis, if he is going to retire, he is certainly doing it with a burst of fireworks," Brandeis's wife, Alice, wrote on reading the press reaction to his nomination. The fireworks continued to burst from that time to the day five months later when she proudly greeted her husband, returning from his law office to their Dedham home, with "Good evening, Mr. Justice Brandeis." Progressives and conservatives waged a battle over the nomination all the more bitter for being partly under cover. Financial and industrial interests opposed the "people's lawyer" on the public grounds of lack of judicial temperament and the like, but in fact attacked this radical—and a Jewish radical, to boot—because they did not want his economic and social views represented on the High Court.

Brandeis himself, while publicly standing mute, supplied his supporters with reams of material to rebut the opposition, wrote a partial brief defending his own "high reputation," and personally and secretly lobbied two Democratic members of the Senate Judiciary Committee. Boston Brahmins, headed by Brahmin-in-chief A. Lawrence Lowell, circulated an anti-Brandeis petition. Brandeis's supporters, including Rabbi Stephen Wise and Henry Morgenthau, threw themselves into the battle. Brandeis's young friend Felix Frankfurter wrote unsigned editorials for the *New Republic;* Walter Lippmann campaigned day after day on Capitol Hill. Following this counterattack, and a public statement by Wilson that constituted one of the most generous endorsements of an Administration nominee in presidential history, the Senate voted for confirmation, 47 to 22, with only one Democrat deserting the President and his nominee.

During the spring and summer months of 1916, Wilson shifted steadily toward a progressive stance in both politics and policy. In part, he was moving into the void left by the disintegrating Progressive party. Not only had the Democrats lost seats in the 1914 elections—predictably for the party in power—but the Bull Moosers too suffered setbacks across the country, though the indomitable Hiram Johnson won reelection as governor of California. Progressive leadership was more divided than ever, as Theodore Roosevelt edged back toward the GOP and Pinchot progressives eyed the liberalizing Democracy with rising hopes. A great Democratic party opportunity was beckoning.

Wilson realized that policy, not rhetoric, would be the acid test of his own shift toward progressivism. By early summer 1916, he was not only supporting a rural credits bill and a child labor bill but personally lobbying members of Congress. As the President moved left, progressives increasingly flocked to his standard: Jane Addams, John Dewey, Lillian Wald, Herbert Croly, Lincoln Steffens, and a host of other national and grassroots leaders of progressivism. Wilson met with another convert, Walter Lippmann, to mutual enchantment.

The President had virtually dished the Bull Moosers by the time they convened in Chicago early in June 1916, at the same time as the Republicans and only a mile away. Under pressure from Taft and other Old Guard leaders, the GOP drafted Supreme Court Justice Charles Evans Hughes as the ideal compromise candidate who might unite the fractured ranks of Republicanism. Since Taft's preconvention stance was "anyone but Roosevelt," and TR's "anyone but Taft or Root," the old rivals could at least unite behind the mildly progressive candidacy of the former New York governor—and behind their ultimate war cry, "anyone but Wilson."

The end came for the Bull Moosers during the Republican convention.

From his home in Oyster Bay, Roosevelt had been negotiating with Republican leaders, using the only leverage he had left—his threat to run again under the Bull Moose banner. But his heart was not in it; by now he was far more interested in the nation's foreign and war policies. At the last moment, after the indignant and frustrated Progressive convention nominated Roosevelt anyway, he declined the honor—and then had the audacity to urge his old comrades to draft Senator Henry Cabot Lodge, a moderate standpatter and the Colonel's longtime confidant. Two weeks later, the Progressive party leadership disbanded the party, but progressivism would not die. Early in August, a rump of the Progressive party held a new convention in Indianapolis, repudiated Roosevelt, and endorsed Wilson.

The Democratic convention in St. Louis was a far happier affair and a far more momentous one. For at this convention the antiwar forces in the Democracy spoke up with a power and passion the party leadership could not ignore. It had been planned not as a peace convention but as a patriotic one. The President had directed that "Americanism" and "preparedness" be the keynotes, and the flag-bedecked hall was full of spread-eagle symbolism. When the keynoter, Governor Martin Glynn of New York, dutifully sounded these themes, however, the response seemed so tepid that Glynn decided to hurry through pages of his address that listed historical precedents when the United States did *not* go to war. But this was the red meat the crowd wanted, and as he began to recite the provocations that the nation had not converted into war, the crowd picked up the refrain, chanting again and again: "What did we do? What did we do?" and Glynn roared back: "We didn't go to war! We didn't go to war!"

The convention delegates—leaders in their own precincts but relegated to mere followership at these party conclaves—were exerting a leadership of their own. Other speakers responded with thunderous peace oratory. The delegates called Bryan from his seat in the press gallery—the Peerless Orator had been denied a convention seat—and Bryan thanked God that the people had a President who did not want war. Wilson, the "peace President," was nominated by acclamation.

Sounding the peace theme, and passing a strongly progressive platform that Wilson had largely framed, the Democratic convention set the tone of the fall contest. The President, who had been preaching both peace and preparedness, both Americanism and internationalism, now moved strongly toward the stance that would make his 1916 campaign famous: "He kept us out of war." Pamphlets by the millions and newspaper ads by the thousands amplified the keynote of peace. Hughes not only made tactical errors—most notably tying himself to the Republican Old Guard in California and unwittingly snubbing the prickly Hiram Johnson—but he failed to work out an effective strategy beyond carping at the Administration record. His potential big break came in early September after Wilson, in order to head off a nationwide rail strike, forced through Congress the Adamson Act requiring an eight-hour day on interstate railroads. Hughes quite reasonably seized on this as a campaign issue, protesting that Wilson had given in to organized labor to win its votes, but the Republican candidate may have done little more than polarize the contest, as more businessmen moved to his side and more laborites and progressives to Wilson's.

The 1916 election would long be remembered for its poignant election night: Hughes went to bed expecting to wake up as President, and Wilson retired expecting to awaken as a lame duck. The Republican candidate had had good reason to be optimistic, for early returns showed him sweeping the Northeast, save for Ohio, and the Democratic New York *World* conceded victory to him. Then the West and of course the South came in heavily Democratic, with California's thirteen votes proving decisive for Wilson in the final 277 to 254 electoral college outcome. California's popular margin for Wilson was by 4,000 out of 928,000. Snubbing an old Bull Mooser, the pundits pontificated, could be costly.

Wilson's photo finish portended ill for the Democratic party. A popular President, riding the tide of peace and progressivism, had barely beaten an inept campaigner hardly known in much of the nation. The barely reunited Republican party had reestablished its hammerlock on the big industrial states of the East, awakening horrendous Democratic memories of McKinley's trouncings of Bryan. The shape of the nation's political future was forecast far more in the GOP's party victory than in Wilson's personal one. And, after a decade of national debate and ferment over issues of industrial democracy, perhaps a hint of the nation's ideological future lay in the Socialist Party vote in 1916, which dropped off almost 40 percent from its high point of four years before.

*   *   *

The charge leveled by Bryan and others, that the Administration was increasingly pro-Allied, had some truth to it. Certainly Walter Hines Page, the U.S. envoy in London, was so outspoken in his pro-British views that Wilson thought he needed to be brought home for "a bath in American opinion." Robert Lansing, too, Bryan's successor at the State Department, seemed to be working for an Allied victory. He had watered down Bryan's protests against British abuses on the high seas while toughening the language of notes to Germany, had advised Wilson to cut off German radio traffic with America, and had drafted the legal rulings that enabled the Allied governments to obtain credit in the United States.

This last point was of special importance, for strong financial ties were growing between American industry and the Allied war effort. By April of 1917, American firms had advanced Britain and France $2.3 billion, and were doing almost $3 billion in trade each year with the Allied countries. The war was working a revolution in global economic relations, making New York the financial capital of the world in place of London. The American economy, meanwhile, was stimulated to new heights of prosperity by the Europeans' war expenditures.

Bryan would allege, in 1917, that America finally entered the war at the behest of "Eastern financiers" determined to "make their investments in the war loans of the Allies profitable." "We are going into war upon command" of Wall Street "gold," Senator Norris charged. Echoed by such respected historians as Walter Millis and Charles Beard, that theory later gained wide acceptance in the 1920s and '30s, although more recent writers have rebutted it. By the end of 1916, according to John Milton Cooper, Wilson was brandishing the money club over the Allied heads; "if Senator Norris's 'command of gold' existed, the United States held it and exercised it."

The one man who surely could influence Wilson was Edward Mandell House. The self-styled Texas "colonel" had the President's ear and his confidence; he also was one of Wilson's prime sources of information on European politics after his two trips to the Continent in 1914 and 1915. According to House's diary, Wilson assured him on the eve of his second mission to Europe that "we are of the same mind and it is not necessary to go into details with you." The President entrusted House with the task of bringing Europe's leaders around to his ideas for a compromise peace.

If Wilson really believed that he and House thought alike—a possibility, given the pains House took to hide his true feelings from others—then the President was mistaken. While Wilson was trying to force the Germans to honor the *Arabic* pledge and Bryan was working for the Gore-McLemore resolutions, House composed a secret plan to bring America into the war on the side of the Allies. He proposed that, after obtaining the consent of the British, Wilson call for a peace conference, with America to join the fight against Germany if the Berlin government refused. House refined this plan in a series of secret discussions with the British Foreign Secretary, Sir Edward Grey, and then formalized it in the so-called House-Grey Memorandum.

That Wilson accepted the House-Grey Memorandum in early 1916 has mystified many observers since. Certainly the President had not abandoned his belief that the "worst thing that could possibly happen *to the world,"* as he confided to his new wife, "would be for the United States to be drawn into this contest." Wilson made several important changes in House's memorandum, noting that he would use every diplomatic measure available to bring Germany to the peace table and that should those fail America's entry into the war was only "probable." Still, Wilson was running a great risk by endorsing the plan, a risk he could justify to himself only with the possible reward of ending the fighting in Europe.

Ironically, the British refused to take up Wilson's half-commitment to intervene on their side. Several times during the spring and summer of 1916 Wilson, through House, asked the British for their consent to his calling a peace conference, but each time he was rebuffed. It eventually became clear to House and Wilson that the British wanted to win more than they wanted peace. When no Allied victories followed, the House-Grey Memorandum was allowed to lapse.

The failure of House's secret diplomacy, plus the sneaking suspicion that the Colonel may have been duped all along by the British, may have been the first step in the weakening of Wilson's ties to his Texan advisor. In the past, the President had always sought to keep House close at hand; now he offered to send him to London as U.S. ambassador. Yet if the President may have been a little disillusioned with House, his disgust with the British was clear and manifest. In the fall, he informed Lord Grey "in the strongest terms" that the feeling of the American people was "as hot against Great Britain as it was at first against Germany and likely to grow hotter still against an indefinite continuation of the war." Conventional diplomacy had failed to secure peace; so had secret machinations. Once the election of 1916 was safely won, Wilson resolved to strike out on his own, through the public and oratorical means that had served him so well in domestic politics.

Wilson's peace offensive in the winter of 1916–17 met resistance from every side. The President originally intended to demand an immediate armistice and to repeat his offer of mediation. House, however, persuaded him to limit his statement to a call for both sides to reveal their war aims. Even this move was sabotaged by Lansing, who of his own accord told reporters, on the day Wilson's peace note was published, that America was on the "verge of war." The President, furious, made Lansing retract his remarks and came close to firing him, but the damage was already done. The British, now even more hopeful of imminent American support, announced war aims that included transfers of territories and colonies which clearly were unacceptable to the Central Powers.

Berlin, however, did not publish its own demands, calling instead for

peace talks at which both sides would state their case. This was the slim
hope to which Wilson clung, not knowing that the Germans had already
secretly resolved against peace. In the meantime Wilson laid out, in an
address to the Senate, his own design for "a peace without victory."

Victory for one side or the other, Wilson argued, would not bring true
peace. It "would leave a sting, a resentment, a bitter memory upon which
terms of peace would rest, not permanently, but only as upon quicksand."
A lasting peace would have to rest on respect for the rights of small
nations, on freedom of the seas, upon the free self-determination of subject peoples such as the Poles.

"I am proposing, as it were, that the nations should with one accord
adopt the doctrine of President Monroe as the doctrine of the world: that
no nation should seek to extend its polity over any other nation or people.
. . . I am proposing that all nations henceforth avoid entangling alliances
which would draw them into competitions of power, catch them in a net
of intrigue and selfish rivalry. . . .

"I am proposing government by the consent of the governed . . . freedom of the seas . . . moderation of armaments. . . . These are American
principles, American policies. We could stand for no others. And they are
also the principles and policies of forward-looking men and women everywhere, of every modern nation, of every enlightened community. They are
the principles of mankind and must prevail."

The Senate greeted Wilson's elevating statement of ideals with thunder-
ous applause. The President's speech, however, changed no minds in
Berlin, where the military commanders had already browbeaten Kaiser
Wilhelm into unleashing Germany's submarines for an all-out attack on
Britain's vital sea links. In Washington, Ambassador von Bernstorff, himself desperate to prevent war between the United States and Germany, fed
Wilson's hopes with positive replies to the President's suggestions while
bombarding Berlin with telegrams begging for reconsideration. At last, on
January 31, von Bernstorff was forced to tell Wilson that unrestricted
submarine warfare would resume the next day. Allied, American, and other
neutral ships would be sunk indiscriminately. The chance for peace was
lost.

The collapse of all his hopes shocked Wilson deeply. He felt, he confided
to House, "as if the world had suddenly reversed itself . . . and he could
not get his balance." He severed relations with Germany and on February
26 asked Congress for the power to put navy gun crews on American
merchant ships, hoping that these actions would force the German government to reverse itself. Instead, the toll of sinkings in the North Atlantic
mounted, until Wilson finally was forced to call Congress back into session.

On April 2, he went before both houses and called for a declaration of war against Germany.

How could a country fervently committed to neutrality, led by a President with a sweeping vision of the benefits to be derived from peace, choose to go to war? Part of the explanation lay in the dire and intolerable nature of the German provocations. As one historian put it: "Britain's violations of neutral rights provoked delay and argument, but claims for damages could eventually be settled peacefully; Germany's procedure presented a threat to important economic interests and also threatened life itself, a matter not subject to amicable arbitration." After February 1, 1917, as the Germans continued to sink American ships and kill American citizens, the consensus for peace among American voters had rapidly unraveled.

A period of confusion might have followed, but instead the German government made a critical diplomatic blunder. The new German Foreign Secretary, Arthur Zimmermann, had cabled to Mexico a proposal for a military alliance, under which the Latin republic would join in attacking America in return for Texas, New Mexico, and Arizona. The British had intercepted the telegram and forwarded it to the State Department, which made it public on February 28. Touching a sensitive nerve, the Zimmermann telegram crystallized national opinion. Editors castigated Germany's actions as "sneaking and despicable." There was a national outcry, but no stampede toward war—most Americans were still yearning for both honor *and* peace.

At this point, Wilson demonstrated his power to lead, as the members of the House and Senate overwhelmingly embraced his call to fight "for the ultimate peace of the world and for the liberation of its peoples, the German people included: for the rights of nations great and small . . . to choose their way of life" so that the world could be "made safe for democracy." Individual legislators like Robert La Follette and George Norris— whom Wilson denounced as members of a "little group of willful men, representing no opinion but their own"—did honestly differ with the President as to how those ideals might be translated into policy. But for one dramatic moment in American history, public emotion and private vision were fused into national action.

Others took a quite different view—notably V. I. Lenin. And he was right, to a degree; the bonds of trade and travel did help draw the United States into the war. But much more was involved. Wilson's search for a road to peace rather than war cannot be gainsaid. As Devlin has noted, the President was prepared, just prior to Germany's shift to unrestricted submarine warfare, to stop trading with the Allies rather than extend them formal loans and thus compromise America's neutral stance. Even after February 1, the policy of retreat and noninvolvement advocated by Bryan was still an option.

Ultimately, Wilson's choice of war over isolation turned on one compelling point. "This was that, if he and America with him chose the path of submission," according to Devlin, "his ideals, his hopes, and his dreams of bringing in the new world to regenerate the old would be destroyed." Wilson did not want war—particularly not this war. Yet every ideal that he cherished impelled him to seek a democratic world order in place of the old order that Europe's war had razed. The President's intimates have testified to the agony of indecision he endured in those last two months of neutrality.

In effect, Wilson called for a revolution on April 2. He summoned Americans to rally, not around the flag, but around a radical extension of the American experiment, a goal as different from Lenin's as it was from those of supporters of the old order in both Europe and the United States. If he could mobilize Americans for war while still keeping their eyes fixed on his higher vision of peace, Wilson could yet make his ideal into reality.

MOBILIZING THE WORKSHOP

The streets of Petrograd, February 23, 1917: Thousands of Russian workers riot over food shortages. Soldiers from the city garrison join the protest and fire on police. Within days Czar Nicholas abdicates, the Duma establishes a provisional government, and councils—soviets—of soldiers and workers spring up across the country. France and Britain extend formal recognition to the Duma's representatives, but it is on the soviets that Lenin's Bolsheviks pin their hopes. Lenin, meanwhile, leaves Switzerland in a special train provided by the Germans, and makes his way back to Petrograd.

Allied commanders on the western front were uncertain how to regard the Russian February Revolution. A democratic government might revitalize the Russian army, bringing new pressure to bear on the Germans; on the other hand, with the monarchy gone Russia might collapse altogether or even, as Lenin vociferously advocated, withdraw from the war. Britain's General Sir Douglas Haig and his French counterpart, Robert Nivelle, decided to wait on neither the Russians nor the newly entered Americans. Overriding the protests of Winston Churchill and the unvoiced fears of the new Prime Minister, David Lloyd George, Haig launched a full-scale assault on German positions near Passchendaele.

After a ferocious artillery bombardment, British troops lumbered across the Belgian mud toward the enemy trenches—and were stopped almost immediately. For three months, Haig kept up the attack, eventually sacrificing 300,000 men to gain just 10,000 yards of shell-blasted swamp. Of the British dead, some 56,000 sank into the muck and could never be recovered for burial.

The Nivelle offensive also ended in failure, and in its aftermath fifty divisions of the French army mutinied. Brought in as the new French commander, General Henri Pétain eventually resolved most of the soldiers' grievances and quelled the mutiny. In the meantime, he vowed that no new offensives would be launched. "We will wait," he promised, "for the tanks and the Americans."

The war hit the American capital like a tidal wave—literally, a tidal wave of people. Within weeks, an estimated 40,000 soldiers, office-seekers, businessmen, clerks, scientists, and foreign dignitaries descended on Washington. Some were transients, but many more stayed to participate in the confusing welter of war work. "Life seemed suddenly to acquire a vivid scarlet lining," wrote one old-time resident. "The one invariable rule seemed to be that every individual was found doing something he or she had never dreamed of doing before."

Peacetime laws and the tiny federal bureaucracy could not cope with the demands of total war. General William Crozier of the Ordnance Department, charged with arming a force of 1 (eventually 3) million men, was prohibited from acquiring new offices or even hiring new clerks without specific authorization from Congress. In time, the regulations were changed, and Crozier's command grew from less than a hundred men to 68,000 soldiers and 80,000 civilians, but it was among the "slowest mobilizations of the war."

Wilson's response to the confusion was to try to sweep it aside with direct presidential intervention. At his instigation, Senator Lee Overman introduced a bill in Congress authorizing the President to "make such redistribution of functions among executive agencies . . . and . . . make such regulations and issue such orders as he may deem necessary." Despite charges from Republicans that the measure "pointed the way toward absolutism," Congress complied with his request.

From the Overman bill and other congressional grants of power, Wilson created a series of wartime agencies to direct mobilization. The first need was for men to fill out the ranks of the proposed army in France. When only 32,000 men volunteered in the first weeks after the declaration of war, Wilson called for a draft and established the Selective Service Administration. The actual work of registering, ranking, and exempting potential recruits was delegated to local draft boards appointed by the state governors; thus the federal apparatus was kept relatively small.

During the Civil War, the draft had sparked riots and desertions, and some political leaders feared that it would again. Senator James Reed of Missouri warned Secretary of War Newton Baker, who would draw the first number of the draft, "You will have the streets of our American cities running with blood on registration day." But no riots or large-scale protests materialized. The draft boards registered 24 million young men, of whom just over 2 million were inducted into the army.

Feeding and warming 2 million men was another unprecedented task for the government. Herbert Hoover of the Food Administration and Harry Garfield of the Fuel Administration sought to meet the army's needs by both increasing production and limiting domestic consumption. Neither agency had any coercive powers and so had to rely on voluntary compliance with the quotas and rations that they established. Hoover launched a massive publicity campaign to promote "meatless" and "wheatless" days each week, limit sugar consumption, and encourage families to plant "victory gardens." Domestic use of food and fuel did change marginally, but market forces worked the biggest transformations. With increased demand from both the U.S. government and the Allies, prices soared and production was boosted. For farmers and miners, patriotism went hand in hand with undreamed-of profits.

Less visible was the work of the Shipping Board. German submarines were sinking Allied shipping at a phenomenal rate—900,000 tons in April of 1917 alone—and without ships no American men or even supplies would reach Europe. The board met the need by building, buying, and renting vessels, eventually assembling a merchant marine of over 3.5 million tons. To fight the U-boat menace, the Allies organized merchant ships into convoys protected by destroyers. American shipyards ceased work on battleships and instead concentrated on convoy escorts, several hundred of which were launched by the end of the war. The convoy system proved so effective in reducing ship losses and sinking German submarines that one military historian has described it as the turning point of the war.

Riding herd over these and other wartime agencies was the War Industries Board headed by Bernard Baruch. Wilson charged the WIB with general oversight of production for both the war effort and the domestic market—an assignment both vague and demanding. Baruch was particularly adept at persuading businessmen voluntarily to join the board in reordering production and prices—thus, his biographer concludes, making the government party to a "conspiracy in restraint of trade for reasons of national security." The war forced Wilson and Baruch to adopt policies reminiscent of the collectivist aspects of Roosevelt's New Nationalism.

Industrialists initially were highly suspicious of Baruch and his agency. No businessman wanted government control of his firm; one vowed to "go out of business before I'll let them come into my shop and run it." Instead, Baruch wielded indirect power. In essence, the WIB left companies free to make whatever products they wanted, but it fixed early delivery dates —on a graduated scale of priorities—for war-related goods. Since the government oversaw rail traffic, coal production, and myriad other facets of the economy, in theory it could cut off the fuel and raw materials of any factory that failed to meet its priority deadlines. In fact, however, Baruch seldom had to invoke that threat. In general, the workshops shouldered their war burdens with alacrity.

With one dramatic exception: America's entire mobilization effort depended on the railroads, but the giant firms controlling the transport lines proved unequal to the challenge. Massive bottlenecks developed as 1917 wore on. In eastern ports, loaded freight cars piled up because the ships they were supposed to be unloaded into could not sail, the ships could not sail because they could get no fuel, and the fuel could not get to the ships because of the jam of waiting cars. As the tie-ups spread and winter approached, half the country faced the prospect of being cut off from coal shipments.

The problem stemmed partly from Washington's priority system, which played havoc with orderly freight schedules. Perhaps the worst bottleneck developed around the steel mills of Pittsburgh, where 85 percent of all cargoes carried priority tags. In the end, Wilson was forced to break the logjam by direct intervention. He appointed his Treasury Secretary and son-in-law, William G. McAdoo, to head the U.S. Railroad Administration, which in turn simply took over the lines. Gradually, government coordination of traffic and a new "permits" system designed to ensure the timely unloading of cargoes ended the crisis. McAdoo also was able to pool repair efforts on the tracks, add new rolling stock, and expand facilities at crucial freight terminals like Pittsburgh and Chicago.

Perhaps the main beneficiaries of federal control were the railway workers. The government allowed freight rates to increase 28 percent and passenger fares 18 percent, but railroad wages rose even higher. By executive order, McAdoo instituted equal pay for woman employees and attacked some forms of discrimination against blacks. Railroad unions won government recognition, an eight-hour day, and centralized grievance procedures. The government's wage commission, meanwhile, recommended a pay settlement based upon "a measure of justice, consideration for the needs of the men, whether organized or unorganized, whether replaceable or not replaceable." Labor strife on the railways subsided for the first time in years.

*　　*　　*

The intricacy of the wartime directed economy was staggering, and its accomplishments were breathtaking—especially when compared to the primitive organization of the Civil War or the brief headlong rush of 1898. Ammunition production alone required a national effort. From the cotton fields of Mississippi, cellulose for smokeless powder traveled up the Illinois Central to the great federal explosives plant in Nashville. Wood pulp crossed the Great Lakes by barge, was loaded into freight cars in Chicago, and then was carried along the Chesapeake & Ohio to another powder mill in Charleston, West Virginia. Toluol, crucial to making TNT, was extracted from the coke ovens of Pittsburgh and Birmingham and then shipped to California along the Union Pacific or the Southern Pacific. In Los Angeles, scientists "cracked" more toluol from crude oil and sent some of it to Wisconsin via the Chicago & North Western. Sulfur, for sulfuric acid, came from Texas and Louisiana along J. P. Morgan's Southern line. Nitrates too were vital; they reached eastern ports from Chile via the Panama Canal.

Once the explosives were made they had to be bagged or packed into shells. The smokeless powder again was loaded onto trains, traveling eastward this time over the Pennsylvania or Baltimore & Ohio lines to bagging plants in New Jersey, Pennsylvania, and Virginia. The TNT also was shipped to New Jersey, site of the main artillery shell factories. There booster charges, fuses, and adjusters were added—more components, from more parts of the country. At last the ammunition was ready for use. Trainloads fanned out to army bases and navy installations, or to Atlantic ports for shipment to France.

Over the course of their production the shells and explosives were handled by increasing numbers of female workers. The bagging of smokeless powder, for example, was done almost exclusively by women, in huge new government-run plants. The railroads saw a massive increase in the employment of women, rising from 31,000 in 1917 to 101,785 in the last month of the war. Women serviced engines, moved freight with electric lift trucks, and coupled cars, as well as working in railroad offices across the country.

Overall female employment, however, did not rise dramatically during the World War. The number of woman workers increased only 6.3 percent, not much higher than the increases of prewar years. The dramatic changes that *did* occur were in the nature of women's work: females were able to secure more interesting and higher-paying jobs, some in fields once exclusively the domain of men. In previous years, women had begun moving from domestic service and piecework to jobs in offices, schools, restaurants, factories, and telephone exchanges; the war merely accelerated this trend. Some of women's more spectacular gains—such as the Railroad Administration's Women's Service Section, which successfully fought sexual harassment and discrimination—disappeared after the war. The hostility of organized labor to woman workers remained largely unchanged. The shift in female employment would continue into peacetime, however.

The wartime demands that opened new job opportunities for women also helped change the lives of many Southern blacks. Over the war years more than 400,000 black men and women traveled north in search of work, most of them settling in cities along the trunk rail lines. For many, their first jobs were provided by the railroads themselves; the Pennsylvania and Erie lines, among others, actively recruited Southern blacks for such menial tasks as road work and car-cleaning. The majority of blacks, however, were able to take advantage of the war boom in employment once the railroads had taken them north. There were job openings in a variety of places and fields: the steel mills of Pennsylvania, Massachusetts war plants, the wire factories and brick yards of New Jersey.

One Connecticut city, Hartford, received 3,000 black immigrants in 1917 alone. The new climate and culture, coupled with an acute housing shortage, took its toll. "Unused to city life," one magazine wrote of the new arrivals, "crowded into dark rooms, their clothing and utensils unsuitable, the stoves they have brought being too small to heat even the tiny rooms they have procured . . . shivering with the cold from which they do not know how to protect themselves, it is small wonder that illness has overtaken large numbers." Various religious and voluntary organizations attempted to meet the housing crisis, but the more basic problem—that black workers received lower wages than whites and were forced to pay higher rents—went largely unaddressed.

The mobilization of women and the migration of blacks were great changes, but even these paled in comparison to the upheaval of sending 2 million draftees and nearly a million more soldiers, sailors, Guardsmen, and Marines to war. For this vast legion of men, 1917 was a time of tedious drilling in camps all across America; only a handful reached the fighting in France before year's end.

In July, the first token U.S. force, a division of army regulars and a battalion of Marines, debarked in St. Nazaire. Two months later, the first volunteers arrived—men wearing spring parade uniforms, uncertain how

to fire their rifles, and with just ten rounds of ammunition apiece. "To have
sent us to the front at that time," one soldier recalled, "would have been
murder." General John J. Pershing, commander of the budding American
Expeditionary Force, wisely held his men back for several more months of
training and then committed the first regiments to a quiet sector of the
front. On November 3, the Germans tested the mettle of the newcomers:
the enemy hit an American platoon in a night trench raid, killing three of
the "doughboys" and capturing eleven while leaving three of their own
dead behind. The Americans had neither run nor won; their first taste of
the war was of bloody stalemate. One way or another, however, the deadlock in France was about to end.

"Nous Voilà, Lafayette!"

On November 6, 1917, just three days after the first clash between
German and American troops in Alsace, Lenin's Bolsheviks had seized
control of the Russian capital and declared the formation of a Marxist
Soviet regime. Although he had only tenuous control of a few major cities,
Lenin had taken immediate steps to secure the "just and democratic"
peace the Bolsheviks had promised. Lev Davidovich Trotsky, a principal
Bolshevik lieutenant, met with German representatives at Brest-Litovsk
and reluctantly accepted the draconic terms that they imposed. Thereafter,
while Russia lapsed into civil war between Lenin's forces and various
opposing factions, the Germans had been able to transfer a million men
to the western front. With them General Erich Ludendorff hoped to win
the war before America could make its weight felt.

On the morning of March 21, 1918, out of a fog of smoke shells and
poison gas, sixty-three German divisions attacked the British forces near
St. Quentin and Arras. Hitting the Allied line at its weakest point, the
Germans broke through for the first time since 1914. Forced out of their
trenches, the British reeled back, losing 100,000 men and a thousand
cannon in a single week. German troops reached the rail center at Amiens,
threatening to cut the British off from the French and drive them into
the sea.

When the British checked his first thrust at Arras and Amiens, Ludendorff launched two more attacks. The first hit the British at Ypres; the
second broke through the French lines at Chemin des Dames. In this
moment of crisis, with the British in retreat and German columns only fifty
miles from Paris, General Pershing relented his insistence on keeping the
American divisions together to fight as an independent army. The American commander dispatched two units to support the British at Amiens and

sent a third to bolster the French at Château-Thierry. The U.S. 2nd Division, meanwhile, marched toward the Belleau Wood, there to meet the spearhead of the German advance on Paris.

The 2nd U.S. was a composite division, a brigade of doughboys paired with a brigade of Marines. The Americans reached Belleau Wood on June 1, only to be told by French officers on the spot that they would have to retreat. "Retreat, hell," replied Marine Captain Lloyd Williams, "we just got here!" The lone U.S. unit stopped five German divisions on the far side of the woods; then, on June 6, the Americans attacked. More than fifty percent of the American troops were killed or wounded in the frontal assault on the German positions, but the Germans were driven out of the woods and forced to retreat. The threat to Paris was over.

Ludendorff had been set back again, but he still had enough fresh troops to launch two more offensives. One drive, on Amiens, was quickly thwarted by a French counterattack. The other, however, thrust across the Marne, surrounding the 38th U.S. Infantry Regiment on three sides. Then the new Allied Supreme Commander, General Ferdinand Foch, counterpunched with a mixed force of Frenchmen, Americans, and Moroccans. Again the Germans were driven back; from then on, the strategic initiative belonged to the Allies.

The German spring offensive of 1918 may have been a blessing in disguise for the novice American troops. Pershing had originally believed that he could break the German lines with attacks by "stalking, stealthy" riflemen—the kind of tough, individualistic fighters he had commanded on the western plains, in Cuba, in Mexico. But against German artillery and machine guns, Pershing's expert riflemen would have been slaughtered en masse, just as similar French and British assaults had failed from 1914 to 1917. Even at Belleau Wood, where the Germans had had little time to fortify their positions, that sort of impromptu attack had cost the Americans enormous casualties. In the open field, however, against German columns thinned from breaking through the Allied trenches, Pershing's aggressive infantry tactics paid off.

The AEF also benefited from the "Iron Commander's" emphasis on drill and discipline. "The standards of the American Army will be those of West Point," Pershing declared in an early order. He put particular pressure on the junior officers, weeding out scores of volunteer and National Guard commanders who failed to measure up. As a result, the AEF was left with a cadre of superlative tactical leaders, young men of the caliber of Douglas MacArthur, George Patton, and George Marshall.

More than from marksmanship or discipline, the Americans drew strength from their brash self-confidence. These fresh divisions of dough-

boys—each twice as large as the war-worn Allied and German units—
marched to battle bedecked with flowers by the dazzled French. When one
frightened peasant shouted to the Marines that the war was lost, a college
linguist turned leatherneck shot back, *"Pas finie,"* thereby giving the Marne
front its name.

The Americans lost their freshness, if not their insouciance, in the
fighting at Château-Thierry and Belleau Wood. Ludendorff himself was
forced to acknowledge the toughness of his new foes. On the Marne, five
platoons of the 38th U.S. were all but annihilated in hand-to-hand fighting
with rifle butts, grenades, pistols; still the regiment held, and broke up the
German attack. When the first American division had marched through
Paris the previous summer, Colonel Charles Stanton had stopped to salute
Lafayette's tomb with the cry, "Nous voilà, Lafayette!"—"Lafayette, we are
here!" Now the hardened survivors of Ludendorff's attacks quipped,
"We've paid our debt to Lafayette; who the hell do we owe now?"

*   *   *

As late as January 1918, Wilson had not given up his hopes for a compromise peace based on the principles of democracy and international cooperation. He instructed Colonel House to assemble a panel of experts to
advise him on peace terms. In consultation with Felix Frankfurter, House
brought together a team of researchers and intellectuals that included Dr.
Isaiah Bowman of the American Geographical Society and Walter Lippmann. This informal body, dubbed "The Inquiry" by the newspapers,
assembled memos, testimony, maps—in all, more than 2,000 documents
—on questions that might be discussed at a peace conference.

More than intellectuals, events in far-off Russia affected the lives of
American soldiers, scholars, and President alike in 1918. Even before they
made peace with the Germans, the Bolsheviks denounced and published
the czarist regime's wartime treaties with the Allies. As Lenin intended,
these secret agreements, which contemplated the division of territories of
the Central Powers among Russia and its was partners, seriously embarrassed the efforts of the British and French to depict their side in the war
as just and nonimperialistic.

The publication of the secret treaties reinforced Wilson's determination
to stand aloof from the British and French, as an "associated" power rather
than as a formal member of their alliance. It also put pressure on him to
clarify America's own terms for peace. The American people, he wrote
House, had to be reassured that they were not fighting "for any selfish aim
on the part of any belligerent . . . least of all for divisions of territory such
as have been contemplated in Asia Minor." With preliminary reports from

the Inquiry in hand, Wilson outlined the fourteen points of his tentative peace terms in an address to Congress.

Wilson took the Congress and the audience of Allied diplomats by surprise with his Fourteen Points speech. About half of the points were concrete terms for the territorial settlement of the war: evacuation of Belgium, Russia, France, and the Balkans; return of Alsace-Lorraine to France; self-determination for the peoples of the Ottoman and Austro-Hungarian empires; independence for Poland; adjustment of the borders of Italy. Six points, however, reached beyond the immediate conflict to address the problems that had troubled Europe over the past decades.

Wilson acknowledged the challenge posed by the Bolsheviks. "There is . . . a voice calling for these definitions of principle and of purpose which is, it seems to me, more thrilling and more compelling than any of the many moving voices with which the troubled air of the world is filled. It is the voice of the Russian people. . . ." The President then outlined a sweeping series of reforms: open diplomacy; freedom of the seas; an end to trade barriers between nations; international arms reductions; adjustment of colonial disputes in the interests of the native populations. In the fourteenth point he declared, "A general association of nations must be formed under specific covenants for the purpose of affording mutual guarantees of political independence and territorial integrity to great and small states alike."

The Fourteen Points formed the basis of what historians would later call the "liberal" peace program, the general set of ideals that progressives throughout Western Europe and America were agreed upon. The German government, however, responded with a sneer at the "demagogic artifices" of "this American busybody." In the Treaty of Brest-Litovsk the Germans demonstrated their own idea of fair peace terms, stripping Russia of 34 percent of its population, 32 percent of its farmland, half of its factories, and virtually all its coal mines. The final German answer to the Fourteen Points was Ludendorff's spring offensive in the West.

The ferocious German attacks in France sapped some of Wilson's idealism. He targeted the German government as the enemy; the war had to bring the "destruction of every arbitrary power anywhere that can . . . disturb the peace of the world." Otherwise, he warned a cheering crowd in Baltimore, "Everything that America has lived for and loved and grown great to vindicate . . . will have fallen in utter ruin." Wilson offered but one response to the German breakthroughs on the western front: "Force, Force to the utmost, Force without stint or limit, the righteous and triumphant Force which shall make Right the law of the world."

By July, more than a million American soldiers had been sent to France.

In August, the Allies turned to attack all along the front. At Amiens the British broke through with four hundred tanks, the mechanical "land battleships" that Churchill had sired for the Royal Navy. The Americans too had tanks—a single brigade of borrowed French Renaults, led by a young cavalry major named Patton. With this handful of lightly armored vehicles Patton spearheaded an assault on the German salient at St. Mihiel. The Germans were already beginning to withdraw, so the Americans advanced with ease, clearing the enemy positions in just two days.

The tanks of the First World War were unromantic offspring of the industrial revolution. Slow, squat, underarmed, almost unbearably hot, they nonetheless accomplished their purpose of cutting through enemy trench lines. The same could not be said, however, of the other grand technical innovation of the war, the airplane.

Aviation was the one genuinely romantic service in this otherwise businesslike, butcherous war. René Fonck of France, Canada's William Bishop, the von Richthofen brothers of Germany, Raoul Lufberry in the Lafayette Escadrille—these were the conflict's truly glamorous figures, the handful of men who could literally rise above the mass carnage of the trenches and engage each other in single combat. To be sure, the march of military technology injected more and more prosaic elements into the lives of flyers: their planes began to mount more and better weapons with which to kill their fellow aviators from "the other side of the hill"; photo reconnaissance gave way to bombing missions against enemy troops and, for German zeppelin pilots, against enemy cities; ground artillery began to take its toll on the flyers, supposedly killing even the legendary Red Baron, young Manfred von Richthofen. The wartime public, however, and many of the flyers too, chose not to look beyond the knightly façade. Winston Churchill was learning to fly during the war. Theodore Roosevelt, too, might have given it a try if Wilson had not explicitly barred him from military service. Roosevelt's son Quentin did join the army's Aviation Section (still officially part of the Signal Corps) and died in his second week of action over the Marne.

For all the attention they received, however, the aviators had relatively little impact on the war's course. When the Americans mounted their first independent bombing mission of the war, they could muster only eight borrowed British planes, six of which were downed and none of which bombed its assigned target. Later raids had many more planes and proportionally fewer casualties, but the results of air bombardment remained disappointing.

In the end, Pershing's riflemen carried the brunt of the fighting for the Americans. After the relatively easy conquest of St. Mihiel, Pershing massed almost his entire force before the Argonne Forest, a tangle of fortified ridges and woods that formed the hinge of Germany's Hindenburg Line. The Americans jumped off on September 26, quickly gained three miles, and then ran into the main line of the Germans' defenses. Thereafter the battle degenerated into a welter of individual fights, with small units on each side lunging through the smoke-filled woods, trading grenades and machine-gun bursts, attacking and defending individual strong points. Once again the freshness and numbers of the doughboys outweighed their relative inexperience. Slowly the Germans were driven back toward the vital rail center of Sedan.

Even before that city fell, the will of the German leadership broke. Ludendorff, meeting with Kaiser Wilhelm on September 29, was forced to admit that his armies were in retreat all along the western front. Caught between a starving civilian population and a collapsing army, abandoned by the generals who had frog-marched him through the war, unnerved by Bolshevik agitators in his fleet and desperate calls for peace from his formerly docile Reichstag, Wilhelm gave up. On October 6, Wilson received a telegram, relayed from Berlin, requesting an immediate armistice.

The Germans had directed their appeal to Wilson in the hope of securing peace on the relatively generous terms of the Fourteen Points. The British, French, and Italian leaders gave their general consent to a settlement along those lines, with a few reservations designed to protect their special interests, only after House had rushed to Europe to threaten them with the prospect of a separate American peace. However, Foch and the other Allied military commanders—including Pershing—were agreed that the Germans had to be prevented from using a truce to regroup for further resistance. Foch persuaded the Allied governments that, as a precondition to negotiations, the German army had to evacuate Belgium, France, and the Rhineland, and that it must turn over to the Allies vast stores of military equipment. The generals would leave the Germans with enough arms to put down any Bolshevik-inspired uprising at home, but not enough to continue the war.

When the end finally came, it was quick. October 30: The Turks surrender to the British. November 3: Sailors of the German fleet mutiny over orders to sortie for a final suicide battle; they kill a number of their officers and refuse to leave port. On the same day, Austria accedes to terms laid down by Italy. November 7: Foch dictates his terms to the German peace commissioners. November 9: The Reichstag proclaims a republic in Germany, overthrowing the Kaiser. November 10: Wilhelm flees to the Netherlands, Ludendorff to Sweden.

On the morning of November 11, the armistice was signed at Foch's headquarters, a converted railroad car near Compiègne. Just before noon, the guns fell silent from the English Channel to the Swiss border; it was the first moment of calm in over four years. In the tangle of the Meuse-Argonne, corpses of German and American boys continued to rot side by side. Gas still wisped from shell craters along the Somme. Trench scars still defaced the landscape around shattered Verdun; they would still be there decades later.

There was no quiet in New York City on November 11. News of the armistice reached the city at 3 A.M. and within minutes the air-raid sirens were blaring. Ships in the harbor replied with their foghorns. Factory whistles added to the cacophony. Throughout the day, people swarmed in the streets, slapping each other on the back and echoing cheers. Impromptu parades snarled traffic. Society matrons, news vendors, shipwrights, and stenographers all rubbed elbows in the joyous throngs. There were cheers for Wilson and for the doughboys, catcalls for the Kaiser, good-natured denunciations of food rationing. Underlying the immediate relief over the war's end was a dim realization that while America was untouched, or even stronger, because of the conflict, Europe lay on the edge of—as one paper put it—"Disaster . . . Exhaustion . . . Revolution."

OVER HERE: LIBERTY AND DEMOCRACY

War has its own trajectory and momentum. It gorges on heavy industrial goods and starves others; accelerates certain economic trends and diverts or suppresses others; levels some class barriers and creates new ones; sharpens national loyalties and stifles diversity; summons new leadership and bypasses old. In early 1917, America lay slack, loose-jointed, divided in loyalty, hazy in ideology amid the mobilized great powers. Some eighty years earlier, Tocqueville had observed that an "aristocratic nation" that did not succeed quickly in "ruining" a democratic one ran the risk of being conquered by it. He also warned that a protracted war would "endanger the freedom of a democratic country." Would Americans conquer autocracy only to be conquered by it?

For a time after the April 1917 declaration, Americans had appeared to remain passive, as though confused or even disgruntled. Even the leadership seemed uncertain; when a senator was told that $3 billion was needed to send an army to France, he reportedly exclaimed, "Good Lord! You aren't going to send soldiers over there, are you?" Fighting a war 3,000 miles away seemed almost incomprehensible.

Then the momentum of war took over. Americans rallied around their flag, their soldiers, their commander-in-chief. They burst into patriotic song; people who had been singing the pacifist song "I Didn't Raise My Boy to Be a Soldier," six months later, as Ernest May remarked, were singing George M. Cohan's stirring "Over There." Americans knit sweaters for soldiers overseas, volunteered their services to hospitals, the Red Cross, the YMCA, the Salvation Army. Children collected peach stones to be converted into charcoal for gas masks. Hosts of people came out of retirement for war work. Families observed meatless and even wheatless days. Fidgety boys were told, "Chew your food."

Above all, Americans seemed ready to part with their money for the cause. War bonds, sold at immense rallies sparked by celebrities like Douglas Fairbanks, Geraldine Farrar, and Ignace Jan Paderewski, went by the hundreds of millions of dollars. Voluntary purchases of Liberty and Victory bonds, war savings certificates, and "thrift stamps" reached $23 billion, according to May, from a population with an average annual income of less than $70 billion. Americans accepted a jump in the federal personal income tax from a 1-to-7 percent to a 4-to-67 percent graduation, on all incomes over $1,000. It was a time for patriotic self-discipline.

Under Wilson's direction a young California newspaperman, George Creel, established the most powerful propaganda agency the nation had known. His Committee on Public Information mobilized artists like Howard Chandler Christie and James Montgomery Flagg to design war posters for liberty loans and recruiting, including Flagg's famous "I Want *You* for the U.S. Army." Creel organized the nation's orators into a 75,000-strong army, the "Four Minute Men," who carried the Administration's messages to millions of Americans in grange halls, lodge meetings, schools, synagogues, churches, movie theaters, and he drafted novelists such as Mary Roberts Rinehart and hosts of historians and other scholars. Creel not only mobilized the mind of America; he opened offices in world capitals to relay his war news and Wilson's war messages to millions of Europeans and Asians, especially Chinese.

As the voices of war were piped out of Washington and amplified by the media, the attitudes of millions of Americans focused and hardened and fortified one another in an orgy of Americanism and chauvinism. Before the war, the United States had developed a "crazy quilt anti-radical pattern," in William Preston's words, that closed the nation to aliens if they advocated certain radical doctrines, and provided for the deportation of aliens within five years of entry if they were guilty of certain "wrong" beliefs. At this time, while the repression had not touched great numbers of persons, it had ominous potentials. "The vague terminology of deportation legislation, the removal of time limits, the withering away of due process in immigration procedure, the bureaucratic ignorance of radical ideology, and the administrative mind conditioned by its dealings with defenseless undesirables" had come to characterize Washington's practices by 1917.

As war hysteria mounted during that year, the people and their leaders turned their jingoism and their fear against the more defenseless targets —immigrants, aliens, radicals, pacifists, German-Americans. In the rising paranoia, local epidemics were blamed on German spies contaminating the local water supply. A high Red Cross official warned that hospital bandages were being poisoned by plotters. Armed uprisings were rumored in Milwaukee and other German-American centers. Violinist Fritz Kreisler was barred from playing a concert in East Orange, New Jersey. Brown University revoked a degree given earlier to the German ambassador to the United States.

The juiciest target of all was the IWW, which had publicly and provocatively stuck to its stand against "war and capitalism" following America's entrance. In the popular mind, the Wobblies stood for radicalism, aliens, strikes, industrial sabotage, threats to private property, and everything else that was opposed to 100 percent Americanism. Vigilantes in Arizona mining towns shipped hundreds of Wobblies and suspected sympathizers out into the desert. Western governors, reflecting logging, mining, and farm interests, petitioned the Wilson Administration to intern in remote camps Wobblies suspected of treason or of hindering "the operation of industries, or the harvesting of crops necessary to the prosecution of the war."

Who would hold out against the war hysteria? Not the federal government, which finally opposed internment but called for increased state vigilance and state suppression of IWW propaganda. Not the religious leadership, which typically showed little Christian tolerance: a Congregational minister called the Lutheran Church in Germany "not the bride of Christ, but the paramour of Kaiserism," and another favored hanging anyone who lifted his voice against American entrance into the war. Not judges, who often denounced Wobblies from the bench, or juries—the designated defenders of citizens against their government—who often came in with anti-Wobbly verdicts within an hour of retiring. Not the AFL leadership, which despite its own experience with antilabor bias in the courts seemed only too pleased with the persecution of the IWW.

Early in September 1917, federal agents swooped down on the Chicago IWW headquarters, seizing membership lists, leaflets, buttons, books, office equipment. The authorities seemed intent on destroying the IWW leadership. The following June, two weeks after a deliberately provocative speech by Eugene Debs in Canton, Ohio, a federal grand jury indicted him under the Espionage Act of 1917, which provided heavy penalties for persons aiding the enemy, obstructing recruiting, or causing disloyalty, and under the May 1918 sedition amendment, which banned "disloyal, profane, scurrilous, or abusive language" against the American form of government, the Constitution, the flag, the armed forces, or necessary war production.

In court, Debs invoked the memories of the "rebels of their day" like Tom Paine and Sam Adams, of Wendell Phillips and William Lloyd Garrison and other fighters for justice. "You are teaching your children to revere their memories," Debs told the jury, "while all of their detractors are in oblivion." Promptly found guilty, Debs affirmed on sentencing his "kinship with all living beings." As the impassive judge stared down at him, he said, "While there is a lower class, I am in it; while there is a criminal class, I am of it; while there is a soul in prison, I am not free." The judge condemned those "who would strike the sword from the hand of this nation while she is engaged in defending herself against a foreign and brutal power." His sentence: ten years in jail.

"Once lead this people into war," President Wilson was reported to have said before American entrance into the conflict, "and they'll forget there ever was such a thing as tolerance. To fight you must be brutal and ruthless, and the spirit of ruthless brutality will enter into the very fiber of our national life." Given this insight, why did not Wilson himself swing his presidential influence more strongly against the intolerance of 1917–19? He had been raised in the tradition of civil liberty and free speech. Liberty for him, as for millions of Americans, was the very linchpin of democracy. To a people who feared government and repression, the Bill of Rights was the essence of the Constitution. Once again from the crucible of war, however, liberty emerged as a misty symbol for most Americans and their leaders rather than a concrete guide to public and private action.

For some Americans, the worst wartime loss of liberty was their right to take the swig of their choice. By 1917, twenty-six states had prohibition laws; about half of these were "bone-dry." Converted into a win-the-war measure by the Anti-Saloon League, a constitutional amendment banning the "manufacture, sale or transportation" of intoxicating liquors won congressional approval by the end of that year, and passed the required number of states during the following year, just in time to serve as a welcome-home present to the doughboys returning from the vineyards of France.

Not only did Prohibition constitute the kind of governmental intrusion into personal life that Americans had fought since the days of the *Mayflower*. It was also a *federal* intrusion. But many a lawmaker who had declaimed for years about states' rights and individual liberty swallowed without a murmur an act that challenged all the ancient war cries about individualism, personal choice, family responsibility, and local option.

*   *   *

Amid the jingoism and intolerance and repression of the war to save democracy, some Americans fought a heroic battle at home that would produce a vital step in the democratization of American life and politics. This was the battle for woman suffrage.

Not since Civil War days had a body of Americans faced such an intimidating set of political and intellectual problems as had the suffragists during the progressive years. Not only did they confront the most impossible problem of all—how to gain the right to vote without having the vote itself as a weapon to gain it—but they had to conquer a political system loaded with booby traps, minority checks, devices of delay and devitalization, group and individual vetoes. They had to work with Southerners who were anti-Negro, with Californians who were anti-Oriental, with Northerners who were anti-immigrant, with businessmen who were antilabor.

And by now the women leaders were politically bone-tired after seventy-five years of almost ceaseless struggle. Again and again in their letters, they refer to their fatigue, the overwork that was making "physical wrecks" of women, the racking journeys by train and trolley and auto, the late-night speeches and conferences. Elizabeth Cady Stanton talked of the "wrangles, pitfalls, and triumphs" of the suffrage leaders.

"Have I not served out my sentence," Anna H. Shaw asked in 1914, at the age of sixty-seven. "Has the cause any right to ask more of me? Why may I not go home, home, the one quiet spot in all the world, and with my books and trees and flowers and birds, rest away from all antagonisms, and fruitless misunderstandings." But Anna Shaw would labor for another five years, then die of pneumonia while on one more speaking tour.

Despite the decades of grinding battles, some women leaders believed that victory was just a matter of time and persistence. Women continued to move into factory jobs; perhaps more importantly, they were entering professional and office positions long reserved for men, while a few more men were taking "women's jobs" such as cooking and baking. Industrialization, along with its human evils, was generating money and leisure that freed some women to confront such evils. Women leaders were highly conscious of these trends. "Little by little, very slowly, and with most unjust and cruel opposition," sociologist Charlotte Perkins Gilman had written in 1898, "at cost of all life holds most dear, it is being gradually established by many martyrdoms that human work is woman's as well as man's."

By the turn of the century, these leaders had to confess failure in their campaign for the vote, save in a handful of states. By 1913, through this state-by-state approach, women could still vote for only seventy-four presidential electors. The problem facing women strategists was not only political but intellectual and moral: To what extent should they be concerned with the rights of blacks, immigrants, illiterates, factory workers, and Indians, rather than exclusively the right of women, to vote—never forgetting that each of those groups included women? One advantage of the state-by-state suffrage strategy was that it let legislatures decide suffrage issues on the basis of local attitudes. But the moral price was high, as lawmakers yielded to regional biases.

The cardinal issue was, of course, black voting in the South. Women abolitionists had joined with men in the searing struggle before the Civil War, and a postwar alliance of voteless women and still-deprived Negroes seemed both a moral and political necessity; at the same time, suffragists still resented the fact that Southern blacks alone were granted citizenship. During Reconstruction, Isabella Beecher Hooker, one of Susan B. Anthony's Washington correspondents, had reported that she had gone in to see Charles Sumner and other senators with the first copy of a new suffrage pamphlet. She continued:

"I told him I heard him comment almost with tears in the Senate the day before on the case of a black man refused hotel accommodations in the middle of a stormy night—& my tears of indignation blinded my eyes & sent me out of the Senate chamber—because women had been treated thus over & over again. . . ." Sumner asked if more Democrats might support suffrage. "When I told him that Southern democrats were really coming to think that if niggers voted it was high time their wives and mothers should—he said 'Well that party isn't a big thing in the south you know.' No Sir—said I—but a disaffected republican is about as good as a democrat —isn't he?" Sumner seemed to agree. "Well then," she continued, "if we can get some of the democrats & the disaffected republicans to unite with some of the labor people & some of the temperance people, this might be a bigger thing than you speak of—& he didn't even laugh or attempt a joke."

Forty years later, suffragist leaders had not only failed to forge a full coalition of the deprived—many were also resentful of immigrants, whom Elizabeth Cady Stanton had publicly pictured as "coarse, ignorant beings" fresh from the steerage, protected by the police in their right to cast a vote, usually a vote purchased by the bosses. She resented the "ignorant native vote" of uneducated workers, even—in South Dakota—of "Indians in blankets and moccasins" who were "engaged in their ghost dances," while "the white women were going up and down the State pleading for the rights of citizens." Still, by the end of the progressive and reform years many women leaders were fighting both for the suffrage and for the full panoply of human rights for all Americans—especially after horrifying episodes like the 1911 Triangle fire, in which 146 women garment workers perished and which suggested that women needed safe working conditions if they were even to live to vote.

Human rights for all Americans save—as always—for the Southern black woman and man. By 1915, it was clear that women could neither pressure suffrage through the Southern-dominated committee system of Congress, nor through the Southern state legislatures, in the face of the defenders of states' rights, Anglo-Saxon civilization, and the "Southern way of life." The problem was growing acute, for the Republican party was increasingly falling under the leadership of antisuffragists like Henry Cabot Lodge, and the Democracy under the leadership of liberals and progressives—but always there loomed the Southern Democratic lawmakers. The national suffrage movement was losing some of its ablest Southern leaders to the antiblack claims of the region.

Suffrage leaders faced other political problems of intellectually baffling complexity. To what extent should the woman's movement try to work through either or both major parties, or exert leverage between them, or form its own party as of old? How strongly should it link with labor and consumers and even farmers—and with their causes and demands, some of them distant from the needs of women as such? What political tactics should be used—electioneering (when only a minority of women had the vote), propaganda, personal influence, militancy, even violence? And how deal with the two male leaders who still dominated the political scene— Theodore Roosevelt, who had taken a strong position for a federal amendment in 1912 but seemed to be backsliding ever since, and Woodrow Wilson, who was a master of rhetoric about democracy and women's rights but somehow could not bring himself to make a clear and eloquent statement for the federal—the "Susan B. Anthony"—amendment?

Slowly during 1914–16, letter by letter, speech by speech, conference by conference, setback by setback, suffragist leaders felt and thought their way through the political murk. The issue was not whether to take a new stand but whether to stick to the federal amendment route despite enticing temptations to yield unduly to "states' rights." The decision was to stand firm "for Susan." Several forces converged at this point. A new cadre of leaders had arisen in the movement. Elizabeth Cady Stanton had died in 1902, Anthony herself four years later, and Anna Shaw, longtime head of the National American Woman Suffrage Association—a brilliant orator but a poor administrator—had been succeeded in 1915 by Carrie Chapman Catt, a woman of enormous organizational energy, political skill, and fierce determination to mount a final assault for suffrage. Moreover, a more militant woman's organization had sprung up to challenge the NAWSA— the Congressional Union for Woman Suffrage, headed by Alice Paul, who as an American student had been jailed in Britain for suffrage militancy and who felt that the time had come for suffragists to be less genteel and to hold the Democratic party—the "party in power"—strictly accountable for carrying out its campaign promises. It was also becoming evident by this time that the state-by-state movement was slowing down, that many suffragists even in the South were now favoring the federal amendment, and that the power of women who already had gained the vote in some states should be mobilized for one final push for "Susan B."

So the target now was the United States Congress—and one man, Woodrow Wilson, who would have no vote in the long amending process but could have ample influence. The suffragists had about given up on TR, who refused to use his personal influence with Lodge and the other Republican irreconcilables in Congress. But would Wilson use his presidential and personal influence with *his* Southern irreconcilables in House and Senate?

By no means did all women support woman suffrage; some organized against it and sought to influence Wilson. "The men should stand fast & protect us, protect ourselves as a father refuses his child something he knows that child is better without," Mary Wilson Thompson urged in a letter to the President. "In the eyes of the world you are the Father of this great United States & you personally know that Suffrage ought not to be granted through Federal Amendment & that it never will by the States individually, that the women of this country are not fitted for the vote & that it will not come if you hold firm. Therefore I ask you to be true to your ideals of States Rights & of womanhood."

To suffragists, the President was both attractive and exasperating. Originally antisuffrage, he "passed through successive phases in which he pleaded that he could do nothing until his party acted," though he had led it on the most factious issues; "that he could do nothing until Congress acted and could not invade the province of a Congressional Committee," though he had often done so; and finally, "that the issue was one solely up to the several states," in Eleanor Flexner's summary. Late in 1915, he journeyed to Princeton to cast a vote for woman's suffrage in a New Jersey referendum. But this was the old state-by-state approach. When, if ever, would the President support "Susan B." in the face of intense "states' rights" feeling in his party?

The woman leaders supplied their own answer through a marvelous combination of skill, persistence, and luck. In January 1917, militants began picketing the White House. Standing motionless outside the gates, they held banners demanding, "MR. PRESIDENT, WHAT WILL YOU DO FOR WOMAN SUFFRAGE?" and "HOW LONG MUST WOMEN WAIT FOR LIBERTY?" As the weeks passed and the slogans became more provocative, passers-by tore the banners from their hands, and police began arresting the pickets rather than the troublemakers. Thrown into a notorious workhouse nearby in Virginia, women protested their brutal treatment, went on hunger strikes, underwent forced feeding—and became martyrs.

While the militants catalyzed public sentiment, the more genteel leadership of the NAWSA exerted influence inside the White House gates. While Catt mobilized the state groups, her lobbyists pressured lawmakers on the Hill. Her ablest lieutenant by far was Helen Gardener, an affluent Washingtonian who had the good luck—if such it was—to live next to Speaker Champ Clark. Occasionally she had her cook make up Southern delicacies and hand them to the Clarks' cook over the back fence. Mrs. Gardener was not above waiting inside her front door, with hat and coat on, until she spied Clark on his front steps; then she "chanced by."

Helen Gardener also had access to Woodrow Wilson—a resource she used to the hilt. As a crucial House vote neared in late 1917, she played on the President's newest and strongest motivation by urging him to support suffrage as a war measure. Soon she asked Wilson to intervene with a wavering Tennessee congressman. In January of 1918, the combined efforts of the President, the militants, the organizers, the mobilizers, and the inside operators paid off when the House of Representatives passed the Susan B. Anthony amendment by exactly the required two-thirds majority, with Champ Clark's "yea" held in reserve in case of a deadlock.

Next the Senate—and now Helen Gardener redoubled her White House operation. Flattering Wilson with the observation that he had linked the cause of human liberty and democracy with the end of government by "male domination," she persuaded him again and again to intervene with vacillating senators. In September 1918, on her urging and those of Administration officials including McAdoo, Wilson staked his prestige on a sudden personal appearance before the Senate. Coming before the upper chamber on only half an hour's notice, the President gave one of his most eloquent speeches. "This is a people's war," he said; "democracy means that women shall play their part in affairs alongside men and upon an equal footing with them. . . .

"We have made partners of the women in this war; shall we admit them only to a partnership of suffering and sacrifice and toil and not to a partnership of privilege and right?" And women were vital to winning the peace as well.

Eloquent words, wise words—and they did not change a single vote. After a heartbreaking loss by two votes in the Senate, the indomitable suffrage leaders returned to the battle they had fought now for three-quarters of a century—and in another year they won that battle in the Senate. It would take the movement yet another year to push the amendment through three-quarters of the states, but the two-thirds votes in House and Senate, the voting power already achieved in key states, and women's grass-roots efforts brought victory in time for the election of 1920. Nine Southern states and Delaware refused to ratify.

The final victory was a splendid one for women and all Americans, a victory too for liberty and equality, though a victory so delayed as to lose some of its savor for the exhausted suffrage workers. It was also a flawed victory. Women had succeeded through expediency as well as conviction, making deals, forming coalitions, lobbying like any votemonger of old. All this was necessary in a veto-ridden political system. But they had failed to form firm linkages with labor or immigrants or with blacks, with Democrats or Republicans, with a third party or a party of their own. Lacking such linkages, women might be hard put to use their newly won vote to realize the humane goals that had validated their long struggle.

All this would be settled in the future. At the very least, the Nineteenth Amendment stood as a monument to the transforming leadership of five generations of women. And it was a monument as well to a President who, amid the cares and distractions of war, was willing to spend political capital on a cause that he viewed as linked to a fundamental aim of that war—the expansion of liberty and equality, and thus the enlargement of American democracy.

CHAPTER 13

The Fight for the League

T HE SS *George Washington* pulled away from the flag-draped pier in the late morning of December 4, 1918. Warships in New York Harbor fired salutes to the little liner, once German-owned and now part of the spoils of war. Crowds were gathered at Battery Park and on Staten Island to see the ship off. As she passed the submarine net and the old Civil War ironclad that guarded the Narrows, passengers on board could make out children waving flags all along the shore. Once in the lower harbor, the *George Washington* was met by her escort: the battleship *Pennsylvania,* a dozen destroyers, plus airplanes and a navy dirigible. They all had assembled to see President Woodrow Wilson off for Europe on what all expected would be a historic mission.

The President had decided to break all precedent and personally represent the United States at the peace conference convening in Paris. Wilson was convinced, as he told reporters aboard the ship, that the Allied heads of state had already decided together to impose "a peace of loot or spoliation" upon Germany, and that only his on-the-spot intervention could redirect the conference to a program for lasting peace. Beyond that reason, however, was Wilson's obvious, burning desire to participate in what promised to be the most important international meeting in over a century. "The plot is thickening," he told newsmen with obvious relish. Wilson could no more have stayed away from Paris than Theodore Roosevelt could have sat out the 1912 election.

The President brought with him to Europe only a relatively small entourage: his second wife, Edith Galt Wilson; his physician, Admiral Cary Grayson; two typists; and most of the members of the Inquiry. As formal Peace Commissioners, Wilson appointed Colonel House and General Tasker Bliss (Wilson's able liaison to the Allied Supreme War Council), who already were in Europe. The other two commissioners accompanied him—Secretary of State Lansing and Henry White, a nominal Republican and experienced diplomat long friendly with Roosevelt and Lodge.

Life aboard ship quickly settled down to routine. Most of the time the President remained isolated, talking and dining only with the members of his immediate circle. George Creel was on board, personally supervising the movie that the Committee on Public Information was making about the peace mission. Evenings Wilson and his wife joined the other passengers to enjoy the film exploits of Charlie Chaplin and Douglas Fairbanks before returning to affairs of state.

The President had only one extensive conference with the members of the Inquiry during the trip. He was quite frank and specific in laying out his views and goals. While the Americans had no selfish objectives to pursue at Paris, he said, the Allied leaders were bound to each other by a web of secret deals and thus "did not represent their own people." He discussed animatedly his ideas for a league of nations. A permanent league, whose exact political structure could evolve with experience, was in his view the only guarantee of both "elasticity and security" in the wake of the World War. He foresaw this league deterring future aggressors by cutting them off from trade and communications while world public opinion was roused against them; military force would be necessary only as a last resort. In the meantime, the organization would promote international commerce and administer the colonies of the defeated Central Powers.

Wilson heartened his advisors by calling on them to guide him on the specific economic and territorial issues involved. "Tell me what's right and I'll fight for it," he concluded.

His associates tried to take the measure of this American scholar-turned-politician who sought to redirect the destiny of the world with the hammer blows of his ideals. James Shotwell, a historian attached to the peace commission, was struck by the contradictions in Wilson's appearance and actions. Close up the President had warm eyes and an engaging smile, but from the side his face appeared severe and determined. Wilson remained aloof from the other officials on the ship, yet on Sunday he unself-consciously joined the sailors singing hymns in their mess hall. Watching Wilson watch a movie, Shotwell saw powerful emotions being held under tight control.

Escorted by Allied warships, the *George Washington* moved through mists as it approached the coast of France; then the skies cleared and the liner pulled into Brest harbor in mid-December 1918. The President and his party went immediately to the train that was waiting to carry them to Paris, but Shotwell took a few minutes to walk around the town. He noticed the slate-roofed stone houses, the many women dressed in black among the crowds, and the groups of American soldiers everywhere waiting for orders to sail for home. Most of all, Shotwell was struck by the wall placards that announced the coming of Wilson. One, a "red splash of color on a gray stone wall," called upon "one and all, without distinction of party" to praise the leader who had arrived "to found a new order on the rights of peoples, and to stop forever the return of an atrocious war. . . ."

THE MIRRORED HALLS OF VERSAILLES

No American President had ever before met with a foreign leader while in office. Grant and Roosevelt, after they left the White House, did visit a number of heads of state during their travels, but those were social calls rather than serious diplomatic missions. Now Wilson was about to meet with the assembled premiers and foreign ministers of every European power—except defeated Germany and Bolshevik Russia—as well as leaders from nations on five continents. They had gathered to address issues of sovereignty, disarmament, and trade that spanned the globe.

The global problems were staggering. The war had left 50 million soldiers and civilians dead or maimed; blasted into ruin large stretches of France, Belgium, and Eastern Europe; sent 13 million tons of shipping to the bottom of the sea. Now starvation and typhus—which would kill another 6 million people over the next year—stalked Europe in its first winter of peace since 1914. Nor was there even peace in the east, where Poles clashed with Czechs, Bolsheviks with czarist Whites, Slavs with Italians, Turks with Greeks, and Arabs with Jews amidst the ruins of the old autocratic empires. The leaders of Europe's three powerful democracies—Britain's David Lloyd George, France's Georges Clemenceau, and Italy's Vittorio Orlando—had been united by the war but now were divided on how best to cope with its chaotic aftermath. The three were hard-pressed to make common cause with one other; how would they deal with the professor-politician-president from the west?

Clemenceau was the first to greet the American President. The French premier—still vigorous at seventy-eight, broad of chest, with short legs and a yellowish complexion that struck Lansing as the "face and figure [of] a Chinese mandarin"—had earned the nickname "Le Tigre" for his tenacious attacks on any and all political opponents. It had been Clemenceau who had published Emile Zola's impassioned defense of Alfred Dreyfus, kept the "Affaire Dreyfus" alive year after year in the French press and Chamber of Deputies, and finally won exoneration for the wronged Jewish officer. A cold, ruthless idealist, not much liked but infinitely respected, Clemenceau had been uncompromising in prosecuting the war against the Central Powers, and now he called for peace terms that would prevent Germany from ever again being strong enough to invade France.

The first meeting between Wilson and Clemenceau went surprisingly well, mainly because both leaders strove to be conciliatory. Much to the annoyance of Colonel House, who still hoped to head the American delegation, Wilson convinced the Frenchman that the President should sit in on the peace talks as America's chief spokesman; in return, Wilson happily agreed that Clemenceau should preside over the conference. Neither professed to see any conflict between their main aims—for Clemenceau French security, for Wilson the league—and both later took House aside to express their delight at the way things had begun.

With some days still remaining before the conference opened, Wilson's next stop was Britain. There he met with the Royal Family, paraded through the streets of London, and joined the leaders of Britain's Liberal party in following the returns of the elections in progress. Lloyd George, Wilson's host, was tremendously heartened by the results as they were telegraphed in to the group gathered around the Cabinet table at 10 Downing Street. The white-maned Prime Minister—devious in his political dealings but unshakable in his commitment to his working-class constituents—was receiving a tremendous popular mandate for his party's promise to squeeze Germany "until the pips squeak." Any private doubts Lloyd George might have had about the wisdom of a punitive peace were not visible that night—but Wilson's were, as he glumly sat watching the British politicians celebrate.

From England, Wilson traveled to Italy, for his most enthusiastic public greeting of all. The cheering crowds, however, could not dispel the tension in Rome. Italy's leaders—the short, tenacious Orlando and his Foreign Minister, the "protractedly unreliable" Baron Sidney Sonnino—were determined to gain major concessions of territory as their price for Italy's fighting on the Allied side. Wilson had already balked at some of their demands, and now the President sparred with his hosts about travel plans and access to the Italian public.

To varying degrees, therefore, the four democratic leaders—soon dubbed "the Big Four"—were divided by their aims before the talks even began. Once the conference convened, the confusions and cross-purposes were multiplied a hundredfold as each nation and group arose to plead its case. Lawrence of Arabia was on hand to speak for the Iraqis; Ho Chi Minh tried vainly to gain a hearing for Vietnamese independence; the Czechs and Poles sent representatives to argue over the coal mines of Teschen. British diplomat Sir Harold Nicolson remembered the bedlam of "the machine-gun rattle of a million typewriters, the incessant shrilling of telephones, the clatter of motor bikes . . . the cold voices of interpreters . . . and throughout the sound of footsteps hurrying" down the mirrored halls of Versailles. It reminded him, Nicolson wrote, of a "riot in a parrot house."

Amidst the multiplicity of issues, Wilson did not take his eye off his main concern for a league of nations. Within a week of the conference's formal opening, he arose to advocate "that a League of Nations be created to promote international cooperation, to ensure the fulfillment of accepted international obligations, and to provide safeguards against war." Speaking from a draft resolution prepared in consultation with the British, the President declared that the "League should be created as an integral part of the general Treaty of Peace, and should be open to every civilized nation. . . ." The conference voted unanimously to establish a committee, with Wilson as its head, to draft a constitution for the League.

Over the next two weeks, Wilson attended the general meetings of the conference and also chaired the League committee. In drawing up the covenant of the League, the President worked closely with Colonel House and Lord Robert Cecil of Britain, both ardent advocates of the proposed organization. Even more, Wilson relied on his own ability to lead debate and shape compromise. "The President excels in such work," House recorded in his diary. "He seems to like it and his short talks in explanation of his views are admirable. I have never known any one to do such work as well." High praise indeed from a self-styled master of quiet political manipulation—yet House's opinion seemed warranted. Wilson made important concessions, giving up his own proposal for a statement on religious tolerance (and helping to beat down a Japanese plank on racial equality), and in turn blocked a French call for an international standing army. Overall, the nineteen-man committee took on the air of a college seminar, with several of the brighter pupils making important contributions—Cecil provided a working draft of the covenant, and Jan Smuts of South Africa devised the mandate procedure—but the terms of the discussion clearly being set by Professor Wilson.

After just ten meetings, the committee's work was done. On February 14, Wilson addressed the general session of the conference, reading and commenting upon the finished covenant. "A living thing is born," he concluded. "It is definitely a guarantee of peace." H. Wickham Steel wrote in the Paris *Daily Mail* that Wilson's presentation had "lifted" the affairs of the world "into new dimensions. The old dimensions of national individualism, secrecy of policies, competitive armaments, forcible annexations . . . were raised, if only for an instant, to a higher plane on which the organized moral consciousness of peoples, the publicity of international engagements and of government by the consent of and for the good of the governed, became prospective realities."

The only question, wrote Steel, was "How long will the instant last?"

*   *   *

While Wilson framed his plan for the League, the other American delegates and experts were left largely to their own devices. With the President's consent and some general supervision by House, the Inquiry members gradually became negotiators, in their own right, on the questions falling within their special spheres of expertise. Shotwell and the others found themselves engaged in days of exhausting but exhilarating work on issues of finance, navigation and trade, territorial adjustment, and the like.

Amidst the "whirlpool of political intrigue" slowly engulfing the delegates, the issue of Russia loomed large. None of the Western democracies had yet extended recognition to the Bolshevik regime in Moscow. Instead, France and Britain were helping to finance various of Lenin's adversaries in the civil war engulfing the country. The Allies maintained a blockade of Russia's ports and even landed troops to fight the Bolsheviks. While the World War was still on, the British and French had persuaded Wilson to send a small expeditionary force to northern Russia and a second force to Vladivostok on the Pacific—an intervention by the United States that was, in one scholar's words, both "extremely reluctant and severely restrained," though from Moscow's standpoint, of course, a flagrantly hostile act. With public clamor to bring their troops home increasing, the Allies and Americans now sought a way out of the imbroglio in the East, a way out of the intervention of which George F. Kennan would say later, "never, surely, in the history of American diplomacy has so much been paid for so little."

On January 22, Wilson proposed that the various warring factions in Russia meet with Allied representatives at Prinkipo, in Turkey, to attempt to hammer out their differences. The Bolsheviks hedged their reply to Wilson's proposal, but the anti-Bolsheviks rejected it outright. Then young William Bullitt stepped into the breach. Meeting with House and with Lloyd George's private secretary, Philip Kerr, Bullitt won approval for a fact-finding mission to Moscow. Accompanied by Lincoln Steffens and two military men, and armed with a set of general proposals suggested by Kerr and House, Bullitt left Paris on February 22.

One week earlier Wilson too had left, traveling in the opposite direction. The Congress was about to end its session, requiring him to return to Washington to sign legislation. Even more important, the League Covenant was completed, ready for presentation to the American people. Already the President was hearing in Paris echoes of opposition to the League building among politicians back home, and he sought to forestall his critics from organizing the public against his proposal. Before sailing from France, Wilson cabled the members of the Foreign Relations Committees of both houses of Congress, inviting them to meet with him at the White House to discuss the League Covenant.

Wilson clearly needed to mend his fences with the Congress—particularly with those Republicans whose votes would be necessary if the League were to gain two-thirds approval in the Senate—largely owing to his own political miscalculation. The previous October, in an effort to strengthen his hand before the Paris negotiations opened, Wilson had called upon the public to return a Democratic majority in the upcoming congressional elections. The call backfired, galvanizing Republican opposition; the GOP swept into control of the House by fifty seats, and acquired a precarious majority of two in the Senate. That slim majority elevated Wilson's archopponent Henry Cabot Lodge to the chairmanship of the Senate Foreign Relations Committee.

Debate on the Covenant began while Wilson was still in transit, with opponents labeling it everything from "an international quilting society" to "the most impudently un-American proposal ever submitted to the American people by an American President." Landing in Boston on February 23, Wilson fired back at the critics, saying that in defense of this cause it was a pleasure to indulge his "fighting blood." Three days later, however, he adopted a conciliatory tone in meeting over dinner with the congressional leaders. Those who had come to the White House determined not to be convinced by Wilson went away unmoved; Senator Frank Brandegee of Connecticut described the session as a "tea with the Mad Hatter." Another Republican, however, John Jacob Rogers of Massachusetts, carried away a much more favorable impression.

"I thought the President appeared extremely well," Rogers wrote to Henry White in Paris. "He submitted himself to quite rigorous cross-examination for two hours, answering every question, easy or difficult, as fully as possible and with apparent candor. . . . There was no suggestion of a feeling of militant arrogance about him. He apparently tried to give the impression that he really was one of the circle in the East Room, who was answering rather than asking questions only because he had been so recently in Paris, and had been a factor in the preparation of the instrument under discussion." Even Lodge admitted to Henry White that Wilson had patiently answered questions for two hours—but added, "We learned nothing."

Where would Lodge stand on the President's proposal? The senator's personal antipathy toward Wilson was well known; so too, however, were his wartime statements in favor of the general idea of an international council or league. During the early stages of the Paris negotiations, Lodge hedged on the question, pleading ignorance of the President's intentions, while touching base behind the scenes with TR and other Republican leaders inclined to distrust Wilson. Now, two days after the White House conference, he stated his position to the Senate. Lodge noted that America was being asked "to give up in part our sovereignty and independence and subject our own will to the will of other nations." He continued: "I am not contending now that these things must not be done. . . . What I ask, and all I ask, is consideration, time, and thought."

Fair words, spoken in a moderate tone—but Lodge had already made up his mind. At the suggestion of Brandegee, he now drew up a resolution urging that "the constitution of the league of nations in the form now proposed to the peace conference should not be accepted by the United States." Securing in a single feverous day the signatures of thirty-seven senators—enough to block the passage of any treaty—Lodge rose in the Senate just before midnight on March 3 to read his "Round Robin" into the record. Next morning, the editors of the New York *Sun* chortled: "Woodrow Wilson's League of Nations died in the Senate tonight. Henry Cabot Lodge . . . read the death warrant of the League."

Wilson's response to the Senate Round Robin was swift. Previously he had tended to slight the efforts of ex-President Taft and other Republicans who had been stumping the country in support of an international peace-keeping body; now Wilson telegraphed Taft, asking that he appear with the President to speak in favor of the League. The Republican leader raced northward by train to New York, meeting Wilson just hours before he was scheduled to sail back to France. The two then addressed a cheering crowd of League supporters gathered at the Metropolitan Opera House. Taft spoke first, calling the League "the living evidence of the united power of Christian civilization to make this treaty a real treaty of peace." Wilson then followed with a combative defense of his plan. To Lodge's suggestion that the League be considered separately from the peace treaty, Wilson replied, "Gentlemen on this side will find the Covenant not only in it, but so many threads of the treaty tied to the Covenant that you cannot dissect the Covenant from the treaty without destroying the whole vital structure."

The next two months were to be among the most difficult of Woodrow Wilson's life. Immediately upon his return to Paris, he received a nasty jolt: during his absence the Europeans and House, for reasons of their own, had proceeded to detach the League plan from the peace treaty—just as Lodge had suggested. With Ray Stannard Baker, the President drew up a statement reiterating his commitment to making the Covenant an integral part of the treaty, a statement so strong that Baker feared it would "break up the Conference then and there."

Over the next weeks, the differences between Wilson and the European leaders became starkly apparent. In particular, the rigid Clemenceau clashed repeatedly with the idealistic President. Relations between the two men, which had once seemed so promising, reached such a low that at one point Wilson prepared to abandon the talks and return to America. Gone were the happy days of the League-committee "seminar." The conference now revolved around the daily meetings of the Big Four, and their increasingly acrimonious debates over military and territorial questions. During part of this time, Wilson was prostrated by an attack of influenza, the debilitating effects of which lingered through the spring and summer. He also became increasingly distant from Colonel House, whom he began to suspect of pursuing his own separate program at the conference. "I seldom or never have a chance to talk with him seriously," House lamented, "and, for the moment, he is practically out from under my influence."

At this critical juncture, Bullitt returned from Moscow, afire with a proposal from Lenin for a truce in the Russian Civil War and negotiations to resolve the Bolsheviks' differences with the West. Wilson, in the thick of a fight to keep his Covenant in the treaty, could spare only brief attention for Bullitt's report. More important, the young emissary's two original supporters, House and Lloyd George, now backed away from the prospect of dealing directly with Lenin. The Russian offer was allowed to lapse; when Bullitt repeated it to Harold Nicolson, the Englishman "blinked politely." Wilson, meanwhile, went ahead with a unilateral withdrawal of the American forces in northern Russia, and with the promotion of his supreme goal of the League.

In the end, Wilson preserved the Covenant by compromising on a number of issues less important to him. He accepted some of Clemenceau's proposals for weakening Germany, agreed to British suggestions on disarmament and reparations, yielded to the Commonwealth nations on mandates, and let the Japanese retain control of Shantung. At the same time, in spite of the defiant speech he had made in New York, Wilson took steps to placate his Republican critics at home. Through Taft and some Democratic sources, Wilson learned of four basic changes that most of the signers of the Round Robin seemed to desire; in exchange for his concessions to Clemenceau and the others, Wilson was able to write three of those alterations into the Covenant. Even so, Lodge told Henry White, these were not good enough.

The final Treaty of Versailles, signed on June 28, did not completely satisfy anyone, and certainly not Wilson. But at least it included a strong, well-defined League of Nations. Throughout the talks the President had put so much emphasis on the League because, in part, he believed that eventually it could correct any other mistakes embodied in the peace settlement. He had succeeded in committing the European and other leaders to this great experiment in international democracy; now he had to persuade his own countrymen.

THE BATTLE FOR THE TREATY

On July 10, 1919, just one day after his return from France, President Wilson drove to Capitol Hill to present the completed Treaty of Versailles to the Senate. In his address Wilson reviewed the causes of America's entry into the war, the diplomatic commitments that the Allies had made to one another before America joined them, and the compromises that he had been forced to make in Paris. The treaty was not perfect, he conceded, but it did give international sanction to American principles of individual liberty, free trade, and the peaceful resolution of disputes.

The proposed League of Nations formed the core of Wilson's address. If the League was to fulfill its promise of bringing disarmament and peace, the President urged, then America must join it. The weaker nations trusted the good intentions of the United States, which after the Spanish-American War had honored its pledge to evacuate Cuba and begin giving self-rule to the Philippines. Leadership of the League, and thus of the world, was being offered America. "Dare we reject it and break the heart of the world?"

Wilson answered his own question with a stirring peroration: "The stage is set, the destiny disclosed. It has come about by no plan of our conceiving, but by the hand of God who has led us in this way. We cannot turn back. We can only go forward, with lifted eyes and freshened spirit, to follow the vision. It was of this that we dreamed at our birth. America shall in truth show the way. The light streams upon the path ahead, and nowhere else."

Wilson's eloquence reverberated through a press and public that already were bestirring themselves to debate the treaty. Thanks in part to the work of ex-President Taft and the League to Enforce Peace, public opinion in general was favorable to the idea of a League of Nations. Such diverse papers as the Boston *Globe,* the Philadelphia *Inquirer,* and the Des Moines *Register* applauded Wilson's League as a "broadening out of the Monroe Doctrine" to cover the entire world. Only an "international despot or an international pariah" could object to the League concept of collective security, the New York *World* opined. The Baltimore *Sun* unconsciously paraphrased James Madison's language in Federalist 51, saying that the League of Nations would not "make nature angelic" but would be a large stride toward that goal. The *Register* put it more succinctly: "The alternative of the league of nations is an armed America."

In April, the *Literary Digest,* in an effort to gauge public sentiment, asked newspaper editors across the country whether they favored the proposed League. Of the 1,377 editors who replied to the poll, 718 answered yes, 181 no, and 478 indicated conditional agreement. If these papers represented the views of their readers, then Democrats overwhelmingly supported the League, and even the vast majority of Republicans favored some international organization. A breakdown of the replies by region shows that the South was solidly behind the League, while conditional supporters were concentrated in the Northeast and New England. In no area did outright opponents number even 20 percent of the responses.

But while across the country League opponents may have been few and divided, in the U.S. Senate they were powerful, concentrated, and organized. While Wilson was still in Paris, Henry Cabot Lodge and his allies had agreed to launch a public campaign against the League. With funds provided by Henry Clay Frick and by the Pennsylvania industrialist Andrew Mellon, the opponents set up their own league—the League for the Preservation of American Independence—which ran advertising and sponsored meetings nationwide. William Randolph Hearst was also persuaded to throw his vast chain of newspapers into the fight against Wilson's proposal. Meanwhile, the New York *Sun* declared that "greater even than the Monroe Doctrine is the Washington Doctrine," which warned America against entangling "our peace and prosperity in the toils of European ambition, rivalship, interest, honor or caprice."

Lodge himself entertained hopes that the efforts of the League critics would eventually turn the public against Wilson's plan, to the advantage of the Republicans in the next presidential election. Indeed, the senator made a conspicuous contribution to the public campaign by engaging Harvard president A. Lawrence Lowell in a much-publicized debate of the League's merits before a capacity crowd in Boston's Symphony Hall.

The real debate, however, was to occur in the Senate. The Founding Fathers had feared both a runaway majority and an overweening chief executive, so they had fragmented power throughout the structure of American government—and Lodge never for a moment lost sight of the fact that the Constitution gave the upper chamber the ultimate power of decision to accept or reject a treaty. "The only people who have votes on the treaty are here in the Senate," he reassured a friend. A consummate dealer in the transactions of legislative politics, Lodge relied from the first on defeating Wilson and the treaty through a legislative strategy.

Lodge's first task was to ensure that the Republicans controlled the

Senate. The election of 1918 had given the GOP a majority of two in the upper house, but Lodge had to keep in line Idaho's William E. Borah and several old Bull Moosers who had become "irreconcilable" opponents of the treaty. While the majority of Senate Republicans agreed that some sort of league was desirable, although not necessarily the one presented by Wilson, Borah and his allies seemed willing to bolt the party rather than vote for any international organization that might infringe upon American sovereignty. Before Wilson's return, Lodge had met with Borah and struck a deal. The irreconcilables would cooperate with the other Republicans in organizing the Senate and amending the treaty, and then would be free to vote against the pact in the final roll call. In return, Lodge would give Borah ample opportunity to promote his arguments for isolationism. Thus Borah could be sure that, even if the treaty did pass, it would be thoroughly "Republicanized."

The Lodge-Borah arrangement worked. The Republicans took control of the Senate, elevating Lodge to the post of majority leader—and, more important, to the chairmanship of the Foreign Relations Committee, to which Wilson now had to submit the treaty. Lodge proceeded to stack the committee with irreconcilables, and with less ideological skeptics like Senator Warren G. Harding of Ohio. In particular, the new chairman denied a seat to Frank Kellogg of Minnesota, one of the foremost Senate spokesmen for the Taft wing of the party, when Kellogg refused to cooperate with Lodge's plans.

Lodge acted in large part out of partisan considerations: if Wilson and the Democrats were allowed to take credit for creating an international organization that outlawed war, Lodge feared, they could reap a harvest of votes in the next election and undermine for years to come the tenuous Republican majority across the country. Personal factors were also at work —the two men in fact loathed each other. "I never expected to hate anyone in politics with the hatred I feel toward Wilson," Lodge had written Theodore Roosevelt long before the League fight. Even Jefferson was a better man than Wilson, the senator wrote another friend; "he could not have been worse." Soon Lodge was calling the President "the most sinister figure that ever crossed the country's path." His venom arose in part from his indignation that Wilson should be regarded as the foremost intellectual in American politics—this *Princeton* man with his popular writings, as compared with his own classical education at Harvard. Wilson, for his part, simply viewed Lodge with cold contempt.

At the core of the hostility, however, lay genuine differences of outlook and principle. For nearly three decades, Lodge had been a leading spokesman for an aggressive, unilateralist foreign policy backed by a stronger military establishment. In the 1880s and 1890s, he had led Theodore Roosevelt and a few other young Republicans in calling for a naval buildup and the acquisition of colonies overseas. He had supported, as matters of paramount national interest, the war with Spain, the annexation of the Philippines, the building of the Panama Canal, and most of the interventions in Latin America carried out by Roosevelt and Taft. In 1919, Lodge hoped for a peace settlement that would strengthen America's international influence vis-à-vis the European powers, and also in the Western Hemisphere. Wilson's "idealistic" internationalism left Lodge cold, and he viewed the idea of collective security that was at the heart of Wilson's League as a distinct threat to American freedom of action.

The President and the senator, therefore, were engaged in a battle over two conflicting foreign policy strategies. Wilson's concept had its intellectual origins largely in his personal moral values; Lodge's sprang mainly from traditional power considerations. The President placed his faith in the collegial good sense of an international parliament that he had taken great pains to craft; the senator proposed to rely on the nationalist economic and military policies that he had promoted for decades.

When the debate was cast in these terms, Lodge was able to rally some support in the Senate and in the country, yet seemingly not enough to block the treaty. In order to defeat Wilson, Lodge had to win and keep the backing of senators who opposed the treaty for a variety of other reasons, some of them not very admirable. Indeed, the struggle over the League of Nations aroused some of the basest prejudice and hate-mongering in American politics. James Reed of Missouri declared that "dark" peoples would outnumber whites three to one in the League assembly, while Senator Lawrence Sherman of Illinois alleged that the Catholic majority in the League would make it a tool of the Vatican. Other senators engaged in the traditional sport of twisting the lion's tail, claiming that the British would use the League to send American boys to suppress freedom-fighters in Ireland.

With these and other legislators, Lodge acted as a traditional power broker, agreeing to tolerate or support their objections to the treaty in return for their supporting his. Slowly Lodge worked to knit the treaty opponents into a coherent group that would act together to amend or kill Wilson's proposal. Hiram Johnson of California came over when Lodge agreed to support Johnson's objection to Canada, Australia, and other British dominions having an independent vote in the League. At the same time, Lodge conducted delicate negotiations with Senator Porter McCumber, one of the mildest reservationists on the treaty, to find some common ground for an amendment to Article 10—Wilson's Covenant.

The League's opponents needed time to organize their coalition in the Senate and to convey their message to the general public. Lodge used parliamentary maneuvers to secure that time, first by tying up the Foreign Relations Committee with a two-week, word-for-word reading of the entire 268-page treaty, and then by inviting every conceivable opponent of the pact to testify at length against it. Lodge's delaying tactics, however, did not redound exclusively to his side's advantage. Wilson was also able to use the extra time to round up votes, for he too was pursuing a legislative strategy.

* * *

Soon after the President returned from Europe, several of his advisors suggested that he immediately tour the country to arouse further public support for the League. Other political insiders, however, most notably Herman Kohlsaat and Senator Gilbert Hitchcock, calculated that Wilson could do more good by staying in Washington to deal directly with the Senate. He heeded the advice of the latter; for six weeks he talked with senators individually and in small groups, wrote private letters to wavering Republicans, and submitted evidence—although not as much as Lodge requested—to the Foreign Relations Committee. One historian concludes that Wilson's "approach to senators was flexible, not dogmatic and doctrinaire, not rigid and unbending." The President answered questions and expounded on the League Covenant, but he also listened to the senators' reservations and weighed their advice. Both Democrats and Republicans informed him that, despite the compromises that Wilson had made in Paris, the treaty would not gain the support of two-thirds of the Senate as it stood. Finding himself in a "perplexed and somewhat distressing situation," the President nonetheless resolved to compromise once more in order to achieve his main goal of leading the United States into the League.

The key to Wilson's strategy of conciliation lay with a small group of Republican senators, led by Kellogg, who had proposed a set of four moderate revisions to the treaty. If Wilson and Kellogg could rally a large enough coalition around those reservations, which were mainly interpretive in nature, they could beat Lodge at his own game. The contest settled into a battle of parliamentary tactics. Wilson persuaded Kellogg to submit his interpretive reservations as a separate resolution, requiring a two-thirds majority for passage, to be considered at the same time as the treaty itself. As Wilson explained the plan to his supporters, a coalition strong enough to pass Kellogg's resolution would be strong enough to pass the treaty. By accepting Kellogg's compromise, Wilson hoped to maneuver the Republican moderates into voting for the League.

Lodge recognized at once that Wilson's tactics threatened his own efforts at coalition-building. The senator insisted that reservations to the treaty had to be submitted as amendments to the text itself, to be approved or rejected by a simple majority vote. Lodge could rally a potential majority behind his grab-bag of amendments, but not a two-thirds majority. The parliamentary arithmetic was plain: if Wilson won on the procedural question of what form reservations should take, the moderate Republicans would probably rally around Kellogg's resolution as the best possible compromise and the treaty would pass substantially as Wilson wanted it.

The real climax of the legislative battle, therefore, came on August 20 when Democratic Senator Key Pittman moved that reservations to the treaty be passed in a contemporaneous resolution. Lodge met the challenge head-on, appealing to his fellow Republicans to stand together as a majority and thus retain control over consideration of the treaty. Faced with the prospect of dividing their party to the ultimate advantage of a Democratic President, most of the moderate Republicans sided with Lodge and the irreconcilables on the procedural question. Pittman was forced to delay his motion for a week while Wilson's allies sought in vain to rally the mild reservationists back to their side. Finally, on August 27, the President conceded defeat in his tactical struggle with Lodge.

So Lodge had won—in the Senate. He had won because he had carried out one of the most brilliant feats of transactional leadership in the Senate's history. He had controlled both his Senate majority and his committee with consummate skill. When a senator threatened to drift off the reservation, Lodge spared no pains to persuade the right man to get in touch with the right politicians who could bring the man back into the fold. Day after day he brokered and traded with both the reservationists and the anti-League extremists in his own party. He played the game like a chess master, arraying his men, calculating his tactics, exploiting time, coldly analyzing his foe's moves, keeping his queen and his king—his committee chairmanship and his majority leadership—intact and in command.

Wilson too played a strong game in the Senate, mustering all his presidential and personal influence, using face-to-face persuasion, pulling back when need be, always holding his Senate Democrats in line. But the Senate was Lodge's chessboard, not his. It was Lodge's two-thirds rule for ratifying treaties, Lodge's majority rule for amending treaties, not his.

Wilson's strength lay in a much wider field, the national electorate. Lodge, to be sure, had not neglected this field: several hundred thousand copies of his key Senate speech were sent to his Senate friends for grassroots distribution; anti-League propaganda organs were busy; Lodge turned to Irish and other ethnic groups for support. But Wilson would transcend all this. By appealing to the nation he could transform the very ground on which the battle was being fought—and transform global politics in the process.

On the same day that he conceded Senate defeat to Lodge, the President announced his intention of appealing to the country.

*   *   *

On the evening of September 3, the presidential special rolled out of Washington's Union Station. The engine drew only seven cars: quarters for the servants, reporters, Secret Service men, and the train crew that accompanied Wilson; a dining car; and, last in line, the President's blue-painted private coach, the *Mayflower*. As they sat together in the lounge of the final car, Wilson's three chosen companions for the journey—his wife Edith, his devoted secretary Joseph Tumulty, and the uneasy doctor Cary Grayson—eyed the President anxiously.

Wilson had never seemed to recover fully from his bout of influenza in Paris. For weeks he had suffered daily from mind-numbing headaches. The strain of his constant negotiations with the Senate showed in every line on his face, every irritable word and clipped gesture. Grayson, familiar with Wilson's history of periodic physical breakdowns under stress, was vehemently opposed to the trip. But the President was determined to make his appeal to the country, to circumvent by force of eloquence and will the constitutional impasse that threatened to nullify his diplomatic craftsmanship. He believed that American leaders, like British parliamentarians, should "take their case to the people."

When the train arrived next morning in Columbus, Ohio, the President seemed to brighten somewhat. The cheering crowds, though not as large or as reverential as those in Europe, were plainly a tonic to him. He opened his first speech of the tour with words of relief: "I have long chafed at confinement in Washington and I have wanted to report to you and other citizens of the United States."

Public speaking as the enunciation of moral principles in clear ringing terms was Wilson's first love, his greatest political asset. As the audiences responded to his verbal magic, some of Wilson's frustration at the near-checkmate in the Senate began to ease away. He reached out to touch the issue closest to the hearts of his listeners. If the treaty could be passed, he declared with a beat of his hands, then "men in khaki will not have to cross the seas again!" He also reached upward, to the high ideals that were the staple of his political philosophy. "America was not founded to make money," he told businessmen in St. Louis, "it was founded to lead the world on the way to liberty."

The swing around the country was not destined to be a triumphant march of idealism, however. The President's visits triggered opposition as well as applause. In Missouri, a minister countered Wilson by denouncing the League as a Wall Street plot. A Milwaukee socialist labeled the President's plan a "capitalist scheme" to bring "more wars and more armaments."

Lodge, meanwhile, was not idle. Although he remained firmly committed to his legislative strategy, he did dispatch several of his allies from among the irreconcilables to counter Wilson in the battle for public opinion. Hiram Johnson arrived in the Midwest shortly after Wilson left and brought an anti-League rally to its feet with charges that England hoped to use the international pact to send a hundred thousand American soldiers to fight in Constantinople. James Reed stumped New England, where doubts about the League and suspicions of Britain were most concentrated. Reed played to the hilt his assigned role of twisting the lion's tail; "the bloody footprints of John Bull," he exclaimed in speech after speech on the treaty, were "all over the dastardly document." But it was back in Washington that Lodge landed the most telling blow, against both the League and against Wilson personally. The senator summoned William Bullitt, still smarting over what he regarded as Wilson's betrayal of the peace mission to Russia, to testify about Secretary of State Lansing's true attitude toward the treaty. Bullitt told the Foreign Relations Committee that Lansing had been less than candid in publicly stating his support for the treaty, that privately the Secretary believed the League was "entirely useless" and should "unquestionably be defeated." When quizzed by the press, Lansing refused to deny that he had made such remarks to Bullitt.

The rising echoes of opposition that pursued Wilson denied him the release he had sought in the speaking tour. As the special moved westward, the President telescoped his schedule of speeches, canceled the days that had been set aside for rest, harangued crowds at every whistle-stop from the rear platform of his train. His headaches and nausea grew worse. Grayson feared that Wilson was trying to kill himself.

As the strain mounted, Wilson strove to answer the attacks on the treaty point by point. The people were being "deliberately misled," he charged in Oakland, especially about the plan for collective security. In Reno and elsewhere, he laid out the rationale behind Article 10, the League Covenant that he himself had composed.

"Article 10 is the heart of the enterprise. Article 10 is the test of the honor and courage and endurance of the world. Article 10 says that every member of the League, and that means every fighting power in the world . . . solemnly engages to respect and preserve as against external aggression the territorial integrity and existing political independence of the other members of the League. If you do that, you have absolutely stopped ambitious and aggressive war. . . ."

The pressure on Wilson drove him again and again to an emotional prophecy: "I have it in my heart that if we do not do this great thing now, every woman ought to weep because of the child in her arms. If she has a boy at her breast, she may be sure that when he comes to manhood this terrible task will have to be done once more. Everywhere we go, the train, when it stops, is surrounded with little children, and I look at them almost with tears in my eyes, because I feel my mission is to save them. These glad youngsters with flags in their hands—I pray God that they may never have to carry that flag upon the battlefield."

The campaigner was fighting his heart out on his own battlefield. On September 25, as the train was pulling out of Pueblo, Colorado, the first premonitory stroke hit the President, temporarily leaving his whole left side numb and practically useless. Wilson pleaded for a chance to continue the journey, to show Lodge and the others that he was not a quitter, but Grayson rallied Tumulty and Edith to dissuade him. The train sped back to Washington, where Wilson suffered an even more massive stroke on the night of October 1. For the next weeks he wavered on the edge of death. By crusading for the League, Wilson had indeed nearly thrown his own life away—yet he had not succeeded in changing a single vote in the Senate.

Wilson lay imprisoned in his White House sickroom for more than two months after his strokes. His left side was paralyzed, his speech blurred, his vision drastically reduced. Cutting the President off from visitors, Grayson and Mrs. Wilson concealed from the country the seriousness of his condition. With the help of Tumulty and the White House staff, they handled the routine business of the government until Wilson insisted he was well enough to work. He was barely able to receive Senator Hitchcock, the Democratic floor leader, for a few brief consultations as the final vote on the treaty drew near.

The debate over the treaty culminated on November 19, when the Senate finally voted on the package of fourteen amendments Lodge had assembled. Among them was the reservation Lodge himself had composed to delete Article 10, the League's collective security pact: "The United States assumes no obligation to preserve the territorial integrity or political independence of any other country or to interfere in controversies between nations," except when Congress, in each individual case, agreed to do so. Wilson had always opposed Lodge's attack on Article 10. From his sickbed, just two days before the final vote, he told Hitchcock that it

was "a nullification of the Treaty and utterly impossible," the moral equivalent of South Carolina's nullifying ordinances of the 1830s. "That cuts the
heart out of the Treaty; I could not stand for those changes for a moment."
By letter Wilson instructed the Senate Democrats to vote against the treaty
as amended by Lodge.

In the Senate, three factions squared off for the showdown. The Democrats and the irreconcilables voted down Lodge's reservations by 39 to 55;
then the Republican moderates joined the irreconcilables to defeat Wilson's unamended treaty by 38 to 53. On the surface it was a straight party
vote. Only four Democrats supported Lodge's final bill, and only one
Republican backed Wilson's. In fact, however, it had taken Lodge months
of adroit maneuvering to bring about this ultimate result. The Treaty of
Versailles was dead, and it was Wilson's Democrats who were forced to
administer the final blow.

For decades scholars have asked why Wilson allowed the treaty to go
down in defeat, why he did not just swallow hard and accept the Lodge
reservations as one more necessary concession. One doctor who has done
an exhaustive analysis of Wilson's medical and emotional history maintains
that the massive stroke he suffered in the fall of 1919 was the decisive factor
in the situation. "It is almost certain," writes Edwin A. Weinstein, "that
had Wilson not been so afflicted, his political skills and his facility with
language would have bridged the gap" between the Democrats and the
Republican reservationists. Weinstein notes that Wilson's judgment was
clouded by "cerebral dysfunction" in the wake of the stroke, and that his
access to information necessary for rational political calculation was being
severely limited by his wife and physician. As recently as February 1919,
Wilson had shown himself to be an able compromiser; the change, Weinstein concludes, must have stemmed from the President's physical collapse.

This analysis assumes that the Republican moderates were still amena-
ble to compromise as the final vote approached. In fact, however, Wilson
had already tried to conciliate the reservationists but had lost their support
by the end of August; hence the swing around the country. Moreover,
Wilson *did* make one more stab at compromise from his sickbed. His
instructions to the Senate Democrats focused on the key Lodge reservation
to Article 10. One could conclude that the other reservations were negotia-
ble as long as the attack on the League's covenant of collective security was
deleted. Lodge, however, had by November woven too tight a legislative
coalition for Wilson to sunder. None of the reservationists dared to desert
Lodge's amendment lest they see their own pet changes also struck down.
Thus Wilson's famous remark to Hitchcock, that it was up to Lodge to

make a move toward compromise, was reasoned political analysis rather than the petulance of a sick man.

The peculiarities of Wilson's character were well known during his lifetime and have been subjected to endless analysis since. That Wilson's self-esteem was damaged in his childhood, with important consequences for his adult behavior, has been commonly accepted by scholars. It still is legitimate to ask, however, whether Wilson was as much the prisoner of those psychological problems as some authors have made him out to be. Time and again in his political career, Wilson in fact was able to transcend his personal limitations. Certainly in the process of drafting and defending the Treaty of Versailles the President made repeated, skillful concessions in order to preserve the essence of his vision of a world parliament for peace. Even when paralyzed and nearly blind, he was able to lead the fight for the League from his darkened sickroom.

Wilson's mistakes in the League fight—if mistakes they were—seemed to stem more from intellectual strategy than from mental illness. Throughout his life, Wilson held as his leadership ideal the minister, the teacher, the orator. In politics he sought to practice the arts of persuasion and inspiration, to some neglect of the structural, transactional aspects of party politics. He seemed, to both friend and foe, to care little for the gritty tasks of government beyond his own agenda for reform. Also, Wilson's focus on inspirational leadership caused him to miss opportunities for tactical alliances—such as with the League to Enforce Peace—that could have promoted the very causes he espoused. One scholar detects in Wilson the self-styled transforming leader an "egocentricity," a "desire for glory," that marred his political career. Wilson could write eloquently about Cabinet government, but too often his unwillingness to share credit for accomplishments prevented him from exercising true collective leadership.

In the battle for the treaty, however, policy and not personality was the crucial factor. Wilson finally would compromise no further because the League—with a binding American commitment to it—was the irreducible core of his program. He seemed willing to accept almost anything else as long as he could preserve his plan for collective security, but that was precisely the one thing Lodge was unwilling to grant him. If the League fight is compared to the famed graduate-school controversy at Princeton, in which Wilson became locked in a bitter personal quarrel with Dean Andrew West, we then see a dramatic and ironic reversal of Wilson's role. In the dispute at Princeton, Wilson was unwilling to accept any of the compromises West offered, whereas in the treaty fight it was Wilson who made concession after concession, only to be rebuffed by the Republicans.

Ultimately, Wilson's League was not killed by him, by the Senate Demo-

crats who voted as Wilson instructed them, by the irreconcilables, or even
by Lodge. It was thwarted by a political system that chopped up Wilson's
idealism, diluted public sentiment for his cause, atomized his efforts for
reform. Lodge, it is true, manipulated that system brilliantly, but he had
only inherited it. In the struggle over the Treaty of Versailles, the American system of checks and balances worked as the Founding Fathers intended that it should. The President was unable to bring about a radical
alteration in American foreign policy through a simple vote of the Senate.

Wilson, however, was not about to give up trying. Already, as his tour
of the country had presaged, he was looking for another political lever with
which to move the nation.

1920: The Great and Solemn Rejection

Defeated in the Senate, where a two-thirds vote was required from a
body he considered both unrepresentative and oligarchical, and with his
direct appeal to the people cut short by illness, Woodrow Wilson looked
now to one last alternative—to the presidential electoral college, where an
approximate majority of the people would render the final verdict. Early
in January 1920 he wrote the Democratic party leadership that he did not
accept the action of the Senate as the decision of the nation. "If there is
any doubt as to what the people of the country think on this vital matter,
the clear and single way out is to submit it for determination at the next
election to the voters of the Nation, to give the next election the form of
a great and solemn referendum. . . ."

For Wilson, "going to the country" was far more an expression of
personal conviction and philosophy than a mere political tactic. His faith
in representative democracy, in majority rule, in the ultimate wisdom of
the people went to the very core of his being. His ultimate value—individual liberty—could be secure only in a democratic system. While still a
Princeton undergraduate he had written that "*representative* government,"
at its highest development, was that form "which best enables a free people
to govern themselves." He admired parliamentary systems—especially the
British—where leaders could appeal directly to the people for decision and
support. He favored not the "disintegrate ministry" of a checks-and-bal-
ances system but strong executive leadership directly linked to the people
through political parties. He even proposed that the Constitution be
amended so that members of Congress might join the Cabinet without
surrendering their seats in House or Senate. He believed that Presidents
should *if necessary* appeal to the voters over the heads of the legislators, as
he had done in 1918, and even appeal to peoples of foreign countries over

the heads of their leaders, as he had done in Europe as a world leader. By the same token, he felt that leaders who had lost the confidence of the people should resign instantly, as he had planned to do if he had lost to Hughes in 1916.

And now he would stake all on a colossal throw of the electoral dice. Doubters abounded even in his official family. How could treaty ratification be made the single issue in an election involving many questions? Lansing asked in his private diary. How could the people render a decision on several grades of League reservations, "interpretive, slightly modifying, radical, and nullifying?" The whole idea of obtaining a popular judgment by election or referendum was "absurd and utterly unworkable."

1920 was hardly shaping up as a year for isolating and testing even a transcendent issue like the League. The end of the war seemed to bring not peace but heightened social tensions. It was a time of race riots—in Chicago, Gary, Omaha, even Washington itself; of radical and revolutionary unrest in the streets of New York and other metropolises; of a rash of labor disputes; of a resurgence of the Ku Klux Klan; of food shortages and price rises; of thousands of ex-servicemen searching for jobs; of "red hunts," by Wilson's Attorney General, A. Mitchell Palmer, culminating in the arrest of several thousand suspected radicals in New York on New Year's Day, 1920. The world prospect seemed much worse. "Europe is in the throes of great changes," wrote socialist Seymour Stedman, "class wars, nationalistic wars, revolutions, repudiation of debts, starvation, revenge, subjugation, outbursts of the oppressed, strikes, the fall of kings and cabinets; and Asia is shaking as she stretches to arise." Everywhere recession, radicalism, repression, revolt seemed to herald a new age of the Four Horsemen.

And who would carry the League issue to the country? As Wilson looked over the field of Democratic presidential aspirants, he could see little to inspire hope. Palmer he had had to restrain, urging him, "Do not let the country see red." The trouble was, the country already had. Then there was McAdoo, the President's son-in-law, brilliant but not a veteran of the hustings. Out in the hinterland, one could dimly perceive the figure of James Cox, an Ohio newspaper editor, and even of William Jennings Bryan. Impossible! Who but the President himself could go to the people, could fight for vindication? They had never failed him when *he* was the nominee.

The idea of Woodrow Wilson as a third-term candidate seemed incredible, shocking, even to persons in Wilson's entourage—indeed, most of all to them, for they saw him close up, while the public hardly knew of his condition. Months after his stroke, Wilson could walk only by using a cane and someone's helping arm, and by dragging his left leg forward. Still unable to work more than a few hours a day, he looked gaunt and old, his white hair thin and wispy above the cavernous face, his voice often weak and faltering, his left arm still dangling at his side. Mrs. Wilson no longer isolated him, and he was meeting with his aides and Cabinet, but only irregularly. Visitors were still shocked by the inert, reclining figure; they remembered the man who had always leaned forward as though tensed for a footrace. But the President was slowly learning to walk again—and if he could walk, why could he not run?

*   *   *

In the spring of 1920, the Republicans appeared to be as united and resolute as the Democrats seemed divided and leaderless. The Grand Old Party could blame all the ills of the nation, if not of Europe, on the Wilson Democracy. It could benefit from the tides of postwar reaction and race and ethnic hostility sweeping the nation. It had a simple goal—to eradicate Wilsonism root and branch. It could boast of a galaxy of leaders—seasoned national campaigners like Taft and Hughes, Senate gladiators like Lodge and Hiram Johnson, favorite sons like Governor Calvin Coolidge of Massachusetts and reform governor Frank Lowden of Illinois, Old Guard politicos in Senate and House, even a military hero, the TR protégé and Rough Rider General Leonard Wood, who had been kept out of the fighting in France, it was said, precisely because Wilson still hated Roosevelt men.

The GOP was divided, however, between its old presidential wing and its congressional leadership entrenched in the committee system on Capitol Hill—between the moderately liberal, internationalist party headed or symbolized by Abraham Lincoln, TR, Taft, and Hughes, and the more conservative, "unilateralist" party headed by Lodge and his fellow reservationists. Each party was bottomed in its own voting constituency, entrenched in its own governmental structures, inspired by its own memories, principles, and heroes. While the Democracy also embraced two leadership structures, its congressional party had been overshadowed by Wilson's driving presidential leadership. The presidential parties usually dominated presidential elections—but 1920 loomed as an exceptional year in which the militant, anti-League congressional Republicans might hold unprecedented influence over the Republican nomination.

Already some party leaders were counseling compromise between the Taft-Hughes leadership and the Senate Old Guard, but most of the potential nominees seemed to be lined up with one side or the other. Could a compromise candidate be found who was not a cipher? Some wondered if Senator Warren Gamaliel Harding would fill the bill. The Ohio senator had always been a party man—as a most partisan editor of the Marion *Star*, as an Ohio politico and officeholder, and as a conciliator who yet in 1912 had stuck with the party nominee, Taft, against the usurper back from Africa. Elected to the Senate in 1914, in Ohio's first experience with the statewide direct primary and the direct election of senators, he had served a term distinguished mainly by his ability to win friends in all Republican factions.

But it was—it would always be—too easy to caricature Harding, as a mere glad-hander, an easygoing, fun-loving, poker-playing politician, a small-town man with a small-town mind and outlook. Although brought up in a severe and pious home—or perhaps because of it—he had a reputation as an occasional cutup, hard drinker, womanizer. He had no convictions, it was said, no set of principles, no quality of leadership. His mind, somebody would quip, was like stellar space—a huge void filled with a few wandering clichés. At least he had the becoming virtue of modesty. He did not, he wrote a friend, "possess the elements of leadership or the widespread acquaintances" essential to the "ideal leadership of our Party in 1920."

Such was the basis of the legends that would sprout about Harding—that he did not want to be nominated for President, that he made no effort for the nomination, that he was the pawn of corporate interests seeking power, that he was a country yokel, a dumbbell, a spread-eagle orator who liked to "bloviate," doze in his office, or relax around the poker table with his Ohio cronies.

In fact Harding had convinced himself by the summer of 1920 that he wanted to be President, that he would at least be better than the other hopefuls, and that he must work for it. While his friend Harry Daugherty made the rounds asking otherwise committed delegates to make Harding their second or third choice at the convention, he campaigned in several states. Harding was barely able to stave off an invasion by Leonard Wood in the Ohio primary, however, and he was shellacked in Indiana. By the time the first ballot was held at the broiling June convention in Chicago, Harding was far behind the front-runners, Wood, Lowden, and Johnson.

What happened in Chicago that June was simple in essence and complex in mechanics. The three front-runners deadlocked in ballot after ballot, while the steaming delegates, sometimes politicking in temperatures over 100 degrees, grew more and more weary and impatient. Late in the week, a group of senators who considered themselves the real leaders of the party gathered at the Blackstone Hotel to see if they could resolve the stalemate. It looked like a Senate cabal—Reed Smoot of Utah was there, and James Watson of Indiana, Medill McCormick of Illinois, Henry Cabot Lodge and former senators Crane and Weeks of Massachusetts. But this was no ,cabal, with an agreed-on strategy. All through the evening politicians drifted in and out of the smoke-filled Blackstone suite, pouring themselves drinks, sending up small trial balloons, bickering and dickering. Someone said that the room seemed like the Senate in miniature, with Lodge sitting back in his chair and biting off brief comments, while the others indulged in what one senator, stalking off, called a "footless conversation."

The senators continued to ruffle through possible dark horses "like a deck of soiled cards," in Francis Russell's words, but however many times "the political cards were shuffled and dealt and discarded, somehow the Harding card always remained." Senators who knew Harding had little respect for his intellect, his convictions, or his qualities of leadership. But he came from a pivotal and symbolically important state, he was the right age at fifty-five, he *looked* like a President, and above all he was a party man who would follow the Republican senators' lead on policy, especially on the League. He seemed perfectly to fill the party slot. Still, the few stalwarts remaining in the Blackstone suite came to no final conclusion—essentially they agreed to give Harding a run for his money for a few ballots the next day, and if the Ohioan did not click with the delegates, to try some other compromise possibility.

That evening Harding was not sitting in a hotel room awaiting the call to greatness. He was roaming the Blackstone corridors, unshaven, unkempt, liquored up a bit, buttonholing any man he could meet. Gradually word leaked out to reporters—and to Harding—that he was the group's trial horse. Next day, many of the senators in the "cabal" stuck to their earlier commitments over several ballots. But the delegates, eager to go home, knew that Harding now more than ever was "available." Slowly they edged toward him, as Daugherty scurried around the convention floor calling in those second-chance promises, while the fading front-runners desperately tried to patch together a stop-Harding coalition. No one would run as his rival's running mate. On the tenth ballot the man from Marion went over the top amid a burst of enthusiasm and relief.

Already a legend was sprouting—that a cabal of determined, likeminded senators had gathered at the Blackstone with the single determination to make an obscure colleague their President, and their patsy. Weeks before the convention Daugherty, in a euphoric moment, had predicted to two reporters, in New York's Waldorf-Astoria, that "about eleven minutes after two o'clock on Friday morning of the convention, when fifteen or twenty men, bleary-eyed and perspiring profusely from the heat, are sitting around a table . . . at that decisive time the friends of Senator Harding can suggest him and can afford to abide by the result." He might suggest Harding himself, Daugherty added brightly. And now the prophecy was resurrected, even though Daugherty had not attended the smoke-filled proceedings and the cabal had been far more a cloudiness than a conspiracy.

The truth was simpler and more significant—that the anti-League, conservative Republicans at the convention had wrested control from the old presidential leadership; that its leaders—primarily senators but including also national party leaders and local party bosses—had rummaged through their "soiled cards" and found their man; and that the actions of the first-cadre leaders in smoke-filled rooms had largely turned on their estimates of how hundreds of second- and third-cadre leaders on the floor of the stink-filled convention would react. Ultimately, Harding was the delegates' choice—a party choice. And if anyone doubted the capacity of the rank-and-file delegates to work their will, they showed their power by brushing aside establishment candidates for Vice-President and nominating that law-and-order man from Massachusetts, Calvin Coolidge, as Harding's running mate.

So, as the whole national party rallied behind Harding in its common hatred of Wilsonism, the Ohio senator sallied forth in his front-porch campaign as a party man, in the McKinley tradition. And it was as a party man that he harmonized the wings of his party, stuck to the party platform, and equated Republicanism with Americanism. The League continued to be the overriding issue. Every time Harding made a strong anti-League statement, he heard from internationalists like Herbert Hoover. When he softened his stand, Johnson and Borah descended on him like furies. Teetering back and forth, concealing his position behind clouds of platitudes, Harding skillfully held his party together until election day.

The Democrats too sought a candidate who could unite the party—and also exploit the Wilson heritage without being overburdened by it. For thirty-eight ballots McAdoo, Cox, and Palmer waged a stand-off battle at the party's convention in San Francisco, until Palmer pulled out, Cox picked up a majority of his delegates, and the Ohio Democrat won by acclamation on the forty-fourth ballot. Refusing to desert their leader languishing in the White House, the party paid fulsome tribute to Wilson in their platform, endorsed his League, and reaffirmed Wilson's New Freedom. But they would not renominate the President, who waited at the White House through ballot after ballot, hoping that the party might still turn to him. When word came to the President of Cox's nomination Wilson burst into a stream of profanities and obscenities, according to his valet.

The President was hardly mollified by the choice for Vice-President of young Franklin D. Roosevelt, who had something of a reputation in Washington for being independent and a bit bumptious, but the delegates liked him for his youth and vigor—especially after his spirited seconding speech for Al Smith for President, during which FDR said that the Democrats' choice would not be made in a hotel room at two in the morning—and above all they loved him for his last name.

So Cox and Roosevelt, backed by a dispirited party, sallied forth on their quest like Don Quixote and Sancho Panza, and with about as much objective chance of success. Almost quixotically—at least in the minds of hardened Democratic politicos—they resolved that they would campaign for Wilson's League. The two men visited the White House.

"Mr. President," Cox said, "I have always admired the fight you made for the League."

"Mr. Cox," said Wilson, "that fight can still be won."

After a few moments Cox went on: "Mr. President, we are going to be a million per cent with you and your Administration, and that means the League of Nations."

"I am very grateful," the President said in a faltering voice. "I am very grateful."

Cox and Roosevelt lived up to their promise, campaigning vigorously throughout the nation. Cox backslid only slightly on the League, saying that he would accept a reservation to Article 10 stating that the United States would not send its armed forces into action unless authorized by Congress in each case. But it was too late for compromise. Harding swept all the states outside the South, many of the far-northern states by two-to-one and three-to-one majorities. The omen of 1916 had been realized: the Democrats had been forced back on their shrunken base. And so had the omen of 1918: the Republicans now commanded top-heavy majorities in both House and Senate.

*   *   *

The President's life had settled down to a routine by the late fall of 1920. Each day he struggled to take a few steps, saw as many visitors as he could, perhaps took a drive. One of his pleasures was almost daily movies in a White House parlor. One day Ray Stannard Baker joined the President, Mrs. Wilson, and one or two others for a film on the President's first trip to Europe.

The projector clattered and whirred, and suddenly, Baker remembered, "we were in another world; a resplendent world, full of wonderful and glorious events"—President Wilson sailing into Brest amid beflagged ships and soldiers marshaled upon the quay, "smiling upon the bridge, very erect, very tall, lifting his hat to shouting crowds." The film ground on: Wilson driving down the Champs-Elysées, Wilson crossing the Channel escorted by warships, Wilson riding down from Buckingham Palace with the King of England, "behind noble horses flanked by outriders flying pennants"—always amid bands and flags and shouting crowds.

The film sputtered and ended. The little company sat silent in the darkness for a moment. Then Wilson was helped to his feet. He turned slowly and shuffled out of the room, without a word.

PART V
The Culture of Democracy

CHAPTER 14

The Age of Mellon

H*enry Ford's Rouge plant, a working day in the early 1920s.* A massive ship loaded with iron ore steams into a turning basin off the River Rouge, swings ponderously to starboard, and slides into a slip next to Henry Ford's concrete holding bins. Hulett unloaders rumble down the tracks alongside the slip, pause, plunge their huge arms down into the ship's hold, scoop out ten-ton bites of ore, and swing around to dump their loads into the bins behind. Within the day, the ore is rolling on bottom-dumping railroad cars from bins to blast furnaces; within hours, molten metal moves from furnace to foundry, to be cast into engine blocks, and to the machining rooms, where the engines pass through thirty or more machine-tool operations.

In the vast assembly rooms, vehicles begin to take shape as castings, pistons, axles, springs, and thousands of other parts and pieces flow into the central assembly line. Coming in at right angles are the conveyors feeding in the parts via buckets, belts, rollers, monorails, and "scenic railways." A seven-leafed car-spring has passed through its own assembly line—punch press, bending machine, nitrate bath, bolt insertion, painting, inspection—before joining the central procession. Roofs, wheels, windows, bumpers are clamped into place. A tall, black Model T triumphantly emerges at the end of the long line. Kindled into life by a gallon of gasoline, the car roars off in a cloud of exhaust to a railway siding and the awaiting freight train. The whole process, from ore to car, has taken perhaps a day. . . .

The men standing at the moving assembly lines and toiling in the rolling mill, powerhouse, blast furnaces, and foundry were considered the elite of American industry, well paid, well housed, well treated by a benevolent employer. Life at the Rouge was not easy. They were part of an army— 75,000 men worked at the sprawling facility by 1926—and they were treated much like soldiers. Amid an ear-splitting roar, they fought their daily battle of production standing often shoulder to shoulder, absolutely dominated by the flow of work, just as the flow of work had been carefully adjusted to them. Each man had enough space to do his work, no more. Men did not move; only materials. Each work unit, wrote an admiring observer, was "a carefully designed gear which meshes with other gears

479

and operates in synchronism with them, the whole forming one huge, perfectly-timed, smoothly operating industrial machine of almost unbelievable efficiency."

The whole plant seemed in motion as parts flowed from scores of tributaries into the mighty central stream. Men seemed in constant motion from the waist up as they drilled, inserted, bolted, clipped, plucked parts from small bins at their side, moved in a precise series of steps to an exact and demanding time sequence. Mass production, according to company doctrine, reduced the "necessity for thought on the part of the worker and . . . his movements to a minimum." Thus workers were expected to act as efficiently and automatically as machines. Plant bosses, on the other hand, were not only allowed to move about but required to. They were given desks without chairs so that they had to work standing up, or preferably on the move. Casual conversations were frowned upon. An air of anxiety hung over the whole place as workers labored and bosses scrambled to meet the company injunction—produce, produce, produce.

The man most in motion at the Ford works was Henry Ford himself. Still lean and sinewy as he entered his sixties, almost handsome, with his black eyes and slightly curling hair, he was bored by executive meetings, hardly able to sit still for more than a few minutes. Restlessly he toured his plants and yards, his bins and his foundries, sharp to spot men engaged in idle chatter or executives stuck to their desks, praising or upbraiding with brief words and rapidly gesturing hands. Even on holidays he was restless, hurrying. Camping in the Smokies with his old friend Thomas Edison, he was surprised when the inventor felt his hip pocket. "What are you looking for?" Said Edison: "I figure you always carry a lighted bunch of firecrackers in your clothes somewhere. Slow to a walk for a while, will you? I get tired of motion pictures."

By the early twenties, Henry Ford was already a legend, both in the popular press and in the automobile industry. The public drank in the stories—how as a young genius mechanic he had experimented with light-car Models A and B and K at a time when automobiles were big and their owners wealthy; how he had worked out audacious mass-production techniques for building hundreds of thousands of Model Ts; how he had fought off Wall Street bankers who were trying to dominate the automobile industry through patent control; how he had sent a Peace Ship to Europe in 1915 to end the war; how he had fought off his own associates and stockholders so that he could establish personal control of his company; how he had made several hundred million—or was it a billion?—dollars; and how, above all, he had suddenly announced in 1914 that every Ford worker would receive at least five dollars a day, to the delight of auto workers and the consternation of his rivals.

What impressed Americans most was Ford's independence. In an age of monopoly and trusts, he steered clear of combination and stuck to his last —making cars and tractors. In an age that preached individualism more than it practiced it, he was the supreme individualist—a man who could tell bankers, suppliers, union bosses, rivals to go to hell. This perception was accurate. Thwarted by strikes against his glass and steel suppliers, and by miners and railroad workers, he resolved to control the source of his raw materials—of the timber that went into his car bodies, the iron mines that produced ore for wheels and axles, the glass that made car windows, the leather for interiors, the coal that fed his towering furnaces. By 1915, with his Highland plant a huge success, he had resolved on building a far bigger works at Rouge—an integrated works that would combine a multitude of auto-building processes, resting on a vertical organization of production. Raising colossal amounts of capital from his own profits, and some from bankers, Ford simply bought up enormous tracts of land, timber, iron fields, waterpower rights, limestone, and silica sand.

So that ore-bearing vessel easing into the slip belonged personally to Henry Ford, as did the cargo ship headed out to Europe and South America packed with his cars and tractors, as did canals and railroads and ports and harbors. He planned for the future, too, requiring that branch plants be set up next to waterways in case other men's railroads should fail him. Ford wanted independence because that to him meant power—power to do as he wished. And he had few doubts about what he could do through his own talents if only rivals or incompetents did not stand in his way.

Ford would control not only raw materials but men's lives as well—and not only their working lives but, to a degree, their home lives, too. To make sure that his five-dollars-a-day wage would not be wasted—or worse—Ford established the Sociological Department, whose main task was to encourage workers toward "thrift, honesty, sobriety, better housing, and better living generally." At this time, the company was employing thousands of immigrants from Poland, Russia, Romania, Italy, and other less industrialized areas of Europe. Over a hundred staff members from the Sociological Department visited workers' homes to inspect for uncleanliness, bad habits, congestion, undernourished children, drunkenness, gambling. "Employees should use plenty of soap and water in the home, and upon their children, bathing frequently," a Ford pamphlet advised. "Notice that the most advanced people are the cleanest."

The result was a clash of cultures—between the immigrants' pre-industrial living and working habits and Ford's Puritan ethic of hard work, clean living, and efficiency. Ford's paternalism reflected a pervasive fear that the immigrants would not only waste their five dollars a day but flaunt it. A veiled warning came in a condescending verse from the Detroit poet Edgar Guest about "Giuseppe," who goes out promenading with white collar, silk hat, cane, and Ford badge on his lapel:

> He smok' da cigar weath da beega da band,
> Da "three-for-da-quart" ees da kind;
> Da diamond dat flash from da back of hees hand,
> Eez da beegest Giuseppe could find. . . .
> For Giuseppe, he work at da Ford.

If the company's "sociologists" had limited impact on the workers' home lives, Ford had more control of their working time. Within his plants he established "Americanization" classes that taught English, table manners, cleanliness, proper attire, and even etiquette, as well as Ford shop practices. "Graduation" took the form of a pageant depicting immigrants descending from a boat down a gangway into a fifteen-foot-wide "melting pot" representing the Ford English School. But the clash of cultures could not be resolved; and, inevitably, Ford's paternalism had its ugly side. Vexed above all by absenteeism, the company sacked almost a thousand Greek and Russian workers who as Orthodox Christians celebrated Christmas thirteen days after the regular holiday under their own Julian calendar. "If these men are to make their home in America," a Ford official stated, "they should observe American holidays."

Still, as historians noted, immigrants tended to cling to their ways—to the crowded tenements, the noisy sociability, the relaxed hours, even the "squalor." After a few years, the sociological and Americanization programs were dropped. While these programs did have a certain impact on the wider social scene—the 16,000 workers who graduated from the Ford schools served as models for many local and national "Americanization" efforts directed at immigrants—Ford, in the end, found that he had less power over men than over machines.

All told, however, Henry Ford had emerged by the mid-1920s as one of the country's supreme transforming leaders. He belonged, concluded a biographer, "to that small company of historical personalities who literally transformed the world of their time." Not only did he make it possible for millions of Americans to own cars, not only did he develop the moving assembly line as a fundamental part of the total production process, help put the nation on wheels, and force a vast expansion of the highways his "flivvers" rode on; he also reshaped the home locations, recreation habits, social intercourse, even the language of tens of millions of working people.

THE AGE OF MELLON

Thus he "altered the contours of society" as much as he "permanently changed the topography of cities and nations."

It was not that Ford had a direct influence on politics or government. On the contrary, on almost every occasion where he moved outside his industrial orbit he failed, sometimes dramatically. Thus his Peace Ship— a 1915 cruise to Europe with Jane Addams and other pacifists—not only failed but made him something of a laughingstock. An ardent supporter of Woodrow Wilson, he moved with the President from pacifism to war mobilization, in which he had a prominent role, and then went down with Wilson and the League. He rashly accepted the Democratic nomination for United States senator from Michigan, only to be beaten by what he viewed as "Wall Street money" and by a free-spending Republican candidate who later was found guilty of violating the federal corrupt practices act. He published his own weekly, the Dearborn *Independent,* but this venture turned sour when Ford used it for anti-Semitic propaganda, in part because for a time he imagined a "Jewish control" of banking. His most bizarre and humiliating experience resulted from a libel suit he launched against Colonel Robert R. McCormick's Chicago *Tribune* for calling him an unpatriotic "anarchist" during the war. After a long proceeding, during which Ford was put on the stand and exposed as ignorant of American history, a jury of farmers found the *Tribune* guilty but fined it six cents— a deliciously satisfying verdict for the Colonel.

Like many transforming leaders, Ford was a bundle of contradictions. He believed in "pragmatic," ad hoc, day-to-day decision-making, and yet carefully and brilliantly planned one of the biggest and most complex production layouts in the world. He demanded absolute discipline from the work force, but made a special effort to employ not only unlettered immigrants but handicapped persons and ex-convicts. He led his company into historic advances but also setbacks, such as refusing to paint Model Ts anything save black, long delaying the shift from the Model T to the Model A, and holding an almost obsessive bias against hydraulic brakes. He practiced centralized and disciplined management, but preached old-fashioned smallness and, indeed, during the early twenties built a number of small factories—called Village Industries—to produce sub-assembly parts. He was almost impossible to work with or under, but he brought to industrial leadership a number of men who would become giants in the automotive industry—notably William S. Knudsen and Charles E. Sorensen. Ford, someone said, was able to assemble everything except himself.

"Ford runs modern society and not the politicians who are only screens," F. Scott Fitzgerald wrote in 1924. The novelist was only partly right. Ford enormously influenced social and political attitudes through his Model Ts, his pervasive company propaganda, and his own example. His influence was worldwide; Europeans coined the term "Fordismus" for the idea of mass production, industrial efficiency, and cheap consumer goods, and even the Russians hailed him and his tractors as symbols of the kind of modern industry needed to build socialism. But the automaker found out the hard way that economic power was not directly convertible into political power. A financial loner, a political independent, an erratic innovator, Ford was far more a throwback to the days of the Carnegies and Rockefellers than a forerunner of the modern capitalist in politics. The future lay with the bankers and businessmen and brokers who would make up the transactional leadership of mid-twentieth-century America.

"THE BUSINESS OF AMERICA . . ."

During the 1920s the Republican leaders and the business leaders of the nation—often the same men—conducted a crowning experiment in America's capitalistic brand of conservatism. Assured and determined, for ten years they had the almost unfettered opportunity to convert their individualistic rhetoric, pro-business beliefs, and corporate power into public policy and governmental action. No opponent could obstruct them as they worked in their economic and political laboratory. The conservative leaders did not, of course, view their efforts as experimental; on the contrary, they assumed that they were bringing the nation back to "normalcy"—back to old moorings, established wisdoms, and the proper conduct of affairs after the radical Wilson years. Hence the period was not a mere interregnum between the New Freedom and the New Deal, but witnessed a major venture with its own powerful impact on American history and American democracy.

An extraordinary political continuity and consistency marked that decade. Throughout, Republicans remained firmly in control. Whether the Democrats nominated a moderate liberal and internationalist in 1920, or a conservative in 1924, or an Irish-Catholic city man in 1928, the Grand Old Party racked up its nearly two-to-one popular majorities and its three- or four-to-one electoral college majorities throughout the decade. The Republicans kept control of Congress, even during the "off-year" House and Senate elections of the 1920s.

The Republicans nominated and elected three Presidents, each with a distinctive image and style. Harding in the White House continued to be very much the same man as in the Senate—a poker-playing, golf-addictive, tobacco-chewing, mistress-keeping, whiskey-drinking politico who concealed a good deal of political sophistication and grasp of policy behind an affable, glad-handing front, and a quick intelligence and lazy, undisciplined mind behind his Hollywood-presidential appearance—silvery hair, square jaw, expressive mouth, big frame, high paunch. Calvin Coolidge seemed almost his opposite—a small, spare man, as austere and hard-looking as some of his native Vermont granite, taciturn in public though garrulous enough when he wanted to be. Herbert Hoover, who had won warm admiration from Republicans and Democrats alike, and from acute observers such as Brandeis and Lippmann, for his competent and compassionate handling of wartime relief, was a remarkable administrator, both well organized and imaginative, who could launch major new ventures and write a sophisticated tract, as he did on individualism, with equal skill. All three men had small-town origins, but they had been shaped by diverse subcultures—Harding by the boom town of Marion, Coolidge by the staid political and business world of Northampton, Hoover by years as an engineer and promoter overseas and at home.

In broad political outlook, on the other hand, the three Presidents were much alike. At his first Cabinet meeting after Harding's death in August 1923, and later to press and Congress, Coolidge stated that he would continue all his predecessor's policies. Hoover in turn carried on most of Coolidge's initiatives, at least until new imperatives arose. All three chief executives were under the same institutional constraints. The presidency had its own direction and dynamics, as foreign demands and bureaucratic pressures played on the White House. Even the easygoing Harding was moving toward a more modern and coherent program in the last year of his brief presidency, and Coolidge, in Robert Murray's words, was able to be the President that Harding would have liked to have been. Undergirding all three Administrations, moreover, was the power of the Republican party. No single "boss" could tell Presidents what to do, but the collective leadership, triumphant self-confidence, and policy and patronage demands of the Grand Old Party set the course of all three Administrations.

Presidential Republican rule showed the most continuity in its top executive leadership. Secretary of State Hughes served during both the Harding and early Coolidge years, as did a number of other Cabinet officers. Coolidge as Vice-President sat in Harding's Cabinet, Hoover as Secretary of Commerce in both Harding's and Coolidge's. After the long patronage drought during the Wilson years, GOP leaders in Congress and the country put intense pressure on all three Presidents for Republican appointments. But of all the forces for continuity through the 1920s, nothing could compare, in intensity and effect, with that of Andrew William Mellon.

Andrew Mellon. The star of no leader was to shine so brightly in the

1920s, nor fade so quickly into darkness thereafter. Born in 1855, Mellon had grown up in a Pittsburgh banking family drenched in affluence, education, gentility, conservatism, and Republicanism. Everything Mellon touched, as he rose in banking and industry circles, turned to money. Taking over his father's bank at the age of twenty-seven, Andrew helped establish the Aluminum Company of America, Gulf Oil, and Union Steel, then moved on into manufacturing, shipbuilding, public utilities. He helped Marshall-McClintick become world-famous as builder of the Panama Canal locks, the Hell Gate and George Washington bridges, the Waldorf-Astoria Hotel. But at heart he always remained a banker. By 1920, he was reputed to be one of America's richest men—perhaps the richest—with a fortune of several hundred millions.

He was an austere figure amid the flamboyant politicos of the day—reticent, soft-voiced, with a long narrow head and chilly gray-blue eyes on top of a small, slight frame tightly buttoned into a dark suit. It was considered a master stroke on Harding's part when the new President was able to persuade this diffident multimillionaire to come to Washington as Secretary of the Treasury. Coolidge, who admired wealth, was delighted to keep him on as Treasury Secretary, as was Hoover despite earlier disagreements with him in the Cabinet. He rivaled all three Presidents in his influence over economic policy.

Above all Mellon symbolized the unity between corporate power and the Grand Old Party. No chasm separated his Republicanism from his business conservatism. However much he disdained truck with ordinary politicos, touching their hands only with the tips of his fingers, organizational Republicanism was part of his life. Leaders of the Pennsylvania Cameron-Quay machine had often dropped in to see his father; later, Mellon consorted with Boies Penrose, Philander Knox, and other heads of one of the most conservative state parties in the country. Corporate control of the Republican party had long been a staple of muckraking journalists and progressive orators. They drew a picture of politicians as pawns of the corporations. But big business did not have to exert conservative influence *on* most Republican regulars; that influence was already *in* them, inculcated by heritage, family, education, occupation, class status, social environment, and party ideology.

So Harding really meant it when he said, "This is essentially a business country. We hear a vast deal about 'big business,' but the big business of America is nothing but the aggregate of the small businesses. That is why we need business sense in charge of American administration, and why the majority of America has for more than half a century been a Republican majority." He denounced the "hampering restrictions and bullying methods" used against business. Coolidge not only issued his famous pronunciamento: "The business of America is business," but, flinty Vermonter though he was, waxed euphoric: the man "who builds a factory," he said, "builds a temple, the man who works there worships there, and to each is due not scorn and blame, but reverence and praise." Herbert Hoover said in 1928: "Given a chance to go forward with the policies of the last eight years we shall soon with the help of God be in sight of the day when poverty will be banished from this nation." Every "expansion of government in business," he said, "poisons the very roots of liberalism—that is, political equality, free speech, free assembly, free press, and equality of opportunity."

In the election of 1928 the voters granted Hoover's wish to continue the essential program of the previous eight years—to proceed with the Republicans' venture in a businesslike and business-loving regime. The Grand Old Party could claim all credit for the continuing success of the grand old experiment in rugged individualism, laissez-faire, materialism, social stability, corporate influence, and business power.

*   *   *

Thus for a solid decade conservative belief dominated the public affairs of the nation. Not since the triumphant Republicanism of the turn of the century had a party majority so firmly established its power and leadership in Congress and the presidency, but the stakes were much higher now because of the expanded role of the federal government. Refurbishing its electoral majorities throughout the decade, the leadership of the Grand Old Party carried through its policies and programs not only in Washington but in a host of state capitals outside the South. It was government by compact majority.

It was precisely this kind of majority that the Founding Fathers had feared in drafting the new constitution in 1787. As good republicans they believed in majority rule—rule by a majority of the fraction of the people who could vote at the time, that is—but as men wanting order and stability, they proposed to curb majorities, especially majorities composed of turbulent mobs and unruly populaces. Thus James Madison recognized the old and "fundamental principle of Republican government—that the majority who rule are the safest Guardians both of public good and private rights." But—"If a majority be united by a common interest, the rights of the minority will be insecure." By dividing up powers among different sets of leaders, by making these leaders elected by and responsible to diverse and conflicting constituencies, and by staggering elections over a period of time, the Framers sought to tame the unruly beast of majority power.

The Founders recognized, nonetheless, that popular majorities ultimately would take control of the new federal government if such majorities
could remain large and united enough to win a series of presidential and
legislative elections. Here was where they played their trump constitutional card. By establishing presidential selection and Senate confirmation
of federal judges, they tied the judiciary into the republican system; but by
giving judges lifetime tenure, along with some power of judicial review,
they created a judicial leadership that institutionally would be "behind the
times"—that is, responding to the presidential and legislative majorities of
a decade or even a generation back. This meant a virtual guarantee of
continuity and stability: the judiciary would represent a kind of consensus
among shifting factions, parties, and ideologies.

Somehow this logical arrangement did not seem to be working in the
early twentieth century. It might have been expected that when Harding
came to the White House in March of 1921, the Supreme Court in particular would strike a balance between the conservative presidencies of McKinley and Taft and the progressive presidencies of Roosevelt and Wilson. But
history played one of its tricks. Taft had the pleasure of making as many
Supreme Court appointments in his four years in the White House as
Wilson and TR did in their combined fifteen years. This was not wholly
by chance; retiring justices had long since learned the art of waiting out
Presidents.

So the Republicans returning to power in 1921 happily found likeminded brethren on the bench. Their luck continued when, two months
after he took office, Harding could bestow the highest gift in a President's
hands—the chief justiceship. It was not only luck: Chief Justice White had
held out until the GOP returned, repeatedly telling Taft, as the former
President said later, that "he was holding the office for me and that he
would give it back to a Republican administration." It was Taft's crowning
moment, too, for this was above all else the post he craved, while serving
in practically every other. There was a slight problem, since Harding had
promised a place on the Court to his campaign brain-truster George Sutherland, but this was straightened out—Sutherland was told to wait for the
next vacancy—and by summer 1921, William Howard Taft, as spry and
genial as ever and less plump, was seated at the center of the High Court.

That Court had for some years been a center of controversy. During the
heyday of progressivism, liberals and radicals complained that the reactionary bench was upholding corporate property rights and thwarting state
and federal regulation of the economy. In 1908, three years after *Lochner*
v. *New York*, the court in *Adair* v. *U.S.* invalidated the Erdman Act, which
had outlawed the notorious "yellow-dog" contract that made union non-

membership a condition of employment. The Court held that the act impaired both the employer's and the worker's freedom of contract, and that the commerce power of Congress did not extend to the act, for labor relations had no "real or substantial relation" with commerce. A few years later, the Court struck down a *state* law against yellow-dog contracts. During the progressive era, the Court upheld a couple of Oregon laws limiting hours of work, as well as other regulatory legislation. But then came *Hammer* v. *Dagenhart* (1918), invalidating a child labor act that had been the direct product of efforts by Florence Kelley and other progressive activists. Congress, the Court held in a five-to-four verdict, lacked power to exclude goods from interstate commerce unless they were themselves intrinsically harmful. No matter, as Oliver Wendell Holmes said in dissent, that the goods were the "product of ruined lives."

Would the new Chief Justice—genial, moderate, kind Will Taft—make a difference? An early answer came in the second child labor case in 1922. Thwarted by *Hammer* v. *Dagenhart,* Congress had passed a new act against child labor, this time using its taxing power. Taft not only voted with the Court to invalidate; he wrote the decision. Then came *Adkins* v. *Children's Hospital.*

Congress had passed a minimum-wage law for women in the District of Columbia, partly on the ground of a relationship between wages and the health and morals of women. The High Court was expected to sustain the act, on precedent of the Oregon cases, but the Court was now packed with more conservative justices. Writing for the Court, Justice Sutherland, who had finally been elevated late in 1922, based his decision voiding the law on the liberty-of-contract doctrine. Taft produced a moving dissent but could not sway his colleagues. Using as precedent the *Lochner* and *Adair* decisions, Sutherland held that in principle "there can be no difference between the case of selling labor and the case of selling goods." As Max Lerner later pointed out, "by treating the labor contract like any commodity purchase-and-sale," Sutherland had borne out the contention of Karl Marx that "under capitalism labor has become a mere commodity." From Marx's grave in Highgate cemetery in London might have come a thin peal of cynical laughter.

For a time under Taft's leadership the Court followed a wavering centrist course, issuing a number of antiunion labor decisions while upholding various state regulatory laws and federal programs. Later in the 1920s, its conservatism seemed to harden. In vain left-liberals denounced the "reactionary" course of the Court. For most Americans, the High Court was still above politics and above ideology, handing down decisions from some rarefied summit, interpreting a sacred document, simply "finding" the law, not making it. In fact, the Court could hardly have been more partisan and ideological. Taft used his personal and political skills in "massing the court," as he strove to make it appear more united than it was. Sometimes, justices would reluctantly go along with the majority in order to lessen internal conflict. Taft even held Sunday afternoon caucuses in his home, described by his friendly biographer as "extra-curricular conferences" at which "plans were made to block the liberal machinations."

Taft and his Court occupied the best of political worlds. Benefiting from both the popular worship of the Constitution and the "cult of the robe," the justices seemed above the battle at the same time that they in fact were deeply involved in politics. Ironically, in a system designed to thwart majorities, they held a majority that worked, that delivered. In a system that so often thwarted the wishes of masses of voters, they had the votes.

The compact majority produced. As President, Congress, and Court worked smoothly together, despite occasional sputterings, a conservative party and government churned out conservative legislation and administrative and judicial decisions. Following a rash of railroad and coal strikes in the summer of 1922, Harding allowed Harry Daugherty, now his Attorney General, to gain a sweeping restraining order from a federal judge against the rail strikers. The failed strikes left railroad labor furious with the Administration, and divided to boot, as tens of thousands of shopmen were required to sign agreements with vindictive managements, forcing them into company unions.

Toward farmers the Harding Administration took a more generous line. The Packers and Stockyards Act of 1921 forbade discriminatory practices in livestock, poultry, and dairy transactions, especially the manipulation of prices, and next year the Capper-Volstead Act exempted farmers and their organizations from the reach of the antitrust laws. But what most farmers most keenly wanted was control of farm surpluses and stabilization of prices. When a 1923 credit act easing loans for crop financing proved inadequate, farm organizations rallied behind the McNary-Haugen bill, an elaborate scheme to buy the annual surplus of certain crops during times of high output and keep it off the domestic market. Defeated time and again in House or Senate, the bill finally passed Congress in 1927, only to be vetoed by Coolidge.

The Grand Old Party seemed powerful enough to resist the demands of poorer members of its grand old coalition of farmers and workers. It was equally casual toward a third and historic bastion of Republicanism—black Americans. Harding had been treading a wary course between those Republicans who wanted the GOP to recognize burgeoning black power in Northern cities, and others who sought to curb the Republican "black-

and-tan" organizations in the South in order to create a "lily-white" party that could appeal to Southern whites. But Harding wanted the Negro to have the right to vote. "Let the black man vote when he is fit to vote," he told a Birmingham audience; "prohibit the white man voting when he is unfit to vote." And he wanted the black man to have the right to life. He proposed a federal anti-lynching law, only to see it filibustered to death by Southern Democrats in the Senate. Under Lodge's leadership the Republican caucus decided to give up efforts to overcome the filibuster, handing black leaders the excuse blacks would hear again and again—the anti-lynching bill had to yield to "more important" business in the Senate.

That important business was a ship subsidy bill, and the Republicans throughout the decade pushed through subsidies for a variety of business interests despite their vaunted belief in laissez-faire. But the most powerful Republican thrust came in the field of taxation. This was Treasury Secretary Mellon's domain. The financier was quite direct and emphatic in his approach to taxation. The income tax and war demands had shifted the tax burden too heavily onto the upper-income classes, he believed, impairing their capacity to risk capital for the expansion of production. Soon after his appointment, Mellon appeared before the House Ways and Means Committee to urge repeal of the excess-profits tax and reduction of the maximum surtax rate from 65 percent to 32 percent.

Harding fully backed his Secretary, though he was hardly of much help intellectually. "I can't make a damn thing out of this tax problem," he exploded to an aide. "I listen to one side and they seem right, and then —God!—I talk to the other side, and they seem just as right." But Mellon did not need Presidents; he had himself. With the help of Penrose and other Old Guard members of Congress, he pushed through the first of his revenue bills by the end of 1921. Unappeased, he pressed for further reductions in personal income taxes on the rich and in inheritance taxes, gaining these in the revenue acts of 1926 and 1928 under Coolidge. Mellon backed up both Harding and Coolidge in vetoing veterans' bonus bills, and he worked closely with Harding's budget director, Charles Dawes, on government economy. By the time Mellon left Hoover's Cabinet for the Court of St. James's in early 1932, the Mellon-Harding-Coolidge-Hoover fiscal program had long been firmly in place.

Only one thing seemed to threaten continued Republican ascendancy throughout the decade—scandal. Rumors of malfeasance on the part of an "Ohio gang," climaxed by the suicide of an old friend of Harding and Daugherty, began circulating through Washington early in 1923. The President had been suffering from high blood pressure and other ills for some time, and his concern over the reports probably hastened his death, apparently from an embolism, during a long trip back from Alaska early in August that year. For months, indeed years, following Harding's death, Washington was titillated by revelations of fraud and bribery in the Veterans Bureau, of secret leases of Teapot Dome oil reserves to oil men in exchange for their "loans" to Harding's Interior Secretary, Albert B. Fall. Attorney General Daugherty, who was accused of conspiracy, refused to testify, charged that "Red labor" was plotting against him, and got off with a hung jury, some three years after Coolidge had sacked him.

For all the publicity, the scandals had little effect on Republican presidential victories. In large part, this was due to Coolidge's probity and his distance from the "Ohio gang." Coolidge also possessed a gift that Harding lacked—luck. He had luck in small ways: the news of Harding's death came to him while he happened to be in his rustic home town in Vermont, resulting in marvelous newspaper stories of his swearing-in by his father, a notary public, in the little parlor of the Coolidge household. If Harding had died a day later, the news would have come to Coolidge while he was stopping at the baronial New Hampshire estate of a rich Boston friend. He had luck in big ways too: the "Coolidge boom" roared all through the five and a half years of his presidency.

Coolidge boom? This was just what Andrew Mellon had planned.

BANKERS AND BATTLESHIPS

The Republican "compact majority" was far less united over foreign policy than domestic. Businessmen could agree on tax, labor, subsidy, and similar issues, but the business community fragmented in the face of world needs and demands. Ideologically they divided into isolationists, unilateralists, and internationalists; economically they divided into importers and exporters, competing regional producing interests, investment bankers like the House of Morgan favoring financial and commercial cooperation with London, and industrialists like the Rockefellers pressing for aggressive American investment abroad. Politically they divided into factions in the GOP, in Congress, and in the presidency. The conservatism that dominated the decade's thought seemed to falter at the water's edge.

The result was a foreign policy of zigzag, of "fits and starts, of hesitancy and of timid advance," in L. Ethan Ellis's words. At times, envoys to Washington could hardly find a foreign policy. Editors sardonically suggested that the American Secret Service or even Scotland Yard be dispatched to locate it.

Harding's Cabinet epitomized the Republican disunity. On the President's right sat Secretary of State Charles Evans Hughes, ardent spokesman for the dwindling band of GOP internationalists. Across from him was the imperious Andrew Mellon, who had bankrolled the unilateralists' campaign against Wilson's League. Between them was Commerce Secretary Herbert Hoover, whose main goal now was to promote American exports while limiting imports. Alongside these men sat the knavish party regulars and domestic policy brokers, Albert Fall and Harry Daugherty. These regulars linked with the conservative congressional party centered in the Senate, where Lodge continued to press for a foreign policy expressive of American power, and where Borah and his fellow isolationists now opposed Lodge as tenaciously as they had fought Wilson.

Washington seemed headed for a dull and squalid unilateralism as the Republicans dropped any pretense of fulfilling Harding's vague promise of an "association of nations" in place of the spurned League. Then came a historic zigzag.

A deadly spiral of naval shipbuilding had begun as the British, once America had opted out of the League, wished to reassert their traditional command of the seas, as the Japanese undertook their own buildup, and as American watchdogs called for escalation. But there were calls too for an end to the arms race. Borah, moving to head up the disarmament movement, proposed a simple halving of naval construction by the three maritime superpowers. Lodge earlier had buried two such resolutions, but Borah proved his match in legislative maneuver. Moreover, the Borah Resolution captured the imagination of the public, which hailed it as the "Model 'T'" of diplomatic proposals for its simplicity and practicality. A sizable portion of the business community, concerned that the cost of the naval arms race—in an era when an estimated 93 percent of all federal expenditures went to military or veterans' programs—would interfere with Mellon's planned tax cuts and business subsidies, quietly rallied behind the peace movement.

In this thrust toward peace, women leaders were now playing their part. Fresh from their success in helping secure female suffrage, members of the League of Women Voters made disarmament the first issue on which to demonstrate the power of the woman's vote. Carrie Chapman Catt roused the LWV convention in April 1921 with a hard-hitting call to action: "Everybody at this time is extremely careful about being nonpartisan. I don't care a rap about it. I am for disarmament. I believe in taking action. . . . We are the appointed ones to lead in this question." The women coordinated an alliance of church groups, unions, business and academic spokespeople in favor of arms control.

Lodge and Harding succumbed to the mounting public pressure; on July 10, Secretary of State Hughes invited the Japanese, British, and six other powers to send representatives to Washington to discuss naval armaments and political problems in the Far East. Hughes saw in the negotiations an opportunity to revive the internationalist wing of the Republican party. Throughout the summer he consulted with a group of young naval officers and administrators, led by Assistant Secretary of the Navy Theodore Roosevelt, Jr., and together they hammered out an audacious proposal to end the arms race.

Although Harding appointed him as one of the four American negotiators, Lodge at first put little stock in the conference. "I do not for a moment believe that either Japan or England will accept any disarmament proposals," he confided to his diary just days before the talks opened, "but . . . we shall have made our position clear and will lay the responsibility where it will belong—with them."

In mid-November 1921, the negotiators and their advisors assembled in Continental Memorial Hall for the first session of the naval talks. Only the handful of American experts who had been working with Hughes suspected that they were about to witness one of the most dramatic acts of individual leadership in the history of peace. The crowd of distinguished guests—senators and congressmen, Holmes and Brandeis from the Supreme Court, Vice-President Coolidge, British pacifist spokesman H. G. Wells—heard President Harding make a vapid introductory speech and then applauded politely as the Secretary of State took the floor.

It was the moment of a lifetime. Hughes, erect and gray-bearded at the podium, shocked the audience by calling for an immediate end to all naval construction, and went on to spell out in exquisite detail a plan for stopping the construction of capital ships for at least ten years. As the foreign negotiators sat bolt upright in disbelief, Hughes listed the ships that each power would have to cancel or scrap—seventy-eight battleships in all, totaling nearly 2 million tons. In the gallery, William Jennings Bryan, still the leader of American pacifists, sat with tears of joy in his eyes.

Hughes had instantly riveted world attention on the Washington Conference, making it difficult for any of the delegates to challenge the American proposal. Though weeks of hard negotiating still followed, the Secretary's task was made considerably easier by the cryptologists of the Navy's "Black Chamber," who broke Japan's diplomatic codes and so were able to learn the Japanese negotiating positions in advance. But it was Hughes's benign persistence, coupled with his willingness to link the arms talks to the resolution of the political problems pending in the Far East, that finally turned the tide. The Americans' flexibility in mixing diplomatic, territorial, and arms compromises, Hughes said later, "alone made possible the success of the Conference."

A broad-ranging series of agreements grew out of the Washington talks. The British and Japanese accepted Hughes's ten-year freeze and a ratio of 5:5:3 in battleships between their fleets and the U.S. Navy. Japan settled for the short end of the ratio, but in return Britain and America promised not to build or fortify any new bases in the Western Pacific. France and Italy also agreed to limit the number of their capital ships, as long as smaller vessels were exempted from the treaty. Limits were set on the tonnage and armament of all remaining warships. On the political front, Japan and Britain replaced their military alliance with a four-power nonaggression pact that included France and the United States, thus laying to rest American fears of a possible joint Anglo-Japanese attack. Lodge was able to secure Senate approval of all these agreements, although the isolationists balked at the Four-Power Treaty, which barely passed with help from Senate Democrats. The final fruit of the negotiations was a nine-power treaty in which all the nations with interests in the Far East bound themselves to uphold the independence and territorial sovereignty of China. After more than twenty years, John Hay's Open Door proposal had finally been transformed into an international covenant.

A triumph for American ideals and interests, the Washington Conference also proved to be the swan song of the Republican internationalists. Over the rest of the decade, the leaders of the GOP proceeded to undermine or fritter away the gains that the talks had brought them. Relations between Japan and America began to improve after the conference, only to be poisoned by the xenophobic Immigration Act of 1924. Sponsored by Lodge and by California's Hiram Johnson, the bill closed the United States to immigrants from the Orient—a mortal insult in the eyes of the Japanese. Partly as a result of rising anti-American and anti-Western sentiments in Japan, a second round of arms talks, convened in Geneva in 1927, ended in failure.

Another set of negotiations, held in London in 1930, did produce an agreement to limit all vessels, not just battleships, but only at the price of major new concessions to Japan. The London talks, moreover, foreboded a bleak future for arms control. The French and Italian delegates walked out of the conference, and the Japanese government suffered a wave of assassinations and mass protests when it ratified the new treaty.

On other fronts as well the Republicans failed to capitalize on the openings made by Hughes. After years of coaxing, the Senate in 1925 agreed to America's joining the World Court, but only with a series of reservations that the court administrators in Geneva declined to accept. The United States also joined an international movement, led by Columbia professor James Shotwell, to "outlaw" war. The resulting Kellogg-Briand Pact, which twenty-six nations signed in 1928, had no enforcement mechanism —and just to be sure, the Senate appended a list of occasions when the United States would not be bound by it. One senator labeled it "an international kiss."

*   *   *

If the Republicans stood divided in their response to internationalism, on the economics of foreign affairs they were somewhat more united. The economic thrust of American policy in the 1920s was set by Andrew Mellon and Herbert Hoover, who despite occasional disagreements over tactics basically concurred. The Treasury and Commerce secretaries promoted a business approach to international affairs. Drawing on their experiences in private enterprise, the two focused on "fostering the use of experts, on finding apolitical solutions, on encouraging private voluntary and cooperative action, and on enlarging but circumscribing the role of government." They would rely on private trade, buttressed by federal data-gathering and voluntary international cooperation, to advance American interests abroad. Most of all, they would rely on Mellon's old colleagues, the staid Republican investment bankers.

The help of the bankers was especially needed to untangle the international financial mess left by the World War and the peace settlement. The war had disrupted the old, London-based network of financial ties between Europe and the rest of the world. The Allies had been forced to borrow billions of dollars from the United States, and the various European states needed billions more to rebuild their economies when the fighting ended. When Harding entered the White House, the American government had loans out to seventeen European nations totaling more than $10 billion. The main debtors, Britain and France, made their repayment contingent on receiving reparations from Germany.

Here the Republicans reaped one of the unintended fruits of their failure to ratify the Treaty of Versailles. In Paris, Wilson and Lloyd George had agreed to leave unspecified the amount to be paid by Germany, as they expected that later the British and American representatives on the reparations committee would work out a fairly moderate sum. When America rejected the treaty, however, the French were left as the dominant power on the committee, and in 1921 they presented Germany with a bill for the astronomical sum of $32 billion. After the Germans refused to pay, the specter of international debts unsettled efforts to stabilize European currencies and economies.

Mellon's banking instincts urged him toward a moderate solution to the growing debt/reparation crisis. "If we insist on too difficult terms," we would "receive nothing," he noted. But he was unwilling to have the American government simply write off $10 billion in supposed assets which would then have to be replaced out of the pockets of bondholders and taxpayers. His solution was to renegotiate the loans, granting the Europeans lower interest rates and longer terms of repayment. Using the leverage provided by Treasury Department oversight of private loans to foreign powers—the bankers seldom risked a loan not approved by Mellon and Hoover—the Republican banker-in-chief brought country after country to the bargaining table. Slowly the loan tangle was resolved, in the finance ministries and the banking houses. For the press and the public, however, the issue remained an acrimonious one; Coolidge's bland and perhaps apocryphal "they hired the money, didn't they," rather than Mellon's strategy of enlightened self-interest, seemed to define the American position on the debts.

Sound American business sense was also needed to help defuse the explosive question of German reparations. France's attempt to bludgeon the Germans into paying by occupying the Ruhr in 1923 only helped wreck the German economy, unleash wild inflation that pauperized the country's middle class, and encourage political extremists on both the left and the right. Two Americans, the Chicago banker Charles Dawes and General Electric chairman Owen Young, helped shape a solution under which Germany's reparation payments were fixed at a reasonable yearly sum. Meanwhile private American capital flowed into Germany, helping restore prosperity to that country and indeed to much of Europe.

The cycle of private loans, reparation payments, and rescheduled war debts seemed to some a "financial merry-go-round," as the United States collected in debt payments approximately the same amount the bankers lent to Germany. But in fact the cycle of payments seemed to be fulfilling the Republicans' goals. With the structure of international credit restored, prosperity returned to both sides of the Atlantic. Urged on by the American banks, Britain and other European powers went back onto the gold standard. Stable prices, sound currencies, steadily growing trade—the Republican millennium appeared to be at hand as Hoover moved from the Commerce Department to the White House in 1929.

The real source of the international recovery, however, was the expansion of trade, and here the Republicans' business sense would eventually play them false. But, for a time, Hoover's efforts to promote American sales and investment abroad gleaned tremendous dividends. Yankee investment in Latin America tripled, and commerce with the region grew by 87 percent. Even while Congress—over Hoover's objections—offended Japan with exclusionary immigration laws, trade with the island kingdom swelled. In revolution-torn China, where the United States government maintained a brigade of Marines from 1927 on, Model T Fords shared streets with rickshaws, and the Standard Oil refinery was one of the largest employers in Tientsin.

It was dollar diplomacy—but with a difference. Throughout the decade, the Republicans worked steadily to placate anti-American feelings triggered by previous heavy-handedness. In 1924 Coolidge withdrew the Marines from the Dominican Republic; in 1925 the occupation of Nicaragua ended, although a year later American troops returned to that country to battle the guerrilla forces of the legendary General Sandino.

The most dramatic improvement came in relations with Mexico. The Mexican government had aroused both American Catholics by its anticlerical policies and American oil companies—which controlled 70 percent of Mexico's oil—by its nationalization of foreign oil holdings. Talk of war even bubbled up on both sides of the Rio Grande until Coolidge moved to head off the building crisis by appointing his old friend Dwight Morrow, of the House of Morgan, as envoy to Mexico City. Morrow's tact and infectious good nature won him the friendship of Mexican officials, and he sponsored a visit to Mexico by the aviation hero Charles Lindbergh (soon to be his son-in-law) that helped turn public attitudes toward the United States around. Morrow helped negotiate a reconciliation between the government and the church in the Latin republic and he worked out a businesslike compromise on the question of oil. In the next year, Hoover put the presidential seal of approval on the tenuous new friendship with Latin America by undertaking a seven-week goodwill tour of the region just before his inauguration.

As the decade closed, the earlier rifts in the GOP seemed to have yielded to the party's general pro-business consensus. With Hughes heading for the Supreme Court and Lodge dead, the League a political cipher, and the drama of disarmament drained by the very success of the Washington Conference, the way was at last clear for a moderate foreign economic policy. Then the GOP took another leap—backwards—as it turned in 1929 to write into law the last facet of Mellon's economic program: a high, across-the-board protective tariff. President Hoover viewed with misgivings his party's rally around upward tariff revision. Few men recognized better than Hoover the importance of international trade to America's continuing prosperity, or more feared tariff retaliation by other nations.

"Break this chain" of trade, Hoover declared during the 1928 campaign, "and the whole machine is thrown out of order. . . . Cease exporting automobiles to South America or Europe, and automobile workers are thrown out of work in Michigan. The suffering does not stop there. . . . The steel mills slacken in Pennsylvania and Indiana. The mines employ fewer workers at Lake Superior. And every farmer in the United States suffers from diminished purchasing power."

Thus Hoover had serious private doubts about the Smoot-Hawley bill that the Republicans in Congress enacted in early 1930. In public, however, the President emphasized the handful of concessions the legislative leaders had granted him. The fusillade of antitariff protests from academics and from Democrats—although many of the latter had joined in the orgy of log-rolling as Smoot-Hawley took final form—also apparently stiffened Hoover's resolve to follow his party and accept the bill. In June 1930 the President signed the tariff into law, hailing it as the fulfillment of "the repeated demands of statesmen and industrial and agricultural leaders over the past twenty-five years."

The ghosts of John Sherman, Mark Hanna, and Nelson Aldrich no doubt smiled down in approval.

THE VOICES OF PROTEST

Smoot-Hawley towered as a party achievement, the culmination of a century of Whig and Republican economic nationalism, the climactic act of the 1920s' "compact majority." At the end of that decade of conservative business rule, as at the start, the party had its way, despite the misgivings of Herbert Hoover and the fears of internationalists in both parties. James Madison's old checks and balances, designed to delay and fragment "naked majority rule," still seemed to be suspended. By 1931, the Republicans had achieved what no liberal or progressive leadership had brought about at least since Reconstruction—ten solid years of party government. The voices of protest were shrill and scattered, minority opposition weak and divided.

If the Framers' anti-majoritarian Constitution could not protect minority interests, what could? The American people had supplied their own answer within a dozen years of adopting the 1787 charter, by establishing a Jeffersonian party opposition to challenge the Federalist incumbents. That opposition went on to take office in 1800. The flowering of the party system had nurtured a "loyal opposition" ready to critique, challenge, and balance the party in power. As parliamentary systems grew in Europe during the nineteenth century, the idea of the militant but loyal opposition grew with them. By 1930, the labor movement in Britain, for example, and German socialists, had long since been challenging the established parties.

Emboldened by their midterm gains of 1922 and the "Ohio gang" scandals the next year, the Democrats marched into 1924 with high hopes of ousting the GOP. With a host of promising leaders, including such veterans as Oscar Underwood and former Treasury Secretary McAdoo and rising young figures like Governor Alfred E. Smith of New York, the Democracy's prospects looked good, as they assembled in Manhattan for the quadrennial conclave. But everything fell apart in their convention hall, "Tex" Rickard's old Madison Square Garden. Even the place was wrong—a red-brick edifice used to host circuses and six-day bike races and adorned by a ten-story tower (in which the architect Stanford White had been murdered), and located in the middle of Al Smith territory—urban, polyglot, and very "wet." McAdoo arrived breathing fire against the city itself—"the city of privilege," he called it, "reactionary, sinister, unscrupulous, mercenary, and sordid," rooted in corruption and dominated by greed. At the convention, when the keynote speaker declaimed that what this country "needs is Paul Revere," he was greeted with a round of boos because the delegates thought he said what the country needed was "real beer." During a demonstration by the Georgia delegation, the convention band struck up with "Marching Through Georgia," thinking it was a beloved Southern song, instead of Sherman's victory march.

But the main trouble in the convention was the old Democratic party divisions between the congressional leadership and the presidential, between the South and the North, between the wets and the drys, between the country and the city—plus the two-thirds requirement for nomination. The convention was so divided that it failed even to censure the Ku Klux Klan. In the early-summer heat, roll call followed roll call as the Smith and McAdoo forces checked each other. Days dragged by. On the 99th ballot McAdoo led Smith by half a vote. The exhausted leadership finally worked a compromise on the 103rd ballot, by nominating for President John W. Davis, a conservative corporation lawyer in the Cleveland tradition, and for Vice-President Charles W. Bryan, brother of the Commoner, part populist and part socialist. This ticket was not balanced but, in David Burner's term, "schizoid."

The nation's labor and progressive leaders had long before recognized the feebleness of the divided Democracy. Throughout the early twenties, AFL and rail labor leaders, farm-laborites, old and new Progressives, and socialists had been planning independent action for 1924. Out of these activities had grown the Conference for Progressive Political Action, which sponsored a Progressive party convention in 1924. Robert La Follette, older, wearier, was both the unifier and the hero of the CPPA. At its convention in Chicago, he won the united support of 1,200 delegates embracing labor, farmers, students, a few women, and virtually no blacks. La Follette gained the plaudits of both liberals and socialists with a demand that monopolies be "crushed." Senator Burton K. Wheeler of Montana, declaring that when "the Democratic party goes to Wall Street for a candidate" like Davis, he must refuse to go with it, accepted the nomination for Vice-President.

Once again La Follette found that launching a third party is one of the most difficult ventures in American politics. It was hard enough to foster unity among the fragmented elements of the left. The Socialist party fell in line, formally endorsing La Follette, while the Communists and other radical parties castigated the La Follette Progressives as even more reactionary than the two major parties. But the strategic problem lay deeper. The La Follette leadership hoped that the Progressive thrust in 1924 would break through existing party alignments and clear the way for a true split by 1928 between a right and a left party. In the meantime, though, La Follette did not want to jeopardize the reelection of Borah, Norris, and other Progressives. Many socialists, on the other hand, wanted a third party that would push for its own Senate and state candidates, even against liberal Democrats and Republicans, if need be, in order to build a labor-left party that could some day take over the whole sprawling governmental system. La Follette insisted on running solo. As it turned out, the Idaho Progressive party endorsed Borah, who later backed Coolidge; Norris ran as a Republican but renounced Coolidge.

The Republicans held probably the dullest convention in the nation's history. Hiram Johnson, who opposed the Administration's tax reduction program and many of its foreign policies, might have enlivened the proceedings, but he lost out early against Coolidge's party organization and patronage. In any event, the GOP leadership wanted a bland convention and a quiet campaign. It publicized slogans such as "Keep Cool with Coolidge" and "Coolidge or Chaos." The myth of cautious Cal, of silent Cal, was building. Middle-class Americans liked him for his nutshell philosophy, "Work and save." They liked him for his honesty and simplicity, for his willingness to put on Indian headdresses out west, all the while looking as though he had been weaned on a pickle, as Alice Roosevelt Longworth would claim she had not said.

Americans liked him in 1924, giving him a huge vote of endorsement, 15.7 million votes to Davis's 8.4 million and La Follette's 4.8 million. La Follette carried only his own Wisconsin, though he ran second to Coolidge in half the mountain and all three Pacific states. The GOP carried the congressional elections, and Borah and Norris retained their seats and returned to Washington to carry on the fight within the party. Progressivism seemed to be stalled as a national movement. The 1912 progressives had split with the Taft party and met defeat at the hands of a united

Democracy. The 1924 progressives had failed to unite with the Democrats, and both parties had been shellacked by a united GOP.

It was clear to the Democratic party leaders—including young Franklin Roosevelt, now slowly regaining some mobility after a crippling polio attack—that the Democracy must move more firmly to the still-burgeoning urban and immigrant masses and toward industrial labor. Their candidate for 1928 was at hand. Al Smith had emerged from the sidewalks of New York, educated at no college other than the Fulton Fish Market, politically savvy, able above all to learn from experience. Elected to the state legislature, he gained a seat on the Banking Committee after having entered a bank only once—to serve a jury notice—and on the Forest Committee, though he had never been in a forest. He learned much from Tammany and from rebelling against Tammany; he learned from the Triangle fire that women were cheap, property sacred. Democratic hopes for Al Smith and his party soared when Silent Cal, vacationing in the Black Hills in August 1927, summoned the press and handed each reporter a little slip: "I do not choose to run for President in 1928."

Most Americans knew little about Al Smith except for one big fact: he was a Catholic. Survivors of the McAdoo-Smith convention duel of 1924 knew that a Smith nomination in 1928 would set off a religious war. Could a rational debate on the issue forestall irrational confrontation? In April 1927, the *Atlantic Monthly* published an "open letter" from Charles C. Marshall to Smith questioning whether a Catholic's dual allegiance to his Church and Constitution should bar him from the presidency. The *Atlantic* printed Smith's reply in the next issue:

"Taking your letter as a whole and reducing it to commonplace English, you imply that there is a conflict between religious loyalty to the Catholic faith and patriotic loyalty to the United States." No such thing could be true. "I have taken an oath of office in this State nineteen times. Each time I swore to defend and maintain the Constitution of the United States." He had never known any conflict between his official duties and his religious belief. And, rebutting Marshall, Smith contended that no such conflict could exist in education, religious tolerance, appointments, foreign policy.

"I summarize my creed as an American Catholic. I believe in the worship of God according to the faith and practice of the Roman Catholic Pope and I recognize no power in the institutions of my Church to interfere with the operations of the Constitution of the United States or the enforcement of the law of the land. I believe in absolute freedom of conscience for all men and in equality of all churches, all sects, and all beliefs before the law as a matter of right and not as a matter of favor. I believe in the absolute separation of Church and State. . . ."

In vain. Americans were not yet ready for a rational debate over church and state. As the Democratic nominee, Smith ran into a hurricane of religious bigotry, misunderstanding, sectional chauvinism. It was a religious war and much more—a culmination of the cultural war between big city and small town, immigrants and nativists, wets and drys, North and South, East and West, Irish and English, on a battlefield of ignorance and intolerance. Smith, moreover, refused to pretend that he was not what he was, in Oscar Handlin's words—"a Catholic, a grandson of Irish immigrants, a poor boy off the sidewalks of New York." Against the advice of the media experts of the day he went right on wearing his brown derby and big cigar, saying "horspital" over the "raddio," attacking Prohibition, refusing to restrict immigration: "I have lived among these people all my life" and "I can't shut the door in their faces."

Al Smith received the news of his defeat sitting in the Seventy-first Regimental Armory, an unlighted cigar clamped in his teeth. He had won 87 electoral votes against Hoover's 444, 15 million popular votes against Hoover's 21.4 million. "Well," he later said, "I guess the time has not yet come when a man can say his beads in the White House."

Once again the Democrats had failed to build an electoral coalition that could even come close to beating the GOP. Once again the loyal opposition had failed to come up with a credible alternative. Excuses there were aplenty, but perhaps even the Democrats did not comprehend the full power of the Republicans' "compact majority." Corporate business had more than an efficient party working for it; it had an ideology rooted in the modern American experience, grounded in fundamental American beliefs and attitudes, fortified by "scientific ideas" such as Social Darwinism, operationalized through an experienced political leadership, and above all expressive of the nation's industrial and financial power. The only strategy for a party and electoral opposition was to shape an ideology, a party, and a leadership so sharply different from the "ins" as to pose a constant challenge and thereby offer some hope of winning in the future. The Democrats failed to do this; even Smith, with his ties to big business and his innate social conservatism, offered no clear-cut alternative. Election studies later revealed that the 1928 presidential contest was far more a reflection of the politics of the 1920s than a forerunner of the political alignments to come.

*　　*　　*

If Democrats, progressives, liberals, laborites, and their allies could not overcome the "compact majority" of corporate and Republican power and leadership, at least the minority had the right to exist, speak up, challenge the ins, and seek to oust them at the polls. What about opposition from more radical elements? The Founding Fathers had sought to protect the rights of small minorities as well as large, of tiny sects, rebellious movements, individual dissenters. They had bequeathed this protection in the checks and balances and in the Bill of Rights, and they and their successors had institutionalized that protection by allowing dissenters recourse to the judges, who were expected to be aloof, protected by lifetime tenure from the gusts of intolerance and passion that swept the populace.

Toward "seditionists," draft obstructionists, and the like, a conservative Supreme Court took a hard line during wartime. In the *Schenck* case Oliver Wendell Holmes spoke for the entire Court in upholding Charles T. Schenck's conviction for mailing impassioned anti-draft letters to draftees. "The most stringent protection of free speech," Holmes wrote, "would not protect a man in falsely shouting fire in a theatre and causing a panic." But Holmes set a stern test for future restrictions on First Amendment liberties. "The question in every case is whether the words used are used in such circumstances and are of such a nature as to create a clear and present danger that they will bring about the substantive evils that Congress has a right to prevent. It is a question of proximity and degree. When a nation is at war many things that might be said in time of peace are such a hindrance to its effort that their utterance will not be endured so long as men fight. . . ."

Eugene Debs fared no better than Schenck, however, under this wartime test. Holmes spoke for the Court in sustaining Debs's conviction for obstructing the recruiting service in the socialist leader's now famous Canton speech. Privately Holmes seemed defensive about his position. Referring to a "lot of jaw about free speech," he wrote his friend Sir Frederick Pollock about "people who pitched into the Court for sending Debs to prison." He hoped that Wilson would pardon him "and some other poor devils with whom I have more sympathy." He went on: "The greatest bores in the world are the come-outers who are cocksure of a dozen nostrums. The dogmatism of a little education is hopeless."

Jacob Abrams, a Russian emigrant, was sentenced under the Espionage Act to twenty years' imprisonment for throwing down from a loft in the garment district some leaflets urging workers to produce no arms for American intervention in Russia at a time when Americans were not at war with Russians. The Court held that the necessary result of this incitement was to hamper the war with Germany. Holmes and Brandeis dissented. Abrams's action was only indirect, Holmes argued; there was no clear and present danger in the publication of such a "silly leaflet." Holmes concluded with words that would become etched in American constitutional history:

"But when men have realized that time has upset many fighting faiths, they may come to believe even more than they believe the very foundations of their own conduct that the ultimate good desired is better reached by free trade in ideas—that the best test of truth is the power of the thought to get itself accepted in the competition of the market. . . . That, at any rate, is the theory of our Constitution. It is an experiment, as all life is an experiment. . . ." What about free speech when the nation was *not* at war? The "red scare" of 1919, coming on the heels of the Bolshevik Revolution in Russia and a rash of communist uprisings elsewhere in Europe, left a scar on the popular mind that lasted well into the twenties and later. Extremism had fed on extremism; alarming labor actions like the Boston police strike, the furious factional quarrels among communists and between communists and socialists, and the bombings, had been matched by the reckless arrests and imprisonments, mass deportations, and demands by such as Billy Sunday that "wild-eyed Socialists and I.W.W.'s" be stood up before firing squads.

Amid the whipped-up fear and hysteria, each side stereotyped the other and lost any capacity to discriminate. Fanatics placed or mailed bombs that mainly hurt the poor and vulnerable—one mail bomb blew off the hands of a Southern senator's maid—while missing their targets; Tennessee's Senator Kenneth McKellar wanted to send American radicals to penal colonies in the middle of the Pacific, and South Carolina's James F. Byrnes asked federal help to thwart an alleged plot of communists to foment a black uprising in the South. The New York State Assembly denied their seats to five socialists who obviously had chosen the democratic electoral process over "red rebellion."

In the postwar hysteria Benjamin Gitlow, a left-wing socialist, had been arrested and convicted under New York's Criminal Anarchy Act of 1902 for writing pamphlets that urged proletarian "struggle." The Court upheld his conviction, Holmes and Brandeis dissenting. Holmes and Brandeis agreed with the majority on one crucial point—that the freedom of speech guaranteed by the First Amendment was part of the "liberty" of the Fourteenth Amendment and thus guaranteed against state infringement. The dissenters, moreover, saw no clear and present danger in Gitlow's pamphlet. Incitement? Holmes asked in response to the Court's depiction of the pamphlet. "Every idea is an incitement." He added: "If in the long run the beliefs expressed in proletarian dictatorship are destined to be accepted by the dominant forces in the community, the only meaning of free speech is that they should be given their chance and have their way."

And in the *Schwimmer* case, upholding the right of a pacifist to become naturalized as a United States citizen, he reminded the Court that the most vital principle of the Constitution was that of free thought, including freedom for the thought "we hate."

Still, this was only the loyal opposition speaking. The compact majority on the Court, under Taft's unifying leadership, turned out decision after decision against dissent—or at least against dissenters. To some it seemed odd that a Court so clearly representing conservative thought in the country, so clearly committed to laissez-faire and against governmental regulation, should crumble so easily when government attacked individual liberty to dissent. The High Bench seemed far more devoted to property rights than to civil liberties. This view was bottomed on a major and very articular premise—that in America's hierarchy of liberties, economic liberty stood at the top. Faith in Algerism was still running strong in the 1920s.

However thwarted by their minority status, the dissenters found other ways to influence political opinion and action. Holmes and Brandeis and their numerous political friends such as the La Follettes, former law clerks, intellectual correspondents, and faithful acolytes constituted a powerhouse of ideas, criticisms, ruminations, explorations, and proposals. Brandeis and Holmes struck sparks off each other; Brandeis wrote Felix Frankfurter of Harvard Law School almost every day, passing on political and judicial gossip, asking for legal and other information, and often suggesting ideas, proposals, and comments for Frankfurter in turn to pass on to the *New Republic* or—later—the New York *World*. Through Frankfurter also, Brandeis made his private political views known to a wider circle. The justice paid his young associate several thousand dollars a year to help him work for causes they both favored.

Holmes and Brandeis were tourist attractions on the High Court, in the little Capitol room in which the Court still met—the former with his swath of white hair, mustachios, and imperial presence; the latter with his "piercing blue eyes," abundant gray hair, and creased cheeks, looking, according to one of his clerks, "like a combination of Hebrew prophet and Abraham Lincoln." But even between the two of them there was a division in the intellectual powerhouse. Holmes did not share Brandeis's almost undiscriminating opposition to "bigness." Holmes's approach to free speech was based on claims of utility rather than of morality, in Philippa Strum's words, while "Brandeis saw free speech as an end as well as a means," and believed in it as an absolute truth, along with his insistence upon experimentation. Agreed in practice on most legal questions, the two men differed on key issues of principle and philosophy.

Nor did left-liberal thinkers outside the Court achieve much intellectual unity. Philosophers, historians, and economists seemed more interested in perfecting their crafts than in trying to match the brilliant innovations of the progressive era or, in the European fashion, to frame comprehensive doctrines that could undergird political programs. Vernon Parrington worked on the third volume of his architectonic *Main Currents in American Thought,* which he would never complete. Thorstein Veblen, a founding member of the New School for Social Research in New York, had fled from the "higher learning in America" that he had derided in 1918 only to see some of his work popularized and cheapened. Neither man would outlive the decade. Charles and Mary Beard published a best-selling history of the United States. Walter Lippmann, writing first for the *New Republic* and then for the New York *World,* had moved by the late 1920s so far toward the lively political center that after the *World* was sold off to Scripps-Howard, he was offered jobs by William Randolph Hearst, Roy Howard, the *New York Times,* and the Republican New York *Herald-Tribune;* Lippmann chose the *Trib.*

Certainly no creed arose in the 1920s to challenge Sumner's Social Darwinism or Herbert Hoover's *Individualism;* no radical movement or party arose that could mobilize popular support in the fashion that the Republican party did. While the weakness of the left was partly political—the socialists, for example, were unable truly to engage with the "masses"—the failure was primarily intellectual. Few demanded of Hoover how far he would go if he really believed that everyone should be given the chance to develop "the best with which he has been endowed in heart and mind." If life chances were to be equalized, if everyone, in Hoover's words, was to be given an equal place at the starting line, where would that starting line be established? Who would provide the "life chances": only one's parents or employers, or also schools, literacy projects, vocational programs, health and welfare agencies—in short, *government?*

"Equality of opportunity" was becoming the catchword of corporate conservatism—its formula for combining liberty and equality. But how much genuine equality was implied in this slogan, and what kind, and when? How much liberty, not only of property but of speech, ideas, dissent?

CHAPTER 15

The Commercialized Culture

M ORE than any other decade since the Civil War, the 1920s quickly settled into the American memory as a distinctive era in the nation's history. Perhaps the reason was simply that the years seemed clearly bracketed by the coming of Harding and the economic crisis under Hoover. Or perhaps it was because the decade was studded by events that took on enormous symbolic importance even though they appeared later as of little historical significance. Unlike the first dozen years of the century, which would be remembered as the age of muckraking, TR, and the Square Deal, or of the second decade—the New Freedom, Wilson, the war—the 1920s seemed to have had no shape, no hero in the presidency, no long-run impact.

Yet the twenties would become the most unforgettable of decades, the most sentimentalized and scorned, evoked and rejected. America could never quite get the era out of its hair. It began to apply labels to the decade even before it was over.

It was, first and last, the Dollar Decade. Real national income soared during the period; real earnings of workers—at a time of relative price stability—rose sharply; millionaires multiplied. From its cornucopia the huge American workshop showered goods onto eager buyers. Industrial production almost doubled between the recession year of 1921 and the boom year of 1929. Spending skyrocketed—on cars, telephones, cigarette lighters, oil furnaces, fresh fruit and vegetables from distant parts. The smell of money hung in the air. A big electric sign blinked out the message over New York's Columbus Circle: YOU SHOULD HAVE $10,000 AT THE AGE OF 30; $25,000 AT THE AGE OF 40; $50,000 AT 50.

It was the Age of Ballyhoo, with enormous promotion of prizefights, football contests, parlor games, movie stars—the age of fads, crimes, trials, Gene Tunney and Jack Dempsey, Mah-Jongg and crossword puzzles, Red Grange and Bobby Jones, the marriage of Gloria Swanson to a marquis and the funeral of Rudolph Valentino, which was promoted as heavily as an opening night. The winds of publicity blew capriciously: the slow and closely followed death of one man, Floyd Collins, in a Kentucky cave-in won a three-column headline from the *New York Times,* while the deaths of fifty-three miners in a North Carolina cave-in a month later attracted only routine notice. Thousands craned their necks as Shipwreck Kelly sat on a Baltimore flagpole for twenty-three days and seven hours; while the morbid watched, marathon dancers shuffled night and day, day and night, in an agony of fatigue.

It was the Jazz Age. This new music was fast, loud, feverish, exciting. A verb entered the popular vocabulary—to "jazz" or "jazz up." The new music was all the more delicious because the establishment opposed it: jazz would drive out opera, claimed the Italian composer Mascagni; it was insane, boring, brainless, said others. It was the day of the saxophone; Mark Sullivan said a skillful player "could achieve titillating arpeggios, glissandos, every sort of musical coruscation; he could toot and he could tootle, he could blare and blast, could bleat and blat, he could chatter, he could coo." Proclaimed Paul Whiteman: "I sincerely believe that jazz is the folk-music of the machine age."

It was the Roaring Twenties, by which people meant flaming youth, illegal liquor, dancing the Charleston, singing the blues, joyriding in the family Wills Saint Claire, partying through the night. They also meant factories working round the clock, the booming stock market, the passion for size and speed. Above all they meant sex—petting parties, the twosome with a flask in the rumble seat, people dancing as if glued together, cheek to cheek, body to body. Women smoking, women with rouge, women abandoning corsets, women getting "blotto"—these were the big issues.

"The low-cut gowns, the rolled hose and short skirts are born of the Devil and his angels," warned the president of the University of Florida, "and are carrying the present and future generations to chaos and destruction."

For some, it was the worst of decades. Millions of people remained in poverty and squalor amid the boom. Countless middle-class innocents were swindled out of their life's savings by con artists like the fabled Charles Ponzi of Boston. Tens of thousands of blacks who had migrated north found that settling in and becoming "neighbors" did little to mitigate intolerance and discrimination. Blacks were still mobbed, shot, beaten, and stabbed in riots or individual encounters. Reorganized and reinvigorated, the Ku Klux Klan under Wizards and Goblins and Kleagles sold memberships at ten dollars a head, recruiting, according to one estimate, over 4 million persons by the mid-twenties. Long after the 1920 expulsion of five socialist members of the New York State Assembly on the grounds of "disloyalty," the anti-red and anti-radical hysteria continued to flare. Middle-class Catholics and Jews suffered more subtle kinds of discrimination, often as a result of WASP "gentlemen's agreements."

For some, it was the best of decades. Millions of Americans realized their dream of owning an automobile and a home. Big industry cut the hours of work, giving its employees more time with their families and for recreation. A construction boom provided laborers with jobs building highways, bridges, and skyscrapers. The consumption of entertainment—sports, films, plays, games, trials—reached new highs.

Amid this boom in money and stocks and things, one epic adventure transcended the intolerance and the self-seeking. On the evening of May 19, 1927, a twenty-five-year-old stunt flyer named Charles A. Lindbergh took off from Long Island into drizzling skies and headed out over the Atlantic. For thirty-three hours the nation held its breath. Lindbergh's arrival in Paris unloosed a flood of relief, joy, and ballyhoo. He was young and lean and tousle-haired and modest. President Coolidge sent a cruiser to fetch him back, commissioned him a colonel, presented him with the Congressional Medal of Honor. New York dumped 1,800 tons of torn-up paper on his triumphal procession. Streets and schools were named for him. Nor did the adulation cease. Hero-worshippers packed the roads around his New Jersey farm on weekends; laundries kept his shirts for souvenirs; medals, tributes, dollars were showered on him.

Why? For years men had been flying the Atlantic, in both directions; Lindbergh's distinction was only to be the first to do it alone. The explanation was simple, wrote Frederick Lewis Allen as the decade came to an end. "A disillusioned nation fed on cheap heroics and scandal and crime was revolting against the low estimate of human nature which it had allowed itself to entertain." The flyer seemed to be a modern Galahad. He "did not accept the moving-picture offers that came his way, he did not sell testimonials, did not boast, did not get himself involved in scandal, conducted himself with unerring taste—and was handsome and brave withal. The machinery of ballyhoo was ready and waiting to lift him up where every eye could see him."

The flight was a triumph of individual daring and enterprise; it was also the "climax of the co-operative effort of an elaborately interlocked technology," noted John W. Ward. In pinning the Distinguished Flying Cross on Lindbergh, President Coolidge expressed his delight that the flyer, who liked to use the term "we," gave equal credit to his plane—for which, Coolidge asserted, "more than 100 separate companies furnished materials, parts or service in its construction."

This "silent partner," declared the President, "represented American genius and industry."

THE WORKSHOP OF EDUCATION

Soon Lindbergh's portrait was adorning thousands of school classrooms, side by side with Washington and Lincoln, Edison and Ford. It was a tribute to Lindy's enterprise and heroism that he was admitted to the pantheon of portraiture, for even small changes such as this were not made lightly in the nation's schools. The elementary school was one of the most immobile institutions in America.

Exploring the work of the seventh grade in Muncie, Indiana, the sociologists Robert and Helen Lynd noted that reading, writing, arithmetic, language, spelling, drawing, music, and geography, which had comprised the essential curriculum of that grade in 1890, still did so thirty-four years later, though civic training, history and civics, and manual arts for boys and home economics for girls had been added.

Nor had the life of the school changed much in those thirty-four years. "The school, like the factory, is a thoroughly regimented world," reported the Lynds. "Immovable seats in orderly rows fix the sphere of activity of each child. For all, from the timid six-year-old entering for the first time to the most assured high school senior, the general routine is much the same. Bells divide the day into periods. For the six-year-olds the periods are short (fifteen to twenty-five minutes) and varied. . . ." They were free to move about except during "recitation," but as they grew older "the taboo upon physical activity becomes stricter, until by the third or fourth year practically all movement is forbidden except marching from one set of seats to another" and brief exercise.

The teachers of Muncie children also provided continuity. They were predominantly women brought up in Indiana; in Middletown, as in the nation, the percentage of male teachers had dropped by more than half in two generations. All were high school graduates, but less than half had attended college or even "normal school." They shared little in Muncie community life, much less any broader one. Middletown, the Lynds discovered, paid the people to whom it entrusted its children about what it paid retail clerks, and otherwise rather ignored them.

The nation's high schools gave promise in the 1920s of turbulence and change, if only as a result of skyrocketing numbers of youths entering secondary school. Enrollments in the four public high school years doubled during the 1920s, from 2.2 million in 1920 to 4.4 million ten years later. Immense high school buildings were overflowing within a few years of construction. The buildings themselves "reflected the ideology of mid-1920s prosperity and power," Edward Krug has observed. "Massive and overwhelming on the outside, coldly ostentatious on the inside, they fit well the impersonal dignity of institutions that daily processed several thousand students with efficiency and dispatch." Behind the school explosion lay major social trends: rising middle-class and business stress on education as the key to success, lessened child labor in industry since 1910, and, to some degree, tougher school attendance laws. Still, for every student enrolled in high schools in 1920, two teenagers were not.

Out of these teeming numbers in school rose the image of flaming youth. Not only in college but in high school the "Wild Young People" proceeded to shock their elders—even more so by charging that the "older generation," as one of the self-proclaimed wild ones said, "had certainly pretty well ruined this world before passing it on to us." The elders—especially the educators—hunted for scapegoats: drink, lurid magazines and novels, the sensationalist press, films like *The Mad Whirl, Sinners in Silk, Mad Hour, Unguarded Women, A Perfect Flapper.* An Illinois high school teacher blamed jazz for loose speech, morals, and dress; Wisconsin county superintendents condemned it by formal vote. Conservative students at the University of Minnesota, blaming improper dancing, passed out cards to offenders: "We do not dance cheek to cheek, shimmy, or dance other extreme dances. You must not."

It was a picture of wild abandon, untrammeled sex, unabashed self-indulgence. It led to even wilder expectations. "Institutions everywhere are in flux," wrote Miriam Van Waters. "In morals the old is not dead and the new is not strong enough to stand," as "youth dances into the streets, eager and untaught. . . ." In fact the picture was wildly exaggerated. Behind the hullabaloo, conservative attitudes in secondary education in the 1920s hardly changed. The schools of the 1920s were many times more effective as bulwarks of the existing order than as challengers to it.

"As a public agency," wrote an educator early in the decade, "the schools of this democracy have in every age reflected the current political and social philosophy, the dominant social theory and aim of the day. . . . That aim today is social efficiency through mass conservation. Consequently, layman and educator alike are no longer defining education in terms of personal accomplishment or political rights, but in terms of social necessity, social efficiency, social conservation, social adjustment." In practice this meant playing up patriotism and the flag, assimilating and homogenizing immigrants and other students who were "different," teaching them not only English but "American" English, emphasizing vocational education as preparation for practical work, trimming down the classics, both ancient and later, in favor of courses that could lead directly into the world of business, discouraging dissent in thought, speech, or action.

Business exerted influence not by a heavy hand from the top circles of corporate capitalism—education was too decentralized and locally controlled for that—but through a widely shared perception that schools should teach youth how to get ahead in the practical world. The Indiana and Muncie educational leaders, the Lynds noted, stressed that history should teach reverence for law and for private property, that other social studies should emphasize respect for "fundamental institutions of society: private property, guaranteed privileges, contracts, personal liberty, right to establish private enterprises." A solid education, said Treasury Secretary Andrew Mellon, would teach Americans to lose their fear of stocks, Wall Street, banks, and large corporations, so that even women would find that "the symbols of the ticker tape are not Sanskrit after all."

Few worried that education for "social efficiency" or for "life adjustment" could be profoundly hostile to the intellect—hostile to the free play of the mind, exploration of new ideas, vigorous controversy over fundamentals, learning for its own sake. There were few protests against anti-intellectualism, even within the teaching community. Elmer Ellis of the University of Missouri argued for "making modern life comprehensible to the individual so that he can act intelligently in relation to it," but far more typical was the New York committee of principals and teachers who complained that certain textbooks were written from the point of view "of a critical historian" rather than from the point of view of teachers.

Nor was there a genuine youth revolt in the twenties, or even a youth movement. Although countercultural philosophy was available in the works of Randolph Bourne and others, most young people, as usual, reflected the conventional attitudes of their parents. "The image that teases the historical imagination," according to Paula Fass, "is of a rebellious youth, iconoclastic, irreverent, frivolous, lost to social responsibility, and even more lost to traditional values and beliefs." It was in fact "a portrait carefully constructed by contemporaries in the twenties—in the creative literature, popular journals, and volumes of social analysis by educators, judges, and poets."

*　　*　　*

College youth had an even more distorted reputation than high school students. After all, college was where flaming youth really congregated, with its raccoon coats, hip-pocket flasks, fraternity parties, rumble-seat petting, ear-splitting jazz. But here too the noisy, gaudy façade cloaked the reality of apathy, a dash of cynicism, a touch of revolt, and a structure of conservative Republicanism.

Like the high school students, the college generation in the twenties seemed lively and rebellious in large part because of sheer numbers. The number of men students receiving bachelor's degrees during the decade doubled; the number of women graduates, after rising steadily since 1890, tripled in the same decade. But in general, the students seemed to bring their home lives and attitudes with them. They joined fraternities and sororities dominated by the same middle-class virtues they had learned at their parents' knees. "We are all more or less self-centered residents of Main Street," said a Trinity College editor. Fraternities, with their booster-ism and their absorption in athletics and socializing, were easy way-stations to postgraduate membership in the Kiwanis and Rotary Club. College youth read the *Saturday Evening Post, Ladies' Home Journal,* and *Cosmopolitan,* just as their parents did; they also read Sinclair Lewis, and perhaps even glimpsed their futures in *Babbitt.*

"George F." Babbitt Jr. "is going to college," said an Ohio State University editor, "and he is even more secure in college than in the world of business, if we are to believe our eyes and ears and the college papers."

Politically, college students outside the South were heavily Republican. A large, moderately representative poll of students in 120 institutions in October 1924 gave Coolidge 30,000 "votes" to fewer than 14,000 for Davis and 7,500 for La Follette. Women were no less conservative than men. Coolidge, who as Vice-President had called eastern women's colleges hotbeds of radicalism and Bolshevism, "carried" Wellesley by 76 percent of the vote, Smith by 73, Vassar and Bryn Mawr each by 54. La Follette made a decent showing only at Barnard.

College students in the twenties, on the other hand, were by no means lacking in a measure of idealism, or at least old-fashioned liberalism. On issues that did not clearly affect their future pocketbooks they could take advanced positions. They were often tolerant of dissent, intolerant of intolerance as embodied in the Ku Klux Klan, protective of civil liberties and academic freedom. But they saw little linkage between such issues and party politics. "The only subjects that are getting any attention from the 'political minded,' " observed an editor at the University of California at Los Angeles in 1926, "are Prohibition, Birth Control and the Bible Issue, none of which are in the least related to politics or political wisdom." The simmering issue of racial justice was largely ignored, except when a campus incident produced a quick but fleeting expression of concern.

On the fringes of campus life, small groups of students spoke up for socialism or liberalism or black rights or academic liberty or—especially in the immediate post–World War I years—pacifism and internationalism and disarmament. Here and there a student editor or group might speak up against United States policy in Latin America or the efforts of an American Legion post to get a normal-school teacher fired for radical views. But college students formed no general political movement, headed toward no confrontation with their teachers or their elders. There was, it is true, one issue on which concerned students were relatively consistent—the supreme issue in America of individual liberty. Thus, when the New York State legislature proposed to purge socialist and communist teachers from the schools, an editor of the *Cornell Sun* demanded: "Has the panic caused by Bolshevism and socialism so befuddled the college graduate [in the legislature] that he can urge the investigation of the beliefs of every member of the Cornell faculty, and the discharge of every man whose views do not coincide with his own? Since when, may we ask, has any group of citizens been granted the power of determining what a man may think in order that he may secure a livelihood?" But such occasional challenges as these, in the 1920s, merely reinforced the views of those who chose to believe that the colleges were hotbeds of subversion as well as sex.

Most college youth of the 1920s had shared educational experiences outside the classroom. They were graduates of American Protestantism, the products of Sunday school and church pews, of YMCAs and YWCAs, during the years when the Protestant Establishment had been at the height of its numbers, momentum, and apparent influence. Protestantism encompassed diverse tendencies—this was part of its strength—both theological conservatism and the powerful Social Gospel movement, both old-fashioned fundamentalist orthodoxy and liberal reformism. It was learning to live with a Roman Catholic community that was developing the "largest private educational system in the world."

Having developed historically in intimate embrace with capitalist ideals and institutions, dynamic Protestantism might have seemed poised at the start of the twenties for another great period of expansion. Yet by 1921, notes Winthrop Hudson, "much of the contagious enthusiasm exhibited by the churches in the prewar years had begun to be dissipated. By 1925 the usual indices of institutional strength—church attendance, Sunday school enrollment, missionary giving—showed a downward trend that was to continue for at least a decade." Perhaps nothing better indicated Protestantism's loss of verve and idealism during the twenties than the fact that 2,700 students applied for foreign missionary service in 1920, 252 eight years later.

Most serious of all for the Protestant churches in the 1920s, according to Sydney Ahlstrom, "was a pervasive thinning out of evangelical substance, a tendency to identify religion with the business-oriented values of the American way of life." Much of the leadership of the church, instead of countering the conservatism, commercialism, and complacency of the decade, succumbed to these tendencies.

The most glaring sign of the churches' surrender to the commercial spirit was the effort to "merchandise" religion. In part, this was due to the need to compete with films and radio, with the automobile that made whole families mobile on weekends, with burgeoning entertainments and recreation; in part it was due to the role of businessmen in promoting and financing churches; most of all, probably, it was due to the prevailing commercial ethos of the twenties. Ministers "are salesmen with a wonderfully fine 'line' to sell their congregations," a Methodist paper editorialized. "Selling Religion—that is the only business of the Church," advised the clerk of the Presbyterian General Assembly. Promoters and preachers concocted teasing slogans and sermon topics: "Worship Increases Your Efficiency" or "Business Success and Religion Go Together."

By far the most successful promoter of Protestantism was Bruce Barton, onetime muckraker and radical, later a sensationally successful Manhattan advertising executive and publicist for the Republican party. In 1925, he published *The Man Nobody Knows*, a portrait of Jesus Christ as master salesman, vigorous executive, and creator of the best twelve-member management team of all time. Critics charged that Barton ignored Christ's divinity and even remade Jesus in the author's own image, but the work headed the nonfiction best-seller lists for many months. Barton was in fact a sophisticated and thoughtful conservative, and *The Man Nobody Knows* was by no means a crass defense of capitalism; rather, in Otis Pease's words, its "principal thrust was to urge business-minded Americans, concerned with success, to model their lives on a man who, Barton insisted, exemplified humaneness, sociability, service to others, the leadership to inspire ordinary people to rise above themselves, a capacity to love everyone as persons. . . ." But these finer points tended to become lost in the decade's ballyhoo.

There was little protest against conservatism and commercialism in the churches, except on the part of a few liberals and radicals in the theological schools and the religious press. No strong movement appeared on the religious left. Opposition, on the contrary, rose on the "rural right" from the old fundamentalist, revivalist sectors of Protestantism. The new fundamentalist militancy in the 1920s took two distinct forms, according to Ahlstrom: an effort to stop public schools and colleges from teaching scientific theories thought to be contrary to traditional interpretations of the Bible, and an effort to halt liberal theology and critical scholarship within the churches. Protestant unity soon was shattered by bitter fundamentalist-modernist disputes.

Fundamentalism in the twenties embraced some ministers of great congregations in the North, not merely the rural South and West, but the movement came to be characterized—and caricatured—by some of its more spectacular leaders. Billy Sunday, a former professional baseball player, had become a super-evangelist who could attract a million-and-a-half attendance in a ten-week campaign. He also denounced "hireling" ministers who forgot Jesus Christ in their effort to please their liberal parishioners. While Sunday had reached the peak of his influence before the war, both his revival rhetoric and his rescuing of the fallen at two dollars a soul cast their spell over the evangelists of the 1920s. The most unforgettable of these was Aimee Semple McPherson, proprietor of the Angelus Temple in Los Angeles. Presented in her $1.5 million temple, attired in virginal white, McPherson made a continuous wedding service of entertainment, commerce, and evangelism. "There is no way to understand how a jejune and arid pulpit has become a dynamic of literally National proportions," said a rival Los Angeles minister, "but to hear and see the woman." And that was just what Aimee Semple McPherson wanted.

What the modernist-fundamentalist conflict needed in the 1920s was a drama with a morality theme, and this was provided by the trial of John Scopes in Dayton, Tennessee, in July 1925, for teaching evolution in defiance of the laws of the state. Over one hundred newspaper journalists telegraphing 2 million words of newspaper reportage brought an audience of tens of millions into the morality play. Eagerly they followed the principals and the scenario: young Scopes, struggling through his first year of high school teaching; Clarence Darrow, the famed attorney for the defense; William Jennings Bryan, who had helped draft an anti-evolution resolution passed by the Florida legislature; and then the tragicomic encounter between Darrow and Bryan, as the attorney led the old Commoner into detailing an absurdly literal interpretation of the Bible. Day after day, in killing heat, the ordeal continued, with Scopes found guilty—and Bryan found dead a few days later.

Not reported was one arresting aspect of the "monkey trial": the whole issue had arisen in Dayton because a group of local businessmen wanted to stage an event that would spark the town's economic development. Even the most spectacular ideological confrontation of the 1920s had not escaped the commercial taint.

The Press as Entertainment

The one hundred or more newspeople who reported the Scopes trial were not a high number for the coverage of courtroom dramas in the 1920s. The Hall-Mills murder trial—the bodies of a minister and his church's choir leader had been found together under a New Jersey crab-apple tree—attracted twice as many reporters. The *New York Times* printed 528,000 words on the trial and 435 pictures; the New York *American,* 347,000 words and 2,691 pictures; the *Daily News,* 223,000 words and 2,962 pictures. For the *Times,* half a million words on the trial was almost literally all the news fit to print.

Doubtless the press felt it deserved such self-indulgence, for it had ballyhooed the case into sensationalism in the first place. Indeed, after a grand jury had refused to indict, a tabloid had gotten the case reopened on the basis of flimsy evidence, and then reaped circulation benefits by its avid coverage of the subsequent trial. The press corps at the later murder trial of a corset salesman included Mary Roberts Rinehart and Billy Sunday, and D. W. Griffith and Peggy Joyce did special interpretations. It received more play than the sinking of the *Titanic;* the press assigned 120 reporters to this case, "more than represented all the American newspapers and news agencies in the Far East," Silas Bent observed.

Sensationalism was nothing new in the American press, but the 1920s was indeed the age of ballyhoo. The reason was in part economic. For half a century the newspapers had undergone rising costs and circulation wars. The indispensable Linotype machine now cost $18,000. Newsprint had soared from 2 1/4 cents to 6 cents a pound during the war. Printers' and pressmen's wages had doubled since 1910, to $50 a week during the twenties. But newspapers were still selling for the smallest coin of the realm. Until recently, Walter Lippmann wrote in *Public Opinion,* the public had accustomed itself "to paying two and even three cents on weekdays, and on Sundays, for an illustrated encyclopedia and vaudeville entertainment attached, we have screwed ourselves up to paying a nickel or even a dime."

More than ever this cost-price gap was being filled by advertising, which by the 1920s was generating two-thirds of the newspaper revenue and, in metropolitan newspapers, appropriating three columns for every two of reading matter. The cost of advertising in English language newspapers tripled between 1915 and 1929, amounting to $860 million in the latter year. Earlier, Ivory Soap had boasted, "It Floats"; now Maxwell was urging installment buyers of autos to "Pay As You Ride"; the railroads were exhorting travelers to "See America First"; Listerine was warring on halitosis and Life Buoy Soap on "B.O."

In the frenzied search for advertising and hence for circulation, the newspapers offered entertainment and diversion—scandal, crime, fashion notes, puzzles, society gossip, recipes, beauty hints, astrology, chess, whist, bridge, gardening, palmistry, advice to the lovelorn. "The newspaper offers a mart wherein the commodity factory may shriek its wares, and exploit its own workers, who spend more and more of their surplus on newly-created wants," Silas Bent wrote during mid-decade. "The newspaper offers to the literate but uneducated workers an escape, an entertainment, a thrill, an opiate."

Nothing combined all these qualities more graphically than the comics, which had originated earlier as day-to-day gags but came into their own as continuity strips at the start of the twenties. Millions followed the lives and times of Andy Gump, Toots and Casper, Skeezix, Winnie Winkle, Barney Google, Tillie the Toiler, Moon Mullins, and Blondie. Accident-prone, crisis-ridden, vociferous, funny, they let their eager public identify itself with their family squabbles and personal foibles. "If historians of the next century were to rely upon the comic strip," Stephen Becker has observed, "they would conclude that we were a peaceful lot of ruminant burghers from 1920 to 1929, with only flashes of inspired insanity, and that our social conflicts and national crises were settled by family conferences at the dinner table."

No ideological pattern emerged from the zany characters and their doings. Cartoonist Harold Gray's conservatism, individualism, and philosophy that "only the good have rights" expressed itself in Little Orphan Annie's millionaire protector Daddy Warbucks, but most of the comic characters of the 1920s are notable only for their human vanities and failings. The comics represented commercialism more than conservatism. Publishers knew that the comic strips were by far the most read of all their features, and their artists were among the best paid of all who worked for newspapers.

More than ever before, the big papers were big business, sharing the powers and vicissitudes of big business. Newspaper proprietors, it was said, had to be "reelected" every day, as customers casually chose among a dozen competing papers at a newsstand. One response to "destructive competition" was consolidation. Strong newspapers swallowed up weak ones; morning and evening papers combined, thus keeping a single plant running twenty-four hours; papers merged to keep or gain the precious Associated Press franchise. Consolidation intensified during the war years and continued into the twenties.

The monarch of mergers in the 1920s was surely Frank A. Munsey. A Horatio Alger figure who had started out at thirteen as a clerk, he rose to fame and riches by buying, selling, merging, or discontinuing a large number of newspapers. After buying the New York *Press* and merging it with the *Sun,* a penny paper, he poured $2 million in it by 1920 without much effect on circulation. He then bought the *Herald,* a venerable paper that with the *Sun* had set high standards in American journalism. After neither turned a profit, Munsey eyed the *Tribune,* another excellent and unprofitable organ. When the Reid family refused to sell this living legacy of their late father, Munsey abruptly sold them the *Herald.* The result was the *Herald Tribune.*

Munsey did not sentimentalize over the seven New York dailies or the eleven magazines that he merged, sold, killed off, or renamed. "The same law of economics applies in the newspaper business that operates in all other important business to-day," he said. "Small units in any line are no longer competitive factors." The mergers that made newspapers scarcer made Munsey richer, to the tune of $20 million.

*   *   *

At the start of the twenties, Upton Sinclair threw down his gauntlet before the working press. "The Brass Check is found in your pay-envelope every week—you who write and print and distribute our newspapers and magazines. The Brass Check is the price of your shame—you who take the fair body of truth and sell it in the market place, who betray the virgin hopes of mankind into the loathsome brothel of Big Business."

Strong words, but Walter Lippmann granted that Sinclair spoke for a large body of Americans. How answer such a charge? Lippmann could hardly defend the accuracy of the press, for he and a colleague were just completing a test of the *New York Times*'s coverage of the Russian Revolution and concluding that the "news about Russia is a case of seeing not what was" but rather what reporters and editors "wished to see." But Lippmann would not blame the big publishers as big businessmen. The problem lay elsewhere—in the fact that news and truth were by no means the same thing. The press could report only palpable events, "like the beam of a searchlight that moves restlessly about, bringing one episode and then another out of darkness into vision." It could not report underlying, tangled, "social truth." That could be done only through a system of intelligence, a machinery of knowledge.

Others traced the failure to economics and technology. "The industrialization of the news gathering process," according to a recent study, "had inevitably required further and further division of labor. From a colonial institution in which one man wrote, edited and printed the entire newspaper, the press had developed into a complex operation in which the facts in any one story were transmitted from one person to another in an expanding chain. An overseas story might go from reporter to rewrite man to editor of the originating paper in the United States and thence through wire or syndicate editors to hundreds of other papers for handling by still other rewrite men and editors. The process provided limitless possibilities for honing and focusing news, but it also made possible a good deal of misunderstanding and re-interpretation."

Perhaps the critical change had taken place in the nature of public opinion itself. Trying to collect news from a chaos of sights and sounds, reporters lacked a shaping framework in which to conduct their work. In earlier days, at least in their political reporting, they had operated in a party environment and worked for partisan newspapers. Public opinion was largely party opinion. Parties were already declining in the 1920s under the impact of the anti-party reforms of earlier in the century, however, and the number of party-affiliated newspapers had dropped dramatically—from 801 Republican and 732 Democratic dailies in 1899 to 505 Republican and 434 Democratic dailies by 1929. More party independence did not free the press from political or economic controls, but simply made reporters dependent on other influences and moorings.

To some degree, publicity agents filled the party gap—a clear sign, Lippmann noted, that "the facts of modern life do not spontaneously take a shape in which they can be known. They must be given a shape by somebody." Also interpreting events were syndicated political columnists, who came into their own during the twenties. Arthur Brisbane's column "Today" was syndicated by Hearst's Washington *Times*. Mark Sullivan, Walter Winchell, and Will Rogers appeared in scores of papers; Heywood Broun's "It Seems to Me" appeared in the New York *Tribune* and then in the New York *World* until he clashed with his employers and moved to the New York *Telegram*. And when the *World* disappeared into the *World-Telegram* in 1931, the dispossessed Walter Lippmann moved to the *Herald Tribune*, where for years he would help "shape the news."

Henry Luce, recently of Yale, had his own ideas as to how to sculpture the news. With his friend Britton Hadden, he founded *Time* in 1923, with a prospectus claiming that Americans were on the whole poorly informed. Luce and Hadden proposed to offer a blend of fact and opinion, on the premise that anyone who thought he was objective was deceiving himself. Luce urged newspapers to drop their separate editorial page and feature "intelligent criticism, representation and evaluation" of leaders. *Time* itself had no editorial page; critics held that all its pages were editorial. Luce believed in free enterprise, free speech, hard competition, and the "American Way." Even more conservative, at least on economic issues, was the *Reader's Digest,* which began in 1922 as a pocket-sized monthly composed of articles condensed from other publications. Both these journals ended the decade with sizable circulations; in 1930, Time Inc. spawned *Fortune,* a monthly for affluent businessmen.

To such publications there was, however, no counterpart on the left, no substantial adversary press. The Yiddish-language *Daily Forward* had a decent circulation, but most socialist and communist journals struggled through the gay twenties. The trade union press consisted mainly of provincial, craft-oriented papers. At the start of World War I, the United States could boast of more than 1,200 foreign-language newspapers, 500 of them printed in German; New York alone had ten German-language newspapers. But many German-language presses were stopped during the war, never to run again. Socialist papers such as the Milwaukee *Leader* and the New York *Call* were denied the use of the mails; the *Leader*'s editor, Victor Berger, was barred from his seat in Congress; the editors of Philadelphia's *Tageblatt* went to jail for criticizing the war effort.

The native Indian newspapers, which under the leadership of the *Cherokee Advocate* had thrived during the previous century, entered a dark age. The *Advocate*'s Cherokee-language type was handed over to the Smithsonian, and its press sold as junk. Other journals such as the *American Indian Magazine* printed work by leading Indian writers but lasted only a few years. A number of black newspapers, on the other hand, flourished during the twenties; even the radical Chicago *Defender* had a circulation of 93,000, and W. E. B. Du Bois's *Crisis,* the organ of the NAACP, enjoyed a marked influence. Northern black papers were said to have helped inspire the continuing Negro migration to Northern cities.

Nonetheless, all these minority or dissenting papers combined—and, in contrast to mainstream papers, they did not seek to combine—could in no way be considered to constitute a strong adversary or opposition press.

The major challenge to the established press lay outside the press, in an innocuous little box that was showing up in more and more American parlors. This was the radio, the "Furniture That Talks," as comedian Fred Allen dubbed it.

"I have in mind," twenty-five-year-old David Sarnoff had written in 1916, "a plan of development which would make radio a 'household utility' in the same sense as the piano or phonograph. . . . The receiver can be designed in the form of a simple 'Radio Music Box' and arranged for several different wave lengths." Five years later, after becoming general manager of the new Radio Corporation of America, Sarnoff persuaded RCA to enter radio broadcasting. Five years after that, he helped launch the National Broadcasting Company.

Everything turned on that box in the parlor. By 1922 sales of radio sets and parts had reached $60 million; within two more years sales were almost six times that figure. Stations quickly proliferated—28 were licensed in 1921; by July 1922 this number had swelled to 430. A whole new industry was getting under way. Radio magazines appeared with broadcasting schedules. Technology, programming, professionalism all improved. At first the stations tended to feature European classical music. Then they discovered the swinging music of New Orleans, called jazz or "race music." Because the saxophone was considered an immoral instrument, this kind of music was not to be found on the airwaves until the mid-1920s—and by then the listener could hear little else.

Radio had a particular impact on the nation's farmers, a million of whom were receiving programs from five hundred stations. Some large firms like the Gurney Seed and Nursery Company in South Dakota bought not only time but whole stations. Soon the little boxes were offering religion, politics, Fibber Magee and Molly on Chicago's WMAQ, and Henry Ford's old-time square-dance music on Detroit's WBZ. It was estimated that 25 million people heard Calvin Coolidge's Inaugural Address in 1925.

The Bill of Rights forbade regulation of the press, but what about radio, which used the nation's airwaves? The federal government, through activist Secretary of Commerce Herbert Hoover, began to regulate radio by assigning wavelengths. Some small stations refused to stick to their allotted place, wandering instead through the radio spectrum in search of clear air. When Hoover sealed the chronically offending station of Aimee Semple McPherson, she replied with a tart telegram: "PLEASE ORDER YOUR MINIONS OF SATAN TO LEAVE MY STATION ALONE. YOU CANNOT EXPECT THE ALMIGHTY TO ABIDE BY YOUR WAVE LENGTH NONSENSE."

Minor controversy broke out as to whether radio should be federally regulated at all, but only regulation of wavelengths could prevent chaos, and radio recognized no state boundaries. Virtually no one even raised the question of whether government should own the airwaves or control the contents of radio broadcasts, even though during the 1920s Britain under a Conservative government established the nationalized British Broadcasting Corporation. So radio was turned over to private enterprise, which inevitably competed to offer entertainment.

ENTERTAINMENT AS SPECTATORSHIP

The movies had a history something like that of radio. In each "a crude toy became an industry; fierce patent struggles erupted; public acceptance skyrocketed; business combinations won domination; anonymous idols exploded into fame." There was a difference in degree of spectatorship between radio and film, however, that amounted to a difference in kind. People could interact face-to-face with stump speakers; they could heckle, applaud, boo, and hiss, and speakers could respond to these cues. Audiences could interact with actors in the "legitimate theater," registering their feelings and even eliciting subtle responses from the stage. Radio listeners could talk among themselves, or at least turn to another wave band. But moviegoers sat in relative isolation; they could not communicate with the silent actors on the silver screen; they could not easily talk among themselves or quit the theater. Spectatorship was complete.

The earliest movies had typically been either ludicrous farces or stiffly filmed stage plays. Then films increasingly became rich in spectacle, allegory, and melodrama. The blazing power of huge battle was combined with close attention to detail in both these and domestic scenes. D. W. Griffith's *The Birth of a Nation,* with its pioneering film technique, was a landmark of art and of finance. Some viewers were furious over the film's portrayal of idyllic life on an antebellum Southern plantation, villainous abolitionists, and the evils of miscegenation—and also because many of the blacks in the huge cast were played by white actors. But Griffith's film went on making money, at the then-unheard-of price of two dollars a seat, with the producer proclaiming his audience to be the leisured elite, not the impecunious who had filled the nickelodeons.

As people demanded to see more feature films like Griffith's, as big-name stars, better scripts, lavish sets and costumes became more expensive, the scattered film enterprises were transformed into a major industry. By 1920, studios were vast businesses, embracing real estate, production plants, towering sets, well-paid screen writers, film stock, animals, carpenters, electricians, cameras, laboratories, promoters and advertisers, and performers. As in all businesses, distribution was another huge expense, involving everything from posters and theaters to usherettes and popcorn sellers. It was also a key to domination of the whole industry.

This key was in the hands of entrepreneurial producers like Adolph Zukor. Under Zukor's leadership, Paramount Pictures abandoned the old method of renting films to many theaters simultaneously and substituted a method of classifying picture houses. The first exclusive showing at a

prestigious theater would cost more than later runs. Following lavish promotion of a new film, Zukor insisted that a theater owner who wanted it
would have to take his studio's entire year's output. After experimenting
with three kinds of pictures—artsy, star-studded, and cheap-and-quick—
Zukor discovered that the films with stars were the most popular. With
actors like Mary Pickford and William S. Hart, he was in a commanding
position.

Prestigious films with celebrated actors and actresses required fitting
movie theaters. Fifty years earlier, the cathedrals of American business had
been magnificent railroad stations; now they were "movie palaces," the
legendary master of which was Samuel L. Rothafel, known to the public
as "Roxy." In the mid-twenties he built in New York City his dream show-
place, modestly called the Roxy. "Three hundred plasterers were gathered
to work their rococo magic on every available inch," according to a breath-
less report. "The Roxy also utilized Renaissance details of gold filigree and
vivid red. The rotunda was supported by twelve marble columns, and rose
five stories above a magnificent oval rug which weighed over two tons,
measured fifty-eight feet by forty-one feet, and cost $15,000. Amber glass
windows, crystal chandeliers, and enormous urns decorated the immense
6,214-seat auditorium." Roxy and other impresarios built strings of rococo
palaces across the nation, and Roxy reached his own pinnacle with the
Radio City Music Hall. Charlie Chaplin, Noel Coward, Irving Berlin, and
William Randolph Hearst were among the celebrities attending the opening night.

Titanic battles were fought to control theaters, films, and stars. Theater
owners, cut off from control by impresarios like Zukor, banded together
to take over film production, contracting with stars like Chaplin. Zukor
responded by building some six hundred first-run theaters for Paramount,
including some of the rococo cathedrals. Film artists too sought to control
their own product. Griffith, Chaplin, Pickford, and Douglas Fairbanks
formed United Artists in 1919 to distribute their films. Each of them had
a separate production unit, thus insuring their independence. United Artists survived, despite the power of the goliaths, and became a model for
independent producers in later decades.

But the true czars were the producers who owned or controlled movie
theaters, and America had never seen a group of entrepreneurs quite like
the first generation of czars. Typically Jewish immigrants from Central and
Eastern Europe, with little formal education, they plunged into the American business maelstrom, sometimes running amusement parks where they
converted their arcades into nickelodeons. As the movie business prospered, these producers typically built a few more theaters until they owned

a chain. One of the most famous was Louis B. Mayer, who as a child had emigrated from Minsk with his Russian family in the late 1880s. He bought his first nickelodeon with his last fifty dollars, then moved up the ladder to fame and fortune. Volatile, ruthless, melodramatic, Mayer was innovative in seeking an appealing story, rather than depending on the popularity of stars.

Temperamental producers often battled with their temperamental stars. "Remember it was I who first had the vision!" Zukor said to Chaplin. "Who swept out your dirty nickelodeon? Who put in your plush seats? It was I who built your great theaters, who raised prices and made it possible for you to get large grosses for your pictures."

As in other industries, the Hollywood studios could always fall back on mergers. Marcus Loew's ailing Metro studio, Sam Goldwyn's heavily indebted Goldwyn Company, and Louis Mayer's thriving studio combined in 1924 in a lasting merger. Metro-Goldwyn-Mayer billed itself "The Home of the Stars," proving it with such big names as Buster Keaton, Lillian Gish, and Lon Chaney. Much of MGM's success was due to a shy, talented young businessman from Brooklyn, Irving Thalberg, whose instinct for film, for the right scene, gave him the reputation of defining the quintessential "MGM film."

But what Americans saw was not the industry but the stars, and during the twenties they were flocking to watch the mishaps of Charlie Chaplin, the acrobatics of Buster Keaton, the antics of Harold Lloyd, the licit sex appeal of Clara Bow, the brooding, heavy-lidded eyes of Theda Bara, the dark passion of Rudolph Valentino. A host of movie magazines told in intimate detail, issue after issue, of the working lives and good times and tragedies of such stars, of their romances, marriages, divorces, of their clothes, hairdos, cars. A nation of spectators watched a handful of stars.

The censors also were watching. Hollywood had taken on the flavor of sin after comedian "Fatty" Arbuckle's involvement in the death of a starlet, the mysterious murder of director William Desmond Taylor, and Cecil B. De Mille's *Male and Female*—the film version of James M. Barrie's *The Admirable Crichton*—which had allowed a fleeting glimpse of Gloria Swanson's breasts. Several states had passed censorship laws by 1920. More ominously, the United States Supreme Court had held that prior censorship of motion pictures was within the constitutional authority of the states. The guarantee of free opinion and speech, the Court ruled, need not encompass the profit-making business of exhibiting films.

With their usual resourcefulness, the Hollywood moguls hit upon a winning formula in the face of these threats—films that were paeans to the resistance of temptation, yet showed in lurid detail the temptations resisted. But the industry's main defense was to form a new trade organization, the Motion Picture Producers and Distributors Association. Chosen as first president was a man of impeccable moral and political credentials, Will H. Hays, former Postmaster General under Harding, former chairman of the Republican National Committee, Presbyterian elder from Pennsylvania. Functioning as a glorified press agent, Hays managed, through speeches, articles, and committee sessions, both to placate the guardians of morality and to celebrate the role of film in American life. Although movies still depicted nudity and debauchery, with Hays at the helm the studios were able to persuade the upright that the films were purer than ever—chiefly by rewarding virtue at the end of the film.

This myth—Hollywood as virtuous—was only one of the illusions manufactured by the magical image-makers of the film industry. By the end of the decade, Hollywood had become a worldwide symbol of the lights and shadows cast on the silver screen, avidly followed by a nation of voyeurs.

*   *   *

Entertainment as spectatorship reached its apogee in the 1920s with the confluence of two great forces—nationwide media and professional athletics. Newspapers had been paying more and more attention to big-league baseball; a New York editor commented that "no single classification of news . . . sells more papers than sports." Film and the set-piece sports event seemed made for each other, as evidenced in the Pathé and other newsreels that preceded the feature film in theaters; the feature itself might deal with a sports hero. And the graphic broadcasts of Grantland Rice, Graham McNamee, and others sometimes made the play sound better over the radio than it looked on the field.

Few aspects of American life were changing so fast as sports participation and spectatorship. During much of the nineteenth century American sports had been palpably class-oriented. The social elites, city and country, had gone in heavily for individual and often expensive recreation: riding, yachting, rowing, billiards, and later, tennis, polo, golf. The urban rich grouped together in country clubs and athletic clubs that set them apart from the sports-minded masses. The New York Athletic Club was founded in 1866, the Westchester Polo Club in the late seventies, the Amateur Athletic Union in 1888, the Intercollegiate Athletic Association in 1905. As usual, the elites had their internal squabbles. The New York Athletic Club was rent by conflict between the Old Guard, who believed in sports for sport's sake, and an element that was suspected of using the club as a stepping-stone to high social status. Some of the old sports gaffers resigned when they lost this battle.

Middle-class men and women had shared in some upper-class sports activities, but to a limited degree. Genteel women were not expected to be physically active or participate in games; they often shunned dancing or even card-playing. The working classes, in factory and field, had more than enough exercise on the job, but they might hunt or fish, or repair to a secluded livery stable to watch a cockfight, goat fight, or "ratting"—wagering on how long it would take a dog to kill a pit full of rats. But late in the century "urbanization, technological innovations, rising per capita incomes, and the new social and cultural milieu combined in complex ways to trigger a sports revolution and a new era of American sport, 'The Age of the Players,'" according to Benjamin Rader. The players "took the initiative in organizing, managing, and financing" the sports of the upper and middle classes. And these sports were still player-centered.

Many were still excluded from this tight circle, but the "outsiders" found points of entry or, more often, developed their own sports events. Caledonian Scots put on contests in footracing, tug-of-war, hurdling, pole-vaulting, throwing the hammer, and other games brought over from the old country. The Turner Societies held gymnastics competitions modeled after festivals in Frankfurt and other German cities. As usual, blacks encountered the worst exclusion. Marshall W. "Major" Taylor, acclaimed as the "Fastest Bicycle Rider in the World," encountered rivals who together sought to knock him off his cycle, box him in, or attack him.

The 1920s brought, in Rader's terms, the "age of the spectator"—the heyday of the modern sports hero, celebrated teams, big-time promoters, athletic specialization, expert coaching; in short, the triumph of mass spectator sports. This did not mean the end of participatory sport, of course. For a time, indeed, it seemed possible that hosts of new players might match the number of spectators. Over a million persons were playing tennis by the end of the decade, and 2 million had taken up golf. But the most popular sports were organized for the watchers rather than the players. Never before had sports in America offered such an array of spectacles, or been so lucrative for their promoters.

The age of the football hero began. The game in a single decade was transformed from a college pastime to a national fascination. In the first thirteen minutes of one game against Michigan, "Red" Grange scored four touchdowns for Illinois in four carries. One hundred thousand persons gathered from throughout the nation to watch Grange play his last game for Illinois in 1925. Thereafter, as a professional, he earned as much as $35,000 a game, netting himself a million dollars and enabling him to retire while still in his twenties. What Grange was to playing, Knute Rockne was to coaching. Piloting Notre Dame to football greatness, he promoted the forward pass, which broke up the old static defense formations, boosted scores, and brought new excitement to the game.

Tennis had its own hero, in the versatile stroking machine known as Big Bill Tilden. After years of tirelessly practicing the mechanics of each shot and return, he won the singles championship at Wimbledon as an unknown, and for the next six years he dominated the game. Golf too had its brilliant technician in Bobby Jones. Dubbed "Robot, the Mechanical Man of Golf," Jones first mastered his own self-destructive temper and then perfected the loveliest swing in the game. On the links, thousands of fans pursued him, chanting "Bobby! Bobby!" between strokes.

But the hero of heroes, in part because he played in the game of games, was George Herman Ruth, Jr. He had risen to fame and fortune out of adversity: given up by his parents at the age of nine as incorrigible, raised in a Catholic reform school, he moonlighted as a bartender and bouncer in his father's saloon during his first season on the diamond. Benefiting from the abolition of the "spitball" and the development of a more resilient baseball, he hit fifty-four home runs in 1920—twice the previous record—and batted a smashing .376 for the season. The Ruth legend was born. Guided by his personal manager Christy Walsh—"the first modern athletic business agent"—the Babe lent his name to newspaper articles, clothing, sports products, even automobiles.

There was plenty of money to go around. In Ruth's first year with the Yankees, attendance at their games doubled, topping the 1 million mark. Through the twenties, a team could expect to take in around $10 million a year in gate receipts and concessions, of which nearly 20 percent was profit. The owners were able to build huge ballparks in the hearts of the major cities. Yankee Stadium, the "House That Ruth Built," cost nearly $2.5 million and seated more than 60,000 spectators. City bosses and businessmen rushed to invest in this newest and most lucrative of urban franchises. It was better even than the stock market. Ruth himself picked up the rags-to-riches theme. "The great thing about this country," he said, "is the wonderful fact that it doesn't matter which side of the tracks you were born on, or whether you're homeless or homely or friendless. The chance is still there. . . ."

But for crack baseball players born on the wrong side of the color line, the chance was not there, not in the big leagues. Baseball, indeed, had an inflated reputation as the poor man's sport. Immigrants tended to ignore the game, blacks had to play in their own league, and high ticket prices kept many poor people outside the stadium.

The fans adored Babe Ruth despite his roguish qualities—or perhaps because of them. But about the other great sports hero from the working classes, Jack Dempsey, they remained divided. The press branded him—falsely—as a draft dodger and wife-beater; churchmen denounced him as the symbol of the American relapse into "paganism." Dempsey was in fact neither a rogue nor a villain. A shy, uneducated man, the son of poor Colorado pioneers, he had made a meager living from impromptu fights in Rocky Mountain saloons and mining camps. Seeing the potential in the sinewy young boxer, the gambler-turned-promoter "Tex" Rickard arranged for Dempsey to fight Jess Willard, the world heavyweight champion. After the aggressive, snarling Dempsey beat his bigger foe bloody in three rounds, Rickard unleashed a blizzard of publicity for the new champion, "Jack the Giant Killer."

Rickard promoted not only Dempsey but boxing. He made prizefighting respectable, taking it out of smoke-filled rooms and staging it before upper- and middle-class audiences in big, scrubbed-up auditoriums. Purses of fifty and one hundred thousand dollars added piquancy for both spectator and contestant. Dempsey became such a celebrity that he made half-a-million annually from vaudeville and movie appearances without accepting a single fight in three years. But the fans—and the promoters—wanted him back in the ring. The obvious contender was Harry Wills of New Orleans. But he was black. Earlier, lynchings and race riots had followed in the wake of Jack Johnson's winning of the heavyweight crown, and Rickard was not willing to run this risk again.

So Dempsey fought Gene Tunney and made sports history—twice. Tunney was a different kind of boxer from most of the fighters Dempsey had met. For years he had studied and practiced his craft, mastering combinations of blows and footwork that he was certain could overcome Dempsey's savage power. In a result that astonished everyone else, Tunney absorbed and evaded the champion's blows, slowly wore him down, and won on points.

Tunney might have walked out of a Scott Fitzgerald novel. A onetime clerk and Marine, he aspired to an educational and social status that might have seemed beyond the reach of his Irish working class and took a most unusual route to attain it. In a Scott Fitzgerald story there would have been a rematch, and there was. With movie cameras whirring above Chicago's Soldier Field, Graham McNamee narrating for the radio fans, and 100,000 spectators in their seats, once again Dempsey threw himself into every punch, once again Tunney danced and jabbed. Knocked flat by a powerful punch, Tunney waited out a delayed count to nine, outpointed Dempsey in each of the remaining rounds, and won by unanimous decision of the judges. Tunney retired rich afterwards, married an heiress, and lived happily ever after.

"I have no alibis to offer," Dempsey said. "I lost to a good man, an American—a man who speaks the English language."

*   *   *

There had always been a seamy side to sports in America. Rough-and-tumble fighting on the frontier often ended in kneeing, biting, hair-pulling, eye-gouging, or even "balloching," or emasculation. Horse racing attracted gamblers, touts, tricksters, and prostitutes. Slaveowners were reported to have pitted their best fighting slaves against those from nearby plantations. A ratting or a cockfight in a livery stable might end with a boxing match between two women naked above the waist.

In 1919 the World Series itself was fixed, when seven White Sox players accepted $5,000 to $10,000 to let Cincinnati win. To cleanse baseball's public image the owners hired the theatrical Judge Kenesaw Mountain Landis as baseball czar. Landis cut a highly visible swath through organized baseball, fining or firing players, barring them from the game, vowing an open war on gambling. Landis played too, his critics said—to his audience.

Corruption in sports helped establish the twenties in the popular mind as the time of the great crime wave. In fact, there was no such crime wave, aside from the millions of Americans who drank illegal liquor. Public perception of crime turned largely on the mobsters who moved in on the illicit liquor traffic and the "speakeasies." The decade also introduced a new figure into American culture, the big-time gangster hero. As the press sensationalized the sordid exploits of Al Capone and his ilk, and Edward G. Robinson immortalized the mobster in *Little Caesar,* crime became another spectator sport.

Some of the spectators were not amused. President Hoover and Secretary Mellon were said to have conferred repeatedly on federal efforts to prosecute Capone. The Justice Department's Prohibition Bureau set up a special unit to get him. Tax sleuths also investigated him. Under pressure the Chicago gangster slipped, was convicted of tax evasion, was sentenced to ten years, and later died of syphilis. But that was long after this antihero hero, bullet-headed and weasel-eyed, with his florid suits and string of grisly murders, had captured the imagination of the country.

THE WORKSHOP AND THE DEMOS

If more and more Americans were becoming spectators in a commercialized society, what did they see? Crammed with political and economic pieties from birth, steeped in Social Darwinist ideology, conditioned by a conservative and sensationalist press, lulled by religious orthodoxy,

opiated by heavily promoted sports and other entertainments, what *could*
they see? Some observers contended that the people were conditioned to
see nothing except the glories of capitalism—that Jack Dempsey, for example, by being made a hero helped to perpetuate conservative values,
such as white superiority, or the mythology of a simple boy's rise from
nowhere to fame and riches. Others, following more a confusion theory
than a conspiracy theory, held that the effect of mass spectatorship was
to divert workers' attention away from social and political matters to recreation and entertainment. Diversion was easy, for the intellectual challenge was harsh.

The prime intellectual issue still facing the American people in the 1920s
was the compatibility of a rapidly centralizing system of corporate capitalism with an old-fashioned, divided constitutional system—a republic that
institutionalized civil liberties, a broad electorate, checks and balances, and
minority vetoes. The key political question was which system could better
satisfy people's wants and needs, expectations and demands.

The bemused and distracted American people hardly recognized the
problem, however, much less the solution. Even if they had focused their
attention they might not have seen that they had a choice between the two
systems. Many felt that they had done well under capitalism, or hoped to
do well in the future, or had concluded that if they had not done well it
was their fault and not the system's. In many aspects the economic system
remained harsh and inhuman, but compared to the old days, when the
industrial titans could let the public be damned, an army of publicists and
promoters were decking out "free enterprise" in the rosiest of colors. Even
more, the system *was* changing a bit, as some of the bigger firms began to
provide free legal services, group insurance, profit-sharing, medical clin-
ics, or other forms of welfare capitalism; Owen D. Young of General
Electric shocked his Harvard Business School audience by calling for
"great business organizations" that would actually belong to the workers
"who are giving their lives and their efforts to them."

It was also evident by the 1920s that business could not mobilize the kind
of naked economic power that the tycoons had wielded almost casually a
half century before. Business—industrial, financial, commercial business—
was too divided within itself, too localized and regionalized and specialized, to present a common front, except in final defense of property. The
translation of economic into political power was not all that easy, moreover, especially in a system of dispersed authority between nation and
states, between executives and legislatures and judiciaries, among public
and private agencies. The growing body of regulatory legislation—federal
laws passed during the days of TR and Wilson, and state measures spon-

sored by La Follette and other progressive governors—established rough constraints on the economic and political power of business.

What business had been supremely successful at doing was to maintain an ideology of free enterprise that made opposition to capitalism appear wrongheaded at best and subversive at worst. Thus the issue returned full circle to the question of whether the people as a whole could see through the propaganda, the stereotypes, the prejudices surrounding corporate power and privilege, so as to achieve a realistic grasp of affairs. The answer of leading pundits of the day was: no, they could not.

H. L. Mencken had no doubts on the matter. The Sage of Baltimore had long dismissed the typical American as "homo boobiens." Public opinion? It gushed out from mob fears, was "piped to central factories," there "flavoured and coloured, and put into cans." The average man? He did not want to be free, only to be safe in a well-managed penitentiary. Democracy? A fraud perpetrated by the upper class, full of delusion, sentimentality, envy, bamboozlement.

Walter Lippmann's view of democracy was more considered but almost as pessimistic. In *Public Opinion,* written at the start of the decade, he had used the parable of Plato's cave to contend that average people mistook the pseudo-environment they saw for reality. The world had become too complex and remote for the mass public to understand. By the mid-twenties Lippmann was taking an even bleaker view of the situation. In *The Phantom Public,* he asserted that the "ideal of the omnicompetent, sovereign citizen" was a "false ideal," and that none of the educational, ethical, populist, or socialist remedies for the situation could possibly work. Mencken welcomed Lippmann to the ranks of those who viewed the masses as ignorant and unteachable.

Lippmann made one vital concession to the ideal of self-government. He granted that the mass public did have the capacity to make decisions between clearly visible leaders, issues, parties. The public could not creatively make complex policy, but to "support the Ins when things are going well; to support the Outs when they seem to be going badly, this, in spite of all that has been said about tweedledum and tweedledee, is the essence of popular government." Lippmann betrayed his own growing conservatism when he added that the difference between the Ins and the Outs should not be profound; otherwise "the defeated minority would be constantly on the verge of rebellion." Surely in the 1920s the problem was not too much conflict between parties, leaderships, and programs but too much blandness and consensus.

Still, Lippmann posed the issue: Were the deprived people of the 1920s —nonunion workers, jobless women, blacks North and South, middle-class people unprepared for the competitive scramble, among others—capable of perceiving and defending their own interests against the compact majority of the Republicans? Were they able to see through the fog of stereotypes, self-promotion, and self-satisfaction surrounding the corporate elites?

The answer depended first of all on the extent to which the opposition was organized and militant. This could hardly have been said of the Democratic party during the twenties. Irresolute, divided, underorganized, the Democracy did little to mobilize the masses; it seemed content to hold lengthy national conventions, sometimes help and sometimes oppose the GOP in Congress, and serve as an arena for bitter primary contests among Democratic aspirants. Nor did organized labor, the other great potential countervailing force against business power, assume the task of militant opposition. On the contrary, total union membership dwindled from almost 5 million in 1921 to less than 3.5 million in 1929; AFL rolls fell by a million during that period; even John L. Lewis's mine workers shrank from 400,000 dues-paying members to about a fifth of that. Under William Green's benign leadership, the AFL was far more interested in business unionism than in militant opposition or even vigorous industrial unionism. Women and Northern blacks had the right to vote but continued to be politically underorganized.

Though united by common concerns and vibrant memories, women also remained divided over priorities and tactics. "Hard core feminists" stressed above all women's rights, while "social feminists" made social reform their first priority. Women active in the National Woman's Party favored independent political action, while female Democratic and Republican activists worked through their respective parties. Tension developed between the Women's Joint Congressional Committee, essentially a lobbying vehicle, and the League of Women Voters, more oriented toward its grass-roots organizations. Women who had opposed their own suffrage continued to fight the movement and its legislative goals. Still, the women's groups—through arduous lobbying and grass-roots efforts, and despite charges of "communism" and "socialism" from women's groups as well as men's—were able in 1921 to push through a lethargic Congress the Sheppard-Towner maternity and infancy bill, designed to aid the states in attacking the alarming level of maternal and infant mortality in the United States. It was in part a measure of the weakness of women's political organization, however, that the act was allowed to expire by the end of the decade.

The main hope for the Outs in the 1920s lay in the realm of ideas, and here the picture was far more mixed. The political opposition in America, no matter how defined, had sharply limited common ideology, core of ideas, or psychological basis of unity. If the literary and political world had no equivalent to England's Bloomsbury circle, with its fecund and eclectic concepts and conceits, American workers also had nothing to compare with Britain's Workers Educational Association, with its grass-roots teaching of trade unionists by some of the finest university minds. The American left could find little basis for unity; not only did socialists, communists, and La Follette progressives attack one another doctrinally, but factions within each of these groupings fought among themselves with the kind of bitterness reserved for renegades. Writers on the left seemed to war on one another with even greater fury than did the radical politicos.

The most biting attacks on American culture came less from socialists or social scientists than from novelists. After his years at Yale, in Greenwich Village and as a reporter and free-lance writer for popular magazines, Sinclair Lewis touched an American nerve with *Main Street* in 1920, and stung that nerve with *Babbitt* two years later. In these novels, Lewis satirized in merciless detail the flat, sluggish, and supremely dull lives of the conventional middle-class people he had known while growing up in Sauk Centre, Minnesota. His characters' voices were often his own—for example, that of Carol Kennicott in *Main Street,* reflecting on the contrast between the portrait of small-town life in popular fiction—friendly, honest people, etc.—and reality: a "savorless people, gulping tasteless food, and sitting afterward, coatless and thoughtless, in rocking-chairs prickly with inane decorations, listening to mechanical music, saying mechanical things about the excellence of Ford automobiles, and viewing themselves as the greatest race in the world."

In his speech accepting the Nobel Prize—an award he coveted even at the earlier time when he had declined a Pulitzer—Lewis excoriated the American literary establishment and especially the "writers for the popular magazines who in a hearty and edifying chorus chant that the America of a hundred and twenty million population is still as simple, as pastoral as it was when it had but forty million; that in an industrial plant with ten thousand employees, the relationship between the worker and the manager is still as neighborly and uncomplex as in a factory of 1840, with five employees; that the relationships between father and son, between husband and wife, are precisely the same in an apartment in a thirty-story palace today, with three motor cars awaiting the family below and five books on the library shelves and a divorce imminent in the family next week, as were those relationships in a rose-veiled five-room cottage in 1880. . . ."

Back home, as Mark Schorer said, dudgeon was high after this address.

Lewis had never feared to state—often to overstate—his case, and he would not stop now, at the pinnacle of success. Nor had the establishment feared to take him on. In *Elmer Gantry*, *Time* said, Lewis had made "another large roundup of grunting, whining, roaring, mewing, driveling, snouting creatures," whom he could "beat, goad, tweak, tail-twist, eye-jab, belly-thwack, spatter with sty-filth and consign to perdition." But the most telling attack on Lewis came from Walter Lippmann, who was so upset by Harcourt Brace's ballyhoo for *Elmer Gantry* that he broke off his relationship with the publisher. In *Men of Destiny*, Lippmann wrote off Lewis as puerile, shallow, overrated, propagandistic, and a greater bigot than the characters in his novels. The big question, Lippmann concluded, was whether Lewis would reach maturity or remain arrested in adolescent rebellion.

Lippmann's attack on Lewis typified the hostility among literary men during the twenties. Though Lewis made generous references to Dreiser and other fellow authors in his Nobel and other addresses, he attacked them in personal talk and correspondence. Solidarity was almost wholly lacking within the American literary firmament. The writers were isolated and, in part because they were isolated, they were vulnerable to the very forces they caricatured in their writings—the censors, the puritans, the bluestockings. And, typically, fiction writers scorned politics except for occasional causes.

John Dos Passos brilliantly limned persons in their economic struggles and class positions, and in his middle years he took a militant role in left-wing causes, but he did little to explore the implications of his graphic writings for class struggle or political action. There was little on politics in his first great success, *Manhattan Transfer*. "The book," Granville Hicks wrote, "is directed against a way of life, not a political or economic system—against greed and conformity and pretentiousness." It was said later that Dos Passos had omitted only the external class struggle and that within his characters the class struggle was waged constantly, but this inclusion still left his characters with crises of individual morality rather than the catharsis of collective communication and political action.

Dos Passos's views flowed far more from Whitman and Veblen than from Marx, as he admitted. Whitman's faith in the capacities of individual man and Veblen's faith in the value of workmanship seemed to stay with Dos Passos throughout his life. Yet, as with Jefferson's individualism, this faith could co-exist with a variety of diverse social attitudes and political strategies. Dos Passos was the first major American writer, according to Jack Diggins, "to develop a purposely fragmented narrative style in order to convey the frantic tone and mechanical temper of modern technological society." He hated establishments, left and right, and establishment leaders like Woodrow Wilson. In *The 42nd Parallel,* the first volume of his trilogy *U.S.A.,* he began to develop his master portrait of Americans caught in the rhythms, machinery, organizations, and structures of the Machine Age. But there seemed no way out, whether through individualism or communism—both of which Dos Passos simultaneously embraced.

Many other novelists in the twenties were sensitive to class differences and social prejudice but silent about possible political implications. Like Edith Wharton earlier, F. Scott Fitzgerald had a love-hate attitude toward the world of the rich and established. "Let me tell you about the very rich," he wrote in his story "The Rich Boy" in 1926. "They are different from you and me. They possess and enjoy early, and it does something to them, makes them soft where we are hard, and cynical where we are trustful, in a way that, unless you were born rich, it is very difficult to understand. They think, deep in their hearts, that they are better than we are because we had to discover the compensations and refuges of life for ourselves. Even when they enter deep into our world or sink below us, they still think that they are better than we are. They are different. . . ."

The rich for Fitzgerald were nevertheless careless and even brutal, as well as vacuous and vulgar: Daisy's voice "full of money," Gatsby reverently displaying his fancy imported shirts, the "diamond as big as the Ritz," Gatsby's weekend entertainments full of champagne and yacht trips and Rolls-Royces, the eight servants and "extra gardener" required on Mondays to clean up his estate after the ravages of the night before. Still, this was nothing to campaign against. Life was largely a personal affair. The question of politics hardly existed for even the class-conscious writers; as Fitzgerald himself said, it was "characteristic of the Jazz Age that it had no interest in politics at all." A character in *The Beautiful and Damned* tried to imagine himself in Congress "rooting around in the litter of that incredible pigsty," associating with mediocre men spouting puerile ideas and copybook ambitions in "the lustreless and unromantic heaven of a government by the people. . . ."

Government by the people. At the very least, this meant a government by majority rule that respected personal liberties, due process, the rights of unpopular minorities and individuals. In August 1927, at the height of the Gay Twenties, there occurred an event that shook people's faith in American justice. This was the execution of Nicola Sacco and Bartolomeo Vanzetti, Italian aliens, draft-registration evaders, and admitted anarchists, who had been convicted of murder after a trial that violated fundamental tenets of procedural and substantive justice. Challenged by the liberal and labor press (though not at first by the communists), out-argued by Felix

Frankfurter, who presented the case against the government in the *Atlantic,* deplored even by Walter Lippmann in the *World,* the government of the Commonwealth of Massachusetts, with the backing of a governor's advisory committee headed by President Lowell of Harvard, moved inexorably to the final solution. Before and after the execution, bombs exploded in foreign capitals, demonstrators marched on the American embassy, workers rioted. Dos Passos, Edna St. Vincent Millay, and other writers were jailed for demonstrating in Boston.

So the American conservative establishment, even at its most manifestly callous, appeared as complacent in ideology and as effective in action as it was secure against attacks from the left. Dos Passos wrote:

"they are stronger   they are rich   they hire and fire the politicians the newspapereditors the old judges the small men with reputations the collegepresidents the wardheelers (listen. . . . America will not forget her betrayers). . . .

all right we are two nations"

CHAPTER 16

The Vacant Workshop

L ATE in the 1920s, as the Soviets' first Five-Year Plan was getting under way, Russian fourteen-year-olds were given a school text called *New Russia's Primer*. While the little volume focused on the glories of the plan, its author, a young Soviet engineer named M. Ilin, had America very much on his mind. "America has many large factories, many more than we have," he wrote. There factories turned out four automobiles a minute; there a million tractors worked in the fields.

"The Americans are proud of their machines, of their factories. But how do these factories work? According to some general plan, do you suppose? No, they work without a general plan." And, with clever illustrations, the author offered the parable of Mr. Fox, the capitalist.

"Mr. Fox acquires money—one million dollars. But money must not remain idle." Mr. Fox consulted newspapers, friends, agents. "At last a business is found. Hats! That is what one should make. Hats sell; men get rich." Mr. Fox promptly builds a hat factory.

"The same idea occurs at the same time to Mr. Box, and Mr. Crox, and Mr. Nox. And they all begin to build hat factories simultaneously." Soon shops are bursting with hats. But the factories continue to work at full speed.

"And here something happens that neither Mr. Fox, nor Mr. Box, nor Mr. Nox, nor Mr. Crox anticipated. The public stops buying hats." Fox et al. cut prices, slash wages, close their factories. Thousands of workers are idle, new machines grow rusty, factory buildings are sold. Then a year or two passes, the hats wear out, people return to the shops, hat prices go up.

"And now, not Mr. Fox, but a certain Mr. Doodle, thinks of a profitable business"—hats, of course. "The same idea also enters the heads of other wise and business-like people—Mr. Boodle, Mr. Foodle, and Mr. Noodle. And the old story begins over again.

"The experience with hats is repeated with shoes, with sugar, with pig iron, with coal, with kerosene. Factories are blown up like soap bubbles and burst. One would think people had lost their minds."

This picture of American capitalism, drawn at the height of Soviet euphoria over planning and before sinister aspects of Soviet leadership be-

539

came evident, was not wholly a caricature of the American economy in the
1920s. The Florida land boom was not all that different from Comrade
Ilin's hat story. In the early twenties the scrublands and everglades of the
"Friendly State" lay open for draining and development, thanks to better
roads and railroads, a benevolent climate, and the testimonials of William
Jennings Bryan, who made his home there, the Ringling circus brothers,
Roger W. Babson, the stock market forecaster, and a host of promoters,
speculators, and developers. Inflamed by get-rich-quick stories pouring
out of Florida, thousands of the gullible bought "prime beachfront property" in towns with such beguiling names as Boca Raton, Coral Gables,
Hollywood-by-the-Sea. Never mind that they bought options from a blueprint and did not trouble to look at their land, which might be part of a
pestiferous swamp or at the bottom of a lake.

The speculative fever and the enticing stories fed on each other. There
were tales—some even true—about the poor woman who had bought a
piece of land near Miami in 1896 for $25 and sold it in 1925 for $150,000,
about the New York lawyer who turned down $240,000 for a strip along
Palm Beach, finally accepted $800,000 in 1923, only to see the strip broken
into building lots and sold for a total of $1.5 million, with the value rising
later by another $2 million or so at the height of the boom.

Then, in a single day, the bubble burst. A hurricane ripped through
southern Florida, smashing buildings, killing several hundred persons,
shredding the illusions of the survivors. Even without the storm, the land
boom would soon have collapsed. It had been a pyramid game, with each
speculator buying not property but a promise, a piece of paper, with which
to entice another buyer. Nine buyers out of ten, it was estimated, purchased their options with only one purpose—to resell.

Some of the get-rich-quick schemes were bogus from the start. Charles
Ponzi of Boston, a convicted felon, gulled people into giving him more
than $15 million on the claim that he could make vast profits through deft
manipulation of foreign exchange rates. In fact, he used the money of later
investors to pay off the earlier ones—a classic pyramid scheme. Ponzi
seems to have deluded even himself. When he was finally arrested for mail
fraud, it was discovered that he had stolen very little for himself; most of
the millions he netted had quite unintentionally trickled through his
fingers to the investors in his "business."

Speculative fever spread across the nation in the late twenties and
peaked in the "Great Bull Market." The myth developed that farmers and
window washers and maids entered the market in droves, but they did this
more as spectators than participants. The number of actual players was
probably less than 1 percent of a population of 120 million; as in the past,

speculation remained almost exclusively the preserve of the financial elite. But there was an ominous change in who among the elite were playing. Relatively few industrialists and businessmen had participated in past booms, but now much of the money pouring into the stock market came from the capital reserves of manufacturing corporations. With returns from stock speculation exceeding 12 percent through 1928 and early 1929, how could a corporation head resist such alluring profits? When General Motors bought out the plants of the seven Fisher brothers, the automotive pioneers transferred their fortune to Wall Street and became full-time speculators. This industrial money might otherwise have gone into dividends, wage hikes, or capital improvement.

Indeed, the economic leadership of the country seemed to sponsor a market surge that in earlier days would have been discouraged by the likes of Andrew Mellon. Even the former high priests of fiscal conservatism, the directors of the House of Morgan, formed their own investment trust as stock prices skyrocketed. Columnist Arthur Brisbane, himself heavily involved in speculation, wrote glowing accounts of stock prospects for the Hearst chain. President Coolidge opined that Wall Street was "absolutely sound" and that stocks remained "cheap at current prices." The Democrats chose the market operator John J. Raskob as their National Committee chairman.

The bull market pounded through 1928 and thundered into 1929. Trading on the New York Stock Exchange rose from 3.8 million shares a day to more than 6.6 million during 1928. Brokers' loans—a measure of the activity of persons buying stock "on margin," putting up only part of the purchase price—grew from around a billion dollars in the early 1920s to $5.7 billion in 1928, even as interest rates on them doubled. Few found it worth remarking that brokers' loans had reached a total larger than the amount of actual currency circulating in the country. Herbert Hoover, who had entered the White House with vague intentions of trying to curb the boom, quietly abandoned his effort in the face of opposition from banking and business leaders.

In the summer of 1929, the speculative fever turned into a frenzy. Every market indicator shot up to unprecedented heights. Time and again the ticker in the New York Exchange fell an hour or more behind. Then, at the beginning of September, the upward surge suddenly halted. It was mysterious; there seemed to be no reason. For more than a month prices hovered shakily, as speculators debated whether to cut and run, or to wait in the hope that the boom would pick up again. Slowly, in the Wall Street psychology that had replaced economics and politics, the market edged downward as one investor after another sold out.

Life in the Depression

The stock market debacle of fall 1929 came not in one dramatic crash but in a series of sickening collapses and cruelly delusive rallies. The stock market broke early in September, recovered strongly, then weakened erratically over the next weeks. This period of uncertainty ended with sudden panic on Thursday, October 24—"Black Thursday." Almost 13 million shares passed over the Wall Street counter that day, often at fractions of their previous prices. The forces building up the market earlier in the decade now went into reverse, destroying stock values at a geometric rate. The need to meet margin calls forced more and more speculators to sell at a loss, which fed the rising panic.

At noon of that day, word spread that Charles E. Mitchell, Thomas W. Lamont, and several other banking czars were meeting at the 23 Wall Street offices of J. P. Morgan and Company. This was immensely reassuring, for the elder Morgan, who had died in 1913, was reputed to have averted the panic of 1907. His son was in Europe, but Lamont was Morgan's senior partner. There "has been a little distress selling on the Stock Exchange," Lamont told reporters, "due to a technical condition of the market." Prices already were firming. Then Richard Whitney—not present at the Lamont meeting—strode confidently onto the Exchange floor and moved conspicuously from post to post, buying shares. Brokers breathed easier. A sharp recovery followed.

Would the big bankers' dam hold? Prices steadied during Friday and the short Saturday session, but plunged again on Monday. Once again the bankers met, but now their mood had changed. In the face of the panic to sell, the bankers now wished to protect themselves. No optimistic statements came out of the meeting; no Whitney appeared jauntily on the Exchange floor. There was an ominous silence.

On Tuesday, October 29, the hurricane struck. It was, John Kenneth Galbraith would write, "the most devastating day in the history of the New York stock market, and it may have been the most devastating day in the history of markets. It combined all of the bad features of all of the bad days before." Under a four-column headline next day, the *New York Times* summed up the crisis in its lead story: "From every point of view, in the extent of losses sustained, in total turnover, in the number of speculators wiped out, the day was the most disastrous in Wall Street's history. Hysteria swept the country. . . ."

"The fundamental business of the country, that is production and distribution of commodities, is on a sound and prosperous basis," said President Hoover during these October days. His statement was intended mainly to reassure investors, but Hoover's emphasis on production reflected his own economic philosophy. As a "practitioner of industrial rationalization" and a prophet of enlightened industrialism, he had seen the strength of the nation in its vast and efficient manufacturing capacity, and its economic weakness in unbridled speculation. Now he was presiding over an economy in which reckless investors—stock purchasers and sellers —appeared to be dragging industry into the chasm with them.

But industry was still the fundamental strength of the nation; Hoover and the economic leadership assumed that the financial panic would pass, after a healthful cleansing, and then the economy would right itself. This is what had always happened in the past. But, to the bewilderment of Administration and business leaders, this was dramatically not happening in 1930. On the contrary, the first half of that year brought a massive drop in consumer spending that in turn closed shops and factories. The Gross National Product, the measure of all goods produced in the country, fell from $103.1 billion in 1929 to $90.4 billion in 1930, $75.8 billion in 1931, and $58 billion in 1932. Unemployment in the same years rose from 1.55 million in 1929 to 4.34 in 1930, 8.02 in 1931, 12.06 million in 1932. National income, $81 billion in 1929, shrank to $68 to $53 to $41 billion in 1932. The three years 1930–32, according to Dixon Wecter, "took a toll of eighty-five thousand business failures with liabilities of four and a half billion dollars and the suspension of five thousand banks. Nine million savings accounts were wiped out. . . ."

The nation's great industrial centers—the sinews and pride of American capitalism—were especially hard hit. By 1932, a million were jobless in New York City, 660,000 in Chicago; in Cleveland, 50 percent of the working force lacked work, in Akron 60 percent, in Toledo 80 percent. It was estimated that, during the three years after the crash, an average of 100,-000 workers were laid off every week. The huge steel furnaces were banked down; the automobile industry by 1932 was operating at one-fifth of its 1929 capacity.

Farmers were hit even harder. Agriculture had been ailing long before the crash, as prices of farm products declined steadily through the decade while maintaining a precarious parity with the fall of other price levels in the economy. But not for years had farmers faced such a cataclysm as 1930. Within a year the price of December wheat at Chicago plummeted from $1.35 to 76 cents a bushel, of July wheat from $1.37 to 61 cents. Millions of farmers plunged deeper into debt, many of them into bankruptcy. And as usual in depressions, it was the weakest, poorest people on America's farmlands—tenant farmers, migratory workers, blacks, women—who were most vulnerable.

President Hoover had been neither uncaring nor inactive in the days following the crash. He summoned to meetings the leaders of the "solid" part of the economy—top industrialists, railway and utility managers, farm spokesmen, union heads. To halt the deflationary spiral, he asked the industry leaders to agree not to cut wages or payrolls. His guests responded with optimistic statements, pep talks, and promises. Henry Ford, acting with his usual well-publicized boldness, left with Hoover a pledge to hike auto workers' pay to seven dollars a day. In the hope of expanding the supply of credit enough to offset the contraction, the President took steps toward tax reduction, increased spending on public works, and a Federal Reserve cut in the discount rate.

Hoover also tackled the psychological aspect of the problem. So earnestly did he believe in the importance of confidence, according to David Burner, that he "attended a World Series game in Philadelphia simply to make an example of his own serenity." And he made a point of using the term "depression" because he feared people would be frightened by such blunt words as "panic" or "crisis."

When the stock market recovered in the winter of 1930, it appeared that Hoover's policies might be working. "I am convinced we have passed the worst and with continued effort we shall rapidly recover," said the President. Then the market slide resumed, week after week, month after month. Skepticism rose. Hoover's tax reductions, it was noted, grossly favored the rich. The industrialists forgot the promises they had made in Washington when they returned to their bleak factory towns. Congress resisted measures that might unbalance the federal budget.

Increasingly, people saw an economic crisis and called it that. And they were less and less concerned about Hoover's serenity, which appeared intact, than about his wisdom and compassion.

*   *   *

In later years, memories of the Great Depression would take their shape from photographs of long breadlines, people selling apples, men living in shacks called Hoovervilles, emaciated women and children, the jobless clustering by the hundreds in front of factory gates. But perhaps the most remarkable aspect of the depression at the time was its invisibility. Walking through an American city, Frederick L. Allen wrote, you "might notice that a great many shops were untenanted, with dusty plate-glass windows and signs indicating that they were ready to lease; that few factory chimneys were smoking; that the streets were not so crowded with trucks as in earlier years, that there was no uproar of riveters to assail the ears, that beggars and panhandlers were on the sidewalks in unprecedented numbers (in the Park Avenue district of New York a man might be asked for money four or five times in a ten-block walk). Traveling by railroad, you might notice that the trains were shorter, the Pullman cars fewer—and that fewer freight trains were on the line. Traveling overnight, you might find only two or three other passengers in your sleeping car." Otherwise things might seem to be going on much as usual.

Nor were people as militant and activist as later generations might have expected. The desperate men lined up quietly in the soup lines. People were evicted from their homes or farms and resignedly went off somewhere. The unemployed demonstrated, but only infrequently. Some workers struck, but no more than before; the number of strikes remained about the same during the depression, and union membership even declined. Workers gathered before factory gates not to take over the plant, or to burn it down, but in hope of a job. The dominant emotion was not anger or hostility but resignation or fear. Instead of rising up, people hunkered down. People in Cincinnati wore buttons: "I won't talk depression." During the depression, billboards appeared reading, "Wasn't the Depression Terrible?"

This social passivity rested on the profoundest of psychological forces that swept pervasively through the population—loss of security and lack of self-esteem. A wiped-out bank account did not send people out onto the streets or even to the bank; it was too devastating. Losing a job, seeking a job, being denied a job—these meant constant blows to self-esteem. "Anonymous" wrote for *Outlook* magazine about how "I Lost My Job." In the spring of 1929, he had left a $65-a-week staff job with a New York newspaper to become a public relations man for a big eastern railroad at three times that pay. A year later the public relations department was wiped out in a merger.

What Anonymous then endured would come to be familiar to millions of families: dispossession from his apartment for failure to pay the rent—moving with his wife and baby into the home of her family, to the latter's intense annoyance—getting ample free advice from the family to sell brushes or silk stockings—studying the Help Wanted columns and starting the dolorous rounds of nonemployment—borrowing on insurance policies—earning a few dollars by selling Christmas cards, mainly to kind friends—losing his final cash reserve in the closing of the Bank of the United States—earning $30 on jury duty—watching his job application blank torn up by a clerk when he had the temerity to inquire about the job—contem-

plating suicide but lacking the courage—having to move his father from
a home into a "poorhouse"—appealing for help to relatives he hardly
knew on his mother's side of the family—receiving $10 from them—taking
a furnished room with wife and baby—left with $12 at the time of writing
his article.

Some took the drastic way out that Anonymous flirted with. Reports of
bankrupted millionaires jumping out of skyscraper windows after the crash
became part of the legend of the Great Crash. The suicide rate was relatively low in late 1929, but it did rise during the next three years. But it
was not brokers but unemployed workers who were more likely to contemplate or threaten suicide, like the former Youngstown steel operative who,
begging for a job in 1932, said, "If you can't do something for me, I'm
going to kill myself."

As usual, women were highly vulnerable to economic threat, whether as
wives or workers or both. Marriage, divorce, and birth rates all fell sharply
in the early 1930s. It was often too expensive to get a divorce or to have
children. There was evidently a decline in sexual relations owing to fear
of pregnancy, psychological demoralization following loss of a job, and
women fatigued by having to work both outside and inside the home.
Married women were tempting targets for legislators and organizations.
Of 1,500 school systems contacted in 1930–31, over three-quarters would
not hire married women and almost two-thirds dismissed women teachers
if they were married. Although the unemployment rate for women was 4.7
percent in 1930 compared to 7.1 percent for men, this was partly because
many women held low-income jobs for which men could not or would not
compete.

And as usual, blacks were most vulnerable of all. They had little seniority
and only a weak, semiskilled status at best. Working mainly in service and
unskilled industries, they were the classic "last hired, first fired." When
skilled white workers lost their jobs, they often slid into the dirtier, more
demeaning jobs, displacing blacks. A social worker in Atlanta noted that
white men "have taken over such positions as elevator operators, tradesmen, teamsters, expressmen, bill posting, city sanitary wagon drivers
. . . stewards, cooks, waiters and bell boys in hotels, hospital attendants,
mechanics at filling stations, delivery boys from drug stores" and even
chauffeurs and maids. Sometimes whites forced blacks out of jobs through
intimidation, sometimes through force. In the southwestern division of the
Illinois Central, black firemen were lured from their cabs with flares and
then shot down.

The desperate jobless, blighted women, intimidated blacks—these and
millions of other fearful, poverty-stricken Americans might have formed a

mighty army of the wretched, a coalition of the deprived. But misery did not seem to like company. The depression exacerbated tensions among the wretched of the earth as blacks and whites fought for jobs, women lost jobs because their husbands had them, and jobless workers competed to be first in line at the employment office.

In his textbook for Soviet schoolchildren M. Ilin had described how, in a country "boasting millions of machines, storerooms are bursting with goods; corn is burned in place of coal; milk is poured into the river." Ilin had quoted stories from the 1920–21 recession. Already, as he wrote, he was hearing reports of a new depression, new spilling of milk.

"What does this mean?" he asked. "Who profits by it?

"It is profitable to the Foxes and the Boxes. Mr. Fox burns a few train-loads of grain in order to raise the price of corn. Mr. Box gives orders to spill tens of thousands of bottles of milk into the river in order that milk may not be sold too cheaply. And in the mean time school physicians in New York report that one out of every four children in the city is under-nourished." The fact that farmers, not capitalists, were destroying grain and milk might not have daunted Mr. Ilin; these were kulaks, and kulaks too were capitalists.

THE CRISIS OF IDEAS

Americans entered the decade of the thirties with their economy half paralyzed, their family and individual lives impoverished, their hopes and expectations blighted. With the poet Carl Sandburg they might ask, "Where to? What next?" Their only hope lay in thinking their way out of the crisis, and acting on the basis of that thought. But this was an intellectual capacity that leaders of established wisdom found utterly lacking in the people as a whole. The Enlightenment idea, Lippmann had written in *Public Opinion* ten years before, that assumed humankind had direct experience and understanding of the complex world around it, was false for a mass society. People were governed by stereotypes, prejudice, propaganda. A few years later, in *The Phantom Public*, Lippmann had taken an even stronger position. "The public will arrive in the middle of the third act and will leave before the last curtain, having stayed just long enough perhaps to decide who is the hero and who the villain of the piece."

The best hope, Lippmann believed, lay with the experts, armed with the latest inside information—experts who could rise above narrowness and bias. Who in times of crisis could better assume that role than the experienced insiders who had actually run American industry and finance, who could now tell what was wrong and put the economy back on track?

Innovators and enterprisers, they would not be mired in the failed ideas of the past.

Surely the big industrialists in particular would be a fount of fresh wisdom during the crisis—and their potent propaganda and political arm, the National Association of Manufacturers, providentially happened to be in annual session assembled when Wall Street was experiencing one of its first panics in the fall of 1929. Confronting this "financial" crisis caused by upstart speculators, the NAM stuck to its ancient wisdom about economics and politics. The test would come as the depression deepened and it became clear that the nation was caught in a general industrial and business crisis and not merely a Wall Street dip.

But the citadel of NAM conservatism remained unpenetrated. A few weeks after the market crash, the NAM president, John E. Edgerton, congratulated Hoover on his conference of business leaders and assured the President that "complete confidence will very soon be restored, if, as you advised, everybody goes to work and quits talking about the securities of our economic future, and, if there are no attempts made among the people to capitalize for personal or group advantage a situation which lends itself so readily to publicity." Evidently the NAM shared Lippmann's doubts about the competence of the people, though perhaps for different reasons.

A year later, in the face of sharply mounting unemployment, Edgerton was holding his ideological fort. The most important cause of poverty, he said, lay in the failings of the unemployed themselves. Poverty "results not alone from involuntary unemployment, but more often from voluntary unemployment, thriftlessness, sin in various forms, disease, and other misfortunes." Fred W. Sargent, railroad president and director of the Chamber of Commerce, gave his answer: "We should go back to the policies that have thus far made us great; to stop petitions for public improvement far beyond our means to afford; to realize that we cannot solve our problems of governmental finance by easy expedients, and to admit that nothing can take the place of collective thrift, self-denial and intelligent citizen participation in government."

Citizen participation in government? Were the leaders of industry urging the mass public to go into politics to protect its own interests? Only if it was *intelligent* participation—that is, not harmful to property and social stability. Noting that "there are already formulated and in process a variety of legislative proposals on public unemployment insurance, old age pensions, and similar measures for the consideration of the Legislatures which are to meet in 1931," Edgerton warned that all such proposals were intended "in the name of expediency and social progress to shift individual responsibility to the already overburdened shoulders of government and industry and thereby take us a long step further towards the Socialistic goal, the abolition of private property."

Was there no role, then, for government in the crisis? Yes, there was a role—to fight crime. This was government's greatest responsibility; there was no need, Edgerton said, "for it to become more concerned with or to look for other tasks." Indeed, a sincere and successful attack on crime would promptly end the depression itself! "Driving crime from its appalling entrenchments in this land of boasted civilization" would itself "mean food to the hungry, clothes for the naked, jobs for the unemployed, peace in industry, and security to all."

At this point—when industry leaders were proposing to solve the great depression through crime-fighting—this leadership was clearly losing touch with economic reality. But the NAM did not speak for all or even most of industry—there were enlightened business leaders, and the most powerful and convinced of these was sitting in the White House—the "Great Engineer," former Secretary of Commerce, now President, Herbert Hoover.

Hoover saw his presidency as an exercise in moderate, rational government. "Our program," he said later, "was one of deliberate purpose to do everything possible to uphold general confidence which lies at the root of maintained initiative and enterprise; to check monetary, security, and commodity panics in our exchanges; . . . to accelerate construction work so as to absorb as many employees as possible from industries hit by decreased demand; to hold up the level of wages by voluntary agreement and thus maintain the living standards of the vast majority who remain in employment; to avoid accelerating the depression by the hardship and disarrangement of strikes and lockouts; and by upholding consuming power of the wage earners to in turn support agriculture."

To the extent that he could deal with problems in an orderly, temperate manner, Hoover was reasonably successful with some of these policies. His troubles arose whenever the compelling needs of the time required him to move toward, or away from, ideas on which he was inflexible. Thus he had an overpowering faith in voluntary cooperation, local initiative, efforts by the Red Cross and charities, and if necessary governmental action by the states and localities—a faith he simply would not give up many months after it was clear that voluntarism of these sorts could not possibly break the grip of the depression. He maintained a zealous opposition to direct federal relief to the poor and the jobless because, he said, it would rob them of their character and initiative, and he stuck to this position long after no alternative to the "dole," as Hoover preferred to call it, seemed feasible.

If Hoover had shared Andrew Mellon's conservative ideology, he might have stuck to orthodox finance, rigorous economy, and pro-business policies until the economy, purged of its waste and inefficiency, could return to rigorous capitalistic rules and norms. That was Mellon's strategy; the Treasury Secretary, Hoover would remember, "had only one formula: 'Liquidate labor, liquidate stocks, liquidate the farmers, liquidate real estate. . . . purge the rottenness out of the system.' " But Hoover was too much the moderate, the liberal Republican, the critic of big finance to do this, and hence he was unable to embrace the kind of forthright alternative that a stronger leader might have followed in similar circumstances.

Hoover, as an engineer, had very definite views on specific policies. He had strong moral beliefs about such things as wastefulness, indolence, governmental paternalism. But he possessed no general philosophy—no moral code—that linked broad principles to operating strategies, and these in turn to social and economic programs and specific policies. Hence he often seemed lost, even bewildered, desperate over the failure of his policies to turn the tide, yet too frozen in his pieties to be able to execute a major shift in strategy. Hence, too, he kept searching for the origins or causes of the depression—a search economists would be conducting for another half century at least—and changing his mind as to whether the main source was irresponsible financial policies at home, or faulty economic actions in Europe, or big business, or some failure in the American people.

Nothing tested Herbert Hoover's policy consistency and economic principle more sharply than the tariff issue, and here he simply failed. Having pledged in the 1928 campaign that he would aid farmers by seeking higher duties on agricultural imports, he called a special session of Congress a few weeks after his Inaugural for the "selective" revision of the tariff. He might have predicted that he could not control a Congress that opened the Pandora's box of tariff revision, and, sure enough, he lost his legislative leadership as senators and representatives went in for an orgy of tariff-raising. The resulting Smoot-Hawley bill was the highest tariff rise in history.

Would the President sign it? He had long preached economic internationalism. He was angered by some of the high schedules in the measure. Internationalist business and political leaders in both parties urged him to veto it. More than 1,000 economists denounced the bill. Hoover signed it because he liked some of its provisions, because it was politically expedient, because other nations were adopting nationalistic policies. In doing so, Herbert Hoover aligned himself with the Republican Old Guard more clearly and controversially than by any other act of his Administration.

As he reached his midterm, the President did begin to change some of his positions. In particular, he concluded that a greater federal recovery effort was necessary. In December 1930 he asked Congress for an additional $100 to $150 million for public works. In January 1932 he obtained from Congress a bill to establish the Reconstruction Finance Corporation, empowered to provide emergency financing to banks, railroads, life insurance companies, and other institutions, to the maximum extent of $2 billion. But Hoover's position on the tariff, along with his opposition to direct federal relief to *persons,* sharpened the popular image of a rigid, doctrinaire President.

                            *   *   *

Hoover and the Republican leadership had a powerful political and moral argument for sticking to their convictions—they had won a mandate in 1928, they were carrying out that mandate, and they needed four years to make it work. They could boast, moreover, that they had won a renewed vote of confidence in the 1930 midterm election, gaining over 54 percent of the popular major-party vote for House seats—down only 3.3 percent from that of 1928—and retaining control of the Senate, if only by a paper-thin majority. It was not, after all, the job of the party in power to attack its own program. Let the opposition do that.

But where was the opposition? The most striking political fact of the depression era was not the failure of the Republican government—the GOP was simply going down in the face of the economic storm, its doctrinal pennant still waving bravely—but the feebleness, the cowardice, indeed the near-invisibility of the opposition.

Labor was the main case in point. The days of the militant Knights of Labor and IWW appeared to be over. The dominant national organization of trade unionists, the American Federation of Labor, entered the depression clinging strongly to its old doctrine of "voluntarism"—the concept of organized labor as a private enterprise to be promoted through bread-and-butter unionism, limited government, and opportunistic political tactics of "aiding labor's friends and opposing labor's enemies." With the depression, though, "massive unemployment, declining wage rates, falling membership, and hopeless strikes demonstrated that history had outsped Gompers," in Irving Bernstein's summary. How long could the AFL stick to Gompersism? The answer came in a series of annual AFL conventions as the delegates discussed the issue of unemployment insurance, which was becoming the litmus test for voluntarism.

Gompers had denounced unemployment insurance as "socialism." To craft unions with their own insurance programs, the proposal did seem like unfair competition from government. Voluntarism won overwhelmingly at the 1930 AFL convention. Opponents of unemployment insurance called it a "dole." Should workers' liberty be sacrificed, demanded one delegate, to afford workers a little "unemployment relief under government supervision and control"? The next year, in the face of rising joblessness, the convention again debated the issue. More individual unions were sending delegates to the national convention endorsing unemployment insurance, but voluntarism still won the voice vote. The time had not yet arrived for it, said AFL president William Green. Finally, in the 1932 session—a few weeks *after* the presidential election—the AFL came out for insurance, both state and federal.

Over toward the left, the Socialist Party made its first gains in almost a decade, doubling its membership in just three years, raising money on a national scale, and organizing a speaker's bureau to spread the message of radical reform. Still, the movement remained puny; there were scarcely more than 16,000 members in 1932. Moreover, the party had changed drastically since the days of Eugene Debs, loosening its ties with labor and becoming largely an organization of college-educated, middle-class reformers. The old leadership of the Socialists faced repeated challenges from the new recruits, who tended to be younger, more radical, and impatient with a doctrinaire approach to reform. Socialist successes in electing a few local officials, and Norman Thomas's impressive showing in his two New York mayoralty races, stemmed more from the individual reputations of the candidates than from any ground swell of support for socialism in itself.

The most impatient reformers abandoned socialism altogether. Joining the Socialist Party, John Dos Passos said, "would have just about the same effect on anybody as drinking a bottle of near-beer." The moment of the Communist Party would seem to have come. Yet the American communists failed altogether to engage—either intellectually or politically—with the crisis gripping the United States. Instead, William Z. Foster and his followers set their party line by the dictates of factional fights in Moscow, paying more attention to purging their ranks of "Trotskyites" and "Bukharinites" than to organizing the unemployed millions in the United States. Although Dos Passos urged the Communist Party to "Marxianize the American tradition" or else "Americanize Marx," no home-grown Lenin arose with a program equivalent to the "Peace, Land, and Bread" of the Russian Revolution. The American workers were interested in immediate solutions, not in eventual revolutions, and here the communists, like the socialists, failed them.

In a two-party democracy, the burden of opposing the "ins" lies ultimately on the main opposition party. Shut out from the White House for more than a decade, the Democratic party in the early 1930s seemed to have an unparalleled opportunity to put the depression squarely on the backs of the Republicans. But thoughtful Americans expected more from the Democracy than blind opposition, and here the Democrats ran into trouble. They were too fundamentally divided to offer a coherent and credible opposition to the GOP.

The hand of the past rested heavily on the Democratic party. Al Smith, the 1928 candidate, appeared to be moving to the right as Franklin D. Roosevelt, his dynamic successor in the governor's chair in Albany, came up with liberal, or at least fresh, ideas and policies. John W. Davis, the Democrats' 1924 candidate, attacked Hoover in 1931 for "following the road to socialism at a rate never before equaled in time of peace." Even James Cox, the Wilsonian 1920 candidate, demanded a balanced budget and a sales tax, in a speech at the Democracy's Jackson and Jefferson Day dinners of 1932. These were the *Northern* Democrats; much of the Southern leadership of the Democratic party lay to the right of the Republicans on economic policy and far to the right of it on racial issues.

In Congress the Democracy claimed some conspicuous liberals, such as Senators Robert Wagner of New York, Thomas Walsh of Montana, and Burton Wheeler of Montana, but the party as a whole, in Otis Graham's summary, "had no ideological center. Every four years its national nominating convention briefly encompassed diverse elements—Jeffersonian states' righters, liberal intellectuals and planners, urban bosses, Wilsonian idealists, midwestern soft money men, conservative labor leaders, Wall Street bankers. Party structure was appropriate to this doctrinal babel of tongues." The party had an impoverished headquarters in New York, shared its "fund-raising duties and its powerlessness" with the Senate and House campaign committees, and tried to preside over forty-eight state parties, countless city and county organizations, and a few thousand party "leaders" going their separate ways.

Could a party like this put up an effective opposition? A battle over taxes left the issue in doubt. Desperately seeking a balanced budget in a time of shrinking revenue, Hoover proposed a sales tax as part of the 1932 revenue legislation. It was a classic issue on which the Democrats could pose as the "party of the people," except that most of the Democratic leadership in Congress, as well as Smith, Cox, Davis, Raskob, and Bernard Baruch, backed the bill. Opposition fell into the hands of Fiorello La Guardia, a fiery maverick Republican from Manhattan, and rank-and-file Democratic leaders. Castigating the bill as "grinding the face of the poor," La Guardia and his Democratic allies aroused a House coalition that defeated the measure. But the fractured Democracy had denied itself a party victory.

If the party could not oppose, could it govern? Could it indeed even choose a winning candidate for the presidency? The two-thirds requirement for nomination encouraged candidates to appeal to factions and ideas across the whole spectrum of the party from left to right. In January 1932, Roosevelt threw his hat into the ring; a few days later, Al Smith announced his availability. Several favorite sons eyed the race, hoping for a deadlock between the current and former New York governors. For a time it seemed they might have their wish. With the help of the astute James A. Farley, New York Democratic party chairman, and the prestige of his own record-breaking majority in winning reelection two years before, Roosevelt had become the Democratic front-runner. But he met a series of setbacks in the spring of 1932 when Smith won a big bloc of Tammany-ites, every delegate from Massachusetts, Rhode Island, and Connecticut, and a sizable chunk of the California delegation. Smith had become the candidate of the Democratic right. After FDR charged Hoover with neglecting the "little fellow" in favor of big business, Smith declared that he would "take my coat off" and enter the ring against any candidate for the presidency who persisted "in any demagogic appeal to the masses of the working people." At the same time, some liberal Democrats attacked FDR for embracing conservative policies.

Battered from left and right, Roosevelt straddled as many issues as he could, and this in turn strengthened attacks on him as a cynical opportunist. No one pursued this line more assiduously than Walter Lippmann, who prided himself on being a connoisseur of leadership. Charging Roosevelt with failure to offer true national leadership, Lippmann remarked, as the campaign year opened, that the "art of carrying water on both shoulders is highly developed in American politics, and Mr. Roosevelt has learned it." Roosevelt, he concluded, "is no crusader. He is no tribune of the people. He is no enemy of entrenched privilege. He is a pleasant man who, without any important qualifications for the office, would very much like to be President." Lippmann much preferred former Secretary of War Newton D. Baker to Roosevelt, but Baker too—and with Lippmann's help —had softened his old fervor for the League of Nations in order to disarm his isolationist foes.

If FDR was really just a political broker, as others besides Lippmann believed, brokerage paid off handsomely at the Democratic national convention in Chicago late in June. Apparently stalled after leading on the first three ballots, the Roosevelt forces strove desperately to keep their delegates in line while they sought the additional votes needed to reach the magical two-thirds. Joseph P. Kennedy reached William Randolph Hearst and warned him that Baker, whom Hearst detested, would gain the nomination if FDR went down. Hearst was the key to shifting the California delegation. When California was reached on the fourth roll call, William G. McAdoo stepped to the podium and announced: "California came here to nominate a President of the United States; she did not come to deadlock the Convention or to engage in another devastating contest like that of 1924." Thus the ghosts of the past hovered over the Democratic conclave as delegation after delegation broke toward Roosevelt and gave him the nomination with enthusiasm—but not with unanimity, for the embittered Smith refused to release his delegates. Then the Democrats, still divided, prepared to attack the Republican redoubt.

"ONCE I BUILT A RAILROAD, MADE IT RUN"

The imperious locomotives still thundered through town. If the express slowed down a bit coming round the bend, you could stand at the depot and look into brightly lit interiors as the Broadway Limited or the Twentieth Century Limited flashed by—actually see people reclining in their palatial diners, luxurious club cars, ornate drawing rooms. A century earlier Ralph Waldo Emerson had seen in the rails a magician's rod with the power "to evoke the sleeping energies of land and water." Railroads had become the nation's first big industry, a sinew of war, a spearhead of urban change, a transformer of the environment. Through it all, Americans had never forsaken their romance with the rails, even when gouging and monopolistic railroads had forsaken them.

Now the railroads seemed forsaken. American Locomotive had been selling six hundred of its great steam engines a year during the 1920s; in 1932 it sold one. Between 1929 and 1932, rail employees had dropped from 1.7 million to less than 1 million, freight tons carried from 1.419 billion to 679 million, dividends from $500 million to one-fifth of that. You could stand for hours at the depot and not see a train come through.

1932 was the worst year yet by far. The gross national product fell from $103.1 billion in 1929 to $58 billion in 1932. Automobile production dropped from 411,000 cars a month in the same period to 89,000; oil production sagged from a billion barrels to less than 800 million; contracts for new residential buildings shrank 86 percent; farm income fell from $6.2 billion to $2 billion. U.S. Steel was operating at 19 percent capacity. Retail sales declined, but the number of retail stores *increased*—a measure of inflated hopes and frustrated expectations.

There was no human misery index as accurate as the economic. Psychologically, middle-class people probably were hit hardest. They made up a

good part of the 273,000 families evicted during 1932. Some fought back
as best they could. They opened small businesses at home—beauty parlors, laundries, grocery stores, ice cream booths, antique shops often filled
with items from forced sales of farms. People resharpened safety razors,
bought day-old bread, rolled their own cigarettes, renewed the shoulder
straps of bras, perused chapters in cookbooks called *New Dishes from Left-
overs.* The wife of a middle-aged broker, living with her husband in a posh
New Jersey residential hotel, was within a few months of the crash working
in the hotel laundry.

Workers in heavy industry were especially hard up, except where they
had some union protection. Wages of unorganized laborers fell far more
rapidly than union workers' pay during 1931–32 and by 1933 a wage
differential of 30 percent separated the two groups. A Kentucky miner
wrote that "we have been eating wild greens" such as violet tops, wild
onions, and "forget-me-not wild lettuce." Strikes and demonstrations
were rarely very effective when so many men were competing for jobs. In
the late winter of 1932, several thousand Detroit workers, under militant
leaders, marched toward the employment office of Henry Ford's Rouge
works, crown of the Ford industrial empire. Pushing past the Dearborn
police, the marchers, waving placards and banners, encountered contin-
gents of Detroit security forces. The nature of the wild melee that followed
was never clear, but the upshot was twenty-four demonstrators killed or
wounded, a good number of police injured by bricks, stones, and clubs.

A large new class had come into being—a class of the unemployed, the
reliefers, the transients, the homeless, the vagabonds, the hoboes. Many
of the jobless, according to Caroline Bird, "simply could not bear going
home and headed for a freight train instead." They followed rumors of
jobs, often false ones. "Once footloose, it did not much matter where they
went. Hope of warm weather, word of a friend, memory of relatives perhaps never actually known, was excuse for a jaunt across the continent."
Many headed home after a spell of wandering. Home, Robert Frost had
written, was "the place where, when you have to go there, they have to take
you in." It was estimated that only 10 percent of the transients were
"professional bums."

How could local communities cope with armies of transients? Many
could not. Queried by a Senate subcommittee, some mayors reported that
they variously pushed the transients on, "[got] them out of town as soon
as possible," "flatly refused to help," helped "a little." Others responded:
"one good meal and more if they work" . . . "bunked in barracks—fed at
jail" . . . "merchants taking care of" . . . "work them in the wood yard"
. . . "let them sleep in flop houses; give a bowl of soup in the morning and

order them out of town." Tucson posted a sign on its outskirts: "Warning to Transients. Relief funds for local residents only. Transients, do not apply."

* * *

Three score and nine years earlier, Abraham Lincoln had asked whether a nation conceived in liberty and dedicated to equality could long endure. He had consecrated the nation to a continuing experiment in freedom and justice. Was the experiment over? In a new crisis, when the leadership in neither party appeared to have achieved the Emancipator's courage and resolution, many were answering, "Yes!"

In September 1932, fifty-three intellectuals and artists published an open letter that denounced the two major parties as hopelessly corrupt, repudiated the socialists as do-nothings, and announced their support for the Communist Party. The manifesto proclaimed the fatal contradictions of capitalism, the futility of socialist "reformism," the menace of fascism. It rejected "the disorder, the lunacy spawned by grabbers, advertisers, speculators, salesmen, the much-adulated, immensely stupid and irresponsible 'business men.' " It urged writers, artists, scientists, teachers, engineers, and "all honest professional workers" to support the "frankly revolutionary Communist Party" and its candidates.

One of the signatories of this letter was the literary critic Edmund Wilson, and his political odyssey epitomized the leftward movement of the intelligentsia. Like many of his comrades, he was no ivory-tower intellectual but had observed poverty firsthand in West Virginia, in Harlan County, Kentucky, and in California. The depression had convinced him of "the incurable swinishness and inertia of human nature which automatically leads to class war." He expected Roosevelt to be "largely controlled by the profit-squeezing class," just as Hoover was, and he saw the socialists as identifying themselves with the owning classes. While he had misgivings about the Communists' insistence on ideological discipline, he concluded that they alone were working impressively "to educate and organize our wage-earning classes for the defeat of the capitalist system."

And the capitalists themselves? By mid-1932, they were alternating between a foolish optimism and deep frustration and bewilderment. "If you can't think yourself into a job, work yourself into one," advised the financial seer Roger Babson. "Insist on working even without pay." "We cannot squander ourselves into prosperity," declaimed Herbert Hoover. Said Henry Ford of young vagabonds: "Why, it's the best education in the world for those boys, that traveling around! They get more experience in a few months than they would in years at school."

Behind such zany views, however, lay a hardening class attitude. A deputy to General Douglas MacArthur in May 1932 proposed to ship "leading malefactors," including "important public officials," to a sparsely inhabited Hawaiian island where they could "stew in their own filth." Two months later, MacArthur led four troops of cavalry, four companies of infantry, a mounted machine-gun squadron, and six tanks down Pennsylvania Avenue past big crowds. His troops crossed the Anacostia Bridge and attacked thousands of the "Bonus Army" veterans, their wives and children, with tear gas and bayonets, burning their encampment and killing two veterans, fatally injuring a baby, and partially blinding an eight-year-old boy. The bonus marchers, nearly two-thirds of whom had served in Europe during World War I and one-fifth of whom had been disabled, were described by an Assistant Secretary of War as "a polyglot mob of tramps and hoodlums, with a generous sprinkling of Communist agitators."

Many Americans recoiled with shame. Reporter Thomas L. Stokes wondered if this might be the end of the country as he knew it. "The United States Army turned on to American citizens—just fellows like myself, down on their luck, dispirited, hopeless. My mood was one of despair." But the American public did not know the worst. MacArthur had disobeyed Hoover's order to "use all humanity" in dispersing the veterans, yet the President did not discipline his general or even protest. The following day the White House announced to the press that "the President was pleased."

If an experiment was ending in late 1932, it was not the grand American experiment of the Framers, of Jefferson and Lincoln. It was an experiment in rule by industrialists and financiers. They had by no means been all-powerful. In case after case—as in the example of Henry Ford's political activities—they had found it impossible to convert economic power into social control. But American business held two strong cards. It could accomplish through the Republican party, and the broad coalition it represented, what it could not effect through economic means alone. And it had long been represented by a "compact majority" that united the separated institutions of government behind pro-business measures.

If the compact majority had held power, it had also to assume responsibility. But assumption of responsibility was impossible unless there was a "compact opposition" to put the failures of leadership directly on the shoulders of the Hoover Administration. As the campaign of 1932 got under way, no such compact opposition was evident. No one could quite place Franklin Roosevelt. Sometimes he almost talked socialism, sometimes he promised to balance the budget. The nation waited.

The transients waited, killing time, moving ever on, hunkering down at night in "hobo jungles," reduced to the primal wants of food and shelter. In the silence of the railroad tracks they rarely burst into song; they had little to sing about. But a plaintive ditty began to catch on:

> Once I built a railroad, made it run,—
> Made it race against time.
> Once I built a railroad, now it's done—
> Brother can you spare a dime?
>
> Once in khaki suits, gee, we looked swell
> Full of that Yankee Doodle-de-dum.
> Half a million boots went sloggin' thru Hell,
> I was the kid with the drum.
> Say don't you remember, they called me Al—
> It was Al all the time
> Say, don't you remember, I'm your Pal!
> Buddy, can you spare a dime?

Notes
Acknowledgments
Index

Notes

1. THE WAR OF LIBERATION

p. 3 [*Lincoln's trip to Gettysburg*]: Carl Sandburg, *Abraham Lincoln: The War Years* (Harcourt, Brace, 1939), vol. 2, pp. 462–63; George M. Hart, Director of the Railroad Museum of Pennsylvania, supplied technical and historical information on the type of train Lincoln rode to Gettysburg; see also Edwin P. Alexander, *Down at the Depot* (Clarkson N. Potter, 1970), pp. 58–59; William E. Barton, *Lincoln at Gettysburg* (Peter Smith, 1950), pp. 58–59. The wood most probably used to fire the engine was hardwood, and in the Gettysburg region that implies walnut or cherry, the smoke of which would be blue. See also Philip Kunhardt, *A New Birth of Freedom* (Little, Brown, 1983), pp. 68 ff.

3–4 [*Washington, November 18, 1863*]: *New York Times*, November 19, 1863, pp. 1–4; Howard K. Beale, ed., *Diary of Gideon Welles* (W. W. Norton, 1960), vol. 1, pp. 479–80; Sandburg, vol. 2, p. 461.

4–5 [*Ceremonies at Gettysburg*]: Barton, pp. 72–79; Clark E. Carr, *Lincoln at Gettysburg* (A. C. McClurg, 1906), pp. 36–56; Sandburg, vol. 2, pp. 465–68; Massachusetts Historical Society, *Edward Everett at Gettysburg* (Massachusetts Historical Society, 1963); David C. Mearns, "Unknown at This Address," in Allan Nevins, ed., *Lincoln and the Gettysburg Address* (University of Illinois Press, 1964).

5 [*Text of Everett's oration*]: Barton, pp. 211–54.

5–6 [*Text of Gettysburg Address*]: Newspaper version, in Roy P. Basler, ed., *The Collected Works of Abraham Lincoln* (Rutgers University Press, 1953), vol. 7, pp. 19–21.
[*Lincoln's delivery of Address*]: Barton, pp. 80–81; Carr, pp. 56–57, 70.

Manning the Front

6 [*Bull Run survivors in Washington*]: Margaret Leech, *Reveille in Washington* (Harper & Bros., 1941), pp. 102–6; Benjamin P. Thomas, *Abraham Lincoln* (Alfred A. Knopf, 1952), pp. 271–73.

6–7 [*Lincoln's strategic plan*]: "Memoranda of Policy Suggested by Bull Run Defeat," July 23, 27, 1861, in Basler, *op. cit.*, vol. 4, pp. 457–58, quoted at p. 457.

7 [*Southern military advantages*]: James M. McPherson, *Ordeal by Fire: The Civil War and Reconstruction* (Alfred A. Knopf, 1982), pp. 184–86.
[*"Highways of invasion" into the South*]: *ibid.*, p. 186.
[*Lincoln on his Indian War service*]: Thomas, pp. 33–34.
[*Confederate defensive strategy*]: Address to the Confederate Congress, April 29, 1861, in Dunbar Rowland, ed., *Jefferson Davis, Constitutionalist: His Letters, Papers and Speeches* (J. J. Little and Ives, 1923), vol. 5, p. 84.

8 [*Lincoln on outcome of Fredericksburg*]: quoted in McPherson, p. 306.
[*Vallandigham*]: Thomas, pp. 379–80.
[*Desertion in the Army of the Potomac*]: Bruce Catton, *Glory Road: The Bloody Route from Fredericksburg to Gettysburg* (Doubleday, 1952), pp. 111–12, 116.
[*Lincoln finds a general*]: T. Harry Williams, *Lincoln and His Generals* (Alfred A. Knopf, 1952), pp. 271–99; see also Kenneth P. Williams, *Lincoln Finds a General*, 5 vols. (Macmillan, 1949–59).

9 [*Lincoln on Grant*]: quoted in Bruce Catton, *Grant Moves South* (Little, Brown, 1960), p. 371.
[*Confederate general on Grant*]: General Richard Ewell, quoted in Robert Leckie, *The Wars of America* (Harper & Row, 1968), pp. 412–13.

9 [*Union officer on Grant*]: Catton, *Grant Moves South,* p. 420.
9–10 [*Vicksburg campaign*]: Samuel Carter III, *The Final Fortress: The Campaign for Vicksburg, 1862–1863* (St. Martin's Press, 1980), *passim;* Catton, *Grant Moves South,* pp. 405–70; Shelby Foote, *The Civil War: A Narrative* (Random House, 1963), vol. 2, pp. 323–427, 606–14; *Battles and Leaders of the Civil War* (Century, 1888), vol. 3, pp. 462–570.
9 [*Grant on the need for a decisive victory*]: quoted in Carter, p. 109.
10 [*Sherman's jubilation*]: quoted in Catton, *Grant Moves South,* p. 448.
[*Lincoln's reaction to Chancellorsville*]: quoted in Catton, *Glory Road,* p. 230.
10–11 [*Generalship of Robert E. Lee*]: Thomas L. Connelly, *The Marble Man: Robert E. Lee and His Image in American Society* (Alfred A. Knopf, 1977), pp. 4–8; Foote, vol. 1, pp. 128–31.
11 [*Confederate strategic planning and Lee's plan*]: McPherson, p. 324; Foote, vol. 2, pp. 424–33.
[*Lee's army the true objective*]: Lincoln to Hooker, telegram, June 10, 1863, in Basler, vol. 6, p. 257.
[*Battle of Gettysburg*]: Catton, *Glory Road,* pp. 289–344; see also Sandburg, *op. cit.,* vol. 2, pp. 340–47.
12 [*Lincoln's whaling metaphor*]: quoted in Sandburg, vol. 2, p. 21.
[*The discouragement of Lincoln*]: *ibid.,* vol. 2, p. 351; Beale, *op. cit.,* vol. 1, p. 371.
[*Battle of Chattanooga*]: Foote, vol. 2, pp. 685–94, 708–68; see also Bruce Catton, *Grant Takes Command* (Little, Brown, 1968), pp. 30–93.
[*The ebbing of Confederate hopes*]: Davis to General E. K. Smith, letter, July 14, 1863, in Rowland, vol. 5, p. 554.
[*Despair of Confederate veterans*]: quoted in McPherson, p. 333.
[*Mary Chesnut*]: C. Vann Woodward, ed., *Mary Chesnut's Civil War* (Yale University Press, 1981), pp. 519, 502, 501, 523.

Forging the Sword

13 [*Meeting of Lincoln and Grant*]: Catton, *Grant Takes Command, op. cit.,* pp. 124–27, Lincoln quoted at p. 125.
[*Southerners evaluate Grant*]: quoted in Woodward, *op. cit.,* p. 520.
14 [*The draft*]: Eugene C. Murdock, *One Million Men: The Civil War Draft in the North* (State Historical Society of Wisconsin, 1971), pp. 6–8, 24–25; see also, Albert B. Moore, *Conscription and Conflict in the Confederacy* (Macmillan, 1924).
[*Rich man's war*]: quoted in Murdock, p. 6.
[*New York draft riots*]: Albon P. Man, Jr., "Labor Competition and N.Y. Draft Riots, 1863," *Journal of Negro History,* vol. 36, no. 4 (October 1951); see also, Henry Steele Commager, ed., *The Blue and the Gray* (Bobbs-Merrill, 1950), vol. 2, pp. 714–19.
[*Disappointment of Northern draft*]: Allan Nevins, *The War for the Union* (Scribner's, 1960–71), vol. 2, pp. 464–66, quoted at p. 464; see also, Bruce Catton, *A Stillness at Appomattox* (Doubleday, 1954), pp. 23–31; Peter Levine, "Draft Evasion in the North During the Civil War," *Journal of American History,* vol. 67, no. 4 (March 1981), pp. 816–34.
14–15 [*Draft as stimulus to volunteering*]: Nevins, vol. 2, p. 465.
15 [*Southern opposition to draft*]: T. Harry Williams, *The History of American Wars: From 1745 to 1918* (Alfred A. Knopf, 1981), p. 224; Moore, pp. 229–304.
[*Numbers mobilized, North and South*]: Williams, p. 225; Thomas L. Livermore, *Numbers and Losses in the Civil War in America, 1861–1865* (Houghton, Mifflin, 1901).
[*Sudden mobilization and demand for war supplies*]: A. Howard Meneely, *The War Department, 1861: A Study in Mobilization and Administration* (Columbia University Press, 1928), *passim;* see also, Fred Albert Shannon, *Organization and Administration of the Union Army,* 2 vols. (Arthur H. Clark, 1928); Frederick Phisterer, *Statistical Record of the Armies of the United States* (Scribner's, 1883).
[*Records of quartermaster*]: Nevins, vol. 2, p. 473.
[*Lincoln on the national resources*]: Annual Message to Congress, December 6, 1864, in Basler, *op. cit.,* vol. 8, p. 151.
[*Improved production of shoes*]: Frank A. Taylor, "Lyman Reed Blake," in Allen Johnson, ed., *Dictionary of American Biography* (Scribner's, 1929), vol. 2, pp. 344–45; Nevins, vol. 2, pp. 492–94.
15–16 [*Southern industrial weaknesses*]: Williams, p. 228.

16 [*Centralized Confederate war effort*]: Emory M. Thomas, *The Confederate Nation, 1861–1865* (Harper & Row, 1979), pp. 206–14.
[*Rifles of the Civil War*]: Nevins, vol. 1, pp. 342–50.
[*The effect of canister or grape shot*]: term employed by McPherson, *op. cit.*, p. 192.
[*Erie Canal traffic*]: Richard B. Morris, ed., *Encyclopedia of American History* (Harper & Bros., 1961), p. 516.
[*Horses for the Army of the Potomac*]: Nevins, vol. 2, p. 475.

16–17 [*Prosperity of Northern railroads*]: ibid., pp. 501–3, 505, Tribune quoted at p. 501; see also, Thomas Weber, *The Northern Railroads in the Civil War, 1861–1865* (King's Crown Press, 1952), pp. 15, 43–93.
[*Spanning the Potomac Creek*]: George Edgar Turner, *Victory Rode the Rails* (Bobbs-Merrill, 1953), pp. 149–53, Turner quoted at p. 152, Lincoln at p. 153.

17–18 [*Emerson's plight*]: Emerson to William Emerson, January 21, 1862, in Ralph L. Rusk, ed., *The Letters of Ralph Waldo Emerson* (Columbia University Press, 1939), vol. 5, pp. 263–64.

18 [*Financing the war*]: Sidney Ratner, *American Taxation: Its History as a Social Force in Democracy* (W.W. Norton, 1942), pp. 67–110; Nevins, vol. 2, pp. 212–14; Robert P. Sharkey, "Commercial Banking," in David T. Gilchrist and W. David Lewis, eds., *Economic Change in the Civil War Era* (Eleutherian Mills—Hagley Foundation, 1965); Morris, pp. 239–40, 530.
[*Jungle of laissez-faire*]: Bray Hammond, *Banks and Politics in America* (Princeton University Press, 1957), p. 675.
[*Party and intra-party divisions on finance*]: Robert P. Sharkey, "Money, Class and Party: An Economic Study of Civil War and Reconstruction," *Johns Hopkins University Studies in Historical and Political Science* (Johns Hopkins Press, 1959), pp. 279–84.

19 [*Women's labor*]: McPherson, p. 376; see also, Cindy Aron, " 'To Barter Their Souls for Gold': Female Clerks in Federal Government Offices, 1862–1890," *Journal of American History*, vol. 67, no. 4 (March 1981), pp. 835–53.
[*Women's wages*]: Sharkey, "Money, Class and Party," p. 181; and see Emerson David Fite, *Social and Industrial Conditions in the North during the Civil War* (Frederick Ungar, 1963), p. 184.
[*Labor union response to war*]: quoted in T. V. Powderly, *Thirty Years of Labor: 1859 to 1889* (Excelsior, 1890), p. 35.
[*Myth of economic impact of Civil War*]: Charles A. Beard and Mary R. Beard, *The Rise of American Civilization* (Macmillan, 1927–42), vol. 2, pp. 53, 54.

20 [*War and financiers*]: Sharkey, "Money, Class and Party," p. 295.
[*Economic impact of war*]: Gilchrist and Lewis; Ralph Andreano, ed., *The Economic Impact of the American Civil War* (Schenkman, 1967).

The Society of the Battlefield

21 [*Soldiers' low spirits*]: John N. Moulton to his homefolk, February 1, 1863, quoted in Bell Irvin Wiley, *The Life of Billy Yank* (Bobbs-Merrill, 1951), p. 279.
[*Moulton's tiredness*]: Moulton to his homefolk, March 16, 19, 1863, quoted in *ibid.*, p. 280.
[*Enthusiasm and disappointment*]: Levi Ross to his father, February 3, 1863, quoted in *ibid.*
[*Soldiers sick of battle*]: M. N. Collins to C. H. Bell, December 22, 1862, quoted in *ibid.*, p. 279.
[*Soldiers' fear*]: John N. Moulton to his homefolk, February 1, 1863, quoted in *ibid.*, p. 279.
["*Fantom of hope*"]: M. P. Larry to his sister, December 23, 1862, quoted in *ibid.*, p. 280.
[*Incompetent leadership*]: Edward L. Edes to "Charlotte," December 28, 1862, quoted in *ibid.*, p. 279.

21–2 [*Soldiers on slaves and emancipation*]: *ibid.*, p. 281.

22 [*Participation of blacks*]: Benjamin Quarles, *The Negro in the Civil War* (Russell & Russell, 1968), quoted at p. 199; Dudley Taylor Cornish, *The Sable Arm: Negro Troops in the Union Army, 1861–1865* (W. W. Norton, 1966); Ira Berlin, ed., *Freedom, A Documentary History of Emancipation, 1861–1867: The Black Military Experience* (Cambridge University Press, 1982).
["*Heartily sick of war*"]: Edward L. Edes to "Charlotte," December 28, 1862, quoted in Wiley, p. 279.

22 [*Desire for compromise*]: Levi Ross to his father, February 3, 1863, quoted in *ibid.*, p. 280.
   [*Peace and soldiers' defeatism*]: Crittenden to his wife, February 20, 1863, quoted in Bell Irvin Wiley, *The Life of Johnny Reb* (Bobbs-Merrill, 1943), p. 131.
   [*Confederacy "done whiped"*]: John R. Hopper to his brother, September 9, 1863, quoted in *ibid.*
   [*Going home*]: William R. Stillwell to his wife, August 13, 1863, quoted in *ibid.*
22–3 [*Methods of encouraging reenlistment*]: *ibid.*, pp. 132–33.
23 [*Daily routine*]: John Beatty, *Memoirs of a Volunteer* (W. W. Norton, 1946), p. 40.
   [*Soldiers' rations and supplements*]: Nevins, *The War for the Union, op. cit.*, vol. 2, p. 479; and see Commager, *op. cit.*, vol. 1, p. 293; Wiley, *Reb*, pp. 90–107.
23–4 [*Improvisation and the influence of army life*]: Wiley, *Yank*, chs. 2, 12; Catton, *Stillness at Appomattox, op. cit.*, pp. 219–25, 241–43; F. H. Mason, *The Forty-Second Ohio Infantry* (Cobb, Andrews, 1876), pp. 78–79.
24 [*Organization and the war*]: Nevins, vol. 1, p. v, and vol. 3, chs. 7–8; Jacob D. Cox, *Military Reminiscences of the Civil War* (Scribner's, 1900), vol. 1, pp. 169–79.
24–5 [*The field of battle*]: Leander Stillwell, *The Story of a Common Soldier, 1861–1865* (Franklin Hudson, 1920), p. 44; and see Commager, vol. 2, p. 603; Wiley, *Yank*, ch. 3.
25 [*Fondness for war*]: quoted in Nevins, vol. 2, p. 347 footnote.
   [*"Nobody sees a battle"*]: quoted in Wiley, *Yank*, p. 77.
   [*Loading muskets*]: McPherson, *op. cit.*, p. 196.
   [*Disposition of dead after battle*]: quoted in T. Harry Williams, *History of American Wars, op. cit.*, p. 257.
26 [*Medical treatment for wounded*]: McPherson, p. 384.
   [*Sanitary conditions and disease*]: *ibid.*, p. 383; Wiley, *Yank*, p. 125.
26–7 [*Sanitary Commission*]: Nevins, vol. 1, pp. 283–85, 416, and vol. 3, pp. 317–19; George M. Fredrickson, *The Inner Civil War* (Harper & Row, 1965), ch. 7; *United States Sanitary Commission Documents*, 2 vols. (1866).
27 [*Patent Office into hospital*]: Eliza Woolsey Howland, "The Top of the Patent Office Became a Hospital," in Sylvia G. L. Dannett, ed., *Noble Women of the North* (Thomas Yoseloff, 1959), pp. 81–83, quoted on soldier at p. 83.
   [*Prison conditions*]: William B. Hesseltine, *Civil War Prisons* (Frederick Ungar, 1930); and see Commager, vol. 2, pp. 685–707.
28 [*"Battle Hymn" in Libby Prison*]: Laura E. Richards and Maud Howe Elliot, *Julia Ward Howe* (Houghton Mifflin, 1915), vol. 1, pp. 188–89.

"Let Us Die to Make Men Free"

28–9 [*The threat to Washington and the Shenandoah Valley campaign*]: Catton, *Stillness at Appomattox, op. cit.*, pp. 255–75, 279–88, 295–317; McPherson, *op. cit.*, p. 429.
29 [*Atlanta campaign*]: Samuel Carter III, *The Siege of Atlanta, 1864* (St. Martin's Press, 1973); B. H. Liddell Hart, *Sherman: Soldier, Realist, American* (Dodd, Mead, 1930), pp. 231–307.
   [*"Atlanta is ours"*]: quoted in Carter, p. 318.
   [*The view from Richmond*]: see Morris, *op. cit.*, p. 290.
30 [*"Loathsome wounds"*]: Woodward, *op. cit.*, p. 641.
   [*"I am First Texas"*]: quoted in *ibid.*, p. 637.
   [*Wounded soldiers in Washington, D.C.*]: Leech, *op. cit.*, pp. 325–26.
   [*Louisa May Alcott in Washington, D.C.*]: *ibid.*, pp. 222–24.
   [*"Getting worse, worse, worse"*]: letter of April 5, 1864, in Whitman, *The Correspondence*, Edwin Haviland Miller, ed. (New York University Press, 1961–69), vol. 1, p. 208.
   [*Lincoln on cooperation with successor*]: quoted in Stephen B. Oates, *With Malice Toward None* (Harper & Row, 1977), p. 395.
31 [*Lincoln as politician*]: David Donald, *Lincoln Reconsidered* (Vintage Books, 1961), pp. 57–81, 103–27; Don C. Seitz, *Lincoln: The Politician* (Coward-McCann, 1931).
   [*1862 cabinet crisis*]: Burton J. Hendrick, *Lincoln's War Cabinet* (Little, Brown, 1946), Book 5, ch. 1; James MacGregor Burns, *The Vineyard of Liberty* (Alfred A. Knopf, 1982), pp. 626–27, Lincoln on "pumpkins" quoted at p. 627.

31 [*Pressure for Seward's resignation*]: James W. White to William Butler, January 12, 1863, Chicago Historical Society.
[*Lincoln's advice to general*]: Lincoln to J. M. Schofield, May 27, 1863, Lincoln Collection, Chicago Historical Society.

31-2 [*Lincoln and foreign policy*]: Brian Jenkins, *Britain and the War for the Union* (McGill-Queen's University Press, 1974); Martin Duberman, *Charles Francis Adams, 1807–1886* (Stanford University Press, 1960), chs. 21–22; Thomas A. Bailey, *A Diplomatic History of the American People* (F. S. Crofts, 1941), ch. 22; Philip Van Doren Stern, *When the Guns Roared* (Doubleday & Co., 1965), ch. 38; Norman Graebner, "Northern Diplomacy and European Neutrality," in Armin Rappaport, ed., *Essays in American Diplomacy* (Macmillan, 1967), pp. 106–20.

32 [*Absence of loyalty to Lincoln*]: quoted in Donald, p. 62.
[*Republican critics on Lincoln*]: ibid.
[*Advisability of second term questioned*]: ibid., p. 63.
[*Adams on Davis and Lincoln*]: Charles Francis Adams to Richard Henry Dana, Jr., April 8, 1863, R. H. Dana Papers, Massachusetts Historical Society.
[*Republican radicals and Lincoln:*] T. Harry Williams, *Lincoln and the Radicals* (University of Wisconsin Press, 1941), esp. ch. 12; Donald, ch. 6; Hans L. Trefousse, *The Radical Republicans: Lincoln's Vanguard for Racial Justice* (Alfred A. Knopf, 1968); Mark E. Neely, Jr., *The Abraham Lincoln Encyclopedia* (McGraw-Hill, 1982), pp. 251–54 ("Radical Republicans").
[*Lincoln's use of patronage*]: Harry J. Carman and Reinhard H. Luthin, *Lincoln and the Patronage* (Columbia University Press, 1943), ch. 10.

33 [*1864 conventions and campaign*]: Harold M. Hyman, "Election of 1864," in Arthur M. Schlesinger, Jr., ed., *History of American Presidential Elections, 1789–1968* (Chelsea House, 1971), vol. 2, pp. 1155–78; Oates, pp. 387–99.
[*"A view to an ultimate convention"*]: Democratic platform reprinted in Schlesinger, vol. 2, pp. 1179–80, quoted at p. 1179.
[*Richmond Examiner on McClellan's platform*]: quoted in Nevins, *The War for the Union, op. cit.*, vol. 4, p. 101.
[*Copperheads in 1864*]: Wood Gray, *The Hidden Civil War* (Viking Press, 1942), ch. 8.
[*Election results, 1864*]: Schlesinger, vol. 2, p. 1244.
[*Lincoln's movement to the left*]: McPherson, p. 477.

34 [*Peace initiatives*]: Basler, *op. cit.*, vol. 7, pp. 517–18.
[*Lincoln's leadership*]: see Isaiah Berlin, *The Hedgehog and the Fox* (Simon and Schuster, 1953).
[*Sherman's march through Georgia*]: McPherson, p. 460; and see Liddell Hart, pp. 331–35.

35 [*Lee on his army*]: quoted in Douglas Southall Freeman, *R. E. Lee* (Scribner's, 1934–36), vol. 4, p. 84.
[*Surrender at Appomattox*]: ibid., vol. 4, pp. 117–48.
[*Union colonel on Lee*]: Stephen Minot Weld, *War Diary and Letters* (Massachusetts Historical Society, 1979), p. 396.
[*News of Lee's surrender reaches Washington*]: Oates, p. 422.
[*Welles on jubilation in Washington*]: Beale, *op. cit.*, vol. 2, p. 278.

36 [*The legend of Lincoln begins*]: adapted in part from Max Lerner, *Ideas for the Ice Age* (Viking Press, 1941), pp. 396–97.
[*Experiment of the Confederacy*]: E. Merton Coulter, *The Confederate States of America: 1861–1865* (Louisiana State University Press, 1950); Clement Eaton, *A History of the Southern Confederacy* (Macmillan, 1954); Hudson Strode, *Jefferson Davis* (Harcourt, Brace & World, 1955–64), vols. 1 and 2; Frank Lawrence Owsley, *State Rights in the Confederacy* (University of Chicago Press, 1925).
[*The end of an experiment*]: William B. Hesseltine, *Lincoln and the War Governors* (Alfred A. Knopf, 1948); Harold M. Hyman, *Lincoln's Reconstruction: Neither Failure of Vision Nor Vision of Failure* (Louis A. Warren Lincoln Library and Museum, 1980).

37 [*Lincoln's peroration*]: Basler, vol. 8, p. 333.
[*Lincoln's funeral trip*]: Sandburg, *op. cit.*, vol. 4, ch. 76.
[*"When lilacs last in the dooryard bloom'd"*]: Walt Whitman, *The Complete Writings of Walt Whitman* (Putnam's, 1920), vol. 2, pp. 94, 96.

2. THE RECONSTRUCTION OF SLAVERY

38 [*Euphoria at the bush spring*]: Laura S. Haviland, *A Woman's Life-Work* (Arno Press, 1969), pp. 414–15.

38–9 The leading source on reactions and perceptions of slaves and former slaves, drawn largely from oral interviews and histories made many years after the event, is George P. Rawick, ed., *The American Slave: A Composite Autobiography* (Greenwood Press, 1972), 19 vols. See also Leon F. Litwack, *Been in the Storm So Long* (Alfred A. Knopf, 1979); John W. Blassingame, *Slave Testimony* (Louisiana State University Press, 1977); Norman R. Yetman, ed., *Voices from Slavery* (Holt, Rinehart and Winston, 1970); Paul D. Escott, *Slavery Remembered* (University of North Carolina Press, 1979).

40 [*Myrta Lockett Avary on her father's talk to his slaves*]: Myrta Lockett Avary, *Dixie After the War* (Doubleday, Page, 1906), pp. 183–85; see also, James Roark, *Masters Without Slaves* (W. W. Norton, 1977), esp. part 3.

41 [*Blacks' song in Bexar County*]: quoted in Litwack, p. 217.

Bound for Freedom

41–2 [*Political situation and attitudes following Civil War*]: Michael Les Benedict, *A Compromise of Principle* (W. W. Norton, 1974), chs. 5–6; David Donald, *Charles Sumner and the Rights of Man* (Alfred A. Knopf, 1970); Kenneth M. Stampp, *The Era of Reconstruction, 1865–1877* (Alfred A. Knopf, 1975), ch. 3; Fawn M. Brodie, *Thaddeus Stevens, Scourge of the South* (W. W. Norton, 1959), chs. 18, 19.

43 [*Mantell on Republican leadership*]: Martin E. Mantell, *Johnson, Grant, and the Politics of Reconstruction* (Columbia University Press, 1973), p. 5.
[*Andrew Johnson*]: Lately Thomas, *The First President Johnson* (William Morrow, 1968); Howard K. Beale, *The Critical Year: A Study of Andrew Johnson* (Harcourt, Brace & World, 1930); Eric L. McKitrick, ed., *Andrew Johnson* (Hill and Wang, 1969).
["*Fine feathers and gewgaws*"]: quoted in Margaret Shaw Royall, *Andrew Johnson—Presidential Scapegoat* (Exposition Press, 1958), p. 51.

43–4 [*Wade-Johnson mutual assurances*]: Brodie, p. 223; David Donald, *The Politics of Reconstruction, 1863–1867* (Louisiana State University Press, 1965), p. 19.

44 [*Historians' shifting views of Reconstruction*]: Harold M. Hyman, ed., *The Radical Republicans and Reconstruction, 1861–1870* (Bobbs-Merrill, 1967), introduction, pp. xvii–lxviii; see also Mark W. Summers, *Railroads, Reconstruction, and the Gospel of Prosperity* (Princeton University Press, 1984).

45 [*Keller on new nationalized and centralized system*]: Morton Keller, *Affairs of State* (Belknap Press of Harvard University Press, 1977), pp. vii–viii, 4, 17ff.

46 ["*The only safety of the nation*"]: quoted in Beale, p. 27.
[*Amnesty and other measures, late spring 1865*]: Stampp, pp. 62–64.
[*Sumner's confidence in Johnson*]: quoted in Donald, *Sumner*, p. 222 (italics in original).

47 [*Johnson's break with radicals, other Reconstruction developments*]: Stampp, ch. 3 and *passim*; Hyman; Mantell, chs. 1–5; Howard P. Nash, Jr., *Andrew Johnson: Congress and Reconstruction* (Fairleigh Dickinson University Press, 1972); LaWanda Cox and John H. Cox, *Politics, Principle, and Prejudice* (Free Press, 1963).
[*Schurz's tour of the South*]: Stampp, pp. 73–80, quoted at p. 78.

47–8 [*Sumner's exchange with Johnson*]: quoted in Donald, *Sumner*, p. 238; see Eric McKitrick, *Andrew Johnson and Reconstruction* (University of Chicago Press, 1960), pp. 142–52.

49 [*Proposed terms of Fourteenth Amendment*]: quoted in Stampp, p. 136.
[*Sumner's oration on "The Equal Rights of All"*]: *Congressional Globe: The Debates and Proceedings of the First Session of the Thirty-ninth Congress* (F. & J. Rives, 1866), February 6, 1866, p. 687.

50 [*Clara Barton's testimony*]: quoted in Brodie, p. 244.
["*Irresponsible central directory*"]: quoted in Stampp, p. 112.
[*National Union Convention*]: Benedict, pp. 191–96.

51 [*Warning to Johnson against "swing around the circle"*]: quoted in Thomas, p. 484.
[*Johnson's campaign*]: ibid., pp. 485–99, quoted at pp. 489, 491.
[*Election results, 1866*]: Brodie, p. 288; Stampp, pp. 117–19.

A Revolutionary Experiment

52 [*Reconstruction Congress as querulous, distracted, etc.*]: Timothy Otis Howe, quoted in Benedict, *op. cit.*, p. 239.
[*Stevens on the floor*]: Brodie, *op. cit.*, pp. 309–10.
[*Marx on Johnson*]: quoted in Keller, *op. cit.*, p. 63.
53 [*Chronology of Radical Reconstruction*]: Stampp, *op. cit.*, pp. 144–48.
[*Reconstruction Act of March 2, 1867*]: *ibid.*, pp. 144–45.
[Ex parte Milligan]: 4 *Wallace* 2 (1866), quoted at p. 124.
54 [*Stevens on* Milligan]: quoted in W. R. Brock, *An American Crisis: Congress and Reconstruction* (St. Martin's Press, 1963), p. 186.
[*Brock on* Milligan]: *ibid.*
[*Measure limiting Supreme Court jurisdiction*]: Charles Warren, *The Supreme Court in United States History* (Little, Brown, 1932), vol. 2, pp. 456–64.
[*Court rulings against Southern states seeking to enjoin executive enforcement of the Reconstruction Acts*]: State of Georgia v. Stanton, 6 *Wallace* 50 (1867); State of Mississippi v. Johnson, 4 *Wallace* 475 (1867); and see Warren, vol. 2, pp. 465, 472–84, 487–88.
[*Chase's warning against "collision"*]: quoted in Keller, p. 76.
55 [*Impeachment of Andrew Johnson*]: Michael Les Benedict, *The Impeachment and Trial of Andrew Johnson* (W. W. Norton, 1973); Hans L. Trefousse, *Impeachment of a President* (University of Tennessee Press, 1975); James E. Sefton, *Andrew Johnson and the Uses of Constitutional Power* (Little, Brown, 1980); Raoul Berger, *Impeachment: The Constitutional Problems* (Harvard University Press, 1973).
[*Letter to Garfield on constitutional implications of impeachment*]: Burke A. Hinsdale to Garfield, September 30, 1867, in Mary L. Hinsdale, ed., *Garfield-Hinsdale Correspondence: Correspondence between James Abram Garfield and Burke Aaron Hinsdale* (University of Michigan Press, 1949), pp. 107–8.
[*Johnson's opposition to black suffrage in the South*]: see esp. George F. Milton, "The Tennessess Epilogue," excerpted from Milton, *The Age of Hate* (Coward-McCann, 1930), reprinted in McKitrick, ed., *Andrew Johnson, op. cit.*, pp. 193–218; Benedict, *Compromise of Principle*, ch. 5.
56 [*Johnson on being compelled to stand on his rights*]: quoted in Stampp, p. 149.
[*Johnson in the impeachment experience*]: Thomas, *op. cit.*, pp. 541–607; Albert Castel, *The Presidency of Andrew Johnson* (Regents Press of Kansas, 1979), and sources cited therein; McKitrick, *Andrew Johnson and Reconstruction, op. cit.*, pp. 486–509.
[*Grant, Johnson, and the Tenure of Office Act*]: William S. McFeely, *Grant* (W. W. Norton, 1981), pp. 262–73.
56–7 [*Surratt episode*]: Thomas, pp. 349–52, 538–40.
57 [*Foreknowledge of balloting on Johnson's removal*]: Trefousse, p. 169; see also, Ralph J. Roske, "The Seven Martyrs?," *American Historical Review*, vol. 64, no. 2 (January 1959), pp. 323–30.
57–8 [*Trumbull on possible implications of impeachment*]: quoted in Stampp, p. 153; Stampp's comment on same, *ibid.*
58 [*Johnson's burial*]: Milton in McKitrick, pp. 216–17.
[*Election of 1868*]: Mantell, *op. cit.*, chs. 6–9; William B. Hesseltine, *Ulysses S. Grant—Politician* (Frederick Ungar, 1935), chs. 5–6; John Hope Franklin, "Election of 1868," in Arthur M. Schlesinger, Jr., *History of American Presidential Elections* (Chelsea House, 1971), vol. 2, pp. 1247–1300.
[*Grant on the summer of 1868*]: quoted in Mantell, p. 129.
59 [*1868 Republican platform*]: reprinted in Schlesinger, vol. 2, pp. 1270–71, quoted at p. 1270.
[*1868 election results*]: Mantell, pp. 143–49; Schlesinger, vol. 2, p. 1300.

"I'se Free. Ain't Wuf Nuffin"

60 [*Sumner upon his reelection*]: quoted in Donald, *Sumner, op. cit.*, p. 348.
[*Implications of election results of 1867*]: Benedict, *Compromise of Principle, op. cit.*, pp. 272–75; James M. McPherson, *The Struggle for Equality* (Princeton University Press, 1964), pp. 378, 382, 412.

60 [American Freedman *editorial*]: quoted in McPherson, p. 399.
[*Passage of the Fifteenth Amendment*]: William Gillette, *The Right to Vote* (Johns Hopkins Press, 1965).

60-1 [*Henry Wilson on Republican struggle to give equal rights*]: quoted in Benedict, p. 326, which is also the source of the statement of the other Republican senator (Samuel C. Pomeroy).

61 [*Benedict on the political fortunes of the Republican party*]: *ibid.*, p. 327.
[*Iowa editor on Phillips*]: Keokuk *Gate City*, quoted in McPherson, p. 368.
[New York Times *and* World *on the radicals*]: *ibid.*

61-2 [*American Anti-Slavery Society on Fifteenth Amendment*]: *ibid.*, p. 427.

62 [*Child on Fifteenth Amendment*]: *ibid.*, p. 428.
[*Southern politics in Reconstruction*]: Stampp, *op. cit.*, ch. 6, quoted on black leaders at p. 167.
[*Reaction of planters to new prestige and power of freedmen*]: Litwack, *op. cit.*, pp. 553-54.

62-3 [*Bryce on corruption in the South*]: James Bryce, *The American Commonwealth* (Macmillan, 1924), vol. 2, pp. 498-99.

63 [*Results of black-and-white rule in South*]: Stampp, p. 172.
[*South Carolina constitution*]: *ibid.*, pp. 172-73.
[*McPherson on education of black schoolchildren*]: McPherson, p. 394.

63-4 [*Education and black children*]: *ibid.*, pp. 386-407; W. E. B. Du Bois, *Black Reconstruction* (Russell & Russell, 1935), ch. 15; Luther P. Jackson, "The Educational Efforts of the Freedmen's Bureau and Freedmen's Aid Societies in South Carolina," *Journal of Negro History*, vol. 8, no. 1 (January 1923), pp. 1-40; James M. Smallwood, *Time of Hope, Time of Despair: Black Texans During Reconstruction* (Kennikat Press, 1981), ch. 4; Gerda Lerner, ed., *Black Women in White America: A Documentary History* (Pantheon Books, 1972), pp. 92-118.

64 [*Comments of Louisiana legislator and Southern white woman on schooling for blacks*]: quoted in Litwack, pp. 485, 486.
[*Paducah* Herald *on ruining blacks as laborers*]: quoted in McPherson, p. 395.
[*Mayor of Enterprise on teacher's arrest*]: quoted in Litwack, p. 487.
["*Forty acres and a mule*"]: McPherson, pp. 407-16; Smallwood, ch. 3; Eric Foner, "Reconstruction and the Crisis of Free Labor," in Foner, *Politics and Ideology in the Age of the Civil War* (Oxford University Press, 1980), pp. 97-127; Foner, "Thaddeus Stevens, Confiscation and Reconstruction," in Foner, pp. 128-49; Escott, *op. cit.*, pp. 150-51.
[*South Carolina black, black preacher, Virginia black on land*]: quoted in Litwack, pp. 392, 402, 403, respectively.

65 [*Black leaders' emphasis on liberal, middle-class values*]: *ibid.*, pp. 520-22; Harold M. Hyman, ed., *New Frontiers of the American Reconstruction* (University of Illinois Press, 1966), pp. 73-74, 79; Eugene Genovese, *In Red and Black: Marxist Explorations in Southern and Afro-American History* (Pantheon Books, 1971), esp. pp. 139-42; Howard M. Shapiro, "Land Reform During Reconstruction: A Case Study in the Sociology of History," Williams College, 1981.

65-6 [*Means of keeping blacks from voting*]: William Gillette, *Retreat from Reconstruction, 1869-1879* (Louisiana State University Press, 1979), chs. 2, 12.

66 [*Gibson County, Tennessee*]: *ibid.*, p. 29.
[*The Klan and federal action*]: see Allan W. Trelease, *White Terror: The Ku Klux Klan Conspiracy and Southern Reconstruction* (Harper & Row, 1971), *passim*.
[*Dwindling of voting prosecutions and convictions*]: Gillette, *Retreat*, pp. 42-45.

67 [*Hayes and the South*]: Gillette, *Retreat*, ch. 14; C. Vann Woodward, *Reunion and Reaction* (Little, Brown, 1951).
[*White Georgian on "negro's first want"*]: quoted in Litwack, p. 448. This statement is a paraphrase made by a *New York Times* correspondent (see *New York Times*, January 7, 1866, p. 3) who does not name the quoted Georgian.
[*One-sided black-planter bargains*]: *ibid.*, p. 409.

68 [*Phillips on the need for a social revolution*]: quoted in McPherson, pp. 370, 373.
[*Henry Wilson on freedom*]: quoted in Stampp, p. 88.
[*Congressman Hoar on suffrage without education*]: Gillette, *Retreat*, p. 215.
[*Phillips on how to make "the negro safe"*]: quoted in Benedict, p. 258.

69 [*Stampp on radicals' lack of knowledge of "sociology of freedom"*]: Stampp, p. 129.
    [*Gillette on the kind of leadership needed*]: Gillette, *Retreat*, p. 184.
69–70 [The Nation *on governing well*]: quoted in Alan Pendleton Grimes, *The Political Liberalism of the New York Nation* (University of North Carolina Press, 1953), p. 10; see also Edwin Lawrence Godkin, *Problems of Modern Democracy*, Morton Keller, ed. (Harvard University Press, 1966), *passim.*
70 [*Sumner on human rights as constitutional*]: quoted in Grimes, p. 6.
    [*Sea Islands land distribution*]: Litwack, pp. 400–407; Willie Lee Rose, *Rehearsal for Reconstruction: The Port Royal Experiment* (Bobbs-Merrill, 1964).
    [*Black woman and Alabama freedman on freedom*]: quoted in Litwack, pp. 226, 328, respectively.

3. THE FORCES OF PRODUCTION

73 [*John Adams on studying politics*]: James Truslow Adams, *The Adams Family* (Little, Brown, 1930), p. 67.
    [*Charles Francis Adams, Jr.*]: *Diary* of Charles Francis Adams, Jr., Massachusetts Historical Society; Charles Francis Adams, *An Autobiography* (Houghton Mifflin, 1916); Edward Chase Kirkland, *Charles Francis Adams, Jr.: The Patrician at Bay* (Harvard University Press, 1965).
    [*Adams following the locomotive engine*]: *Diary*, August 21, 1887.
74 [*American patents*]: see U.S. Bureau of the Census, *Historical Statistics of the United States: Colonial Times to 1970* (U.S. Government Printing Office, 1975), Part 2, pp. 957–59 (Series W 96–106).
    [*Observer on machinery, 1844*]: Thomas A. Devyr, in the *Working Man's Advocate*, March 30, 1844, cited in John R. Commons and Associates, *History of Labour in the United States* (Macmillan, 1918–35), vol. 1, p. 491.
75 [*Charles Francis Adams on his "blue" day*]: *Diary*, February 2, 3, 5, 6, 7, 1883.
    [*Marx on the forces of production*]: Karl Marx and Frederick Engels, *The German Ideology, Parts I and III*, R. Pascal, ed. (International Publishers, 1947), pp. 16, 28, 29.
    [*Marx and Engels on revolutionizing the instruments of production*]: Karl Marx and Frederick Engels, "Manifesto of the Communist Party," in David Fernbach, ed., *Karl Marx: Political Writings* (Random House, 1973–74), vol. 1, pp. 67–98, quoted at p. 70.
    [*Americans' knowledge of Marx and Marxism*]: Howard H. Quint, *The Forging of American Socialism: Origins of the Modern Movement* (University of South Carolina Press, 1953), p. 4; David Herreshoff, *American Disciples of Marx* (Wayne State University Press, 1967).
    [*Marx on Lincoln*]: Karl Marx and Friedrich Engels, *The Civil War in the United States* (International Publishers, 1937), p. 281.
76 [*Marx's American journalism*]: Henry M. Christman, ed., *The American Journalism of Marx & Engels* (New American Library, 1966).
    [*Life of Marx*]: Christman, p. xii; and see Maximilien Rubel and Margaret Manale, *Marx Without Myth* (Harper & Row, 1975); Werner Blumenberg, *Karl Marx*, Douglas Scott, trans. (New Left Books, 1972).
    [*The "wretchedness of existence"*]: see Blumenberg, p. 109.
    [*Marx on "feverish and youthful" America*]: Karl Marx, "The Eighteenth Brumaire of Louis Bonaparte," in Fernbach, vol. 2, p. 155.
    [*America as "outside history"*]: see Herreshoff, p. 13.
    [*Marx on "wonders" of bourgeois production*]: quoted in *ibid.*, p. 20.

Innovators: The Ingenious Yankees

[*Hoosac Tunnel*]: Gary S. Brierly, "Construction of the Hoosac Tunnel 1855 to 1876," *Journal of the Boston Society of Civil Engineers Section, American Society of Civil Engineers*, vol. 63, no. 3 (October 1976); Carl R. Byron, *A Pinprick of Light* (Stephen Greene Press, 1974); J. L. Harrison, *The Great Bore* (Advance Job Print Works, 1891); William B. Browne, "Tunnel Days in the Tunnel City" (unpublished manuscript, Williamsiana Collection, Williams College).
77–8 [*Progress in coal and iron mining*]: John W. Oliver, *History of American Technology* (Ronald Press, 1956), pp. 315–17.

79 [*Automatic turret lathe*]: Nathan Rosenberg, *Perspectives on Technology* (Cambridge University Press, 1976), p. 21.

[*Late-nineteenth-century innovators*]: W. Paul Strassmann, *Risk and Technological Innovation: American Manufacturing Methods during the Nineteenth Century* (Cornell University Press, 1959), pp. 130–33, 142–45.

[*American iron and steel industry*]: ibid., ch. 2; Oliver, ch. 22; Peter Temin, *Iron and Steel in Nineteenth Century America* (M.I.T. Press, 1964), ch. 8.

[*Bessemer converters*]: Temin, ch. 6; Oliver, p. 318; see also James M. Swank, *History of the Manufacture of Iron in All Ages, and Particularly in the United States from Colonial Times to 1891* (American Iron and Steel Association, 1892), chs. 45, 46.

80 [*Bridges*]: D. B. Steinman, *The Builders of the Bridge* (Harcourt, Brace, 1945); David Plowen, *Bridges: The Spans of North America* (Viking Press, 1974).

[*Eads and the St. Louis bridge*]: Joseph Gies and Frances Gies, *The Ingenious Yankees* (Thomas Y. Crowell, 1976), ch. 22.

81 [*Twine binder*]: Oliver, pp. 366–67; William T. Hutchinson, *Cyrus Hall McCormick: Harvest, 1856–1884* (D. Appleton-Century, 1935), vol. 2, ch. 13.

[*Chronology of progress after the Civil War*]: adapted from Lawrence Urdang, ed., *The Time-Tables of American History* (Simon and Schuster, 1981), pp. 223–47.

82 [*Sawyer on technological development*]: quoted in Strassmann, p. 184.

[*American investment in education*]: Nathan Rosenberg, *Technology and American Economic Growth* (M. E. Sharpe, 1972), p. 35.

[*Marx on competition and technological progress*]: Karl Marx, "Wage Labour and Capital," in Karl Marx and Frederick Engels, *Selected Writings* (International Publishers, 1968), p. 90.

[*Jefferson on practicality*]: Jefferson to Cooper, July 10, 1812, in H. A. Washington, ed., *The Works of Thomas Jefferson* (Townsend, MacCoun, 1884), vol. 6, p. 73.

83 [*Practical man on "our greatest thinkers"*]: John Milton Mackie, *From Cape Cod to Dixie and the Tropics* (Putnam, 1864), pp. 200–201, as quoted in Rosenberg, *Technology and Growth*, p. 33.

[*Tocqueville on limits to American mind*]: Alexis de Tocqueville, *Democracy in America*, Henry Reeve, trans., 4th ed. (Sever and Francis, 1864), pp. 40, 48, 53.

[*Experiments in electricity*]: Strassmann, pp. 159–60; Malcolm MacLaren, *The Rise of the Electrical Industry during the Nineteenth Century* (Princeton University Press, 1943); Harold Passer, *The Electrical Manufacturers, 1875–1900* (Harvard University Press, 1953).

[*Joseph Henry*]: J. G. Crowther, *Famous American Men of Science* (W. W. Norton, 1937), ch. 2.

[*Davenport*]: Carl W. Mitman, "Thomas Davenport," in Allen Johnson and Dumas Malone, eds., *Dictionary of American Biography* (Scribner's, 1930), vol. 5, pp. 87–88.

[*Alexander Graham Bell*]: Herbert N. Casson, *The History of the Telephone* (A. C. McClurg, 1910); Robert V. Bruce, *Alexander Graham Bell and the Conquest of Solitude* (Little, Brown, 1973); Gies and Gies, ch. 24; Oliver, ch. 30.

84 [*"Mr. Watson—come here"*]: quoted in Bruce, p. 181.

[*Edison*]: Crowther, ch. 4; Matthew Josephson, *Edison* (McGraw-Hill, 1959); Oliver, ch. 24.

85 [*Edison's search for a filament*]: quoted in Oliver, p. 349.

Investors: Eastern Dollars and Western Risks

[*Adams's boredom and frustration*]: Adams, Jr., *Diary, op. cit.*, January 21, 22, February 16, March 4, 1869; see also Kirkland, *op. cit.*, p. 127.

86 [*Adams's visit to Stock Exchange*]: *Diary*, April 14, 1869.

[*New Year's greeting*]: quoted in Edward Chase Kirkland, *Men, Cities and Transportation: A Study in New England History, 1820–1900* (Harvard University Press, 1948), p. 92.

[*Michigan copper*]: William B. Gates, Jr., *Michigan Copper and Boston Dollars* (Harvard University Press, 1951); Angus Murdock, *Boom Copper* (Macmillan, 1943).

[*"Trial-and-error fumbling"*]: Gates, p. 30.

[*Lodes at Calumet and Hecla*]: Russell B. Adams, Jr., *The Boston Money Tree* (Thomas Y. Crowell, 1977), pp. 160–67, Agassiz quoted at p. 163; Gates, pp. 43–45, 57.

87 [*Dividends from Calumet and Hecla*]: Adams, *Boston Money Tree*, p. 166.
[*The "general entrepreneur"*]: Thomas C. Cochran, *Railroad Leaders 1845–1890: The Business Mind in Action* (Harvard University Press, 1953), pp. 9–12; see also Adams, *Boston Money Tree*, pp. 136–46.
[*Chapin*]: Cochran, pp. 19–20, 288–89.
[*Higginson*]: Adams, *Boston Money Tree*, pp. 183–88 and *passim*.
[*Nathan and Thomas Gold Appleton*]: Frederic C. Jaher, "Businessman and Gentleman: Nathan and Thomas Gold Appleton—An Exploration in Intergenerational History," *Explorations in Entrepreneurial History*, 2nd ser., vol. 4, no. 1 (Fall 1966), pp. 17–39.
[*Capital tied up in family trusts*]: *ibid.*, p. 34.
88 [*Growth of New York City as capital market*]: William J. Schultz and M. R. Caine, *Financial Development of the United States* (Prentice-Hall, 1937), pp. 192, 239, 249.
[*Lowell on the Lowells*]: quoted in Cleveland Amory, *Proper Bostonians* (E. P. Dutton, 1947), p. 44.
[*Barker*]: Fritz Redlich, *The Molding of American Banking: Men and Ideas* (Johnson, 1968), Part 2, pp. 60–61; see also Richard Sylla, "American Banking and Growth in the Nineteenth Century: A Partial View of the Terrain," *Explorations in Economic History*, vol. 9, no. 2 (Winter 1971–72), pp. 197–227.
[*Girard*]: Redlich, Part 2, pp. 61–63.
[*Jay Cooke*]: Ellis P. Oberholtzer, "Jay Cooke," in Johnson and Malone, *Dictionary of American Biography, op. cit.*, vol. 4, pp. 383–84; Stuart Bruchey, "Jay Cooke," in John A. Garraty, ed., *Encyclopedia of American Biography* (Harper & Row, 1974), pp. 217–18.
89 [*Redlich on Cooke*]: Redlich, Part 2, p. 356.
[*Post–Civil War banking*]: *ibid.*, p. 74 ff.
[*J. P. Morgan*]: George Wheeler, *Pierpont Morgan & Friends: The Anatomy of a Myth* (Prentice-Hall, 1973).
[*Morton, Bliss and Co.*]: George Bliss Papers, Miscellaneous correspondence (Letterpress), 1876–79, New-York Historical Society.
90 [*Bliss on "our position with the new administration"*]: Bliss to Grenfell, March 6, 1877, in *ibid.*
[*Communist Manifesto on entrepreneurs*]: Marx and Engels, "Manifesto," in Fernbach, *op. cit.*, vol. 1, p. 72.
[*Schumpeter on the entrepreneurial function*]: Joseph A. Schumpeter, *Capitalism, Socialism, and Democracy*, 3rd ed. (Harper & Bros., 1947), p. 132 (emphasis added).
90–1 [*Veblen on failure to innovate*]: Thorstein Veblen, *Absentee Ownership and Business Enterprise in Recent Times: The Case of America* (B. W. Heubsch, 1923), pp. 80–103; see also J. D. Bernal, *Science and Industry in the Nineteenth Century* (Routledge and Kegan Paul, 1953).
91 [*Investment and innovation in late nineteenth-century capitalism*]: see Strassmann, *op. cit.*; Rosenberg, *Technology and Growth, op. cit.*; Rosenberg, *Perspectives, op. cit.*
[*Daniel Drew*]: Allan Nevins, "Daniel Drew," in Johnson and Malone, *Dictionary of American Biography*, vol. 5, pp. 450–51; Charles Francis Adams, Jr., "A Chapter of Erie," in Charles Francis Adams, Jr., and Henry Adams, *Chapters of Erie and Other Essays* (James R. Osgood, 1871), pp. 1–99, quoted at p. 5.
92 [*"Commodore" Vanderbilt*]: Wheaton J. Lane, *Commodore Vanderbilt: An Epic of the Steam Age* (Alfred A. Knopf, 1942).
[*Harlem Railroad corner*]: Nevins in Johnson and Malone, p. 450.
[*Jay Gould*]: Julius Grodinsky, *Jay Gould: His Business Career, 1867–1892* (University of Pennsylvania Press, 1957); Richard O'Connor, *Gould's Millions* (Doubleday, 1962).
[*James Fisk*]: Robert H. Fuller, *Jubilee Jim: The Life of Colonel James Fisk, Jr.* (Macmillan, 1928).
[*"Instincts of fourteen"*]: Henry Adams, "The New York Gold Conspiracy," in Adams, Jr., and Adams, p. 104.
93 [*Adams on Fisk and Gould*]: Kirkland, *Charles Francis Adams, Jr.*, pp. 41, 62.
[*Adams and bribery*]: *ibid.*, p. 110; Adams, Jr., *Autobiography, op. cit.*, pp. 191–96; see also Paul Goodman, "Ethics and Enterprise: The Values of a Boston Elite, 1800–1860," *American Quarterly*, vol. 18, no. 3 (Fall 1966), pp. 437–51.

Entrepreneurs: The Californians

93 [*Lake Donner*]: Alonzo Delano ("The Old Block"), *The Central Pacific Railroad, or '49 and '69* (White and Bauer, 1868), p. 18; Collection Bancroft Library, University of California.

94 [*Winter of 1866–67*]: Sacramento *Union*, December 28, 1866; Testimony of James Strobridge before the Pacific Railway Commission (Government Printing Office, 1887), vol. 5, p. 3150; Statement of L. M. Clement, civil engineer, Pacific Railway Commission, vol. 5, p. 2577; Alexander Saxton, *The Indispensable Enemy* (University of California Press, 1971), p. 64.

   [*Conditions*]: *Chinese-American Workers, Past and Present: An Anthology of Getting Together Magazine* (Getting Together, 1970), pp. 6–7; Wesley Griswold, *A Work of Giants* (McGraw-Hill, 1962), p. 120.

   [*Twenty-seven-inch record*]: James McCague, *Moguls and Iron Men* (Harper & Row, 1964), p. 159.

   [*Reluctance to use Chinese laborers*]: Testimony of James Strobridge, *Report of the Joint Special Committee to Investigate Chinese Immigration*, 2nd Session, 44th Congress, 1876–77 (Government Printing Office, 1877), Report No. 689, p. 723; McCague, pp. 103–4.

   [*Chinese hired as potential strikebreakers*]: Saxton, p. 62; McCague, pp. 103–4.

   [*Early agitation for railroad*]: Robert S. Cotterhill, "Early Agitation for a Pacific Railroad, 1845–1850," in *Mississippi Valley Historical Review*, vol. 5, no. 4 (March 1919), pp. 396–414, esp. p. 397.

95 [*Federal approval*]: Norman E. Tutorow, *Leland Stanford: Man of Many Careers* (Pacific Coast Publishers, 1971), pp. 70, 72.

   [*Big Four*]: *ibid.*, pp. 70–75.

   [*Judah*]: Collection of pamphlets on Theodore Judah, Bancroft Library, University of California, Berkeley.

   [*Stanford at GHQ*]: Leland Stanford Correspondence, vol. 3, October 21, 1868, Stanford University Archives.

   [*Crocker in the field*]: Charles Crocker, "Facts . . . regarding . . . identification with the Central Pacific Railroad," dictated to H. H. Bancroft, Bancroft Library, University of California, Berkeley, pp. 49–52.

   [*Chinese strike*]: *Alta California*, July 1, 3, 1867; Testimony of Charles Crocker, *Report of the Joint Committee to Investigate Chinese Immigration*, p. 669.

96 [*Railroad rivalry*]: John Debo Galloway, *The First Transcontinental Railroad* (Simmons-Boardman, 1950), p. 88; "The Last Spike," pamphlet (not dated), Bancroft Library, University of California, Berkeley; Testimony of Leland Stanford, Pacific Railway Commission, vol. 5, p. 2523; Strobridge Testimony, Pacific Railway Commission, vol. 5, pp. 2580–81; General Grenville M. Dodge (chief engineer of the Union Pacific Railway), "How We Built the Union Pacific Railway," in Henry Steele Commager and Allan Nevins, eds., *The Heritage of America* (Little, Brown, 1939), pp. 835–37.

   [*Last spike*]: Dodge, in Commager and Nevins, p. 837; Tutorow, pp. 90, 91, 98.

   ["*You brag of the East*"]: "What the Engines Said," in Bret Harte, *Poems* (Fields, Osgood, 1871), pp. 38–39.

   [*Emerson trip*]: James Bradley Thayer, *A Western Journey with Mr. Emerson* (Little, Brown, 1884; reprinted by Kennikat Press, 1971), pp. 39–43, quoted at p. 42.

97 [*Sights of gold mining*]: Thayer, pp. 113–14; Albert D. Richardson, *Beyond the Mississippi: From the Great River to the Great Ocean* (American Publishing, 1867), pp. 391–92.

   [*Urchins panning gold*]: Charles Nordhoff, *California: A Book for Travellers and Settlers* (Harper & Bros., 1872), pp. 98–99.

   [*Windmills*]: Thayer, p. 119.

   [*John Muir*]: *ibid.*, pp. 88–109.

98 [*Traveling south through Central Valley, past land of Spanish and Indians*]: Nordhoff, pp. 119–24, 150–57, 238–45, quoted at pp. 123, 157, 152, 242 respectively.

99 [*Los Angeles market produce*]: Nordhoff, p. 136.

   [*Railroad in Los Angeles*]: Glenn S. Dumke, *The Boom of the Eighties in Southern California* (Huntington Library, 1944), pp. 19–21.

99 [*Shipping*]: Iris Higbie Wilson, *William Wolfskill* (Arthur H. Clarke, 1965), pp. 176–77; Andrew F. Rolle, *California: A History*, 2nd ed. (Thomas Crowell, 1969), pp. 359–60.
[*Phineas Banning*]: Banning Papers, Huntington Library, San Marino, California; Dumke, pp. 19–20.

100 [*"Stanford's Palace"*]: Tutorow, pp. 206–7.
[*Lucy Jones*]: Diary of Lucy S. Jones, 1874–75, Bancroft Library, University of California, Berkeley.
[*Chinatown*]: San Francisco *Alta* (1870), quoted in William N. Camp, *Port of Gold* (Country Life Press, 1947), p. 264; Hubert Howe Bancroft, *History of California* (The History Co., 1890), vol. 7, pp. 336, 340, 691–92, footnote 37.
[*Absentee landlords*]: Nordhoff, p. 91.

100–1 [*Anti-Chinese agitation and legislation*]: Elmer Clarence Sandmeyer, *The Anti-Chinese Movement in California* (University of Illinois Press, 1973), p. 52; Ira B. Cross, *A History of the Labor Movement in California* (University of California Press, 1935), pp. 74–87.

101 [*Democratic planks*]: Sandmeyer, p. 46.
[*Anti-Chinese sentiment within labor movement*]: Frederick L. Ryan, *Industrial Relations in the San Francisco Building Trades* (University of Oklahoma Press, 1936), p. 15; Lucile Eaves, *A History of California Labor Legislation* (University of California Press, 1910), pp. 6, 105, quoted in Sandmeyer, p. 40; Cross, pp. 74–75.
[*Mass meetings, Workingmen's Party*]: Sandmeyer, pp. 47, 66.
[*Invalidity of constitutional provisions*]: *ibid.*, p. 74.
[*San Francisco's cultural life*]: Rolle, p. 450; Lucy Jones Diary, Bancroft Library; Franklin Walker, *San Francisco's Literary Frontier* (Alfred A. Knopf, 1939), pp. 8, 116, 127, 316, 352; Lawrence Ferlinghetti and Nancy J. Peters, *Literary San Francisco* (City Lights Books and Harper & Row, 1980), pp. ix–xi, 29–32, 42–44, 64–66, 75–84.

Industrialists: Carnegie, Rockefeller, and the Two Capitalisms

102 [*Carnegie*]: Joseph Frazier Wall, *Andrew Carnegie* (Oxford University Press, 1970), *passim*, Irishman quoted at p. 151.
[*"I can get nae mair work"*]: quoted in Harold C. Livesay, *Andrew Carnegie and the Rise of Big Business* (Little, Brown, 1975), p. 11.
[*Carnegie making the trains run*]: Andrew Carnegie, *Autobiography of Andrew Carnegie* (Houghton Mifflin, 1920), pp. 70–72.
[*Carnegie burning wrecked freight cars*]: Wall, p. 151.

104 [*Carnegie on lime and coke*]: quoted in *ibid.*, p. 342.
[*Wall on Carnegie and cost-cutting*]: Joseph F. Wall, "Andrew Carnegie," in Garraty, *op. cit.*, p. 176.
[*"We were boys together"*]: J. Edgar Thomson, quoted in Livesay, p. 162.
[*Growth and economies*]: *ibid.*, pp. 155–56.
[*"Beyond this never earn"*]: quoted in Wall, *Carnegie*, pp. 224–25.
[*"Gospel of Wealth"*]: *ibid.*, pp. 805–15.
[*The "other" Carnegie in England*]: *ibid.*, ch. 14; see also Carnegie, chs. 22–25.

105 [*John D. Rockefeller and his family*]: David Freeman Hawke, *John D.* (Harper & Row, 1980), ch. 1.

105–6 [*Rockefeller's youthful enterprises*]: *ibid.*, p. 12.

106 [*Rockefeller on competition and combination*]: a composite of paragraphs of conversations of John D. Rockefeller with William O. Inglis, quoted in *ibid.*, pp. 153–55.

107 [*Philanthropy of Carnegie and Rockefeller*]: Burton J. Hendrick, "Andrew Carnegie," in Johnson, *Dictionary of American Biography, op. cit.*, vol. 3, p. 505; Wall, *Carnegie*, ch. 22; Allan Nevins, *John D. Rockefeller: The Heroic Age of American Enterprise* (Scribner's, 1941), vol. 2, chs. 48, 49, and p. 712.
[*Marxist definition of need*]: Agnes Heller, *The Theory of Need in Marx* (St. Martin's Press, 1974), *passim*.
[*Production in the late nineteenth century*]: Edwin Frickey, *Production in the United States: 1860–1914* (Harvard University Press, 1947), especially pp. 7–15 (Table 1); John A. Garraty, *The New Commonwealth, 1877–1890* (Harper & Row, 1968), pp. 82–85.

107 [*Manufactured goods index*]: Garraty, *New Commonwealth*, p. 80; see also David A. Wells, *Recent Economic Changes* (D. Appleton, 1899).
108 [*Innovation in 1886-95*]: Urdang, *op. cit.*, pp. 244-58.
109 [*Scientific man versus inventor*]: Edison in Brooklyn *Citizen*, November 4, 1888, quoted in Robert Conot, *A Streak of Luck* (Seaview Books, 1979), p. 460.
[*"My business is* thinking"]: *ibid.*, p. 456.
[*Edison as a transitional figure*]: Norbert Wiener, *The Human Use of Human Beings: Cybernetics and Society* (Houghton Mifflin, 1950), p. 127.

Philadelphia 1876: The Proud Exhibitors

[*Philadelphia Centennial Exposition*]: Gies and Gies, *op. cit.*, pp. 3-9; Oliver, *op. cit.*, pp. 300-302; Marshall Davidson, *Life in America* (Houghton Mifflin, 1974), vol. 1, pp. 538-41; J. S. Ingram, *The Centennial Exposition* (Hubbard Bros., 1876).
110 [*"Sober black iron monsters"*]: Gies and Gies, p. 7.
[*Bell at the Centennial*]: *ibid.*, pp. 327-28; Bruce, *op. cit.*, p. 197.
[*"Centennial Hymn"*]: *The Complete Poetical Works of John Greenleaf Whittier* (Houghton Mifflin, 1895), p. 234, stanza 1.

4. THE STRUCTURE OF CLASSES

111 [*Chicago stockyards*]: W. Joseph Grand, *The Illustrated History of the Union Stock Yards, Chicago, Ill.* (Thomas Knapp, 1896); "The Meat Industry of America," *Scientific American*, vol. 100, no. 4 (January 23, 1909), pp. 84-86 and no. 5 (January 30, 1909), pp. 99-102; Rudolf A. Clemen, *The American Livestock and Meat Industry* (Ronald Press, 1923); Lewis Corey, *Meat and Man* (Viking Press, 1950).
[*Everything used but the squeal*]: quoted in Bessie L. Pierce, *A History of Chicago* (Alfred A. Knopf, 1957), vol. 3, p. 123.
[*Uses of the cow*]: Finley Peter Dunne, quoted in *ibid.*, vol. 3, p. 124.
112 [*Alienation in capitalist production*]: Karl Marx, *Capital*, Samuel Moore and Edward Aveling, trans. (Charles H. Kerr, 1915), p. 708.
[*Capital as dead labor*]: *ibid.*, p. 257.
[*Labor robbed of its value*]: *ibid.*, pp. 202-3.
[*Gutman on London*]: Herbert G. Gutman, *Work, Culture, and Society in Industrializing America* (Alfred A. Knopf, 1976), p. 40.

Upper Classes: The New Rich and the Old

113 [*The Chicago rich*]: Wayne Andrews, *Battle for Chicago* (Harcourt, Brace, 1946); Harper Leech and John Charles Carroll, *Armour and His Times* (Appleton-Century, 1938); Pierce, *op. cit.*, vols. 2 and 3; Dixon Wecter, *The Saga of American Society* (Scribner's, 1937), pp. 143-48.
[*Armour's routine*]: Andrews, pp. 86-87, quoted at p. 87.
[*Armour on making money*]: quoted in *ibid.*, p. 87.
[*Ethics according to* David Harum]: Edward N. Wescott, *David Harum* (D. Appleton, 1899), p. viii.
114 [*Elites generally*]: see Frederic Cople Jaher, ed., *The Rich, The Well Born, and the Powerful* (University of Illinois Press, 1973); Frederic Cople Jaher, "Nineteenth Century Elites in Boston and New York," *Journal of Social History*, vol. 6, no. 1 (Fall 1972), pp. 32-77; Maury Klein and Harvey Kantor, *Prisoners of Progress* (Macmillan, 1976), esp. ch. 7; Gustavus Myers, *History of the Great American Fortunes* (C. H. Kerr, 1909).
[*Palmer House*]: Andrews, pp. 75-78, quoted at p. 76.
[*McCormick's fresco*]: *ibid.*, p. 112.
[*Boston elites*]: Cleveland Amory, *The Proper Bostonians* (E. P. Dutton, 1947); Lucius Beebe, *Boston and the Boston Legend* (Appleton-Century, 1935).
[*Chicagoans and Mr. Smith*]: Amory, p. 11.
115 [*Intermarriage in Boston high society*]: *ibid.*, p. 20.
[*Mrs. Jack Gardner*]: *ibid.*, ch. 6; Beebe, ch. 17.
[*Beacon Hill lady on being "already here"*]: quoted in Amory, p. 23.

115 [*Jaher on Brahmin power*]: Jaher, "Nineteenth Century," p. 60.
116 [*Philadelphia elites*]: E. Digby Baltzell, *Philadelphia Gentlemen: The Making of a National Upper Class* (Collier-Macmillan, 1966); Nathaniel Burt, *The Perennial Philadelphians: The Anatomy of an American Aristocracy* (Little, Brown, 1963).
    [*"Different, aloof and apart'"*]: Baltzell, p. 188.
    [*Pepper on Walnut Street*]: quoted in *ibid.*, p. 185.
117 [*New York elites*]: John A. Kouwenhoven, *The Columbia Historical Portrait of New York* (Doubleday, 1953); Lloyd Morris, *Incredible New York* (Random House, 1951); Mrs. John King van Rensselaer, *The Social Ladder* (Henry Holt, 1924).
    [*McAllister on standards*]: quoted in Klein and Kantor, p. 221.
    [*The "Four Hundred"*]: *ibid.*, pp. 225–26; Morris, ch. 12; Ward McAllister, *Society As I Have Found It* (Cassell, 1890).
118 [*American society managed by women*]: quoted in Klein and Kantor, p. 231; see also Wecter, ch. 8.
    [*Ambitious hostesses*]: Klein and Kantor, p. 226.
    [*The Vanderbilts*]: Wayne Andrews, *The Vanderbilt Legend* (Harcourt, Brace, 1941).
    [*Vanderbilt, Astor hostilities*]: *ibid.*, pp. 254–55; Harvey O'Connor, *The Astors* (Alfred A. Knopf, 1941), pp. 195–98.
    [*Vanderbilt Hyde Park mansion*]: Charles W. Snell, *Vanderbilt Mansion* (National Park Service Historical Series No. 32, 1960).
119 [*New Haven class structure*]: Robert E. Dahl, *Who Governs?: Democracy and Power in an American City* (Yale University Press, 1961), Books 1, 2.
    [*Springfield*]: Michael Frisch, *Town into City: Springfield, Massachusetts, and the Meaning of Community, 1840–1880* (Harvard University Press, 1972).
    [*Patriarchal chauvinism*]: see O'Connor, pp. 193, 194.

The Middle Classes: A Woman's Work

[*Details of home life*]: Helen Smith Jordan, *Love Lies Bleeding: The Life in Letters of Mary Abigail Abell* (1979), at Schlesinger Library, Radcliffe; Mary E. Howard, "The Changing Household, 1865–1900," paper presented to Radcliffe Women's Archives Workshop, 1952–53, Schlesinger Library; Robert S. Lynd and Helen Merrell Lynd, *Middletown* (Harcourt, Brace, 1929), ch. 12, p. 167 footnote 17; Philip C. Dolce, ed., *Suburbia: The American Dream and Dilemma* (Anchor Books, 1976), pp. 5–7; Earl Lifshey, *The Housewares Story* (National Housewares Manufacturers Association, 1973), pp. 124, 126; Richard Sennett, "Middle-Class Families and Urban Violence: The Experience of a Chicago Community in the Nineteenth Century," in Stephan Thernstrom and Richard Sennett, eds., *Nineteenth Century Cities* (Yale University Press, 1969); Doreen Yarwood, *Costume of the Western World* (St. Martin's Press, 1980).
119–20 [*Laundry tasks*]: *Diary of Annie Thompson* (unpublished manuscript in private collection, Chicago), quoted at p. 117; Howard, *passim*.
120 [*Housecleaning*]: Claudia L. Bushman, *A Good Man's Poor Wife* (University Press of New England, 1981), pp. 112–13.
    [*"Hattie's 'opera cape'"*]: Harriet Hanson Robinson, quoted in *ibid.*, p. 113.
    [*Journals read by women*]: Frank Luther Mott, *A History of American Magazines* (Harvard University Press, 1930–68), vol. 3, ch. 4; vol. 4, ch. 21 and supplement; collection, New York Historical Society.
121 [*Domestic help*]: U.S. Department of the Interior, Census Office, *Statistics of the Population of the United States of the Tenth Census (June 1, 1880)* (Government Printing Office, 1883), p. 729; Theresa M. McBride, *The Domestic Revolution* (Holmes & Meier, 1976), pp. 18–19; David M. Katzman, *Seven Days a Week: Women and Domestic Service in Industrializing America* (Oxford University Press, 1978); Jordan; Bushman, pp. 109–12; Lillian Pettingill, *Toilers of the Home* (Doubleday, 1903); Harriet Prescott Spofford, *The Servant Girl Question* (1881; reprinted by Arno Press, 1977); Faye E. Dudden, *Serving Women* (Wesleyan University Press, 1983).
    [*Housewives' complaints*]: Harriet Hanson Robinson, quoted in Bushman, pp. 109, 110, 109 respectively; see also Katzman, pp. 16–17.
    [*Domestic science, domestic feminism*]: Catharine E. Beecher and Harriet Beecher Stowe, *The American Woman's Home: or Principles of Domestic Science* (J. B. Ford, 1869; reprinted, 1874,

as *The Housekeeper's Manual*); Edith Hoshino Altbach, *Women in America* (D. C. Heath, 1974), pp. 8, 33; Kathryn Kish Sklar, *Catharine Beecher: A Study in American Domesticity* (Yale University Press, 1973), pp. 96–97, 158–67, and *passim;* Mary P. Ryan, "The Power of Women's Networks: A Case Study of Moral Reform in Antebellum America," *Feminist Studies,* vol. 5, no. 1 (Spring 1979), pp. 66–85; Barbara Ehrenreich and Deirdre English, *For Her Own Good* (Anchor Press, 1978), ch. 5.

121 [*Training of daughters*]: Edna Ormsby, *Journal* (Schlesinger Library), February 12, 1895, p. 73; *ibid.,* February 20, 1896, p. 84; Bushman, p. 112; Jordan, *passim;* Thompson, *passim.*

121–2 [*Sexuality*]: Linda Gordon, *Woman's Body, Woman's Right* (Penguin Books, 1977), pp. 23–25; Ronald G. Waters, *Primers for Prudery: Sexual Advice to Victorian America* (Prentice-Hall, 1974), pp. 65–78; see also Stephen Kern, *Anatomy & Destiny: A Cultural History of the Human Body* (Bobbs-Merrill, 1975), ch. 9; G. J. Barker-Benfield, *The Horrors of the Half-Known Life: Male Attitudes Toward Women and Sexuality in Nineteenth Century America* (Harper & Row, 1976).

122 [*"The full force of sexual desire"*]: William Sanger, *The History of Prostitution: Its Extent, Causes and Effects Throughout the World* (Harper & Bros., 1858), pp. 488–89, in Waters, p. 67.
[*Fashion*]: Yarwood, pp. 52, 54.
[*Corsets*]: Andrew Sinclair, *The Better Half: The Emancipation of the American Woman* (Harper & Row, 1965), pp. 103–5, Stanton quoted at p. 105.
[*English visitor on corseted American women*]: Ada S. Ballin, *The Science of Dress in Theory and Practise* (Low, Marston, Searle & Rivington, 1885), p. 160, in Kern, p. 13.
[*Beecher on cares of marriage*]: Catharine Beecher, "On Female Health in America," from *Letters to the People on Health and Happiness* (Harper & Bros., 1855), in Nancy F. Cott, ed., *Roots of Bitterness* (E. P. Dutton, 1972), p. 263.
[*"Like a man a-mowing"*]: Anonymous wife, quoted in Gordon, p. 105.
[*"Unaccommodating and capricious"*]: *ibid.,* p. 125.
[*Women's network*]: Carroll Smith-Rosenberg, "The Female World of Love and Ritual: Relations Between Women in Nineteenth Century America," in Linda K. Kerber and Jane De Hart Mathews, eds., *Women's America: Refocusing the Past* (Oxford University Press, 1982), pp. 156–79.

123 [*Contraception and control of family size*]: Gordon, chs. 5–6; Daniel Scott Smith, "Family Limitation, Sexual Control, and Domestic Feminism in Victorian America," in Nancy F. Cott and Elizabeth H. Pleck, *A Heritage of Her Own* (Simon and Schuster, 1979), pp. 222–45.
[*Comstock law*]: reprinted in Kerber and Mathews, p. 438; and see Gordon, pp. 24, 167.
[*Abortion*]: James C. Mohr, "Abortion in America," in Kerber and Mathews, pp. 179–89.
[*Stanton on Whitman and women*]: Harriet Stanton Blatch and Theodore Stanton, eds., *Elizabeth Cady Stanton* (Arno Press, 1969), vol. 2, p. 210 (diary entry, September 6, 1883).
[*Burton on love*]: Harriet Burton Laidlaw, *Diary,* Harriet B. Laidlaw Papers, Schlesinger Library.
[*Survey of women's attitudes toward sex*]: Dr. Clelia Duel Mosher, "Hygiene and Physiology of Women" (Mosher Papers, Stanford University), vol. 10, in Carl N. Degler, "What Ought to Be and What Was: Women's Sexuality in the Nineteenth Century," *American Historical Review,* vol. 79, no. 5 (December 1974), pp. 1467–90, quoted at p. 1487.
[*Gilman's illness*]: Charlotte Perkins Gilman, *The Living of Charlotte Perkins Gilman* (Harper Colophon Books, 1975), p. 92.
[*Women's depression*]: Ehrenreich and English, pp. 1–4; and ch. 4, esp. p. 95.

124 [*Alice James on the "receptive attitude"*]: Alice James to William James, January 3–7, 1886(?), in Ruth Bernard Yeazell, *The Death and Letters of Alice James* (University of California Press, 1981), p. 107.
[*Beecher on "decay of female health"*]: Beecher, "On Female Health in America," in Cott, pp. 263–70, quoted at p. 263.
[*Woman as "chief ornament"*]: Thorstein Veblen, *The Theory of the Leisure Class: An Economic Study of Institutions* (Modern Library, 1934), p. 180.
[*Gilman on wife's role*]: Charlotte Perkins Gilman, "Are Women Human Beings?," *Harper's Weekly,* May 25, 1912, p. 11, in Aileen S. Kraditor, ed., *Up from the Pedestal* (Quadrangle, 1975), pp. 325–31; see also Charlotte Perkins Gilman, *Women and Economics* (Small, Maynard, 1898).

124 [*Doctors and women*]: Ehrenreich and English, pp. 35–88, also ch. 4.

[*Henry Ward Beecher*]: Clifford E. Clark, Jr., *Henry Ward Beecher: Spokesman for a Middle-Class America* (University of Illinois Press, 1978); William G. McLoughlin, *The Meaning of Henry Ward Beecher: An Essay on the Shifting Values of Mid-Victorian America, 1840–1870* (Alfred A. Knopf, 1970).

125 [*Victoria Woodhull*]: Emanie Sachs, *"The Terrible Siren"* (Harper & Bros., 1928); Johanna Johnston, *Mrs. Satan* (Putnam's, 1967).

[*Woodhull & Claflin's Weekly*]: Mott, vol. 3, pp. 443–53; extensive (though incomplete) collection of the *Weekly* in New-York Historical Society.

125–6 [*Woodhull on freeing women from sexual slavery*]: *Woodhull & Claflin's Weekly*, October 1, 1870, p. 11.

126 [*Woodhull's appearance in Steinway Hall*]: Sachs, pp. 135–36; see also the *Weekly*, January 2, 1875, p. 2.

[*Woodhull's exposé of the Beecher-Tilton relationship*]: *Weekly*, November 2, 1872, pp. 9–13; see also Robert Shaplen, *Free Love and Heavenly Sinners* (Alfred A. Knopf, 1954).

127 [*Beecher as spokesman for the middle class*]: Clark, prologue.

The Farmer's Lot

[*Department of Agriculture study of farm wife's work*]: cited in John Mack Faragher, "The Midwestern Farming Family, 1850," in Kerber and Mathews, *op. cit.*, pp. 114–29, quoted at p. 123.

[*Farm women's routine*]: John Ise, *Sod and Stubble: The Story of a Kansas Homestead* (University of Nebraska Press, 1967), ch. 3.

128 [*E.B.'s complaint and rejoinders*]: from *The Household*, 1878–79, 1883, in Norton Juster, *So Sweet to Labor: Rural Women in America, 1865–1895* (Viking Press, 1979), pp. 145–51, quoted at pp. 145, 146, 149.

[*Migration into the Plains states*]: Fred A. Shannon, *The Farmer's Last Frontier* (Holt, Rinehart and Winston, 1961), p. 38; see also Page Smith, *Daughters of the Promised Land* (Little, Brown, 1970), esp. ch. 15.

[*Creating new counties and communities*]: John D. Hicks, *The Populist Revolt* (University of Minnesota Press, 1931), p. 18.

[*Homestead Act*]: ibid., pp. 9–10.

129 [*Sod houses and living conditions*]: Ise, *passim;* Hicks, p. 30.

[*Farmers' financial plight*]: Lawrence Goodwyn, *Democratic Promise: The Populist Moment in America* (Oxford University Press, 1976), p. 114; Hicks, pp. 89–90; Norman Pollack, ed., *The Populist Mind* (Bobbs-Merrill, 1967), p. 34; Ise, p. 17.

130 [*Farmers, middlemen, and trusts*]: Shannon, pp. 174, 179, 192–93; Hicks, p. 61.

[*Downgrading "number one" wheat*]: Lewis Walker, Jr., "Abuses in the Grain Trade of the Northwest," in *Annals of the American Academy of Political and Social Science*, vol. 18 (November 1901), pp. 488–90, quoted at p. 490.

[*The small farmer's high costs of transportation*]: Hicks, pp. 61–65.

[*Migration back to the East*]: ibid., p. 84; Shannon, p. 146.

130–1 [*Susan Orcutt's appeal*]: quoted in Pollack, p. 36 (June 29, 1894).

131 [*Condition of Southern farmers, post–Civil War*]: Roger L. Ransom and Richard Sutch, *One Kind of Freedom: The Economic Consequences of Emancipation* (Cambridge University Press, 1977), p. 151.

[*The cotton mania*]: Charles H. Otken, *The Ills of the South* (Putnam's, 1894), ch. 7, quoted in Hicks, p. 49.

[*Conditions in Alabama, Louisiana, and Mississippi*]: C. Vann Woodward, *Origins of the New South, 1877–1913* (Louisiana State University Press, 1951), p. 177.

[*Political leaders on farmers' conditions*]: quoted in ibid., pp. 187–88.

132 [*"Working on halves"*]: Ransom and Sutch, pp. 89–90.

[*"Slavery under a new name"*]: Robert Preston Brooks, "The Agrarian Revolution in Georgia, 1865–1912," in *Georgia Studies: Selected Writings of Robert Preston Brooks* (University of Georgia Press, 1952), p. 101.

[*Ned Cobb on his labor as a boy*]: quoted in Theodore Rosengarten, *All God's Dangers: The Life of Nate Shaw* (Alfred A. Knopf, 1974), p. 15.

132–3 [*Washington on living conditions of sharecroppers*]: Booker T. Washington, *Up from Slavery:*

An Autobiography (Corner House, 1971; originally published 1900, 1901), pp. 112–16.

134 [*Ownership of land by black farmers*]: Woodward, p. 205; Arnold H. Taylor, *Travail and Triumph: Black Life and Culture in the South Since the Civil War* (Greenwood Press, 1976), p. 72.

[*Pride of ex-slaves in owning land*]: George P. Rawick, ed., *The American Slave: A Composite Autobiography* (Greenwood Press, 1972), vol. 6, p. 192, quoted in Taylor, p. 69.

[*Conditions of white sharecroppers*]: Shannon, p. 99.

134–5 [*Farm family's income*]: *ibid.*, quoted at p. 115.

[*Woodward on the crop lien system*]: Woodward, p. 180.

[*Otken on credit system*]: quoted in Ransom and Sutch, p. 164.

135–6 [*Merchant-debtor relationship*]: Goodwyn, p. 31; see also Thomas D. Clark, "The Furnishing and Supply System in Southern Agriculture Since 1865," *Journal of Southern History*, vol. 12, no. 1 (February 1946), pp. 24–44.

136 [*"No cotton, no credit"*]: Goodwyn, p. 31.

[*Matt Brown*]: Clark, "Furnishing and Supply System," pp. 41–42.

Working Classes: The Conditions of Existence

137 [*Transformation of Lynn*]: John T. Cumbler, *Working-Class Community in Industrial America* (Greenwood Press, 1979), quoted at p. 17.

[*Inside view of a tenement*]: Jacob A. Riis, *How the Other Half Lives* (Scribner's, 1890), p. 43.

[*Death rate of children*]: *ibid.*, p. 36.

138 [*Death of a baby*]: *ibid.*, pp. 43–44.

[*Divisions between ethnic groups*]: *ibid.*, pp. 24–25.

[*Sweatshops*]: John Dewitt Warner, "The 'Sweating System' in New York City," *Harper's Weekly*, vol. 39, no. 1990 (February 9, 1895), p. 135, as cited in Milton Meltzer, *Bread—and Roses: The Struggle of American Labor, 1865–1915* (Alfred A. Knopf, 1967), p. 41.

139 [*Testimony of Fannie Harris*]: quoted in Robert W. Smuts, *Women and Work in America* (Schocken Books, 1971), pp. 43–44; on child labor, see also Jacob A. Riis, *The Children of the Poor* (Scribner's, 1902).

[*Richardson*]: Dorothy Richardson, *The Long Day: The True Story of a New York Working Girl as Told by Herself* (Century, 1905), as cited in Smuts, pp. 70–72, Richardson quoted on owner at p. 72.

[*"A few hard chairs"*]: Rose Cohen, quoted in Katzman, p. 12.

[*Domestics' grievances*]: Helen Campbell, *Prisoners of Poverty* (Little, Brown, 1900), pp. 222–31, excerpted in Cott, pp. 322–26, quoted at pp. 323, 324.

[*Domestic work*]: Smuts, pp. 79–80, quoted at p. 80.

140 [*Wage data*]: Clarence D. Long, *Wages and Earnings in the United States, 1860–1890* (Princeton University Press, 1960), pp. 61–68, 109–10.

[*Incomes of the wealthy*]: Dumas Malone, ed., *Dictionary of American Biography* (Scribner's, 1929), vol. 1, p. 348 ("Philip Danforth Armour"), and vol. 3, pp. 500, 503 ("Andrew Carnegie"); Jules Abels, *The Rockefeller Billions* (Macmillan, 1965), p. 179.

[*Life in a steel works*]: Charles Rumford Walker, *Steel: The Diary of a Furnace Worker* (Atlantic Monthly Press, 1922), p. 16; John A. Fitch, *The Steel Workers* (Russell Sage Foundation, 1911), Part 1.

[*Accidents in a steel mill*]: Fitch, p. 64.

141 [*"I live in the mills"*]: quoted in *ibid.*, p. 201.

[*Home life in a mill town*]: *ibid.*, p. 203.

[*Homes of steel workers*]: Stefan Lorant, *Pittsburgh* (Author's Edition, Inc., 1980), p. 212.

[*Steel wages*]: Fitch, ch. 12; see also Paul Underwood Kellogg, ed., *Wage-Earning Pittsburgh* (Survey Associates, 1914), ch. 3.

[*Social evils of the urban environment*]: Riis, *The Other Half*, p. 3.

142 [*The Pullman experiment*]: Stanley Buder, *Pullman: An Experiment in Industrial Order and Community Planning, 1880–1930* (Oxford University Press, 1967), p. 41; and see also Meltzer, pp. 148–52.

Social Class and Social Outcast

142 [*Aristotle on the class system as universal*]: Aristotle, *Politics*, Benjamin Jowett, tr. (Modern Library, 1943), quoted at pp. 190, 191, 192.
[*Postwar disparity in income*]: Jeffrey G. Williamson and Peter H. Lindert, *American Inequality: A Macroeconomic History* (Academic Press, 1980), quoted at p. 75; see also J. R. Pole, *The Pursuit of Equality in American History* (University of California Press, 1978), p. 208.

143 [*Myth of "rags to riches" in Pittsburgh*]: John N. Ingham, *The Iron Barons: A Social Analysis of an American Urban Elite, 1874–1965* (Greenwood Press, 1978), quoted at p. 5; see also, Gutman, *op. cit.*, ch. 4.
[*Social and cultural forces in the industrial working class, and their political implications*]: see Melvin Rader, *Marx's Interpretation of History* (Oxford University Press, 1979); John M. Maguire, *Marx's Theory of Politics* (Cambridge University Press, 1978); Harry Cleaver, *Reading Capital Politically* (University of Texas Press, 1979); Gutman, *passim.*
[*Gutman on transformations of working class*]: Gutman, p. 15.

144 [*Eastern Europeans at Carnegie*]: David Brody, *Steel Workers in America: The Nonunion Era* (Harvard University Press, 1960), ch. 5, esp. p. 96.
[*"Nothing job, nothing job"*]: "Song of an Italian Workman," Rochester (N.Y.) *Post-Express*, n.d., reprinted in Gutman, p. 31.

145 [*Caste and class and race in the United States*]: Anthony de Reuck and Julie Knight, *Caste and Race: Comparative Approaches* (J. & A. Churchill, 1967); Celia S. Heller, ed., *Structured Social Inequality* (Macmillan, 1969); Reinhard Bendix and Seymour Martin Lipset, eds., *Class, Status, and Power* (Free Press, 1953).
[*Dimensions of caste*]: Max Weber, "Class, Status, Party," reprinted in Bendix and Lipset, pp. 63–75.
[*Jewish upper class in Manhattan*]: Stephen Birmingham, *"Our Crowd": The Great Jewish Families of New York* (Harper & Row, 1967), *passim;* John Higham, *Send These to Me* (Atheneum, 1975), esp. ch. 8; John Higham, "Anti-Semitism in the Gilded Age: A Reinterpretation," *Mississippi Valley Historical Review*, vol. 43, no. 4 (March 1957), pp. 559–78; see also Judith Rita Kramer and Seymour Leventman, *Children of the Gilded Ghetto* (Anchor Books, 1969).
[*Jewish aristocracy*]: Birmingham, p. ix.

146 [*Hierarchy within the Jewish community*]: *ibid.*, pp. 154–55; and see also Nathan Glazer, *American Judaism* (University of Chicago Press, 1957).
[*Jews and the Statue of Liberty*]: Birmingham, p. 128.
[*Ghetto to ghetto*]: Irving Howe, *World of Our Fathers* (Harcourt Brace Jovanovich, 1976), chs. 1–3, quoted at p. 67.
[*East Side living and working conditions*]: Howe, ch. 3, quoted at p. 88; and see Riis, *The Other Half, op. cit.*, chs. 10, 11.

147 [*"Jewtown"*]: Riis, *The Other Half*, p. 104.
[*Jews indifferent to abuse*]: *ibid.*, p. 42.
[*Nineteenth century immigration*]: Richard B. Morris, ed., *Encyclopedia of American History* (Harper & Bros., 1961), pp. 471–72.

148 [*Blacks in Washington*]: James Borchert, *Alley Life in Washington* (University of Illinois Press, 1980).
[*A "vile place"*]: quoted in *ibid.*, pp. 26–27.
[*Color line in Manhattan*]: Riis, *The Other Half*, p. 150.
[*Ethnic cleanliness*]: *ibid.*
[*"Once a colored house"*]: quoted in *ibid.*, p. 151.
[*Welshman on Southern blacks*]: John R. Williams to William Thomas, letter of November 10, 1895, in Mortimer S. Adler, ed., *The Negro in American History: A Taste of Freedom, 1854–1927* (Encyclopaedia Britannica Educational Corporation, 1969), pp. 137–41, quoted at pp. 139, 140.

149 [*Black cowhands*]: Kenneth W. Porter, "Negro Labor in the Western Cattle Industry, 1866–1900," in Milton Cantor, ed., *Black Labor in America* (Negro Universities Press, 1969), pp. 24–52.
[*Vardaman on official Southern racism*]: quoted in E. Franklin Frazier, *The Negro in the United States* (Macmillan, 1949), p. 157; and see C. Vann Woodward, *The Strange Career of Jim Crow* (Oxford University Press, 1974).

149 [*Kansas Exodus*]: Charles H. Wesley, *Negro Labor in the United States, 1850–1925* (Russell & Russell, 1967), pp. 213–15.
149–50 [*Cheyennes vs. the Union Pacific*]: Angie Debo, *A History of the Indians of the United States* (University of Oklahoma Press, 1970), pp. 185–86.
150 [*Ten Bears against settling*]: quoted in *ibid.*, pp. 187–88.
    [*The Sioux*]: Ruth Underhill, *Red Man's America* (University of Chicago Press, 1953), ch. 8; see also George Bird Grinnell, *When Buffalo Ran* (University of Oklahoma Press, 1966); Royal Hassrick, *The Sioux: Life and Customs of a Warrior Society* (University of Oklahoma Press, 1972); and Warren K. Moorehead, *The American Indian in the United States: Period 1850–1914* (Andover Press, 1914).
    [*Sioux Ghost Dance*]: Alvin M. Josephy, Jr., *The Indian Heritage of America* (Alfred A. Knopf, 1968), p. 121; Underhill, p. 159.
    [*Sioux preparation for the hunt*]: Grinnell, p. 19.
    [*The hunt*]: Underhill, p. 156.
    [*The agriculturalists of the Southwest*]: E. E. Dale, *The Indians of the Southwest* (University of Oklahoma Press, 1949); Josephy, ch. 16; Underhill, ch. 9; Clark Wissler, *Indians of the United States* (Doubleday, 1966), ch. 22.
151 [*Hopi snake dance*]: Wissler, p. 220.
    [*The pueblo*]: *ibid.*, p. 225.
    [*The Navajos and Apaches*]: Underhill, ch. 10.
    [*Kwakiutl competitiveness and cannibalism*]: Phillip Drucker, *Cultures of the North Pacific Coast* (Chandler, 1965), ch. 8; Josephy, p. 77; Wissler, p. 119.

5. THE POWER OF IDEAS

152 [Times *on liberty*]: *New York Times,* October 29, 1886, p. 1.
152–3 [*Creation and dedication of the Statue of Liberty*]: Marvin Trachtenberg, *The Statue of Liberty* (Penguin Books, 1976); Rodman Gilder, *The Battery* (Houghton Mifflin, 1936), pp. 219–20.
153 [*Cleveland's acceptance of the Statue*]: quoted in *New York Times,* October 29, 1886, p. 2.
    [*Liberty*]: Christian Bay, *The Structure of Freedom* (Stanford University Press, 1958); Sidney Hook, *The Paradoxes of Freedom* (University of California Press, 1964); Louis Hartz, *The Liberal Tradition in America* (Harcourt, Brace, 1955).
    [*Webster on Liberty and Union*]: *Register of Debates* (Gales and Seaton, 1830), vol. 6, 21st Congress, 1st session, January 27, 1830, p. 80.
    [*Adams on liberty and property*]: from John Adams, *A Defense of the Constitutions of the Governments of the United States,* quoted in Francis W. Coker, *Democracy, Liberty, and Property* (Macmillan, 1942), p. 125.
    [*Emerson's liberty*]: see James MacGregor Burns, *The Vineyard of Liberty* (Alfred A. Knopf, 1982), pp. 483, 491.
154 [*Marx on bourgeois liberty*]: Karl Marx, "On the Jewish Question," in Robert C. Tucker, ed., *The Marx-Engels Reader* (W. W. Norton, 1972), p. 40.

Dinner at Delmonico's

155 [*Liberty and laissez-faire*]: R. L. Meek, *The Economics of Physiocracy* (Harvard University Press, 1963).
    [*Malthus*]: T. R. Malthus, *Principles of Political Economy,* 2nd ed. (W. Pickering, 1836).
    [*Ricardo*]: David Ricardo, *On the Principles of Political Economy and Taxation,* 3rd ed. (John Murray, 1821).
    [*Wayland*]: *The Elements of Political Economy* (Gould, Kendall and Lincoln, 1837).
156 [*Individualism, late nineteenth-century America*]: Irvin G. Wyllie, *Self-Made Man in America* (Rutgers University Press, 1954); Kenneth S. Lynn, *Dream of Success: The Modern American Imagination* (Little, Brown, 1955); Theodore P. Greene, *America's Heroes* (Oxford University Press, 1970); Moses Rischin, ed., *The American Gospel of Success* (Quadrangle, 1965); Richard M. Huber, *The American Idea of Success* (McGraw-Hill, 1971).
    [*The "Great Train Robbery"*]: Clinton Rossiter, *Conservatism in America* (Alfred A. Knopf, 1955), p. 221.
    [*Conservatism in nineteenth-century America*]: Sidney Fine, *Laissez Faire and the General-Wel-*

fare State: A Study of Conflict in American Thought, 1865–1901 (University of Michigan Press, 1956), *passim,* from whom Atkinson (p. 52), J. S. Mill (p. 9), the theologian, Roswell D. Hitchcock (p. 121), and Burgess (p. 94), respectively, are quoted; see also Rossiter, esp. chs. 3 and 4; Vernon Louis Parrington, *The Beginnings of Critical Realism in America* (Harcourt, Brace and World, 1958), vol. 3 of *Main Currents in American Thought.*

157 [*Darwin vs. the creationists*]: Ralph Henry Gabriel, *The Course of American Democratic Thought,* 2nd ed. (Ronald Press, 1956), ch. 14.

[*The "Vogue of Spencer"*]: Richard Hofstadter, *Social Darwinism in American Thought,* rev. ed. (Beacon Press, 1955), ch. 2; Andrew Carnegie, *Autobiography* (Houghton Mifflin, 1920), esp. pp. 333–39; John Fiske, *Edward Livingston Youmans* (D. Appleton, 1894), esp. pp. 502–51.

[*Spencer on true liberty*]: Herbert Spencer, *Social Statics* (D. Appleton, 1865), quoted in Fine, p. 33.

[*Spencerism and its influence*]: Herbert Spencer, *An Autobiography,* 2 vols. (D. Appleton, 1904); for recent analyses of Social Darwinism see Robert C. Bannister, *Social Darwinism: Science and Myth in Anglo-American Social Thought* (Temple University Press, 1979); Greta Jones, *Social Darwinism and English Thought: The Interaction Between Biological and Social Theory* (Humanities Press, 1980); Gertrude Himmelfarb, *Darwin and the Darwinian Revolution* (W. W. Norton, 1962); Jack Jones, "Social Darwinism Reconsidered," *Political Psychology* (Spring–Summer 1981–82), pp. 239–66.

158 [*Hofstadter on Spencer*]: Hofstadter, p. 32.

[*American sales of Spencer's books*]: *ibid.,* p. 34.

[*James on Spencer*]: Fine, p. 41.

[*Professors agreeing on free competition*]: J. F. Normano, *The Spirit of American Economics* (John Day, 1943), p. 61, quoted in Fine, pp. 11–12; see also Joseph Dorfman, *The Economic Mind in American Civilization* (Viking Press, 1946–59), vol. 2; Anna Haddow, *Political Science in American Colleges and Universities, 1636–1900* (D. Appleton-Century, 1939), Part 4.

[*Sumner*]: Hofstadter, ch. 3; Stow Persons, ed., *Social Darwinism: Selected Essays of William Graham Sumner* (Prentice-Hall, 1963); Bruce Curtis, *William Graham Sumner* (Twayne, 1981).

[*Sumner on "strong" and "weak"*]: quoted in Hofstadter, p. 57.

[*Sumner on the natural selection of millionaires*]: *ibid.,* p. 58.

159 [*Student exchange with Sumner*]: William Lyon Phelps, "When Yale Was Given to Sumnerology" (review of Harris E. Starr, *William Graham Sumner*), *Literary Digest International Book Review,* vol. 3, no. 10 (September 1925), pp. 661–63, quoted at p. 661.

[*Clergymen on success and property*]: quoted in Fine, pp. 118–19.

[*Edwin Lawrence Godkin on government intervention and corruption*]: quoted in Parrington, vol. 3, p. 162.

160 [*Horatio Alger, Jr.*]: John Tebbel, *From Rags to Riches* (Macmillan, 1963); Ralph D. Gardner, *Horatio Alger, or the American Hero Era* (Wayside Press, 1964); Herbert R. Mayes, *Alger* (Macy-Masius, 1928).

]*Huber on Alger's heroes*]: Huber, p. 46.

[*Greene on Munsey*]: Greene, quoted at p. 99.

["*Riches, power*"]: quoted in *ibid.,* p. 99.

[*White on Munsey*]: *ibid.,* p. 102.

[McGuffey Reader *on trying*]: quoted in Rischin, p. 45.

161 [*Carnegie on Spencer*]: quoted in Joseph F. Wall, *Andrew Carnegie* (Oxford University Press, 1970), p. 381.

[*Dinner at Delmonico's*]: Spencer, *Autobiography,* vol. 2, p. 478; *New York Times,* November 10, 1882, p. 5; Carnegie, pp. 335–37; Wall, pp. 387–89; Lately Thomas, *Delmonico's* (Houghton Mifflin, 1967); Ethel F. Fisk, ed., *The Letters of John Fiske* (Macmillan, 1940), p. 478.

162 [*Wall on other speakers*]: Wall, p. 388.

[*Beecher's qualified endorsement of evolution*]: quoted in *New York Times,* November 10, 1882, p. 5.

The Bitch-Goddess Success

162 [*Dinner at Delmonico's for Henry George*]: *New York Times*, October 22, 1882, p. 9; Perry Belmont, *An American Democrat* (Columbia University Press, 1940), pp. 296–97.
[*Henry George*]: Henry George, Jr., *The Life of Henry George* (Robert Schalkenbach Foundation, 1960); Charles Albro Barker, *Henry George* (Oxford University Press, 1955).
163 [*Henry George on man's right to the free gifts of nature*]: quoted in George, Jr., p. 223.
[*Bellamy*]: Sylvia E. Bowman, *The Year 2000: A Critical Biography of Edward Bellamy* (Bookman Associates, 1958), esp. pp. 107–52.
164 [*Bellamy on his purpose in writing* Looking Backward]: Edward Bellamy, "How I Wrote *Looking Backward,*" *Ladies' Home Journal*, vol. 2, no. 5 (April 1894), quoted in A. E. Morgan, *Edward Bellamy* (Columbia University Press, 1944), pp. 229–30.
[Looking Backward]: Edward Bellamy, *Looking Backward, 2000–1887* (Houghton Mifflin, 1888).
[*The metaphor of the coach*]: ibid., pp. 10–12.
164–5 [*Dialogue between Julian West and Edith*]: Edward Bellamy, *Equality* (D. Appleton, 1897), pp. 4–13.
166 [*Lloyd*]: Chester McArthur Destler, *Henry Demarest Lloyd and the Empire of Reform* (University of Pennsylvania Press, 1963).
[*Destler on Lloyd*]: ibid., p. 301.
166–7 [*George on* Looking Backward]: quoted in Barker, p. 540.
167 [*Lloyd on George*]: quoted in Destler, p. 136.
[*Bellamy, nationalizing and "Nationalism"*]: Bowman, pp. 122–38, 308–14.
[*Bellamy-George exchange*]: quoted in Morgan, pp. 392–93.
[*Bellamy on the word* socialist]: quoted in John A. Garraty, *The New Commonwealth, 1877–1890* (Harper & Row, 1968), p. 319; see also, Bellamy, *Looking Backward*, p. 252.
[*"Prince of muddleheads"*]: quoted in Garraty, p. 319.
[*Marx on George as theorist*]: quoted in Barker, p. 356.
[*Lloyd on Marx's determinism*]: quoted in Destler, pp. 180, 508.
[*Gladden*]: see Washington Gladden, *Applied Christianity: Moral Aspects of Social Questions* (Houghton Mifflin, 1886), esp. pp. 103 ff; Washington Gladden, *Tools and the Man* (Houghton Mifflin, 1893).
[*Morris on* Looking Backward]: quoted in Parrington, *op. cit.,* vol. 3, pp. 311–12.
167–8 [*Post–Civil War New England culture*]: Van Wyck Brooks, *New England: Indian Summer, 1865–1915* (E. P. Dutton, 1940); Parrington, vol. 3, *passim;* see also F. O. Matthiessen, *American Renaissance* (Oxford University Press, 1941).
[*Parrington on nostalgia for Federalism*]: Parrington, vol. 3, p. 50.
[*Adams on Boston*]: Henry Adams, *The Life of George Cabot Lodge* (Houghton Mifflin, 1911), quoted in Brooks, p. 199 footnote.
[*Twain on his Boston audience*]: quoted in ibid., p. 8.
[*Brooks on exhaustion of old reformers*]: ibid., p. 120.
169 [*Henry Adams*]: Ernest Samuels, *Henry Adams*, 3 vols. (Belknap Press of Harvard University Press, 1948–64); Henry Adams, *The Education of Henry Adams* (Houghton Mifflin, 1918).
[*Adams trying to drive away students*]: quoted in Brooks, p. 254 footnote.
[*Mrs. Lightfoot Lee and power*]: Henry Adams, *Democracy* (Farrar, Straus and Young, n.d.), p. 10.
[*Henry James*]: Leon Edel, *Henry James* (J. B. Lippincott, 1953–72), vol. 1; Maxwell Geismar, *Henry James and the Jacobites* (Houghton Mifflin, 1963).
170 [*James's alleged lampooning of Peabody*]: Edel, vol. 3, pp. 142–43.
[*Parrington on James's concern only with nuances*]: Parrington, vol. 3, p. 241.
[*James as "pragmatizing"*]: quoted in Brooks, p. 228.
[*James's (not necessarily intended) "figure in the carpet"*]: Geismar, pp. 137–39.
[*"Best and brightest"*]: quoted in Brooks, p. 188.
[*Howells*]: Kenneth S. Lynn, *William Dean Howells: An American Life* (Harcourt Brace Jovanovich, 1971).
[*Twain*]: Justin Kaplan, *Mr. Clemens and Mark Twain* (Simon and Schuster, 1966); Roger B. Salomon, *Twain and the Image of History* (Yale University Press, 1961); Philip S. Foner, *Mark Twain: Social Critic* (International Publishers, 1958).

171 [*Huck on the Mississippi*]: Mark Twain, *The Adventures of Huckleberry Finn* (American Publishing, 1903), p. 161.
[*Huck's escapism*]: Albert E. Stone, Jr., *The Innocent Eye: Childhood in Mark Twain's Imagination* (Yale University Press, 1961), esp. ch. 5.
[*Huck on Aunt Sally's effort to "sivilize" him*]: Twain, p. 375.
[*"I'd got to decide, forever"*]: ibid., p. 279. On Huck's decision, see also Leo Marx, *The Machine in the Garden* (Oxford University Press, 1964), pp. 337–38.
[*"NOTICE" to the reader*]: Twain, p. iii.
[*Norris*]: Ernest Marchand, *Frank Norris* (Octagon Books, 1981); William B. Dillingham, *Frank Norris: Instinct and Art* (University of Nebraska Press, 1969).
[McTeague]: Frank Norris, *McTeague: A Story of San Francisco* (Doubleday, Doran, 1928).
172 [The Octopus]: Frank Norris, *The Octopus; The Epic of the Wheat: A Story of California* (P. F. Collier, 1901), quoted at p. 473.
[*Huck on the steamboat smashing through the raft*]: Twain, p. 133.

"Toiling Millions Now Are Waking"

173 [*De Leon on the Declaration of Independence*]: quoted in David Herreshoff, *American Disciples of Marx* (Wayne State University Press, 1967), pp. 167–68.
[*Marx on wages labor as a probational state*]: quoted in Stuart Bruce Kaufman, *Samuel Gompers and the Origins of the American Federation of Labor, 1848–1896* (Greenwood Press, 1973), p. 28.
[*Early development of American socialism*]: Howard H. Quint, *The Forging of American Socialism* (University of South Carolina Press, 1953), esp. ch. 1; Herreshoff, chs. 3–4.
174 [*Woodhull & Claflin's Weekly*]: most issues in New-York Historical Society; *Communist Manifesto* in issue of December 30, 1871; see also, Herreshoff, pp. 83–84, 86.
175 [*National Labor Union*]: Gerald N. Grob, *Workers and Utopia* (Northwestern University Press, 1961), ch. 2.
[*Socialists on letting "wage slavery" go on*]: Kaufman, p. 85.
[*Union membership, 1878*]: see Philip S. Foner, *History of the Labor Movement in the United States* (International Publishers, 1947–65), vol. 1, pp. 439–40.
[*Labor troubles of 1870s*]: Philip S. Foner, *The Great Labor Uprising of 1877* (Monad Press, 1977); Garraty, *op. cit.*, ch. 4; Jeremy Brecher, *Strike!* (South End Press, 1972), ch. 1; Herbert Gutman, *Work, Culture and Society in Industrializing Ame.ica* (Alfred A. Knopf, 1976), ch. 6.
[*Molly Maguires*]: Louis Adamic, *Dynamite* (Viking Press, 1934), ch. 2.
176 [*Adams on railroad strikes*]: Edward Chase Kirkland, *Charles Francis Adams, Jr.* (Harvard University Press, 1965), pp. 54–55.
[*National trade unions*]: Norman J. Ware, *The Labor Movement in the United States, 1860–1895* (D. Appleton, 1929); Lloyd Ulman, *The Rise of the National Trade Union* (Harvard University Press, 1955); John Philip Hall, "The Knights of St. Crispin in Massachusetts, 1869–1878," *Journal of Economic History*, vol. 18, no. 2 (June 1958), pp. 161–75.
[*Knights of Labor and the strikes of 1884 and 1886*]: Brecher, ch. 2; Grob, chs. 3, 4; Gerald N. Grob, "The Knights of Labor and the Trade Unions, 1878–1886," *Journal of Economic History*, vol. 18, no. 2 (June 1958), pp. 176–92; Foner, *History of the Labor Movement*, vol. 1, ch. 21, pp. 504–12 and vol. 2, chs. 3–5; James MacGregor Burns, "Labor's Drive to Majority Status," unpub. dissertation, Williams College, 1939.
[*Garraty on Powderly*]: Garraty, p. 162.
[*Powderly on the word "class"*]: quoted in Harold C. Livesay, *Samuel Gompers and Organized Labor in America* (Little, Brown, 1978), p. 77.
[*"Toiling millions now are waking"*]: quoted in Adamic, p. 62.
177 [*Haymarket Massacre*]: Henry David, *The History of the Haymarket Affair* (Farrar & Rinehart, 1936); Adamic, ch. 6; Philip S. Foner, *The Autobiography of the Haymarket Martyrs* (Humanities Press, 1969).
[*Anarchist circular*]: reprinted in Adamic, p. 70.
[*"Then we'll all go home"*]: quoted in *ibid.*, p. 73.
178 [*David on the Haymarket "martyrs"*]: David, p. 534.
[*The American Federation of Labor*]: Livesay; Kaufman; Foner, *History of the Labor Movement*, vol. 2, chs. 9, 12; Grob, *Workers and Utopia*, chs. 8, 9; John Laslett, "Reflections on the

Failure of Socialism in the American Federation of Labor," *Mississippi Valley Historical Review*, vol. 50, no. 4 (March 1964), pp. 634–51.

178 [*Strasser's dialogue with the senator*]: quoted in Garraty, p. 170.

179 [*Gompers's early life and apprenticeship*]: Samuel Gompers, *Seventy Years of Life and Labor* (E. P. Dutton, 1925), vol. 1, book 1; Livesay, chs. 1–3.
[*"Study your union card, Sam"*]: Karl Laurrell, quoted in Gompers, vol. 1, p. 75.
[*Gompers on improving material conditions*]: quoted in Kaufman, p. 174.

180 [*"The only desirable legislation for the workers"*]: Twentieth Century Fund, *Labor and the Government* (McGraw-Hill, 1935), pp. 14–15.
[*Gompers and Social Darwinism*]: Gompers, vol. 2, ch. 26; George B. Cotkin, "The Spencerian and Comtian Nexus in Gompers' Labor Philosophy: The Impact of Non-Marxian Evolutionary Thought," *Labor History*, vol. 20, no. 4 (Fall 1979), pp. 510–23.

The Alliance: A Democracy of Leaders

[*"Largest democratic mass movement"*]: Lawrence Goodwyn, *The Populist Moment* (Oxford University Press, 1978), p. vii.

181 [*Crop lien system*]: Lawrence Goodwyn, *Democratic Promise: The Populist Moment in America* (Oxford University Press, 1976), pp. 26–31.
[*"Laboring men of America"*]: W. Scott Morgan, *History of the Wheel and Alliance and the Impending Revolution* (W. Scott Morgan, 1889), p. 24, quoted in Martha A. Warner, *Kansas Populism: A Sociological Analysis* (M.A. thesis, University of Kansas, 1956), p. 94.

182 [*Founding and structure of Farmers' Alliance*]: Goodwyn, *Democratic Promise*, pp. 33–40; Topeka *Advocate*, July 22, 1891; John D. Hicks, *The Populist Revolt* (University of Nebraska Press, 1961), pp. 128–29; Homer Clevenger, "The Teaching Techniques of the Farmers' Alliance," *Journal of Southern History*, vol. 11, no. 4 (November 1945), pp. 504–18.
[*Lamb*]: Goodwyn, *Democratic Promise*, pp. 40–41; Roscoe C. Martin, *The People's Party in Texas: A Study in Third Party Politics* (reprint; University of Texas Press, 1970), pp. 44–45.
[*Great Southwest Strike and the Alliance*]: Goodwyn, *Democratic Promise*, pp. 54–65.
[*Growth of Alliance membership*]: *ibid.*, pp. 65, 73.
[*Cleburne convention and demands*]: *ibid.*, pp. 77–83, demands quoted at p. 79; Hicks, pp. 105–6.

183 [*Macune*]: Hicks, pp. 106–9; Goodwyn, *Democratic Promise*, pp. 83–86; Annie L. Diggs, "The Farmers' Alliance and Some of Its Leaders," *The Arena*, no. 29 (April 1892), pp. 598–600; C. Vann Woodward, *Origins of the New South, 1877–1913* (Louisiana State University Press, 1951), p. 190.
[*"Freedom from the tyranny of organized capital"*]: quoted in Goodwyn, *Democratic Promise*, p. 90.
[*Waco, 1887*]: *ibid.*, pp. 89–91; Hicks, pp. 107–9.
[*Farmers like "ripe fruit"*]: William L. Garvin and S. O. Daws, *History of the National Farmers' Alliance and Cooperative Union of America* (J. N. Rogers, 1887), pp. 49–50, quoted in Hicks, p. 110.

184 [*Georgia Alliance and the "jute trust"*]: C. Vann Woodward, *Tom Watson: Agrarian Rebel* (Macmillan, 1938), pp. 136, 141–42; Alex M. Arnett, *The Populist Movement in Georgia* (Columbia University Press, 1922; reprinted by AMS Press, 1967), p. 100; see also Steven Hahn, *The Roots of Southern Populism* (Oxford University Press, 1983).
[*Kansas Alliance and the "twine trust"*]: Goodwyn, *Democratic Promise*, pp. 94–107; W. F. Rightmire, "The Alliance Movement in Kansas," *Kansas State Historical Society Collections*, vol. 9 (1906), pp. 3–4; W. P. Harrington, "The Populist Party in Kansas," *Kansas State Historical Society Collections*, vol. 16 (1925), pp. 405–6; *American Nonconformist* (Winfield, Kansas), April 4, 11, 1889.
[*Sectionalism of postwar Democratic and Republican parties*]: Goodwyn, *Democratic Promise*, pp. 4–10.
[*Kansas People's Party*]: Topeka *Advocate*, June 18, 1890; Rightmire, p. 5; Harrington, pp. 410–11; Hicks, pp. 155–56.

185 [*Simpson*]: Paul Dean Harper, *The Speechmaking of Jerry Simpson* (M.A. thesis, Kansas State College of Pittsburg, 1967), pp. 30–44; O. Gene Clanton, *Kansas Populism* (University Press of Kansas, 1969), pp. 82–87.

185 [*Simpson on debate with Hallowell*]: quoted in Clanton, p. 86.

[*Diggs on Alliance women*]: Annie L. Diggs, "The Women in the Alliance Movement," *The Arena*, no. 32 (July 1892), pp. 163–64.

[*Diggs*]: Ross E. Paulson, "Annie LePorte Diggs," in Edward T. James, ed., *Notable American Women, 1607–1950* (Belknap Press of Harvard University Press, 1971), vol. 1, pp. 481–82; Walter T. K. Nugent, *The Tolerant Populists: Kansas Populism and Nativism* (University of Chicago Press, 1963), p. 135.

[*Lease*]: Diggs, "Women in the Alliance Movement," pp. 165–67; Clanton, pp. 73–78; *American Nonconformist*, September 25, 1890.

[*"Pinning sheets of notes"*]: Clanton, p. 74.

186 [*"A golden voice"*]: William Allen White, *The Autobiography of William Allen White* (Macmillan, 1946), p. 218.

[*Diggs on Lease's voice*]: Diggs, "Women in the Alliance Movement," p. 166.

[*"Less corn and more Hell!"*]: quoted in Elizabeth Barr, "The Populist Uprising," in William E. Connelley, *History of Kansas: State and People* (American Historical Society, 1928), vol. 2, p. 1166.

[*Kansas Populists in the elections of 1890 and 1892*]: Goodwyn, *Democratic Promise*, pp. 200–201, 317–18; Nugent, pp. 91–93, 123–24.

[*"First People's party government on earth"*]: Clanton, p. 129.

[*"Incendiary Haymarket inaugural"*]: quoted in *ibid.*, p. 131.

[*Kansas tug-of-war*]: *ibid.*, pp. 131–36; Barr in Connelley, pp. 1184–98.

187 [*Goodwyn on the People's Party*]: Goodwyn, *Populist Moment*, pp. 126–27.

[*Woodward on complexities of race*]: Woodward, *Watson*, p. 220.

[*Populism and American blacks*]: Goodwyn, *Democratic Promise*, ch. 10; Norman Pollack, ed., *The Populist Mind* (Bobbs-Merrill, 1967), part 4, ch. 2.

[*Watson*]: Woodward, *Watson*, *passim*.

188 [*"I did not lead the Alliance"*]: quoted in *ibid.*, p. 140.

[*Watson's 1890 campaign for Congress*]: *ibid.*, pp. 146–50, 156–61; Arnett, pp. 113–14.

[*"Nebuchadnezzar's furnace"*]: quoted in Arnett, p. 114.

[*Watson in Congress*]: Woodward, *Watson*, ch. 12.

[*Watson on economic basis for black-white division*]: Watson, "The Negro Question in the South," *The Arena*, no. 35 (October 1892), pp. 540–50, in Pollack, pp. 361–74, quoted at p. 371.

[*Watson's 1892 electoral defeat*]: Woodward, *Watson*, pp. 227–43; Arnett, pp. 143–55.

[*Texas Alliance Exchange*]: Goodwyn, *Democratic Promise*, pp. 125–42.

189 [*Subtreasury as instrument of political revolt*]: *ibid.*, p. 243.

[*Founding of People's Party of Texas*]: *ibid.*, pp. 285–91; Martin, pp. 36–41.

[*Donnelly's St. Louis address*]: quoted in Goodwyn, *Democratic Promise*, p. 265.

[*Omaha convention*]: *ibid.*, pp. 270–72; George B. Tindall, "The People's Party," in Arthur M. Schlesinger, Jr., ed., *History of U.S. Political Parties* (Chelsea House, 1973), vol. 2, pp. 1714–16.

[*People's Party platform, 1892*]: Pollack, pp. 60–66, quoted at pp. 63, 64.

[*Populist campaign and election results*]: Tindall in Schlesinger, vol. 2, pp. 1716–18; Theodore Saloutos, *Farmer Movements in the South, 1865–1933* (University of California Press, 1960), pp. 133–35.

[*"A regular walking omelet"*]: quoted in Barr in Connelley, p. 1183.

6. The Brokers of Politics

192 [*"Government . . . for the benefit of Senators"*]: Henry Adams, *Democracy* (Farrar, Straus and Young, n.d.), pp. 22–23.

[*Emerson and Burroughs on Whitman's eyes*]: quoted in Mark Van Doren, "Walt Whitman," in Dumas Malone, ed., *Dictionary of American Biography*, vol. 20 (Scribner's, 1936), p. 146.

[*Parrington on Whitman*]: Vernon L. Parrington, *Main Currents in American Thought* (Harcourt, Brace, 1927), vol. 3, p. 69.

[*Whitman's familiarity with Mill and Tocqueville*]: see Roger Asselineau, *The Evolution of Walt Whitman* (Harvard University Press, 1960–62), vol. 2, pp. 331–32.

[*Whitman on "our great experiment"*]: quoted in Parrington, vol. 3, p. 72.

192–3 [*"I chant . . . the common bulk"*]: quoted in Asselineau, vol. 2, p. 154.

193 [*"Divine average"*]: see "Starting from Paumanok," in Whitman, *Leaves of Grass* (Double-day, Doran, 1929), p. 17.
[*Whitman on Whitman, "a kosmos"*]: "Song of Myself," in *ibid.*, pp. 43–44.
[*Whitman in the Brooklyn* Eagle]: Whitman, *The Gathering of the Forces*, Cleveland Rodgers and John Black, eds., 2 vols. (Putnam's, 1920).
[*Whitman on equality, including female*]: "Preface to 1855 Edition," in *Leaves of Grass*, p. 491. See also F. O. Matthiessen, *American Renaissance* (Oxford University Press, 1946), ch. 13.
[*"Pride, competition, segregation"*]: *Democratic Vistas* (1871) in Whitman, *Prose Works, 1892*, Floyd Stovall, ed. (New York University Press, 1963–64), vol. 2, pp. 361–426, quoted at p. 422.
[*"The People!"*]: *ibid.*, p. 376.
[*"Pervading flippancy and vulgarity"*]: *ibid.*, p. 372.
[*Whitman on need for natural leaders*]: see Asselineau, vol. 2, pp. 154–55.
194 [*Marx on class flux in the United States*]: "The Eighteenth Brumaire of Louis Bonaparte," in Robert C. Tucker, ed., *The Marx-Engels Reader* (W. W. Norton, 1972), p. 444.
[*Mr. Gore and Mrs. Lee on democracy in America*]: Adams, pp. 53, 54.

The Ohioans: Leaders as Brokers

194-5 [*Republican convention, 1868*]: quoted in Arthur M. Schlesinger, Jr., ed., *History of U.S. Political Parties* (Chelsea House, 1973), vol. 2, pp. 1337, 1340.
195 [*Journalist on Ohio "conspiracy"*]: Rollin Hartt, "The Ohioans," *Atlantic Monthly*, vol. 84 (1899), p. 690.
[*Pre–Civil War Ohio politics*]: Stephen E. Maizlish, *The Triumph of Sectionalism: The Transformation of Ohio Politics, 1844–1856* (Kent State University Press, 1983).
[*Hartt on Ohio*]: "The Ohioans," p. 682.
196 [*"A neighborly place"*]: Walter Havighurst, *Ohio: A Bicentennial History* (W. W. Norton, 1976), p. 138.
[*Ohio boxing the compass*]: Hartt, p. 684.
[*Ohio cities*]: Havighurst, p. 121.
[*Growth of city populations*]: John Sherman, *Recollections of Forty Years* (Werner, 1895), vol. 1, p. 71.
[*City culture and industry*]: Havighurst, pp. 109–18, 150; William Rose, *Cleveland: The Making of a City* (World, 1950); Writers' Program, *Cincinnati* (Wiesen-Hart Press, 1943; reprinted by Somerset Publishers, 1973).
197 [*Impact of railroads*]: Hartt, p. 680; Sherman, vol. 1, p. 70.
[*"Smoke means business"*]: Hartt, p. 681.
[*Cities and blacks*]: David Gerber, *Black Ohio and the Color Line* (University of Illinois Press, 1976); W. A. Joiner, *A Half Century of Freedom of the Negro in Ohio* (1915; reprinted by Books for Libraries Press, 1977).
[*Basis of old Ohio civilization*]: Havighurst, p. 115.
[*Young Ohio leaders*]: Felice A. Bonadio, *North of Reconstruction: Ohio Politics, 1865–1870* (New York University Press, 1970), pp. 24–27.
198 [*Faith of the new leaders*]: *ibid.*, p. 30.
[*Array of Ohio leadership*]: see William Dean Howells, *Stories of Ohio* (American Book, 1897), chs. 24–25.
[*Ohio's "treacherous" politics*]: Bonadio, p. 22. On Ohio leadership and politics generally, see collections in Ohio Historical Society, especially the Charles Kurtz Papers and the William Henry Smith Papers.
[*"Every man for himself"*]: Cox to Aaron Perry, January 25, 1867, quoted in Bonadio, p. 73.
[*Garfield*]: Margaret Leech and Harry J. Brown, *The Garfield Orbit* (Harper & Row, 1978); Allan Peskin, *Garfield* (Kent State University Press, 1978); Theodore Clarke Smith, *The Life and Letters of James Abram Garfield* (Yale University Press, 1925), vol. 1; James D. Norris and Arthur H. Shaffer, eds., *Politics and Patronage in the Gilded Age: The Correspondence of James A. Garfield and Charles E. Henry* (State Historical Society of Wisconsin, 1970).
199 [*Sherman*]: Theodore E. Burton, *John Sherman* (Houghton Mifflin, 1906); Sherman, *Recollections*.

200 [*Hayes*]: Harry Barnard, *Rutherford B. Hayes and His America* (Bobbs-Merrill, 1954); H. J. Eckenrode, *Rutherford B. Hayes: Statesman of Reunion* (Dodd, Mead, 1930).
[*"Not too much hard work"*]: quoted in Barnard, p. 242.
[*Hayes on reform of appointments*]: diary entry of March 28, 1875, in Charles R. Williams, ed., *Diary and Letters of Rutherford Birchard Hayes* (Ohio State Archaeological and Historical Society, 1922–26), vol. 3, p. 269.
[*"Grantism"*]: William S. McFeely, *Grant: A Biography* (W. W. Norton, 1981), chs. 24–25; Thomas A. Bailey, *A Diplomatic History of the American People*, 9th ed. (Prentice-Hall, 1974), pp. 379, 383.
[*Waite*]: Peter C. Magrath, *Morrison R. Waite: The Triumph of Character* (Macmillan, 1963).
201 [*Hayes on push and shove*]: quoted in Bonadio, p. 27.
[*The election of 1876 and the Compromise of 1877*]: C. Vann Woodward, *Reunion and Reaction* (Little, Brown, 1951); Keith Ian Polakoff, *The Politics of Inertia* (Louisiana State University Press, 1973); Allan Peskin, "Was There a Compromise of 1877?," *Journal of American History*, vol. 60, no. 1 (June 1973), pp. 63–75; C. Vann Woodward, "Yes, There Was a Compromise of 1877," *ibid.*, pp. 215–23.

Politics: The Dance of the Ropewalkers

203 [*Huntington's direct action*]: Woodward, *Reunion and Reaction, op. cit.*, pp. 235–36.
[*Josephson on the talkers and the actors*]: Matthew Josephson, *The Politicos* (Harcourt, Brace, 1938), p. vii.
[*Constriction of the Fourteenth Amendment*]: *U.S.* v. *Cruikshank*, 92 U.S. 542 (1876), quoted at pp. 545–55; Civil rights cases, 109 U.S. 3 (1883).
[*Origins of the Fourteenth Amendment*]: Howard Jay Graham, "The Early Antislavery Backgrounds of the Fourteenth Amendment," *Wisconsin Law Review* (May 1950), pp. 479–661; Jacobus tenBroek, *The Antislavery Origins of the Fourteenth Amendment* (University of California Press, 1951); Raoul Berger, *Government by Judiciary* (Harvard University Press, 1977); Joseph B. James, *The Framing of the Fourteenth Amendment* (University of Illinois Press, 1956).
204 [*Conkling's interpretation of Fourteenth Amendment*]: Kenneth Stampp, *The Era of Reconstruction: 1865–1877* (Alfred A. Knopf, 1975), pp. 137–38.
[*Women and the Fourteenth Amendment*]: Ellen C. Du Bois, *Feminism and Suffrage* (Cornell University Press, 1978), pp. 58–62, 65; Bettina Aptheker, *Woman's Legacy* (University of Massachusetts Press, 1982), ch. 2.
[*Anthony's vote and arrest*]: Alma Lutz, *Susan B. Anthony: Rebel, Crusader, Humanitarian* (Beacon Press, 1959), pp. 198–213, quoted at p. 201.
[*Virginia Minor case*]: *Minor* v. *Happersett*, 88 U.S. 162 (1875).
[*Hopes for a new North-South party of property*]: Woodward, ch. 2.
[*Raleigh* Observer *on reviving the Whig Party*]: April 4, 1877, quoted in *ibid.*, p. 39.
205 [*Continuing strength of the Democratic party*]: Jerome Mushkat, *The Reconstruction of the New York Democracy* (Fairleigh Dickinson University Press, 1981).
[*Nature of party cleavages*]: James L. Sundquist, *Dynamics of the Party System* (Brookings Institution, 1973), quoted at pp. 93–94.
206 [*Factional stability*]: Polakoff, *op. cit.*, p. 321.
[*Republican party subdivisions*]: David Donald, *The Politics of Reconstruction* (Louisiana State University Press, 1965), p. 76.
[*Continuing Ohio Republican leadership*]: Joseph B. Foraker Papers, Library of Congress, Container 1.
[*George A. Myers*]: George A. Myers Papers, Ohio Historical Society; John A. Garraty, ed., *The Barber and the Historian: The Correspondence of George A. Myers and James Ford Rhodes, 1910–1923* (Ohio Historical Society, 1956); Felix James, "The Civic and Political Career of George A. Myers," *Journal of Negro History*, vol. 58, no. 2 (April 1973), pp. 166–78.
207 [*The Liberal Republicans*]: John G. Sproat, *"The Best Men"* (Oxford University Press, 1968), quoted at p. 81.
208 [*Greenback party*]: Paul Kleppner, "The Greenback and Prohibition Parties," in Schlesinger, *op. cit.*, vol. 2, pp. 1549–1697; Sundquist, pp. 98–101, and state studies cited therein; Irwin Unger, *The Greenback Era* (Princeton University Press, 1964).
[*Third parties*]: Murray S. Stedman, Jr., and Susan W. Stedman, *Discontent at the Polls*

(Columbia University Press, 1950); Steven J. Rosenstone, Roy L. Behr, Edward H. Lazarus, *Third Parties in America* (Princeton University Press, 1984), ch. 3.

208 [*Woman suffragist movement, post–Civil War*]: Eleanor Flexner, *Century of Struggle* (Harvard University Press, 1975), esp. ch. 10; Edith Hoshino Altbach, *Women in America* (D. C. Heath, 1974); Aptheker, ch. 2.
[*Stanton on blacks and foreigners*]: quoted in Flexner, p. 147.
208–9 [*Douglass on blacks' and women's rights*]: ibid.
209 [*Patrons of Husbandry*]: Solon Justus Buck, *The Granger Movement, 1870–1880* (Harvard University Press, 1913); D. Sven Nordin, *Rich Harvest: A History of the Grange, 1867–1900* (University Press of Mississippi, 1974).
210 [*Party continuity*]: party histories cited above; also Horatio Seymour Papers, New-York Historical Society.
[*Presidential election of 1884*]: Mark D. Hirsch, "Election of 1884," in Arthur M. Schlesinger, Jr., ed., *History of American Presidential Elections* (Chelsea House, 1971), vol. 2, pp. 1561–1611; Allan Nevins, *Grover Cleveland* (Dodd, Mead, 1932), ch. 11.
[*Campaign taunts*]: quoted in Nevins, p. 177.
211 [*Pastor on "Rum, Romanism and Rebellion"*]: quoted in Hirsch in Schlesinger, *Elections*, vol. 2, p. 1578.
[*"Royal Feast"*]: October 30, 1884, reprinted in *ibid.*, pp. 1604–5.

The Poverty of Policy

[*Washington in the 1880s*]: Frank G. Carpenter, *Carp's Washington* (McGraw-Hill, 1960), quoted at pp. 8–9; see also Charles Hurd, *Washington Cavalcade* (E. P. Dutton, 1948), pp. 127–43; Constance M. Green, *Washington: Capital City 1879–1950* (Princeton University Press, 1963), chs. 2–6; David L. Lewis, *District of Columbia* (W. W. Norton, 1976), *passim*.
[*"City of rest and peace"*]: S. Reynolds Hole, quoted in Green, p. 77.
[*Grigsby on comfort in Post Office*]: ibid.
212 [*Pennsylvania Railroad vs. Pennsylvania Avenue*]: *ibid.*, pp. 52–53; Hurd, p. 127.
[*Tariff controversy*]: Tom E. Terrill, *The Tariff, Politics, and American Foreign Policy, 1874–1901* (Greenwood Press, 1973); Morton Keller, *Affairs of State* (Belknap Press, 1977), esp. ch. 12; John A. Garraty, *The New Commonwealth* (Harper & Row, 1968), *passim*.
[*Newspapers and tariffs*]: Terrill, p. 35.
213 [*Terrill on tariff politics*]: *ibid.*, p. 10.
[*Cleveland on tariff reduction*]: "President's Annual Message," December 6, 1887, *Congressional Record*, 50th Congress, 1st session (Government Printing Office, 1888), vol. 19, part 1, pp. 9–11, quoted at p. 11.
[*Currency legislation*]: Margaret G. Myers, *A Financial History of the United States* (Columbia University Press, 1970), ch. 9; Don C. Barrett, *The Greenbacks and Resumption of Specie Payments, 1862–1879* (Harvard University Press, 1931); Clarence A. Stern, *Golden Republicanism* (Edwards Bros., 1970); Frank W. Taussig, *The Silver Situation in the United States* (Putnam's, 1893); Allen Weinstein, *Prelude to Populism: Origins of the Silver Issue, 1867–1878* (Yale University Press, 1970).
[*Diffusion of interests on silver issue*]: Robert P. Sharkey, "Money, Class, and Party: An Economic Study of Civil War and Reconstruction," *The Johns Hopkins University Studies in Historical and Political Science* (Johns Hopkins Press, 1959), series 77, no. 2, pp. 286, 301; Robert Wiebe, *The Search for Order, 1877–1920* (Hill and Wang, 1967), pp. 13, 21, 300; Stanley Coben, "Northeastern Business and Radical Reconstruction: A Re-examination," *Mississippi Valley Historical Review*, vol. 46, no. 1 (June 1959), pp. 67–90.
214 [*Government of maneuver and drift*]: Wiebe, pp. 35, 43.
[*Railroad policy*]: Thomas C. Cochran, *Railroad Leaders, 1845–1890* (Harvard University Press, 1953), ch. 14; Keller, pp. 422–30; see also Gabriel Kolko, *Railroads and Regulation 1877–1916* (Princeton University Press, 1965), chs. 1–3; Robert W. Harbeson, "Railroads and Regulation, 1877–1916: Conspiracy or Public Interest?," *Journal of Economic History*, vol. 27, no. 2 (June 1967), pp. 230–42; Albro Martin, "The Troubled Subject of Railroad Regulation in the Gilded Age—A Reappraisal," *Journal of American History*, vol. 61, no. 2 (September 1974), pp. 339–71.
215 [*Failure of state and federal supervision*]: Keller, p. 430.

215 [*The Big Four*]: Leland Stanford Correspondence, Stanford University Archives; Collis P. Huntington Papers, Bancroft Library; Huntington–Mark Hopkins Correspondence, Stanford Archives; Norman E. Tutorow, *Leland Stanford: Man of Many Careers* (Pacific Coast Publishers, 1971), esp. pp. 70–75.
[*Stanford on "question of might"*]: quoted in Stuart Daggett, "Leland Stanford," in Dumas Malone, ed., *Dictionary of American Biography* (Scribner's, 1935), vol. 17, p. 504.
[*"Battle" for the mountain passes*]: Stewart H. Holbrook, *The Age of the Moguls* (Doubleday, 1953), p. 123.
215–16 [*Huntington's comments and instructions*]: New York *Sun*, December 29 and 30, 1883, from letters dated January 17, 1876; November 9, 1877; February 28, 1878 (the letters were from court records of a suit against Huntington).
216 [*Lord Bryce on combination*]: James Bryce, *The American Commonwealth*, rev. ed. (Macmillan, 1921), vol. 2, pp. 591–92.
[*Background and passage of Sherman Antitrust Act*]: Hans B. Thorelli, *The Federal Antitrust Policy* (Johns Hopkins Press, 1955); Keller, pp. 436–37.
[*Antitrust Act*]: quoted in Thorelli, p. 610.
217 [*Attacking the surplus*]: James R. Tanner, quoted in Richard B. Morris, ed., *Encyclopedia of American History* (Harper & Bros., 1961), p. 261.
[*Indian policy*]: Loring B. Priest, *Uncle Sam's Stepchildren* (Rutgers University Press, 1942); Henry E. Fritz, *The Movement for Indian Assimilation, 1860–1890* (University of Pennsylvania Press, 1963); Grant Foreman, *The Last Trek of the Indians* (University of Chicago Press, 1946), part 2; Katherine C. Turner, *Red Men Calling on the Great White Father* (University of Oklahoma Press, 1951), chs. 9–12; Richard H. Pratt, *Battlefield and Classroom*, Robert M. Utley, ed. (Yale University Press, 1964); Sean D. Cashman, *America in the Gilded Age* (New York University Press, 1984), ch. 8.
[*Church officials and Indians*]: Priest, esp. ch. 3.
[*Congressional debate on Indians*]: Wiebe, p. 11.
218 [*Indian wars*]: Robert M. Utley, *Frontier Regulars: The United States Army and the Indian, 1866–1890* (Macmillan, 1973); Robert Leckie, *The Wars of America* (Harper & Row, 1968), pp. 534–38.
[*Sitting Bull*]: Utley, *Frontier Regulars*, p. 236.
219 [*"A match for any man"*]: General George Crook, quoted in *ibid.*, p. 72.
[*Life of frontier regulars*]: *ibid.*, ch. 6, self-description quoted at p. 80.
219–20 [*U.S. foreign policy, 1865–1877*]: Bailey, *Diplomatic History, op. cit.*, chs. 24–26; McFeely, *op. cit.*, ch. 21.
220 [*New interest in foreign affairs*]: Robert Beisner, *From the Old Diplomacy to the New, 1865–1900* (Thomas Y. Crowell, 1975); Walter LaFeber, *The New Empire: An Interpretation of American Expansion, 1860–1898* (Cornell University Press, 1963); Milton Plesur, *America's Outward Thrust: Approaches to Foreign Affairs, 1865–1890* (Northern Illinois University Press, 1971).
[*Grant's world tour*]: McFeely, ch. 26.
221 [*Americans abroad*]: Plesur, *passim;* Foster Rhea Dulles, *Americans Abroad* (University of Michigan Press, 1964), chs. 8–10.
[*James on tourists*]: quoted in Dulles, p. 111.
222 [*Economic expansion and foreign affairs*]: Plesur, pp. 28ff.
[*"Th' hand that rules th' wurruld"*]: quoted in *ibid.*, p. 31.
[*Foreign service a "humbug and a sham"*]: quoted in Leckie, p. 539.
[*Developments in naval policy*]: Walter R. Herrick, Jr., *The American Naval Revolution* (Louisiana State University Press, 1966); Ronald Spector, *Admiral of the New Empire: The Life and Career of George Dewey* (Louisiana State University Press, 1974), pp. 21–32; see also Hyman G. Rickover, *How the Battleship* Maine *Was Destroyed* (Department of the Navy, 1976), pp. 1–3, 18–21.
223 [*Arthur on need to rebuild navy*]: quoted in Herrick, p. 25.

Showdown 1896

[*Carnegie on* Triumphant Democracy]: quoted in Keller, *op. cit.*, p. 440.
224 [*Condition of labor, 1892*]: John R. Commons et al., *History of Labour in the United States* (Macmillan, 1918–35), vol. 2, part 6, ch. 13; Walter A. Wyckoff, *The Workers, An Experiment in Reality: The West* (Scribner's, 1899), *passim.*

224 [*Fears of class warfare*]: H. Wayne Morgan, *From Hayes to McKinley: National Party Politics, 1877–1896* (Syracuse University Press, 1969), p. 441 and note.
[*Populists and blacks*]: Robert Saunders, "Southern Populists and the Negro, 1893–1895," *Journal of Negro History*, vol. 54, no. 3 (July 1969), pp. 240–61.
[*Fraud in Watson elections*]: C. Vann Woodward, *Tom Watson, Agrarian Rebel* (Macmillan, 1938), pp. 270–77.
[*Homestead strike*]: Joseph F. Wall, *Andrew Carnegie* (Oxford University Press, 1970), ch. 16; see also Andrew Carnegie, *Autobiography* (Houghton Mifflin, 1948), ch. 17.
[*Frick*]: George Harvey, *Henry Clay Frick: The Man* (Scribner's, 1928), *passim;* Wall, pp. 478–536.
225 [*Carnegie's and Frick's attitudes toward unions*]: Wall, p. 544.
[*Berkman's attack upon Frick*]: Harvey, pp. 136–40.
[*Press revilement of Carnegie following Homestead*]: Wall, pp. 571–73.
[*St. Louis* Post-Dispatch *contrasting Frick and Carnegie*]: quoted in *ibid.*, p. 573.
225–6 [*Frick's intransigence*]: Harvey, ch. 11, quoted at p. 151; Wall, pp. 566–69.
226 [*Carnegie on Cleveland's victory*]: Carnegie to Frick, November 9, 1892, quoted in Harvey, p. 157.
[*Cleveland's rejection of "paternalism"*]: Inaugural Address, March 4, 1893, reprinted in *Inaugural Addresses of the Presidents of the United States* (U.S. Government Printing Office, 1974), quoted at p. 165.
[*Depression of the nineties*]: Charles Hoffman, *The Depression of the Nineties: An Economic History* (Greenwood Publishing, 1970), esp. ch. 2 and appendix to ch. 2; Morris, *Encyclopedia of American History, op. cit.,* p. 539; see also Rendig Fels, *American Business Cycles, 1865–1897* (University of North Carolina Press, 1959), chs. 10–12.
[*Cleveland's response to the crisis*]: Allan Nevins, *Grover Cleveland: A Study in Courage* (Dodd, Mead, 1932), chs. 29, 31; Morgan, pp. 451–65, 473–76.
[*Living petition*]: Resolution of Oak Valley Alliance, Nebraska, May 5, 1894, quoted in Norman Pollack, *The Populist Response to Industrial America* (W. W. Norton, 1966), p. 50.
[*"Petition in boots"*]: Donald L. McMurry, "Jacob Sechler Coxey," in John A. Garraty, ed., *Encyclopedia of American Biography* (Harper & Row, 1974), p. 235.
[*Coxey and Coxey's army*]: Norman Pollack, ed., *The Populist Mind* (Bobbs-Merrill, 1967), pp. 342–47; George P. Tindall, ed., *A Populist Reader* (Harper & Row, 1966), pp. 160–65; Elizabeth Barr, "The Populist Uprising," in William E. Connelley, *History of Kansas: State and People* (American Historical Society, 1928), vol. 2, pp. 1199–1200; Pollack, *Populist Response,* pp. 48–52; McMurry in Garraty, pp. 234–35.
227 [*The Pullman Palace Car Company in 1894*]: Thomas G. Manning, *The Chicago Strike of 1894* (Holt, Rinehart and Winston, 1960), p. 1.
[*Flowers and lawn in the model town*]: Pullman pamphlet, quoted in Milton Meltzer, *Bread —and Roses: The Struggle of American Labor, 1865–1915* (Alfred A. Knopf, 1967), p. 148.
[*Pullman paternalism*]: Almont Lindsey, "Paternalism and the Pullman Strike," *American Historical Review*, vol. 44, no. 2 (January 1939), pp. 272–89.
[*"We are born in a Pullman house"*]: quoted in Meltzer, p. 151.
[*Strike*]: Stanley Buder, *Pullman: An Experiment in Industrial Order and Community Planning* (Oxford University Press, 1967), chs. 12–15; Manning, *passim;* Meltzer, ch. 14; Christopher Lamb, "Eugene Debs, the A.R.U., and the Failure of Radical Labor" (typescript, Williams College, 1981); Louis Adamic, *Dynamite: The Story of Class Violence in America* (Viking Press, 1934), ch. 11.
[*Railroad boycott*]: Meltzer, pp. 153–54.
227–8 [*Effect on congressional elections in the nineties of economic and social pressures*]: Samuel T. McSeveney, *The Politics of Depression: Political Behavior in the Northeast, 1893–1896* (Oxford University Press, 1972), pp. vii–ix.
[*Reed on the unknown Democratic dead*]: quoted in Paul W. Glad, *McKinley, Bryan, and the People* (Lippincott, 1964), p. 91.
228 [*Cleveland, federal finances and the syndicate*]: Nevins, pp. 652–66.
[*"I hate the ground that man walks on"*]: Senator John T. Morgan, quoted in *ibid.*, p. 568.
[*Democratic factionalism*]: Glad, pp. 91–94, 113–22; Morris, p. 264.
[*Internal populist crisis over silver*]: John D. Hicks, *The Populist Revolt* (University of Nebraska Press, 1961), pp. 316–19; Pollack, *Populist Response,* pp. 109–10; Topeka *Advocate*, May 8, 1895.

228 [*Watson on free silver*]: C. Vann Woodward, *The Origins of the New South, 1877–1913* (Louisiana State University Press, 1951), p. 282.

229 [*Pre-presidential McKinley*]: see Margaret Leech, *In the Days of McKinley* (Harper & Bros., 1959), chs. 1–3.
[*Governor McKinley's debt*]: H. Wayne Morgan, *William McKinley and His America* (Syracuse University Press, 1963), pp. 169–76.
[*Morgan on McKinley*]: Morgan, *Hayes to McKinley*, pp. 492–93.
[Bryan]: Louis W. Koenig, *Bryan* (Putnam's, 1971); Paolo E. Coletta, *William Jennings Bryan: Political Evangelist, 1860–1908* (University of Nebraska Press, 1964).

229–30 [*McKinley and Bryan compared*]: Glad, ch. 1 and pp. 32–36, quoted at p. 15.

230 [*La Follette on Bryan's appearance*]: quoted in Morgan, *Hayes to McKinley*, p. 496.
[*The convention and the speech*]: Koenig, ch. 13; Coletta, ch. 8.

230–1 [*Text of Bryan's "Cross of Gold"*]: William Jennings Bryan, *The First Battle: A Story of the Campaign* (W. B. Conkey, 1896), pp. 199–206, reprinted in Schlesinger, *Parties, op. cit,* vol. 2, pp. 1080–85, quoted at pp. 1080, 1081, 1085.

231 [*Lloyd on Populist dilemma*]: quoted in Woodward, *Watson*, p. 303.
[*1896 Populist convention*]: Robert F. Durden, *The Climax of Populism: The Election of 1896* (University of Kentucky Press, 1965), pp. 23–44; Woodward, *Watson*, pp. 302–31.
[*The fall campaign*]: Keller, pp. 582–84; Glad, ch. 8; Gilbert Fite, "Election of 1896," in Schlesinger, *Elections, op. cit.,* vol. 2, pp. 1787–1825.

232 [*Bryan's concession and challenge*]: quoted in Morgan, *Hayes to McKinley,* p. 521.
[*Watson on death of Populist party*]: Woodward, *Watson*, p. 330.

Triumphant Republicanism

[*Significance of 1896 election*]: Sundquist, *Dynamics of the Party System, op. cit.,* esp. ch. 7; Walter Dean Burnham, *Critical Elections and the Mainsprings of American Politics* (W. W. Norton, 1970), esp. ch. 4; Jerome M. Clubb, William H. Flanigan, and Nancy H. Zingale, *Partisan Realignment* (Sage Publications, 1980); V. O. Key, Jr., "A Theory of Critical Elections," *Journal of Politics,* vol. 17, no. 1 (February 1955), pp. 3–18; Allan J. Lichtman, "Critical Election Theory and the Reality of American Presidential Politics, 1916–1940," *American Historical Review,* vol. 81, no. 2 (April 1976), pp. 317–51, esp. pp. 320–23, 339–44; Fite in Schlesinger, *Elections, op. cit.,* vol. 2, pp. 1787–1825.

232–3 [*County results in the Midwest*]: Sundquist, p. 151.

233 [*Sundquist on "another R"*]: ibid., p. 150.
[*Kleppner on the redeveloped Republican party*]: Paul Kleppner, "From Ethnoreligious Conflict to 'Social Harmony': Coalitional and Party Transformations in the 1890s," in Seymour Martin Lipset, ed., *Emerging Coalitions in American Politics* (Institute for Contemporary Studies, 1978), pp. 41–59, quoted at p. 42.
[*Farm support for McKinley, 1896*]: Gilbert C. Fite, "Republican Strategy and the Farm Vote in the Presidential Campaign of 1896," *American Historical Review,* vol. 65, no. 4 (July 1960), pp. 787–806.
[*Labor support for McKinley*]: Morgan, *McKinley and His America, op. cit.;* see also Irving Bernstein, ed., "Samuel Gompers and Free Silver, 1896," *Mississippi Valley Historical Review,* vol. 29, no. 3 (December 1942), pp. 394–400.

234 [*The McKinley administration*]: Morgan; Leonard D. White, *The Republican Era: 1869–1901* (Macmillan, 1958); Keller, *op. cit.,* esp. ch. 16.
[*1896 Republican platform on lynching*]: quoted in Schlesinger, *Elections,* vol. 2, p. 1834.
[Plessy v. Ferguson]: 163 U.S. 537 (1896).
[Williams v. Miss.]: 170 U.S. 213 (1898).
[*Washington on segregation*]: Booker T. Washington, *Up From Slavery* (1901), in Louis R. Harlan and John W. Blassingame, eds., *The Booker T. Washington Papers* (University of Illinois Press, 1972–82), vol. 1, pp. 209–385, quoted at p. 342.
[*Carnegie on Washington and blacks*]: quoted in Wall, *op. cit.,* pp. 972–74.
[*Carnegie on "Triumphant Democracy"*]: ibid., p. 469.
[*Carnegie on freedom*]: ibid., p. 396.

234–5 [*Carnegie's economic and social views*]: Andrew Carnegie, *Triumphant Democracy* (Scribner's, 1893); Carnegie, *Autobiography, op. cit.;* Robert Green McCloskey, *American Conservatism in the Age of Enterprise* (Harvard University Press, 1951), esp. ch. 6.

235 [*Wall on the have-nots*]: Wall, p. 459.
[*The* Maine *in Havana*]: Rickover, *op. cit.*, ch. 4.
[*Spanish-Cuban-American war*]: Bailey, *Diplomatic History, op. cit.*, ch. 31; Philip S. Foner, *The Spanish-Cuban-American War and the Birth of American Imperialism, 1895–1902* (Monthly Review Press, 1972), vol. 1, *passim;* Ernest R. May, *Imperial Democracy: The Emergence of America as a Great Power* (Harper & Row, 1961), parts 4–5; Morgan, chs. 15–17.
[*The Hearst-Pulitzer war*]: W. A. Swanberg, *Citizen Hearst* (Scribner's, 1961), part 3; Leckie, *op. cit.*, pp. 544–45.

236 [*McKinley and Cuba*]: Lewis L. Gould, *The Presidency of William McKinley* (Regents Press of Kansas, 1980); Foner, vol. 1, chs. 11–12.

237 [Journal *on the* Maine *disaster*]: February 17, 1898, quoted in Swanberg, p. 136.
[*Roosevelt on Spanish "treachery"*]: Roosevelt to Benjamin Diblee, February 16, 1898, in Elting E. Morison, ed., *The Letters of Theodore Roosevelt* (Harvard University Press, 1951–54), vol. 1, p. 775.
[*1898 Navy Department study*]: Rickover, *passim.*
[*1898 court of inquiry report on the* Maine]: quoted in *ibid.*, p. 70.
[*Foraker on "aggressive conquest of territory"*]: *Congressional Record,* 2nd Session (Government Printing Office, 1898), vol. 31, part 4, p. 3780 (April 13, 1898).

238 [*American military effort*]: Graham Cosmas, *An Army for Empire* (University of Missouri Press, 1971); David F. Trask, *The War with Spain in 1898* (Macmillan, 1981); Foner, vol. 2, ch. 15; Leckie, pp. 546–63; Spector, *op. cit.*, chs. 2–3.

239 [*"Damned Yankees on the run"*]: quoted in Leckie, p. 556.
[*"The poor fellows are dying"*]: *ibid.*, p. 562.
[*McKinley's strategy*]: see Trask, *passim.*

239-40 [*Diplomatic resolution of the war*]: H. Wayne Morgan, ed., *Making Peace with Spain: The Diary of Whitelaw Reid, September–December, 1898* (University of Texas Press, 1965); Morgan, *McKinley and His America*, pp. 400–414.

240 [*Annexation as "consummation"*]: quoted in Bailey, p. 435.
[*Debate over imperialism*]: Morgan, *McKinley and His America*, pp. 415–23 and ch. 19; Daniel B. Schirmer, *Republic or Empire: American Resistance to the Philippine War* (Schenkman, 1972); Richard E. Welch, Jr., *Response to Imperialism: The United States and the Philippine-American War, 1899–1902* (University of North Carolina Press, 1979); see also Walter L. Williams, "United States Indian Policy and the Debate over Philippine Annexation: Implications for the Origins of American Imperialism," *Journal of American History*, vol. 66, no. 4 (March 1980), pp. 810–31.
[*Carnegie on McKinley's leadership*]: quoted in Wall, p. 693.
[*"Triumphant Despotism"*]: *ibid.*, p. 694.
[*Hoar on the "downfall" of the republic*]: quoted in Schirmer, p. 109.
[*Lodge on passage of the treaty*]: *ibid.*, p. 122.

241 [*Philippine insurrection*]: John M. Gates, *Schoolbooks and Krags: The United States Army in the Philippines, 1898–1902* (Greenwood Press, 1973); Bonifacio S. Salamanca, *The Filipino Reaction to American Rule, 1901–1913* (Shoe String Press, 1968), chs. 1–3.
[*Election of 1900*]: Coletta, *op. cit.*, ch. 12; Koenig, *op. cit.*, chs. 18–19; Morgan, *McKinley and His America*, ch. 21; Walter LaFeber, "Election of 1900," in Schlesinger, *Elections*, vol. 3, pp. 1877–1962.
[*Imperialism as "paramount" issue*]: quoted in LaFeber in Schlesinger, vol. 3, p. 1878.
[*Carnegie's support of McKinley*]: Wall, p. 710.
[*Donnelly on "shooting negroes"*]: quoted in LaFeber in Schlesinger, vol. 3, p. 1883.
[*"President of the whole people"*]: quoted in Morgan, *McKinley and His America*, p. 508.
[*"Timekeepers of progress"*]: *ibid.*, p. 517.
[*Assassination of McKinley*]: A. Wesley Johns, *The Man Who Shot McKinley* (A. S. Barnes, 1970); see also James W. Clarke, *American Assassins: The Darker Side of American Politics* (Princeton University Press, 1982), pp. 39–62.

7. THE URBAN PROGRESSIVES

245 [*Origins of progressivism*]: Irwin Unger and Debi Unger, *The Vulnerable Years: The United States, 1896–1917* (New York University Press, 1978), ch. 4; Richard L. McCormick, "The Discovery That Business Corrupts Politics: A Reappraisal of the Origins of Pro-

gressivism," *American Historical Review*, vol. 86, no. 2 (April 1981), pp. 247–74; Arthur A. Ekirch, Jr., *Progressivism in America* (New Viewpoints, 1974); Richard Hofstadter, *The Age of Reform: From Bryan to F.D.R.* (Alfred A. Knopf, 1955), chs. 4, 5; John D. Buenker, "The Progressive Era: A Search for a Synthesis," *Mid-America*, vol. 51, no. 3 (July 1969), pp. 175–93; David P. Thelen, "Social Tensions and the Origins of Progressivism," *Journal of American History*, vol. 56, no. 2 (September 1969), pp. 323–41; Peter G. Filene, "An Obituary for 'The Progressive Movement,'" *American Quarterly*, vol. 22, no. 1 (Spring 1970), pp. 20–34; Robert H. Wiebe, *Businessmen and Reform: A Study of the Progressive Movement* (Harvard University Press, 1962); Samuel P. Hays, *The Response to Industrialism, 1885–1914* (University of Chicago Press, 1957).

245 [*Hofstadter on class anxieties*]: Hofstadter, p. 137.

246 [*Ungers on development of progressivism*]: Unger and Unger, pp. 101–2.
[*Immigration, migration, and population increases*]: Richard B. Morris, ed., *Encyclopedia of American History* (Harper & Row, 1976), pp. 647–62.

246–47 [*Urban crowding*]: Joel Arthur Tarr, "From City to Suburb: The 'Moral' Influence of Transportation Technology," in Alexander B. Callow, Jr., ed., *American Urban History*, 2nd ed. (Oxford University Press, 1973), pp. 205–6; John A. Garraty, *The New Commonwealth* (Harper & Row, 1968), pp. 188–93.

247 [*Chicago stink and stench*]: quoted in Garraty, p. 193.

248 [*Industrialization of large American cities*]: Maury Klein and Harvey A. Kantor, *Prisoners of Progress: American Industrial Cities, 1850–1920* (Macmillan, 1976); Blake McKelvey, *The Urbanization of America* (Rutgers University Press, 1963); Sam Bass Warner, Jr., *The Urban Wilderness* (Harper & Row, 1972), ch. 4; Allan R. Pred, *The Spatial Dynamics of U.S. Urban-Industrial Growth, 1800–1914: Interpretive and Theoretical Essays* (MIT Press, 1966).
[*McKelvey on shift from commercial to industrial cities*]: McKelvey, p. 48.

248–49 [*Aspects of the industrializing city*]: Stephan Thernstrom, "Reflections on the New Urban History," *Daedalus*, vol. 100, no. 2 (Spring 1971), pp. 359–75.

The Shape of the City

249 [*Railroad terminals*]: Carroll L. V. Meeks, *The Railroad Station: An Architectural History* (Yale University Press, 1956).
[*Louis Sullivan on the Chicago station*]: quoted in *ibid.*, p. 108.
[*Central business district*]: Martyn J. Bowden, "Growth of the Central Districts in Large Cities," in Leo F. Schnore, ed., *The New Urban History* (Princeton University Press, 1975), pp. 75–109.

250 [*City transport*]: Charles N. Glaab and A. Theodore Brown, *A History of Urban America* (Macmillan, 1967), pp. 147–52; Klein and Kantor, *op. cit.*, pp. 146–51; McKelvey, *op. cit.*, ch. 5.
[*Mark Twain on hanging on by eyelashes*]: quoted in Glaab and Brown, p. 149.
[*Estimate of manure left on streets*]: Joel A. Tarr, "Urban Pollution—Many Long Years Ago," *American Heritage*, vol. 22, no. 6 (October 1971), pp. 65–106.
[*Sprague on the "Edison legend"*]: F. J. Sprague to S. H. Libby, October 10, 1931, in Roger Burlingame, *Engines of Democracy* (Scribner's, 1940), p. 198.

251 [*Elevators*]: Glaab and Brown, pp. 144–45; Burlingame, pp. 88–89.
[*Traveler on sensations of an express ride*]: Julian Ralph, quoted in Glaab and Brown, p. 145.
[*Cast-iron and steel buildings*]: Siegfried Giedion, *Space, Time and Architecture* (Harvard University Press, 1954), pp. 193–98.

252 [*Sullivan on the power of height*]: quoted in Klein and Kantor, p. 158.
[*Woolworth Tower*]: *ibid.*, pp. 159–60.
[*Appearance of the grid pattern*]: *ibid.*, p. 127.
[*Bryce on monotony*]: quoted in *ibid.*

253 [*The balloon frame*]: Giedion, pp. 345–53, G. E. Woodward quoted at p. 347.
[*Sewerage and water*]: Klein and Kantor, pp. 165–68; Glaab and Brown, pp. 164–66.
[*Cleveland's open sewer*]: quoted in Garraty, *op. cit.*, p. 192.

254 [*Waring on filth as cause of disease*]: quoted in Glaab and Brown, p. 165.
[*Urban parks*]: Galen Cranz, *The Politics of Park Design* (MIT Press, 1982).
[*Mumford on rectangular street platting*]: Lewis Mumford, *The Culture of Cities* (Harcourt, Brace, 1938), quoted at p. 189.

The Life of the City

255 [*Social topography of the Lower East Side*]: Moses Rischin, *The Promised City: New York's Jews, 1870–1914* (Harvard University Press, 1962), pp. 76–94; see also Irving Howe, *World of Our Fathers* (Harcourt Brace Jovanovich, 1976), ch. 2; and, more generally, John Higham, *Send These to Me: Jews and Other Immigrants in Urban America* (Atheneum, 1975).

256 [*Bennett on the architecture "sweating humanity"*]: Arnold Bennett, *Those United States* (Martin Secker, 1912), p. 239.
[*Cultural and psychological shocks of migration*]: Oscar Handlin, *The Uprooted,* 2nd ed. (Little, Brown, 1973), esp. chs. 9, 10.

257 [*Howe on role of religion*]: Howe, p. 70.
[*Italian immigrants*]: Robert F. Foerster, *The Italian Emigration of Our Times* (Harvard University Press, 1919); Andrew F. Rolle, *The Immigrant Upraised* (University of Oklahoma Press, 1968); Oscar Handlin, ed., *Immigration as a Factor in American History* (Prentice-Hall, 1959), pp. 29–31, 77–84, 133–35.
[*Italian immigrants in Chicago*]: Humbert S. Nelli, *Italians in Chicago, 1880–1930* (Oxford University Press, 1970).
[*Italian immigrants adapting to the urban language*]: Joseph Lopreato, *Italian Americans* (Random House, 1970), p. 57.

258 [*Nelli on the role of the* padrone]: Nelli, p. 63.
[*Prices charged by* padroni]: Carroll Wright, "Ninth Special Report of the Italians in Chicago," *United States Department of Labor Bulletin,* no. 13 (November 1897), p. 727.
[*Pressures on Chicago community life*]: Richard Sennett, "Middle-Class Families and Urban Violence: The Experience of a Chicago Community in the Nineteenth Century," in Stephan Thernstrom and Richard Sennett, eds., *Nineteenth-Century Cities* (Yale University Press, 1969), pp. 386–420.
[*Smith on transporting of man*]: Herbert G. Gutman, "Work, Culture, and Society in Industrializing America, 1815–1919," *American Historical Review,* vol. 78, no. 3 (June 1973), pp. 531–87, quoted at p. 547.

259 [*Communist Manifesto on factories as industrial armies*]: in Robert C. Tucker, ed., *The Marx-Engels Reader* (W. W. Norton, 1972), quoted at pp. 341, 342.
[*Immigrants celebrating old-time holidays*]: Gutman, pp. 547–48.
[*Jews moving upward*]: Bernard D. Weinryb, "Jewish Immigration and Accommodation to America," in Marshall Sklare, ed., *The Jews: Social Patterns of an American Group* (Free Press, 1958), pp. 4–22.
[*Irish-American upward mobility*]: William V. Shannon, *The American Irish* (Macmillan, 1966), chs. 6, 9; Carl Wittke, *The Irish in America* (Louisiana State University Press, 1956); Oscar Handlin, *Boston's Immigrants, 1790–1865* (Harvard University Press, 1941).

260 [*MacShinnegan coat of arms*]: *The Argonaut,* quoted in Shannon, p. 88.
[*Marx and Engels on the impact of industrialization and the industrial city*]: *The German Ideology,* in Tucker, quoted at pp. 149–50; I have made minor changes in punctuation.
[*Marx and class consciousness*]: Norman Birnbaum, "Afterword," in Thernstrom and Sennett, pp. 421–30.

260–61 [*Thernstrom on continuity of class membership in one setting*]: Stephan Thernstrom, "Urbanization, Migration, and Social Mobility in Late Nineteenth-Century America," in Callow, *op. cit.,* p. 405.

261 [*Communist Manifesto on proletarianization*]: in Tucker, pp. 341–42.
[*Changes in the home*]: Elizabeth M. Bacon, "The Growth of Household Conveniences in the U.S. from 1865 to 1900," Ph.D. dissertation, Radcliffe College, 1942.
[*Domestic science movement*]: Barbara J. Harris, *Beyond Her Sphere: Women and the Professions in American History* (Greenwood Press, 1978), p. 135; *Diary of Annie Thompson,* private collection; Catharine Esther Beecher, *The American Woman's Home; or, Principles of Domestic Science* (J. B. Ford, 1869).
[*Alcott on making a battering-ram of her head*]: quoted in Marjorie Worthington, *Miss Alcott of Concord* (Doubleday, 1958), p. 83.
[*Bradwell*]: *Bradwell v. Illinois,* 83 U.S. 130 (1873), quoted at 141; Harris, pp. 110–12.

262 [*The club movement*]: Karen J. Blair, *The Clubwoman as Feminist: True Womanhood Redefined, 1868–1914* (Holmes & Meier, 1980).
[*Maine delegate on fashionable clubwomen*]: quoted in *ibid.,* pp. 95–96.

262 [Scientific American *on assimilation or extermination*]: June 9, 1869, quoted in Gutman, p. 584.
[*"Forget your past"*]: quoted in *ibid.*, p. 582.
[*The "clock in the workshop"*]: reprinted in *ibid.*, p. 547. I have added the word "to" to the last line.

The Leaders of the City

263 [*Boss Plunkitt's day*]: William L. Riordon, *Plunkitt of Tammany Hall* (E. P. Dutton, 1963), pp. 91–93.
[*Tammany Hall*]: Gustavus Myers, *The History of Tammany Hall* (Boni & Liveright, 1917); M. R. Werner, *Tammany Hall* (Doubleday, Doran, 1928); John W. Pratt, "Boss Tweed's Public Welfare Program," *New-York Historical Society Quarterly*, vol. 45, no. 4 (October 1961), pp. 396–411.

264 [*Tammany structure and function*]: Robert K. Merton, *Social Theory and Social Structure* (Free Press, 1957), pp. 71–82; Eric L. McKitrick, "The Study of Corruption," *Political Science Quarterly*, vol. 72, no. 4 (December 1957), pp. 502–14; Seymour J. Mandelbaum, *Boss Tweed's New York* (John Wiley, 1965).
[*Other city "machines"*]: Harold F. Gosnell, *Machine Politics: Chicago Model* (University of Chicago Press, 1968); Zane L. Miller, *Boss Cox's Cincinnati* (Oxford University Press, 1968); George M. Reynolds, *Machine Politics in New Orleans, 1897–1926* (Columbia University Press, 1936); Walter Bean, *Boss Ruef's San Francisco* (University of California Press, 1952).

265 [*Lomasney on getting help*]: quoted in Lincoln Steffens, *Autobiography* (Chautauqua Press, 1931), p. 618.
[*Glaab and Brown on machine as "avenue of advance"*]: Glaab and Brown, *op. cit.*, p. 225.
[*Merton on corporations and the "economic czar"*]: Robert K. Merton, "Latent Functions of the Machine," in Callow, *op. cit.*, pp. 220–29, quoted at p. 223.

266 [*Boyer on cities replicating the moral order of the village*]: Paul Boyer, *Urban Masses and Moral Order in America, 1820–1920* (Harvard University Press, 1978), p. viii.
[*Reformers*]: Geoffrey Blodgett, "Reform Thought and the Genteel Tradition," in H. Wayne Morgan, ed., *The Gilded Age*, 2nd ed. (Syracuse University Press, 1970), pp. 55–76; John G. Sproat, *"The Best Men": Liberal Reformers in the Gilded Age* (Oxford University Press, 1968); Geoffrey Blodgett, *The Gentle Reformers: Massachusetts Democrats in the Cleveland Era* (Harvard University Press, 1966).
[*Boss Tweed*]: Alexander B. Callow, Jr., *The Tweed Ring* (Oxford University Press, 1966); Merton in Callow, *American Urban History;* Mandelbaum.

267 [*"What are you going to do about it?"*]: quoted in Callow, *The Tweed Ring*, p. 9.
[*Plunkitt on reform movements as "mornin' glories"*]: Riordon, p. 17.

267–68 [*Plunkitt on politics as a business*]: *ibid.*, p. 19.

268 [*Steffens on businessmen and corruption*]: quoted in Klein and Kantor, *op. cit.*, p. 357.
[*Wiebe on reformers' dependence on business*]: Robert H. Wiebe, *The Search for Order, 1877–1920* (Hill and Wang, 1967), p. 174.

269 [*Choate on the danger to liberty*]: quoted in Callow, *The Tweed Ring*, p. 265.
[*Doubts of some reformers about universal suffrage*]: *ibid.*, ch. 17; Melvin G. Holli, *Reform in Detroit* (Oxford University Press, 1969), pp. 171–78.
[*Times on the "dangerous classes"*]: *New York Times*, July 16, 1871, p. 4.
[*E. L. Godkin on ignorant and corrupt voters*]: quoted in Callow, *The Tweed Ring*, p. 267.
[*"Expert's" prediction of abandonment of universal suffrage*]: Frank Goodnow, quoted in Holli, p. 174.

The Reformation of the Cities

[*Union for Concerted Moral Effort and National Union for Practical Progress*]: Boyer, *op. cit.*, p. 163.

270 [*Hull House*]: Jane Addams, *Twenty Years at Hull House* (Macmillan, 1910).
[*Jane Addams on transforming cities*]: quoted in Boyer, pp. 222–23; see also, Jane Addams, *The Spirit of Youth and the City Streets* (Macmillan, 1909); Addams, *A New Conscience and an Ancient Evil* (Macmillan, 1912).

270 [*Mary Richmond on settlement house workers*]: quoted in Boyer, p. 156.
271 [*City Beautiful movement*]: Jon A. Peterson, "The City Beautiful Movement: Forgotten Origins and Lost Meanings," *Journal of Urban History*, vol. 2 (August 1976), pp. 415–34; Klein and Kantor, *op. cit.*, pp. 423–30.
[*City planning*]: John W. Reps, *The Making of Urban America: A History of City Planning in the United States* (Princeton University Press, 1965); Frederick Law Olmsted, Jr., "The Town-Planning Movement in America," *Annals of the American Academy of Political and Social Science*, vol. 51 (January 1914), pp. 172–81; Boyer, ch. 18; Mumford, *op. cit., passim.*
272 [*Pingree and Detroit*]: Holli, *op. cit., passim.*
[*"I'm too busy making shoes"*]: quoted in *ibid.*, p. 17.
273 [*Pingree's achievements*]: *ibid.*, pp. 157–58, quoted at p. 158.
[*"Golden Rule" Jones*]: Jack Tager, *The Intellectual as Urban Reformer* (Case Western Reserve University Press, 1968), ch. 4; Samuel M. Jones, *The New Right: A Plea for Fair Play Through a More Just Social Order* (Eastern Book Concern, 1899); Brand Whitlock, *Forty Years of It* (D. Appleton, 1914); Samuel M. Jones, "The New Patriotism: A Golden Rule Government for Cities," *Municipal Affairs Magazine* (September 1899), pp. 455–61, in Charles N. Glaab, ed., *The American City: A Documentary History* (Dorsey Press, 1963), pp. 406–13.
[*Jones on "the ideal society"*]: Jones, *The New Right*, p. 66.
[*Johnson*]: Tom Loftin Johnson, *My Story* (B. W. Huebsch, 1911).
274 [*Johnson on municipal ownership*]: quoted in Glaab and Brown, *op. cit.*, p. 215.

Women: The Progressive Cadre

275 [*Lathrop*]: Jane Addams, *My Friend Julia Lathrop* (Macmillan, 1935); Ray Ginger, "The Women at Hull-House," in Linda K. Kerber and Jane De Hart Mathews, *Women's America* (Oxford University Press, 1982), pp. 265–66.
[*Kelley*]: Josephine Goldmark, *Impatient Crusader* (University of Illinois Press, 1953); Ginger, pp. 263–64.
[*Goldman*]: Richard Drinnon, *Rebel in Paradise* (University of Chicago Press, 1961).
[*Addams*]: Jane Addams, *Twenty Years at Hull House, op. cit.*; Allen F. Davis, *American Heroine: The Life and Legend of Jane Addams* (Oxford University Press, 1973); Anne Firor Scott, "Jane Addams," in Edward T. James, ed., *Notable American Women, 1607–1950* (Belknap Press of Harvard University Press, 1971), vol. 1, pp. 16–22.
276 [*German's response to Christian Scientist*]: quoted in Ginger, p. 269.
[*Addams's only cigarette*]: Ginger, p. 271.
[*Kelley's arrival at Hull-House with children*]: Davis, pp. 76–77.
[*Addams and Powers*]: quoted in Ginger, p. 270; Davis, pp. 121–25.
277 [*Addams and Lathrop as midwives*]: Davis, pp. 81–82.
[*Addams's activities in organizations*]: Lauren Ribardo, "Jane Addams: A Guiding Woman in a Man-Made World," typescript, Williams College, November 1983, pp. 11, 14.
[*Davis on Addams*]: Allen F. Davis, "Jane Addams," in John A. Garraty, *Encyclopedia of American Biography* (Harper & Row, 1974), p. 18.
[*Addams's reputation*]: see Davis, *American Heroine*, ch. 11.
[*Women and reform efforts*]: see Allen F. Davis, *Spearheads for Reform* (Oxford University Press, 1967).
278 [*Zimmerman on professionally trained women*]: Joan G. Zimmerman, "Women as Interpreters of Social Scientific Knowledge: A Professional Approach to Progressive Reform, 1880–1925," paper presented at the University of Maryland, College Park, Maryland, October 1981, to the Chesapeake Area Group of Women Historians.
[*Hofstadter on Addams*]: Hofstadter, *op. cit.*, p. 208.
[*Political action for laws protecting women and children*]: see Davis, *Spearhead*, ch. 7.
[*Wald*]: Robert L. Duffus, *Lillian Wald* (Macmillan, 1938); Blanche Wiesen Cook, "Female Support Networks and Political Activism: Lillian Wald, Crystal Eastman, Emma Goldman," in Nancy F. Cott and Elizabeth H. Pleck, eds., *A Heritage of Her Own* (Simon and Schuster, 1979), pp. 412–44; Lillian D. Wald, *The House on Henry Street* (Henry Holt, 1915).
279 [*WCTU*]: Ruth B. Bordin, *Woman and Temperance: The Quest for Power and Liberty 1873–1900* (Temple University Press, 1981); Barbara Epstein, *The Politics of Domesticity: Women,*

Evangelism and Temperance in Nineteenth-Century America (Wesleyan University Press, 1981), chs. 4–5.

279 [*"Do Everything"*]: see Epstein, pp. 120–21.

[*Sanger*]: David Kennedy, *Birth Control in America: The Career of Margaret Sanger* (Yale University Press, 1970); James Reed, "Margaret Sanger," in *Notable American Women*, vol. 4, pp. 623–27.

[*Sanger on "the basic freedom"*]: Sanger, *Woman and the New Race* (Brentano's, 1920), p. 94.

280 [*Women in nonagricultural pursuits*]: see Janet M. Hooks, "Women's Occupations Through Seven Decades," *Women's Bureau Bulletin*, no. 218, U.S. Department of Labor (U.S. Government Printing Office, 1947), esp. Appendix, Table IIa.

[*Women and unions*]: Alice Kessler-Harris, "Where Are the Organized Women Workers?," in Cott and Pleck, pp. 343–66; Kessler-Harris, *Out to Work: A History of Wage-Earning Women in the United States* (Oxford University Press, 1982), pp. 151–64. See also Susan Levine, "Labor's True Woman: Domesticity and Equal Rights in the Knights of Labor," *Journal of American History*, vol. 70, no. 2 (September 1983), pp. 323–39.

281 [*WTUL*]: Kessler-Harris, *Out to Work*, pp. 164–71, 203–10; Robin Miller Jacoby, "The Women's Trade Union League and American Feminism," *Feminist Studies*, vol. 3 (Fall 1975), pp. 126–38, quoted at p. 128; Nancy S. Dye, "Creating a Feminist Alliance: Sisterhood and Class Conflict in the New York Women's Trade Union League," *Feminist Studies*, vol. 2, no. 2/3 (1975), pp. 24–38.

[*"I am a good democrat in theory"*]: quoted in Jacoby, p. 132.

[*Justice on Kelley*]: Felix Frankfurter, "Foreword," in Goldmark, p. v.

282 [*AFL under Gompers*]: Harold C. Livesay, *Samuel Gompers and Organized Labor in America* (Little, Brown, 1978); Bernard Mandel, *Samuel Gompers: A Biography* (Antioch Press, 1963); Lewis Reed, *The Labor Philosophy of Samuel Gompers* (Columbia University Press, 1930).

[*Haywood*]: Joseph R. Conlin, *Big Bill Haywood and the Radical Union Movement* (Syracuse University Press, 1969); Peter Carlson, *Roughneck* (W. W. Norton, 1983); Eric Sears Stein, "Reform and Revolutionary Leadership: A Study of Samuel Gompers and William Haywood," typescript, Williams College, December 1983.

283 [*IWW*]: Paul Frederick Brissenden, *The IWW: A Study of American Syndicalism* (Columbia University, Studies in History, Economics and Public Law, 1920); Melvyn Dubofsky, *We Shall Be All: A History of the Industrial Workers of the World* (Quadrangle, 1969).

[*IWW on labor unity among races*]: Brissenden, pp. 84, 208; see also, Milton Meltzer, *Bread —and Roses* (Alfred A. Knopf, 1967).

[*Debs*]: Nick Salvatore, *Eugene V. Debs: Citizen and Socialist* (University of Illinois Press, 1982); Bruce Rogers, comp., *Debs: His Life, Writings and Speeches* (The Appeal to Reason, 1908).

[*Goldman*]: Drinnon; Emma Goldman, *Living My Life*, 2 vols. (Alfred A. Knopf, 1931); Terry M. Perlin, ed., *Contemporary Anarchism* (Rutgers University Press, 1979); Alan Ritter, *Anarchism: A Theoretical Analysis* (Cambridge University Press, 1980); William Reed Sawyers, "Emma Goldman: Anarchist as Leader," typescript, Williams College, November 1983.

284 [*Washington*]: Louis R. Harlan, *Booker T. Washington: The Making of a Black Leader* (Oxford University Press, 1972); Louis R. Harlan, *Booker T. Washington: The Wizard of Tuskegee* (Oxford University Press, 1983); Booker T. Washington, *Up from Slavery* (1901) in Louis R. Harlan, ed., *The Booker T. Washington Papers* (University of Illinois Press, 1972–82), vol. 1, pp. 209–385; Rayford W. Logan, *The Betrayal of the Negro* (Collier Books, 1969); E. Davidson Washington, ed., *Selected Speeches of Booker T. Washington* (Doubleday, Doran, 1932).

[*Washington on "questions of social equality"*]: "The Standard Printed Version of the Atlanta Exposition Address," September 18, 1895, in *Washington Papers*, vol. 3, p. 586.

285 [*Du Bois*]: Francis L. Broderick, *W. E. B. Du Bois* (Stanford University Press, 1959); Rayford W. Logan, ed., *W. E. B. Du Bois: A Profile* (Hill and Wang, 1971); W. E. Burghardt Du Bois, *Black Folk Then and Now* (Octagon Books, 1973); see also William Toll, *The Resurgence of Race* (Temple University Press, 1979).

[*Du Bois on his son*]: quoted in Eric Goldman, *Rendezvous with Destiny* (Alfred A. Knopf, 1952), p. 178.

[*Du Bois's interchangeable use of terms "Negro," "black," "colored"*]: Logan, *Du Bois*, p. xiii.

285 [*Mary Harris Jones*]: *Autobiography of Mother Jones* (Charles H. Kerr, 1925).
286 [*Women's networks*]: Cook, in Cott and Pleck, *passim*.

8. THE MODERNIZING MIND

287 [*Mr. Dooley on history*]: quoted in Mark Sullivan, *Our Times* (Scribner's, 1926–35), vol. 1, p. 243 footnote.
[*Gould on "intriguing interplay"*]: Lewis L. Gould, ed., *The Progressive Era* (Syracuse University Press, 1974), p. 9.
[*1893 Chicago Fair*]: Sullivan, vol. 1, pp. 188–93, Ernest I. Lewis quoted at p. 192 footnote.
[*Even Henry Adams*]: Adams, *The Education of Henry Adams* (Houghton Mifflin, 1927), pp. 339–43; and see also Adams to Elizabeth Cameron, October 8, 1893, in Worthington Chauncey Ford, ed., *Letters of Henry Adams* (Houghton Mifflin, 1930–38), vol. 2, p. 33, footnote 1.
[*Gibson girls, shirtwaists, and bicycles*]: Sullivan, vol. 1, pp. 193–96, 13–14, 240–43, respectively.
288 [*American production, 1900*]: ibid., p. 33.
[*Negro spiritual*]: quoted in *ibid.*, p. 38 footnote.
[*Black petition for passage to Liberia*]: *ibid.*, pp. 591–92.
[*Comstock report on improper pleasures*]: 37th Annual Report of the New York Society for the Suppression of Vice, January 1911, in Theodore Roosevelt Papers, Reel 98, Library of Congress.
289 [*Kathleen Norris on women's dress*]: quoted in Sullivan, vol. 1, p. 390.
[*Dominance of the "invisible" machine*]: Oscar Handlin, "Science and Technology in Popular Culture," in Gerald Holton, ed., *Science and Culture* (Houghton Mifflin, 1965), esp. p. 194.
[*Marx on technology and the productive processes*]: Nathan Rosenberg, "Karl Marx on the Economic Role of Science," in Rosenberg, *Perspectives on Technology* (Cambridge University Press, 1976), pp. 126–38.
[*Michelson*]: Bernard Jaffe, *Men of Science in America* (Simon and Schuster, 1949), ch. 15.
[*Willson*]: Robert Multhauf, "Industrial Chemistry in the Nineteenth Century," in Melvin Kranzberg and Carroll W. Purcell, Jr., eds., *Technology in Western Civilization* (Oxford University Press, 1967), vol. 1, pp. 468–89, esp. p. 478.
[*Gooch*]: Ralph G. Van Name, "Frank Austin Gooch," in National Academy of Sciences, *Biographical Memoirs*, vol. 15, 3rd memoir (1934), pp. 105–35.
290 [*Acheson*]: Edward G. Acheson, *A Pathfinder* (Press Scrap Book, 1910).
[*Morley*]: Howard R. Williams, *Edward Williams Morley* (Chemical Education Publications, 1957).
[*Sabine*]: Daniel J. Kevles, "Wallace Clement Ware Sabine," in Charles C. Gillespie, ed., *Dictionary of Scientific Biography* (Scribner's, 1970–80), vol. 12, p. 54.
[*Submersibles*]: Allen Hoar, *The Submarine Torpedo Boat* (Van Nostrand, 1916).
[*Flying machines*]: Tom D. Crouch, *A Dream of Wings: Americans and the Airplane, 1875–1905* (W. W. Norton, 1981).
[*Langley*]: Jaffe, ch. 14.
[*Charles and Frank Duryea*]: G. N. Georgano, ed., *Encyclopedia of American Automobiles* (E. P. Dutton, 1971), pp. 67–68 ("Duryea").
[*Gibbs and Steinmetz*]: Jaffe, ch. 13; J. W. Hammond, *Charles Proteus Steinmetz* (Century, 1924).
[*Osborn*]: Edwin H. Colbert, *Men and Dinosaurs: The Search in Field and Laboratory* (E. P. Dutton, 1968), pp. 147 ff.
[*Boas and Wissler*]: Melville J. Herskovits, *Franz Boas: The Science of Man in the Making* (reissue; Augustus M. Kelley, 1973).
[*Morgan*]: Garland E. Allen, *Thomas Hunt Morgan: The Man and His Science* (Princeton University Press, 1978).
291 [*Pattern of development in science*]: Thomas S. Kuhn, *The Structure of Scientific Revolutions*, 2nd ed. (University of Chicago Press, 1970).
[*James on pragmatism's "precipitation"*]: William James, *Pragmatism, and Four Essays from The Meaning of Truth* (Meridian Books, 1950), p. 13.

The Pulse of the Machine

291–92 [*William James in New York and at Columbia*]: James to Henry James and William James, Jr., February 14, 1907, in Elizabeth Hardwick, ed., *The Selected Letters of William James* (Farrar, Straus and Cudahy, 1960), pp. 227–29; Gay Wilson Allen, *William James* (Viking Press, 1967), pp. 457–58.

291 [*James on Twain*]: letter, February 14, 1907, in Hardwick, pp. 228–29.

292 [*James on New York*]: *ibid.*, pp. 228, 229.

[*James's earlier life, and relationship with Peirce*]: Ralph Barton Perry, *The Thought and Character of William James*, vols. 1 and 2 (Little, Brown, 1935), esp. chs. 32, 75, 76.

[*Peirce*]: Charles Hartshorne, Paul Weiss, and Arthur Burks, eds., *The Collected Papers of Charles Sanders Peirce*, 8 vols. (Harvard University Press, 1931–58); Philip P. Weiner and Frederic H. Young, eds., *Studies in the Philosophy of Charles Sanders Peirce* (Harvard University Press, 1952).

292–93 [*James's lectures on pragmatism*]: reprinted "as delivered," according to the author, in James, *Pragmatism, op cit.*

293 [*James on the "tender-minded" and the "tough-minded"*]: *ibid.*, p. 22. Other quotations from the lectures: *ibid.*, pp. 19, 21, 23, 24, 27, 49, 45, 47, respectively.

[*Reception of pragmatism*]: see Perry, vol. 2, ch. 78; James on the evening discussions quoted in Hardwick, p. 229.

294 [*James's sudden "fear of my own existence"*]: quoted in Edward C. Moore, *American Pragmatism: Peirce, James, and Dewey* (Columbia University Press, 1961), p. 115.

[*Reaction of philosophers and others to James's* Pragmatism]: H. Münsterberg to James, July 1, 1906, in Perry, vol. 2, pp. 471–72; C. S. Peirce to James, March 7, 1904, in *ibid.*, p. 430; see also p. 465.

[*Pragmatism as humanism*]: F. C. S. Schiller, *Studies in Humanism* (Macmillan, 1907); see corr. between James and Schiller, in Perry, *passim.*

[*Derivation of "pragmatism"*]: Philip P. Wiener, ed., *Dictionary of the History of Ideas* (Scribner's, 1973), vol. 3, p. 554.

295 [*Holmes to James on* Pragmatism]: Perry, vol. 2, p. 462. Earlier comments on James's articles on pragmatism: Holmes to James, March 24, 1907, *ibid.*, pp. 459–61; Holmes to James, April 1, 1907, *ibid.*, pp. 461–62.

[*Holmes on the "life of the law"*]: Oliver Wendell Holmes, Jr., *The Common Law* (Little, Brown, 1881), p. 1. See also Note, "Holmes, Peirce and Legal Pragmatism," *Yale Law Journal*, vol. 84, no. 5 (April 1975), pp. 1123–40.

[*Lochner v. New York*]: 198 U.S. 45 (1905), quoted at 75; see also Max Lerner, ed., *The Mind and Faith of Justice Holmes* (Little, Brown, 1943), pp. 143–50.

[*Holmes on letting slaughterhouses be built*]: quoted in Eric F. Goldman, *Rendezvous with Destiny* (Alfred A. Knopf, 1952), p. 136.

296 [*Rostow on Holmes's opinions*]: Eugene V. Rostow, "The Realist Tradition in American Law," in Arthur M. Schlesinger, Jr., and Morton White, eds., *Paths of American Thought* (Houghton Mifflin, 1970), p. 205.

[*Holmes on Brandeis as a crusader*]: quoted in Perry, vol. 1, p. 518.

[*Aspects of pragmatism*]: Morton White, *Social Thought in America: The Revolt Against Formalism* (Beacon Press, 1947); Charles Morris, *The Pragmatic Movement in American Philosophy* (George Braziller, 1970); Morton White, *Pragmatism and the American Mind* (Oxford University Press, 1973); Gail Kennedy, ed., *Pragmatism and American Culture* (D. C. Heath, 1950); Andrew J. Reck, *Introduction to William James* (Indiana University Press, 1967), esp. chs. 5–6.

297 [*Pratt on James's pragmatism*]: James Bissett Pratt, *What Is Pragmatism?* (Macmillan, 1909).

[*James on bringing out the cash value of each word*]: *Pragmatism*, p. 46.

The Critics: Ideas vs. Interests?

298 [*Hofstadter on the newly rich*]: Richard Hofstadter, *The Age of Reform* (Alfred A. Knopf, 1955), p. 137.

[*Protestant ministry's "massive" front*]: Henry F. May, *Protestant Churches and Industrial America* (Harper & Bros., 1949), p. 91.

[*Shift of Protestant clergy and of legal profession*]: Hofstadter, ch. 4.

299 [*Turner on the frontier*]: Frederick Jackson Turner, *The Frontier in American History* (Henry Holt, 1920); see also Frederick Jackson Turner, *Frontier and Section: Selected Essays*, Ray A. Billington, ed. (Prentice-Hall, 1961); Wilbur R. Jacobs, ed., *Frederick Jackson Turner's Legacy* (Huntington Library, 1965).
[*Other progressive historians*]: Orin Grant Libby, "The Geographical Distribution of the Vote of the Thirteen States of the Federal Constitution, 1787–1788," in *Bulletin of the University of Wisconsin, Economics, Political Science and History Series*, vol. 1, no. 1 (1934); J. Allen Smith, *The Spirit of American Government* (Macmillan, 1907).
[*Beard's economic interpretation*]: *An Economic Interpretation of the Constitution of the United States* (Macmillan, 1913).
[*Beard's early years*]: Richard Hofstadter, *The Progressive Historians* (Alfred A. Knopf, 1968), ch. 5; Goldman, *op. cit.*, pp. 149–51.
300 [*Beard's conclusions*]: *Economic Interpretation*, pp. 324–25.
[*Response to Beard's* Interpretation]: quoted in Goldman, pp. 153–54.
[*Lerner on Beard's* Interpretation]: Max Lerner, *Ideas Are Weapons* (Viking Press, 1939), p. 154.
301 [*Madison on ideas and interests*]: *The Federalist*, Jacob E. Cooke, ed. (Wesleyan University Press, 1961), no. 10, quoted at pp. 57–59.
[*Holmes on Beard's* Interpretation]: quoted in Hofstadter, *The Progressive Historians*, pp. 212–13.
On Charles A. Beard and his *Interpretation* in general, see John Patrick Diggins, "Power and Authority in American History: The Case of Charles A. Beard and His Critics," *American Historical Review*, vol. 86, no. 4 (October 1981), pp. 701–30.
302 [*Beard as a theorist*]: Harold J. Laski, "Charles Beard: An English View," in Howard K. Beale, ed., *Charles A. Beard: An Appraisal* (University of Kentucky Press, 1954), pp. 9–24.
302-3 [*Veblen's personality and background*]: Joseph Dorfman, *Thorstein Veblen and His America* (Viking Press, 1934); David Riesman, *Thorstein Veblen* (Scribner's, 1953); Max Lerner, ed., *The Portable Veblen* (Viking Press, 1948), "Introduction" by Lerner.
303 [*Veblen chrestomathy*]: Thorstein Veblen, *The Theory of the Leisure Class* (Modern Library, 1934), pp. 274, 170–71, 141, 143, 140, respectively.
[*Veblen's basic philosophy*]: Bernard Rosenberg, *The Values of Veblen* (Public Affairs Press, 1956); Stanley Matthew Daugert, *The Philosophy of Veblen* (King's Crown Press, 1950).
[*Veblen on the subordination of women*]: John P. Diggins, *The Bard of Savagery* (Seabury Press, 1978), ch. 8.
[*Veblen and Marx*]: Diggins, *Bard of Savagery*, part 2; Veblen, "The Socialist Economics of Karl Marx and His Followers," in Veblen, *Veblen on Marx, Race, Science and Economics* (Capricorn Books, 1969), pp. 409–56; J. A. Hobson, *Veblen* (Chapman and Hall, 1936).
304 [*Dobriansky on Veblen*]: Lev E. Dobriansky, *Veblenism: A New Critique* (Public Affairs Press, 1957), esp. ch. 9.
[*Veblen's failure to offer comprehensive social alternative*]: Arthur K. Davis, "Sociological Elements in Veblen's Economic Theory," *Journal of Political Economy*, vol. 53, no. 2 (June 1945), pp. 132–49.
[*Irish gardener to Adams*]: *Education of Henry Adams*, *op. cit.*, p. 16.
[*Adams in Washington*]: Van Wyck Brooks, *New England: Indian Summer* (E. P. Dutton, 1940), ch. 17.
305 [*Henry Adams, life and ideas*]: Henry Brooks Adams Papers, Massachusetts Historical Society; Ernest Samuels, *Henry Adams: The Major Phase* (Harvard University Press, 1964); R. P. Blackmur, *Henry Adams* (Harcourt Brace Jovanovich, 1980); David R. Contosta, *Henry Adams and the American Experiment* (Little, Brown, 1980); John J. Conder, *A Formula of His Own* (University of Chicago Press, 1970); William Dusinberre, *Henry Adams: The Myth of Failure* (University Press of Virginia, 1980).
[*Kelvin on modern biologists*]: quoted in Samuels, p. 476.
[*James on not understanding Adams's theory*]: *ibid.*, p. 485.
[*Adams on power, Roosevelt, and trusts*]: *Education of Henry Adams*, pp. 418, 500.
306 [*Brooks Adams's views*]: Brooks Adams, "Introductory Note," in Henry Adams, *The Degradation of the Democratic Dogma* (Macmillan, 1920), pp. v–xiii; Brooks Adams, *The Law of Civilization and Decay* (Swan Sonnenschein, 1895).
[*Charles Francis Adams on being bored*]: Charles Francis Adams, Jr., to Henry Adams,

January 15, 1908, Henry Brooks Adams Papers, Massachusetts Historical Society; see also, Ford, *Letters of Henry Adams, op. cit.,* vol. 2, pp. 487–88 (Henry Adams to Charles Francis Adams, Jr., January 17, 1908).

Art: "All That Is Holy Is Profaned"

306 [*Greenwich Village, early 1900s*]: Arthur Frank Wertheim, *The New York Little Renaissance* (New York University Press, 1976); John A. Kouwenhoven, *The Columbia Historical Portrait of New York* (Doubleday, 1953), Group Six; Frederick J. Hoffman, *The Twenties* (Viking Press, 1955), ch. 1.

307 [*"Everybody was freeing themselves"*]: Floyd Dell, quoted in Goldman, *op. cit.,* p. 224.
[*Washington Square boardinghouse of the great*]: Gilbert Tauber and Samuel Kaplan, *The New York City Handbook* (Doubleday, 1966), p. 467.
[*A bastard and the "bourgeois pigs"*]: quoted in Goldman, p. 225.

308 [*Luhan's voice*]: Maurice Sterne, quoted in Wertheim, p. 91.
[*The Luhan salon*]: Mabel Dodge Luhan, *Movers and Shakers,* vol. 3 of *Intimate Memoirs* (Harcourt, Brace, 1933–36), p. 83.
[*Reed on Luhan*]: quoted in Wertheim, p. 91.
[*"Melt, You Women!"*]: *ibid.*
[*Marx on the bourgeois epoch*]: quoted in Justin Kaplan, review of Marshall Berman, *All That Is Solid Melts into Air* (Simon and Schuster, 1982), *Harvard Magazine* (March–April 1982), pp. 8–9.
[*The American art establishment, late nineteenth century*]: Alan Trachtenberg, *The Incorporation of America: Culture and Society in the Gilded Age* (Hill and Wang, 1982), esp. ch. 5, quoted at pp. 144–45; Robert M. Crunden, *Ministers of Reform* (Basic Books, 1982), pp. 102–3.

309 [*"And I dislike unrest"*]: Sir Purdon Clarke, quoted in Herbert J. Seligmann, "291: A Vision Through Photography," in Waldo Frank et al., *America & Alfred Stieglitz* (Aperture, 1975), p. 60.
[*New currents in art, late nineteenth century*]: Oliver W. Larkin, *Art and Life in America* (Holt, Rinehart and Winston, 1960), book 4; Theodore E. Stebbins, Jr., Carol Troyen, and Trevor J. Fairbrother, *A New World: Masterpieces of American Painting, 1760–1910* (Museum of Fine Arts, Boston, 1983), chs. 8–9; Trachtenberg, *passim.*
[*Homer*]: Gordon Hendricks, *The Life and Work of Winslow Homer* (Harry N. Abrams, 1979); Lloyd Goodrich, *Winslow Homer* (Whitney Museum of American Art–Macmillan, 1945).
[*"Exactly as it appears"*]: quoted in James T. Flexner, *That Wilder Image* (Little, Brown, 1962), pp. 345–46.
[*Eakins*]: Gordon Hendricks, *The Life and Times of Thomas Eakins* (Grossman, 1974); Sylvan Schendler, *Eakins* (Little, Brown, 1967).
[*"Physiology from top to toe"*]: quoted in Larkin, p. 277.

310 [*"Drunks and slatterns"*]: *Outlook,* quoted in *ibid.,* p. 336.
[*"Paint the ugly"*]: *ibid.*
[*The Eight*]: Bernard B. Perlman, *The Immortal Eight* (Exposition Press, 1962); Ira Glauckens, *William Glauckens and the Ashcan Group* (Crown, 1957); Wertheim, pp. 131–36.
[*Henri*]: William Innes Homer, *Robert Henri and His Circle* (Cornell University Press, 1969); Perlman, pp. 39–64 and *passim.*
[*Henri's convictions about painting*]: Crunden, p. 104.
[*Stieglitz*]: Dorothy Norman, *Albert Stieglitz: An American Seer* (Random House, 1960); Sue Davidson Lowe, *Stieglitz: A Memoir/Biography* (Farrar, Straus & Giroux, 1983); Sara Greenough and Juan Hamilton, eds., *Alfred Stieglitz: Photographs and Writings* (Callaway Editions, 1983); Waldo Frank et al.

311 [*"Not very elevating"*]: W. B. McCormick, quoted in Norman, p. 72.
[*Armory Show*]: Larkin, ch. 28. I have drawn heavily from Larkin in describing the exhibits, especially the "American room," quoted from Larkin at p. 363.
[*Century review of Armory Show*]: *ibid.,* p. 364.

312 [*Roosevelt on the Armory Show*]: quoted in Crunden, p. 114.
[*Loss of continuity between art and experience*]: Larkin, p. 348.
[*Mumford on Stieglitz assimilating the machine*]: Mumford, "The Metropolitan Milieu," in Waldo Frank et al., p. 32.

313 [*Wright on the uglification of America*]: quoted in Crunden, pp. 158–59.
[*Wright on the machine and Democracy*]: *ibid.*, p. 157.

Writing: "Venerable Ideas Are Swept Away"

[*Sloan and* The Masses]: Wertheim, *op. cit.*, pp. 37–44; Bruce St. John, ed., *John Sloan's New York Scene, from the Diaries, Notes and Correspondence, 1906–1913* (Harper & Row, 1965); Crunden, *op. cit.*, pp. 111–12.
[*Art Young*]: Young, *Art Young: His Life and Times*, John N. Beffel, ed. (Sheridan House, 1939), esp. ch. 26.
[*Eastman*]: Daniel Aaron, *Writers on the Left* (Harcourt, Brace & World, 1961), ch. 1 and *passim;* William O'Neill, *The Last Romantic* (Oxford University Press, 1978), esp. ch. 2; Max Eastman, *Enjoyment of Living* (Harper & Bros., 1948), esp. parts 6 and 7; Wertheim, pp. 34–35.
[*Eastman's appointment*]: Young, p. 275.
314 [*"We live on scraps"*]: quoted in Wertheim, p. 43.
[*Secession at* The Masses]: *ibid.*, pp. 43–44, Young quoted at p. 43.
[The Seven Arts]: *ibid.*, pp. 173–83, Oppenheim quoted at p. 174; James Oppenheim, "The Story of the *Seven Arts*," *The American Mercury*, vol. 20, no. 78 (June 1930), pp. 156–64.
[*Bourne*]: Louis Filler, *Randolph Bourne* (American Council on Public Affairs, 1943); Max Lerner, "Randolph Bourne and Two Generations," *Twice a Year*, vols. 5–6 (double number: Fall–Winter 1940 and Spring–Summer 1941), pp. 54–78.
[*Oppenheim on Bourne*]: "The Story of the *Seven Arts*," p. 163.
[*Mencken and* The Smart Set]: Wertheim, ch. 12; C. L. Bode, *Mencken* (Southern Illinois University Press, 1969), esp. ch. 5. The six-volume "series" of *Prejudices* (Alfred A. Knopf, 1919–27) offers a selection, with some revisions, of Mencken's contributions to *The Smart Set*.
315 [*Mencken's ambition for* The Smart Set]: quoted in Wertheim, p. 197.
[*"Poet's Free Lunch"*]: *ibid.*, p. 196; Bode, p. 71.
[*Mencken and the new poets*]: Mencken, "The New Poetry Movement," in Mencken, *Prejudices: First Series* (Alfred A. Knopf, 1919), pp. 83–96.
[Others]: Wertheim, pp. 102–8.
[Poetry]: Harriet Monroe, *A Poet's Life* (Macmillan, 1938), esp. chs. 24–27; Dale Kramer, *Chicago Renaissance: The Literary Life in the Midwest, 1900–1930* (Appleton-Century, 1966), ch. 15; "Bastien von Helmholtz" (Ezra Pound), "Review: *Poetry: A Magazine of Verse*," *The Egoist* (reprinted by Kraus Reprint), vol. 1, no. 11 (June 1, 1914), p. 215.
[*Monroe circular*]: quoted in Monroe, p. 251.
[*"Keenest young literary group"*]: *ibid.*, p. 259.
316 [*Pound's letter to Monroe*]: August 18, 1912, in D. D. Paige, ed., *The Letters of Ezra Pound, 1907–1941* (Harcourt, Brace, 1950), pp. 9–10, quoted at p. 10.
[*Principles of Imagism*]: "F. S. Flint" (Ezra Pound), "Imagisme," *Poetry*, vol. 1, no. 6 (March 1913), p. 199.
[*"Image" defined*]: Pound, "A Few Don'ts by an Imagiste," *ibid.*, p. 200.
[*Dreiser and Mencken*]: W. A. Swanberg, *Dreiser* (Scribner's, 1965), pp. 124–27, Dreiser quoted at p. 126; Bode, pp. 103–5.
317 [*Dreiser's family*]: Swanberg, ch. 1.
[*Dreiser's years before* Carrie]: *ibid.*, pp. 23–81.
[*Dreiser as first important American writer from a non-Anglo-Saxon, lower-class background*]: John Lydenberg, "Theodore Dreiser: Ishmael in the Jungle," in Lydenberg, ed., *Dreiser: A Collection of Critical Essays* (Prentice-Hall, 1971), p. 24.
318 [*Ford on Dreiser*]: Ford, "Theodore Dreiser," *The American Mercury*, vol. 40, no. 160 (April 1937), p. 495.
[*Doubleday and* Carrie]: Swanberg, pp. 85–90.
[*Early reviews of* Carrie]: *ibid.*, pp. 91–92; Donald Pizer, ed., *Critical Essays on Theodore Dreiser* (G. K. Hall, 1981), pp. 157–68.
[*"Mr. Dreiser can not punctuate"*]: Harriet Merton Lyon, "Theodore Dreiser's 'Sister Carrie'" (1907), in Pizer, p. 163.

319 [*Markels on Dreiser*]: Markels, "Dreiser and the Plotting of Inarticulate Experience," in Pizer, p. 186.
[*"Bitter, brutal insistence"*]: Dreiser, *The 'Genius'* (Horace Liveright, 1923), p. 231.
[*"Old, mournful Carrie"*]: Dreiser, *Sister Carrie* ("The Pennsylvania Edition": University of Pennsylvania Press, 1981), p. 487.
[*"Rubber-stamp formulae"*]: Mencken, "The Dreiser Bugaboo," *The Seven Arts* (reprinted by AMS), vol. 2 (August 1917), p. 517.
[*Young Edith Jones*]: Edith Wharton, *A Backward Glance* (D. Appleton-Century, 1934), chs. 1–4; R. W. B. Lewis, *Edith Wharton* (Harper & Row, 1975), chs. 2–3.
[*Father's library*]: *Backward Glance*, pp. 64–72.
[*First literary effort*]: ibid., p. 73.
[*Trilling on Wharton*]: Diana Trilling, "*The House of Mirth* Revisited," in Irving Howe, ed., *Edith Wharton: A Collection of Critical Essays* (Prentice-Hall, 1962), p. 105.
[*Kazin on function of genteel women*]: Kazin, *On Native Grounds* (Doubleday, 1956), p. 55.
321 [*"What marriage was really like"*]: quoted in Lewis, p. 53.
322 [*Archer on emancipating his wife*]: Wharton, *The Age of Innocence* (Modern Library, 1920), p. 196.
[*Roosevelt on cleaning out the stable*]: *Age of Innocence*, pp. 348–49.
[*Best-sellers, 1901–1908*]: Richard B. Morris, ed., *Encyclopedia of American History* (Harper & Row, 1976), p. 858.
[*Sales of* Age of Innocence]: Lewis, p. 429.
[*Dreiser on discovering America*]: quoted in Kazin, p. 68.
323 [*Generous illusions and mean truths*]: Wharton, *The House of Mirth* (Berkley Books, 1981), p. 71.

"All That Is Solid Melts into Air"

[*Paterson strike and pageant*]: John Reed, "War in Paterson," in William L. O'Neill, ed., *Echoes of Revolt: The Masses, 1911–1917* (Quadrangle, 1966), pp. 143–47; William D. Haywood, *Bill Haywood's Book* (International Publishers, 1929), pp. 261–64; Joyce L. Kornbluh, *Rebel Voices: An I.W.W. Anthology* (University of Michigan Press, 1964), ch. 7; Wertheim, *op. cit.*, pp. 51–57.
[*Bourne on pageant*]: Randolph Bourne, "Pageantry and Social Art," in Bourne, *The Radical Will: Selected Writings, 1911–1918*, Olaf Hansen, ed. (Urizen Books, 1977), p. 519.
324 [*Flynn's judgment of pageant*]: Flynn, "The Truth about the Paterson Strike," address given January 13, 1914, reprinted in Kornbluh, pp. 215–25, esp. pp. 221–22.

9. THE REFORMATION OF ECONOMIC POWER

325 [*Roosevelt's pre-presidential career*]: Edmund Morris, *The Rise of Theodore Roosevelt* (Coward, McCann & Geoghegan, 1979); David McCullough, *Mornings on Horseback* (Simon and Schuster, 1981); Elting E. Morison, ed., *The Letters of Theodore Roosevelt* (Harvard University Press, 1951–54), vol. 1.
326 [*Roosevelt's personality and views*]: John Morton Blum, *The Republican Roosevelt* (Harvard University Press, 1967); Edward Wagenknecht, *The Seven Worlds of Theodore Roosevelt* (Longmans, Green, 1958); John M. Blum, "Theodore Roosevelt: The Years of Decision," appendix 9, in Morison, *Letters*, vol. 1, pp. 1484–94; Morris; McCullough.
[*Roosevelt's killing of neighbor's dog*]: Morris, p. 98.
[*Roosevelt on Irish fellow legislators*]: Theodore Roosevelt, "Diary of Five Months in the New York Legislature," in Morison, *Letters*, vol. 2, appendix 1, pp. 1469–73, quoted at p. 1470.
[*"Wealthy criminal class"*]: quoted in Wagenknecht, p. 217.
[*Roosevelt and Social Darwinism*]: William Henry Harbaugh, *Power and Responsibility* (Farrar, Straus and Cudahy, 1961), pp. 62, 92, 99, 140.
[*Roosevelt on self-help and struggle*]: quoted in Morris, pp. 348, 571.
[*Roosevelt on the "best classes" and on sterilizing the criminal and the feebleminded*]: quoted in Wagenknecht, p. 86.
327 [*Roosevelt's reading*]: Blum in Morison, vol. 1, pp. 1488–91.
[*Roosevelt on social critics*]: quoted in *ibid.*, p. 1491.

327 [*Roosevelt's qualified admiration of Tolstoy*]: Harbaugh, p. 460.

[*Roosevelt on Longfellow*]: Roosevelt to Arlo Bates, September 29, 1897, in Morison, *Letters*, vol. 1, p. 695.

[*Roosevelt on Chaucer*]: Roosevelt to Cecil Arthur Spring Rice, May 3, 1892, in *ibid.*, vol. 1, p. 277.

[*Roosevelt in his biographies of Benton and Cromwell*]: Morris, pp. 332-35, 705.

[*Adams on Roosevelt*]: Adams, *The Education of Henry Adams* (Houghton Mifflin, 1974), p. 417.

[*Roosevelt's anger over query as to his presidential ambition*]: Lincoln Steffens, *The Autobiography of Lincoln Steffens* (Harcourt, Brace, 1931), pp. 258-60, Roosevelt quoted at pp. 259, 260.

328 [*"The Man with the Hoe"*]: quoted in Mark Sullivan, *Our Times* (Scribner's, 1926-35), vol. 2, p. 239.

The Personal Uses of Power

[*"I was a sickly and timid boy"*]: Roosevelt to Edward Sanford Martin, November 26, 1900, in Morison, *Letters, op. cit.*, vol. 2, pp. 1442-45, quoted at pp. 1442, 1443.

329 [*Roosevelt on history*]: *ibid.*, p. 1444.

[*"Deep and damnable alliance"*]: quoted in William Allen White, *The Autobiography of William Allen White* (Macmillan, 1946), pp. 297-98.

[*White on Roosevelt*]: *ibid.*, p. 298.

[*Franchise tax bill*]: Morris, *op. cit.*, p. 698.

330 [*Program of "moderately positive action"*]: Harbaugh, *op. cit.*, pp. 155-57, quoted at p. 155.

[*Mr. Dooley on Roosevelt's antitrust policy*]: quoted in Elmer Ellis, *Mr. Dooley's America: A Life of Finley Peter Dunne* (Alfred A. Knopf, 1941), p. 170.

[*Aldrich and Quay*]: Nathaniel W. Stephenson, *Nelson W. Aldrich* (Scribner's, 1930); James A. Kehl, *Boss Rule in the Gilded Age: Matthew Quay of Pennsylvania* (University of Pittsburgh Press, 1981).

[*Hanna on Roosevelt as "madman" and as "cowboy"*]: quoted in Henry F. Pringle, *Theodore Roosevelt: A Biography* (Harcourt, Brace, 1931), p. 223; and in H. H. Kohlsaat, *From McKinley to Harding* (Scribner's, 1923), p. 101.

331 [*Reed's retirement*]: Samuel W. McCall, *The Life of Thomas Brackett Reed* (Houghton Mifflin, 1914), ch. 20.

[*"Go slow"*]: quoted in Harbaugh, p. 155.

[*Robinson's warning to Roosevelt about business confidence*]: quoted in *ibid.*, pp. 153-54.

[*Roosevelt's reply*]: Roosevelt to Douglas Robinson, October 4, 1901, in Morison, *Letters*, vol. 3, pp. 159-60.

[*Morgan*]: Frederick Lewis Allen, *The Great Pierpont Morgan* (Harper & Bros., 1949); Herbert L. Satterlee, *J. Pierpont Morgan* (Macmillan, 1939).

332 [*Early prosecutions under the Sherman Antitrust Act*]: Hans B. Thorelli, *The Federal Antitrust Policy* (Johns Hopkins Press, 1955), esp. chs. 7 and 8.

[*Roosevelt on corporate control as question of presidential and popular power*]: Thorelli, pp. 423-24; Theodore Roosevelt, *An Autobiography*, as quoted in Harbaugh, p. 149.

[*Morgan-Roosevelt relationship*]: Roosevelt to William Thomas O'Neil, November 12, 1882, in Morison, *Letters*, vol. 1, p. 58, footnote 2; Roosevelt to Elihu Root, December 5, 1900, in *ibid.*, vol. 2, p. 1450; Allen, ch. 11; Satterlee, *passim*.

[*Morgan-Knox-Roosevelt dialogue and Roosevelt's subsequent reflections*]: quoted in Joseph B. Bishop, *Theodore Roosevelt and His Time* (Scribner's, 1920), vol. 1, pp. 184-85.

333 [*Coal strike, 1902*]: Robert J. Cornell, *The Anthracite Coal Strike of 1902* (Catholic University of America Press, 1957); Robert H. Wiebe, "The Anthracite Strike of 1902: A Record of Confusion," *Mississippi Valley Historical Review*, vol. 48, no. 2 (September 1961), pp. 229-51; Harbaugh, ch. 10.

[*Baer on the rights of laboring men*]: quoted in Harbaugh, p. 173.

[*Roosevelt on behavior at White House conference*]: quoted in Pringle, p. 272.

[*Campaign of 1904*]: William E. Harbaugh, "Election of 1904," in Arthur M. Schlesinger, Jr., ed., *History of American Presidential Elections* (Chelsea House, 1971), vol. 3, pp. 1965-2046.

334 [*Roosevelt and the admission of three new states*]: George E. Mowry, *The Era of Theodore Roosevelt* (Harper & Bros., 1958), p. 126.

334 [*Harbaugh on campaign shenanigans*]: Harbaugh, *Power and Responsibility*, p. 217.
[*Roosevelt on no third term*]: quoted in *ibid.*, p. 232.
[*Blum on "central issue"*]: Blum, *The Republican Roosevelt, op. cit.*, p. 86.
[*Roosevelt on transportation*]: *Congressional Record*, 59th Congress, 1st Session (vol. 40, part 1), December 5, 1905, pp. 91–105, quoted at p. 93.
335 [*Rail reform legislation*]: Blum, *Republican Roosevelt*, ch. 6.
[*Roosevelt to Lodge on Holmes*]: reprinted in William M. Goldsmith, ed., *The Growth of Presidential Power* (Chelsea House, 1974), vol. 2, pp. 1160–62; see also John Garraty, "Holmes' Appointment to the Supreme Court," *New England Quarterly*, vol. 22, no. 3 (March 1949), pp. 291–303; Max Lerner, ed., *The Mind and Faith of Justice Holmes* (Little, Brown, 1943), pp. xxxi–xxxvi, 217–31.
[*Roosevelt on Holmes's lack of "backbone"*]: quoted in Harbaugh, *Power and Responsibility*, p. 162.

Foreign Policy with the TR Brand

336 [*Correspondence, Roosevelt-style*]: Morison, *Letters, op. cit.*, vol. 3, pp. 651, 625, 599, respectively. See also Wagenknecht, *op. cit.*, p. 9.
337 [*Interview with Roosevelt*]: Diary of Sir Mortimer Durand, quoted in Eugene P. Trani, *The Treaty of Portsmouth: An Adventure in American Diplomacy* (University of Kentucky Press, 1969), pp. 15–16.
[*Panama Canal diplomacy*]: Thomas A. Bailey, *A Diplomatic History of the American People*, 9th ed. (Prentice-Hall, 1974), ch. 33; Lawrence O. Ealy, *Yanqui Politics and the Isthmian Canal* (Pennsylvania State University Press, 1971), chs. 4–6; Walter LaFeber, *The Panama Canal: The Crisis in Historical Perspective* (Oxford University Press, 1978), ch. 2; David McCullough, *The Path Between the Seas* (Simon and Schuster, 1977), chs. 10–14.
[*Hay on "ignorance and spite"*]: quoted in Bailey, p. 488.
338 [*Volcanic inscription*]: *ibid.*, p. 489.
[*Herrán's fear of Roosevelt*]: quoted in McCullough, p. 332.
339 [*Roosevelt on Panamanian independence*]: Roosevelt to Albert Shaw, October 10, 1903, in Morison, *Letters*, vol. 3, p. 628.
[*Denunciations of U.S. role in Panama insurrection*]: quoted in McCullough, p. 381, and Ealy, p. 61. See also Bailey, p. 495.
340 [*Republican platform on canal success*]: quoted in Ealy, p. 65.
[*Roosevelt on Colombian canal banditry*]: quoted in G. Wallace Chessman, *Theodore Roosevelt and the Politics of Power* (Little, Brown, 1969), pp. 99–100.
[*Roosevelt Corollary*]: quoted in Bailey, p. 505. See also Cecil V. Crabb, Jr., *The Doctrines of American Foreign Policy* (Louisiana State University Press, 1982), pp. 38–40.
[*Roosevelt on the superiority of fighting men*]: quoted in Wagenknecht, p. 248.
[*Competition of races*]: see Robert Dallek, *The American Style of Foreign Policy: Cultural Politics and Foreign Affairs* (Alfred A. Knopf, 1983), pp. 6–7.
341 [*Roosevelt's preference for Japan*]: letter of February 10, 1904, in Morison, *Letters*, vol. 4, p. 724.
[*Roosevelt's annoyance with the Russians*]: *ibid.*; and Roosevelt to Cecil A. Spring Rice, December 27, 1904, *ibid.*, vol. 4, p. 1085.
342 [*Roosevelt on Japanese contempt for "white devils"*]: *ibid.*, pp. 1085–86.
[*Portsmouth negotiations*]: Trani, *passim*, and sources cited therein.
[*Roosevelt's frustration with Portsmouth negotiators*]: Roosevelt to Kermit Roosevelt, August 25, 1905, in Morison, *Letters*, vol. 4, pp. 1316–17.
342–43 [Morning Post *on Roosevelt as diplomatist*]: quoted in Trani, p. 61.
[*Roosevelt's fear of disorder*]: Morison, *Letters*, vol. 5, p. xvi.
[*Roosevelt's mastery of "uncontrollable forces"*]: Dallek, p. 51.
[*Roosevelt on work*]: Roosevelt to Frederic René Coudert, July 3, 1901, in Morison, *Letters*, vol. 5, p. xv.
[*Roosevelt at the Canal*]: McCullough, pp. 492–502.
[*Roosevelt on "one of the great works of the world"*]: quoted in Ealy, p. 66.
[*California school segregation*]: Bailey, pp. 521–23, Roosevelt quoted at p. 522.
344 [*Tour of the "Great White Fleet"*]: Robert A. Hart, *The Great White Fleet* (Little, Brown, 1965), fleet commander (Adm. Robley D. Evans) quoted at p. 45; see also Harbaugh,

Power and Responsibility, op. cit., pp. 300–301; Howard K. Beale, *Theodore Roosevelt and the Rise of America to World Power* (Johns Hopkins Press, 1956), pp. 328–32.

Reform: Leadership and Power

345 [*The new breed of reformers*]: Louis Filler, *Crusaders for American Liberalism* (Harcourt, Brace, 1939), esp. chs. 5–7.
[*Mr. Dooley on reform magazines*]: Finley Peter Dunne, "National Housecleaning," in Finley Peter Dunne, *Mr. Dooley: Now and Forever,* Louis Filler, ed. (Academic Reprints, 1954), pp. 244–45.
[*Roosevelt's personal relationships with reformers*]: Morison, *Letters, op. cit., passim.*

346 [*White on Roosevelt as "reform in a derby"*]: quoted in Eric F. Goldman, *Rendezvous with Destiny* (Alfred A. Knopf, 1952), p. 165.
[*Rise of the "ten-cent magazine"*]: Frank Luther Mott, *A History of American Magazines* (Harvard University Press, 1957), vol. 4, chs. 1, 4.
[*Profusion of magazines*]: *ibid.,* vol. 4, p. 11.
[*Comment of* Philosophical Review]: quoted in *ibid.,* vol. 4, p. 10.
[*"Magazines, magazines, magazines!"*]: *National Magazine,* November 1897, quoted in *ibid.,* p. 11.
[*Rise of McClure's*]: Harold S. Wilson, *McClure's Magazine and the Muckrakers* (Princeton University Press, 1970); Mott, vol. 4, pp. 589–607.
[*McClure's philosophy*]: quoted in Mott, vol. 4, p. 594.
[*Goldman on McClure*]: Goldman, p. 172.

347 [*Steffens*]: Steffens, *Autobiography, op. cit.;* Justin Kaplan, *Lincoln Steffens* (Simon and Schuster, 1974).
[*Tarbell and Standard Oil*]: Filler, *Crusaders,* ch. 9.
347-48 [*Filler on Tarbell's Standard Oil series*]: *ibid.,* p. 104.
348 [*Aldrich on food and drug regulation*]: quoted in Sullivan, *Our Times, op. cit.,* vol. 2, p. 532.
[*Sinclair*]: Upton Sinclair, *The Autobiography of Upton Sinclair* (Harcourt, Brace, 1962).
[*Roosevelt to Sinclair on the perils of socialism*]: March 15, 1906, in Morison, *Letters,* vol. 5, pp. 178–80, quoted at pp. 178, 180.
[*Food and drug legislation*]: Harbaugh, *Power and Responsibility, op. cit.,* pp. 255–60.

349 [*Roosevelt's proposals of December 1906*]: Annual Message of the President to the Congress, in *Congressional Record,* 59th Congress, 2nd Session (vol. 41, pt. 1), December 4, 1906, pp. 22–36, quoted at p. 26.
[*Roosevelt trying to keep the left center together*]: Mowry, *op. cit.,* p. 211.
[*Conservation*]: William D. Lewis, *The Life of Theodore Roosevelt* (John C. Winston, 1919), ch. 19.
[*Cannon on "scenery"*]: quoted in Harbaugh, p. 321.

350 [*Roosevelt's refusal of 1904 Standard Oil contribution*]: Harbaugh, pp. 228–29.
[*Roosevelt and corporate heads*]: see, e.g., Roosevelt to Charles Joseph Bonaparte, January 2, 1908, in Morison, *Letters,* vol. 6, pp. 883–90, and *ibid.,* vol. 5, pp. 755, 797, 845, 856, 859.
[*Panic of 1907 and the merger*]: Harbaugh, pp. 311–16.
[*Roosevelt's assurance to Gary and Frick*]: Roosevelt to Charles Joseph Bonaparte, November 4, 1907, in Morison, *Letters,* vol. 5, pp. 830–31.

351 [*Roosevelt's congratulations to "conservative and substantial businessmen"*]: Roosevelt to George Bruce Cortelyou, October 25, 1907, in *ibid.,* vol. 5, pp. 822–23.
[*Annual Message, 1907*]: in *Congressional Record,* 60th Congress, 1st Session (vol. 42, pt. 1), December 3, 1907, pp. 68–84.
[*Roosevelt's special message of January 1908*]: Message of the President to the Congress, in *Congressional Record,* 60th Congress, 1st Session (vol. 42, pt. 2), January 31, 1908, pp. 1347–53, quoted at pp. 1349, 1353, 1350, 1351, respectively; Harbaugh, p. 343; see also Mowry, p. 220.

352 [*Roosevelt's denunciation of "muckrakers"*]: quoted in Mowry, p. 206.
[*Roosevelt's confrontation with senators at the Gridiron Club*]: *ibid.,* p. 213.
352-53 [*Roosevelt on not being able to restrain himself*]: Roosevelt to John Burroughs, March 12, 1907, in Morison, *Letters,* vol. 5, p. 617.

353 [*The "fakir" on Roosevelt as "naturalist"*]: Rev. William J. Long, quoted in Harbaugh, p. 309.
[*Brownsville*]: John D. Weaver, *The Brownsville Raid* (W. W. Norton, 1970); Ann J. Lane, *The Brownsville Affair: National Crisis and Black Reaction* (Kennikat Press, 1971).
[*Roosevelt's attitude toward blacks*]: Roosevelt to Owen Wister, April 27, 1906, in Morison, *Letters*, vol. 5, pp. 221–30; Wagenknecht, *op. cit.*, pp. 230–36; see also Seth M. Scheiner, "President Theodore Roosevelt and the Negro, 1901–1908," *Journal of Negro History*, vol. 47, no. 3 (July 1962), pp. 169–82; Thomas G. Dyer, *Theodore Roosevelt and the Idea of Race* (Louisiana State University Press, 1980), ch. 5.
354 [*Mr. Dooley on American people "batin' a carpet"*]: Dunne, "National Housecleaning," in Dunne, pp. 246, 248.

10. THE CAULDRON OF LEADERSHIP

355 [*Eve of March 4, 1909, at the White House*]: William Manners, *TR and Will* (Harcourt, Brace & World, 1969), ch. 1; Philip Jessup, *Elihu Root* (Dodd, Mead, 1938), vol. 2, pp. 137–38.
[*Roosevelt and Taft "at one"*]: Roosevelt to George Otto Trevelyan, June 19, 1908, in Elting E. Morison, ed., *The Letters of Theodore Roosevelt* (Harvard University Press, 1951–54), vol. 6, p. 1085.
355–56 [*Roosevelt to Sullivan on Taft*]: quoted in Mark Sullivan, *Our Times* (Scribner's, 1926–35), vol. 4, pp. 331–32.
356 [*Taft on "my storm"*]: quoted in Paolo Coletta, *The Presidency of William Howard Taft* (University Press of Kansas, 1973), p. 47.

Taft, TR, and the Two Republican Parties

[*Taft as party man*]: Donald F. Anderson, *William Howard Taft* (Cornell University Press, 1973), pp. 99–104, 162–67.
[*Taft and the two Republican parties*]: James MacGregor Burns, *The Deadlock of Democracy* (Prentice-Hall, 1963), ch. 5; I have borrowed occasional sentences and paragraphs in this section from this earlier work; I have also used the sources cited therein (pp. 354–55).
357 [*Party developments during progressive era*]: James L. Sundquist, *Dynamics of the Party System*, rev. ed. (Brookings Institution, 1983), ch. 8; Paul T. David, *Party Strength in the United States, 1872–1970* (University Press of Virginia, 1972); David Burner, "The Democratic Party, 1910–1932," in Arthur M. Schlesinger, Jr., *History of U.S. Political Parties* (Chelsea House, 1973), vol. 3, pp. 1811–1936; William H. Harbaugh, "The Republican Party, 1893–1932," in *ibid.*, pp. 2069–255.
[*The struggle over Cannonism*]: Blair Bolles, *Tyrant from Illinois* (W. W. Norton, 1951), chs. 13–15; Alfred Lief, *Democracy's Norris* (Stackpole, 1939), ch. 4; Randall B. Ripley, *Majority Party Leadership in Congress* (Little, Brown, 1969), pp. 136–44.
[*Roosevelt on Taft's "bungling leadership"*]: Coletta, *op. cit.*, pp. 106–7; see in general, Morison, *Letters, op. cit.*, vol. 7, *passim*.
358 [*Taft's stubbornness*]: quoted in Henry Pringle, *The Life and Times of William Howard Taft* (Farrar & Rinehart, 1939), vol. 2, p. 762.
[*Taft's indolence and corpulence*]: Judith Icke Anderson, *William Howard Taft* (W. W. Norton, 1981), ch. 1.
[*Mowry on TR's "catlike touch"*]: George E. Mowry, *The Era of Theodore Roosevelt* (Harper & Row, 1958), p. 245.
[*Taft's "love letters" to Hale and Aldrich*]: quoted in Pringle, vol. 1, p. 415.
[*Taft-Depew exchange*]: quoted in Judith Anderson, p. 28.
[*Taft's early legislative victories*]: see Coletta, chs. 3, 6.
[*Roosevelt's return home, June 1910*]: Joseph L. Gardner, *Departing Glory* (Scribner's, 1973), ch. 9.
[*Lodge on Pinchot*]: Lodge to Roosevelt, January 15, 1910, in *Selections from the Correspondence of Theodore Roosevelt and Henry Cabot Lodge* (Scribner's, 1925), vol. 2, p. 358.
[*Roosevelt to Root on unpleasant summer*]: letter of October 21, 1910, in Morison, *Letters*, vol. 7, p. 148.
[*Roosevelt's indignation against Taft*]: George E. Mowry, *Theodore Roosevelt and the Progressive*

Movement (University of Wisconsin Press, 1947), pp. 137–42; see also Morison, *Letters,* vol. 7, pp. 93–156.

359 [*Roosevelt's dismissal of Taft as good first lieutenant*]: see, for example, Roosevelt to Henry Cabot Lodge, April 11, 1910, in Morison, *Letters,* vol. 7, p. 69.

[*Grass-roots calls on Roosevelt to run for the presidency*]: reels 96–97, Theodore Roosevelt Papers, Library of Congress (January 1911); reel 122, *ibid.* (January 1912).

[*Roosevelt's "noncandidacy" but possible availability in 1911*]: Morison, *Letters,* vol. 7, *passim;* Roosevelt to Benjamin Barr Lindsey, December 5, 1911, in *ibid.,* pp. 450, 451.

360 [*Root on Roosevelt as a "thirsty sinner"*]: Root to Roosevelt, February 12, 1912, in *ibid.,* vol. 7, p. 504, footnote 1.

[*La Follette and his progressives*]: David P. Thelen, *Robert M. La Follette and the Insurgent Spirit* (Little, Brown, 1976); Kenneth W. Hechler, *Insurgency* (Columbia University Press, 1940); Belle Case La Follette and Fola La Follette, *Robert M. La Follette* (Macmillan, 1953), vol. 1; Robert M. La Follette, *La Follette's Autobiography* (Robert M. La Follette Co., 1913).

[*Norris to Roosevelt on Roosevelt's noncandidacy*]: Norris to Roosevelt, January 5, 1912, reel 122, Theodore Roosevelt Papers, Library of Congress.

[*La Follette's Philadelphia speech*]: La Follette's version of the text is in the appendix of his *Autobiography,* pp. 762–97.

362 [*Taft's forcing of the issue with Roosevelt, 1911*]: Norman M. Wilensky, *Conservatives in the Progressive Era,* University of Florida Monographs, *Social Sciences,* no. 25 (Winter 1965), esp. ch. 2.

[*Taft on Roosevelt as surrounded by sycophants*]: Taft to Horace Taft, February 15, 1912, quoted in Donald Anderson, p. 182.

[*Taft on judicial recall as causing anarchy*]: quoted in Mowry, *Roosevelt and the Progressive Movement,* p. 216.

[*1912 Republican primaries*]: Gardner, pp. 228–35, primary results given at p. 235 (figures have been rounded off).

363 [*Demagogue and fathead*]: quoted in Mowry, *Roosevelt and the Progressive Movement,* p. 234.

[*Roosevelt on Root as "representative of reaction"*]: quoted in Sullivan, *op. cit.,* vol. 4, p. 498.

[*Mr. Dooley on the forthcoming Republican convention*]: quoted in Mowry, *Roosevelt and the Progressive Movement,* pp. 243–44.

[*1912 Republican convention*]: Gardner, ch. 12; Burner in Schlesinger, vol. 3, pp. 2090–91.

[*"We stand at Armageddon"*]: quoted in Sullivan, vol. 4, p. 509.

Wilson and the Three Democratic Parties

[*Wilson at New Jersey Democratic convention, 1910*]: Arthur S. Link, *Wilson: The Road to the White House* (Princeton University Press, 1947), pp. 166–68; John Milton Cooper, Jr., *The Warrior and the Priest* (Harvard University Press, 1983), pp. 164–66.

364 [*Wilson's address to New Jersey convention*]: quoted in Link, p. 167.

[*Wilson on influencing public opinion*]: John Morton Blum, *Woodrow Wilson and the Politics of Morality* (Little, Brown, 1956), p. 21.

[*"All the renewal of a nation"*]: quoted in Cooper, p. 128.

364–65 [*Wilson on leadership*]: Arthur S. Link, ed., *The Papers of Woodrow Wilson* (Princeton University Press, 1966–83), vol. 6, pp. 646–71 ("Leaders of Men" address dated June 17, 1890); vol. 12, p. 365 ("A Memorandum on Leadership," May 5, 1902); T. H. Vail Motter, ed., Woodrow Wilson, *Leaders of Men* (Princeton University Press, 1952), esp. pp. 41–42.

365 [*Wilson's childhood and youth*]: Alexander L. George and Juliette L. George, *Woodrow Wilson and Colonel House* (John Day, 1956), chs. 1–2; Sigmund Freud and William C. Bullitt, *Thomas Woodrow Wilson* (Houghton Mifflin, 1967); Robert C. Tucker, "The Georges' Wilson Reexamined: An Essay on Psychobiography," *American Political Science Review,* vol. 71, no. 2 (June 1977), pp. 606–18.

[*Georges on Wilson's leadership*]: George and George, p. 320.

[*Wilson's transformation of Princeton*]: Cooper, p. 101; Henry W. Bragdon, *Woodrow Wilson: The Academic Years* (Harvard University Press, 1967), part 3.

366 [*Governor Wilson*]: Link, *Road to the White House,* chs. 7–9.

[*Bryan's shift to the left*]: David Burner, *The Politics of Provincialism* (Alfred A. Knopf, 1968),

p. 7; Paul W. Glad, *The Trumpet Soundeth: William Jennings Bryan and His Democracy, 1896–1912* (University of Nebraska Press, 1960), esp. ch. 5.

367 [*Democratic party divisions*]: Ralph M. Goldman, *Search for Consensus: The Story of the Democratic Party* (Temple University Press, 1979); Wilfred E. Binkley, *American Political Parties: Their Natural History* (Alfred A. Knopf, 1947); Herbert Agar, *The Price of Union* (Houghton Mifflin, 1950), chs. 27–33; Sundquist, *op. cit.*, chs. 6, 7.

[*Cleveland on silver Democrats*]: Cleveland to Charles S. Fairchild, April 2, 1897, Grover Cleveland Papers, New-York Historical Society.

[*Response of Democratic party to industrialization*]: Everett Carll Ladd, *American Political Parties: Social Change and Political Response* (W. W. Norton, 1970), ch. 4.

[*Ladd on the Republicans*]: *ibid.*, p. 150.

[*Populist "outcries"*]: quoted in *ibid.*, p. 152.

368 [*Socialist party, early twentieth century*]: Nathan Fine, *Labor and Farmer Parties in the United States, 1828–1928* (Rand School of Social Science, 1928), esp. ch. 8; David A. Shannon, *The Socialist Party of America* (Macmillan, 1955), ch. 3; Ira Kipnis, *The American Socialist Movement, 1897–1912* (Columbia University Press, 1952), chs. 6–11, 16.

[*Debs and associates*]: Nick Salvatore, *Eugene V. Debs: Citizen and Socialist* (University of Illinois Press, 1982), chs. 7, 8; Sally M. Miller, *Victor Berger and the Promise of Constructive Socialism, 1910–1920* (Greenwood Press, 1973), chs. 2–3.

[*Socialist party membership and budget*]: Kipnis, pp. 364–65.

[*Socialist platform, 1912*]: reprinted in Schlesinger, *op. cit.*, vol. 3, pp. 2486–90.

369 [*Wilson's troubles with his History*]: Link, *Road to the White House*, pp. 381–87.

[*Hearst on Wilson*]: quoted in *ibid.*, pp. 382–83.

[*Democratic convention, 1912*]: *ibid.*, ch. 13.

[*Bryan's resolution and subsequent charge*]: quoted in *ibid.*, pp. 442–43.

Armageddon

371 [*Roosevelt's reception at Progressive party convention*]: Mowry, *Roosevelt and the Progressive Movement, op. cit.*, p. 264.

["*Authentic voice" of Progressive convention*]: Burns, *The Deadlock of Democracy, op. cit.*, p. 117.

["*They were crusaders; he was not*"]: *New York Times*, August 7, 1912, p. 2.

372 [*Roosevelt on having to "drag forward" Addams*]: Roosevelt to Arthur H. Lee, November 5, 1912, in Morison, *Letters, op. cit.*, vol. 7, p. 633.

[*Campaign of 1912*]: George E. Mowry, "Election of 1912," in Arthur M. Schlesinger, Jr., ed., *History of American Presidential Elections* (Chelsea House, 1971), pp. 2135–66; Gardner, *op. cit.*, ch. 13; Link, *Road to the White House, op. cit.*, ch. 14.

[*Taft on his role as a conservative*]: quoted in Mowry in Schlesinger, vol. 3, p. 2158.

[*Taft's attacks on "dangerous changes" and direct democracy*]: "Acceptance Speech," August 2, 1912, in *ibid.*, pp. 2204–19, quoted at pp. 2204, 2208.

[*Debs on making the working class the ruling class*]: quoted in Salvatore, *op. cit.*, p. 263.

[*The "Ohio yell"*]: *ibid.*, p. 264.

373 [*Woodrow Wilson on liberty "never coming from the government"*]: John Wells Davidson, ed., *A Crossroads of Freedom* (Wilson's 1912 campaign speeches) (Yale University Press, 1956), p. 130.

[*Roosevelt's response*]: *ibid.*, pp. 123, 130; Mowry in Schlesinger, vol. 3, p. 2160.

[Journal *cartoon*]: reprinted in Davidson, p. 123.

[*Wilson's shift to acceptance of government*]: *ibid.*, p. 264.

[*Democratic party platform plank on democracy*]: Schlesinger, vol. 3, pp. 2169, 2177.

374 [*Progressive party planks on democracy*]: *ibid.*, pp. 2186–87.

[*Wilson on the referendum*]: Davidson, p. 487.

[*Observer on the secrets of Wilson's "verbal power"*]: William Bayard Hale, quoted in George and George, *op. cit.*, p. 108.

[*Georges on Wilson's mastery of oratorical techniques*]: *ibid.*

[*Democratic party plank on antitrust policy*]: Schlesinger, vol. 3, p. 2168.

[*Progressive party plank on antitrust policy*]: *ibid.*, p. 2190.

375 [*Roosevelt quoting Morgan on not unscrambling an omelet*]: quoted in Cooper, *op. cit.*, p. 196.

[*Deletion of antitrust plank*]: Mowry, pp. 269–71.

[*Brandeis establishing connection with Wilson*]: Philippa Strum, *Brandeis* (Harvard University

Press, 1984), read in manuscript; Melvin I. Urofsky, "Wilson, Brandeis, and the Trust Issue, 1912–1914," *Mid-America*, vol. 49, no. 1 (January 1967), pp. 3–28.

375 [*Brandeis's evaluation of Wilson after first meeting*]: Brandeis to Alfred Brandeis, August 29, 1912, in Melvin I. Urofsky and David W. Levy, eds., *Letters of Louis D. Brandeis* (State University of New York Press, 1971–78), vol. 2, p. 661.

[*Roosevelt's ambivalence on race*]: Thomas G. Dyer, *Theodore Roosevelt and the Idea of Race* (Louisiana State University Press, 1980), esp. chs. 1, 5.

376 [*Maude Malone's confrontation with Wilson*]: quoted in Davidson, p. 472.

[*The wounding of Roosevelt*]: Frank K. Kelly, *The Fight for the White House* (Thomas Y. Crowell, 1961), ch. 11, assailant quoted at p. 244, Roosevelt at pp. 245, 246, 247.

377 [*The candidates' climactic speeches*]: quoted in Cooper, p. 202, and Link, *Wilson Papers, op. cit.*, vol. 25, pp. 493–501, at p. 497.

[*Election results*]: Cooper, pp. 204–5; Schlesinger, vol. 3, p. 2242 (state-by-state totals); Sundquist, *op. cit.*, p. 165.

[*Roosevelt's postelection comment*]: Roosevelt to Arthur Hamilton Lee, November 5, 1912, in Morison, *Letters*, vol. 7, p. 633; Roosevelt to James R. Garfield, November 8, 1912, in *ibid.*, p. 637.

11. THE NEW FREEDOM

381 [*Gary steel-making*]: Stewart H. Holbrook, *Iron Brew: A Century of American Ore and Steel* (Macmillan, 1939), pp. 298–304.

[*Coal mining in Appalachia*]: Carter Goodrich, *The Miner's Freedom: A Study of the Working Life in a Changing Industry* (Marshall Jones, 1925), pp. 19–27, quoted at p. 22.

[*Amoskeag*]: Tamara K. Hareven and Randolph Langenbach, *Amoskeag: Life and Work in an American Factory City* (Pantheon, 1978), pp. 34–38, 41–49 (interview with Mary Cunion, weaver), 196–200 (interview with Yvonne Dionne).

382 [*Mechanization in tire manufacture*]: Alfred Lief, *The Firestone Story* (McGraw-Hill, 1951), pp. 65–66.

[*American socialism during the progressive era*]: Ira Kipnis, *The American Socialist Movement, 1897–1912* (Columbia University Press, 1952).

383 [*Taft's trust-busting and tax backing*]: Donald F. Anderson, *William Howard Taft: A Conservative Conception of the Presidency* (Cornell University Press, 1968), pp. 78–82, 108–10, 230.

[*Wilson on leadership*]: quoted in Arthur A. Ekirch, Jr., *Progressivism in America* (New Viewpoints, 1974), p. 224; see also Woodrow Wilson, "The Study of Administration," *Political Science Quarterly*, vol. 2 (June 1887), pp. 197–222.

[*Wilson on need of concert of purpose*]: "Remarks in Trenton to the New Jersey Electors," January 13, 1913, in Arthur S. Link, ed., *The Papers of Woodrow Wilson* (Princeton University Press, 1966–83), vol. 27, pp. 40–44, quoted at p. 41.

The Engine of Democracy

[*Woodrow Wilson's inaugural*]: Arthur S. Link, *Wilson: The New Freedom* (Princeton University Press, 1956), pp. 57–60; John Morton Blum, *Woodrow Wilson and the Politics of Morality* (Little, Brown, 1956), p. 65.

384 [*Wilson's Inaugural Address*]: "An Inaugural Address," March 4, 1913, in Link, *Papers, op. cit.*, vol. 27, pp. 148–52.

385 [*Wilson's Administration in early years as textbook model of presidential leadership*]: Arthur S. Link, *Woodrow Wilson and the Progressive Era, 1910–1917* (Harper & Bros., 1954), ch. 2; John J. Broesamle, "The Democrats," in Lewis L. Gould, ed., *The Progressive Era* (Syracuse University Press, 1974), pp. 101–3; John Milton Cooper, Jr., *The Warrior and the Priest* (Harvard University Press, 1983), ch. 15.

[*Wilson on President as "prime minister"*]: Wilson to Alexander Mitchell Palmer, February 5, 1913, in Link, *Papers*, vol. 27, pp. 99–100.

[*Wilson's denunciations of tariff lobbyists*]: quoted in Link, *The New Freedom*, p. 187.

[*Wilson on "acid test" for cabinet ministers*]: quoted in *ibid.*, p. 11.

386 [*La Follette on rejection of Brandeis*]: La Follette to Josephine La Follette Siebecker, March 16, 1913, in Belle Case La Follette and Fola La Follette, *Robert M. La Follette* (Macmillan, 1953), vol. 1, p. 462.

386 [*Broesamle on Wilson's personal control of his party*]: Broesamle in Gould, quoted at pp. 102–3.

[*Tariff reform*]: Link, *The New Freedom*, ch. 6.

[*Wilson on stimulating business to be more efficient*]: "An Address on Tariff Reform to a Joint Session of Congress," April 8, 1913, in Link, *Papers*, vol. 27, pp. 269–72, quoted at p. 271.

[*Houston on downward revision*]: David F. Houston to W. H. Page, September 12, 1913, quoted in Link, *The New Freedom*, p. 194.

387 [*Banking and currency reform*]: *ibid.*, ch. 7.

[*Wilson on the variety of judgments on banking*]: quoted in Cooper, p. 233.

[*Ekirch on money trust viewed as a spider web*]: Ekirch, *op. cit.*, p. 226.

[*Wilson's message to Congress on currency legislation*]: "An Address on Banking and Currency Reform to a Joint Session of Congress," June 23, 1913, in Link, *Papers*, vol. 27, pp. 570–73, quoted at pp. 572–73.

388 [*Lindbergh and La Follette on Federal Reserve Act*]: quoted in Link, *The New Freedom*, p. 239; see also La Follette and La Follette, vol. 1, pp. 486–87.

[*Link on Federal Reserve Act*]: Link, *The New Freedom*, p. 238.

[*Burleson's advice to Wilson on patronage*]: quoted in *ibid.*, pp. 158–59 (from an interview of Burleson by R. S. Baker, March 17–19, 1927).

[*O'Gorman's thwarting of Wilson*]: *ibid.*, pp. 165–67.

[*Wilson to Burleson on "old standpatters"*]: quoted in Cooper, p. 231.

389 [*Wilson's short-run and long-run strategies*]: Cooper, pp. 231–32; Broesamle in Gould, pp. 104–5; James MacGregor Burns, *The Deadlock of Democracy* (Prentice-Hall, 1963), pp. 131–33; Blum, *passim*.

The Anatomy of Protest

[*Tendencies toward economic concentration*]: John M. Blair, *Economic Concentration: Structure, Behavior and Public Policy* (Harcourt Brace Jovanovich, 1972), esp. ch. 11; G. Warren Nutter and Henry Adler Einhorn, *Enterprise Monopoly in the United States: 1899–1958* (Columbia University Press, 1969), esp. chs. 2, 3; Ralph L. Nelson, *Merger Movements in American Industry, 1895–1956* (Princeton University Press, 1959); Edward S. Herman, *Corporate Control, Corporate Power* (Cambridge University Press, 1981).

[*"A burst of merger activity"*]: Nelson, p. 34.

[*Antitrust legislation*]: Link, *The New Freedom, op. cit.*, ch. 13.

390 [*Hofstadter on the closed system*]: Richard Hofstadter, *The Age of Reform* (Alfred A. Knopf, 1955), p. 227.

[*Wilson on the "powers that have governed us"*]: quoted in Arthur S. Link, *Wilson: The Road to the White House* (Princeton University Press, 1947), p. 514.

[*Rockefeller on petroleum prices*]: testimony before the Committee on Manufactures, *House Report*, no. 3112, 50th Congress, 1st Session (1888), p. 389.

[*Big business's arguments in favor of consolidation*]: Edward C. Kirkland, *Industry Comes of Age* (Holt, Rinehart and Winston, 1961), pp. 310–14.

391 [*Brandeis's economic views*]: Philippa Strum, *Louis D. Brandeis: Justice for the People* (Harvard University Press, 1984), *passim*.

[*Strum on Brandeis and Wilson*]: *ibid.*, p. 221.

392 [*Brandeis's opposition to economic concentration*]: Melvin I. Urofsky, "Wilson, Brandeis and the Trust Issue, 1912–1914," *Mid-America*, vol. 49, no. 1 (January 1967), p. 22.

[*Brandeis on industrial democracy*]: Louis D. Brandeis, testimony before the Commission on Industrial Relations, New York, N.Y., January 23, 1915, Senate Doc. 415, 64th Congress, 1st Session, pp. 7657–81, quoted at pp. 7662, 7659, 7660, 7665, respectively.

[*Croly*]: Charles Forcey, *The Crossroads of Liberalism* (Oxford University Press, 1961), ch. 1 and *passim;* Herbert Croly, *The Promise of American Life* (Macmillan, 1910).

392–93 [*Croly's views on Hamilton and Jefferson*]: Croly, ch. 2.

393 [*Croly on Roosevelt's moral urgings*]: *ibid.*, p. 174.

[*Weyl*]: Forcey, ch. 2; Walter E. Weyl, *The New Democracy* (Macmillan, 1912).

[*Weyl on America's problems*]: Weyl, pp. 1–2.

393–94 [*Weyl on being pragmatic and working for progress through prosperity*]: *ibid.*, chs. 12–13, pp. 268–70, quoted at p. 191.

394 [*Lippmann*]: Ronald Steel, *Walter Lippmann and the American Century* (Little, Brown, 1980); Benjamin F. Wright, *Five Public Philosophies of Walter Lippmann* (University of Texas Press, 1973); Marquis Childs and James Reston, eds., *Walter Lippmann and His Times* (Harcourt, Brace, 1959); Walter Lippmann, *A Preface to Politics* (Mitchell Kennerly, 1913); Walter Lippmann, *Drift and Mastery* (Mitchell Kennerly, 1914).
[*Croly to Hand on Lippmann*]: quoted in Steel, p. 60.

395 [*Steel on* Preface to Politics]: *ibid.*, p. 47.
["*Tabooing our impulses*"]: *Preface to Politics*, p. 49.
["*Chaos of a new freedom*"]: see *Drift and Mastery*, introduction.
[*Failures of liberal and progressive economic thought*]: R. Jeffrey Lustig, *Corporate Liberalism: The Origins of Modern American Political Theory, 1890-1920* (University of California Press, 1982).

396 [*The socialist movement and parties during the Wilson era*]: James Weinstein, *The Decline of Socialism in America, 1912-1925* (Monthly Review Press, 1967), esp. ch. 2; Kipnis, *op. cit.*; Aileen S. Kraditor, *The Radical Persuasion, 1890-1917* (Louisiana State University Press, 1981); Leon Fink, review of Kraditor, *The Radical Persuasion*, in *The Nation*, vol. 236, no. 4 (June 18, 1983), pp. 770-73.
[*De Leon*]: Don K. McKee, "Daniel De Leon: A Reappraisal," *Labor History*, vol. 1, no. 3 (Fall 1960), pp. 264-97; Kipnis, pp. 12-19.
["*Unconditional surrender of the capitalist system*"]: quoted in Kipnis, p. 16.

396-97 [*Socialist Party makeup and evolution*]: Milton Cantor, *The Divided Left* (Hill and Wang, 1978), pp. 23-24, quoted at p. 24; see also David A. Shannon, *The Socialist Party of America* (Macmillan, 1955), esp. chs. 1-3; Nick Salvatore, *Eugene V. Debs: Citizen and Socialist* (University of Illinois Press, 1982); Morris Hillquit, *History of Socialism in the United States*, 5th ed. (Russell & Russell, 1965), chs. 4-5; Sally M. Miller, *Victor Berger and the Promise of Constructive Socialism, 1910-1920* (Greenwood, 1973), esp. ch. 1.

397 [*Debs on running for president to raise social consciousness*]: quoted in Weinstein, p. 11.
[*Kraditor on individualism at core of IWW*]: Kraditor, p. 284.
[*Haywood on the "scum proletariat"*]: quoted in Weinstein, p. 15, footnote.

398 [*De Leon on the Debsites*]: quoted in Kraditor, p. 290.
[*Women, blacks, and socialism*]: *ibid.*, ch. 6; Kipnis, pp. 260-65.
[*Woodward's "Progressivism—For Whites Only"*]: see C. Vann Woodward, *Origins of the New South, 1877-1913* (Louisiana State University Press, 1951), ch. 14.
[*Lenin on trade-union consciousness*]: V. I. Lenin, "What Is to Be Done?," first published in Stuttgart, 1902, reprinted in Lenin, *Collected Works* (Foreign Language Publishing House, 1960-70), vol. 5, pp. 347-529, quoted at p. 375.

Sources on the organizational and especially the intellectual problems of socialism are extremely diverse and scattered; see the model bibliography, Donald Drew Egbert and Stow Persons, eds., T. D. Seymour Bassett, bibliographer, *Socialism and American Life*, vol. 2 (Bibliography: Descriptive and Critical) (Princeton University Press, 1952).

Markets, Morality, and the "Star of Empire"

[*Wilson on "irony of fate"*]: quoted in Arthur S. Link, *Wilson the Diplomatist* (Johns Hopkins Press, 1957), p. 5.

400 ["*We are chosen*"]: quoted in Arthur S. Link, "Woodrow Wilson: Hinge of the 20th Century," in *Woodrow Wilson: A Commemorative Celebration* (The Wilson Center, 1982), p. 21.
["*An engine of liberty*"]: Sidney Bell, *Righteous Conquest: Woodrow Wilson and the Evolution of the New Diplomacy* (Kennikat Press, 1972), p. 22.
[*Wilson on industries bursting their jackets*]: quoted in Jerry Israel, *Progressivism and the Open Door: America and China, 1905-1921* (University of Pittsburgh Press, 1971), p. 104.
[*Wilson on war against money power*]: *ibid.*, p. 107.
["*Star of Empire*"]: quoted in Bell, p. 22.
[*China policy of Taft and Wilson*]: Roy W. Curry, *Woodrow Wilson and Far Eastern Policy: 1913-1921* (Bookman Associates, 1957); Robert Dallek, *The American Style of Foreign Policy: Cultural Politics and Foreign Affairs* (Alfred A. Knopf, 1983), ch. 3; Roberta A. Dayer, *Bankers and Diplomats in China, 1917-1925: The Anglo-American Relationship* (Frank Cass, 1981), ch. 1; Israel, *passim;* Walter V. Scholes and Marie V. Scholes, *The Foreign Policies*

of the Taft Administration (University of Missouri Press, 1970); Harold M. Vinacke, "Woodrow Wilson's Far Eastern Policy," in Edward H. Buehrig, ed., *Wilson's Foreign Policy in Perspective* (Indiana University Press, 1957), pp. 61–104.

400 [*Hay's Open Door notes*]: Thomas A. Bailey, *A Diplomatic History of the American People,* 9th ed. (Prentice-Hall, 1974), pp. 480–83, quoted at p. 482.

400–01 [*Decline of U.S. trade with China*]: Scholes and Scholes, p. 112; Paul A. Varg, "The Myth of the China Market, 1890–1914," *American Historical Review,* vol. 73, no. 3 (February 1968), pp. 742–58, esp. p. 755.

401 [*Taft on "force and pluck"*]: quoted in Scholes and Scholes, p. 21.

[*Taft on U.S. capital in China*]: quoted in Paolo E. Coletta, *The Presidency of William Howard Taft* (University of Kansas Press, 1973), p. 194.

[*Wilson on Chinese movement toward liberty*]: quoted in Curry, p. 16.

402 [*Wilson on awakening of China*]: ibid., p. 23.

[*Need for "evangelical Christian" in Peking*]: ibid., p. 38.

[*Wilson to Eliot on reordering U.S. diplomacy*]: letter of September 17, 1913, quoted in *ibid.,* p. 35.

[*Wilson's withdrawal of American support for consortium*]: ibid., pp. 21–24.

[*George on consortium rejection*]: quoted in Israel, p. 109.

[*Outlook on reform in China*]: September 1, 1915, quoted in *ibid.,* p. 118.

["*Leaving the Firm*"]: Curry, p. 25.

[*Bankers sick of Chinese investments*]: Charles Addis, quoted in Scholes and Scholes, p. 239.

402–03 [*Trade and investment in Latin America*]: Bell, pp. 46–47; Coletta, p. 175.

403 [*Latin American policy*]: Bell, chs. 3–5; Samuel Flagg Bemis, "Woodrow Wilson and Latin America," in Buehrig, pp. 105–40; Sidney Lens, *The Forging of the American Empire* (Thomas Y. Crowell, 1971), chs. 11–13; Scholes and Scholes, part 1; see also Walter LaFeber, *Inevitable Revolutions: The United States in Central America* (W. W. Norton, 1983), ch. 1.

[*Taft on "substituting dollars for bullets"*]: quoted in Coletta, p. 185.

[*Wilson and Mexico*]: Mark T. Gilderhus, *Diplomacy and Revolution: U.S.-Mexican Relations under Wilson and Carranza* (University of Arizona Press, 1977); P. Edward Haley, *Revolution and Intervention: The Diplomacy of Taft and Wilson with Mexico, 1910–1917* (MIT Press, 1970); Linda B. Hall, *Alvaro Obregon: Power and Revolution in Mexico, 1911–1920* (Texas A&M University Press, 1981); Robert E. Quirk, *An Affair of Honor: Woodrow Wilson and the Occupation of Veracruz* (University of Kentucky Press, 1962); Douglas W. Richmond, *Venustiano Carranza's Nationalist Struggle, 1893–1920* (University of Nebraska Press, 1983), chs. 3–4.

404 [*Wilson on "a government of butchers"*]: quoted in Gilderhus, p. 5.

["*Morality and not expediency*"]: quoted in Bailey, p. 556.

[*Policy of "watchful waiting"*]: quoted in Josephus Daniels, *The Life of Woodrow Wilson, 1856–1924* (Will H. Johnston, 1924), p. 179.

[*Wilson's Latin American declaration*]: quoted in Bemis, p. 120.

[*Opposition to Wilson's Mexican policy*]: Bailey, p. 557.

[*Wilson's call for Huerta's surrender*]: quoted in Daniels, p. 179.

[*Wilson on the "vested interests"*]: quoted in Bailey, p. 557.

[*Wilson on self-restraint*]: quoted in Haley, p. 100.

[*Huerta's "saturnalia"*]: John Lind, quoted in *ibid.,* p. 129.

405 ["*Outraged the sovereignty of unwilling nations*"]: Lens, p. 196; see also Scott Nearing and Joseph Freeman, *Dollar Diplomacy* (B. W. Huebsch and the Viking Press, 1926).

[*Wilson on teaching democracy to South America*]: Wilson to Sir William Tyrrell, November 13, 1913, quoted in Bailey, p. 555.

[*Wilson and Villa*]: Clarence C. Clendenen, *The United States and Pancho Villa* (Cornell University Press, 1961); Martin Luis Guzman, *The Eagle and the Serpent,* Harriet de Onis, tr. (Doubleday, 1965); Martin Blumenson, ed., *The Patton Papers, 1885–1940* (Houghton Mifflin, 1972), vol. 1, part 5.

12. OVER THERE

407 [*August 1914*]: William Manchester, *The Arms of Krupp* (Little, Brown, 1964), pp. 280–89; George M. Thomson, *The Twelve Days: 24 July to 4 August 1914* (Hutchinson, 1964); Barbara Tuchman, *The Guns of August* (Macmillan, 1962).

407 ["*Iron dice*" *of war*]: quoted in Tuchman, p. 74.
408 [*Russian war minister on modern weapons*]: General Vladimir Sukhomlinov, quoted in *ibid.*, p. 61.
409 [*Lenin in Zurich*]: Nadezhda K. Krupskaya, *Memories of Lenin* (International Publishers, 1932), vol. 2, pp. 175–97; Adam B. Ulam, *The Bolsheviks* (Collier Books, 1965), pp. 305–13.
[*Lenin on World War I*]: Vladimir I. Lenin, *Imperialism: The Highest Stage of Capitalism* (International Publishers, 1939), p. 9.
[*Industrial concentration in America*]: *ibid.*, pp. 16–17.
410 [*Corporate domination abroad*]: *ibid.*, pp. 70–73.
[*Lenin on monopoly*]: *ibid.*, p. 20.
[*Lenin on railroads*]: *ibid.*, p. 10.

Wilson and the Road to War

[*Congressman on the outbreak of war*]: R. N. Page, quoted in Arthur S. Link, *Wilson: The Struggle for Neutrality, 1914–1915* (Princeton University Press, 1960), p. 7.
[*House's warning from Europe*]: letter of May 29, 1914, quoted in *ibid.*, p. 2; see also Kenneth S. Davis, *FDR: The Beckoning of Destiny, 1882–1928* (Putnam's, 1971), p. 367.
411 ["*Architectural infant asylum*"]: quoted in Constance M. Green, *Washington: Capital City, 1879–1950* (Princeton University Press, 1963), p. 140; see also Frank G. Carpenter, *Carp's Washington* (McGraw-Hill, 1960), p. 125.
[*FDR on apathy toward war*]: FDR to Eleanor Roosevelt, August 2, 1914, quoted in Davis, p. 369.
[*FDR on Bryan*]: *ibid.*, p. 385.
[*Wilson on keeping out of Europe's quarrels*]: quoted in Link, p. 3.
[*Bryan's peace efforts*]: Paolo E. Coletta, *William Jennings Bryan* (University of Nebraska Press, 1964–69), vol. 2, pp. 249–52.
[*Neutrality proclamation*]: quoted in Tuchman, *op. cit.*, p. 337.
[*Wilson's condemnation of the war*]: Wilson to C. R. Crane, August 4, 1914, quoted in Link, p. 50.
412 ["*Only America at peace!*"]: *New York Times*, January 9, 1915, quoted in *ibid.*, p. 55.
[*Tuchman on American neutrality*]: *The Guns of August*, p. 337.
[*Devlin on Wilson and the war*]: Patrick Devlin, *Too Proud to Fight: Woodrow Wilson's Neutrality* (Oxford University Press, 1975), p. vii.
[*Wilson to Tarbell on historian's view of the war*]: quoted in Arthur S. Link, *Woodrow Wilson: Revolution, War, and Peace* (Harlan Davidson, 1979), p. 2.
[*Wilson's early mediation attempts*]: Link, *Struggle for Neutrality*, ch. 7.
413 [*Wilson's despair of a negotiated peace*]: Wilson to House, August 24, 1914, quoted in *ibid.*, p. 50.
[*Bryan and World War I*]: Paolo E. Coletta, "A Question of Alternatives: Wilson, Bryan, Lansing, and America's Intervention in World War I," *Nebraska History*, vol. 63, no. 1 (1982), pp. 33–57; see also Coletta, *Bryan*, vol. 2, chs. 9–12; Louis W. Koenig, *Bryan: A Political Biography of William Jennings Bryan* (Putnam's, 1971), ch. 26.
413–14 [*Coletta on Bryan's principles*]: Coletta, "A Question of Alternatives," p. 33.
414 [*Bryan's "Real Neutrality"*]: Coletta, *Bryan*, vol. 2, p. 313.
415 [*Lansing on the* Falaba *incident*]: quoted in *ibid.*, p. 303.
["*Strict accountability*"]: quoted in Link, *Struggle for Neutrality*, p. 323.
[*Wilson on Bryan's* Lusitania *proposals*]: Wilson to Bryan, May 14, 1915, in Department of State, *Papers Relating to the Foreign Relations of the United States, The Lansing Papers, 1914–1920* (U.S. Government Printing Office, 1939), vol. 1, p. 406.
415–16 [*Bernstorff promise*]: Link, *Struggle for Neutrality*, pp. 582–87.
416 [*House on the* Lusitania]: quoted in *ibid.*, p. 375.
[*Chicago* Standard]: May 13, 1915, quoted in *ibid.*
["*Too proud to fight*"]: quoted in *ibid.*, p. 382.
[*Roosevelt on Wilson's diplomacy*]: Joseph Gardner, *Departing Glory: Theodore Roosevelt as ex-President* (Scribner's, 1973), p. 339; Roosevelt to A. H. Lee, June 17, 1915, in Elting

E. Morison, ed., *The Letters of Theodore Roosevelt* (Harvard University Press, 1951–54), vol. 8, p. 937; Link, *Struggle for Neutrality*, p. 383.

416 [*Wartime propaganda*]: see Link, *Struggle for Neutrality*, pp. 35–43, and sources cited therein.

417 [*Bryan and the Gore-McLemore bills*]: see Devlin, pp. 438, 445–46, Bryan quoted at p. 446.
[*The war in 1916*]: Harvey A. DeWeerd, *President Wilson Fights His War* (Macmillan, 1968), ch. 6.

418 [*Wilson's nomination of Brandeis*]: Alpheus T. Mason, *Brandeis: A Free Man's Life* (Viking Press, 1946), chs. 30–31; Philippa Strum, *Louis D. Brandeis: Justice for the People* (Harvard University Press, 1984), ch. 15.
[*Alice Brandeis on the expected fireworks*]: letter to Alfred Brandeis, January 31, 1916, quoted in Mason, p. 466.

419 [*Brandeis's early involvement in his own defense*]: Brandeis to Norman Hapgood, February 1, 1916, in Melvin I. Urofsky, ed., *Letters of Louis D. Brandeis* (State University of New York Press, 1971–78), vol. 4, pp. 27–29 and *passim*.
[*Lippmann's and Frankfurter's involvement*]: Ronald Steel, *Walter Lippmann and the American Century* (Atlantic–Little, Brown, 1980), pp. 101–2.
[*Wilson's further endorsement of Brandeis*]: Wilson to Senator Charles Allen Culberson, May 5, 1916, in Arthur S. Link, ed., *The Papers of Woodrow Wilson* (Princeton University Press, 1966–83), vol. 36, pp. 609–11.
[*Wilson's shift toward progressivism on domestic policy*]: Arthur S. Link, *Woodrow Wilson and the Progressive Era* (Harper & Bros., 1954), pp. 224–30; Wilson to Newton D. Baker, September 16, 1916, in Link, *Wilson Papers*, vol. 38, p. 178; vol. 38, *passim;* vol. 37, pp. 427–28.
[*Republican and Progressive conventions*]: Arthur S. Link and William M. Leary, Jr., "Election of 1916," in Arthur M. Schlesinger, Jr., ed., *History of American Presidential Elections* (Chelsea House, 1971), vol. 3, pp. 2248–52; George E. Mowry, *Theodore Roosevelt and the Progressive Movement* (Hill and Wang, 1960), ch. 14.
[*Roosevelt's views of the nomination*]: Morison, *Letters*, vol. 8, pp. 1058–74 (esp. Roosevelt's messages to Progressive party "conferees" and leadership, June 10–22, 1916).

420 [*Democratic party convention*]: Link and Leary in Schlesinger, vol. 3, pp. 2252–55.
[*Glynn's keynote address*]: Arthur S. Link, *Wilson: Campaigns for Progressivism and Peace, 1916–1917* (Princeton University Press, 1965), pp. 43–45, quoted at p. 44.
[*Wilson's campaign*]: Link and Leary in Schlesinger, pp. 2258–68; Link, *Wilson Papers*, vol. 38, pp. 165–633. On 1916 campaign in general, see S. D. Lovell, *The Presidential Election of 1916* (Southern Illinois University Press, 1980).
[*Passing a strongly progressive platform*]: Schlesinger, vol. 3, pp. 2271–81.

421 [*Hughes's campaign*]: Betty Glad, *Charles Evans Hughes and the Illusions of Innocence* (University of Illinois Press, 1966), ch. 5; Dexter Perkins, *Charles Evans Hughes and American Democratic Statesmanship* (Little, Brown, 1956), ch. 3.
[*Election results, 1916*]: Schlesinger, vol. 3, p. 2345.
[*Wilson on Page*]: quoted in Devlin, p. 317.
[*Lansing's attitude*]: see Daniel M. Smith, *Robert Lansing and American Neutrality, 1914–1917* (DaCapo Press, 1972).

422 [*American loans and trade during the war*]: Richard B. Morris, ed., *Encyclopedia of American History*, rev. ed. (Harper & Bros., 1961), p. 303.
[*Bryan on Eastern financiers and the war*]: William J. Bryan to Charles W. Bryan, March 26, 1917, quoted in Coletta, "A Question of Alternatives," p. 51.
[*Norris on Wall Street gold*]: John M. Cooper, Jr., "The Command of Gold Reversed: American Loans to Britain, 1915–1917," *Pacific Historical Review*, vol. 45 (1976), pp. 209–30, quoted at p. 209.
[*Revisionists on economic origins of U.S. intervention*]: Charles A. Beard, *The Devil Theory of War* (Vanguard Press, 1936); Walter Millis, *Road to War: America, 1914–1917* (Houghton Mifflin, 1935).
[*Cooper on "command of gold"*]: Cooper, p. 230.
[*Colonel House and the war*]: Alexander L. George and Juliette L. George, *Woodrow Wilson and Colonel House: A Personality Study* (Dover, 1964), chs. 9–10; Devlin, chs. 9, 12–14.

422 [*Wilson's confidence in House*]: quoted in Edwin A. Weinstein, *Woodrow Wilson: A Medical and Psychological Biography* (Princeton University Press, 1981), p. 269.
422-23 [*Wilson on intervention as the worst thing*]: ibid., p. 288.
423 [*Wilson's qualification of House-Grey Memorandum*]: Arthur S. Link, *Wilson: Confusion and Crises, 1915-1916* (Princeton University Press, 1964), p. 138 and footnote 103.
   [*Wilson's protest to Britain*]: quoted in Link, *Progressivism and Peace*, p. 196.
   [*Lansing's sabotage*]: ibid., pp. 221-24, quoted at p. 222.
424 [*"Peace without victory" speech*]: ibid., pp. 265-68.
   [*Resumption of unrestricted submarine warfare*]: ibid., p. 290.
   [*"The world had suddenly reversed itself"*]: House Diary, February 1, 1917, quoted in *ibid.*, p. 294.
425 [*Contrast between British and German neutrality violations*]: Coletta, "A Question of Alternatives," p. 37.
   [*Response to Zimmermann telegram*]: Link, *Progressivism and Peace*, p. 357.
   [*Wilson's statement of war aims*]: quoted in *ibid.*, p. 425.
   [*"Little group of willful men"*]: ibid., p. 367.
425-26 [*Devlin on Wilson's motives*]: Devlin, p. 678.

Mobilizing the Workshop

426 [*Fears of Churchill and Lloyd George in 1917*]: William Manchester, *The Last Lion: Winston Spencer Churchill* (Little, Brown, 1983), p. 616.
   [*Allied offensives of 1917*]: DeWeerd, *op. cit.*, pp. 179-92.
427 [*Pétain on waiting for the Americans*]: quoted in *ibid.*, p. 184.
   [*Washington at war*]: Green, *op. cit.*, pp. 236-40; Helen Nicolay, *Our Capital on the Potomac* (Century, 1924), quoted at pp. 512-13.
   [*Mobilization of the Ordnance Department*]: DeWeerd, pp. 220-23; Crozier is quoted on slowness at p. 221.
   [*Overman bill*]: *Congressional Record*, 65th Congress, 2nd Session (U.S. Government Printing Office, 1918), vol. 56, part 4, p. 3815 (March 21, 1918).
   [*Republican charges of absolutism*]: *New York Times*, February 18, 1918, quoted in George and George, *op. cit.*, p. 180.
   [*Wartime agencies*]: Daniel R. Beaver, *Newton D. Baker and the American War Effort, 1917-1919* (University of Nebraska Press, 1966); Benedict Crowell and Robert F. Wilson, *The Giant Hand* (Yale University Press, 1921); DeWeerd, ch. 10; Francis W. O'Brien, ed., *The Hoover-Wilson Wartime Correspondence* (Iowa State University Press, 1974); Jordan A. Schwarz, *The Speculator: Bernard M. Baruch in Washington, 1917-1965* (University of North Carolina Press, 1981), ch. 2; Mark Sullivan, *Our Times* (Scribner's, 1926-35), vol. 5, chs. 15-21; T. Harry Williams, *The History of American Wars* (Alfred A. Knopf, 1981), pp. 382-98.
428 [*Reed warns of draft riots*]: quoted in Sullivan, vol. 5, p. 296.
   [*Hoover's publicity campaign*]: DeWeerd, pp. 243-44.
   [*Convoys as turning point of war*]: ibid., p. 170.
428-29 [*"Restraint of trade for reasons of national security"*]: Schwarz, pp. 51-52.
429 [*Manufacturer's vow to "go out of business"*]: quoted in Crowell and Wilson, p. 46.
   [*American railroads in World War I*]: Keith L. Bryant, Jr., *History of the Atchison, Topeka and Santa Fe Railway* (Macmillan, 1974), ch. 9; George H. Burgess and Miles C. Kennedy, *Centennial History of the Pennsylvania Railroad Company* (reprint; Arno Press, 1976), pp. 560-72; Richard C. Overton, *Burlington Route* (Alfred A. Knopf, 1965), ch. 16. See also Oliver Jensen, *Railroads in America* (American Heritage, 1981), pp. 284 and 289 for price and profit figures.
   [*Federal direction of railroads*]: Aaron A. Godfrey, *Government Operation of the Railroads, 1918-1920* (San Felipe Press, 1974); Walker D. Hines (Director-General of Railroads, 1919-20), *War History of American Railroads* (Yale University Press, 1928); I. Leo Sharfman, *The American Railroad Problem* (Century, 1921); John F. Stover, *American Railroads* (University of Chicago Press, 1961), ch. 7.
   [*Federal wage recommendations*]: Report of the Lane Commission, quoted in Godfrey, p. 110.
430 [*Production of explosives*]: Benedict Crowell and Robert F. Wilson, *The Armies of Industry*

(Yale University Press, 1921), ch. 8. See also Stover, pp. 160–61, for a map of the principal rail lines.

430 [*Women and war work*]: Crowell and Wilson, *Armies of Industry*, pp. 168–70; Maurine W. Greenwald, *Women, War, and Work* (Greenwood Press, 1980), *passim;* Selig Perlman and Philip Taft, *History of Labor in the United States, 1896–1932: Labor Movements* (Macmillan, 1935), section 3.

431 [*Black labor and migration*]: Sterling D. Spero and Abram L. Harris, *The Black Worker* (Atheneum, 1969), esp. part 4; Emmett J. Scott, *Negro Migration During the War* (reprint; Arno Press, 1969), *passim.*
[*Living conditions of blacks in the North*]: *The Survey*, February 17, 1917, quoted in Scott, p. 140.
[*American military experiences in 1917*]: DeWeerd, pp. 184–85, 193; Robert Leckie, *The Wars of America* (Harper & Row, 1968), vol. 2, pp. 111–17; Laurence Stallings, *The Doughboys* (Harper & Row, 1963), ch. 2.

432 [*Soldier on unprepared American troops*]: Private Leo Bailey, quoted in Stallings, p. 25.

"Nous Voilà, Lafayette!"

[*Lenin's call for peace*]: quoted in Leckie, *op. cit.,* p. 108.
[*German 1918 offensive*]: DeWeerd, *op. cit.,* part 4; Basil H. Liddell Hart, *History of the First World War* (Cassell, 1970), ch. 8; Leckie, pp. 120–27; Manchester, *Last Lion, op. cit.,* pp. 628–42; Stallings, *op. cit.,* chs. 3–7.

433 [*"Retreat, hell"*]: quoted in Robert B. Asprey, *At Belleau Wood* (Putnam's, 1965), pp. 127–28.
[*Pershing's infantry tactics*]: see DeWeerd, pp. 215–16, and sources cited therein.
[*West Point discipline for AEF*]: quoted in *ibid.,* p. 213.

434 [*"Pas finie"*]: Manchester, *Last Lion,* p. 641.
[*"Nous voilà"*]: quoted in Stallings, p. 15.
[*Debt to Lafayette*]: *ibid.,* p. 16.
[*The Inquiry*]: Ray Stannard Baker, *Woodrow Wilson: Life and Letters* (Doubleday, Doran, 1927–39), vol. 7, pp. 254, 275, 352; Arthur Walworth, *America's Moment: 1918* (W. W. Norton, 1977), pp. 76–78. See also Lawrence E. Gelfand, *The Inquiry* (Yale University Press, 1963), *passim.*
[*Wilson on selfish war aims*]: telegram of December 1, 1917, quoted in Baker, vol. 7, p. 387.

435 [*"Fourteen Points" address*]: "An Address to a Joint Session of Congress," January 8, 1918, in Link, *Wilson Papers, op. cit.,* vol. 45, pp. 534–39, quoted at pp. 535, 538; see also Walworth, pp. 275–83 (Appendix A).
[*The "liberal" peace program*]: Link, *Revolution, War, and Peace, op. cit.,* ch. 4.
[*German reply to Wilson*]: *New York Times*, January 11, 12, 1918, quoted in Baker, vol. 7, p. 456, footnote 2.
[*Treaty of Brest-Litovsk*]: see Leckie, p. 120.
[*Wilson on arbitrary power*]: quoted in Sullivan, *op. cit.,* vol. 5, p. 449.
[*Baltimore address*]: April 6, 1918, Baker, vol. 8, p. 76.
[*"Force to the utmost"*]: *ibid.*
[*American tanks at St. Mihiel*]: Martin Blumenson, ed., *The Patton Papers, 1885–1940* (Houghton Mifflin, 1972), ch. 29, Patton quoted at p. 594.
[*Aircraft in World War I*]: Liddell Hart, pp. 457–64; Stallings, ch. 14; Williams, *op. cit.,* pp. 389–92.

435–37 [*The last months of the war*]: DeWeerd, chs. 17–18; Baker, vol. 8, chs. 4–5.

438 [*Armistice celebration in New York*]: Sullivan, vol. 5, pp. 521–27, newspaper (Brooklyn *Eagle*, November 12, 1918) quoted at p. 527.

Over Here: Liberty and Democracy

[*Tocqueville on aristocracies and democracies facing war*]: Alexis de Tocqueville, *Democracy in America,* Philip Bradley, ed. (Vintage Books, 1954), vol. 1, pp. 235–38.
[*Senator on sending an army to France*]: Thomas S. Martin, quoted in Ernest R. May, *War, Boom and Bust* (Time, Inc., 1964), p. 10.

438 [*The momentum of war*]: *ibid.*, pp. 10–14.
[*Creel's propaganda organization*]: George Creel, *How We Advertised America* (Harper & Bros., 1920); Harold D. Lasswell, *Propaganda Techniques in the World War* (Alfred A. Knopf, 1927); James R. Mock and Cedric Larson, *Words That Won the War* (reprint; Russell & Russell, 1968).
[*Chauvinism, war hysteria, war opposition*]: William Preston, Jr., *Aliens and Dissenters* (Harvard University Press, 1963), quoted at pp. 85, 87; see also Sullivan, *op. cit.*, vol. 5, pp. 467–77; H. C. Peterson and Gilbert C. Fite, *Opponents of War, 1917–1918* (University of Wisconsin Press, 1957); Joan M. Jensen, *The Price of Vigilance* (Rand McNally, 1968).

440 [*Western governors' petition for interning of Wobblies*]: quoted in Preston, p. 124.
[*Minister on the Lutheran Church in Germany*]: quoted in Sullivan, vol. 5, p. 467.

440–41 [*Debs's arrest and trial*]: Nick Salvatore, *Eugene V. Debs* (University of Illinois Press, 1982), pp. 294–96, Debs quoted at p. 295, Judge D. C. Westenhaver quoted at p. 296; Peterson and Fite, ch. 22; see also James Weinstein, *The Decline of Socialism in America, 1912–1925* (Monthly Review Press, 1967), ch. 3.
[*Wilson on wartime intolerance*]: Conversation with Frank I. Cobb, in John L. Heaton, *Cobb of "The World"* (E. P. Dutton, 1924), quoted in Link, *Progressivism and Peace, op. cit.*, p. 399. For a discussion of the date of this conversation, see Link, p. 399, footnote 33.
[*Prohibition*]: Joseph L. Gusfield, *Symbolic Crusade: Status Politics and the American Temperance Movement* (University of Illinois Press, 1963); Peter H. Odegard, *Pressure Politics* (Columbia University Press, 1928); James H. Timberlake, *Prohibition and the Progressive Movement, 1900–1920* (Harvard University Press, 1963); Richard Hofstadter, *The Age of Reform* (Alfred A. Knopf, 1955), pp. 287–91.

442 [*Suffragist leaders as "physical wrecks"*]: Carrie Chapman Catt to "My dear precious friend," October 8, 1912, Woman's Rights Collection, The Arthur and Elizabeth Schlesinger Library on the History of Women in America, Radcliffe College.
[*Stanton on "wrangles"*]: Stanton to Ida Harper, September 30, 1902, Harper Manuscripts, Box 4, Henry E. Huntington Library, San Marino, California.
[*Shaw on serving out her "sentence"*]: Shaw to "Dear Friend," June 10, 1914, Woman's Rights Collection, Schlesinger Library.
[*Gilman on human work as woman's work*]: Charlotte Perkins Gilman, *Women and Economics* (Small, Maynard, 1898; reprinted by Harper & Row, 1968), p. 53.

443 [*Progress on woman's suffrage by 1913*]: Eleanor Flexner, *Century of Struggle* (Harvard University Press, 1975), ch. 19.
[*Suffragists and the other dispossessed*]: Aileen S. Kraditor, *The Ideas of the Woman Suffrage Movement, 1890–1920* (Columbia University Press, 1965), chs. 6, 7.
[*Isabella Beecher Hooker's report on her meeting with senators*]: I.B.H. to Susan B. Anthony, January 21, 1871, pp. 1, 10, Stone-Day Foundation, Hartford.
[*Stanton on immigrants and the "ignorant native vote"*]: quoted in Kraditor, pp. 129, 133.
["*Indians in blankets and moccasins*"]: Anna Howard Shaw, quoted in *ibid.*, p. 219.

444 [*Triangle fire*]: Flexner, pp. 251–52.
[*Congressional Union*]: *ibid.*, pp. 274–79; Mari Jo Buhle and Paul Buhle, eds., *The Concise History of Woman Suffrage* (University of Illinois Press, 1978), pp. 417–29.
[*Suffragists and Theodore Roosevelt*]: correspondence of Ida Husted Harper and Theodore Roosevelt, September 16–December 30, 1918, Huntington Library.

445 [*Thompson to Wilson, in opposition to woman's suffrage*]: Link, *Wilson Papers, op. cit.*, vol. 37, pp. 502–4 (July 30, 1916).
[*Flexner on Wilson's shift toward federal amendment*]: Flexner, p. 288.

446 [*Militants at White House gates, January 1917*]: *ibid.*, pp. 292–93.
[*Helen Gardener's personal influence*]: correspondence of Helen Hamilton Gardener, esp. folders 71–73, Woman's Rights Collection, Schlesinger Library; Maud Wood Park, "Supplementary Notes about Helen Gardener" (n.d.), Schlesinger Library. See also Harriet B. Laidlaw Papers, esp. corr. 1917 folder, Schlesinger Library; Minnesota Woman Suffrage Association Papers, esp. boxes 1 and 2, which contain extensive correspondence between Minnesota suffrage leaders and national and other state leaders. See also Adelaide Washburn, "Helen Hamilton Gardener," in Edward T. James, ed., *Notable American Women, 1607–1950* (Belknap Press, 1971), vol. 2, pp. 11–13.

446 [*Wilson's address to the Senate on woman's suffrage*]: quoted in Flexner, p. 322.
447 [*Woman's suffrage movement and third parties*]: see, for example, Susan B. Anthony to Mrs. Colby, July 6, 1894, Huntington Library.

13. THE FIGHT FOR THE LEAGUE

448 [*Voyage of the* George Washington]: Rear Admiral Cary Grayson, *Woodrow Wilson: An Intimate Memoir* (Holt, Rinehart and Winston, 1960), ch. 8; James T. Shotwell, *At the Paris Peace Conference* (Macmillan, 1937), pp. 67–84; Arthur Walworth, *America's Moment: 1918* (W. W. Norton, 1977), pp. 129–36.
[*Wilson on his reasons for attending the conference*]: Grayson, pp. 59–61, quoted at pp. 60, 59 respectively.
[*Wilson's discussion with the Inquiry*]: Shotwell, pp. 75–78, quoted at pp. 76, 77, and 78 respectively.
449 [*Shotwell's observations on Wilson*]: ibid., pp. 70–71, 73.
449–50 [*Poster in Brest*]: ibid., pp. 83–84.

The Mirrored Halls of Versailles

450 [*Europe, winter 1918–19*]: Arno J. Mayer, *Politics and Diplomacy of Peacemaking 1918–1919* (Alfred A. Knopf, 1967); Charles L. Mee, Jr., *The End of Order: Versailles 1919* (E. P. Dutton, 1980); Francis W. O'Brien, ed., *Two Peacemakers in Paris: The Hoover-Wilson Post-Armistice Letters, 1918–1920* (Texas A&M University Press, 1978); Walworth, *op. cit.*
[*Lansing on Clemenceau*]: quoted in Mee, p. 17.
450–51 [*Wilson-Clemenceau meetings*]: Walworth, pp. 144–46; see also Charles Seymour, *The Intimate Papers of Colonel House* (Houghton Mifflin, 1928), vol. 4, pp. 251–54.
451 [*Wilson in Britain and Italy*]: Mee, pp. 29–38.
["*Until the pips squeak*"]: quoted in *ibid.*, p. 34.
[*Lloyd George's doubts about a punitive peace*]: see Shotwell, *op. cit.*, p. 22.
[*Baron Sonnino*]: Harold Nicolson, *Peacemaking 1919* (Houghton Mifflin, 1933), p. 169.
["*Riot in a parrot house*"]: *ibid.*, pp. 152–53.
452 [*Wilson and the League resolution*]: quoted in Seymour, pp. 290–91.
[*House on Wilson's negotiating skill*]: entry of February 7, 1919, in *ibid.*, p. 312.
[*Wilson on the covenant*]: quoted in Jonathan Daniels, *The Time Between the Wars* (Doubleday, 1966), p. 17.
[*Steel on Wilson's presentation*]: Paris *Daily Mail*, February 15, 1919, quoted in Seymour, pp. 318–19.
453 [*Experts as negotiators*]: Shotwell, pp. 153–98.
["*Whirlpool of political intrigue*"]: Eleanor Lansing Dulles, *Chances of a Lifetime* (Prentice-Hall, 1980), p. 66.
[*Historian on American intervention in Russia*]: John W. Long, "American Intervention in Russia: The North Russian Expedition, 1918–19," *Diplomatic History*, vol. 6, no. 1 (1982), pp. 45–67, quoted at p. 47; see also George F. Kennan, *The Decision to Intervene* (Princeton University Press, 1958), quoted at p. 471.
[*Russia and Bullitt*]: Beatrice Farnsworth, *William C. Bullitt and the Soviet Union* (Indiana University Press, 1967), ch. 2; Mayer, ch. 14; Walworth, ch. 12.
[*Wilson's return to America*]: Denna F. Fleming, *The United States and the League of Nations, 1918–1920* (Putnam's, 1932), ch. 5; Alexander L. George and Juliette L. George, *Woodrow Wilson and Colonel House: A Personality Study* (Dover Publications, 1964), pp. 232–39.
454 ["*International quilting society*"]: New York *Sun*, January 27, 1919, quoted in Fleming, p. 118.
[*League as "impudently un-American"*]: *Harvey's Weekly*, February 22, 1919, quoted in *ibid.*, p. 117.
[*Wilson's "fighting blood"*]: *ibid.*, p. 126.
["*Tea with the Mad Hatter*"]: *ibid.*, p. 134. For Wilson's invitation to the meeting, see Joseph Tumulty to Lodge, February 15, 1919, Henry Cabot Lodge Papers, Massachusetts Historical Society, 1919 Boxes (hereafter cited as Lodge Papers).
[*Rogers on conference with Wilson*]: Rogers to Henry White, March 3, 1919, quoted in Allan

Nevins, *Henry White, Thirty Years of American Diplomacy* (Harper & Bros., 1930), pp. 392–93.

454 [*Lodge comment*]: Lodge to Henry White, April 8, 1919, Henry White Papers, Box 53, in the Lodge Papers.
[*Lodge and the League*]: see Henry Cabot Lodge, *The Senate and the League of Nations* (Scribner's, 1925); John A. Garraty, *Henry Cabot Lodge: A Biography* (Alfred A. Knopf, 1953), esp. pp. 349–56.

455 [*Lodge on consideration, time, and thought*]: quoted in Garraty, p. 352.
[*Senate Round Robin*]: ibid., p. 354.
[*Sun on demise of the League*]: March 4, 1919, quoted in Fleming, p. 159.
[*Wilson and Republican League supporters*]: see Ruhl J. Bartlett, *The League to Enforce Peace* (University of North Carolina Press, 1944).
[*Taft on the League*]: quoted in Fleming, p. 160.
[*Wilson on ties between the Covenant and the treaty*]: quoted in George and George, p. 239.
[*Baker's fears about Wilson's statement*]: Ray Stannard Baker, *American Chronicle* (Scribner's, 1945), p. 392.

456 [*Wilson's illness*]: Edwin A. Weinstein, *Woodrow Wilson: A Medical and Psychological Biography* (Princeton University Press, 1981), pp. 336–43.
[*Break between Wilson and House*]: ibid., pp. 334–35, 347–48; see also George and George, ch. 13.
[*House on distance from Wilson*]: quoted in George and George, p. 266.
[*Lenin's peace offer*]: Farnsworth, pp. 40–54.
[*Nicolson's response to Bullitt*]: ibid., p. 54.
[*Unilateral American withdrawal from Russia*]: Long, pp. 65–67.
[*Wilson's compromises*]: Fleming, pp. 179–87; Mee, part 4.
[*Lodge's reaction*]: Lodge to Henry White, April 30, 1919, Henry White Papers, Box 53, Lodge Papers.

The Battle for the Treaty

457 [*Wilson's address to the Senate*]: Fleming, *op. cit.*, pp. 235–37; Arthur S. Link, *Woodrow Wilson: Revolution, War, and Peace* (Harlan Davidson, 1979), p. 107.
[*Efforts of the League to Enforce Peace*]: Bartlett, *op. cit.*, ch. 5; Henry F. Pringle, *The Life and Times of William Howard Taft* (Farrar & Rinehart, 1939), vol. 2, ch. 49.
[*Newspapers on the Monroe Doctrine and the League*]: James D. Startt, "Early Press Reaction to Wilson's League Proposal," *Journalism Quarterly*, vol. 39 (Summer 1962), pp. 301–8, quoted at pp. 302, 304; John A. Aman, "Views of Three Iowa Newspapers on the League of Nations, 1919–1920," *Iowa Journal of History and Politics*, vol. 39 (July 1941), pp. 227–85, quoted at p. 256.
[*New York and Baltimore papers on the League*]: quoted in Startt, pp. 303, 304.

458 [Register *on "an armed America"*]: quoted in Aman, p. 251.
[Literary Digest *poll*]: Fleming, pp. 218–20; Startt, pp. 307–8.
[*Public campaign against the League*]: Fleming, pp. 208–11.
[*Sun on the "Washington Doctrine"*]: quoted in Aman, p. 229.
[*Lodge on the only votes being in the Senate*]: quoted in Garraty, *op. cit.*, p. 370.

459 [*Agreement between Borah and Lodge*]: ibid., pp. 362–63; see also Ralph Stone, *The Irreconcilables: The Fight Against the League of Nations* (University of Kentucky Press, 1970), pp. 90–93; see also Lodge to Frank B. Kellogg, May 28, 1919; Kellogg to Lodge, May 31, 1919, Lodge Papers, Box 51.
[*Lodge's partisan motives for opposing Wilson*]: William C. Widenor, *Henry Cabot Lodge and the Search for an American Foreign Policy* (University of California Press, 1980), ch. 8; see also Garraty, ch. 20; George and George, *op. cit.*, pp. 269–70.
[*Lodge on Wilson*]: Lodge to Theodore Roosevelt (n.d., but evidently 1916 or early 1917); Lodge to Mrs. Winthrop Chanler, August 18, 1919; Lodge to Andrew A. West, August 22, 1919, all in Lodge Papers, Boxes 86, 49, 51, respectively.

460 [*Hate-mongering against the League*]: see Thomas A. Bailey, *The Man in the Street: The Impact of American Public Opinion on Foreign Policy* (Macmillan, 1948), pp. 110, 210.

461 [*Wilson's legislative strategy*]: Kurt Wimer, "Woodrow Wilson Tries Conciliation: An Effort That Failed," *The Historian*, vol. 25, no. 4 (August 1963), pp. 419–38.

461 [*Wilson's flexibility*]: *ibid.*, p. 419; see in general Woodrow Wilson Papers, Reels 157–58 (1919), Library of Congress.
[*Wilson perplexed by opposition to the treaty*]: Wilson to Thomas Lamont, August 1, 8, 1919, quoted in Wimer, p. 425.

462 [*Pittman motion*]: *ibid.*, pp. 432–33.

463 [*Wilson's tour of the country*]: Grayson, *op. cit.*, ch. 14; Gene Smith, *When the Cheering Stopped: The Last Years of Woodrow Wilson* (William Morrow, 1964), ch. 5.
[*"I have long chafed at confinement"*]: quoted in Smith, p. 62.
[*Soldiers never having to cross the seas again*]: *ibid.*
[*"America was not founded to make money"*]: *ibid.*, p. 64.

464 [*Opposition of clergyman and socialist (Victor Berger) to the treaty*]: *ibid.*, p. 66.
[*Attacks by Johnson and Reed*]: *ibid.*, pp. 69–70.
[*Bullitt's testimony against the League*]: Farnsworth, *op. cit.*, pp. 58–63, quoted at p. 62; see also Lodge to Henry White, October 2, 1919, Henry White Papers, Lodge Papers.
[*Wilson on public being misled*]: quoted in Link, p. 114.

464–65 [*Defense of Article 10*]: *ibid.*, p. 115.
[*Wilson's prophecy*]: *ibid.*, p. 118.
[*Failure of the tour*]: see James MacGregor Burns, *The Deadlock of Democracy* (Prentice-Hall, 1963), p. 140.
[*Wilson's illness*]: Weinstein, *op. cit.*, ch. 21; Smith, chs. 6–7.
[*Lodge reservation to Article 10*]: quoted in Link, p. 123.

465–66 [*Wilson on Lodge's reservation*]: quoted in Grayson, pp. 102–3.

466 [*Final vote on the League*]: see tables in W. Stull Holt, "Playing Politics with the League," in Ralph A. Stone, ed., *Wilson and the League of Nations* (Holt, Rinehart and Winston, 1967), pp. 27–35.
[*Doctor on stroke as decisive factor in League defeat*]: Weinstein, pp. 362–63.

467 [*Wilson's psychological makeup*]: see Sigmund Freud and William C. Bullitt, *Thomas Woodrow Wilson: A Psychological Study* (Houghton Mifflin, 1967); George and George; Jerrold M. Post, "Woodrow Wilson Re-examined: The Mind-Body Controversy Redux and Other Disputations," *Political Psychology*, vol. 4, no. 2 (June 1983), pp. 289–306, plus following comments by Weinstein, the Georges, and Michael Marmor; Robert C. Tucker, "The Georges' Wilson Reexamined: An Essay on Psychobiography," *American Political Science Review*, vol. 71, no. 2 (June 1977), pp. 606–18.
[*Wilson's neglect of party politics*]: see Burns, *Deadlock of Democracy*, pp. 142–47.
[*Wilson's desire for glory*]: Tucker, p. 617.
[*Graduate school controversy*]: George and George, esp. ch. 2.

1920: The Great and Solemn Rejection

468 [*Wilson's call for a referendum*]: Richard L. Merritt, "Woodrow Wilson and the 'Great and Solemn Referendum,' 1920," *Review of Politics*, vol. 27, no. 1 (January 1965), pp. 78–104, quoted at p. 97.
[*Wilson's views on relationship of leaders to citizens in a democracy*]: Woodrow Wilson, "Cabinet Government in the United States," *International Review* (August 1879), pp. 146–63; Wilson, *Congressional Government* (Houghton Mifflin, 1885); Wilson, *Constitutional Government in the United States* (Columbia University Press, 1908); A. J. Wann, "The Development of Woodrow Wilson's Theory of the Presidency: Continuity and Change," in Earl Latham, ed., *The Philosophy and Policies of Woodrow Wilson* (University of Chicago Press, 1958), pp. 46–66.
[*Wilson on "representative government"*]: "Cabinet Government in the United States," p. 147.
[*"Disintegrate ministry"*]: *Congressional Government*, p. 102.

469 [*Lansing on absurdity of referendum call*]: quoted in Merritt, pp. 99–100.
[*America in 1920*]: Robert K. Murray, *The Harding Era* (University of Minnesota Press, 1969), ch. 3.
[*Stedman on Europe in chaos*]: Seymour Stedman, "Nine Steps to a New Age," in Arthur M. Schlesinger, Jr., *History of American Presidential Elections* (Chelsea House, 1971), vol. 3, p. 2434.
[*Wilson's warning to Palmer*]: quoted in Smith, *op. cit.*, p. 155.

469 [*Wilson in 1920*]: *ibid.*, chs. 9–10.

470 [*Republican party leadership, 1920*]: Wesley M. Bagby, *The Road to Normalcy* (Johns Hopkins Press, 1962), ch. 1.
[*The four-party system in 1920*]: Burns, *Deadlock of Democracy, op. cit.*, chs. 6–7.

471 [*Editor and Senator Harding*]: Murray, pp. 5–18; Francis Russell, *The Shadow of Blooming Grove* (McGraw-Hill, 1968).
[*Harding on his own inadequacies as leader*]: Russell, pp. 313–15, Harding quoted at p. 313.

472 [*The "smoke-filled room"*]: *ibid.*, ch. 15; Murray, ch. 1; Bagby, ch. 3; William Allen White, *Masks in a Pageant* (Macmillan, 1928), ch. 36.
[*"Footless conversation"*]: Sen. James Wadsworth, quoted in Russell, p. 380.
[*Russell on convention leaders and dark horses*]: *ibid.*, p. 381.
[*Daugherty's prediction*]: quoted in *ibid.*, pp. 341–42.

473 [*Harding campaign*]: *ibid.*, pp. 397–416; Bagby, ch. 5.
[*Democratic convention*]: Donald R. McCoy, "Election of 1920," in Schlesinger, vol. 3, pp. 2361–66; Frank Freidel, *Franklin D. Roosevelt: The Ordeal* (Little, Brown, 1954), ch. 4.

474 [*Cox-Wilson exchange*]: quoted in Freidel, p. 74.
[*Cox campaign*]: Bagby, ch. 5; James M. Cox, *Journey Through My Years* (Simon and Schuster, 1946), chs. 21–24.
[*Presidential election results, 1920*]: Schlesinger, vol. 3, p. 2456.

475 [*Wilson viewing the film*]: Baker, *American Chronicle, op. cit.*, pp. 481–82.

14. THE AGE OF MELLON

479 [*Ford works*]: Allan Nevins and Frank Ernest Hill, *Ford: Expansion and Challenge, 1915–1933* (Scribner's, 1957), ch. 11, John Van Deventer quoted on efficiency of work units at p. 288.

480 [*Thought and motion in mass production*]: Henry Ford, *My Life and Work* (Garden City Publishing, 1922), p. 80. On Ford's views see also, Henry Ford, *My Philosophy of Industry* (Coward-McCann, 1929); Ralph H. Graves, *The Triumph of an Idea* (Doubleday, Doran, 1934).
[*Edison to Ford on slowing down*]: quoted in William C. Richards, *The Last Billionaire* (Scribner's, 1948), p. 378.
[*The Ford legend*]: Nevins and Hill, pp. 607–13.

481 [*Five dollars a day*]: Keith Sward, *The Legend of Henry Ford* (Rinehart, 1948), ch. 4.
[*Creating Rouge*]: Nevins and Hill, ch. 8.
[*Sites of branch plants*]: *ibid.*, p. 256.
[*Ford's Sociological Department*]: Stephen Meyer, "Adapting the Immigrant to the Line: Americanization in the Ford Factory, 1914–1921," *Journal of Social History*, vol. 14, no. 1 (Fall 1980), pp. 67–82, quoted at pp. 70, 71; Allan Nevins, *Ford: The Times, the Man, the Company* (Scribner's, 1954), pp. 551–63, Edgar Guest verse quoted at p. 552; Stephen Meyer, *The Five Dollar Day: Labor Management and Social Control in the Ford Motor Company, 1908–1921* (State University of New York Press, 1981), esp. ch. 6.

482 [*Ford official on observance of "American" holidays*]: quoted in Meyer, "Adapting the Immigrant," p. 74.
[*Ford as transforming leader*]: William Greenleaf, "Henry Ford," in John A. Garraty, ed., *Encyclopedia of American Biography* (Harper & Row, 1974), p. 369.

483 [*Ford in politics*]: Nevins and Hill, pp. 114–22.
[*Ford's anti-Semitism*]: Leo P. Ribuffo, "Henry Ford and *The International Jew*," *American Jewish History*, vol. 69, no. 3 (March 1980), pp. 437–77; Upton Sinclair, *The Flivver King* (Upton Sinclair, 1937), pp. 118–28.
[Tribune *suit*]: Nevins and Hill, pp. 129–42.
[*Ford's personality*]: Ann Jardim, *The First Henry Ford* (MIT Press, 1970); Samuel S. Marquis, *Henry Ford: An Interpretation* (Little, Brown, 1923).
[*Ford and decentralization*]: John Robert Mullin, "Henry Ford and Field and Factory," *Journal of the American Planning Association*, vol. 48 (Autumn 1982), pp. 419–31; Nevins and Hill, pp. 227–30.

483 [*Ford's associates*]: Charles E. Sorensen, *My Forty Years with Ford* (W. W. Norton, 1956); Nevins and Hill, pp. 11–17, 167–70, 269–78.
[*Fitzgerald on Ford*]: quoted in Greenleaf, p. 370.

"The Business of America . . ."

484 [*The 1920s in retrospect*]: Henry F. May, "Shifting Perspectives on the 1920's," *Mississippi Valley Historical Review*, vol. 43, no. 3 (December 1956), pp. 405–27; Burl Noggle, "The Twenties: A New Historiographical Frontier," *Journal of American History*, vol. 53, no. 2 (September 1966), pp. 299–314. For general accounts, see William E. Leuchtenburg, *The Perils of Prosperity, 1914–32* (University of Chicago Press, 1958); David A. Shannon, *Between the Wars, 1919–1941* (Houghton Mifflin, 1965); George Soule, *Prosperity Decade* (Rinehart, 1947); Ellis W. Hawley, *The Great War and the Search for a Modern Order* (St. Martin's Press, 1979).

485 [*Coolidge's pledge to adhere to Harding policies*]: Robert K. Murray, *The Politics of Normalcy* (W. W. Norton, 1973), p. 131.
[*Murray on Coolidge able to be the President Harding wanted to be*]: ibid., p. 143.
[*Harding Administration*]: Robert K. Murray, *The Harding Era* (University of Minnesota Press, 1969); Leuchtenburg, ch. 5; Soule; Eugene P. Trani and David L. Wilson, *The Presidency of Warren G. Harding* (Regents Press of Kansas, 1977).
[*Mellon*]: Andrew W. Mellon, *Taxation: The People's Business* (Macmillan, 1924); Allan Nevins, "Andrew William Mellon," in Robert L. Schuyler, ed., *Dictionary of American Biography*, vol. 22, supplement 2 (Scribner's, 1958), pp. 446–52; Harvey O'Connor, *Mellon's Millions* (John Day, 1933).

486 [*Harding on America as a business country*]: quoted in James Warren Prothro, *Dollar Decade* (Louisiana State University Press, 1954), p. 223.

487 [*Coolidge on factories as temples*]: ibid., p. 224.
[*Hoover on banishing poverty*]: ibid., p. 225.
[*Madison on majority rule*]: Gaillard Hunt, ed., *The Writings of James Madison* (Putnam's, 1900–10), vol. 2, p. 366; Jacob E. Cooke, ed., *The Federalist* (Wesleyan University Press, 1961), p. 351 (Federalist No. 51).

488 [*Post–World War I Supreme Court*]: Charles Warren, *The Supreme Court in United States History* (Little, Brown, 1924), vol. 3; Alpheus Thomas Mason, *The Supreme Court from Taft to Warren* (W. W. Norton, 1964), ch. 2; William F. Swindler, *Court and Constitution in the 20th Century: The Old Legality* (Bobbs-Merrill, 1969).
[*Chief Justice White "holding" the chief justiceship for Taft*]: quoted in Henry F. Pringle, *The Life and Times of William Howard Taft* (Farrar & Rinehart, 1939), vol. 2, p. 955.
[*Adair case*]: *Adair* v. *U.S.*, 208 U.S. 161 (1908), quoted at 178.

488–89 [*State yellow-dog contract case*]: *Coppage* v. *Kansas*, 236 U.S. 1 (1915).

489 [*Child labor case*]: *Hammer* v. *Dagenhart*, 247 U.S. 251 (1918), quoted at 281; Holmes dissent reprinted in Max Lerner, ed., *The Mind and Faith of Justice Holmes* (Little, Brown, 1943), pp. 168–71, quoted at p. 171.
[*Second child labor case*]: *Bailey* v. *Drexel Furniture Company*, 259 U.S. 20 (1922).
[*Adkins case*]: *Adkins* v. *Children's Hospital*, 261 U.S. 525 (1923), quoted at 558.
[*Lerner on Sutherland's treatment of labor as a commodity*]: Lerner, p. 173.

490 [*Taft "massing the court"*]: Mason, pp. 57–58.
[*Taft's Sunday afternoon "caucus"*]: Pringle, vol. 2, pp. 1043–44.
[*Rail and coal strikes of 1922*]: Murray, *Politics of Normalcy*, pp. 80–81.
[*Farmers and the Harding Administration*]: ibid., pp. 50–52, 61–64.
[*Harding and black rights*]: Murray, *The Harding Era*, pp. 397–403, Birmingham address quoted at p. 399; Richard Sherman, "The Harding Administration and the Negro: An Opportunity Lost," *Journal of Negro History*, vol. 49, no. 3 (July 1964), pp. 151–68.

491 [*Tax reductions*]: Murray, *Politics of Normalcy*, pp. 53–55, 57–58, Harding quoted on complexities of "this tax problem" at pp. 54–55.
[*Harding scandals*]: Burl Noggle, *Teapot Dome: Oil and Politics in the 1920's* (Louisiana State University Press, 1962); J. Leonard Bates, *Origins of the Teapot Dome* (University of Illinois Press, 1963).

492 [*Coolidge's luck as to day he heard of Harding's death*]: William Allen White, *A Puritan in Babylon* (Macmillan, 1938), p. 243.

Bankers and Battleships

[*Republican foreign policy in the 1920s*]: L. Ethan Ellis, *Republican Foreign Policy, 1921–1933* (Rutgers University Press, 1968); Betty Glad, *Charles Evans Hughes and the Illusions of Innocence* (University of Illinois Press, 1966), part 3; Murray, *The Harding Era, op. cit.*, ch. 11; Joan Hoff Wilson, *American Business & Foreign Policy, 1920–1933* (University Press of Kentucky, 1971).
[*Ellis on zigzag foreign policy*]: *Republican Foreign Policy*, p. 34.
[*Confusion as to American intentions*]: Benjamin D. Rhodes, "British Diplomacy and the Silent Oracle of Vermont, 1923–1929," *Vermont History*, vol. 50, no. 2 (1982), pp. 69–79.
[*Editors on the mystery of Republican foreign policy*]: Thomas A. Bailey, *The Man in the Street: The Impact of American Public Opinion on Foreign Policy* (Macmillan, 1948), p. 238.
[*Harding's Cabinet*]: see James MacGregor Burns, *The Deadlock of Democracy* (Prentice-Hall, 1963), p. 149.

493 [*Borah Resolution as "Model 'T' "*]: John C. Vinson, *The Parchment Peace* (University of Georgia Press, 1955), p. 52.
[*Business attitude towards arms control*]: Wilson, ch. 2. See also Vinson, p. 46, for cost figures on military spending.
[*Catt on taking action*]: Gaddis Smith, "The First Freeze," *New York Times Magazine*, April 24, 1983, pp. 110–11, 114, quoted at p. 111.
[*Lodge on probable failure of naval talks*]: quoted in John A. Garraty, *Henry Cabot Lodge* (Alfred A. Knopf, 1953), p. 404.
[*Washington Naval Conference*]: Thomas H. Buckley, *The United States and the Washington Conference, 1921–1922* (University of Tennessee Press, 1970); Glad, chs. 17–18; Smith; Vinson. (The conference met in Continental Hall, not Constitution Hall—see Buckley, p. 69.)

494 [*Hughes's speech and reaction to it*]: Buckley, ch. 5.
[*Black Chamber breaks Japanese codes*]: James Bamford, *The Puzzle Palace* (Houghton Mifflin, 1982), pp. 9–10.
[*Hughes on linking political and arms negotiations*]: quoted in Glad, p. 280.

495 [*Immigration Act of 1924*]: Ellis, pp. 14–19.
[*Arms talks in Geneva and London*]: *ibid.*, ch. 5.
[*The Senate and the World Court*]: Thomas A. Bailey, *A Diplomatic History of the American People*, 9th ed. (Prentice-Hall, 1974), pp. 629–31.

495–96 [*Kellogg-Briand Pact*]: L. Ethan Ellis, *Frank B. Kellogg and American Foreign Relations, 1925–1929* (Rutgers University Press, 1961), ch. 7.

496 [*Kellogg-Briand as an "international kiss"*]: James Reed, quoted in Ronald Steel, *Walter Lippmann and the American Century* (Atlantic–Little, Brown, 1980), p. 254.
[*Republican economic policy abroad*]: Melvyn P. Leffler, "Herbert Hoover, the 'New Era,' and American Foreign Policy," in Ellis W. Hawley, ed., *Herbert Hoover as Secretary of Commerce: Studies in New Era Thought and Practice* (University of Iowa Press, 1981), pp. 148–79, quoted at p. 150.
[*Reparations and war debts*]: Soule, *op. cit.*, ch. 12; Wilson, chs. 4–5. See also table in Bailey, *Diplomatic History*, p. 657; Joseph Young Case and Everett Needham Case, *Owen D. Young and American Enterprise* (David R. Godine, 1982).

496–97 [*Mellon on rescheduling debts*]: quoted in Wilson, p. 126.

497 [*Coolidge on war debts*]: Howard H. Quint and Robert H. Ferrell, *The Talkative President* (University of Massachusetts Press, 1964), p. 176.
[*Financial "merry-go-round"*]: Bailey, *Diplomatic History*, p. 664.
[*U.S. trade and investment in Latin America*]: Wilson, pp. 169, 199–200.

498 [*American presence in China*]: Robert M. Leventhal, "China Marine," *Marine Corps Gazette*, vol. 56, no. 11 (1972), pp. 36–44.
[*Relations with Latin America*]: Ellis, *Republican Foreign Policy*, chs. 7–8.
[*Morrow in Mexico*]: *ibid.*, pp. 245, 252.

499 [*Smoot-Hawley tariff*]: Ray Lyman Wilbur, *The Hoover Policies* (Scribner's, 1937), pp. 181–92; Wilson, pp. 93–98; see also Elmer E. Schattschneider, *Politics, Pressures and the Tariff* (Prentice-Hall, 1935).
[*Hoover on international trade*]: quoted in Leffler, p. 152.
[*Hoover on Smoot-Hawley*]: quoted in Wilson, p. 98.

The Voices of Protest

[*Republican party "compact majority"*]: Randall B. Ripley, *Majority Party Leadership in Congress* (Little, Brown, 1969), ch. 4.
[*Rise of the "loyal opposition" party*]: James MacGregor Burns, *The Vineyard of Liberty* (Alfred A. Knopf, 1982), chs. 4–5.
499–500 [*Political developments during the 1920s*]: Jonathan Daniels, *The Time Between the Wars* (Doubleday, 1966), esp. chs. 6–13; Karl Schriftgiesser, *This Was Normalcy* (Little, Brown, 1948).
500 [*1924 Democratic convention*]: David Burner, *The Politics of Provincialism* (Alfred A. Knopf, 1968), pp. 114–28, McAdoo quoted at p. 114; keynote speaker, Sen. Pat Harrison, quoted at p. 116.
[*Burner on 1924 Democratic ticket as "schizoid"*]: ibid., p. 125.
[*Progressive party, 1924*]: Kenneth Campbell MacKay, *The Progressive Movement of 1924* (Columbia University Press, 1947); Belle Case La Follette and Fola La Follette, *Robert M. La Follette* (Macmillan, 1953), vol. 2, chs. 69–71.
501 [*Wheeler on Democratic party*]: Burton Wheeler and Paul F. Healey, *Yankee from the West* (Doubleday, 1962), p. 249.
[*Left-wing parties and the Progressives*]: James Weinstein, *The Decline of Socialism in America, 1912–1925* (Monthly Review Press, 1967), chs. 7–8; David A. Shannon, *The Socialist Party of America* (Macmillan, 1955), ch. 7.
[*1924 election*]: David Burner, "Election of 1924," in Arthur M. Schlesinger, Jr., *History of American Presidential Elections* (Chelsea House, 1971), vol. 3, pp. 2459–2581; J. Leonard Bates, "The Teapot Dome Scandal and the Election of 1924," *American Historical Review*, vol. 60, no. 2 (January 1955), pp. 303–22; Svend Petersen, *A Statistical History of the American Presidential Elections* (Frederick Ungar, 1963), pp. 86–88.
[*1924 election results*]: Schlesinger, vol. 3, p. 2581.
502 [*Roosevelt, Smith, and the future of the Democratic party*]: Burner, *Politics of Provincialism*, ch. 5; Alfred Rollins, Jr., *Roosevelt and Howe* (Alfred A. Knopf, 1962); Frank Freidel, *Franklin D. Roosevelt: The Ordeal* (Little, Brown, 1954), pp. 201–2; Ruth C. Silva, *Rum, Religion and Votes: 1928 Re-examined* (Pennsylvania State University Press, 1962).
[*Al Smith*]: Oscar Handlin, *Al Smith and His America* (Little, Brown, 1958); Leuchtenburg, *op. cit.*, pp. 230–32.
[*1928 election*]: Handlin, ch. 6; Leuchtenburg, ch. 12; Lawrence H. Fuchs, "Election of 1928," in Schlesinger, vol. 3, pp. 2585–2704 (the Marshall-Smith exchange from the *Atlantic* is reprinted in this volume, pp. 2649–60); Silva; Earland J. Carlson, "Franklin D. Roosevelt's Post-Mortem of 1928 Election," *Midwest Journal of Political Science*, vol. 8, no. 3 (August 1964), pp. 298–308; see also Allan J. Lichtman, *Prejudice and the Old Politics: The Presidential Election of 1928* (University of North Carolina Press, 1979).
503 [*Al Smith's refusal to be other than Al Smith*]: Handlin, p. 130.
[*Smith's refusal to "shut the door" in immigrants' faces*]: quoted in Steel, *op. cit.*, p. 248.
[*Election results, 1928*]: Schlesinger, vol. 3, p. 2704.
[*Smith on his loss*]: quoted in Frances Perkins, *The Roosevelt I Knew* (Viking Press, 1946), p. 46.
[*1928 election as reflection of politics in the 1920s*]: Allan J. Lichtman, "Critical Election Theory and the Reality of American Presidential Politics, 1916–40," *American Historical Review*, vol. 81, no. 2 (April 1976), pp. 317–48.
504 [*Civil liberties cases, wartime and postwar*]: Zechariah Chaffee, Jr., *Free Speech in the United States* (Harvard University Press, 1941), chs. 2–4.
[*Oliver Wendell Holmes's opinions and dissents*]: Lerner, *op. cit.*, part 2. See generally, Paul L. Murphy, *The Meaning of Freedom of Speech* (Greenwood Press, 1972), esp. chs. 3–10.

504 [*Holmes's opinion in* Schenck]: *Schenck* v. *United States*, 249 U.S. 47 (1919), quoted at 52; Lerner, pp. 294–97, quoted at pp. 296–97.
     [*Holmes to Pollock on Debs case*]: letters of April 5 and 27, 1919, in Mark DeWolfe Howe, ed., *Holmes-Pollock Letters* (Harvard University Press, 1941), vol. 2, pp. 7, 11.
     [*Holmes's opinion in Debs case*]: *Debs* v. *United States*, 249 U.S. 211 (1919); Lerner, pp. 300–4.
     [*Abrams*]: *Abrams* v. *United States*, 250 U.S. 616 (1919), quoted at 628, 630; Lerner, pp. 307–13, quoted at pp. 310, 312.
505 [*Red scare of 1919–20*]: Robert K. Murray, *Red Scare, 1919–1920* (University of Minnesota Press, 1955); Stanley Coben, "A Study in Nativism: The American Red Scare of 1919–1920," *Political Science Quarterly*, vol. 79, no. 1 (March 1964), pp. 52–75; Paul L. Murphy, "Normalcy, Intolerance, and American Character," *Virginia Quarterly Review*, vol. 40 (Summer 1964), pp. 445–59; Leuchtenburg, ch. 4.
     [*Demands of Sunday, McKellar, and Byrnes for action against radicals*]: Leuchtenburg, p. 66.
     [*Gitlow*]: *Gitlow* v. *New York*, 268 U.S. 652 (1925), quoted at 673; Lerner, pp. 324–25.
506 [*Schwimmer*]: *United States* v. *Schwimmer*, 279 U.S. 644 (1928), quoted at 655; Lerner, pp. 326–28, quoted at p. 328.
     [*Holmes and his correspondents*]: Mark DeWolfe Howe, ed., *Holmes-Laski Letters* (Harvard University Press, 1953), vol. 2; Howe, *Holmes-Pollock Letters*.
     [*Brandeis-Frankfurter relationship*]: Bruce Allen Murphy, *The Brandeis/Frankfurter Connection* (Oxford University Press, 1982), esp. ch. 3; Melvin I. Urofsky and David W. Levy, eds., *Letters of Louis Brandeis* (State University of New York Press, 1971–78), vols. 2–5, *passim;* Philippa Strum, *Louis D. Brandeis: Justice for the People* (Harvard University Press, 1984), *passim*.
     [*Law clerk on Brandeis's appearance*]: H. Thomas Austern, quoted in Strum, p. 358.
     [*Differences between Holmes and Brandeis*]: Strum, p. 317; see also Alpheus Thomas Mason, *Brandeis: A Free Man's Life* (Viking Press, 1946), pp. 572–81.
507 [*Hoover on individualism*]: Herbert Hoover, *American Individualism* (Doubleday, Page, 1922), p. 13; see also David Burner, *Herbert Hoover* (Alfred A. Knopf, 1979), pp. 139–42.

15. THE COMMERCIALIZED CULTURE

508 [*Doubled industrial production*]: George J. Stigler, *Trends in Output and Employment* (National Bureau of Economic Research, 1947), p. 57 (Table A).
     [*Consumer spending*]: Robert S. Lynd and Alice C. Hanson, "The People as Consumers," in The President's Research Committee on Social Trends, *Recent Social Trends in the United States* (McGraw-Hill, 1933), pp. 857–911. Cf. Richard Wightman Fox, "Epitaph for Middletown: Robert S. Lynd and the Analysis of Consumer Culture," in Richard Wightman Fox and T. J. Jackson Lears, eds., *The Culture of Consumption: Critical Essays in American History, 1880–1980* (Pantheon Books, 1983), pp. 101–41.
     [*YOU SHOULD HAVE O$10,000*]: William E. Leuchtenburg, *The Perils of Prosperity, 1914–1932* (University of Chicago Press, 1958), p. 9.
     [*The Age of Ballyhoo*]: Frederick Lewis Allen, *Only Yesterday: An Informal History of the 1920's* (Perennial Library, 1964), pp. 68, 158–62, 186.
509 [*Jazz*]: Gunther Schuller, *Early Jazz: Its Roots and Musical Development* (Oxford University Press, 1968); Marshall W. Stearns, *The Story of Jazz* (Oxford University Press, 1956); Lewis A. Erenberg, *Steppin' Out: New York Nightlife and the Transformation of American Culture, 1890–1930* (Greenwood Press, 1981), ch. 8.
     [*Mascagni on jazz*]: quoted in Mark Sullivan, *Our Times* (Scribner's, 1926–35), vol. 6, p. 481.
     ["*The day of the saxophone*"]: *ibid.*, pp. 483–84.
     [*Whiteman on jazz*]: quoted in *ibid.*, p. 480.
     [*University president on twenties dress as Devil's work*]: quoted in Allen, p. 76.
     [*Ponzi's swindles*]: "Mr. Ponzi and His 'Ponzied Finance,' " *Literary Digest*, vol. 66, no. 8 (August 21, 1920), pp. 44–50.
     [*Blacks in the twenties*]: Louise V. Kennedy, *The Negro Peasant Turns Cityward: Effects of Recent Migrations to Northern Cities* (Columbia University Press, 1930); T. J. Woofter, Jr., "The Status of Racial and Ethnic Groups," in *Recent Social Trends*, pp. 553–601; Alain Locke, ed., *The New Negro: An Interpretation* (Albert & Charles Boni, 1925), esp. part 2.

509 [*The Klan in the twenties*]: Arnold S. Rice, *The Ku Klux Klan in American Politics* (Public Affairs Press, 1962), esp. ch. 2; David M. Chalmers, *Hooded Americanism: The First Century of the Ku Klux Klan, 1865–1965* (Doubleday, 1965); Hiram W. Evans, "The Klan's Fight for Americanism," *North American Review*, vol. 223 (March 1926), pp. 33–63.
[*Anti-red, anti-radical hysteria*]: Zechariah Chaffee, Jr., *Free Speech in the United States* (Harvard University Press, 1941), pp. 269–354.
510 [*Lindbergh*]: Charles A. Lindbergh, *The Spirit of St. Louis* (Scribner's, 1953); Kenneth S. Davis, *The Hero: Charles Lindbergh and the American Dream* (Doubleday, 1959).
[*Allen on Lindbergh*]: Allen, p. 183.
[*Ward on Lindbergh's flight*]: John W. Ward, "The Meaning of Lindbergh's Flight," *American Quarterly*, vol. 10, no. 1 (Spring 1958), pp. 3–16, quoted at p. 14.
[*Coolidge on "this silent partner"*]: quoted in *ibid.*, p. 14.

The Workshop of Education

511 [*Elementary school curriculum*]: Robert Lynd and Helen Lynd, *Middletown: A Study in American Culture* (Harcourt, Brace, 1929), p. 189. See also, Edward A. Krug, *The Shaping of the American High School, 1920–1941* (University of Wisconsin Press, 1972), pp. 55–59.
[*Lynds on the regimented classroom*]: Lynd and Lynd, p. 188.
[*Declining percentage of male teachers*]: *ibid.*, p. 206, footnote 1; see also, Ernest C. Moore, *Fifty Years of American Education: 1867–1917* (Ginn, 1918), pp. 60–61.
[*Education and social status of teachers*]: Lynd and Lynd, ch. 15; Krug, pp. 147–54.
[*High school enrollment, 1920s*]: U.S. Office of Education, "Biennial Survey of Education, 1930–1932," *Bulletin*, 1933, no. 2 (U.S. Government Printing Office, 1934), pp. 46–47, in Robert H. Bremner, ed., *Children and Youth in America: A Documentary Survey* (Harvard University Press, 1970–71), vol. 2, parts 7 and 8, p. 1101.
511–12 [*Krug on high school buildings*]: Krug, pp. 42–43.
512 [*Two of every three teenagers not enrolled*]: *ibid.*, p. 7.
[*Wild one on the "older generation"*]: John F. Carter, Jr., "These Wild Young People," *Atlantic Monthly*, vol. 126, no. 3 (September 1920), pp. 301–4, quoted at p. 302.
[*Search for scapegoats*]: Krug, pp. 21–24, University of Minnesota strictures against improper dancing quoted at p. 23; Paula S. Fass, *The Damned and the Beautiful: American Youth in the 1920's* (Oxford University Press, 1977), pp. 18–25; Joseph F. Kett, *Rites of Passage: Adolescence in America, 1790 to the Present* (Basic Books, 1977), pp. 258–61; Jerome Leon Rodnitzky, "David Kinley: A Paternal President in the Roaring Twenties," *Journal of the Illinois State Historical Society*, vol. 66, no. 1 (Spring 1977), pp. 5–19, esp. pp. 15–16.
[*Van Waters on institutions in flux*]: quoted in Kett, p. 259.
[*Educator on the "aim of today"*]: Charles A. Prosser, quoted in Krug, p. 4.
[*"Americanization" in American schools*]: Bremner, vol. 2, parts 7 and 8, pp. 1324–36.
513 [*The emphases of history and social studies in Muncie*]: Lynd and Lynd, pp. 196–201, quoted at p. 199.
[*Mellon on a solid education*]: quoted in Krug, p. 19.
[*Ellis's plea to make "modern life comprehensible"*]: *ibid.*, p. 82.
[*New York educators on textbooks' point of view*]: *ibid*; see also, E. E. Brossard, ed., *Wisconsin Statutes*, I, 432 (1921), in Bremner, vol. 2, parts 7 and 8, pp. 1330–31.
[*Fass on the "teasing image"*]: Fass, pp. 6, 7.
[*College students, 1920s*]: *ibid., passim;* Kett, pp. 261–64; Joan G. Zimmerman, "College Culture in the Midwest, 1890–1930" (Ph.D. dissertation, University of Virginia, 1978), pp. 252–56.
514 [*Rise in college attendance, 1920s*]: Bureau of the Census, *Historical Statistics of the United States, Colonial Times to 1970* (U.S. Government Printing Office, 1975), part 2, p. 386 (Series H 751–765).
[*Trinity College editor on "self-centered residents of Main Street"*]: quoted in Fass, p. 365.
[*Fraternities, 1920s*]: *ibid.*, pp. 141–67, 235–36; Lawrence R. Veysey, *The Emergence of the American University* (University of Chicago Press, 1965), pp. 292–94.
[*Student reading, 1920s*]: Fass, p. 365.
[*"George F. . . . is going to college"*]: quoted in *ibid.*
[*Student poll, 1924*]: *ibid.*, pp. 343–45.
[*UCLA editor on the "political minded"*]: quoted in *ibid.*, p. 355.

515   [*Cornell editor on "the panic"*]: ibid., p. 349.

[*"Largest private educational system"*]: Winthrop S. Hudson, *Religion in America* (Scribner's, 1965), p. 396.

[*Hudson on decline of Protestantism in 1920s*]: ibid., quoted at p. 357; Robert T. Handy, "The American Religious Depression, 1925–1935," *Church History*, vol. 29, no. 1 (March 1960), pp. 3–16.

[*Applications for foreign missionary service*]: Sydney E. Ahlstrom, *A Religious History of the American People* (Yale University Press, 1972), p. 899.

516   [*Ahlstrom on the "thinning out of evangelical substance"*]: ibid.

[*"Merchandising" of religion*]: Hudson, pp. 375–76, *Zion's Herald* on minister as salesman and Lewis S. Mudge on "the only business of the Church," quoted at p. 375; slogans and sermon topics, quoted at pp. 375–76. See also Ahlstrom, pp. 904–5.

[*Barton*]: Leo P. Ribuffo, "Jesus Christ as Business Statesman: Bruce Barton and the Selling of Corporate Capitalism," *American Quarterly*, vol. 33, no. 2 (Summer 1981), pp. 206–31; Otis Pease, "Bruce Barton," in John A. Garraty, ed., *Encyclopedia of American Biography* (Harper & Row, 1974), pp. 62–63.

[*Pease on* The Man Nobody Knows]: Pease, p. 62.

[*Fundamentalist militancy of twenties*]: Ahlstrom, p. 909. See also, W. B. Riley, "The Faith of the Fundamentalists," *Current History*, vol. 26, no. 3 (June 1927), pp. 434–40, reprinted in Loren Baritz, ed., *The Culture of the Twenties* (Bobbs-Merrill, 1970), pp. 191–201.

517   [*Sunday*]: William G. McLoughlin, Jr., *Billy Sunday Was His Real Name* (University of Chicago Press, 1955); McLoughlin, *Modern Revivalism: Charles Grandison Finney to Billy Graham* (Ronald Press, 1959), ch. 8.

[*"Hireling" ministers*]: quoted in McLoughlin, *Modern Revivalism*, p. 410.

[*O$2 a soul*]: McLoughlin, *Billy Sunday*, ch. 3, esp. p. 116.

[*McPherson*]: Lately Thomas, *Storming Heaven: The Lives and Turmoils of Minnie Kennedy and Aimee Semple McPherson* (William Morrow, 1970); Sheldon Bissell, "Vaudeville at the Angelus Temple," *The Outlook*, vol. 149 (May 23, 1928), pp. 126–27, 158, reprinted in Baritz, pp. 201–9; Carrie McWilliams, "Aimee Semple McPherson: 'Sunlight in My Soul,'" in Isabel Leighton, ed., *The Aspirin Age* (Simon and Schuster, 1949), ch. 3.

[*Rival minister on McPherson*]: Bissell, p. 209.

[*Scopes trial*]: Ray Ginger, *Six Days or Forever? Tennessee v. John Thomas Scopes* (Beacon Press, 1958); James W. Wesolowski, "Before Canon 35: WGN Broadcasts the Monkey Trial," *Journalism History*, vol. 2, no. 3 (1975), pp. 76–79, 86.

[*Bryan's death*]: Ginger, p. 192.

[*Scopes as commercial venture*]: see R. M. Cornelius, "Their Stage Drew All the World: A New Look at the Scopes Evolution Trial," *Tennessee Historical Quarterly*, vol. 40, no. 2 (1981), pp. 129–43.

The Press as Entertainment

518   [*Press coverage of murder trials*]: Silas Bent, *Ballyhoo: The Voice of the Press* (Boni & Liveright, 1927), pp. 192–95, quoted at p. 194.

[*Rising costs of newspaper production*]: Frank Luther Mott, *American Journalism* (Macmillan, 1941), p. 674; Robert A. Rutland, *The Newsmongers: Journalism in the Life of the Nation, 1690–1972* (Dial Press, 1973), pp. 254–55.

[*Lippmann on the price of newspapers*]: Lippmann, *Public Opinion* (Harcourt, Brace, 1922), p. 321.

[*Proportion of ads in metropolitan papers*]: Bent, p. 214.

[*Tripled cost of advertising*]: Mott, p. 712.

518–19   [*Ad slogans*]: ibid., pp. 505, 712, 713.

[*Newspaper features*]: Bent, pp. 227–30.

[*Bent on newspaper offerings*]: ibid., pp. 197–98.

[*Comic strips*]: Stephen Becker, *Comic Art in America* (Simon and Schuster, 1959), ch. 3, quoted at p. 54; Ernest Brennecke, "The Real Mission of the Funny Paper," *The Century*, vol. 107, no. 5 (March 1924), pp. 665–75.

[*"Only the good have rights"*]: Becker, pp. 64–67, quoted at p. 66.

[*Newspaper consolidation*]: Mott, ch. 37; Bent, ch. 10.

520 [*Munsey*]: Mott, pp. 637–40; George Britt, *Forty Years—Forty Millions: The Career of Frank A. Munsey* (Farrar & Rinehart, 1935).
[*Munsey on the "law of economics"*]: quoted in Bent, p. 260.
[*Sinclair on the "Brass Check"*]: Sinclair, *The Brass Check* (Upton Sinclair, 1920), p. 436.
[*Lippmann on the* Times*'s coverage of the Russian Revolution*]: Lippmann and Charles Merz, "A Test of the News," *The New Republic*, vol. 23, no. 296 (August 4, 1920), supplement, pp. 1–41, quoted at p. 3.
[*Lippmann on the press as the "beam of a searchlight"*]: *Public Opinion*, pp. 364–65, quoted at p. 364.
[*Industrialization of news-gathering*]: Cathy Covert, "A View of the Press in the Twenties," *Journalism History*, vol. 2, no. 3 (1975), pp. 66–67, 92–96, quoted at pp. 92–93.
521 [*Decline of partisan papers*]: Alfred M. Lee, *The Daily Newspaper in America* (Macmillan, 1937), p. 182. See also, Silas Bent, "Partisanship in the Press," *The New Republic*, vol. 56, no. 720 (September 19, 1928), pp. 116–18.
[*Publicity agents*]: Michael Schnudson, *Discovering the News: A Social History of American Newspapers* (Basic Books, 1978), pp. 134–41.
[*Lippmann on shaping "the facts of modern life"*]: *Public Opinion*, p. 345.
[*Rise of syndicated columnists*]: Schnudson, pp. 150–51; Mott, pp. 689–94.
[*Founding of* Time]: W. A. Swanberg, *Luce and His Empire* (Scribner's, 1972), pp. 52–56. The prospectus is reprinted at pp. 53–54. See also, Schnudson, p. 149.
[*Luce's proposals for newspaper reform*]: quoted in Swanberg, p. 143.
522 [*Reader's Digest*]: Mott, pp. 732–33; John Bainbridge, "Little Magazine," *The New Yorker*, vol. 21, part 4 ("Profiles" series, November 17–December 15, 1945).
[*Foreign-language papers before World War I*]: Rutland, p. 291.
[*Measures against* Leader, Call, *and* Tageblatt]: ibid., p. 297; Chaffee, *op. cit.*, pp. 86–92, 247–69, 298–305.
[*Indian publications*]: James E. Murphy and Sharon M. Murphy, *Let My People Know: American Indian Journalism, 1828–1978* (University of Oklahoma Press, 1981), esp. ch. 3.
[*Black papers*]: Frederick G. Detweiler, *The Negro Press in the United States* (University of Chicago Press, 1922), ch. 3; Richard Bardolph, *The Negro Vanguard* (Rinehart, 1959), pp. 142–46; Roi Ottley, *The Lonely Warrior: The Life and Times of Robert S. Abbott* (Henry Regnery, 1955).
[*"Furniture That Talks"*]: quoted in Reynold M. Wik, "The Radio in Rural America During the 1920s," *Agricultural History*, vol. 55, no. 4 (October 1981), p. 340.
[*Sarnoff*]: Eric Barnouw, *A Tower in Babel: A History of Broadcasting in the United States* (Oxford University Press, 1966–70), vol. 1, pp. 75–81, Sarnoff's "plan of development" quoted at p. 78; Eugene Lyons, *David Sarnoff* (Harper & Row, 1966).
523 [*Sales of radio sets and parts*]: Barnouw, vol. 1, p. 125.
[*Proliferation of stations*]: ibid., p. 91.
[*Content of musical programming*]: ibid., pp. 126–31.
[*Radio and farmers*]: Wik, pp. 344, 345, 348, 349, and *passim*.
[*Regulation of radio*]: Barnouw, vol. 1, pp. 94–96, 100–101, 121–22, 178–79, 211–19; Wik, pp. 341–42.
[*McPherson's telegram*]: quoted in Barnouw, vol. 1, p. 180.

Entertainment as Spectatorship

524 [*"A crude toy became an industry"*]: Barnouw, *op. cit.*, vol. 1, p. 225.
[Birth of a Nation]: Robert Sklar, *Movie-Made America: A Social History of American Movies* (Random House, 1975), pp. 57–61; Fred Silva, ed., *Focus on* The Birth of a Nation (Prentice-Hall, 1971); Robert M. Henderson, *D. W. Griffith: His Life and Work* (Oxford University Press, 1972), ch. 9.
524–25 [*Studios, Zukor, and block booking*]: Sklar, ch. 9; Lawrence Kardish, *Reel Plastic Magic: A History of Films and Filmmaking in America* (Little, Brown, 1972); Arthur Knight, *The Liveliest Art: A Panoramic History of the Movies* (New American Library, 1957), pp. 107–10.
525 [*The Roxy*]: Lucinda Smith, "Introduction: Before the Final Curtain," in Ave Pildas, *Movie Palaces* (Clarkson N. Potter, 1980), p. 14; see also, Lloyd Morris, *Not So Long Ago* (Random House, 1949), pp. 187–90.
[*United Artists*]: Gerald Mast, *A Short History of the Movies* (Bobbs-Merrill, 1976), p. 121.

525 [*First generation of movie czars*]: Mast, p. 119; Lary I. May and Elaine Tyler May, "Why Jewish Movie Moguls: An Exploration in American Culture," *American Jewish History*, vol. 72, no. 1 (September 1982), pp. 6–25.

526 [*Mayer*]: Bosley Crowther, *Hollywood Rajah: The Life and Times of Louis B. Mayer* (Henry Holt, 1960).
[*Zukor to Chaplin*]: quoted in May and May, p. 21.
["*The Home of the Stars*"]: Crowther, pp. 92–100; Knight, p. 109.
[*Thalberg*]: Crowther, pp. 85–92, 102–4; Kevin Brownlow, *The Parade's Gone By . . .* (Alfred A. Knopf, 1968), pp. 424–27.
[*Film magazines*]: see Sinclair Lewis, *Babbitt* (Harcourt, Brace, 1922), p. 225.
[*Hollywood scandals and censorship*]: Sklar, pp. 77–82, 122–32; Raymond Moley, *The Hays Office* (Bobbs-Merrill, 1945), ch. 1; *Mutual Film Corporation v. Industrial Commission of Ohio*, 236 U.S. 230 (1915); *Mutual Film Corporation v. Hodges, Governor of the State of Kansas*, 236 U.S. 248 (1915).
[*Hollywood response to censorship threats*]: Sklar, pp. 82, 91–95; Moley, ch. 4 and pp. 240–41 (Appendix D); Knight, pp. 112–16.

527 [*Hays*]: Moley, ch. 2; Sklar, pp. 83–85.
[*Editor on sports selling papers*]: W. P. Beazell, quoted in Wayne M. Towers, "World Series Coverage in New York City in the 1920s," *Journalism Monographs*, no. 73 (August 1981).
[*Sports and the elites, nineteenth century*]: Benjamin G. Rader, *American Sports: From the Age of Folk Games to the Age of Spectators* (Prentice-Hall, 1983), ch. 3.
[*Founding of sports clubs and unions*]: ibid., pp. 47, 54.
[*Conflict at the New York Athletic Club*]: ibid., p. 50.

528 [*Women and sports*]: ibid., pp. 164–69.
[*Sports among the working classes*]: ibid., pp. 30–35.
[*Rader on the "sports revolution"*]: ibid., pp. 46, 47.
["*Outsiders" and sports*]: ibid., ch. 5, esp. pp. 90, 91–93, 96.
[*The "age of the spectator"*]: ibid., pp. 172–73.
[*Grange*]: Geoffrey Perrett, *America in the Twenties* (Simon and Schuster, 1982), p. 212; Allison Danzig, *The History of American Football* (Prentice-Hall, 1956), pp. 259–61; W. C. Heinz, "The Ghost of the Gridiron," in Herbert Warren Wind, ed., *The Realm of Sport* (Simon and Schuster, 1966), pp. 315–23.
[*Rockne*]: Perrett, p. 212; Rader, pp. 212–13; " 'Rock' Is of the Ages," *New Republic*, vol. 66, no. 854 (April 15, 1931), pp. 220–22.

529 [*Tilden*]: Frank Deford, *Big Bill Tilden* (Simon and Schuster, 1976); Allison Danzig, "Tilden, Autocrat of the Courts," in Wind, pp. 601–5; William T. Tilden, *The Art of Lawn Tennis* (Methuen, 1920).
[*Jones*]: Perrett, pp. 220–23, quoted at p. 221.
[*Ruth*]: Rader, pp. 177–82; Robert W. Creamer, *Babe* (Simon and Schuster, 1974); Babe Ruth and Bob Considine, *The Babe Ruth Story* (Scholastic Books, 1969); Red Smith, "Babe Ruth: One of a Kind," in Smith, *The Red Smith Reader*, Dave Anderson, ed. (Random House, 1982), pp. 160–65.
[*Technical changes in baseball*]: Towers, p. 2; Harold Seymour, *Baseball: The Golden Age* (Oxford University Press, 1971), ch. 3.
[*Ruth's 1920 season*]: Creamer, ch. 19; Perrett, p. 209.
[*Walsh*]: Rader, pp. 181–92, quoted at p. 181; Creamer, pp. 271–74.
[*Yankee attendance with Ruth*]: Perrett, p. 209; see also, "What Is Babe Ruth Worth to the Yankees?," *Literary Digest*, vol. 104, no. 13 (March 29, 1930), pp. 38–42.
[*Gate receipts and concessions, 1920s*]: Steven A. Riess, *Touching Base: Professional Baseball and American Culture in the Progressive Era* (Greenwood Press, 1980), p. 76.
[*Yankee Stadium*]: ibid., pp. 105–10; Creamer, pp. 276, 277–78.
[*Ruth on "the chance"*]: Ruth and Considine, p. 9.
[*Baseball and the "poor man"*]: Riess, pp. 30–38; Rader, pp. 128–29.

530 [*Dempsey*]: Rader, pp. 186–93; Randy Roberts, *Jack Dempsey: The Manassa Mauler* (Louisiana State University Press, 1979).
[*Dempsey and "paganism"*]: Dr. John Straton, quoted in Roberts, p. 127.
[*Dempsey vs. Willard*]: Roberts, pp. 50–66.
[*Rickard*]: Rader, pp. 186–93; Jack Kofoed, "The Master of Ballyhoo," *North American Review*, vol. 227, no. 3 (March 1929), pp. 282–86.

530 [*Dempsey's non-boxing income*]: Roberts, ch. 10, esp. p. 202.
[*Rickard's denial of a fight to Wills*]: *ibid.*, pp. 141–48, 213–19.
[*Tunney*]: *ibid.*, pp. 219–23; "Corbett to Tunney on 'How to Win the Mob,' " *Literary Digest*, vol. 96, no. 2 (January 14, 1928), pp. 54–60; S. G. S. McNeil, "The Real Gene Tunney," *North American Review*, vol. 226, no. 5 (November 1928), pp. 282–86.
[*Dempsey-Tunney bouts*]: Roberts, chs. 11 and 12; Gene Tunney, "My Fights with Jack Dempsey," in Wind, pp. 212–18.

531 ["*I have no alibis to offer*"]: Randy Roberts, "Jack Dempsey: An American Hero in the 1920's," *Journal of Popular Culture*, vol. 8, no. 2 (Fall 1974), p. 422.
[*Fights on the frontier and the plantations and in the livery stables*]: Rader, pp. 33, 35–36.
[*World Series scandal and Landis*]: Seymour, chs. 15–17 and ch. 19.
[*Twenties crime wave as mythical*]: Perrett, pp. 397–401; Edwin H. Sutherland and C. E. Gehlke, "Crime and Punishment," in *Recent Social Trends, op. cit.*, pp. 1123–39, 1165.
[*The gangster-hero*]: see L. Glen Seretan, "The 'New' Working Class and Social Banditry in Depression America," *Mid-America*, vol. 63, no. 2 (April–July 1981), pp. 107–17.
[*Capone*]: Allen, *Only Yesterday, op. cit.*, pp. 216–20; Perrett, pp. 393–97; John Kobler, *Capone* (Putnam's, 1971).

The Workshop and the Demos

532 [*Dempsey as symbol*]: Roberts, "Jack Dempsey: An American Hero in the 1920's," *op. cit.*, pp. 411–26.
[*Mass spectatorship as diversion*]: see Joel H. Spring, "Mass Culture and School Sports," *History of Education Quarterly*, vol. 14 (Winter 1974), pp. 483–99, esp. pp. 492–93.
[*Welfare capitalism*]: Leo Wolman and Gustav Peck, "Labor Groups in the Social Structure," in *Recent Social Trends, op. cit.*, pp. 843–47; Robert H. Zieger, "Herbert Hoover, the Wage-Earner, and the 'New Economic System,' 1919–1929," *Business Historical Review*, vol. 51 (Summer 1977), pp. 161–89; David Brody, "The Rise and Decline of Welfare Capitalism," in John Braeman et al., eds., *Change and Continuity in Twentieth-Century America: The 1920's* (Ohio State University Press, 1968), pp. 147–78.
[*Young on employee ownership*]: quoted in Josephine Young Case and Everett Needham Case, *Owen D. Young and American Enterprise* (David R. Godine, 1982), p. 374.

533 ["*Homo boobiens*"]: Mencken, *Notes on Democracy* (Alfred A. Knopf, 1926), p. 45. See also, Mencken, "On Being an American," in Mencken, *Prejudices: Third Series* (Alfred A. Knopf, 1922), pp. 9–64.
[*Mencken on public opinion*]: *Notes on Democracy*, p. 192.
[*Mencken on the average man*]: *ibid.*, p. 148.
[*Mencken on democracy*]: *ibid.*, p. 4 and *passim*.
[*Plato's cave in Lippmann*]: Lippmann, *Public Opinion, op. cit.*, esp. ch. 1.
[*Lippmann on the "false ideal"*]: Lippmann, *The Phantom Public* (Harcourt, Brace, 1925), pp. 38–39, quoted at p. 39.
[*Mencken's welcome to Lippmann*]: Mencken, "Katzenjammer" (review of *The Phantom Public*), *American Mercury*, vol. 7, no. 25 (January 1926), pp. 125–26.
[*Lippmann on public support of Ins and Outs*]: *Phantom Public*, pp. 126, 127.

534 [*Democratic party, 1920s*]: David Burner, *The Politics of Provincialism* (Alfred A. Knopf, 1968); James Sundquist, *Dynamics of the Party System* (Brookings Institution, 1973), ch. 9.
[*Union membership, 1920s*]: *Historical Statistics of the United States: Colonial Times to 1970, op. cit.*, part 1, p. 177 (Series D 940–945); Morton S. Baratz, *The Union and the Coal Industry* (Yale University Press, 1955), p. 61.
[*AFL in the twenties*]: James O. Morris, *Conflict Within the AFL: A Study of Craft versus Industrial Unionism, 1901–1938* (Cornell University Press, 1958), chs. 1–5; Philip Taft, *The A.F. of L. from the Death of Gompers to the Merger* (Harper & Bros., 1959).
[*Women's politics in the 1920s*]: J. Stanley Lemons, *The Woman Citizen* (University of Illinois Press, 1973).

535 [*Leftist writers in the twenties*]: Daniel Aaron: *Writers on the Left: Episodes in American Literary Communism* (Harcourt, Brace and World, 1961), chs. 4–7.
[*Lewis*]: Mark Schorer, *Sinclair Lewis: An American Life* (McGraw-Hill, 1961).

535 [*Kennicott on fiction and reality of small-town life*]: Lewis, *Main Street* (Hodder and Stoughton, 1920), p. 265.
[*Lewis's Nobel Prize address*]: reprinted in Lewis, *The Man from Main Street: Selected Essays and Other Writings, 1904–1950*, Harry E. Maule and Melville H. Cane, eds. (Random House, 1953), pp. 3–17, quoted at pp. 6–7.
[*Reaction to Nobel address*]: Schorer, pp. 552–53.

536 [Time *review of* Gantry]: "Bible Boar," *Time*, vol. 9, no. 11 (March 14, 1927), pp. 38–40, quoted at p. 38.
[*Lippmann breach with Harcourt, Brace*]: Ronald Steel, *Walter Lippmann and the American Century* (Atlantic–Little, Brown, 1980), p. 260.
[*Lippmann's judgment of Lewis*]: Lippmann, *Men of Destiny* (Macmillan, 1927), ch. 7.
[*Lewis-Dreiser feud*]: Schorer, pp. 561–64.
[*Hicks on* Manhattan Transfer]: Hicks, "The Politics of John Dos Passos," *Antioch Review*, vol. 10, no. 1 (March 1950), pp. 85–98, quoted at p. 89.
[*Class and individual struggle in Dos Passos*]: Lionel Trilling, "The America of John Dos Passos," in Trilling, *Speaking of Literature and Society*, Diana Trilling, ed. (Harcourt Brace Jovanovich, 1980), p. 108.
[*Influence of Whitman and Veblen*]: Harry Levin, "Revisiting Dos Passos' *U.S.A.*," *Massachusetts Review*, vol. 20 (Autumn 1979), p. 404.
[*Dos Passos's style and the modern temper*]: Jack Diggins, "John Roderigo Dos Passos," in Garraty, *op. cit.*, p. 287. See also, Alfred Kazin, *On Native Grounds* (Doubleday, 1956), pp. 267ff.

537 [*Fitzgerald*]: Arthur Mizener, *The Far Side of Paradise* (Houghton Mifflin, 1965); see also William Wasserstrom, *The Ironies of Progress: Henry Adams and the American Dream* (Southern Illinois University Press, 1984), ch. 8.
[*Fitzgerald's ambivalences towards the rich*]: Henry Dan Piper, *F. Scott Fitzgerald: A Critical Portrait* (Holt, Rinehart and Winston, 1965), pp. 175–77.
["*Let me tell you about the very rich*"]: "The Rich Boy," in *The Bodley Head Scott Fitzgerald* (The Bodley Head, 1959–63), vol. 3, pp. 355–96, quoted at pp. 355–56.
[*Daisy's voice "full of money"*]: *The Great Gatsby* (Scribner's, 1925), p. 144.
[*Eight servants and an "extra gardener"*]: ibid., p. 47.
[*Fitzgerald on the Jazz Age*]: Fitzgerald, "Echoes of the Jazz Age," in Fitzgerald, *The Crack-Up*, Edmund Wilson, ed. (New Directions, 1945), pp. 13–22, quoted at p. 14.
["*That incredible pigsty*"]: Anthony Patch in *The Beautiful and the Damned*, in *Bodley Head Scott Fitzgerald*, vol. 4, quoted at p. 56.
[*Sacco and Vanzetti*]: Herbert B. Ehrmann, *The Case That Will Not Die: Commonwealth vs. Sacco and Vanzetti* (Little, Brown, 1969); David Felix, *Protest: Sacco-Vanzetti and the Intellectuals* (Indiana University Press, 1965).

538 [*Frankfurter in the* Atlantic]: "The Case of Sacco and Vanzetti," *Atlantic Monthly*, vol. 139 (March 1927), pp. 409–32. Frankfurter's *The Case of Sacco and Vanzetti* (Little, Brown, 1927) is an expanded version of the *Atlantic* piece.
[*Lippmann on Sacco-Vanzetti*]: New York *World*, August 8, 12, 19, 24, 1927; Steel, pp. 227–34.
["*they are stronger . . . all right we are two nations*"]: Dos Passos, *The Big Money* (Harcourt, Brace, 1933), pp. 461–62.

16. THE VACANT WORKSHOP

539 [*Soviet primer*]: M. Ilin, *New Russia's Primer: The Story of the Five-Year Plan*, George S. Counts and Nucia P. Lodge, translators (Houghton Mifflin, 1931), pp. 5–9.

540 [*Florida land boom*]: A. M. Sakolski, *The Great American Land Bubble* (Harper & Bros., 1932; reprinted by Johnson, 1966), ch. 16; Frederick Lewis Allen, *Only Yesterday: An Informal History of the Nineteen Twenties* (Harper & Bros., 1931), ch. 11; John Kenneth Galbraith, *The Great Crash: 1929* (Houghton Mifflin, 1954), pp. 8–12; Bruce Bliven, "Where Ev'ry Prospect Pleases," *New Republic*, vol. 38, no. 486 (March 26, 1924), pp. 116–18.
[*Ponzi*]: Geoffrey Perrett, *America in the Twenties* (Simon and Schuster, 1982), pp. 356–57; "Mr. Ponzi and His 'Ponzied Finance,' " *Literary Digest*, vol. 66, no. 8 (August 21, 1920), pp. 44–50.
[*Number of players in the market*]: Galbraith, pp. 82–83; Allen, pp. 314–16.

541 [*Fishers' move to Wall Street*]: Galbraith, p. 19.
[*Morgan investment trust*]: *ibid.*, pp. 55–56.
[*Brisbane*]: *ibid.*, pp. 123–24; Perrett, p. 365.
[*Coolidge on Wall Street*]: quoted in Herbert Hoover, *The Memoirs of Herbert Hoover: The Great Depression, 1929–1941* (Macmillan, 1952), p. 16.
[*Raskob*]: Allen, pp. 302–3.
[*Rise in shares traded, 1928*]: Galbraith, pp. 20, 22.
[*Rise in loans and interest rates*]: *ibid.*, pp. 24–27, esp. pp. 26–27.
[*President Hoover and the boom*]: Hoover, pp. 16–19; David Burner, *Herbert Hoover: A Public Life* (Alfred A. Knopf, 1979), pp. 246–47; Harris G. Warren, *Herbert Hoover and the Great Depression* (Oxford University Press, 1959), pp. 102–3.
[*September halt*]: Galbraith, pp. 87–92.

Life in the Depression

For causes of the Crash and the Depression, see Galbraith, *op. cit.;* Robert Sobel, *Panic on Wall Street: A History of America's Financial Disasters* (Macmillan, 1968), ch. 11; Milton Friedman and Anna Jacobson Schwartz, *The Great Contraction: 1929–1933* (Princeton University Press, 1965); Peter Temin, *Did Monetary Forces Cause the Great Depression?* (W. W. Norton, 1976); Elmus Wicker, "A Reconsideration of the Causes of the Banking Panic of 1930," *Journal of Economic History*, vol. 40, no. 3 (September 1980), pp. 571–83; Ferdinand Pecora, *Wall Street Under Oath* (Simon and Schuster, 1939).

542 [*Trading volume, Black Thursday*]: Galbraith, p. 104.
[*Meeting at Morgan*]: *ibid.*, p. 106; Sobel, pp. 376–77.
[*"A little distress selling"*]: quoted in Galbraith, pp. 106–7.
[*Whitney on the floor*]: *ibid.*, pp. 107–8.
[*The crumbling dam*]: *ibid.*, pp. 110–16.
[*Galbraith on "the most devastating day"*]: *ibid.*, p. 116.
[*Times* on *"the most disastrous" day*]: *New York Times*, October 30, 1929, p. 1.
543 [*Hoover on "a sound and prosperous basis"*]: quoted in Robert S. McElvaine, *The Great Depression* (Times Books, 1984), p. 66.
[*"Practitioner of industrial rationalization"*]: David Burner, "Herbert Clark Hoover," in John Garraty, *Encyclopedia of American Biography* (Harper & Row, 1974), p. 535.
[*Hoover's economic views*]: McElvaine, pp. 56–62, 65–69; J. Joseph Huthmacher and Warren I. Susman, eds., *Herbert Hoover and the Crisis of American Capitalism* (Schenkman, 1973); Peri E. Arnold, "The 'Great Engineer' as Administrator: Herbert Hoover and Modern Bureaucracy," *Review of Politics*, vol. 42, no. 3 (July 1980), pp. 329–48.
[*GNP drop*]: U.S. Bureau of the Census, *Historical Statistics of the United States: Colonial Times to 1970* (U.S. Government Printing Office, 1975), part 2, p. 224 (Series F 1–5).
[*Unemployment rise*]: *ibid.*, part 1, p. 126 (Series D 1–10).
[*National income drop*]: Dixon Wecter, *The Age of the Great Depression: 1929–1941* (Macmillan, 1948), p. 17.
[*Wecter on business failures, bank suspensions, and lost savings accounts*]: *ibid.*
[*Unemployment in the cities*]: William E. Leuchtenburg, *The Perils of Prosperity, 1914–1932* (University of Chicago Press, 1958), p. 247.
[*Weekly layoffs*]: *ibid.*
[*Automobile industry turndown*]: *ibid.*, p. 248.
[*Chicago wheat prices*]: Allen, *Only Yesterday, op. cit.*, p. 343.
544 [*Effect of crash upon the vulnerable*]: see Bernard Sternsher, ed., *Hitting Home: The Great Depression in Town and Country* (Quadrangle, 1970); Mauritz A. Hallgren, *Seeds of Revolt* (Alfred A. Knopf, 1933); Clarence Enzler, *Some Social Aspects of the Depression, 1930–1935* (Catholic University of America Press, 1939), ch. 3; Lorenzo J. Greene, "Economic Conditions Among Negroes in the South," *Journal of Negro History*, vol. 64 (1979), pp. 265–73; Lawrence Gordon, "A Brief Look at Blacks in Depression Mississippi, 1929–1934: An Eyewitness Account," *Journal of Negro History*, vol. 64 (1979), pp. 377–90.
[*Hoover's actions, early days following the Crash*]: Galbraith, pp. 142–46; Hoover, *Memoirs, op. cit.*, ch. 6; Warren, *op. cit.*, ch. 9.
[*Ford's pledge*]: McElvaine, p. 73.

544 [*Burner on Hoover at the World Series*]: Burner, *Hoover: A Public Life, op. cit.*, p. 248.
[*Hoover's use of "depression"*]: ibid.
[*Hoover on passing the worst*]: quoted in Hoover, p. 58.
[*Skepticism and resistance to Hoover*]: see Warren, pp. 120–21.
[*Allen on visible effects of Depression*]: Frederick Lewis Allen, *Since Yesterday: The Nineteen-Thirties in America* (Harper & Bros., 1940), pp. 59–60, quoted at p. 59.

545 [*Decline in strikes and union membership*]: *Historical Statistics*, part 1, pp. 177 (Series D 940–945) and 179 (Series D 970–985); see also Irving Bernstein, *The Lean Years: A History of the American Worker, 1920–1933* (Houghton Mifflin, 1960), pp. 335, 341–42.
[*Buttons and billboards*]: quoted in Sternsher, p. 28.
[*Anonymous on how he lost his job*]: "I Lost My Job," *Outlook*, vol. 160, no. 6 (March 1932), pp. 180–81, 184–85.

546 [*Suicides in the depression*]: Galbraith, pp. 133–37; Enzler, pp. 74–78; "The Depression and Suicide," *Literary Digest*, vol. 114, no. 2 (July 9, 1932), p. 7; Caroline Bird, *The Invisible Scar* (David McKay, 1966), pp. 8–9.
[*"If you can't do something for me"*]: quoted in Robert S. McElvaine, *Down and Out in the Great Depression* (University of North Carolina Press, 1983), p. 18.
[*Women in the depression*]: Susan Ware, *Holding Their Own: American Women in the 1930s* (Twayne Publishers, 1982); Winifred Wandersee, *Women's Work and Family Values* (Harvard University Press, 1981); Maya Angelou, *I Know Why the Caged Bird Sings* (Random House, 1969); Robert S. Lynd and Helen M. Lynd, *Middletown in Transition: A Study in Cultural Conflicts* (Harcourt, Brace, 1937), pp. 54–64, 179–86.
[*Marriage, divorce, birth rates, early thirties*]: Ware, pp. 6–8; Bird, pp. 283–91; Lynd and Lynd, pp. 144–79.
[*Married women in the teaching profession*]: Ware, p. 28.
[*Unemployment among women, 1930*]: ibid., p. 36.
[*Blacks and jobs in the depression*]: Raymond Wolters, *Negroes and the Great Depression: The Problem of Economic Recovery* (Greenwood Press, 1970), esp. pp. 90–94, 113–24; Erwin D. Hoffman, "The Genesis of the Modern Movement for Equal Rights in South Carolina, 1930–1939," in Bernard Sternsher, ed., *The Negro in Depression and War: Prelude to Revolution, 1930–1945* (Quadrangle, 1969), pp. 193–223; John Williams, "Struggle of the Thirties in the South," in *ibid.*, pp. 166–80; Robert Weaver, "Negro Labor Since 1929," *Journal of Negro History*, vol. 35, no. 1 (January 1950), pp. 20–38, esp. pp. 20–23.
[*Social worker on white displacement of blacks*]: Forrester B. Washington, quoted in Wolters, p. 113.
[*Black firemen of the Illinois Central*]: ibid., p. 116.

547 [*Ilin*]: *New Russia's Primer, op. cit.*, pp. 11–12.

The Crisis of Ideas

[*"Where to? What next?"*]: "The People, Yes," in Carl Sandburg, *Complete Poems* (Harcourt, Brace, 1950), pp. 437–617, quoted at p. 617.
[*Lippmann on the arrival and departure of the public*]: Lippmann, *The Phantom Public* (Harcourt, Brace, 1925), p. 65.

548 [*NAM and pre-crash crisis*]: James W. Prothro, *Dollar Decade: Business Ideas in the 1920's* (Louisiana State University Press, 1954), pp. 212–13.
[*Edgerton's assurance to Hoover*]: quoted in *ibid.*, p. 218.
[*Edgerton on the causes of poverty*]: ibid., p. 213.
[*Sargent's prescription for a return to prosperity*]: ibid., p. 217.
[*Edgerton on "Socialistic" legislative proposals*]: ibid., pp. 217–18.

549 [*Edgerton on crime*]: ibid., p. 219.
[*Hoover and his "program"*]: quoted in Warren, *op. cit.*, p. 295.
[*Hoover and voluntarism*]: see Burner, *Hoover, op. cit.*, pp. 259–69; Hoover, *Memoirs, op. cit.*, pp. 53–56, 174–75.

550 [*Hoover on Mellon's proposed purge*]: *Memoirs*, p. 30.
[*Hoover and the tariff*]: Warren, pp. 84–92; Burner, pp. 297–99; Herbert Hoover, *The Memoirs of Herbert Hoover: The Cabinet and the Presidency, 1920–1933* (Macmillan, 1952), ch. 41.

551 [*Public works and the RFC*]: Warren, pp. 142–47, 194; James S. Olson, *Herbert Hoover and the Reconstruction Finance Corporation* (Iowa State University Press, 1972).
[*Voluntarism and unemployment insurance in the AFL*]: Bernstein, *op. cit.*, pp. 91, 345–55.
[*Bernstein on the inadequacies of Gompersism*]: *ibid.*, p. 345.
[*Gompers on unemployment insurance*]: quoted in *ibid.*, p. 347.

552 [*AFL convention debates over unemployment insurance*]: see *Reports of Proceedings* of the 50th (1930), 51st (1931), and 52nd (1932) *Annual Conventions of the American Federation of Labor*, 3 vols. (Law Reporter Printing, 1930–32); Bernstein, pp. 347–54.
[*Delegate on workers' liberty and unemployment relief*]: Victor Olander, quoted in *Report of Proceedings* (1930), p. 311.
[*Green on insurance, 1931*]: *Report of Proceedings* (1931), p. 397.
[*1932 vote for insurance*]: *Report of Proceedings* (1932), pp. 39–44, 325–60.
[*Socialist Party, early Depression*]: David A. Shannon, *The Socialist Party of America* (Macmillan, 1955), ch. 9; Michael Harrington, "The Socialist Party," in Arthur M. Schlesinger, Jr., *History of U.S. Political Parties* (Chelsea House, 1973), vol. 3, pp. 2426–28.
[*Socialist Party membership, 1932*]: Harrington, p. 2427.
[*Dos Passos on Socialist Party*]: quoted in Daniel Aaron, *Writers on the Left: Episodes in American Literary Communism* (Harcourt, Brace and World, 1961), p. 192.
[*Communist Party, early Depression*]: Irving Howe and Lewis Coser, *The American Communist Party: A Critical History (1919–1957)* (Beacon Press, 1957), ch. 5.
[*Dos Passos's advice to the Communist Party*]: quoted in Aaron, p. 192.

553 [*Democratic party, early 1930s*]: David Burner, *The Politics of Provincialism: The Democratic Party in Transition, 1918–1932* (Alfred A. Knopf, 1968), pp. 244–45.
[*Smith's movement to the right*]: Burner, *Politics of Provincialism*, p. 245; McElvaine, *Great Depression, op. cit.*, pp. 123–24.
[*Davis on Hoover's "socialism"*]: Burner, *Politics of Provincialism*, p. 245.
[*Cox's demand for balanced budget and sales tax*]: *ibid.*
[*Graham on Democratic party*]: Otis L. Graham, Jr., "The Democratic Party, 1932–1945," in Schlesinger, vol. 3, pp. 1939–64, quoted at p. 1940.
[*Democrats and the sales tax*]: Burner, *Hoover*, pp. 280–82.
[*La Guardia on sales tax bill*]: quoted in *ibid.*, p. 281.

554 [*1932 campaign for Democratic nomination*]: Burner, *Politics of Provincialism*, pp. 246–50; McElvaine, pp. 123–28; James MacGregor Burns, *Roosevelt: The Lion and the Fox* (Harcourt, Brace, 1956), pp. 123–34.
[*FDR's attack upon Hoover and Smith's retort*]: *New York Times*, April 8, 1932, p. 1; Richard O'Connor, *The First Hurrah: A Biography of Alfred E. Smith* (Putnam's, 1970), p. 251.
[*Lippmann on FDR*]: Lippmann, "Governor Roosevelt's Candidacy," New York *Herald Tribune*, January 8, 1932, reprinted in Lippmann, *Interpretations: 1931–1932*, Allan Nevins, ed. (Macmillan, 1932), pp. 260, 262.
[*Democratic convention, 1932*]: O'Connor, pp. 255–63; Frank Freidel, *Franklin Roosevelt: The Triumph* (Little, Brown, 1956), ch. 20; Michael Beschloss, *Kennedy and Roosevelt: The Uneasy Alliance* (W. W. Norton, 1980), pp. 69–73.

555 [*McAdoo's announcement*]: quoted in Burns, p. 137.

"Once I Built a Railroad, Made It Run"

[*Emerson on the rails*]: Ralph Waldo Emerson, "The Young American," in Emerson, *Nature: Addresses and Lectures* (Houghton, Mifflin, 1903; reprinted by AMS Press, 1979), pp. 363–95, quoted at p. 364.
[*American Locomotive sales*]: William Manchester, *The Glory and the Dream* (Little, Brown, 1974), p. 34.
[*Decline in rail employees*]: Thor Hultgren, *American Transportation in Prosperity and Depression* (National Bureau of Economic Research, 1948), p. 179 (Table 54).
[*Decline in freight tonnage*]: *ibid.*, p. 355 (Table 141).
[*Decline in dividends*]: *ibid.*, p. 336 (Chart 124).
[*Decline in GNP*]: *Historical Statistics of the United States, op. cit.*, part 2, p. 224 (Series F 1–5).
[*Decline in auto production*]: Hultgren, p. 350 (Table 136).
[*Decline in oil production*]: *ibid.*, p. 353 (Table 140).
[*Decline in residential building contracts*]: Warren, *op. cit.*, p. 236.

555 [*Decline in farm income*]: McElvaine, *Down and Out, op. cit.*, p. 27.
[*Decline in steel production*]: Manchester, p. 34.
[*Decline in retail sales*]: see Lynd and Lynd, *op. cit.*, p. 529 (Table 1).
556 [*Families evicted, 1932*]: Manchester, p. 33.
[*Businesses at home*]: Lynd and Lynd, p. 20.
[*Middle-class economies*]: Bird, *op. cit.*, pp. 273–81.
[*Union and nonunion wage decline*]: Bernstein, *op. cit.*, p. 320.
[*Diet of Kentucky miner*]: quoted in "In the Driftway," *The Nation*, vol. 134, no. 3492 (June 8, 1932), p. 651.
[*Rouge demonstration*]: Allan Nevins and Frank Ernest Hill, *Ford: Decline and Rebirth, 1933–1962* (Scribner's, 1962), pp. 32–34; Keith Sward, *The Legend of Henry Ford* (Rinehart, 1948), ch. 18.
[*Bird on transients*]: Bird, p. 67.
[*"They have to take you in"*]: Frost, "The Death of the Hired Man," in Frost, *Selected Poems* (Henry Holt, 1923), pp. 13–20, quoted at p. 18.
[*"Professional bums" among transients*]: statement of Elliot Chapman, *Hearings* of a Subcommittee of the Senate Committee on Manufactures, *Relief for Unemployed Transients*, 72nd Congress, 2nd Session, January 13–25, 1933 (U.S. Government Printing Office, 1933), p. 112.
[*Mayors on treatment of transients*]: "Digest" of mayors' responses, in *ibid.*, quoted at pp. 192, 201, 190, 188, 189, 191, 194, 198, respectively.
557 [*"Transients, do not apply"*]: testimony of Professor A. W. McMillen, in *ibid.*, p. 45.
[*Open letter, September 1932*]: Aaron, *op. cit.*, pp. 196–98, quoted at p. 197.
[*Wilson's firsthand observations*]: see Wilson, *The American Jitters: A Year of the Slump* (Scribner's, 1932); Wilson, *The American Earthquake: A Documentary of the Twenties and Thirties* (Doubleday, 1938); Wilson, *The Thirties*, Leon Edel, ed. (Farrar, Straus and Giroux, 1980), pp. 208–14, quoted at pp. 208, 212.
[*"Insist on working even without pay"*]: quoted in Bird, p. 76.
[*"We cannot squander ourselves into prosperity"*]: quoted in Hoover, *Memoirs: The Great Depression, op. cit.*, p. 134.
[*Ford on vagabonds*]: quoted in Manchester, p. 22.
558 [*MacArthur deputy's proposal*]: Brig. Gen. George Van Horn Moseley, quoted in Burner, *Hoover, op. cit.*, p. 307.
[*Bonus Army*]: *ibid.*, pp. 309–12; Roger Daniels, *The Bonus March* (Greenwood Publishing, 1971); Bernstein, ch. 13; Hoover, *Memoirs: The Great Depression*, pp. 225–32.
[*"A polyglot mob"*]: F. Trubee Davison, quoted in Warren, p. 235.
[*Stokes on Bonus March*]: quoted in Bernstein, p. 454.
[*"Use all humanity"*]: quoted in Daniels, p. 165.
[*"The President was pleased"*]: quoted in Bernstein, p. 454.
559 [*"Brother, Can You Spare a Dime?"*]: lyrics by E. Y. Harburg, music by Jay Gorney, in *100 Best Songs of the 20's and 30's* (Harmony Books, 1973), pp. 271–74. The song was sung and popularized by Rudy Vallee.

ACKNOWLEDGMENTS

In carrying this study of "The American Experiment" on from the Civil War years to the crises of the early 1930s, I have continued to emphasize the role of purposeful leadership in the processes of historical causation. But now my central concern is with economic as well as intellectual and political leadership. The late-nineteenth and early-twentieth centuries were indeed an era of great financial and industrial tycoons—Morgan, Carnegie, Rockefeller, Ford, and many others. I have tried to indicate some of the influence these leaders had on American thought, society, and politics.

As in the first volume, however, I do not conceive leadership as a function merely of the more celebrated persons, but as the product of numberless purposes and actions of leaders of the second and third cadres in many social and political arenas. Even in situations where the top economic leadership—the great industrialists and financiers—appears capable of wielding enormous economic and political power, the "subordinate" leaders in my view have a critical influence on the course of events. Their role also helps to explain why economic power cannot be simply or mechanically converted into political power; for these "lesser" leaders, reflecting as they do the endless social and ideological diversity of the American people, will often tend to lie outside, or even block or divert, the vertical flow of power from the top—and the more numerous and varied such leaders, the greater this tendency. I plan to return to the central problem of the role of concentrated economic power in a democratic republic in the third volume of this trilogy.

Once again I have sought to illuminate the role of second- and third-cadre leaders by sinking "historical drill-holes" in specific sectors and situations, through research in a number of archives and libraries. For their unfailing helpfulness I thank the archivists and librarians at the Baker Library at Harvard Business School, the Buffalo Historical Society, California Historical Society, Columbia University Library, Ford Motor Company, Franklin D. Roosevelt Library, Huntington Library, Kansas State Historical Society, Library of Congress, Louisiana State University Library, Massachusetts Historical Society, Minnesota State Archives, New-York Historical Society, New York Public Library, Ohio Historical Society, Pennsylvania Historical Society, Schlesinger Library at Radcliffe, Stanford University Library and Archives, Stowe-Day Library (Hartford), Williams College Library, and various other, more specialized archives and libraries.

This volume, like *The Vineyard of Liberty,* has been very much a collaborative venture, in which I have had the privilege of working with great and varied talents. Once again I have pitilessly enlisted assistance from my family. My wife and fellow author, Joan Simpson Burns, helped me understand literary and other cultural forces in the late-nineteenth and early-twentieth centuries by sharing with me her ideas on and extensive knowledge of these subjects. I made full use of the versatility of Deborah Edwards Burns, a journalist who helped me with research on women's history and related social history, and who conceived and executed the illustrative endpapers. Trienah Meyers Kuykendall critiqued the whole manuscript, making particular use of her legal background, and I tested my ideas against those of Peter Meyers, a young political theorist. I was especially fortunate to have the creative assistance of Stewart Burns, author of a doctoral dissertation, "The Populist Movement and the Cooperative Commonwealth: The Politics of Non-Reformist Reform" (1984), who generously helped me in placing the role of the Farmers Alliance in a broad historical and theoretical framework, shared with me his data, and collaborated with me in the drafting of the sections on the Alliance, Populism, and related intellectual and political developments.

Because of the emphasis on economic and social history as well as intellectual and political history in this volume, I am especially grateful for help and collaboration from social historians working in these areas. Joan G. Zimmerman gave me indispensable assistance in the fields of Progressive politics, social legislation, and women's education, as did Ellen M. James and Dee Ann Montgomery in women's history, Eric Scheye in intellectual and ethnic history, Fran Burke in the political leadership of women, Anne Margolis in intellectual history, and Philippa Strum, author of a preeminent study of Louis Brandeis, in legal history and politics. Others who provided valued help in specific areas were Eunice Burns, Laurie Burns Gray, Rodger Davis, Lee Farbman, Michael Koessel, and Jay Leibold. Michael Beschloss, Lisl Cade, and Maurice Greenbaum also contributed in important ways. Milton Djuric provided extensive and invaluable editorial assistance at every stage of the book's preparation.

The most important contribution to the volume was made by my good friend, close associate, and former student, Jeffrey P. Trout. Not only did he collaborate with me in planning, researching, and drafting in areas in which he is especially knowledgeable—military, diplomatic, and political history; he also worked closely with me in conceptualizing the whole volume, in organizing the flow of chapters, and in bibliographical research and criticism. His sense of history, enthusiastic participation, and crisis-management have improved every part of the volume.

As with the first volume, I solicited critical reviews of the manuscript from scholars far more expert than I, and I was fortunate in receiving stringent and constructive criticism from David Burner, John Milton Cooper, Jr., Eric Foner, James M. McPherson, Jerome Mushkat, Irwin Unger, and my longtime friend and colleague at Williams, Robert C. L. Scott. At our neighboring North Adams State College, historians W. Anthony Gengarelly, Clark Billings, Richard Taskin, and David Oppenheimer generously shared their specialized knowledge with me. My friends in the Faculty Secretarial Office at Williams literally made possible the production of this work. At Alfred A. Knopf, my editor, Ashbel Green, Betty Anderson, Peter Hayes, Anne Eberle, and Melvin Rosenthal played indispensable roles.

Any errors or deficiencies are solely my responsibility—and I would appreciate being informed of them, at Williams College, Williamstown, Mass. 01267. I wish to thank those who sent in corrections for the first volume. They were: (p. 116) Benjamin Franklin lay mortally ill at this time rather than "lay dying," as he did not die until a year later; (180) it was not Lewis but Clark who had probably met Daniel Boone; (501) Whittier was a Quaker, not a Unitarian (though he did have Unitarian sympathies); (518) Lovejoy was the son of a Congregational minister, not a Presbyterian one, he was a student at Princeton Theological Seminary but did not graduate from it, and he might better be described as an "extremist" than as a "fanatic." These changes have been made in the paperback edition (1983).

As with the first volume, I have borrowed occasional phrases or sentences from my own earlier works in cases where I felt my prose was—or should be made—imperishable.

J.M.B.

Index

abolitionists, and 15th Amendment, 61–2
Abrams, Jacob, 504–5
Acheson, Edward, 290
Adams, Charles Francis, 32, 73, 207
Adams, Charles Francis, Jr., 73, 75, 85–6,
   115
  and railroads, 73, 93, 176
Adams, Henry, vii, 92, 168, 169, 304–6, 326
  Democracy, 169, 192, 194
Adams, John, 73, 153
Adams, Samuel Hopkins, 348
Adamson Act (1916), 421
Addams, Jane, 123, 371–2
  as pacifist, 412, 483
  and Progressive party, 419
  and settlement-house movement,
   270–1, 275–7, 278
advertising, 518–19
AFL, *see* American Federation of Labor
Agassiz, Louis, 81, 86–7
Age of Innocence, The (Wharton), 321, 322
agrarian revolt, 180–91
agriculture:
  in California, 99
  and Civil War, 20–1
  in Depression, 543
  machinery and tools for, 81, 129
  see also farmers
Ahlstrom, Sydney, 516
airplanes, 288, 290
  in World War I, 436
Alaska, 220, 340
Alcott, Louisa May, 30, 261
Aldrich, Nelson, 330, 335, 336, 357
Algeciras Conference (1905), 342
Alger, Horatio, Jr., 159–60
Algerism (rags-to-riches myth), 143,
   144–5, 159–60
  Carnegie and, 102, 161; and McKinley,
   234

Dempsey and, 532
and economic concentration, 390
Frick and, 224
Irish immigrants and, 259–60
La Follette and, 360
and political machines (urban), 265
aliens, deportation and repression of,
   439–40
Allen, Frederick Lewis, 510, 544–5
Altgeld, John P., 227, 276
Amador, Manuel, 339
Amalgamated Iron, Steel and Tin
  Workers, 224–6
Amendments to U.S. Constitution:
  1st, 504, 505
  13th, 37, 48, 60
  14th, 49, 50, 53, 60, 203–4, 505
  15th, 60–2, 204
  18th (Prohibition), 441
  19th ("Susan B. Anthony"), 444–7
  Bill of Rights, 504, 523
American Federation of Labor (AFL),
   178–80, 282
  and Depression, 551–2
  membership of (1920s), 534
  and Pullman boycott (1894), 227
  and SLP, 396
  and women, 280
American Railway Union (ARU), 227
American Woman Suffrage Association, 209
Amiens (France), battles for, 432, 433, 436
ammunition production (World War I), 430
Amory, Cleveland, 115
Ampère, André Marie, 83
Andrews, Stephen P., 125
Anthony, Susan B., 125, 204, 209
antitrust movement, 182, 216
  Brandeis and, 391–2
  of Roosevelt (T.), 332–3, 349–52
  of Wilson, 389–91

PERMISSION ACKNOWLEDGMENTS

The following illustrations have been reprinted with the kind permission of the institutions indicated:

[FRONT ENDPAPER] *Courtesy of Amherst College Library:* Mother ironing with baby in arms, from *Harper's Weekly,* March 22, 1873. *Courtesy of Bancroft Library, University of California, Berkeley:* "Chinese Railroad Laborers Filling in Secrettown Trestle," 1877. *Courtesy of Charles Scribner's Sons:* "The Passing of the Horse," from *The New York Journal,* 1899, reprinted in Mark Sullivan, *Our Times,* vol. I, 1934. *Courtesy of Culver Pictures, Inc.:* "Victoria Woodhull," 1871. *Courtesy of* The Nation: "Fleeing the Storm," reprinted February 7, 1972. *Courtesy of the Library of Congress:* Excerpt from the Gettysburg Address. *Courtesy of the New York Public Library:* "Gettysburg, July 1863," from *Harper's Pictorial History of the Civil War,* 1866 (General Research Division); "Mouth of the Chicago River" and "The City from the Water Works" (Picture Collection); New York City strike, engraved from a drawing by Thure de Thulstrup in *Harper's Weekly,* March 12, 1886 (Picture Collection); "Temperance" by Charles Stanley Reinhart, ca. 1873 (Picture Collection). *Courtesy of Viking Penguin, Inc.:* "Revenge, Working-men, To Arms," from a Haymarket circular, reprinted in Louis Adamic, *Dynamite: The Story of Class Violence in America,* 1931.

[BACK ENDPAPER] *Courtesy of the Atlanta* Constitution: "For President!" by L. C. Gregg in the Atlanta *Constitution,* ca. 1904. *Courtesy of Charles Scribner's Sons, Inc.:* "The Expansion Rooster," reprinted in Mark Sullivan, *Our Times,* vol. I, 1934. *Courtesy of the Detroit Institute of Arts, Founders Society Purchase, Edsel B. Ford Fund and Gift of Edsel B. Ford:* Detail from the North Wall of "The Detroit Industry Frescoes," by Diego Rivera, 1932–33. *Courtesy of* The Nation: "T'Was Ever Thus," F. Opper cartoon, reprinted February 7, 1972. *Courtesy of* the New York Public Library: Cadillac (Picture Collection); "The Grain Movement from the West," from *Frank Leslie's Illustrated Newspaper,* 1877 (Picture Collection); Immigrant woman, by Jacob Riis (Picture Collection); New York City slum children, by Jacob Riis (Picture Collection). *Courtesy of RCA Victor:* Advertisement trademark. *Courtesy of the St. Louis* Post-Dispatch: "The New Man on the Job," by Robert Minor in the St. Louis *Post-Dispatch,* November 25, 1908. *Courtesy of Warner Bros. Music Corp.:* Score from "Brother, Can You Spare a Dime," by E. Y. Harburg and Jay Corney. © 1932, renewed by WB Music Corp. All rights reserved; used by permission.

The endpapers were designed and executed by Deborah Burns and Cecily Dunham.

[PART TITLE ILLUSTRATIONS] *Courtesy of the Atlanta* Constitution: "For President!" by L. C. Gregg in the Atlanta *Constitution,* ca. 1904. *Courtesy of Culver Pictures, Inc.:* Working women marching on May Day, 1912, Brown Bros. *Courtesy of the Detroit Institute of Arts, Founders Society Purchase, Edsel B. Ford Fund and Gift of Edsel B. Ford:* Detail from the North Wall of "The Detroit Industry Frescoes," by Diego Rivera, 1932–33. *Courtesy of the New York Public Library:* "Gettysburg, July 1863," from *Harper's Pictorial History of the Civil War,* 1866. *Courtesy of* The Nation: "Fleeing the Storm," reprinted February 7, 1972.